T0350281

Modern Mathematics and Applications in Computer Graphics and Vision

Modern Mathematics and Applications in Computer Graphics and Vision

Hongyu Guo

University of Houston — Victoria, USA

World Scientific

NEW JERSEY · LONDON · SINGAPORE · BEIJING · SHANGHAI · HONG KONG · TAIPEI · CHENNAI

Published by

World Scientific Publishing Co. Pte. Ltd.

5 Toh Tuck Link, Singapore 596224

USA office: 27 Warren Street, Suite 401-402, Hackensack, NJ 07601

UK office: 57 Shelton Street, Covent Garden, London WC2H 9HE

British Library Cataloguing-in-Publication Data
A catalogue record for this book is available from the British Library.

MODERN MATHEMATICS AND APPLICATIONS IN COMPUTER GRAPHICS AND VISION

ISBN 978-981-4449-32-8
ISBN 978-981-4449-33-5 (pbk)

Printed in Singapore

To Yanping and Alicia

Preface

While I am teaching computer graphics, computer vision and game programming courses, too often I encounter students in classes, who have a great interest and ambition in these fields but only to feel limited by the lacking of proper mathematics preparation. This is because, unlike other areas of computer science, where discrete mathematics is mostly applied, computer graphics and vision, as well as game programming utilize many areas of continuous mathematics. For example, ray tracing in computer graphics rendering is purely the computational simulation of the optical process using laws in physics. The regular university curriculum does not provide proper preparation of the continuous mathematics for these students. Researchers and professionals in these areas have their struggles too. Unlike the students, they do not have a problem with multiplying two matrices. However, more and more modern arsenal of abstract mathematics is utilized in research literature, for example, the concepts of tensors and differentiable manifolds. This book is intended to help them in these areas to better understand and apply the concepts and theories needed in their study and research.

Intended Audience

The intended audience is upper level undergraduate students, graduate students and researchers in computer graphics and vision and related areas. If you are a believer of the saying "A mathematician is a blind man in a dark room looking for a black cat which is not there", probably this book is not for you. You should consider returning the book and getting a refund. If you have been looking for a book with a concise account of a certain topic but only was frustrated because the books for mathematics majors have too many details than you needed, I hope this is the book you have been looking for.

Students and researchers in physics and engineering share most of the arsenal of mathematics with the computer graphics and vision community and therefore this book should help them as well. If you are a math major and want to take a break from math for a moment, you can read this book.

Organization

The book is organized in four parts, Part I Algebra, Part II Geometry, Part III Topology and More, and Part IV Applications. Particular emphasis was given to tensors and manifolds. The intrinsic view of geometry, initiated by Gauss, is also emphasized. Intrinsic geometry is harder for students due to its intrinsic nature, just like the intrinsic beauty of a person is harder to discover than simple good appearance. This book is not intended to be read from the first page to the last page in the sequential order. This is a "get-what-you-want" book. There are minimal dependencies among the parts and chapters, which is illustrated in the chapter dependency chart. The reader is encouraged to start reading from any part, or chapter and he may skip around. Part of the materials of this book come from the lecture notes for two courses that I have taught, Gaming Mathematics at the undergraduate level, and Mathematical Methods in Computer Graphics and Vision at the graduate level, in which I taught the basics of linear algebra, tensor algebra, exterior algebra, quaternion algebra and projective geometry with applications in computer graphics and vision. Part IV Chapter 2 is based on two of my recently published articles. This book can be used for a selected topics course at the undergraduate or graduate level with free choices of topics by the instructor.

The organization of the book is influenced by the structure point of view, which is explained in Chapter 0 as a preliminary. A quick glance of this chapter will benefit in a better understanding of the organization and interrelations of different branches of modern mathematics, as well as the study of each topics. Part I covers some of the algebraic structures, which are discrete structures. Part II covers geometry, which has a mixture of discrete and continuous structures. In the topics in Part III, topological structures, or more generally, continuous structures, play an important role. The topics in Part III are more abstract, compared to Parts I and II. To help the reader, a Venn diagram illustrating the relationship of different structures is provided in the beginning of each chapter in Part III.

Approach and Features

A bottom-up approach is adopted in the treatment of the materials, which is different from many other books. In the history of mathematics development, concrete systems were studied first. In modern times, the focus is on abstract systems. Abstract systems are harder for students to understand. However, the difficulty is eased if we use the concrete systems as examples and prototypes. The bottom-up approach means always starting with a concrete system and then making a transition and generalization to abstract systems. In most of the cases, the Euclidean space, which is our homestead or our Garden of Eden, is our starting point. In one direction, it is generalized to metric spaces and topological spaces (Part III Chap. 1); in another direction, to manifolds (Part III Chap. 2); yet another direction, to Hilbert spaces and Banach spaces (Part III Chap. 3); and the last, to measure spaces and probability spaces (Part III Chap. 4). It is unfortunate that some students are learning modern mathematics in a parrot way. This book aims to help the student develop intuition and avoid learning like a parrot.

Much effort has been made, including not to show the proofs, to make the book easy to read. In some books, if the author wants to omit the proof of a theorem for some reason but feels guilty about it, he often says that the proof is straightforward and is left to the reader as exercise. In this book, all proofs are brazenly omitted and I just had a revelation while writing this book that if the author leaves out a proof, he does not have to leave the "burden of proof" to the reader. I think the students shall be happy about that. I also believe that the readers should not be asked to pay for something they do not read. The proofs are important but they are not the focus of this book with the intended audience. For readers who are interested in the proofs, or having doubt about the truth of a particular theorem, they can find the proofs following the bibliography. However, firstly, this treatment does not mean the discussion lacks rigor. I tried to make the exposition intuitive, but without sacrificing rigor. I deeply believe that making the subject less rigorous is not a shortcut to make it easier. Sloppy exposition only adds more confusion and makes it harder to understand. Secondly, it does not mean that the book is just a simple listing of definitions, theorems and formulas. The concepts are explained with an emphasis on the intuition. Many examples are included to illustrate the concepts. Many categorized remarks discuss possible confusions, provide caution, elaboration, clarification, correction of many common misconceptions, cross links as well as historical and philosophical insight. Definitions are put in boxes with headings. The theorems and important formulas are highlighted with gray shades and a club-suit symbol is used as the delimiter of each example.

Acknowledgments

I wish to express my heartfelt gratitude to all the people who have helped me in various ways in the long process of preparing this text, even though space does not allow me to list all the names. In the preparation of this text,

I found great assistance and inspiration in many books and papers, which are listed in bibliography. I am greatly indebted to all the authors. Many of my colleagues and students read different versions of the manuscript, found errors, and provided feedback and constructive suggestions. I am particularly grateful to Profs. Ricardo Teixeira and Jerry Hu. They committed substantial amount of time reading through most part of the manuscript and provided extremely valuable suggestions. Profs. Pablo Tarazaga, Scott King and Arunava Banerjee read part of an early draft of the manuscript. My students Erin Gabrysch, Srikanth Krishnamachari, Li You, Rui Wang, Druha Chandupatla, Roja Molupoju, Ramya Kurmana and Preethi Chittimalla provided valuable feedback. My thanks go to all of them but the responsibility for any uncaught errors completely remains on myself. I would like to thank Profs. Anand Rangarajan, Alireza Tavakkoli, Ricardo Vilalta, Lee Chao, Jeffery Di Leo and Uppinder Mehan for their encouragement and stimulating discussions. Thanks also go to Prof. Dmitri Sobolev for discussions of color words in Russian.

I am thankful to my students Erin Gabrysch and Kaylee Estrada for posing as models in photographs, which are used in perspective analysis in Part IV Chap. 2.

In addition to the illustrations and photographs made by myself, many images in the public domain contributed to enhance the readability of this book. I thank Artists Rights Society (ARS) and ProLitteris for permission to use captured images from a video showing Markus Raetz's sculpture, which is used in Part IV Chap. 2. I thank Prof. Madhav Nori for the use of a quote from his lectures in the University of Chicago, recorded by one of his students.

I wish to express my appreciation of the staff of World Scientific Publishing, especially the acquisition editor Chunguang Sun, desk editor Steven Patt, senior systems engineer Rajesh Babu and production manager Yolande Koh for their patience and dedication in bring this book out. Special thanks go to Rajesh Babu for his great technical assistance while I was typesetting the book using LaTeX.

Last but not the least, my loving gratitude goes to my family for their patience and support.

Hongyu Guo

guoh@uhv.edu

Brief Contents

Chapter Dependencies

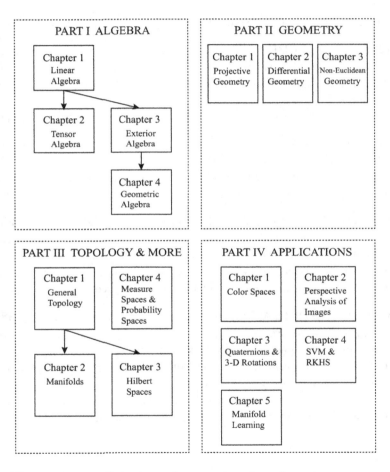

There is an explicit dependency only when there is an arrow shown between the chapters.

Contents

PART III TOPOLOGY AND MORE   235

Symbols and Notations

GENERAL

$\overset{\text{def}}{=}$	equal by definition
$\Rightarrow$	implies
$\Leftrightarrow$, iff	is equivalent to, if and only if
$\wedge$	and
$\vee$	or
$\neg$	not
$\varnothing$	empty set
$x \in A$	x belongs to set A
$x \notin A$	x does not belong to set A
$A \subseteq B$	A is a subset of B
$A \subset B$	A is a proper subset of B
$A \cup B$	set union of A and B
$A \cap B$	set intersection of A and B
$A - B$	set difference of A and B
A^c	set complement of A
$A \times B$	Cartesian product of sets A and B
$\mathbf{P}(A)$	power set of A
$\sim$	equivalence relation
$[x]$	equivalence class represented by x
$\dfrac{A}{R}$, A/R, $A/\sim$	quotient set of A w.r.t. equivalence relation R or $\sim$
$\varphi : X \to Y$	mapping from X to Y
$\varphi : X \to Y; x \mapsto y$	mapping from X to Y, given by $\varphi(x) = y$
$\psi \circ \varphi$	composition of mapping φ and ψ
$|X|$	cardinality of set X
$\mathbb{N}$	set of all natural numbers $\{1, 2, 3, \ldots\}$
$\mathbb{Z}$	set of all integers
$\mathbb{Q}$	set of all rational numbers
$\mathbb{R}$	set of all real numbers
$\overline{\mathbb{R}}$	set of extended real numbers $\overline{\mathbb{R}} \overset{\text{def}}{=} \mathbb{R} \cup \{+\infty, -\infty\}$
$\mathbb{C}$	set of all complex numbers
$\mathbb{H}$	set of all quaternions
$\mathbb{O}$	set of all octonions
$\mathbb{F}_p$	finite field of residue class for prime number p
$\mathbb{R}^n$	n-dimensional real linear space

$\mathbb{C}^n$	n-dimensional complex linear space
S^2	spherical surface (of dimension 2)
S^n	spherical surface of dimension n
$|x|$	absolute value of a real number, complex number or quaternion
$\bar{a}$	conjugate of a complex number or quaternion

ALGEBRA

$$\mathrm{sgn}(\sigma) = \begin{cases} 1 & \text{if } \sigma \text{ is even permutation} \\ -1 & \text{if } \sigma \text{ is old permutation} \end{cases}$$

$\cong$	isomorphic
$\mathrm{char}(F)$	characteristic of field F
$\dim V$	dimension of linear space V
$\mathrm{span}(X)$	linear space spanned by set X
$\mathrm{im}(\varphi)$	image of mapping φ
$\ker(\varphi)$	kernel of linear mapping φ
$\rho(\varphi)$	rank of linear mapping φ
$\nu(\varphi)$	nullity of linear mapping φ
$L(V;W)$	all linear mappings $T : V \to W$
$L(U,V;W)$	all bilinear mappings $\varphi : U \times V \to W$
$F[x]$	all polynomials of single variable x with coefficients in F
$\mathscr{V}_F \langle X \rangle$	free vector space over field F generated by set X
$\mathscr{A}_F \langle X^* \rangle$	free associative algebra over field F generated by set X
$U \oplus V$	direct sum of linear spaces U and V
$U \otimes V$	tensor product of linear spaces U and V
$u \otimes v$	tensor product of vectors $u \in U$ and $v \in V$
$A \otimes B$	Kronecker product of matrices A and B
$u \wedge v$	wedge product of u and v
$u \times v$	cross product of vectors $u, v \in \mathbb{R}^3$
$\{a_i\}_{i=1}^n$	set $\{a_1, a_2, \ldots, a_n\}$
$\begin{bmatrix} a_{11} \cdots a_{1n} \\ \cdots \cdots \cdots \\ a_{m1} \cdots a_{mn} \end{bmatrix}$	$m \times n$ matrix
$\begin{vmatrix} a_{11} \cdots a_{1n} \\ \cdots \cdots \cdots \\ a_{n1} \cdots a_{nn} \end{vmatrix}$	determinant of matrix $\begin{bmatrix} a_{11} \cdots a_{1n} \\ \cdots \cdots \cdots \\ a_{n1} \cdots a_{nn} \end{bmatrix}$
$\det A$	determinant of matrix A
$\mathrm{tr}A$	trace of matrix or operator A

A^t	transpose of matrix A
A^{-1}	inverse of matrix A
$\|v\|$	norm of a vector
$\langle \cdot, \cdot \rangle$	inner product
$\langle u, v \rangle$, $u \cdot v$	inner product of vectors u and v
uv	Gibbs dyad of vectors **u** and **v**
$T_q^p(V)$	tensor space of type (p,q) on linear space V
$T(V)$	tensor algebra on linear space V
$\Lambda^k(V)$	exterior space of degree k
$\Lambda(V)$	Grassmann algebra on linear space V
$Cl(V)$	Clifford algebra on linear space V
$Cl_{p,q}(V)$	Clifford algebra on V with a quadratic form signature (p, q)

GEOMETRY

$\parallel$	parallel
$\perp$	perpendicular
$\angle$	angle
$\triangle ABC$	triangle
$\cong$	congruent
$\sim$	similar
P^2, $P^2(V)$	projective plane, associated with linear space V
P^n, $P^n(V)$	projective space of dimension n, associated with linear space V
y', $\frac{dy}{dx}$	first order derivative of function $y = f(x)$
y'', $\frac{d^2y}{dx^2}$	second order derivative of function $y = f(x)$
$\rho(P_1, P_2)$	Euclidean distance between points P_1 and P_2 in $\mathbb{R}^3$
$\tilde{\rho}(P_1, P_2)$	geodesic distance between points P_1 and P_2 on a surface in $\mathbb{R}^3$
$\dot{\mathbf{r}}$	shorthand for $\frac{d\mathbf{r}}{dt}$, first order derivative of $\mathbf{r}(t)$
$\ddot{\mathbf{r}}$	shorthand for $\frac{d^2\mathbf{r}}{dt^2}$, second order derivative of $\mathbf{r}(t)$
$\mathbf{r}_u$	shorthand for $\frac{\partial \mathbf{r}}{\partial u} = (\frac{\partial x}{\partial u}, \frac{\partial y}{\partial u}, \frac{\partial z}{\partial u})$, tangent vector tangent to the u-line
$\mathbf{r}_{uu}$	shorthand for $\frac{\partial^2 \mathbf{r}}{\partial u^2} = (\frac{\partial^2 x}{\partial u^2}, \frac{\partial^2 y}{\partial u^2}, \frac{\partial^2 z}{\partial u^2})$
$\mathbf{r}_{uv}$	shorthand for $\frac{\partial^2 \mathbf{r}}{\partial u \partial v} = (\frac{\partial^2 x}{\partial u \partial v}, \frac{\partial^2 y}{\partial u \partial v}, \frac{\partial^2 z}{\partial u \partial v})$
n	unit normal vector on a surface
Φ_1	first fundamental form of a surface
Φ_2	second fundamental form of a surface

E, F, G first fundamental quantities of a surface,
$$E = \mathbf{r}_u^2, F = \mathbf{r}_u \mathbf{r}_v, G = \mathbf{r}_v^2$$
L, M, N second fundamental quantities of a surface,
$$L = \mathbf{n} \cdot \mathbf{r}_{uu}, M = \mathbf{n} \cdot \mathbf{r}_{uv}, N = \mathbf{n} \cdot \mathbf{r}_{vv}$$
κ curvature of a plane curve
κ_1, κ_2 principal curvatures of a surface
K Gaussian curvature of a surface
H mean curvature of a surface
Π angle of parallelism

TOPOLOGY AND MORE

$\lim_{n \to \infty} x_n$ limit of sequence x_n
$x_n \to x$ sequence x_n converges to x
$B_\delta(x)$ δ-open ball centered at x
A° interior of point set A
∂A boundary of point set A
A^e exterior of point set A
$\bar{A}$ closure of point set A
A' derived set of point set A
(a, b) open interval in $\mathbb{R}$
$[a, b]$ closed interval in $\mathbb{R}$
$\dot{x}$ shorthand for $\frac{dx(t)}{dt}$
$T_p(M)$ tangent space of differentiable manifold M at point p
$T_p^*(M)$ cotangent space of differentiable manifold M at point p
$T(M)$ tangent bundle of differentiable manifold M
$T^*(M)$ cotangent bundle of differentiable manifold M
$\mathcal{F}(M)$ set of all smooth scalar fields $f : M \to \mathbb{R}$ on M
$\mathfrak{X}(M)$ set of all smooth vector fields X on M
$\nabla_v f$ directional derivative of scalar field f along v
df differential of a scalar field f
$d\varphi$ differential of mapping $\varphi : M \to N$
$[X, Y]$ Lie bracket of vector fields X and Y, or $XY - YX$
g_{ij} Riemannian metric
Γ_{ij}^k connection coefficients, Christoffel symbol (of the second kind)
∇ affine connection, covariant differential
$\nabla_X Y$ covariant directional derivative of vector field Y along X
∇Y covariant differential of vector field Y

∂_k	shorthand for $\frac{\partial}{\partial x_k}$
R	Riemann curvature tensor
$\hat{R}$	Ricci curvature tensor
$\bar{R}$	Ricci scalar curvature
T	torsion tensor
R^l_{ijk}	components of Riemann curvature tensor of type (1,3)
R_{ijkl}	components of covariant Riemann curvature tensor, type (0,4)
$\hat{R}_{ij}$	components of Ricci curvature tensor $\hat{R}$
$\|\cdot\|_p$	p-norm
l^p	p^{th} power summable sequence space
$L^p[a,b]$	Lebesgue space of functions
$\sup(A)$	supremum of $A \subset \mathbb{R}$, least upper bound of $A \subset \mathbb{R}$
$\inf(A)$	infimum of $A \subset \mathbb{R}$, greatest lower bound of $A \subset \mathbb{R}$

Chapter 0

Mathematical Structures

Let X be a set. Call it Y.

— *Mary Ellen Rudin*[1]

---

[1]According to Steven G. Krantz [Krantz (1996)], p. 15.

Reading Guide. This chapter gives a brief overview of mathematical structures. The structure point of view, advocated by the Bourbaki school, is very beneficial in organizing and understanding abstract systems. Take manifolds for example (Part III Chap. 2). A manifold may be endowed with different structures. Manifolds with topological structures alone are the topological manifolds (Chap. 2 §1). They may be endowed with additional structures, like differential structures (Chap. 2 §2 differentiable manifolds), metric structures (Chap. 2 §3 Riemannian manifolds) or other geometric structures (Chap. 2 §4 affinely-connected manifolds).

§1   Branches of Mathematics

Modern mathematics consists of many branches and subbranches organized into a hierarchy. There is a misconception that mathematics is abstract, useless and unrelated to reality, as shown in the saying "A mathematician is a blind man in a dark room looking for a black cat which isn't there." Well, abstract? That part is correct. Useless and unrelated to reality? That is wrong. A simple proof is the fact that you are reading this page in this book, in need of concepts and tools which that "blind man in a dark room" created, to apply them in your work and research in the real world.

To begin a long expedition, it is good to have a bird-eye view of these branches and the organization or classification of mathematics into these branches. We would like to zoom out and have a big picture of the classification of mathematics. We may want to zoom out even further to look at the classification methods at large. What is a classification? Are there different types of classifications? Is there a classification of classifications?

With some observations, we find that there are really two different types of classifications. One is heuristic classification and the other is systematic classification.

Take the film genres for example. The following are some familiar film genres: documentary, drama, biography, romance, western, action, comedy, horror, animation, history, fantasy, family, musical, mystery, spy, detective, science fiction, suspense, war ... This classification is heuristic. There is no strict criterion according to which the movies are classified. This kind of classification is also used in machine learning. It is also called "clustering". In Figure 0.1, we represent each movie with a point. Somehow, we have a vague concept of similarity between two different movies, which is represented by the distance between the points. To classify these movies is to group these points into clusters. The distance between two points in the same cluster tends to be small while the distance between two points in different clusters tends to be bigger. Different clusters may overlap and the boundary between clusters may not be clear-cut . There also may be points that do not fall in any of these clusters. In such a case, an easy remedy would be to establish a new category, named "other", for those outliers.

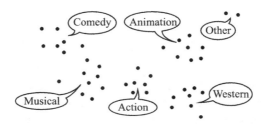

Figure 0.1   Movie genres as clusters.

Traditionally, mathematics is classified to include three big branches: algebra, geometry and analysis. This classification is obviously heuristic. It is very similar to the classification of film genres.

In the early history of human civilization, mathematics started with counting the numbers. So in the very beginning, mathematics was all about numbers. In ancient Greece, Pythagoras has an influential maxim "All things are numbers". The word "mathematics" comes from Greek, meaning learning, study, or science. The word for mathematics in Chinese is *shùxüé*, which literally means the "knowledge of numbers". Basically, algebra is an extension to the study of numbers, where symbols are used to substitute for numbers. The word "algebra" has an Arabic origin, referring to transpose of terms in the process of solving equations. The word "algebra" in Chinese is *dàishù*, literally meaning "substituting for numbers".

The ancient Greeks had a systematic study of geometrical figures and that became part of mathematics, which is very different from the study of numbers. With this addition, mathematics consisted of two branches, algebra and geometry.

This was the case until the 17th century. In the 17th century, Newton and Leibniz invented calculus, motivated by the study of rate of change, like velocity and the tangent of curves. The new study reached a peak in the 18th century and it was known as infinitesimal calculus or infinitesimal analysis, where they make use of something called infinitesimal, which is supposed to be a non-zero quantity that is less than any positive real number (How can this be possible?). The infinitesimal was a kind of vague language at that time but a very powerful tool. For example, it can be used to find the value of π to infinite precision. Before the advent of infinitesimal analysis, ancient cultures took great struggles, and great pride, to find the approximate values of π, to a good precision. Using infinitesimal analysis, many formulas to calculate π using infinite series or infinite product were discovered. Leibniz discovered

$$\pi = \frac{4}{1} - \frac{4}{3} + \frac{4}{5} - \frac{4}{7} + \frac{4}{9} - \frac{4}{11} + \frac{4}{13} - \cdots .$$

The techniques used in infinitesimal analysis are new and they definitely give a quite different flavor from that of algebra or geometry. This field has also become known as mathematical analysis, or just analysis. It deserves to be a third branch. One prominent character of analysis, which distinguishes itself from algebra and geometry, is the utilization of infinite processes and procedures, as demonstrated in the Leibniz's formula for π.

Remark 1. Look Ahead — From Infinitesimals to Topology

In the latter parts of this book, we still occasionally use the term "infinitesimal", like in "infinitesimal neighborhood" and "infinitesimal arc length", because it is more intuitive, rather than pursuing the absolute rigor. The idea of infinitesimal is ingenious and intuitive, although it was not described rigorously at the time of Newton and Leibniz, as criticized by Bishop George Berkeley in 1734. In modern mathematics, this illness has already been treated and cured in late 19th century through the work of Cauchy, Weierstrass, Dedekind, Cantor and others. This was achieved by using the concepts of distance and neighborhood, which are the key concepts in topology, a branch of modern mathematics. The key to avoid the use of infinitesimal neighborhood is to define neighborhood rigorously, because any neighborhood contains all the "infinitesimal neighborhoods" automatically, so that we do not have to mention the "infinitesimal neighborhood" explicitly, although in our minds we are only interested in "infinitesimal neighborhoods". This crystallization of mathematical concepts is a long process in the evolution of mathematics. It is an art to refer to "infinitesimal neighborhood" without using this vague term explicitly and I hope the reader will be able to appreciate this art. Topology takes its roots in analysis, as well as in geometry. We will discuss general topology in Part III Chap. 1. The use of infinitesimals was deserted in late 19th century. However, interesting enough, the infinitesimal reappeared, in a rigorous form, in a new field called "non-standard analysis" in 1960s founded by Abraham Robinson.

Now mathematics consists of three clusters: algebra, geometry and analysis. This heuristic classification is still in use as of today. The American Mathematical Society (AMS) publishes a scheme of Mathematics Subject Classification, which is used by many professional mathematics journals today. This classification scheme is basically the heuristic classification system we discussed above, with algebra, geometry and analysis at the core, with some heuristic expansions. The following is a list of the first level areas in the AMS Mathematics Subject Classification:

(00-03) General / foundations

(05-22) Discrete mathematics / algebra

(26-49) Analysis

(51-58) Geometry and topology

(60-97) Applied mathematics /other

Lo and behold, there you see the category "other"!

The other type of classifications is systematic classification, where we have a clear criterion. Each individual object falls into one and only one category, according to this criterion, and there are no outliers. An equivalence relation can serve as the criterion. Each category is an equivalence class. No two categories overlap and the union of these disjoint categories is the entire universe.

One example of systematic classification is the classification of pure substances. Pure substances are classified into elements and compounds. The criterion is the composition of the substance: an element consists of a single type of atoms, while a compound consists of multiple types of atoms.

Mathematicians have been striving for a systematic classification of mathematics also. Georg Cantor founded the set theory, which serves as the foundation of modern mathematics. David Hilbert advocated the axiomatic method. Beginning in 1930s, a group of French mathematicians under the pseudonym Nicolas Bourbaki started their ambitious plan of reorganizing modern mathematics and published a series of books, the *Elements of Mathematics*. They used a point of view—"mathematical structures", as a thread to organize their books, as well as the content of modern mathematics. Each system in mathematics is a set, equipped with some "structures". These structures usually are mappings or relations. A systematic classification of modern mathematics can be achieved using the concept of mathematical structures. We discuss mathematical structures in more detail in the next section, because the understanding of mathematical structures is essential in understanding any modern abstract mathematics.

Remark 2. Cross Link — Structures and Object-oriented Programming

The idea of structures was reinvented in computer science by programmers in 1970s, in the context of abstract data types and object-oriented programming. Object-oriented programming had become a dominating programming paradigm by 1990s. However, because of the separation of disciplines, mathematicians are not trained for programming and programmers are not trained for abstract mathematics, hardly any one realized the connection between the "objected-oriented" programming and mathematical structures. In fact, objected-oriented programming has everything in the idea of mathematical structures, except the obscure and awkward name. From the perspective of mathematics, "structured" could be a better name for "object-oriented" programming. However, in the computer science jargon, "structured programming" is referred to the old programming paradigm which simply means "not object-oriented".

§2   Mathematical Structures

Modern mathematics is built on the foundations of set theory. The universe in a mathematical system is a set of elements, for example, the set of all real numbers, or the set of all points in the Euclidean space. A mathematical structure $(X, r_1, r_2, r_3, \ldots, r_k)$ is a set X, together with any number of relations $r_1, r_2, r_3, \ldots, r_k$. Each relation r_i could be an n-ary relation with a different n, meaning it could be a binary relation, a ternary relation, etc. Any or all of these relations could be mappings, because mappings are special cases of relations. The set X is called the **universal set** (or **universe**, or **underlying set**) of the structure.

Oftentimes the universal set X is also called the **space** (or **abstract space**), and each element in the set is called a **point**. Note that these terms are borrowed from geometry but they are abstract now. For example, in the case of a complex Hilbert space, each point may be a complex valued function.

A group $(G, +)$ is one example of mathematical structures. G is a set and $+$ is a mapping, or a binary operation $(+) : G \times G \to G$ in this case.

A partially ordered set $(S, \leq)$ is a structure, with S being a set and $\leq$ being a binary relation, which is a partial order.

Sometimes, a structure may have more than one underlying set involved. It is called a **multi-sorted** system. We need to make clear each element is from which set in such a case. For example, a linear space over a field is a structure $(V, F, +, \cdot)$, where V is a set whose elements are called vectors and F is a set whose elements are called scalars. $(+) : V \times V \to V$ is a mapping called vector addition and $(\cdot) : F \times V \to V$ is a mapping called scalar multiplication.

Usually, we stipulate that these relations $r_1, r_2, r_3, \ldots, r_k$ satisfy certain conditions. These conditions are called **axioms**. A mathematical structure with a set of axioms is called a **theory of the structure**. The same structure can be equipped with different axioms and hence to form different theories. One example is that Euclidean geometry and hyperbolic geometry have the same structure but different axioms. They are different theories of the same structure.

With this structural point of view, we have a new, systematic classification of mathematics. The study of each mathematical structure makes a branch of mathematics. Immediately we have a rich and diverse spectrum of branches, but we are comforted with the fact that we have a clear criterion for this classification, which is the structure.

In this way, we have a clutter of hundreds of structures as branches of mathematics. For housekeeping's sake, it helps if we could sort these structures into groups, although this sorting may be heuristic itself.

Bourbaki divides the mathematical structures into three major types: algebraic structures, order structures and topological structures. They call these three types mother structures. This classification of structures is obviously heuristic. I would like to suggest a modification of this scheme: we divide all the mathematical structures into two categories: **discrete structures** and **continuous structures**. Algebraic structures and order structures are examples of discrete structures. Topological structures and measure structures are examples of continuous structures. Geometry in the traditional sense is where discrete structures and continuous structures meet. The formulation of geometries with incidence relations give them the appearance of discrete structures. However, topological structures are often defined and studied in various geometries. Therefore, Euclidean spaces and projective spaces, for example, are also considered topological spaces.

We compare and contrast discrete structures and continuous structures as follows. In a system of discrete structures $(X, r_1, r_2, r_3, \ldots, r_k)$, the relations r_i are defined on X, $X \times X$, $X \times X \times X$, etc.. However, in a systems of continuous structures, (X, r) for example, the relation or mapping is defined on the power set $\mathbf{P}(X)$ of X. The mappings are set functions. In the case of a topological space (X, τ), X is the universal set and τ is the topology, which can be viewed as a mapping $\tau : \mathbf{P}(X) \to \{0, 1\}$. For a subset $U \in \mathbf{P}(X)$, if $\tau(U) = 1$, then we say that U is an open set.

Similarly, in a measure structure (X, μ), the mapping $\mu : \mathbf{M} \to \mathbb{R}$ is defined on $\mathbf{M} \subseteq \mathbf{P}(X)$, a family of subsets of X, called the family of measurable sets. Thus, the measure, μ is a "set function" which assigns a real number to each subset in the family of measurable sets. It makes sense to think that continuous structures provide a means to describe the "congregation" of points, whether they are near to each other, or how much "volume" they occupy, by way of the set functions.

From the perspective of mathematical logic, continuous structures need higher order predicate logic to describe, than discrete structures because they involve subsets.

2.1   Discrete Structures

Algebraic structures and order structures are two examples of discrete structures.

Algebraic Structures

Let X be the universal set. An algebraic structure $(X, \varphi_1, \varphi_2, \ldots, \varphi_k)$ usually has one or more mappings, $\varphi_1, \varphi_2, \ldots, \varphi_k$, most of the times binary operations, in place of those relations in $(X, r_1, r_2, \ldots, r_k)$. A mapping $\varphi : X \times X \to X$ is also called a binary operation. Examples of algebraic structures include groups, rings, fields, linear spaces, algebras over a field, tensor algebras, exterior algebras and geometric algebras.

Order Structures

An order structure is a structure $(X, \leq)$, where $\leq$ is a partial order. The order $\leq$ is in natural numbers as well as in real numbers and many other number systems. Number systems $\mathbb{N}$, $\mathbb{Z}$, $\mathbb{Q}$, and $\mathbb{R}$ all have total orders.

Some systems have a partial order. The partial order must satisfy certain axioms. These order structures include lattices and Boolean algebras.

2.2   Continuous Structures

Topological structures and measure structures are two examples of continuous structures.

Topological Structures

The concept at the center of topology is the concept of continuity. The key concept to describe continuity is "near" or "neighborhood". A topological structure $(X, \mathbf{O})$ is a structure, in which a family $\mathbf{O}$ of "open sets" are specified. Using the concept of open set, all the familiar concepts we have encountered in analysis, like neighborhood, limit, continuous mapping, can be defined.

The topological structure can be viewed as a set function, namely the characteristic function of $\mathbf{O}$, $\tau : \mathbf{P}(X) \to \{0, 1\}$ on the power set $\mathbf{P}(X)$. A subset $U \in \mathbf{O}$ if and only if $\tau(U) = 1$.

Measure Structures

The concept of measure is the generalization of length, area and volume. In a measure space $(X, \mathbf{M}, \mu)$, X is a nonempty set as the universal set.

$\mathbf{M} \subseteq \mathbf{P}(X)$ is a family of "good-natured" subsets of X. Here "good-natured" is in a different sense from that "good-natured" in the context of topology. $\mathbf{M}$ is the family of all measurable sets. $\mu : \mathbf{M} \to \mathbb{R}$ is a set function called the measure, which assigns a real number to each set in $\mathbf{M}$. The specification of the family $\mathbf{M}$ of measurable sets can also be defined by its characteristic function, which is a set function, $m : \mathbf{P}(X) \to \{0, 1\}$. A is a measurable set if and only if $m(A) = 1$.

Topological structures and measure structures are quite different. What they have in common is that these structures are defined on a family of subsets of X, instead of on X itself. That is the reason they are considered as continuous structures. This makes sense with our intuition because the concept of continuity deals with congregation of elements of sets.

2.3 Mixed Structures

Many systems have a mixture of multiple structures. Take the real numbers $\mathbb{R}$ for example. $\mathbb{R}$ has all these types of structures: algebraic structure, order structure, topological structure and measure structure. $\mathbb{R}$ has two binary operations, addition and multiplication. $\mathbb{R}$ has an order structure with a total order $\leq$. $\mathbb{R}$ also has a topological structure, as a complete metric space, with open sets being arbitrary union of open intervals. Furthermore, Lebesgue measure as the measure structure, which is the generalization of length, is defined on $\mathbb{R}$. From the structure point of view, $\mathbb{R}$ can be characterized as "complete Archimedean ordered field".

§3   Axiomatic Systems and Models

Rigor is at the heart of mathematics. All the terms used in mathematics should be precisely defined. However, to define a new term, we need to use old terms. To define the old terms, we need to use even older terms. Albert Einstein once supposedly told a story:

> On a hot summer day, I was walking with a blind friend. I saw a small shop by the roadside. I said: "Why don't we stop by and have a cup of milk?"
> My blind friend asked: "What is milk?"
> "Milk is a white liquid." I answered.
> "Liquid I know. But what is white?"
> "White is the color of the feathers of a swan."
> "Feathers I know. But what is a swan?"

"A swan is a kind of bird with a crooked neck."

"Neck I know. But what is crooked?"

At this point, I grew impatient. I grabbed his arm and said, "Look, this is straight." And then I bent his arm and said: "This is crooked."

"Oh!" My friend uttered. "Now I understand. Let's walk in and have a cup of milk."

This shows that the chain of definitions cannot go on forever indefinitely. We cannot use cyclic definitions either. Look at the following definitions and we know why cyclic definitions won't work:

Definition: The radius of a circle is one half of the diameter.

Definition: The diameter of a circle is two times the radius.

In the *Elements*, Euclid tried to define all the terms. For example, the following are a few definitions from the *Elements*:

A point is that which has no part.

A line is breadthless length.

A straight line is a line which lies evenly with the points on itself.

A surface is that which has length and breadth only.

A plane surface is a surface which lies evenly with the straight lines on itself.

Obviously these are not good definitions without *part, breadthless length,* and *lies evenly* being defined, and Euclid himself did not use any of these definitions in the proofs in the *Elements*. In mathematics, we have to live with the fact that some terms cannot be defined. These terms are called **undefined terms**, or **primitive terms**. All other terms can be defined using these primitive terms. In the Einstein's story, "crooked" is an undefined term, and "milk" is defined using "crooked".

The similar reasoning applies to the proof process. To prove a theorem, we need to use the old proved theorems, and to prove those old theorems, we need even older theorems. This process cannot go on forever and we have to stop somewhere, where we select a group of statements and we assume they are true. This group of hypotheses are called **axioms**.

The ancient view and the modern view of axioms are different. In the ancient times, people thought axioms were self evident truth about the world, which do not need to be proved, like the postulates in Euclid's *Elements*. In modern times, these axioms are viewed as just arbitrary assumptions. It was an interesting new chapter in mathematics history that Lobachevsky and Bolyai negated one axiom, the axiom of parallels in the Euclidean geometry and created a new geometry — hyperbolic geometry.

In the view of formalists, represented by David Hilbert, those terms are just meaningless symbols. According to Hilbert, it would be the same if we replace "points", "lines" and "planes" by "tables", "chairs" and "beermugs". When we associate these abstract symbols with meaning, we have an **interpretation**, or a **model** of the system.

In an axiomatic system, we have a set of undefined terms and a set of undefined relations. For example, in the Hilbert's system of Euclidean geometry—$(P, L, \Pi, r_1, r_2, r_3, r_4, r_5)$, P is the set of "points"; L is the set of "lines" and Π is the set of "planes". These are undefined terms. The undefined relations include r_1: a point "lies on" a line; r_2: a point "lies on" a plane; r_3: a point is "between" two other points; r_4: a line segment is "congruent to" another line segment; and r_5: one angle is "congruent to" another angle.

One question rises. If we keep the fundamental terms undefined, may different people have different understanding of those terms? Will mathematics be built on the foundations of sand?

For example, what is a straight line? It is undefined. What if for a line, some people thinks it is straight while other people think it is curved? Do we debate and fight like politicians do?

We do have tests to determine whether a line is straight or not. We use the axioms. A straight line should behave in a way that is stipulated by the axioms.

This leads to the modern view of axioms. They can be regarded as the definitions of those undefined terms. That is, the axioms are just "disguised definitions". This view is often attributed to Henri Poincaré [Poincaré (1899)], but in fact it was expressed much earlier by José Gergonne [Gergonne (1818)]. Gergonne regarded the axioms as "implicit definitions".

In Euclidean geometry, the axiom of parallels says that in a plane, passing through a point P not lying on a line l, there is at most one line parallel to l. However, in hyperbolic geometry, the axiom of parallels claims there exist at least two such lines passing through P and not intersecting l. Hyperbolic geometry is a sound geometry just as Euclidean geometry is sound. Now we find a reason to explain this. It is simply because that the term of straight line is undefined. The axioms of Euclidean geometry and the axioms of hyperbolic geometry are basically two different definitions of straight lines. The hyperbolic straight lines in hyperbolic geometry are simply curves in the Euclidean sense. This is demonstrated in the many models, like Poincaré disk model, or Gans model. It is also true that the Euclidean straight lines are curves according to the axiomatic definition of hyperbolic geometry.

This is the reason, for example, in group theory, the statements about those operations in a group, like the associative law, etc., are called axioms of groups in some books, while they are called the definition of groups in some other books.

Remark 3. Philosophy — Is Mathematics Discovery or Invention?

In history, there has been an age-long debate: is mathematics discovery or invention? Charles Hermite believed that "numbers and functions of analysis are not the arbitrary result of our minds; I think that they exist outside of us, with the same character of necessity as the things of objective reality, and we meet them or discover them, and study them, as do the physicists, the chemists and the zoologists", while some other mathematicians believed mathematics is an invention of our minds.

Modern mathematics is liberated from the traditional obligation of discovering the absolute truth about the real world we live in. This gives mathematics great freedom to build its own systems as a man-made universe. I personally think now we can put this debate to an end by saying "It is both! Mathematics is both invention and discovery." In modern mathematics we invent those abstract systems first (we do this by abstraction—extracting the essential properties from concrete systems and discard the rest), and then we set out on expedition to discover the structures in the new territories we just created. The invention is easy (or at least it seems to be so. It may not be really so.) However, the easy invention using the method of generalization and abstraction often gives us expansive unknown territory which may take tremendously painstaking effort to discover the structures in these new inventions.

The set of axioms in an axiomatic system need to have some of the following three properties:

(1) Consistency. A set of axioms is consistent if no contradiction can be reached as a logical consequence of these axioms. Now that the axioms have lost their value as absolute truth, consistency seems to be a minimal requirement.

How do we demonstrate, or prove that a set of axioms are consistent? We use models. We can show an axiomatic system is consistent if we can find one model that satisfies the set of all axioms. Here we are talking about the relative consistency. Take plane Euclidean geometry for example. In the analytic geometry, a point in the plane *is represented* by an ordered pair of real numbers (x, y) as coordinates. A straight line *is represented* by the set of all ordered pairs of real numbers (x, y) that satisfy an equation $ax + by + c = 0$. This is a practical technique invented by Descartes. However, when Hilbert studies the axioms of Euclidean geometry, he states a point *is* (or *is interpreted* to be) an ordered pair of real numbers (x, y), and a straight line *is* (or *is interpreted* to be) the set of all ordered pairs of real numbers (x, y) that satisfy an equation $ax + by + c = 0$. With this interpretation (or model), he demonstrates, the points and straight lines so defined (or so interpreted) satisfy all the axioms of Euclidean geometry. Hence if there is any contradiction in Euclidean geometry, this contradiction can be translated to a contradiction in the system of real numbers. Therefore, if we trust that the system of real numbers is consistent, then Euclidean geometry is consistent.

Eugenio Beltrami was the first to give models of non-Euclidean geometry and hence settled the consistency problem of non-Euclidean geometry. It is demonstrated that if Euclidean geometry is consistent, then so is hyperbolic non-Euclidean geometry.

(2) Independence. If we say one axiom is independent of the other axioms in an axiomatic system, we mean that this axiom is not a logical conclusion of other axioms. It is not absolutely necessary to require that all the axioms are independent in an axiomatic system. Requiring each axiom to be independent of others can keep the system minimal. Having the redundant axioms in the system is for more convenience, or better symmetric looking, for mnemonic purposes.

To demonstrate that one axiom A is independent of other axioms in the system, it suffices to show that both A and $\neg$A are consistent with other axioms in the system.

In the history of geometry, mathematicians conjectured that Euclid's fifth axiom, the axiom of parallels, could be a consequence of other axioms, because it is lengthier and does not look like simple and evident truth as other axioms. Great efforts of many great minds were put into the endeavor of proving this conjecture. At the end, it was shown instead that the conjecture was wrong and the axiom of parallels is independent of other axioms. This led to the discovery of a new geometry, non-Euclidean geometry, or hyperbolic geometry.

As an example, in Part I Chap. 1, we choose to show that one of the axioms of linear spaces, $1v = v$, is independent of other axioms by giving a model.

(3) Completeness. We say an axiomatic system is complete, if any statement can be proved, or disproved in the system. Some axiomatic systems are complete, like Euclidean geometry, but some other systems are not, like groups and the Peano system of natural numbers. Completeness is not an absolute requirement for axiomatic systems either. For example, the axioms of groups is not complete and this is just fine, because we have a variety of groups that are not isomorphic to each other. However, for the

Peano system of natural numbers, mathematicians including Hilbert, the advocate of axiomatic methods, rather wished it to be complete to uniquely characterize the natural number system. It was to most mathematicians dismay and disappointment that Kurt Gödel proved that the first order Peano system of natural numbers is incomplete and it cannot be made complete by adding more axioms to it.

That an axiomatic system is incomplete means that there are statements independent of those axioms. Recall that the axioms in a system can be viewed as implicit definitions of the primitive terms. So in an incomplete axiomatic system the definitions are incomplete, or not precise enough to have all the questions regarding the primitive terms to have a definitive "yes" or "no" answer. See Remark 2 in Part III Chap. 3 regarding the independence of continuum hypothesis in ZFC set theory. P. Cohen's explanation of this independence result is that "The notion of a set is too vague for the continuum hypothesis to have a positive or negative answer." Take geometry for another example. Absolute geometry is Euclidean geometry with the axiom of parallels removed. Euclid's axiom of parallels is independent of the axioms of absolute geometry (see Part II Chap. 3). If we take the axioms in absolute geometry as the definition of straight lines, we must say the concept of a straight line as defined by the axioms of absolute geometry is too vague for some questions, like the one that involves the number of parallel lines, to have a definitive answer.

A strong character of modern mathematics is abstract. However, if we look in the history of mathematics, all the abstract systems come from the study of those concrete systems, namely those models. This is similar to abstract art. Pablo Picasso said: "There is no abstract art. You must always start with something. Afterward you can remove all traces of reality." Regarding the methods of learning abstract mathematics, we cannot emphasize enough on the models and examples. The development of abstract theory comes from concrete examples. The concrete examples are also essential in learning and understanding the abstract systems.

PART I
ALGEBRA

William R. Hamilton

(1805 – 1865)

J. Willard Gibbs

(1839 – 1903)

Giuseppe Peano

(1858 – 1932)

G. Ricci-Curbastro

(1853 – 1925)

Hermann Grassmann

(1809 – 1877)

William K. Clifford

(1845 – 1879)

Chapter 1

Linear Algebra

Professor: "Give me an example of a vector space."
Student: "V."

— name unknown

Reading Guide. In case you did not read the preface, the preface chased you down here. That is, I copied a couple of sentences from there to here about how to read this book: This book is not intended to be read from the first page to the last page in the sequential order. You can start with any part, any chapter and feel free to skip around. See the chapter dependency chart in the front of the book. If you are familiar with linear algebra, you may skip this chapter and move on to read other chapters of your interest. You may come back to this chapter for reference on some concepts. This chapter discusses the fundamental concepts of linear spaces and linear mappings. We give a more in-depth discussion of contravariant vectors and covariant vectors in Sections 4 and 5, which will be beneficial to understand the concepts of contravariant tensors and covariant tensors in the next chapter.

§1 Vectors

1.1 Vectors and Their Operations

The concept of vectors comes from quantities which have both a magnitude and a direction, like forces and velocities. They are represented by a line segment with an arrow. The length of the segment represents the magnitude while the arrow represents the direction. When we set up a coordinate system, such a vector can be represented by three components (x_1, x_2, x_3) projected on the three axes, which are called a 3-tuple.

This can be generalized to n ordered numbers, $(x_1, x_2, \ldots, x_n)$, which are called n-tuples. An n-tuple is called a vector, or n-dimensional vector. We will see the meaning of dimension shortly.

Definition 1. Vectors and vector space

Let $v = (x_1, \ldots, x_n)$ be an n-tuple from a field F. We call v a **vector**. The set V of all vectors is called the **vector space** over F, denoted by F^n. An element $a \in F$ is called a **scalar**.

Remark 1. Historical Note — Vectors and Scalars

W. R. Hamilton introduced the terms scalar and vector in 3 dimensions in the context of quaternions.

Most often the field F is the field $\mathbb{R}$ of all real numbers, or the field $\mathbb{C}$ of all complex numbers. In those two cases, the vector space V is called a **real vector space**, denoted by $\mathbb{R}^n$, or a **complex vector space**, denoted by $\mathbb{C}^n$.

We are interested in two operations in the vector space—the addition of two vectors, and the scalar multiplication of a scalar and a vector.

Definition 2. Addition and scalar multiplication of vectors

Let F^n be a vector space over a field F. Let $u = (x_1, \ldots, x_n)$, $v = (y_1, \ldots, y_n) \in F^n$ be two vectors and $a \in F$ be a scalar. The **addition** of the two vectors u and v is defined to be a vector $u + v \overset{\text{def}}{=} (x_1 + y_1, \ldots, x_n + y_n)$. The **scalar multiplication** of scalar a and vector u is defined to be a vector $au \overset{\text{def}}{=} (ax_1, \ldots, ax_n)$.

The vector $\mathbf{0} \overset{\text{def}}{=} (0, \ldots, 0)$ is called the **zero vector**. Notice that we use the boldface $\mathbf{0} \in F^n$ to distinguish it from the zero scalar $0 \in F$. In the future, when we are more relaxed, we will use 0 without the boldface to denote both the zero scalar and the zero vector, which we should be able to distinguish from the context.

For any $v = (x_1, \ldots, x_n) \in F^n$, the vector $-v \overset{\text{def}}{=} (-x_1, \ldots, -x_n)$ is called the inverse of v.

1.2   Properties of Vector Spaces

It is easy to verify that addition and scalar multiplication have the following properties:

Theorem 1. (Properties of vector spaces) *For all $u, v, w \in V$ and $a, b \in F$,*

(1) *Associative law:* $(u + v) + w = u + (v + w)$.
(2) *Identity:* $v + \mathbf{0} = \mathbf{0} + v = v$.
(3) *Inverse in addition:* $v + (-v) = (-v) + v = \mathbf{0}$.
(4) *Distributive law:* $a(u + v) = au + av$.
(5) *Distributive law:* $(a + b)v = av + bv$.
(6) *Associative law for scalar multiplication:* $a(bv) = (ab)v$.
(7) $1v = v$, *where $1 \in F$ is the multiplicative identity in F.*
(8) *Commutative law:* $u + v = v + u$.
(9) $0v = \mathbf{0}$.
(10) $a\mathbf{0} = \mathbf{0}$.
(11) $(-1)v = -v$.
(12) $(-a)v = a(-v) = -(av)$.

§2   Linear Spaces

2.1   Linear Spaces

We take the characterizing properties of vector spaces of n-tuples in Theorem 1 as basic assumptions and the concept of vector spaces can be further generalized.

Definition 3. Linear space

    A **linear space** over a field F is a 4-tuple $(V, F, +, \cdot)$, where V is a nonempty set and F is a field, which is called the **ground field**. $(+)$ is a mapping $+ : V \times V \to V$; $(u, v) \mapsto u + v$, called vector addition. $(\cdot)$ is a mapping $(\cdot) : F \times V \to V$; $(a, v) \mapsto av$, which is called scalar multiplication of a scalar a and a vector v, such that the following **axioms** are satisfied, for all $u, v, w \in V$ and $a, b \in F$.

(1) Associative law: $(u + v) + w = u + (v + w)$.
(2) Identity in addition: there exists an element $\mathbf{0} \in V$ such that $v + \mathbf{0} = v$.
(3) Inverse in addition: for any $v \in V$, there exists $x \in V$ such that $v + x = \mathbf{0}$. We denote $x = -v$.
(4) Distributive law: $a(u + v) = au + av$.
(5) Distributive law: $(a + b)v = av + bv$.
(6) Associative law for scalar multiplication: $a(bv) = (ab)v$.
(7) Identity of scalar multiplication:
$1v = v$, where $1 \in F$ is the multiplicative identity in F.

In the above definition, axioms (1) through (3) state that the vectors form a group with respect to addition. These axioms were first given by G. Peano [Peano (1888)]. Peano also included the commutative law for addition: $u + v = v + u$. Most of modern textbooks still include this, following Peano. V. Bryant points out that this commutative law is redundant as it can be proved using other axioms [Bryant (1971)].

Linear spaces are also called **vector spaces**. There is not a fear of confusion with the vector spaces defined in Definition 1. Linear spaces defined in Definition 3 is more general and abstract. Vector spaces in Definition 1 are special examples of the abstract linear spaces. We will also see very soon that all the finite dimensional abstract linear spaces are isomorphic to vector spaces F^n.

The elements in V are called **vectors**. The elements in F are called **scalars**. A linear space over $\mathbb{R}$ is called a **real linear space**. A linear space over $\mathbb{C}$ is called a **complex linear space**.

Remark 2. Axiomatic Definitions

Definition 3 is the definition of a linear space. The conditions in it are also called axioms of a linear space. So Definition 3 is also called the axiomatic definition of a linear space. In fact, axioms are nothing but the disguised definitions of the undefined terms. Examples of this type of axiomatic definitions include groups, rings, fields, linear spaces, algebras over a field, inner product spaces, normed linear spaces, metric spaces, topological spaces, Hilbert spaces, Banach spaces, measure spaces, affinely-connected manifolds, etc. (see Chap. 0, Section 3).

Remark 3. Methodology — Abstract vs. Concrete Linear Spaces

Apparently the abstract linear space defined by Definition 3 is modeled on the concrete vector spaces F^n of n-tuples, which was defined in Definitions 1 and 2. It is easy to see that the vector space F^n satisfies Definition 3 because Definition 3 contains just part of the properties in Theorem 1. However, Theorem 1 is about the concrete system F^n only and can be proved using Definitions 1 and 2. While linear spaces in the abstract sense is defined by a set of axioms, just like the axioms about "points" and "lines" in Euclidean geometry. The axioms in Definition 3 are a set of assumptions which do not need to and cannot be proved. Any system that satisfies this set of axioms is called a **model** (or **interpretation**) of a linear space. We can immediately see that F^n is a model of the abstract linear space. There exist many other models of linear spaces, which we will show in the following examples. We will also show later in Section 3 that any finite dimensional abstract linear space is isomorphic to F^n, for some n. Isomorphic mappings are structure preserving mappings. We are going to see the precise definition of the term "isomorphic" for linear spaces in Section 3. If two systems are isomorphic to each other, it means that they have the same underlying structure even though their appearances may be different.

Remark 4. Historical Note — Axioms of Linear Spaces

Definition 3 is due to Giuseppe Peano. It is remarkable that he gave these axioms in this modern form as early as 1888 in his book *Geometric Calculus: According to the Theory of Extension of H. Grassmann* [Peano (1888)]. In his book, Peano gave credit to Hermann Grassmann. Peano did not call it a "linear space" in his book, but rather a "linear system". The name "linear space" came much later. Peano was an enthusiastic supporter of David Hilbert's program of axiomization of mathematics. Peano gave axioms to many mathematical systems, including the well-known Peano's axioms for natural numbers. His book did not catch immediate attention while the research in linear systems at that time was still mostly on concrete systems, like Hamilton's quaternions and Cayley's matrices.

In the following, we give examples, namely, models of linear spaces.

Example 1. (Vector spaces F^n) The vector space F^n, defined in Definition 1 becomes a natural model for linear spaces in the abstract sense.   ♣

Example 2. (Arrows in a plane) A vector is interpreted as a directed line segment in a plane. The tail of all the vectors are at the same point O, which is called the origin. We draw an arrow at the head of the vector to indicate the direction. The ground field is $\mathbb{R}$. The addition of two vectors is another vector obtained following the parallelogram rule. For $v \in V$, $a \in \mathbb{R}$ and $a > 0$, av is defined to be a vector in the same direction of v but its length is multiplied by a. If $a < 0$, av is defined as a vector in the opposite direction of v and its length is multiplied by $|a|$. The parallelogram rule was introduced first in physics, as the rule of composition of velocities and forces. It was used by Newton but he did not use the term "vector".   ♣

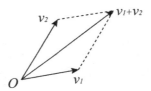

Figure 1.1   Vectors in a plane.

Example 3. (All polynomials) The set of all real coefficient polynomials $\mathbb{R}[x]$ of one variable of any degree form a real linear space with respect to addition and multiplication by a real number.   ♣

Remark 5. Cross Link — Independence of Axioms of Linear Spaces

Property (9) in Theorem 1, $0v = \mathbf{0}$, is similar to Property (7) $1v = v$. Can we use (9) to replace (7) $1v = v$ in Definition 3? The answer is no. We explain why in the following.

In many books, as well as in the latter part of this book, the authors play magician's tricks. They first list some theorems of a concrete system (like Theorem 1, or the triangle inequality of distances in Euclidean spaces), and then say some magic words like "Algebracadabra! We now make these properties axioms and we can generalize to abstract systems!" In the process of generalizing concrete systems to abstract systems, it is not an easy task to decide which properties to choose to make axioms.

To illustrate this difficult distilling process, we listed more properties of the concrete vector space F^n in Theorem 1 than the axioms we chose in Definition 3. Properties (9) and (10) in Theorem 1 can be proved using axioms (1) through (7) in Definition 3. The seven axioms in Definition 3 are independent. Axiom (7) $1v = v$ cannot be proved using (1) through (6) plus (9). To illustrate this, we first show property (9) in Theorem 1 can be proved using axioms (1) through (7) in Definition 3. In fact, we only need axioms (1), (2), (3) and (5).

Property (9) in Theorem 1 says $0v = \mathbf{0}$, where $0 \in F$ on the left-hand-side is the zero scalar, $\mathbf{0} \in V$ on the right-hand-side is the zero vector and $v \in V$ is any vector.

Here is the proof: $0v$ is an element in V. By axiom (3), $0v$ has an inverse, we denote it by x and we have $0v + x = \mathbf{0}$. Therefore,

$$
\begin{aligned}
0v &= 0v + \mathbf{0} && \text{axiom (2)} \\
&= 0v + (0v + x) && \text{axiom (3)} \\
&= (0v + 0v) + x && \text{axiom (1)} \\
&= 0v + x && \text{axiom (5)} \\
&= \mathbf{0}. && \text{axiom (3)}
\end{aligned}
$$

Next we show that axiom (7) $1v = v$ is not provable using axioms (1) through (6). How do we show that a statement is not provable? We use models. If we can construct a model, in which all axioms (1) through (6) are true, but axiom (7) is false, then this shows that axiom (7) is not provable using axioms (1) through (6).

Here is our model: A vector $v \in V$ is interpreted as an ordered pair of real numbers (x_1, x_2). For two vectors, $u = (x_1, x_2)$ and $v = (y_1, y_2)$, we define

$$u + v = (x_1 + y_1, x_2 + y_2).$$

For any real number $a \in \mathbb{R}$, we define

$$av = (0, 0).$$

It can be easily verified, that in this model, axioms (1) through (6) are true while axiom (7) is false because in this model $1v = \mathbf{0}$ for all $v \in V$ instead of $1v = v$.

To play with the axiomatic systems, we can make another axiomatic system by stating as axioms:

axioms (1) through (6) in Definition 3, plus

(7′) $1v = \mathbf{0}$, for all $v \in V$.

We are assured that this system is consistent (meaning free of contradictions) because we have a model. This way, we have created another system, which is different from the Peano system with Definition 3. It may not be an interesting one though, but it is consistent! We could call this system "non-Peano linear space".

The reason we discuss the independence of the axioms of the linear space here is that it can help us better understand non-Euclidean geometry (see Part II, Chap. 3). Non-Euclidean geometry is the geometry created by altering Euclid's axiom of parallels. The reason that non-Euclidean geometry can become a logically consistent system is that the Euclid's parallel axiom is independent of other axioms in Euclidean geometry. We show this independence by constructing models, like Poincaré disc model, Poincaré half plane model and hyperboloid model, among many others.

2.2   Linear Independence and Basis

Definition 4. Linear combination

Let V be a linear space over a field F. A vector $v \in V$ is called a **linear combination** of a set of other vectors $v_1, \ldots, v_k \in V$ if there exist scalars $a_1, \ldots, a_k \in F$ such that v can be expressed as $v = a_1 v_1 + \cdots + a_k v_k$.

Definition 5. Linear independence

Let $v_1, \ldots, v_k$ be k vectors in linear space V. If one of the vectors, for example, v_i is the linear combination of other $k - 1$ vectors, $v_i = a_1 v_1 + \cdots + a_{i-1} v_{i-1} + a_{i+1} v_{i+1} + \cdots + a_k v_k$, then the set of vectors $v_1, \ldots, v_k$ are said to be **linearly dependent**.

A set of vectors $v_1, \ldots, v_k$ are said to be **linearly independent**, if they are not linearly dependent.

The zero vector **0** cannot be in any set of linearly independent vectors because the zero vector is always a linear combination of any nonempty set of vectors. For a set of vectors $\{\mathbf{0}, v_1, \ldots, v_k\}$, we always have $\mathbf{0} = 0v_1 + \cdots + 0v_k$.

Theorem 2. (Linear independence) *Let $v_1, \ldots, v_k$ be k vectors in linear space V. $v_1, \ldots, v_k$ are linearly independent, if and only if, for any $a_1, \ldots, a_k \in F$,*

$$a_1 v_1 + \cdots + a_k v_k = \mathbf{0} \Leftrightarrow a_1 = \cdots = a_k = 0.$$

Definition 6. Dimension

A linear space V is called a **linear space of dimension** n, or n-**dimensional linear space**, if there exists a natural number n such that the following conditions are satisfied.

(1) There exists a set of n vectors in V that are linearly independent.
(2) Any $n + 1$ vectors in V are linearly dependent.

A linear space of any dimension n is called a **finite dimensional linear space**. A linear space which is not finite dimensional is called an **infinite dimensional linear space**.

The linear space F^n has a dimension of n. The linear space of all arrows in a plane in Example 2 has a dimension of 2. The linear space of all polynomials in Example 3 is an infinite dimensional linear space. In Part

III Chap. 3, we will study Hilbert spaces and focus on infinite dimensional linear spaces. In this chapter we focus on finite dimensional linear spaces.

Definition 7. Span

Given a set of vectors $v_1, \ldots, v_k \in V$, the **span** of $v_1, \ldots, v_k$ is defined to be the set of all vectors that are linear combinations of $v_1, \ldots, v_k$, denoted by $\mathrm{span}(v_1, \ldots, v_k)$. Namely, $\mathrm{span}(v_1, \ldots, v_k) \overset{\text{def}}{=} \{a_1 v_1 + \cdots + a_k v_k \,|\, a_1, \ldots, a_k \in F\}$.

Definition 8. Basis

A set of vectors $\{e_1, \ldots, e_n\} \subseteq V$ is called a **basis** of linear space V, if they are linearly independent and they span the linear space V, namely, $\mathrm{span}(e_1, \ldots, e_n) = V$. Each vector in $\{e_1, \ldots, e_n\}$ is called a **basis vector**.

The number of vectors in a basis is equal to the dimension of the linear space. By definition, any vector v in a finite dimensional linear space V can be expressed as a linear combination of the basis vectors, $v = x_1 e_1 + \cdots + x_n e_n$. Given a basis $\{e_1, \ldots, e_n\}$, any vector v can be represented uniquely by an n-tuple of scalars $(x_1, ..., x_n)$. This n-tuple is called the **coordinates** (or **components**) of vector v with respect to basis $\{e_1, \ldots, e_n\}$.

Remark 6. Methodology/Cross Link — Concrete vs Abstract Systems

We started with concrete linear spaces F^n of n-tuples and then generalized it to abstract linear spaces defined by Definition 3. Now we have discovered, when we choose a basis, the vectors in abstract linear spaces can be *represented by* the n-tuples. Have we gone in a circle and come back to the place where we started? The answer is yes and no. The answer is no because now we have two different approaches to study vectors — the abstract approach and the coordinate approach. In the abstract approach, we use a single symbol, like v, to represent a vector. This is the way mostly used in mathematics. The coordinate, or component approach is more often used in physics and engineering. The same is true for tensors. We discuss the abstract approach to tensors in Chap. 2 and compare with the component approach, or the old-fashioned approach in the appendix.

Suppose a vector $v \in V$ has coordinates $(x_1, \ldots, x_n)$ with respect to basis $\{e_1, \ldots, e_n\}$. If we choose a different basis, say $\{\bar{e}_1, \ldots, \bar{e}_n\}$ for V, the same vector v will have different coordinates $(\bar{x}_1, \ldots, \bar{x}_n)$. How are the new coordinates related to the old coordinates? The following theorem answers this question.

We use a shorthand $\{e_i\}_{i=1}^n$ for $\{e_1, \ldots, e_n\}$. When confusion is not feared, we even use a more concise shorthand $\{e_i\}$, with the understanding the index i runs from 1 to n, according to the context.

Suppose the new basis is expressed as

$$\bar{e}_i = \sum_{k=1}^n A_{ki} e_k. \tag{1.1}$$

The matrix A with elements A_{ij} is called the transition matrix from basis $\{e_1, \ldots, e_n\}$ to $\{\bar{e}_1, \ldots, \bar{e}_n\}$. In a compact matrix form this becomes

$$\begin{bmatrix} \bar{e}_1 \cdots \bar{e}_n \end{bmatrix} = \begin{bmatrix} e_1 \cdots e_n \end{bmatrix} A. \tag{1.2}$$

Since both $\{e_i\}$ and $\{\bar{e}_i\}$ are bases for V, the matrix A is invertible.

Theorem 3. (Change of coordinates for vectors) *If the old basis $\{e_i\}$ is changed to a new basis $\{\bar{e}_i\}$ with the transition matrix A defined in Eq. 1.1 or 1.2, the new coordinates $\bar{x}_i$ and the old coordinates x_k of the same vector v are related by*

$$\bar{x}_i = \sum_{k=1}^n \left[A^{-1} \right]_{ik} x_k, \text{ for } i = 1, 2, \ldots, n. \tag{1.3}$$

In the form of column vectors, it becomes

$$\begin{bmatrix} \bar{x}_1 \\ \vdots \\ \bar{x}_n \end{bmatrix} = A^{-1} \begin{bmatrix} x_1 \\ \vdots \\ x_n \end{bmatrix}, \tag{1.4}$$

where A^{-1} is the inverse of A.

Remark 7. Look Ahead — Contravariant Vectors and Tensor Algebra
   Notice the coordinate transformation formula Eq. 1.3 involves the inverse matrix A^{-1} of the transition matrix A. For this reason, the vectors in a linear space are also called **contravariant vectors** in the context of tensor terminology.

Remark 8. Caution — Transition Matrix
   Note that the transition matrix A, which relates the new basis to the old basis, could be defined differently in different books. Caution needs to be taken to be aware

in both Eq. 1.2 and Eq. 1.4, whether the new basis or the old basis is on the left-hand-side, whether the new coordinates or the old coordinates are on the left-hand-side, and whether both equations are written in the column form, or row form, or one in row form and one in column form. For example, the following could be possible alternative but not equivalent definitions of the transition matrix:

$$\bar{e}_i = \sum_{k=1}^{n} A_{ik} e_k, \tag{1.5}$$

or

$$e_i = \sum_{k=1}^{n} A_{ki} \bar{e}_k, \tag{1.6}$$

or

$$e_i = \sum_{k=1}^{n} A_{ik} \bar{e}_k. \tag{1.7}$$

So the transition matrix A defined in one book, could be equivalent to A^t in another book, or A^{-1}, or $(A^{-1})^t$ in other books. We must pay special attention to how A is defined. It helps to call e_i the old basis and x_i the old coordinates, $\bar{e}_i$ the new basis and $\bar{x}_i$ the new coordinates. We illustrate with the first example, Eq. 1.5. This is the same as

$$\begin{bmatrix} \bar{e}_1 \\ \vdots \\ \bar{e}_n \end{bmatrix} = A \begin{bmatrix} e_1 \\ \vdots \\ e_n \end{bmatrix}. \tag{1.8}$$

Then the coordinate transformation Eq. 1.4 should become

$$\begin{bmatrix} \bar{x}_1 \\ \vdots \\ \bar{x}_n \end{bmatrix} = (A^{-1})^t \begin{bmatrix} x_1 \\ \vdots \\ x_n \end{bmatrix}. \tag{1.9}$$

If we write coordinate vectors as row vectors, Eq. 1.9 becomes

$$\begin{bmatrix} \bar{x}_1 \cdots \bar{x}_n \end{bmatrix} = \begin{bmatrix} x_1 \cdots x_n \end{bmatrix} A^{-1}. \tag{1.10}$$

If we write the old coordinates in terms of the new coordinates, Eq. 1.10 becomes

$$\begin{bmatrix} x_1 \cdots x_n \end{bmatrix} = \begin{bmatrix} \bar{x}_1 \cdots \bar{x}_n \end{bmatrix} A. \tag{1.11}$$

2.3 Subspaces, Quotient Spaces and Direct Sums

Linear subspace is also a very important concept, which we define as follows.

Definition 9. Linear subspace

Let $S \subseteq V$ be a subset of a linear space V. If S forms a linear space with respect to vector addition and scalar multiplication in V, then S is called a **linear subspace** (or simply **subspace**) of V.

Theorem 4. *For any number of vectors in a linear space* $v_1, \ldots, v_k \in V$, $\mathrm{span}(v_1, \ldots, v_k)$ *is a linear subspace of* V. *This subspace is called the subspace* **spanned** *(or* **generated***) by vectors* $v_1, \ldots, v_k$.

Definition 10. Quotient space

Given a subspace S of linear space V. We can define an equivalence relation $\sim$. For any $u, v \in V$, we define $u \sim v$ if and only if $u - v \in S$. Denote $[v]$ for the equivalence class of $v \in V$. In the quotient set $V/\sim$, we define

$$[u] + [v] \overset{\text{def}}{=} [u + v]$$
$$a\,[v] \overset{\text{def}}{=} [av],$$

for all $u, v \in V$, $a \in F$. The quotient set $V/\sim$ with addition and scalar multiplication defined above forms a linear space, called the **quotient linear space** (or simply **quotient space**) of V by S, denoted by V/S.

Apparently, S is the zero vector in V/S. If V is a finite dimensional space, then

$$\dim(V/S) = \dim V - \dim S.$$

Let U and V be linear spaces over a field F. We can build a new linear space out of $U \times V$. We call the new linear space the direct sum of U and V.

Definition 11. Direct sum

Let U and V be linear spaces over a field F. In $U \times V$, we define addition and scalar multiplication as follows: for all $(u_1, v_1), (u_2, v_2), (u, v) \in U \times V$ and $a \in F$,

$$(u_1, v_1) + (u_2, v_2) \overset{\text{def}}{=} (u_1 + u_2, v_1 + v_2)$$
$$a(u, v) \overset{\text{def}}{=} (au, av).$$

The set $U \times V$ with addition and scalar multiplication forms a linear

> space, called the (external) **direct sum** of U and V, denoted by $U \oplus V$.

We identify $u \in U$ with $(u, 0)$ and $v \in V$ with $(0, v)$. So we can write $u + v$. It is easy to see that

$$\dim(U \oplus V) = \dim U + \dim V.$$

The linear space U, or the set with elements in the form of $(u, 0)$ forms a subspace of $U \oplus V$. V is another subspace of $U \oplus V$.

§3   Linear Mappings

3.1   Linear Mappings

Definition 12. Linear mapping

Let V and W be linear spaces over a field F. A mapping $T : V \to W$ is called a **linear mapping,** if it satisfies the following conditions.

(1) For all $v_1, v_2 \in U$, $T(v_1 + v_2) = T(v_1) + T(v_2)$.
(2) For all $v \in V$ and $a \in F$, $T(av) = aT(v)$.

A bijective linear mapping $T : V \to W$ is called a **linear isomorphism**. We say that V and W are **isomorphic** to each other, denoted by $V \cong W$, if there exists an isomorphism between V and W.

A linear isomorphism can also be equivalently defined as an invertible linear mapping, because a mapping is invertible if and only if it is bijective.

Under a linear mapping $T : V \to W$, if vector v_1 is mapped to w_1, and v_2 is mapped to w_2, then $v_1 + v_2$ is mapped to $w_1 + w_2$, and av_1 is mapped to aw_1. The difference between a general linear mapping and a linear isomorphism is that a linear isomorphism is required to be invertible and an invertible mapping is always a bijection. We will see shortly that finite dimensional linear spaces V and W are isomorphic to each other, if and only if they have the same dimension.

We have already discussed earlier that in general if two systems are isomorphic to each other, then they have the same underlying structure despite that they may have different appearances. Linear isomorphism preserves linear structures.

A linear mapping $T : V \to V$ is called a **linear transformation** (or **linear operator**).

A linear mapping $T : V \to F$ is called a **linear function** (or **linear functional**, or **linear form**).

Let $T : V \to W$ be a linear mapping. If there exists $v \neq \mathbf{0}$ in V such that $Tv = \mathbf{0}$, then T is called a **singular linear mapping**. Otherwise, it is called a **nonsingular** (or **regular**) **linear mapping**. Namely, T is nonsingular if $v \neq \mathbf{0} \Rightarrow Tv \neq \mathbf{0}$.

Remark 9. Intuition/Cross Link — Active View vs. Passive View

The linear transformations we just introduced are related to the coordinate transformations under basis change (Theorem 3). A linear transformation is a mapping $T : V \to V$ which maps a vector v to another vector $\bar{v}$. This view is called the active view, in which we view the vector v is changed to a new vector $\bar{v}$ by the action of this linear transformation. The coordinate transformations of the same vector under different basis, provide a passive view of linear transformations. Assume T is nonsingular. Under T, the basis $\{e_i\}_{i=1}^n$ is mapped to a new basis $\{\bar{e}_i\}_{i=1}^n$. Notice that the coordinates $(x_1, \ldots, x_n)$ for v and the coordinates $(\bar{x}_1, \ldots, \bar{x}_n)$ for $\bar{v}$ are also vectors. Imagine the inverse transformation T^{-1} of T maps $\bar{v}$ to v, $\{\bar{e}_i\}_{i=1}^n$ to $\{e_i\}_{i=1}^n$, but now $\{e_i\}_{i=1}^n$ is mapped to $\{\bar{\bar{e}}_i\}_{i=1}^n$. If the same vector has coordinates $(x_1, \ldots, x_n)$ under basis $\{e_i\}_{i=1}^n$, then it has coordinates $(\bar{x}_1, \ldots, \bar{x}_n)$ under basis $\{\bar{\bar{e}}_i\}_{i=1}^n$. We could view this as that the vectors are not changed, but their coordinates are changed due to the basis change, or the change of the coordinate system. The active view and passive view apply to affine transformations and projective transformations as well (see Part II Chap. 1).

Definition 13. Addition and scalar multiplication of linear mappings

Let $T_1 : V \to W$ and $T_2 : V \to W$ be two linear mappings from V to W and $a \in F$ is a scalar. The addition of T_1 and T_2 and the scalar multiplication of T_1 by a are defined to be $T \stackrel{\text{def}}{=} T_1 + T_2$, $S \stackrel{\text{def}}{=} aT_1$ such that for all $v \in V$,

$$Tv \stackrel{\text{def}}{=} T_1 v + T_2 v,$$
$$Sv \stackrel{\text{def}}{=} a(T_1 v).$$

It is easy to verify that T and S so defined are also linear mappings and the set of all linear mappings from V to W, denoted by $L(V; W)$, forms a linear space with respect to these two operations.

3.2   Linear Extensions

Given a basis $\{e_1, \ldots, e_n\}$ in linear space V, a vector v can be uniquely represented by its coordinates: $v = a_1 e_1 + \ldots + \alpha_n e_n$. Let $T : V \to W$ be a linear mapping and let $Te_i = t_i$, $i = 1, \ldots, n$. Then T is uniquely determined by t_i, $i = 1, \ldots, n$, because

$$Tv = T(a_1 e_1) + \cdots + T(a_n e_n)$$
$$= a_1 Te_1 + \cdots + a_n Te_n$$
$$= a_1 t_1 + \cdots + a_n t_n.$$

This means that if $T_1 : V \to W$ and $T_2 : V \to W$ are two linear mappings and $T_1 e_i = T_2 e_i$, $i = 1, \ldots, n$, then T_1 and T_2 are identical.

Furthermore, given an arbitrary set of any n vectors in W, we can construct a unique linear mapping $T : V \to W$ such that $Te_1 = w_1, \ldots, Te_n = w_n$. This leads to the following theorem.

Theorem 5. (Linear extension) *Let V and W be linear spaces over a field F. Let $\{e_1, \ldots, e_n\}$ be a basis for V and $\{w_1, \ldots, w_n\}$ be a set of any vectors in W. Then there exists a unique linear mapping $T : V \to W$ such that $Te_1 = w_1, \ldots, Te_n = w_n$.*

This theorem tells us that to determine a linear mapping T, we only need to assign values $w_1, \ldots, w_n$ to the vectors in a basis $\{e_1, \ldots, e_n\}$. The values of this linear mapping on any other vectors can be determined using linear extension.

Definition 14. Image, kernel

Let $T : V \to W$ be a linear mapping. The **image** of T is defined to be $\operatorname{im}(T) \overset{\text{def}}{=} \{T(v) \in W \mid v \in V\}$. The **kernel** of T is defined to be $\ker(T) \overset{\text{def}}{=} \{v \in V \mid T(v) = \mathbf{0}\}$.

Theorem 6. *Let $T : V \to W$ be a linear mapping. Then $\operatorname{im}(T)$ is a subspace of W and $\ker(T)$ is a subspace of V.*

From Theorem 5, the image of linear mapping T is the span of $\{w_1, \ldots, w_n\}$, namely $\operatorname{im}(T) = \operatorname{span}(w_1, \ldots, w_n)$.

Theorem 7. *Let $T : V \to W$ be a linear mapping. Let $\{e_1, \ldots, e_n\}$ be a basis for V and $Te_i = w_i$ for $i = 1, \ldots, n$. Then*

$$\dim(\operatorname{im}(T)) \leq \dim V.$$

The equality holds if and only if $\{w_1, \ldots, w_n\}$ are linearly independent.

The **rank** of linear mapping $T : V \to W$ is defined to be the dimension of its image, denoted by $\rho(T)$. T is said to have **full rank** if $\rho(T) = \dim V$. The **nullity** of T is defined to be the dimension of its kernel, denoted by $\nu(T)$.

Theorem 8. (Rank-nullity) *Let $T : V \to W$ be a linear mapping. Then*

$$\dim V = \dim(\operatorname{im}(T)) + \dim(\ker(T)).$$

Remark 10. Intuition/Look Ahead — Nonsingular Linear Mappings and Tensor Product

We know from Theorem 7 that for a linear mapping, the dimension of the image can never be greater than the dimension of the domain $\dim V$. A nonsingular linear mapping is a linear mapping that keeps its image from collapsing into a lower dimension and hence keeps the dimension of its image maximal. This collapsing happens whenever a nonzero vector is mapped to zero, which is the very definition of a singular linear mapping. The geometric intuition of a singular mapping is that it collapses a straight line to a point; it collapses a plane to a line, or it may even collapse a plane to a point, etc. When we define tensor product, the tensor product mapping is a *bilinear mapping* that keeps the span of its image to a maximal dimension in a similar spirit.

Theorem 9. *Let $T : V \to W$ be a linear mapping. The following statements are equivalent.*

(1) *T is nonsingular.*
(2) *T is injective.*
(3) *$v \neq \mathbf{0} \Rightarrow Tv \neq \mathbf{0}$.*
(4) *$Tv = \mathbf{0} \Rightarrow v = \mathbf{0}$. (contrapositive of (3))*
(5) *T maps linearly independent sets in V to linearly independent sets in W.*
(6) *$\rho(T) = \dim V$. (T has full rank).*
(7) *$\nu(T) = 0$, (or $\ker(T) = \{\mathbf{0}\}$).*
(8) *Factorization property: for any linear space X and any linear map-*

ping $\psi : V \to X$, there exists a linear mapping $\Psi : W \to X$ such that $\psi = \Psi \circ T$.

Theorem 10. *Let $T : V \to W$ be a linear mapping. The following statements are equivalent.*

(1) *T is an isomorphism.*

(2) *T is bijective.*

(3) *T is invertible.*

(4) *T is nonsingular and surjective.*

(5) *$\rho(T) = \dim V = \dim W$.*

(6) *Unique factorization property: for any linear space X and any linear mapping $\psi : V \to X$, there exists a unique linear mapping $\Psi : W \to X$ such that $\psi = \Psi \circ T$.*

Corollary. *Finite dimensional linear spaces V and W are isomorphic to each other if and only if V and W have the same dimension.*

We already had this claim in one of the Remarks in Section 2 by showing each finite dimensional linear space is isomorphic to F^n via using coordinates after choosing a basis.

3.3   Eigenvalues and Eigenvectors

Let $T : V \to V$ be a linear transformation. If there exists a scalar $\lambda \in F$ and a non-zero vector $v \in V$ such that $Tv = \lambda v$, then λ is called an **eigenvalue** (or **proper value**, or **characteristic value**) of T. v is called an **eigenvector** (or **proper vector**, or **characteristic vector**) of T associated with λ.

3.4   Matrix Representations

Let $T : V \to W$ be a linear mapping. Let $\{e_1, e_2, \ldots, e_n\}$ be a basis for V and $\{b_1, b_2, \ldots, b_m\}$ a basis for W. Suppose $Te_i = t_i \in W$. The image t_i of each basis vector e_i has m coordinates under the basis $\{b_1, b_2, \ldots, b_m\}$ and we denote them as τ_{ij}, $i = 1, \ldots, n$, $j = 1, \ldots, m$. Namely,

$$Te_j = t_j = \sum_{i=1}^{m} \tau_{ij} b_i.$$

To write this in the matrix form, it becomes

$$\begin{bmatrix} Te_1 \ Te_2 \ \cdots \ Te_n \end{bmatrix} = \begin{bmatrix} b_1 \ b_2 \ \cdots \ b_m \end{bmatrix} \begin{bmatrix} \tau_{11} & \tau_{12} & \cdots & \tau_{1m} \\ \tau_{21} & \tau_{22} & \cdots & \tau_{2m} \\ \vdots & \vdots & \vdots & \vdots \\ \tau_{n1} & \tau_{n2} & \cdots & \tau_{nm} \end{bmatrix}$$

$$\overset{\text{def}}{=} \begin{bmatrix} b_1 \ b_2 \ \cdots \ b_m \end{bmatrix} [T]. \tag{1.12}$$

The elements τ_{ij}, $i = 1, \ldots, n$ and $j = 1, \ldots, m$ form a matrix, we denote it by $[T]$. Note that

$$[T]_{ij} = (Te_j)_i$$

is the ith coordinate of Te_j under basis $\{b_1, b_2, \ldots, b_m\}$. We call $[T]$ the **matrix associated with** (or **matrix representation of**) **linear mapping** T with respect to bases $\{e_1, e_2, \ldots, e_n\}$ and $\{b_1, b_2, \ldots, b_m\}$. T is uniquely determined by the matrix $[T]$.

Suppose a vector $v \in V$ has coordinates $(x_1, \ldots, x_n)$, and its image Tv has coordinates $(y_1, \ldots, y_m)$, then

$$Tv = \sum_{j=1}^{n} T(x_j e_j) = \sum_{j=1}^{n} x_j Te_j = \sum_{j=1}^{n} \sum_{i=1}^{m} x_j \tau_{ij} b_i = \sum_{i=1}^{m} (\sum_{j=1}^{n} \tau_{ij} x_j) b_i.$$

The coordinates $(y_1, \ldots, y_m)$ of Tv can be obtained by

$$\begin{bmatrix} y_1 \\ y_2 \\ \cdots \\ y_m \end{bmatrix} = [T] \begin{bmatrix} x_1 \\ x_2 \\ \cdots \\ x_n \end{bmatrix}$$

$$= \begin{bmatrix} \tau_{11} & \tau_{12} & \cdots & \tau_{1m} \\ \tau_{21} & \tau_{22} & \cdots & \tau_{2m} \\ \vdots & \vdots & \vdots & \vdots \\ \tau_{n1} & \tau_{n2} & \cdots & \tau_{nm} \end{bmatrix} \begin{bmatrix} x_1 \\ x_2 \\ \cdots \\ x_n \end{bmatrix}. \tag{1.13}$$

The matrix $[T]$ is called the matrix (or **matrix representation**) of linear mapping T with respect to bases $\{e_1, e_2, \ldots, e_n\}$ and $\{b_1, b_2, \ldots, b_m\}$. All the linear mappings $L(V; W)$ from V to W form a linear space of dimension mn. All the $n \times m$ matrices form a linear space of dimension mn. Now by associating a matrix to each linear mapping, we have shown that these two linear spaces are isomorphic to each other.

The matrix associated with a linear transformation $T : V \to V$ is a square matrix. The matrix $[T]$ depends on the choice of basis for V. If $[T]$ is the matrix of T with respect to basis $\{e_1, e_2, \ldots, e_n\}$, the matrix of T would be different, say $[\overline{T}]$, if we choose a different basis $\{\bar{e}_1, \bar{e}_2, \ldots, \bar{e}_n\}$. What is the relationship between the two different matrix representations of the same linear mapping T under two different bases? The following theorem is the transformation law for linear transformations with the change of bases.

Theorem 11. (Change of basis for linear transformations) *Let $T :$ $V \to V$ have a matrix representation $[T] = [\tau_{ij}]$ with respect to basis $\{e_1, \ldots, e_n\}$, and $[\overline{T}] = [\bar{\tau}_{ij}]$ with respect to another basis $\{\bar{e}_1, \ldots, \bar{e}_n\}$. Let A be the transition matrix from $\{e_1, \ldots, e_n\}$ to $\{\bar{e}_1, \ldots, \bar{e}_n\}$ in Eq. 1.2, then the new matrix $[\overline{T}]$ and the old matrix $[T]$ are related by*

$$[\overline{T}] = A^{-1}[T]A. \tag{1.14}$$

---

§4   Dual Spaces

Linear functions are special cases of linear mappings. We defined the addition of two linear mappings and the scalar multiplication of a linear mapping in Definition 13. That definition applies to linear functions also.

All linear functions $f : V \to F$ form a linear space. This space is closely related to the linear space V itself and we call it the dual space of V.

Definition 15. Dual space

Let V be a linear space over a field F. All the linear functions (or linear forms) form a linear space and it is called the **dual space** of V, denoted by V^*.

Remark 11. Cross Link — Covariant Vectors and Tensor Algebra

The vectors in V^* are also called **covectors** (or **covariant vectors**). As a contrast, the vectors in V are called **contravariant vectors** in the context of tensor algebra (see Remark 7). We will see the reason for this naming in the next section when an inner product is introduced and an isomorphism between V and V^* is established with the help of the inner product.

Let $(x, y, z) \in V = \mathbb{R}^3$. A linear function $f \in V^*$ maps (x, y, z) to a real number. In general, $f(x, y, z) = a_1 x + a_2 y + a_3 z$, where $a_1, a_2, a_3 \in \mathbb{R}$. So here the linear function coincide with the linear function in the sense of polynomial function of degree one. We can see here the linear function f can be uniquely represented by a 3-tuple (a_1, a_2, a_3). So f itself is a vector of dimension 3.

Definition 16. Dual basis

Let $\{e_1, \ldots, e_n\}$ be a basis of linear space V. We define a set of linear functions $f_1, \ldots, f_n$ as follows: for any vector $v = a_1 e_1 + \cdots + \alpha_n e_n \in V$, we define $f_i v \stackrel{\text{def}}{=} a_i$ for $i = 1, \ldots, n$. Basically f_i is the projection operator that maps a vector v to its ith coordinate under a given basis. This set of linear functions $\{f_1, \ldots, f_n\}$ is called the (affine) **dual basis** of $\{e_1, \ldots, e_n\}$.

The dual basis so defined is called the **affine dual basis**, to distinguish from the other dual basis, the **metric dual basis** established through an inner product.

It needs to be justified that the "dual basis" defined above is indeed a basis for V^*. Let f be any linear function. Suppose the images of f on the basis vectors $\{e_1, \ldots, e_n\}$ are

$$f e_i = \tau_i, \ i = 1, \ldots, n.$$

For any vector $v = a_1 e_1 + \ldots + a_n e_n$, we have

$$
\begin{aligned}
f v &= f(a_1 e_1 + \cdots + a_n e_n) \\
&= a_1 f(e_1) + \cdots + a_n f(e_n) \\
&= a_1 \tau_1 + \cdots + a_n \tau_n \\
&= \tau_1 f_1(v) + \cdots + \tau_n f_n(v) \\
&= (\tau_1 f_1 + \cdots + \tau_n f_n)(v).
\end{aligned}
$$

This means that f is the linear combination of f_i, $i = 1, 2, \ldots, n$. Namely,

$$f = \tau_1 f_1 + \cdots + \tau_n f_n.$$

The dual space V^* also has dimension n and since all the linear spaces with the same dimension are isomorphic to each other, V^* is isomorphic to V.

Theorem 12. (Dual basis) *Let V be a finite dimensional linear space. The dual space V^* is isomorphic to V and $dimV^* = dimV$. The set of functions $f_1, \ldots, f_n \in V^*$ defined in Definition 16 is a basis for V^* and the following identity holds:*

$$f_i e_j = \delta_{ij} = \begin{cases} 1 & if\ i = j \\ \\ 0 & if\ i \neq j \end{cases}, \tag{1.15}$$

where δ_{ij} is the Kronecker delta.

Notice this theorem is true only when V is finite dimensional. See a good counterexample in [Roman (2005)], p. 84, when V is an infinite dimensional linear space.

If two linear spaces are isomorphic to each other, there are infinitely many different isomorphisms between them. After choosing a basis $\{e_1, \ldots, e_n\}$ for V, an isomorphism $\Psi : V \to V^*$ can be easily constructed. Just define the isomorphism on the basis, $\Psi e_i = f_i$, $i = 1, \ldots, n$, and the mapping can be linearly extended to the entire space V. Since the dual basis is constructed based on projection, we call this isomorphism Ψ **affine duality mapping**. A vector $v \in V$ and $\Psi(v) \in V^*$ are called **affine dual** of each other, $\Psi(v)$ is also denoted by v^* and thus $v^{**} = v$. If $v \in V$ has coordinates $(x_1, \ldots, x_n)$ under basis $\{e_i\}$, then $f = \Psi(v)$ has the same coordinates $(x_1, \ldots, x_n)$ under dual basis $\{f_i\}$. So under affine duality mapping, vectors and covectors with the same coordinates under respective dual bases are identified as the same.

Remark 12. Isomorphisms between V^* and V

Note that the affine dual mapping is defined with respect to a particular chosen basis for V. V^* is isomorphic to V but there is no natural isomorphism between V and V^*. This isomorphism has to be established either by choosing a basis for V (affine dual), or with the help of an inner product (metric dual).

Suppose v is any vector in V and f is any linear function such that $f(v) = a \in F$. v can also be viewed as a linear function on V^*. Namely, $v : V^* \to F$ such that for any $f \in V^*$, define $v(f) \stackrel{\text{def}}{=} f(v) = a$.

Let V and W be two linear spaces, and V^* and W^* be their dual spaces respectively. Let $\Psi : V \to W$ be a linear mapping. We can define the dual mapping of Ψ.

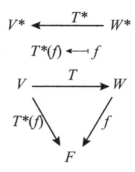

Figure 1.2   Adjoint mapping.

Definition 17. Adjoint mapping of a linear mapping

Let $T : V \to W; v \mapsto w$ be a linear mapping. The **adjoint mapping** (or **transpose mapping**, or **dual mapping**) of T is defined to be a mapping $T^* : W^* \to V^*; f \mapsto T^*f$ such that for all $f \in W^*$ and $v \in V$,

$$(T^*f)\, v \overset{\text{def}}{=} f\,(Tv)\,.$$

See the diagram in Figure 1.2. T^*f is called the **pullback** of f by T^*.

Remark 13. Intuition — Adjoint Mapping and Transpose

The matrix representation of T^* is the matrix transpose of the matrix representation of T. Namely $[T^*] = [T]^t$.

§5   Inner Product Spaces

5.1   Inner Products

We can do a lot of things in a universe as simple as a linear space. However, we still cannot talk about "lengths" and "angles" because we have not built them yet. We now want to add an extra structure in the linear space. That is the inner product. With an inner product, we will be able to discuss the geometrical concepts like "lengths", "distances" and "angles".

An inner product can be defined in a real linear space or a complex linear space, with real linear inner product being a special case of complex inner product space. We discuss real inner product space in this section but complex inner product spaces in Part III Chap. 3.

Definition 18. (Real) Inner product

Let V be a real linear space. A mapping $\langle \cdot, \cdot \rangle : V \times V \to \mathbb{R}$, $(u, v) \mapsto \langle u, v \rangle$ is called a (real) **inner product** (or **dot product**), if it satisfies the following conditions, for all $u, v, u_1, u_2, v_1, v_2 \in V$ and $a_1, a_2 \in \mathbb{R}$.

(1) Bilinear:
   (1a). $\langle a_1 u_1 + a_2 u_2, v \rangle = a_1 \langle u_1, v \rangle + a_2 \langle u_2, v \rangle$.
   (1b). $\langle u, a_1 v_1 + a_2 v_2 \rangle = a_1 \langle u, v_1 \rangle + a_2 \langle u, v_2 \rangle$.
(2) Symmetric: $\langle v_1, v_2 \rangle = \langle v_2, v_1 \rangle$.
(3) Positive definite: $\langle v, v \rangle \geq 0$, and $\langle v, v \rangle = 0 \Rightarrow v = 0$.

Alternatively, $\langle u, v \rangle$ is also denoted by $u \cdot v$. Note, (1b) is not independent and can be derived from (1a) and (2).

A real linear space V together with an inner product $\langle \cdot, \cdot \rangle : V \times V \to \mathbb{R}$ is called a real **inner product space**. A finite dimensional real inner product space is called a **Euclidean Space**.

For any vectors $u, v \in V$, let $\{e_1, \ldots, e_n\}$ be a basis for V and $u = x_1 e_1 + x_2 e_2 + \cdots + x_n e_n$ and $v = y_1 e_1 + y_2 e_2 + \cdots + y_n e_n$. Suppose $\langle \cdot, \cdot \rangle$ is any inner product. We have

$$
\begin{aligned}
\langle u, v \rangle &= \left\langle \sum_{i=1}^{n} x_i e_i, \sum_{j=1}^{n} y_j e_j \right\rangle \\
&= \sum_{i=1}^{n} \sum_{j=1}^{n} x_i y_j \langle e_i, e_j \rangle \\
&= \sum_{i=1}^{n} \sum_{j=1}^{n} x_i y_j g_{ij}
\end{aligned}
\tag{1.16}
$$

where

$$g_{ij} = \langle e_i, e_j \rangle \tag{1.17}$$

are real numbers which form a matrix, denoted by $[g]$. Eq. 1.16 can be written in the matrix form

$$\langle u, v \rangle = \begin{bmatrix} x_1 \cdots x_n \end{bmatrix} [g] \begin{bmatrix} y_1 \\ \vdots \\ y_n \end{bmatrix}$$

$$= \begin{bmatrix} x_1 \cdots x_n \end{bmatrix} \begin{bmatrix} g_{11} & \cdots & g_{1n} \\ \vdots & \vdots & \vdots \\ g_{n1} & \cdots & g_{nn} \end{bmatrix} \begin{bmatrix} y_1 \\ \vdots \\ y_n \end{bmatrix}. \tag{1.18}$$

The matrix $[g]$ is called the **metric matrix** for inner product $\langle \cdot, \cdot \rangle$. $[g]$ must be a symmetric matrix because $\langle e_i, e_j \rangle = \langle e_j, e_i \rangle$. Each inner product has a **matrix representation** just like linear transformations have matrix representations. An inner product is uniquely determined by its metric matrix.

Two vectors u and v are said to be **orthogonal** to each other, if $\langle u, v \rangle = 0$. The concept of orthogonal is the generalization of the geometrical concept of perpendicular. In 2-D or 3-D geometrical vector spaces, two vectors are orthogonal if and only if they are perpendicular. In general, we can define the lengths of vectors and angles between two vectors.

For any $v \in V$, we define the **length** (or the **norm**) of v to be $\|v\| \stackrel{\text{def}}{=} \sqrt{\langle v, v \rangle}$.

For any $u, v \in V$, the distance between u and v induced by the inner product is defined to be

$$d(u, v) \stackrel{\text{def}}{=} \|u - v\| = \sqrt{\langle u - v, u - v \rangle}.$$

The angle between u and v is defined to be

$$\theta \stackrel{\text{def}}{=} \cos^{-1} \frac{\langle u, v \rangle}{\|u\| \, \|v\|}.$$

Let $\{e_1, \ldots, e_n\}$ be a basis for V. If $\langle e_i, e_j \rangle = 0$ for all $i \neq j$, then $\{e_1, \ldots e_n\}$ is called an **orthogonal basis** of V. An orthogonal basis is called an **orthonormal basis**, if $\langle e_i, e_i \rangle = 1$ for all i. $\{e_1, \ldots, e_n\}$ is an orthogonal basis if and only if the matrix of $[g]$ is diagonal with respect to $\{e_1, \ldots, e_n\}$. $\{e_1, \ldots, e_n\}$ is an orthonormal basis if and only if, $g_{ij} = \delta_{ij}$, where δ_{ij} is the Kronecker delta.

5.2 Connection to Dual Spaces

An inner product space V is closely connected to its dual space V^*, because of the inner product structure. We can see this as follows.

First, for any isomorphism from $\Psi : V \to V^*; u \mapsto f_u$ which identifies $u \in V$ with $f_u \in V^*$, we can define a mapping $\langle \cdot, \cdot \rangle : V \times V \to \mathbb{R}$ by assigning $\langle u, v \rangle \overset{\text{def}}{=} f_u(v)$ for all $u, v \in V$. $\langle \cdot, \cdot \rangle$ then becomes an inner product, which is induced by the isomorphism Ψ.

Second, the inner product can induce an isomorphism $\Phi : V \to V^*$. For each $w \in V$, we define a linear function $f_w \in V^*$ such that

$$f_w \overset{\text{def}}{=} \langle w, \cdot \rangle. \tag{1.19}$$

For any $v \in V$, $f_w(v) \overset{\text{def}}{=} \langle w, v \rangle$. This way, an isomorphism $\Phi : V \to V^*; w \mapsto f_w$ is established.

Theorem 13. *Let $(V, \langle \cdot, \cdot \rangle)$ be a Euclidean space. Let $\{e_1, \ldots, e_n\}$ be a basis for V and $\{f_1, \ldots, f_n\}$ be its affine dual basis for V^*.*

(1) *For any $w \in V$, there is a unique $f_w \in V^*$ such that for all $v \in V$,*

$$f_w(v) = \langle w, v \rangle. \tag{1.20}$$

It is easy to see that f_w is determined by

$$f_w = \langle w, \cdot \rangle. \tag{1.21}$$

If we define a mapping $\Phi : V \to V^*; w \mapsto f_w$, then Φ is an isomorphism from V to V^*. The inverse $\Phi^{-1} : V^* \to V; f \mapsto w_f$ is also an isomorphism, which leads to the second part of this theorem.

(2) *For any $f \in V^*$, there is a unique $w_f \in V$ such that for all $v \in V$,*

$$f(v) = \langle w_f, v \rangle. \tag{1.22}$$

In the following theorem, we give the coordinate formulation of the isomorphism $\Phi : V \to V^*$ and its inverse $\Phi^{-1} : V^* \to V$ described in the above theorem.

Theorem 14. *Suppose $v \in V$ and $f \in V^*$ correspond to each other under the isomorphisms $\Phi : V \to V^*$ and $\Phi^{-1} : V^* \to V$ described in Theorem 13. Let $\{e_1, \ldots, e_n\}$ be a basis for V and $\{f_1, \ldots, f_n\}$ be its* *affine dual basis for V^*. Suppose v has coordinates $(x^1, \ldots, x^n)$ under $\{e_1, \ldots, e_n\}$ and f has coordinates $(y_1, \ldots, y_n)$ under $\{f_1, \ldots, f_n\}$, then*

$$y_i = \sum_{k=1}^{n} g_{ik} x^k. \tag{1.23}$$

$$x^i = \sum_{k=1}^{n} g^{ik} y_k, \tag{1.24}$$

where $[g^{ij}]$ is the inverse matrix of $[g_{ij}]$.

Definition 19. Metric duals, metric dual basis

Let $(V, \langle \cdot, \cdot \rangle)$ be a real inner product space and $w \in V$. The covector f_w defined in Eq. 1.21 and $w \in V$ are said to be the **metric dual** of each other. Alternatively, we say that f_w is the **metric representation** of w in V^*, and w is the **metric representation** of f_w in V.

The metric duals of the basis vectors

$$\hat{f}_i \overset{\text{def}}{=} \langle e_i, \cdot \rangle, \ i = 1, \ldots, n, \tag{1.25}$$

form a basis for V^* and it is called the **metric dual basis** for V^* induced by inner product $\langle \cdot, \cdot \rangle$.

Remark 14. Look Ahead — Riesz Representation Theorem in Hilbert Spaces

The part (2) of Theorem 13 is the finite dimensional version of the Riesz representation theorem in Hilbert Spaces (see Part III Chap. 2).

Remark 15. Cross Link — Tensor Algebra, Lowering and Raising the Index

The notation of using upper indices g^{ij} to denote the elements of the *inverse matrix* of $[g_{ij}]$ might be a little confusing, but this is a popular notation in tensor algebra. It gives us a very convenient and unified notation for tensor algebra.

Here we use the notation in tensor algebra: upper indices for contravariant components and lower indices for covariant components. Eqs. 1.23 and 1.24 are known as **lowering and raising the index** in tensor algebra terminology (see Chap. 2 Section 4.4). In fact, they are the coordinate forms of an isomorphism between the linear space and its dual space. This is true for tensor spaces also.

Remark 16. Cross Link — Active View vs. Passive View

In Theorem 13, $f_w \in V^*$ with coordinates $(y_1, \ldots, y_n)$ is viewed as the image of $w \in V$ with coordinates $(x^1, \ldots, x^n)$, under an isomorphic linear mapping Φ. This is the active view.

Alternatively, $(y_1, \ldots, y_n)$ could be viewed as the different coordinates of the same vector $w \in V$ under a different basis — the reciprocal basis $\{\hat{e}_1, \ldots, \hat{e}_n\}$, which we will discuss in the following.

If V is a finite dimensional linear space, then the double dual space V^{**} is isomorphic to V.

Let $\{e_1, \ldots, e_n\}$ be a basis for V and $\{f_1, \ldots, f_n\}$ be the affine dual basis for V^*. Namely,

$$f_i e_j = \delta_{ij} = \begin{cases} 1 & if \ i = j \\ \\ 0 & if \ i \neq j \end{cases}.$$

Definition 20. Reciprocal basis

Let $\hat{e}_1, \ldots, \hat{e}_n$ be the representations in V of the affine dual basis $f_1, \ldots, f_n$ respectively. Namely

$$\langle \hat{e}_i, e_j \rangle \overset{\text{def}}{=} f_i e_j = \delta_{ij}. \tag{1.26}$$

Then $\{\hat{e}_1, \ldots, \hat{e}_n\}$ is a basis for V, and we call it **reciprocal basis** of $\{e_1, \ldots, e_n\}$.

Theorem 15. *The reciprocal basis and the original basis are related by*

$$\hat{e}_i = \sum_{k=1}^{n} g^{ik} e_k,$$

$$e_i = \sum_{k=1}^{n} g_{ik} \hat{e}_k.$$

As a special case, in $\mathbb{R}^3$, the reciprocal basis can be expressed using the cross product and the scalar triple product of vectors.

Let $u = (x_1, x_2, x_3)$ and $v = (y_1, y_2, y_3)$ be two vectors in $\mathbb{R}^3$, the **cross product** of u and v is defined to be

$$u \times v \overset{\text{def}}{=} (x_2 y_3 - x_3 y_2, x_3 y_1 - x_1 y_3, x_1 y_2 - x_2 y_1). \tag{1.27}$$

The **scalar triple product** of three vectors u, v and w in $\mathbb{R}^3$ is defined to be

$$u \cdot (v \times w) \overset{\text{def}}{=} \langle u, v \times w \rangle. \tag{1.28}$$

Remark 17. Historical Note — Inner Product, Cross Product and Scalar Triple Product

These definitions are due to Josiah Willard Gibbs in his book *Elements of Vector Analysis* [Gibbs (1884)], although he used different names, "direct product" and "skew product" for the now called inner product and cross product.

Theorem 16. (Gibbs) *The reciprocal basis of* $\{e_1, e_2, e_3\}$ *in* $\mathbb{R}^3$ *can be expressed as*

$$\hat{e}_1 = \frac{e_2 \times e_3}{e_1 \cdot (e_2 \times e_3)}$$
$$\hat{e}_2 = \frac{e_3 \times e_1}{e_1 \cdot (e_2 \times e_3)}$$
$$\hat{e}_3 = \frac{e_1 \times e_2}{e_1 \cdot (e_2 \times e_3)}.$$

It is easy to verity that $\langle \hat{e}_i, e_j \rangle = \delta_{ij}$ for $i, j = 1, 2, 3$.

Remark 18. Historical Note — Reciprocal Basis

Theorem 16 is due to J. Willard Gibbs. He defined reciprocal basis in the 3-dimensional case [Gibbs (1884)].

5.3   Contravariant and Covariant Components of Vectors

The vectors in a linear space V are also called contravariant vectors. The vectors in the dual space V^*, namely the linear functions on V, are also called covariant vectors. The reason for the names is that in a bases change, the transformation law for contravariant vectors involve the inverse matrix A^{-1} of the transition matrix A, while the transformation law for covariant vectors involve the transition matrix A itself.

The reciprocal basis provides a different perspective to view the covariant vectors. A vector $v \in V$ can be represented by its components $(x^1, \ldots, x^n)$ under the original basis $\{e_1, \ldots, e_n\}$,

$$v = x^1 e_1 + \cdots + x^n e_n = \sum_{k=1}^n x^k e_k. \tag{1.29}$$

The same vector v can also be represented by its components $(x_1, ..., x_n)$ under the reciprocal basis $\{\hat{e}_1, ..., \hat{e}_n\}$,

$$v = x_1 \hat{e}_1 + \cdots + x_n \hat{e}_n = \sum_{k=1}^n x_k \hat{e}_k. \tag{1.30}$$

Definition 21. Contravariant components, covariant components of a vector

The components $(x^1, \ldots, x^n)$ of vector $v \in V$ under the original basis $\{e_1, \ldots, e_n\}$ are called **contravariant components** of v. The components $(x_1, \ldots, x_n)$ of v under the reciprocal basis $\{\hat{e}_1, \ldots, \hat{e}_n\}$ are called the **covariant components** of v.

By equating Eqs. 1.29 and 1.30, we obtain

Theorem 17. *The covariant components $(x_1, \ldots, x_n)$ and contravariant components $(x^1, \ldots, x^n)$ of the same vector are related by*

$$x_i = \sum_{k=1}^{n} g_{ik} x^k, \tag{1.31}$$

$$x^i = \sum_{k=1}^{n} g^{ik} x_k. \tag{1.32}$$

Remark 19. Cross Link — Active View vs. Passive View

Theorem 17 is the passive view of lowering and raising indices. It shows the relationship between the contravariant coordinates and covariant coordinates, viewed as different coordinates of the same vector under different bases.

Remark 20. Special Case — Orthonormal Basis

In the case of orthonormal basis, the reciprocal basis coincides with the original basis and therefore the covariant components also coincide with the contravariant components of the same vector.

Suppose we have a basis change from $\{e_1, \ldots, e_n\}$ to $\{\bar{e}_1, \ldots, \bar{e}_n\}$ and

$$\bar{e}_i = \sum_{k=1}^{n} A_i^k e_k,$$

where A_i^k is the element at the kth row and ith column in the transition matrix A. The new contravariant components under basis $\{\bar{e}_1, \ldots, \bar{e}_n\}$ are

$$\bar{x}^i = \sum_{k=1}^{n} \left[A^{-1}\right]_k^i x^k. \tag{1.33}$$

The new basis $\{\bar{e}_1, \ldots, \bar{e}_n\}$ induces a new reciprocal basis $\{\hat{\bar{e}}_1, \ldots, \hat{\bar{e}}_n\}$.

The new covariant components under basis $\{\hat{\bar{e}}_1, \ldots, \hat{\bar{e}}_n\}$ are

$$\bar{x}_i = \sum_{k=1}^{n} A_i^k x_k. \tag{1.34}$$

We introduced the covariant vectors as linear functions. It is the most economical way to develop the theory but linear functions are more abstract and less tangible to grasp. When the inner product is introduced, we can have isomorphic representations of those covariant vectors in the linear space V itself. Next, we develop some geometric intuitions about contravariant vectors and covariant vectors.

Intuition. (Contravariant and covariant coordinates) The contravariant coordinates (or contravariant components) of a vector are the parallel projections.

The covariant coordinates (or covariant components) of a vector are the perpendicular (orthogonal) projections.

We set up a coordinate system Oxy in the plane. See Figure 1.3. In general, the two axes Ox and Oy are not orthogonal to each other. They make an angle α.

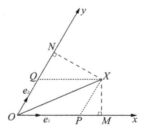

Figure 1.3   Contravariant and covariant components of a vector.

Suppose e_1 has unit length on Ox and e_2 has unit length on Oy. X is a point in the plane. There are two different ways we can equip point X with coordinates—contravariant coordinates or covariant coordinates.

The contravariant coordinates of X are the parallel projections.

Make $XP \parallel Oy$ and $XQ \parallel Ox$. Then the parallel projections (x^1, x^2) are the contravariant coordinates (also called affine coordinates because we only used parallelism but not orthogonality), where

$$x^1 = OP,$$
$$x^2 = OQ,$$

with OP and OQ denoting the signed lengths of segments OP and OQ respectively.

Suppose an inner product is also defined and let $v_1 \cdot v_2$ denote the inner product of two vectors. The matrix of the inner product is

$$[g] \stackrel{\text{def}}{=} \begin{bmatrix} g_{11} & g_{12} \\ g_{21} & g_{22} \end{bmatrix} \stackrel{\text{def}}{=} \begin{bmatrix} \langle e_1, e_1 \rangle & \langle e_1, e_2 \rangle \\ \langle e_2, e_1 \rangle & \langle e_2, e_2 \rangle \end{bmatrix} = \begin{bmatrix} 1 & \cos\alpha \\ \cos\alpha & 1 \end{bmatrix}.$$

With the inner product, we have the concept of orthogonality, or perpendicularity.

The covariant coordinates of X are the perpendicular projections.

We draw $XM \perp Ox$ and $XN \perp Oy$, then the perpendicular projections (OM, ON) are the covariant coordinates for point X.

$$OM = \langle v, e_1 \rangle = \begin{bmatrix} x^1, x^2 \end{bmatrix} \begin{bmatrix} g_{11} & g_{12} \\ g_{21} & g_{22} \end{bmatrix} \begin{bmatrix} 1 \\ 0 \end{bmatrix} = g_{11}x^1 + g_{21}x^2.$$
$$ON = \langle v, e_2 \rangle = \begin{bmatrix} x^1, x^2 \end{bmatrix} \begin{bmatrix} g_{11} & g_{12} \\ g_{21} & g_{22} \end{bmatrix} \begin{bmatrix} 0 \\ 1 \end{bmatrix} = g_{21}x^1 + g_{22}x^2.$$

$$(1.35)$$

We recognize OM and ON are exactly the covariant coordinates (x_1, x_2) as in Eq. 1.31 in Theorem 17.

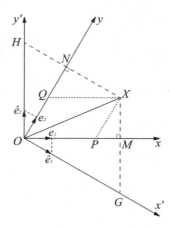

Figure 1.4   Covariant components and reciprocal basis.

Another way to see this is to find out the reciprocal basis $\{\hat{e}_1, \hat{e}_2\}$ explicitly. Draw $Ox' \perp e_2$ and mark $\hat{e}_1$ on the line of Ox'. Similarly, draw $Oy' \perp Ox$ and mark $\hat{e}_{12}$ on the line of Oy', as illustrated in Figure 1.4. Because $\langle \hat{e}_1, e_1 \rangle = \|\hat{e}_1\| \|e_1\| \cos\beta = 1$ and we have assumed $\|e_1\| = 1$, it is easy to see that $\|\hat{e}_1\| \cos \beta = 1$ and

$$\frac{OG}{\|\hat{e}_1\|} = \frac{OM}{\|e_1\|} = OM = x_1.$$

So x_1 is the parallel projection OG of OX onto Ox' but only measured with the reciprocal basis vector $\hat{e}_1$ as a unit vector. Similarly, x_2 is the parallel projection OH of OX onto Oy' but measured with the reciprocal basis vector $\hat{e}_2$ as a unit vector. Namely, $(x_1, x_2) = (OM, ON)$ are the coordinates under reciprocal basis $\{\hat{e}_1, \hat{e}_2\}$.

§6   Algebras

Algebra is the name for a branch of mathematics, as used in "abstract algebra", "linear algebra" or "modern algebra". It is also overloaded to refer to some special mathematical structures, or mathematical entities, as in "tensor algebra", "exterior algebra" or "Grassmann algebra", "geometric algebra" or "Clifford algebra", "Lie algebra", etc.. In this book, in the title of Part I, ALGEBRA, is used in the general sense as a branch of mathematics. The titles of Chap. 1, Linear Algebra is used in this general sense too, as a subbranch. The titles of Chap. 2 through 4 are used for both senses.

A linear space V over a field F is equipped with two operations, the vector addition and the scalar multiplication. If we add one more operation, called vector multiplication $\mu : V \times V \to V$; $(u, v) \mapsto uv$, and the three operations satisfy certain conditions, then it is called an algebra over the field F.

Let us first look at one system, the set of all polynomials with coefficients from a field F. We already know that this system forms a linear space regarding addition and scalar multiplication (Example 3). However, the linear space cannot completely describe the polynomial system because polynomials have another operation which is not present in linear spaces. That is the multiplication of two polynomials. The polynomials with addition and multiplication satisfy the following properties, for all polynomials $u, v, w \in F[x]$, and numbers $a, b \in F$.

(1) Left distributive law: $(u + v)w = uw + vw$.
(2) Right distributive law: $u(v + w) = uv + uw$.
(3) $(au)(bv) = (ab)(uv)$.

This example leads to the definition of an algebra over a field.

Definition 22. Algebra over a field

A linear space V over a field F is called an **algebra** (or **linear algebra**) **over field** F, if V has another operation, called the vector multiplication, $\pi : V \times V \to V$; $(u, v) \mapsto uv$, such that the following conditions are satisfied, for all $u, v, w \in V$ and $a, b \in F$.

(1) Left distributive law: $(u + v)w = uw + vw$.
(2) Right distributive law: $u(v + w) = uv + uw$.
(3) $(au)(bv) = (ab)(uv)$.

The dimension of linear space V is also called the dimension of the algebra.

The three conditions in the above definition is equivalent to that the vector multiplication is bilinear.

Remark 21. Historical Note — Linear Algebras
Benjamin Peirce used the term linear algebra in this sense in 1875 and he used the term linear associative algebra in 1870.

Remark 22. Comparison — Distributive Algebra, Associative Algebra, Commutative Algebra and Division Algebra
The multiplication in polynomial algebra also satisfy associative and commutative laws, which are not required in Definition 22. Distributive laws are the minimal requirement in Definition 22. So the algebra defined in Definition 22 is also called a **distributive algebra** (or **nonassociative algebra**—meaning not necessarily associative). If its multiplication is also associative, then it is called an **associative algebra**. If the multiplication in an associative algebra is also commutative, it is called a **commutative algebra**. Most of the times our study is limited to associative algebras. On rare occasions, we study algebras in which associative laws do not hold, we call them nonassociative algebras. If an algebra is a division ring with respect to addition and multiplication, then it is called a **division algebra**.

Example 4. (Polynomials over field F as commutative algebra) All the polynomials $F[x]$ of a single variable x over a field F is an example of a commutative algebra over field F. The vector multiplication is the usual multiplication of polynomials.   ♣

Example 5. (Square matrices $M_{n,n}$ as associative algebra) All of the $n \times n$ matrices $M_{n,n}$ form a linear space with respect to matrix addition and scalar multiplication. Matrices also have multiplication defined. $M_{n,n}$ forms an algebra with respect to addition, scalar multiplication and matrix multiplication. This algebra is not commutative.   ♣

Example 6. (Cross product algebra as nonassociative algebra) Cross product of two vectors in $\mathbb{R}^3$ is defined in Eq. 1.27. The linear space $\mathbb{R}^3$ with vector cross product as the vector multiplication is a nonassociative algebra over $\mathbb{R}$. The multiplication table for $\mathbb{R}^3$ with vector cross product is shown as follows.   ♣

$\times$	e_1	e_2	e_3
e_1	0	e_3	$-e_2$
e_2	$-e_3$	0	e_1
e_3	e_2	$-e_1$	0

Example 7. (Lie algebra as nonassociative algebra) Let V be an algebra over a field F and $\times : V \times V \to V$ is the vector multiplication. V is called a Lie algebra if the vector multiplication also satisfies the following conditions, for all $x, y, z \in V$ and $a, b \in F$.

(1) Antisymmetry:
$$x \times y = -y \times x.$$
(2) Jocobi identity:
$$x \times (y \times z) + y \times (z \times x) + z \times (x \times y) = 0.$$

The algebra $\mathbb{R}^3$ with vector cross product as vector multiplication is a Lie algebra.   ♣

If we have a linear space, we can define vector multiplication and make it an algebra. To define vector multiplication, it suffices to define vector multiplication on the basis vectors only, and then extend it to all the vectors using bilinear extension. Usually for low dimensional algebras, we can define vector multiplication using a multiplication table for the basis vectors, just like what we did for $\mathbb{R}^3$ with vector cross product in Example 6.

Exercises

1. Using the axioms in Definition 3 (do not use the concrete model F^n in Section 1), prove property (10) in Theorem 1. Namely, $a\mathbf{0} = \mathbf{0}$, where $a \in F$ is any scalar and $\mathbf{0} \in V$ is the zero vector.
2. Using the axioms in Definition 3 (do not use the concrete model F^n in Section 1), prove $(-1)v = -v$, for any vector v, where $-v$ is the additive inverse of v.

3. Using the axioms in Definition 3 (do not use the concrete model F^n in Section 1), prove $(-a)v = -(av)$, for any vector $v \in V$ and scalar $a \in F$.

4. Using the axioms in Definition 3 (do not use the concrete model F^n in Section 1), prove $-(av) = a(-v)$, for any vector $v \in V$ and scalar $a \in F$.

5. Show that the addition group in a linear space must be an Abelian group. That is, the commutative law in property (8) of Theorem 1 can be proved using the axioms in Definition 3. (Hint: use two different ways to expand $(1 + 1)(u + v)$.)

6. Construct models to show that each axiom in Definition 3 is not provable using other axioms (see [Miron and Branzei (1995)]).

7. Let $\mathbf{v}_1 = (1, 3)$, $\mathbf{v}_2 = (5, 2)$. Test if these two vectors are linearly independent.

8. Let $\mathbf{v}_1 = (-1, 0, 2)$, $\mathbf{v}_2 = (-2, 1, 2)$, $\mathbf{v}_3 = (3, 2, -1)$. Test if these three vectors are linearly independent.

9. Let $\mathbf{v}_1 = (0, 2, 1)$, $\mathbf{v}_2 = (2, 1, 1)$, $\mathbf{v}_3 = (1, 3, -1)$ and $\mathbf{v}_4 = (4, 2, 1)$. Write $\mathbf{v}_4$ as the linear combination of $\mathbf{v}_1$, $\mathbf{v}_2$, $\mathbf{v}_3$.

10. Let $M_{2,3}$ be the linear space of all 2×3 real matrices. Find a basis for $M_{2,3}$. What is the dimension of $M_{2,3}$?

11. Let $M_{3,3}$ be the linear space of all 3×3 real matrices, and $S_{3,3}$ be the set of all real matrices A such that the determinant $\det A = 1$. Is $S_{3,3}$ a linear subspace of $M_{3,3}$? Justify your answer.

12. For linear space $\mathbb{R}^4$, let $e_1 = (1,0,0,0)$, $e_2 = (0,1,0,0)$, $e_3 = (0,0,1,0)$, $e_4 = (0,0,0,1)$ be the old basis; and $\bar{e}_1 = (1,0,0,0)$, $\bar{e}_2 = (1,1,0,0)$, $\bar{e}_3 = (1,1,1,0)$, $\bar{e}_4 = (1,1,1,1)$ be the new basis. Find the transition matrix and the coordinate transformation formula for any vector from the old coordinates to the new coordinates.

13. Given a vector $v = (1,1,2,1)$. Find the coordinates of v under basis $e_1 = (1,1,1,1)$, $e_2 = (1,1,-1,-1)$, $e_3 = (1,-1,1,-1)$, $e_4 = (1,-1,-1,1)$.

14. Let $\mathbb{R}[x,n]$ be the linear space of all polynomials with real coefficients of degree at most n, and $T : \mathbb{R}[x,n] \to \mathbb{R}[x,n]$ be the derivative operator. That is, given any polynomial $f \in \mathbb{R}[x,n]$, Tf is the derivative of f.
(a) Show that T is a linear transformation.
(v) Let $T^2 \stackrel{\text{def}}{=} T \circ T$ be the composition of T with itself, $T^3 \stackrel{\text{def}}{=} T \circ T^2$ and $T^n \stackrel{\text{def}}{=} T \circ T^{n-1}$. T^i is the derivative operator of ith order. Show that all T^i, $i = 1, 2, \ldots, n$ are linear transformations.

15. Let $\mathbb{R}[x,n]$ and T^i be defined as in the above problem. Find the matrix representation of T^i with respect to basis $e_0 = 1$, $e_1 = x$, $e_2 = \dfrac{x^2}{2!}, \ldots, e_n = \dfrac{x^n}{n!}$.

16. Let $\mathbb{R}[x, n]$ and T^i be defined as in the above problem. Find the rank and nullity of T^i.

17. Let V be a linear space and $b \in V$ be a constant vector. Define the mapping (translation) $\Phi : V \to V$, for all $v \in V$, $\Phi v = v + b$. Show that the translation is not a linear mapping, if $b \neq 0$.

18. Calculate the angle between the diagonal of a cube and one of its adjacent edges (Hint: use the inner product).

19. Let A, B, C be three points in space with coordinates $(3, -1, 0)$, $(0, 1, 2)$ and $(5, 0, 4)$ respectively. Find $\angle BAC$, $\angle ABC$ and $\angle BCA$. Also find the area of $\triangle ABC$.

20. Three vectors $e_1 = \frac{1}{2}(0, 1, 1)$, $e_2 = \frac{1}{2}(1, 0, 1)$, $e_3 = \frac{1}{2}(1, 1, 0)$ form a basis for $\mathbb{R}^3$. This is used to represent a face-centered lattice in crystallography. Find the reciprocal basis $\{\hat{e}_1, \hat{e}_2, \hat{e}_3\}$. Suppose a vector $\mathbf{v}$ has coordinates $(1, 1, 2)$ under basis $\{e_1, e_2, e_3\}$. What are the coordinates of $\mathbf{v}$ under the reciprocal basis $\{\hat{e}_1, \hat{e}_2, \hat{e}_3\}$?

21. Let $\{e_1, e_2\}$ be a basis for $\mathbb{R}^2$, where $e_1 = (1, 0)$ and $e_2 = (1, 1)$. A vector $\mathbf{v}$ has contravariant coordinates $(5, 3)$. Find its covariant coordinates.

22. Show the three conditions in Definition 22 of an algebra over a field is equivalent to that the vector multiplication is bilinear.

Appendix

A1. Free Vector Spaces and Free Algebras

1. Intuitive Idea

The "free vector space generated by a set X" is a clever and concise way to make the idea of "formal finite linear combinations" rigorous. First, let us look at an example. Let $X = \{\mathbf{a}, \mathbf{b}, \mathbf{c}\}$ with three letters $\mathbf{a}, \mathbf{b}, \mathbf{c}$. We may write the "formal finite linear combinations" of $\mathbf{a}, \mathbf{b}, \mathbf{c}$. Each of these formal finite linear combinations is called a vector. For example,

$$v_1 = 2\mathbf{a} + \mathbf{b} + 3\mathbf{c},$$
$$v_2 = \mathbf{a} - 2\mathbf{b} + \mathbf{c}.$$

We define the addition of two vectors v_1 and v_2 as a formal finite linear combination of $\mathbf{a}, \mathbf{b}, \mathbf{c}$ by combining like terms,

$$v_1 + v_2 = 3\mathbf{a} - \mathbf{b} + 4\mathbf{c}.$$

We define the scalar multiplication of a vector, for example, v_1, and a scalar, for example, 3, as a formal finite linear combination of $\mathbf{a}, \mathbf{b}, \mathbf{c}$ using the distributive law,

$$3v_1 = 6\mathbf{a} + 3\mathbf{b} + 9\mathbf{c}.$$

Then all these formal finite linear combinations form a linear space, called the free vector space generated by a set X and is denoted by $\mathscr{V}_F \langle X \rangle$, where F is a field in which all the coefficients are drawn from. The free vector space $\mathscr{V}_\mathbb{R} \langle X \rangle$ is a three dimensional linear space, which is isomorphic to $\mathbb{R}^3$. The set $X = \{\mathbf{a}, \mathbf{b}, \mathbf{c}\}$ naturally becomes a basis for $\mathscr{V}_\mathbb{R} \langle X \rangle$.

The following is the formal definition that captures this idea.

2. Formal Definition of Free Vector Spaces

Definition 23. Free vector space generated by a set

Let X be a nonempty set and F be a field. The set $\mathscr{V}_F \langle X \rangle$ of vectors is defined to be all the functions $f : X \to F$ that have non-zero values only on finitely many points of X. For $f, g \in \mathscr{V}_F \langle X \rangle$ and $k \in F$, we define the addition $f + g$ and scalar multiplication as follows: for all $x \in X$, define $(f + g)(x) \overset{\text{def}}{=} f(x) + g(x)$, and $(kf)(x) \overset{\text{def}}{=} kf(x)$.

The set $\mathscr{V}_F \langle X \rangle$ forms a linear space with respect to addition and scalar multiplication. $\mathscr{V}_F \langle X \rangle$ is called the **free vector space generated by set** X.

A function $f : X \to F$ is said to have **finite support**, if it takes non-zero values only on finitely many points of X.

For each $x \in X$, we define a function $f_x : X \to F$ such that for any $y \in X$,

$$f_x(y) = \begin{cases} 1 & \text{if } y = x \\ \\ 0 & \text{if } y \neq x \end{cases}.$$

For any function $f \in \mathscr{V}_F \langle X \rangle$, suppose f takes non-zero values at point $x_1, ..., x_n$. Namely $f(x_1) = a_1, ..., f(x_n) = a_n$. Then f can be written as

$$f = a_1 f_{x_1} + ... + a_n f_{x_n}.$$

Hence the set of functions $\{f_x | x \in X\}$ forms a basis for $\mathscr{V}_F \langle X \rangle$. There is a one-to-one correspondence between the elements $x \in X$ and the basis vectors $f_x \in \mathscr{V}_F \langle X \rangle$. When confusion is not feared, we identify x with f_x and hence the set X is exactly a basis for $\mathscr{V}_F \langle X \rangle$. The dimension of $\mathscr{V}_F \langle X \rangle$ is the cardinality of X. If X is a finite set, then $\mathscr{V}_F \langle X \rangle$ is a finite dimensional linear space. Otherwise, it is infinite dimensional.

Remark 23. A free vector space generated by a set X is a special case of a free module generated by a set X. Modules are generalizations of vector spaces. Not all the modules have a basis while all the vector spaces have a basis. A module that has a basis is called a free module. All the vector spaces are free in this sense. A "free-module-generated-by-a-set-X" is a free module in this sense and the set X is a natural basis for the module.

3. Free Algebras

Given any nonempty set X, we can construct an algebra, called the **free associative algebra generated by** X, based on the construction of the free vector space generated by X. To construct an algebra, we need to define multiplication of two vectors. We use the juxtaposition (or concatenation) idea from Gibbs.

Let X be any nonempty set. The elements in X are considered letters and X is called an alphabet. X can be a finite or infinite set. Let X^* be the set of all strings (finite sequences) over the alphabet X. Precisely,

$$X^* = \bigcup_{n=0}^{\infty} X^n,$$

where $X^1 = X$, $X^2 = X \times X$, $X^3 = X \times X \times X$, $\ldots$

For example, let $X = \{a, b, c\}$. **aaa**, **aba**, **cba** are examples of elements of X^3, namely, strings of length 3. $X^0 = \{\varepsilon\}$ is the set of the empty string. We define for a scalar $k \in F$, $k\varepsilon = k$. We can construct a free vector space $\mathscr{V}_F \langle X^* \rangle$ over field F generated by set X^*. We define the multiplication of two strings to be the juxtaposition (or concatenation) of the two strings. For example, **aba** multiplied by **cba** will be **abacba**. The strings are considered "associative". We stipulate the distributive laws regarding multiplication and addition. This way we obtain an associative algebra over F, called the free associative algebra generated by X, denoted by $\mathscr{A}_F \langle X^* \rangle$. It is an infinite dimensional algebra over F. This construction is used to construct tensor algebra.

As an example, let $X = \{x\}$ be a set of a single letter. The free algebra $\mathscr{A}_F \langle X^* \rangle$ is the same as the algebra of all the polynomials $F[x]$ in a single variable x in the form of $a_0 + a_1 x + a_2 x^2 + \cdots + a_n x^n$.

Chapter 2

Tensor Algebra

"In almost all textbooks, even the best, this principle is presented so that it is impossible to understand." (C. Jacobi, Lectures on Dynamics, 1842–1843). I do not choose to break with tradition.[1] — *Vladimir I. Arnold*

[1]Arnold was talking about the principle of least action of Maupertuis (Euler-Lagrange-Jocobi) [Arnold (1997)], p. 246. Books on tensors seem to have a similar tradition.

Reading Guide. What is a tensor? What are contravariant and covariant tensors? The key to answer these questions is tensor product. The tensor product of linear spaces U and V is a new linear space denoted by $U \otimes V$ together with a tensor product mapping $\otimes : U \times V \to U \otimes V$. A tensor product mapping is a bilinear mapping that satisfies the maximal span property. There are different definitions of tensor in different books, the old-fashioned definition and modern definitions. The old-fashioned definition is still used in many books in physics and engineering, while the view of multilinear mapping is used in most of the mathematics textbooks. Lacking an account connecting the two leads to confusions to many students. The old-fashioned definition is difficult for students because it is not rigorous. The modern definitions are difficult for students because they are rigorous, but with a price of being abstract. The reason for the difficulty is in the nature of the concept itself. Tensors involve bilinear and multilinear mappings. Multilinear mappings are significantly more complicated than linear mappings. This also accounts for the reason why it took a long time in history for the definition of tensor to be crystallized from the old-fashioned form to the modern forms. We adopt the modern view while we compare with the old-fashioned definition in the appendix and hope this will connect the dots. The old-fashioned view tends to emphasis that tensors as cubic or higher dimensional matrices are generalizations of vectors and hence more complicated than vectors. Vectors are a special case of tensors. This is a view from the transformation law perspective but the transformation laws of tensors are really not at the root of the concept. What we are going to show is that tensors are not the generalization of vectors but they are vectors themselves living in a bigger vector space. What is new that makes these vectors to be called tensors is their relationship with vectors in another vector space, the base space. The relationship is the tensor product mapping, which is a bilinear mapping, with some extra requirements in order to get what we want out of it.

We discuss bilinear mappings in §2, which will lead to tensor products in §3. We discuss contravariant, covariant and mixed tensor spaces in §4. We introduce tensor algebras in §5, where we can talk about the product of two tensors.

§1   Introduction

The word "tensor" has a root in Latin, "*tensus*", meaning stretch or tension. Literally "tensor" means "something that stretches".

There were two major threads which led to the modern theory of tensors. the dyadics developed by Gibbs and the contravariant and covariant tensors developed by Ricci in the context of absolute differential calculus. We give a brief account of this history in the appendix at the end of this chapter. Tensors have intuition in the theory of elasticity in physics. In fact, the German physicist Woldemar Voigt is credited for being the first to use the term tensor in the modern sense in "The fundamental physical properties of the crystals in an elementary representation" [Voigt (1898)].

Think of the stress forces in liquids and solids. In a liquid, let us single out a small piece of imaginary surface, which separates the liquid on the two sides of the surface, Side A and Side B. Each side exerts a force on the other side (Figure 2.1 (a)). Let us use a vector **S** to represent the surface, where **S** is a normal vector of the surface pointing from Side B to Side A, and the magnitude of **S** represents the area of the surface. Let **F** be the vector representing the force that Side B exerts on Side A through the surface. Because liquids cannot have shear forces, the force **F** must be in the normal direction of the surface, which is the same as **S**. **F** is linearly related to **S**, $\mathbf{F} = \sigma \mathbf{S}$, where σ is a scalar coefficient, which is called the pressure.

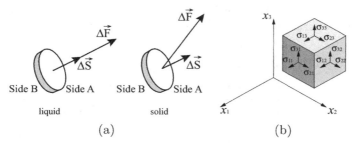

Figure 2.1   (a) Stress in liquids and solids. (b) Stress tensor.

Things are different in solids, like crystals. On a similar imaginary surface **S**, the force **F** that Side B exerts on Side A in general is not in the same direction of **S**. **F** can be decomposed into normal stress, and shear stress (in the tangent direction of the surface). However, **F** is still linearly related to **S**. This relation is a linear transformation: $\mathbf{F} = \Sigma \mathbf{S}$, where Σ is a linear transformation which can be represented by nine components in a matrix $[\Sigma]$:

$$\begin{bmatrix} F_1 \\ F_2 \\ F_3 \end{bmatrix} = \begin{bmatrix} \sigma_{11} & \sigma_{12} & \sigma_{13} \\ \sigma_{21} & \sigma_{22} & \sigma_{23} \\ \sigma_{31} & \sigma_{32} & \sigma_{33} \end{bmatrix} \begin{bmatrix} S_1 \\ S_2 \\ S_3 \end{bmatrix}.$$

Σ is called Cauchy stress tensor. Figure 2.1 (b) represents the nine components of the Cauchy stress tensor.

§2   Bilinear Mappings

Bilinear mappings and multilinear mappings are essential concepts in defining and understanding tensors. In the old-fashioned definition of tensor by

Ricci, the multilinear mapping was implicitly understood but not explicitly stated. In the modern definitions of tensor, the multilinear mapping is made clear and explicit.

2.1   Definitions and Examples

Definition 1. Bilinear mapping

Let U, V and W be linear spaces over a field F. A mapping $\varphi : U \times V \to W$ is called a **bilinear mapping** if it is linear in each variable separately. Namely, for all u, u_1, $u_2 \in U$, v, v_1, $v_2 \in V$ and $a, b \in F$,

$$\varphi(au_1 + bu_2,\, v) = a\varphi(u_1, v) + b\varphi(u_2, v)\,,$$
$$\varphi(u,\, av_1 + bv_2) = a\varphi(u, v_1) + b\varphi(u, v_2)\,.$$

If $W = F$, a bilinear mapping $\varphi : U \times V \to F$ is called a **bilinear form**.

Example 1. (Inner product) Let $u = (x_1, \ldots, x_n)$, $v = (y_1, \ldots, y_n) \in \mathbb{R}^n$. The inner product $\varphi : \mathbb{R}^n \times \mathbb{R}^n \to \mathbb{R}$,

$$\varphi(u, v) \overset{\text{def}}{=} \langle u, v \rangle = x_1 y_1 + \cdots + x_n y_n,$$

is a bilinear form. ♣

Example 2. (Cross product) Let $u = (x_1, x_2, x_3)$, $v = (y_1, y_2, y_3) \in \mathbb{R}^3$. The cross product $\times : \mathbb{R}^3 \times \mathbb{R}^3 \to \mathbb{R}^3$, defined in Eq. 1.27,

$$u \times v \overset{\text{def}}{=} (x_2 y_3 - x_3 y_2,\ x_3 y_1 - x_1 y_3,\ x_1 y_2 - x_2 y_1),$$

is a bilinear mapping. ♣

Example 3. Let $u = (x_1, x_2, x_3) \in \mathbb{R}^3$ and $v = (y_1, y_2, y_3) \in \mathbb{R}^3$. We choose two constant vectors $a = (1, 2, -1) \in \mathbb{R}^3$ and $b = (1, -1, 1) \in \mathbb{R}^3$. Using the inner product in $\mathbb{R}^3$, we define a mapping $\varphi : \mathbb{R}^3 \times \mathbb{R}^3 \to \mathbb{R}$, such that

$$\varphi(u, v) \overset{\text{def}}{=} \langle a, u \rangle \langle b, v \rangle = (x_1 + 2x_2 - x_3)(y_1 - y_2 + y_3).$$

The mapping φ is a bilinear mapping. ♣

Example 4. (Matrix product) Let $M_{m,k}$ be the linear space of all $m \times k$ matrices and $M_{k,n}$ be the linear space of all $k \times n$ matrices. The matrix multiplication $\varphi : M_{m,k} \times M_{k,n} \to M_{m,n}$ is a bilinear mapping. ♣

Example 5. (Product of complex numbers) If the complex numbers $\mathbb{C}$ are viewed as a 2-dimensional linear space $\mathbb{R}^2$ over $\mathbb{R}$, then the complex number multiplication $(\cdot) : \mathbb{R}^2 \times \mathbb{R}^2 \to \mathbb{R}^2$; $(x, y) \mapsto xy$ is a bilinear mapping. If $x = x_1 + ix_2$ and $y = y_1 + iy_2$, then

$$xy = (x_1y_1 - x_2y_2) + i(x_1y_2 + x_2y_1).$$ ♣

Example 6. (Product of column vectors and row vectors) Let $u = (x_1, \ldots, x_m) \in \mathbb{R}^m$ and $v = (y_1, \ldots, y_n) \in \mathbb{R}^n$. We view u and v as column vectors. Namely,

$$u = \begin{bmatrix} x_1 \\ \vdots \\ x_m \end{bmatrix}, \, v = \begin{bmatrix} y_1 \\ \vdots \\ y_n \end{bmatrix}$$

are a $m \times 1$ matrix and a $n \times 1$ matrix respectively.

We define $\varphi : \mathbb{R}^m \times \mathbb{R}^n \to M_{m,n}$, $\varphi(u, v) \overset{\text{def}}{=} uv^t$, where v^t is the transpose of v, which is a row vector, or $1 \times n$ matrix. This is a special case of matrix multiplication in Example 4. The result uv^t is a $m \times n$ matrix with entries $A_{ij} = x_i y_j$. For example,

$$u = (3, 2),$$
$$v = (-1, 4),$$

then

$$\varphi(u, v) \overset{\text{def}}{=} uv^t = \begin{bmatrix} 3 \\ 2 \end{bmatrix} \begin{bmatrix} -1 & 4 \end{bmatrix} = \begin{bmatrix} -3 & 12 \\ -2 & 8 \end{bmatrix}.$$

This mapping φ is a bilinear mapping.

Note that uv^t and $u^t v$ are different. uv^t is a $m \times n$ matrix. u^t and v cannot be multiplied if $m \neq n$. $u^t v$ is a scalar if $m = n$. ♣

Example 7. (Kronecker product of two matrices) Let

$$A = \begin{bmatrix} a_{11} & a_{12} \\ a_{21} & a_{22} \end{bmatrix} \in M_{2,2}$$

be a 2×2 matrix and

$$B = \begin{bmatrix} b_{11} & b_{12} & b_{13} \\ b_{21} & b_{22} & b_{23} \end{bmatrix} \in M_{2,3}$$

be a 2×3 matrix. The Kronecker product $\otimes : M_{2,2} \times M_{2,3} \to M_{4,6}$; $(A, B) \mapsto A \otimes B$ is defined as

$$A \otimes B \overset{\text{def}}{=} \begin{bmatrix} a_{11}B & a_{12}B \\ a_{21}B & a_{22}B \end{bmatrix} \overset{\text{def}}{=} \begin{bmatrix} a_{11}b_{11} & a_{11}b_{12} & a_{11}b_{13} & a_{12}b_{11} & a_{12}b_{12} & a_{12}b_{13} \\ a_{11}b_{21} & a_{11}b_{22} & a_{11}b_{23} & a_{12}b_{21} & a_{12}b_{22} & a_{12}b_{23} \\ a_{21}b_{11} & a_{21}b_{12} & a_{21}b_{13} & a_{22}b_{11} & a_{22}b_{12} & a_{22}b_{13} \\ a_{21}b_{21} & a_{21}b_{22} & a_{21}b_{23} & a_{22}b_{21} & a_{22}b_{22} & a_{22}b_{23} \end{bmatrix}.$$

This is a bilinear mapping. This can be generalized to the Kronecker product of two matrices of any size. If A is an $m \times n$ matrix, B is a $p \times q$ matrix, then $A \otimes B$ is a $mp \times nq$ matrix. ♣

Remark 1. Caution — Differences between Bilinear Mappings and Linear Mappings

Note that although the word "bilinear" has "linear" as a substring in it, and the definition of bilinear mapping is similar to that of linear mapping — a bilinear mapping is a mapping that is linear in each variable separately — there are significant differences between a bilinear mapping and a linear mapping. A linear mapping $f : V \to W$ maps a linear space V to a linear subspace of W. Namely, im$f$ is a linear subspace of W. The geometric picture of this is that a linear mapping f maps a plane to a plane (nonsingular case), or it maps a plane to a straight line or a single point, which is the zero vector (singular case). However, in general the image of a bilinear mapping $\varphi : U \times V \to W$ is not a linear subspace of W. The geometric picture of this is that a bilinear mapping may map a pair of planes to a curved surface or hypersurface in W. In this sense, a bilinear mapping is nonlinear. It is rather like "quadratic". Let us check this with one example that we have given earlier.

In Example 6, bilinear mapping φ is the matrix multiplication of u and v^T. Let us look at the 2-dimensional case, $m = n = 2$. Some 2×2 matrices can be "decomposed" as the product form of uv^T, where u is a column vector and v^T is a row vector but some 2×2 matrices cannot be "decomposed" this way. For example, matrix $\begin{bmatrix} -3 & 12 \\ -2 & 8 \end{bmatrix}$ can be decomposed as

$$\begin{bmatrix} -3 & 12 \\ -2 & 8 \end{bmatrix} = \begin{bmatrix} 3 \\ 2 \end{bmatrix} \begin{bmatrix} -1 & 4 \end{bmatrix}.$$

The matrix $E = \begin{bmatrix} 1 & 0 \\ 0 & 1 \end{bmatrix}$ cannot be decomposed as uv^T. Let us see the reason for this briefly. If a 2×2 matrix

$$A = \begin{bmatrix} a_{11} & a_{12} \\ a_{21} & a_{22} \end{bmatrix}$$

can be decomposed as the product uv^T, where $u = \begin{bmatrix} x_1 & x_2 \end{bmatrix}^T$ and $v = \begin{bmatrix} y_1 & y_2 \end{bmatrix}^T$, then

$$A = \begin{bmatrix} a_{11} & a_{12} \\ a_{21} & a_{22} \end{bmatrix} = \begin{bmatrix} x_1 y_1 & x_1 y_2 \\ x_2 y_1 & x_2 y_2 \end{bmatrix}.$$

If we calculate the determinant of A, we obtain

$$\det A = x_1 x_2 y_1 y_2 - x_1 x_2 y_1 y_2 = 0.$$

This means that any decomposable matrix A must have $\det A = 0$. However, for matrix E, we have $\det E = 1 \neq 0$.

The image $im\varphi$ contain all the 2×2 matrices A such that $\det A = 0$. Hence $im\varphi$ is a 3-D curved hypersurface in a 4-D linear space. It is hard to visualize such a 3-D curved hypersurface but if we fix one variable, say $a_{21} = 1$, then $a_{12} = a_{11} a_{22}$. This can be represented by a curved surface $z = xy$, known as a saddle surface, or a hyperbolic paraboloid in Figure 2.2.

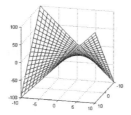

Figure 2.2   The image of one example bilinear mapping is a 3-D hypersurface. This saddle surface is a projection of the hypersurface.

2.2   Bilinear Extensions

The image $\operatorname{im}\varphi$ of a bilinear mapping $\varphi : U \times V \to W$ in general is not a linear subspace of W. However $\operatorname{im}\varphi$ can always span a subspace $\operatorname{span}(\operatorname{im}\varphi)$. What is the dimension of $\operatorname{span}(\operatorname{im}\varphi)$?

Theorem 1. (Bilinear extension) *Let U, V and W be linear spaces over a field F, $\dim U = m$ and $\dim V = n$. Let $\varphi : U \times V \to W$ be a bilinear mapping, $\{e_1, \ldots, e_m\}$ be a basis for U and $\{b_1, \ldots, b_n\}$ be a basis for V.*

A bilinear mapping $\varphi : U \times V \to W$ is uniquely determined by assigning values $w_{ij} \in W$ to mn pairs of vectors $(e_i, b_j) \in U \times V$ $i = 1, \ldots, m$, $j = 1, \ldots, n$, and bilinearly extending it. Namely, for any two vectors $u = \sum_{i=1}^{m} x_i e_i$ and $v = \sum_{j=1}^{n} y_j b_j$, the mapping can be determined by

$$\varphi(u, v) \stackrel{def}{=} \sum_{i=1}^{m} \sum_{j=1}^{n} x_i y_j \varphi(e_i, b_j)$$

$$= \sum_{i=1}^{m} \sum_{j=1}^{n} x_i y_j w_{ij}.$$

Theorem 2. *Let U, V and W be finite dimensional linear spaces and $\varphi : U \times V \to W$ be a bilinear mapping. Then*

$$\dim \operatorname{span}(\operatorname{im}\varphi) \leq \dim U \cdot \dim V.$$

The equality holds if and only if $\{\varphi(e_i, b_j) \in W | i = 1, \ldots, m, j = 1, \ldots, n\}$ are linearly independent, where $\{e_i | i = 1, \ldots, m\}$ is a basis for

U and $\{b_j | j = 1, \ldots, n\}$ is a basis for V.

From Theorem 1, we know that $\mathrm{span}(\mathrm{im}\varphi) = \mathrm{span}(\{w_{ij} | i = 1, \ldots, m,\ j = 1, \ldots, n\})$. If w_{ij} are all independent, then $\dim \mathrm{span}(\{w_{ij} | i = 1, \ldots, m,\ j = 1, \ldots, n\}) = \dim U \cdot \dim V$ and this is when the equality holds in Theorem 2.

Remark 2. Comparison — Bilinear Mappings and Linear Mappings

We see yet another difference between bilinear mappings and linear mappings. A linear mapping $T : V \to W$ can be uniquely determined by assigning values to vectors in a basis for V. A bilinear mapping $\varphi : U \times V \to W$ is determined by assigning values to $\dim U \cdot \dim V$ pairs of vectors. Hence a bilinear mapping can span a much greater space of dimension $\dim U \cdot \dim V$, compared with the dimension of $U \oplus V$ built on $U \times V$, which is $\dim U + \dim V$.

The concepts and theorems about bilinear mappings can be easily extended to multilinear mappings when more than two linear spaces are involved.

Definition 2. Multilinear mapping

Let $V_1, \ldots, V_p$ and W be linear spaces over a field F. A mapping $\varphi : V_1 \times \cdots \times V_p \to W$ is called a **multilinear mapping** (or **p-linear mapping**) if it is linear in each variable separately. If $W = F$, a multilinear mapping $\varphi : V_1 \times \cdots \times V_p \to F$ is called a **multilinear function** (or **multilinear form**, or **p-linear form**).

---

§3   Tensor Products

3.1   Definition and Examples

Recall in Chap. 1, given two linear spaces U and V, we constructed a new linear space called the direct sum $U \oplus V$, using U and V. Here we want to construct another linear space $U \otimes V$, which is called the tensor product of U and V.

There are two different approaches to the tensor product.

One approach [Bourbaki (1942); Roman (2005)] is to construct a new linear space starting from scratch, using U and V, similar to the direct sum space $U \oplus V$ construction process. If we use an analogy, this process is like birds building their nests using twigs. However, the construction of tensor product space is more difficult than the construction of the direct sum, making it more difficult for the beginners to understand. An alternative approach is the axiomatic approach. In the axiomatic approach, we impose some characterizing properties that an existing linear space W and a bilinear mapping $\varphi : U \times V \to W$ are required to have. Then we select those "good" spaces W, together with a "good" bilinear mapping $\otimes$, to be the tensor product. To contrast the bird nest analogy, this approach is like hermit crabs finding existing shells for their homes, instead of building from scratch. Any system $(W, \otimes)$ satisfying those conditions become a model of the tensor product. It can be proved that all these models are isomorphic to each other, and isomorphic to the tensor product space $U \otimes V$ obtained from the (bird nest) construction approach. Hence the tensor product of U and V is unique up to isomorphism and the two approaches are equivalent.

We take the axiomatic approach here, because this is easier for the beginners to understand. Even within each approach, there are many different but equivalent ways to define the tensor product [Wang (1985); Marcus (1973); Greub (1967)].

Definition 3. Tensor product

Let U, V and W be linear spaces. $(W, \otimes)$ is called a **tensor product space** (or simply **tensor product**) of U and V, if $\otimes :$ $U \times V \to W; (u, v) \mapsto u \otimes v$ is a bilinear mapping and satisfies the following conditions.

(1) Maximal span property: If a set of vector X are linearly independent in U, and a set of vectors Y are linearly independent in V, then $X \otimes Y \overset{\text{def}}{=} \{x \otimes y | x \in X, y \in Y\}$ are linearly independent in W.

(2) Generating property: $W = \text{span}(\text{im}\otimes)$.

We also denote $W = U \otimes V$. The vectors in W are called **tensors** over U and V.

Remark 3. Clarification

Note the vectors in $X \otimes Y$ are treated as a *multiset* instead of a regular set, meaning if two vectors in $X \otimes Y$ are equal, they are counted as two distinct vectors. In such a case, the vectors in $X \otimes Y$ are linearly dependent and condition (1) fails. If any $x \otimes y = 0$, condition (1) also fails.

A bilinear mapping $\otimes$ satisfying condition (1) is called a **tensor product mapping** (or simply **tensor product**). The image $x \otimes y$ is also called the **tensor product** of x and y.

I shall call the linear spaces U and V the **factor spaces** of the tensor product space $U \otimes V$. Tensor product is also called **dyadic product**, a term introduced by Josiah Willard Gibbs.

Remark 4. Clarification — The Term "Tensor Product"

The term "tensor product" is used in multiple senses. Computer scientists like to say "The term is overloaded" while mathematicians tend to say "The term is abused". These different meanings are related to one another. So there will not be a confusion under clear context. We give more clarification of these meanings as follows:

(1) The linear space W is called the tensor product space of U and V, or simply **tensor product** of U and V, and denoted by $W = U \otimes V$.

(2) The bilinear mapping $\otimes : U \times V \to W$ satisfying condition (1) in Definition 3 is called a tensor product mapping, or simply **tensor product** for short.

(3) For $x \in U$ and $y \in V$, the image $x \otimes y$, is called the **tensor product** of x and y.

We will find out soon that the tensors in the form of $x \otimes y$ are called decomposable tensors. We should be aware that not all the tensors in the tensor product space $U \otimes V$ are in the form of tensor product $x \otimes y$. Nondecomposable tensors are abundant in $U \otimes V$. The general form of a tensor in $U \otimes V$ is the linear combination of decomposable tensors $x \otimes y$.

Remark 5. Historical Note — Tensor Product

There are many alternative but equivalent modern definitions of tensor product. The early modern definitions of tensor product, not in the same form of Definition 3, were introduced by Whitney [Whitney (1938)] and N. Bourbaki [Bourbaki (1942)], but the ideas trace back to Gibbs and Ricci in late 1800s and early 1900s. We compare with alternative definitions in Appendix A2.

Remark 6. Intuition — Tensor Means "Something that Stretches"

The word "tensor" has its root in Latin and means something that stretches, just like the word tension has to do with stretching. This is the intuition of the concept of tensor.

Theorem 2 states that $\dim \operatorname{span}(\operatorname{im}\otimes) \leq \dim U \cdot \dim V$. That means $\dim U \cdot \dim V$ is the maximal dimension that a bilinear mapping can possibly span. Condition (1) in Definition 3 requires that the tensor product mapping spans this maximal dimension. Intuitively the tensor product stretches to the fullest. Condition (1) is equivalent to

$$\dim \operatorname{span}(\operatorname{im}\otimes) = \dim U \cdot \dim V.$$

Condition (1) implies $\dim W \geq \dim U \cdot \dim V$. Condition (2) and Theorem 2 imply that $\dim W \leq \dim U \cdot \dim V$. Putting it together, we have, for finite dimensional linear spaces U and V,

Theorem 3. *Let U and V be finite dimensional linear spaces. Then* $\dim U \otimes V = \dim U \cdot \dim V$.

The following is an alternative definition which uses the dimensions of the spaces explicitly and hence is limited to finite dimensional spaces.

Definition 4. (Equivalent Definition) Tensor product

Let U, V and W be finite dimensional linear spaces. $(W, \otimes)$ is called a **tensor product space** of U and V, if $\otimes : U \times V \to W$ is a bilinear mapping and satisfies the following conditions:

$$\dim \operatorname{span}(\operatorname{im}\otimes) = \dim W = \dim U \cdot \dim V.$$

Tensor product has no zero divisors.

Theorem 4. *Let $(U \otimes V, \otimes)$ be the tensor product of linear spaces U and V. Then $x \otimes y = 0 \Rightarrow x = 0$ or $y = 0$.*

In the following, we give counterexamples first, followed by examples of tensor products.

Example 8. (Counterexamples of tensor product) Examples 1 through 7 are examples of bilinear mappings. Examples 1 through 5 fail the dimension test, in which the image of φ has a "collapse" in dimension ($\dim W < \dim U \cdot \dim V$) and hence fail to be tensor product. ♣

The bilinear mappings in Examples 6 and 7 are examples of tensor product. Each example becomes a model of tensor product. Examples 6 is an important model of tensor product. We duplicate it in the following. After this we give two other important models of tensor product — Gibbs dyadics and bilinear forms.

Example 9. (Model of tensor product—Matrices $M_{m,n}$) Let $u = (x_1, \ldots, x_m) \in \mathbb{R}^m$ and $v = (y_1, \ldots, y_n) \in \mathbb{R}^n$. We view u and v as column vectors. Namely,

$$u = \begin{bmatrix} x_1 \\ \vdots \\ x_m \end{bmatrix}, \ v = \begin{bmatrix} y_1 \\ \vdots \\ y_n \end{bmatrix},$$

are an $m \times 1$ matrix and an $n \times 1$ matrix respectively. We define $\otimes$: $\mathbb{R}^m \times \mathbb{R}^n \to M_{m,n}$, $u \otimes v = uv^t$, where v^t is the transpose of v, which is a row vector, or $1 \times n$ matrix. This is a special case of matrix multiplication in Example 4. The result uv^t is a $m \times n$ matrix with entries $A_{ij} = x_i y_j$. For example,

$$u = (3, 2),$$
$$v = (-1, 4),$$

then

$$u \otimes v \stackrel{\text{def}}{=} uv^t = \begin{bmatrix} 3 \\ 2 \end{bmatrix} \begin{bmatrix} -1 & 4 \end{bmatrix} = \begin{bmatrix} -3 & 12 \\ -2 & 8 \end{bmatrix}.$$

The mapping $\otimes$ is a tensor product mapping and $(M_{m,n}, \otimes)$ is a tensor product space of $M_{m,1}$ and $M_{1,n}$. ♣

Example 10. (Model of tensor product—Gibbs dyadic tensors) J. Willard Gibbs introduced the dyadics in his book *Elements of Vector Analysis* in 1884. The dyadics are more familiar to physicists and engineers. A tradition in physics and engineering is to write vectors in boldface. We follow this tradition only in this example.

Let U and V be linear spaces over a field F. $\mathbf{a}, \mathbf{b} \in U$ and $\mathbf{p}, \mathbf{q} \in V$ are vectors. For simplicity, we use a special example, instead of the general case. Let $U = V$ be 2-dimensional linear spaces, and $\{\mathbf{e}_1, \mathbf{e}_2\}$ be a basis for U and V. Let $\mathbf{a} = a_1 \mathbf{e}_1 + a_2 \mathbf{e}_2$, $\mathbf{b} = b_1 \mathbf{e}_1 + b_2 \mathbf{e}_2$, $\mathbf{p} = p_1 \mathbf{e}_1 + p_2 \mathbf{e}_2$ and $\mathbf{q} = q_1 \mathbf{e}_1 + q_2 \mathbf{e}_2$. Gibbs defined a **dyad** to be two vectors, one from U and one from V, **juxtaposed** to each other, like $\mathbf{ap}$, $\mathbf{bp}$, $\mathbf{aq}$ and $\mathbf{bq}$ are all dyads. The dyad is just a form. The dyad $\mathbf{ap}$ can be thought of as a "formal product" of $\mathbf{a}$ and $\mathbf{p}$. We can also have the "formal sums" of two dyads, like $\mathbf{ap} + \mathbf{bq}$, and the "formal scalar multiplications" like $k\mathbf{ap}$, where $k \in F$ is a scalar. A "formal linear combination" of dyads is called a **dyadic**, for example $\lambda \mathbf{ap} + \mu \mathbf{bq}$, where $\lambda, \mu \in F$. By "formal", we mean that things are treated as concatenation of strings of symbols while the symbols have no meanings. "+" is just a symbol in the string and has no meaning. We should have used a different symbol, like "$\dotplus$" to distinguish from the real addition. The reason we did not do so, is that under our construction, the real addition and formal addition will coincide.

We define the addition of two dyadics D_1 and D_2 to be the formal sum, which is the concatenation of D_1, " $+$ ", and D_2. Define the scalar multiplication of dyadics D and scalar λ to be the formal scalar multiplication λD, which is the concatenation of λ and D. We stipulate that the formal sum and formal scalar multiplication subject to all the laws of vector operations, including associative law, commutative law and distributive laws. The addition of dyadics is commutative. For example, $\lambda \mathbf{ap} + \mu \mathbf{bq} = \mu \mathbf{bq} + \lambda \mathbf{ap}$. However, the juxtaposition of vectors is not commutative. Namely, $\mathbf{ap} \neq \mathbf{pa}$.

We illustrate these operations with one example in the following.

$$\begin{aligned}
&\lambda \mathbf{ap} + \mu \mathbf{bq} \\
={} & \lambda(a_1 \mathbf{e}_1 + a_2 \mathbf{e}_2)(p_1 \mathbf{e}_1 + p_2 \mathbf{e}_2) \\
& + \mu(b_1 \mathbf{e}_1 + b_2 \mathbf{e}_2)(q_1 \mathbf{e}_1 + q_2 \mathbf{e}_2) \\
={} & (\lambda a_1 p_1 + \mu b_1 q_1)\mathbf{e}_1 \mathbf{e}_1 + (\lambda a_1 p_2 + \mu b_1 q_2)\mathbf{e}_1 \mathbf{e}_2 \\
& + (\lambda a_2 p_1 + \mu b_2 q_1)\mathbf{e}_2 \mathbf{e}_1 + (\lambda a_2 p_2 + \mu b_2 q_2)\mathbf{e}_2 \mathbf{e}_2.
\end{aligned}$$

The dyadics form a linear space with respect to addition and scalar multiplication. The dyads $\mathbf{e}_1 \mathbf{e}_1$, $\mathbf{e}_1 \mathbf{e}_2$, $\mathbf{e}_2 \mathbf{e}_1$ and $\mathbf{e}_2 \mathbf{e}_2$ form a basis for the dyadics space. In fact, the dyadics space is a model of the tensor product space of U and V. The dyadics are also called **dyadic tensors**. In the modern language, the juxtaposition of two vectors is a tensor product mapping and $\mathbf{ap}$ is nothing but $\mathbf{a} \otimes \mathbf{p}$. If we denote the dyadics space by $W = U \otimes V$, then the tensor product mapping is $\otimes : U \times V \to W; (\mathbf{a}, \mathbf{p}) \mapsto \mathbf{ap}$.

The dyadics have a matrix representation. Vectors in U are represented by column matrices and vectors in V are represented by row vectors, like

$$\mathbf{a} = \begin{bmatrix} a_1 \\ a_2 \end{bmatrix}$$

$$\mathbf{p} = \begin{bmatrix} p_1 & p_2 \end{bmatrix}.$$

The dyad $\mathbf{ap}$ is represented by the product of matrices $\mathbf{a}$ and $\mathbf{p}$,

$$\mathbf{ap} = \begin{bmatrix} a_1 p_1 & a_1 p_2 \\ a_2 p_1 & a_2 p_2 \end{bmatrix}.$$

The basis vectors for the dyadics are

$$\mathbf{e}_1 \mathbf{e}_1 = \begin{bmatrix} 1 & 0 \\ 0 & 0 \end{bmatrix}, \ \mathbf{e}_1 \mathbf{e}_2 = \begin{bmatrix} 0 & 1 \\ 0 & 0 \end{bmatrix}, \ \mathbf{e}_2 \mathbf{e}_1 = \begin{bmatrix} 0 & 0 \\ 1 & 0 \end{bmatrix} \text{ and } \mathbf{e}_2 \mathbf{e}_2 = \begin{bmatrix} 0 & 0 \\ 0 & 1 \end{bmatrix}.$$

This matrix representation of dyadics is actually an isomorphism from dyadics space to the matrix space $M_{2,2}$. ♣

Remark 7. Cross Link — Alternative Definitions of Tensor Product
It can be proved that all the models of tensor product $(U \otimes V, \otimes)$ of U and V are isomorphic to each other. So the tensor product $(U \otimes V, \otimes)$ of U and V is unique up to isomorphism. We can use any model as the alternative definition. The Gibbs dyadics is one of the popular definitions as seen in many books [Bourbaki (1942); Roman (2005)], usually using the language of free vector space and quotient space, with no mention of the connection to Gibbs dyadics though. That is the way to define the intuitive ideas of "formal sum" and "formal scalar multiplication" rigorously (see Part I Chap. 1 Appendix A1).

Example 11. (Model of tensor product—Bilinear forms) Let U and V be linear spaces over a field F, and U^* and V^* be the dual spaces. Let $W = L(U, V; F)$ be the linear space of all bilinear forms $\xi : U \times V \to F$. We define a mapping $\otimes : U^* \times V^* \to W$; $(f, h) \mapsto \xi \overset{\text{def}}{=} f \otimes h$ such that for all $x \in U$ and $y \in V$,
$$\xi(x, y) = f(x)h(y).$$
So the linear space of all bilinear forms $L(U, V; F)$ together with mapping $\otimes$ is a tensor product of U^* and V^*.

This is also an economical alternative approach to defining tensor product by using a concrete model, which is used by many books (see Appendix A2). ♣

3.2   Decomposable Tensors

It is important to understand that, in general,
$$\{u \otimes v | u \in U, \, v \in V\} \neq U \otimes V.$$
We have analyzed this in Section 2. This leads to the definition of decomposable tensors.

Definition 5. Decomposable tensor

Let $(U \otimes V, \otimes)$ be a tensor product of U and V. For a tensor $w \in U \otimes V$, if there exist $u \in U$ and $v \in V$ such that $w = u \otimes v$, then w is called a **decomposable tensor**.

In Example 9, the tensor $w_1 = \begin{bmatrix} -3 & 12 \\ -2 & 8 \end{bmatrix} \in M_{2,2}$ is decomposable because w_1 can be expressed as $u \otimes v = (3, 2) \otimes (-1, 4)$. The tensor

$w_2 = \begin{bmatrix} 1 & 0 \\ 0 & 1 \end{bmatrix} \in M_{2,2}$ is not decomposable, because $\det w_2 \neq 0$, which we have discussed earlier. But w_2 can be expressed as the linear combination of decomposable tensors, $w_2 = (1,0) \otimes (1,0) + (0,1) \otimes (0,1)$. This is a special case for $m = n = 2$, where the set of decomposable tensors $\begin{bmatrix} a_{11} & a_{12} \\ a_{21} & a_{22} \end{bmatrix}$ are on a 3-D curved hypersurface $a_{11}a_{22} - a_{12}a_{21} = 0$ in a 4-D space $\mathbb{R}^4$.

Remark 8. Elaboration — Tensor Product Mapping $\otimes$

The existence of nondecomposable tensors indicates that the mapping $\otimes : U \times V \to U \otimes V$ is not surjective in general. It is easy to see $\otimes$ is not injective either.

Remark 9. Intuition — Geometric Picture of the Image of $\otimes$

For the general case of $U = \mathbb{R}^m$, $V = \mathbb{R}^n$ and $U \otimes V = M_{m,n}$, im$\otimes$ is a $m + n - 1$ dimensional curved hypersurface in a mn dimensional linear space $U \otimes V$. This implies that the set of decomposable tensors in the form of $u \otimes v$ is rather "small" and "thin" in $U \otimes V$. im$\otimes$ is "stretched", or rigorously, im$\otimes$ spans to fill the entire mn-dimensional tensor product space $U \otimes V$. For example, if $m = n = 4$, the decomposable tensors live in a 7-dimensional curved hypersurface in a 16-dimensional space. Most of the vectors in $U \otimes V$ are not decomposable.

From Theorem 2 we know that if $\{e_1, \ldots, e_m\}$ is a basis for U and $\{b_1, \ldots, b_n\}$ is a basis for V, then $\{e_i \otimes b_j \,|\, i = 1, \ldots, m, \, j = 1, \ldots, n\}$ forms a basis for $U \otimes V$. Any tensor $w \in U \otimes V$ can be expressed as a linear combination of this basis, as $w = \sum_{i=1}^{m} \sum_{j=1}^{n} w_{ij} e_i \otimes b_j$. The matrix of numbers w_{ij} is called the **coordinates** (or **components**) of tensor w with respect to basis $\{e_i\}$ and $\{b_j\}$. Now we rediscovered the matrix model introduced in Example 1 but here it is a more general case. Due to the uniqueness of tensor product up to isomorphism, any tensor product can be represented by a matrix space $M_{m,n}$. The matrix model $M_{m,n}$ is always a concrete model to help us understand the more abstract structure of tensor product.

In the old fashioned definition of tensor, a tensor is considered a matrix or a cubic or higher dimensional matrix, and a vector is considered a special case of tensors. Here we see that even in the general case, a tensor is nothing but a vector. However, it is that tensor product mapping $\otimes$ that connects the vectors in the tensor product space W to the vectors in the factor spaces U and V. A change of basis in U and V, from $\{e_i\}$ to $\{\bar{e}_i\}$ and from $\{b_j\}$ to $\{\bar{b}_j\}$ will induce a change of basis in $U \otimes V$ from $\{e_i \otimes b_j\}$ to $\{\bar{e}_i \otimes \bar{b}_j\}$, and hence there is a change of coordinates for w.

3.3   Induced Linear Mappings

Definition 6. Induced linear mapping

Let $T_1 : U_1 \to V_1$, $T_2 : U_2 \to V_2$ be linear mappings. There exists a unique linear mapping $T : U_1 \otimes U_2 \to V_1 \otimes V_2$ such that for all $u_1 \in U_1$ and $u_2 \in U_2$,

$$T(u_1 \otimes u_2) = (T_1 u_1) \otimes (T_2 u_2).$$

T is called the linear mapping induced by T_1 and T_2.

3.4   Tensor Product Space of Multiple Linear Spaces

The tensor product can be generalized to multiple linear spaces.

Definition 7. Tensor product space of multiple linear spaces

Let $V_1, \ldots, V_m$ and W be linear spaces. The **tensor product space** of $V_1, \ldots, V_m$ is defined to be a pair $(W, \otimes)$, if $\otimes : V_1 \times \cdots \times V_m \to W$; $(v_1, \ldots, v_m) \mapsto v_1 \otimes \cdots \otimes v_m$ is a multilinear mapping and satisfies the following conditions.

(1) Maximal span property: If a set of vectors X_k are linearly independent in V_k, for $k = 1, \ldots, m$, then vectors in $X_1 \otimes \cdots \otimes X_m$ are linearly independent in W.
(2) Generating property: $W = \text{span}(\text{im}\otimes)$.

W is denoted by $V_1 \otimes \cdots \otimes V_m$.

The following theorem is straightforward.

Theorem 5. Let $V_1, \ldots, V_m$ be finite dimensional linear spaces. Then $\dim(V_1 \otimes \cdots \otimes V_m) = (\dim V_1) \cdots (\dim V_m)$.

§4   Tensor Spaces

4.1   Definition and Examples

One special type of tensor product is especially important in many applications. That is the tensor product of a linear space V itself, or the **tensor power space** (or simply **tensor power**, or **tensor space**) of V. We also consider the tensor powers of the dual space V^*, and the mixture of the two as well. For example, $V \otimes V$, $V \otimes V \otimes V$, *etc.*. These tensor power spaces are also called just tensor spaces on V. I shall call V the **base space** of the tensor space. This is an analogy of the power of a number a^b, where a is called the base. I coined the term "base space" because it is important to indicate the relationship between V and its tensor powers and there is not such a term in the current literature. Lacking this explicit identification of the base space is why the old-fashioned definition causes confusions.

Let V be a linear space and first let us look at three important tensor powers of degree two.

Definition 8. Contravariant, covariant and mixed tensor spaces

$T_0^2(V) \stackrel{\text{def}}{=} V \otimes V$ is called **contravariant tensor space** (of degree 2) on V. The vectors in $T_0^2(V)$ are called **contravariant tensors** (of degree 2).

$T_2^0(V) \stackrel{\text{def}}{=} V^* \otimes V^*$ is called **covariant tensor space** (of degree 2) on V. The vectors in $T_2^0(V)$ are called **covariant tensors** (of degree 2).

$T_1^1(V) \stackrel{\text{def}}{=} V \otimes V^*$ is called **mixed tensor space** (of degree 2) on V. The vectors in $T_1^1(V)$ are called **mixed tensors** (of degree 2).

These tensors get their names, contravariant or covariant, because they obey different coordinate transformation laws when the basis of V is changed from the old basis to a new basis, which we shall see shortly. Covariant tensors get their names because in the coordinate transformation formula, it involves the same transition matrix for basis vectors in V. Contravariant tensors get their names because it involves the inverse of the transition matrix for the basis vectors in V. Vectors in V are called **contravariant vectors** for the same reason. V is also considered a contravariant tensor space of degree 1. Vectors in V^* are called **covariant**

vectors. V^* is also considered covariant tensor space of degree 1. Scalars in F are considered tensors of degree 0. F is also called tensor space of degree 0. (see Chap. 1 Remarks 7, 11 and Chap. 1, Section 5.3).

Example 12. (Matrix space $M_{n,n}$) Matrix space $M_{n,n}$ of all $n \times n$ square matrices is a special case in Example 9. This is a model for contravariant tensor space $T_0^2(V)$. $M_{n,n} = V \otimes V$, where $V = F^n \cong M_{n,1}$. For $x, y \in V$ as column vectors, $x \otimes y = xy^t \in M_{n,n}$. ♣

Example 13. (Space of bilinear forms $L(V, V; F)$) Let V be a linear space and $L(V, V; F)$ be the linear space of all bilinear forms $\xi : V \times V \to F$. This is a special case of Example 13. $L(V, V; F) = V^* \otimes V^*$ is a model for covariant tensor space $T_2^0(V)$. $\otimes : V^* \times V^* \to L(V, V; F)$ is defined as $(f \otimes h)(v_1, v_2) \overset{\text{def}}{=} f(v_1)h(v_2)$, for all $f, h \in V^*$ and $v_1, v_2 \in V$. A bilinear form can also be represented by a matrix. ♣

Example 14. (Space of linear transformations $L(V; V)$) The mixed tensor space $T_1^1(V) = V \otimes V^*$ can be identified with $L(V; V)$, the space of all linear transformations from V to V. The tensor product mapping $\otimes : V \times V^* \to L(V; V)$ is defined as follows: for any $v \in V$ and $f \in V^*$, define $v \otimes f \overset{\text{def}}{=} T \in L(V; V)$ such that for all $x \in V$, $T(x) \overset{\text{def}}{=} f(x)v$. ♣

We have rediscovered linear transformations $T : V \to V$ from a different perspective - the viewpoint of tensors. We have discovered the relationship between linear transformations and square matrices, the relationship between bilinear forms and square matrices, and the relationship between tensors and square matrices. Matrices by themselves are static objects. They are not linear transformations. They are not bilinear forms and they are not tensors. They are representations of linear transformations, or bilinear forms or tensors. They are the coordinates of tensors. The same matrix can represent a contravariant tensor (Example 12), a bilinear form as a covariant tensor (Example 13), or a linear transformation as a mixed tensor (Example 14).

4.2 Change of Basis

Next we consider how the coordinates of tensors change if the basis of the base space changes. Starting now we will use a notational convention to distinguish the coordinates of contravariant tensors and covariant tensors. We use upper indices for contravariant coordinates and lower indices for covariant coordinates.

Let $\{e_1, \ldots, e_n\}$ be a basis of V. Suppose V undergoes a change of basis

$$\bar{e}_i = \sum_{k=1}^{n} A^k{}_i e_k, \tag{2.1}$$

where $A^k{}_i$ is the element at k^{th} row and i^{th} column of matrix A.

Remark 10. Caution — Upper and Lower Index Notations for Tensor Components
We use upper indices for the contravariant components and lower indices for covariant components of tensors. For mixed tensors, when the tensor is treated as a matrix, like the basis transition matrix A, the upper index is the first index—the row index, and the lower index is the second index—the column index. $A^k{}_i$ represents the element at k^{th} row and i^{th} column of matrix A. Eq. 2.1 is the same as Eq. 1.1, and is equivalent to

$$\begin{bmatrix} \bar{e}_1 & \cdots & \bar{e}_n \end{bmatrix} = \begin{bmatrix} e_1 & \cdots & e_n \end{bmatrix} A. \tag{2.2}$$

When V has a change of basis described by 2.1, the dual basis changes as

$$\bar{f}^i = \sum_{k=1}^{n} [A^{-1}]^i{}_k f^k, \tag{2.3}$$

where $\{f^i\}$ is the old dual basis to the old basis $\{e_i\}$ and $\{\bar{f}^i\}$ is the new dual basis to the new basis $\{\bar{e}_i\}$ with $f^i(e_j) = \delta^i_j$ and $\bar{f}^i(\bar{e}_j) = \delta^i_j$, and A^{-1} is the inverse matrix of A.

Theorem 6. (Change of coordinates for contravariant and covariant vectors) *Suppose the base space V undergoes a basis change and let A be the transition matrix.*

A contravariant vector $v \in V$ changes coordinates from $[v^k]_{k=1}^n$ to $[\bar{v}^i]_{i=1}^n$ as follows:

$$\bar{v}^i = \sum_{k=1}^{n} [A^{-1}]^i{}_k v^k. \tag{2.4}$$

A covariant vector $u \in V^*$ changes coordinates from $[u_k]_{k=1}^n$ to $[\bar{u}_i]_{i=1}^n$ as follows:

$$\bar{u}_i = \sum_{k=1}^{n} A^k{}_i u_k. \tag{2.5}$$

Remark 11. Cross Link — Change of Coordinate for Vectors
Compare the matrix in Eq. 2.4 with the matrix in Eq. 2.1, we notice that $\left[A^{-1}\right]^i{}_k$ is the *transpose* of the inverse of matrix A. This agrees with what we obtained in Theorem 3 in Chap. 1, $\bar{v} = (A^{-1})^T v$, but the formula in tensor form is easier to remember because the transpose of the matrix comes naturally in the tensor coordinate notation. Compare

Eqs. 2.1, 2.4 with Chap. 1 Eq. 1.1, 1.3. They are the same thing but here we are using the tensor notation distinguishing upper and lower indices while in Chap. 1 we used plain vector and matrix notations with all the lower indices.

Theorem 7. (Change of coordinates for tensors) *Suppose the base space V undergoes a basis change and let A be the transition matrix.*

A contravariant tensor $\xi \in T_0^2(V)$ changes coordinates from $[\xi^{kl}]_{k,l=1}^n$ to $[\bar{\xi}^{ij}]_{i,j=1}^n$ as follows:

$$\bar{\xi}^{ij} = \sum_{k,l=1}^n [A^{-1}]^i{}_k [A^{-1}]^j{}_l \xi^{kl}. \tag{2.6}$$

A covariant tensor $\zeta \in T_2^0(V)$ changes coordinates from $[\zeta_{kl}]_{k,l=1}^n$ to $[\bar{\zeta}_{ij}]_{i,l=1}^n$ as follows:

$$\bar{\zeta}_{ij} = \sum_{k,l=1}^n A^k{}_i A^l{}_j \zeta_{kl}. \tag{2.7}$$

A mixed tensor $\eta \in T_1^1(V)$ changes coordinates from $[\eta^k{}_l]_{k,l=1}^n$ to $[\bar{\eta}^i{}_j]_{i,j=1}^n$ as follows:

$$\bar{\eta}^i{}_j = \sum_{k,l=1}^n [A^{-1}]^i{}_k A^l{}_j \eta^k{}_l. \tag{2.8}$$

Eq. 2.8 is the same formula in Theorem 11 for the change of matrix associated to a linear transformation when the basis changes. We now rediscovered it in the context of tensors.

Remark 12. Cross Link — Old-fashioned Definition of Tensor

The coordinate transformation laws of tensors in Eqs. 2.6, 2.7 and 2.8 are used in the old-fashioned definition of tensor (see Appendix A2). According to the old-fashioned definition, a tensor is a matrix of numbers that transform according to these transformation laws. A matrix of numbers is not enough to define a tensor, but it also need to be tested by these transformation laws. Even an n-tuple does not guarantee it to be a vector. It needs to be tested whether it obeys the vector coordinate transformation laws. In the context of tensor analysis, the coordinate change happens in the tangent space of a differentiable manifold, which is induced by local coordinate change. In the context of pure algebra, the old-fashioned definition fails to point out how the matrix of numbers are related to the basis and why they change coordinates. In the old-fashioned tensor concept, tensors are generalization of vectors while vectors are a special type of tensors (being degree of one). The difference lies in the different laws of coordinate transformation. In the modern view, tensors are vectors themselves. They live in a higher dimensional linear space $T_0^2(V)$. They are tensors because of the connection between this linear space $T_0^2(V)$ and the base space V through the tensor product mapping $\otimes$. The tensors change coordinates like tensors relative to the basis change in the base space V. However, relative to the basis change of their own space $T_0^2(V)$, the tensors change coordinates just like ordinary vectors.

Similarly we can consider tensor product of a linear space V and its dual space V^* for powers higher than 2.

Definition 9. Tensor spaces of higher degrees

$T_0^p(V) = \underset{p\,factors}{V \otimes \cdots \otimes V}$ is called **contravariant tensor space** (or **contravariant tensor power**) of degree p on V. The vectors in T_0^p are called **contravariant tensors** of degree p.

$T_q^0(V) = \underset{q\,factors}{V^* \otimes \cdots \otimes V^*}$ is called **covariant tensor space** (or **covariant tensor power**) of degree q on V. The vectors in $T_q^0(V)$ are called **covariant tensors** of degree q.

$T_q^p(V) = \underset{p\,factors}{V \otimes \cdots \otimes V} \otimes \underset{q\,factors}{V^* \otimes \cdots \otimes V^*}$ is called **mixed tensor space** (or **mixed tensor power**) of type (p, q) on V. The vectors in $T_q^p(V)$ are called **mixed tensors** of type (p, q).

Remark 13. Look Ahead — Tensors in Riemannian Geometry

In Riemann geometry, the metric tensor in a tangent space at a point on a Riemannian manifold is simply an inner product, which is a bilinear form $g : V \times V \to \mathbb{R}$. The Riemann curvature tensor can take a form of a type $(1,3)$ tensor as $R_{ijk}{}^l$, which is a multilinear mapping $R : V \times V \times V \to V$, or a type $(0,4)$ tensor as R_{ijkl}, which is a multilinear mapping $R : V \times V \times V \times V \to \mathbb{R}$. The curvature tensor is defined as a tensor field though. It is not determined only by the point on the manifold but also its neighborhood.

Remark 14. Elaboration — Different Orders of the Factor Spaces in a Mixed Tensor Space

It is possible to have different orders of the factor space V and V^* in a mixed tensor space, like $V^* \otimes V^* \otimes V^* \otimes V$, or $V^* \otimes V \otimes V^* \otimes V^*$, or $V \otimes V^* \otimes V^* \otimes V^*$. These tensor power spaces are not the same but are isomorphic. When we use indexed notations (or component notations) of tensors, we need to be vary careful about which index comes from which factor space, or dual space. The Riemann curvature tensor of type (1, 3) is exactly this case. Different books have different conventions. Some authors use the component notation R_{ijk}^l, which I call **implicit ordering of mixed indices**. Identification of indices can be resolved using this notation but it is not easy for the eyes to see that upper index l is in what order among the lower index. So some authors use what I call **explicit ordering of mixed indices**, like $R^i{}_{jkl}$, $R_i{}^j{}_{kl}$ or $R_{ijk}{}^l$ to distinguish, which adds much more clarity. See Remark 18 in Part III Chap. 2.

Theorem 8. (Change of coordinates for higher degree tensors) *When V undergoes a change of basis expressed in Eq. 2.1 with transition matrix A, a contravariant tensor $\xi \in T_0^p(V)$ changes coordinates from $[\xi^{j_1 \cdots j_p}]$ to $[\bar{\xi}^{i_1 \cdots i_p}]$ as follows.*

$$\bar{\xi}^{i_1 \cdots i_p} = \sum_{j_1 \cdots j_p = 1}^n [A^{-1}]^{i_1}_{\ j_1} \cdots [A^{-1}]^{i_p}_{\ j_p} \xi^{j_1 \cdots j_p}.$$

A covariant tensor $\zeta \in T_q^0(V)$ changes coordinates from $[\zeta_{j_1 \ldots j_q}]$ to $[\bar{\zeta}_{i_1 \ldots i_q}]$ as follows.

$$\bar{\zeta}_{i_1 \ldots i_q} = \sum_{j_1 \ldots j_q = 1}^n A^{j_1}_{\ i_1} \cdots A^{j_q}_{\ i_q} \zeta_{j_1 \ldots j_q}.$$

A mixed tensor of type (p,q), $\eta \in T_q^p(V)$ changes coordinates from $[\eta^{s_1 \ldots s_p}_{\quad t_1 \ldots t_q}]$ to $[\bar{\eta}^{i_1 \cdots i_p}_{\quad j_1 \ldots j_q}]$ as follows.

$$\bar{\eta}^{i_1 \cdots i_p}_{\quad j_1 \ldots j_q} = \sum_{s_1 \ldots s_p, t_1 \ldots t_q = 1}^n [A^{-1}]^{i_1}_{\ s_1} \cdots [A^{-1}]^{i_p}_{\ s_p} A^{t_1}_{\ j_1} \cdots A^{t_q}_{\ j_q} \eta^{s_1 \ldots s_p}_{\quad t_1 \ldots t_q}.$$

4.3   Induced Inner Product

Definition 10. Induced inner product

Suppose the base space V is equipped with an inner product $\langle \cdot, \cdot \rangle$. There exist a unique inner product in $T_0^p(V)$ satisfying

$$\langle u_1 \otimes \cdots \otimes u_p, v_1 \otimes \cdots \otimes v_p \rangle = \langle u_1, v_1 \rangle \cdots \langle u_p, v_p \rangle.$$

This inner product is called **induced inner product in $T_0^p(V)$.**

If $\{e_1, \ldots, e_n\}$ is an orthonormal basis for V with respect to $\langle \cdot, \cdot \rangle$, then $\{e_{i_1} \otimes \cdots \otimes e_{i_p} \mid i_1, \ldots, i_p = 1, \ldots, n\}$ forms an orthonormal basis for $T_0^p(V)$.

We can define induced inner product for $T_q^0(V)$ and $T_q^p(V)$ in a similar way.

4.4 Lowering and Raising Indices

Let $(V, \langle \cdot, \cdot \rangle)$ be an inner product space. Let $\{e_1, \ldots, e_n\}$ be a basis for V and $g_{ij} = \langle e_i, e_j \rangle$. We have discussed in Chap. 1, Section 5.2, the isomorphism $\Phi : V \to V^*$ such that a vector $v = x^1 e_1 + \cdots + x^n e_n \in V$ is mapped to its metric dual $v^* = y_1 f_1 + \cdots + y_n f_n$, and vice versa, where $\{f_1, \ldots, f_n\}$ is the affine dual basis. The coordinates of the metric dual $(y_1, \ldots, y_n)$ are related to $(x^1, \ldots, x^n)$ as follows:

$$y_i = \sum_{k=1}^{n} g_{ik} x^k,$$

$$x^i = \sum_{k=1}^{n} g^{ik} y_k,$$

(2.9)

where $[g^{ij}]$ is the inverse matrix of $[g_{ij}]$.

Now using the isomorphism $\Phi : V \to V^*$, we can define a linear mapping $\Pi^{\circ\circ}_{\downarrow} : T_0^2(V) \to T_1^1(V)$ such that

$$u \otimes v \mapsto u \otimes v^*.$$

The mapping $\Pi^{\circ\circ}_{\downarrow}$ is a linear isomorphism from $T_0^2(V)$ to $T_1^1(V)$, induced by the identity mapping $\mathrm{id} : V \to V; u \mapsto u$ and $\Phi : V \to V^*; v \mapsto v^*$ (see Section 3.3). $\Pi^{\circ\circ}_{\downarrow}$ maps a contravariant tensor to a mixed tensor.

In coordinate notation, let w have components w^{ij} and $\Pi^{\circ\circ}_{\downarrow}(w)$ have components $w^i{}_j$. They are related by

$$w^i{}_j = \sum_{k=1}^{n} g_{kj} w^{ik}.$$

(2.10)

The inverse of $\Pi^{\circ\circ}_{\downarrow}$, denoted by $\Pi^{\circ\uparrow}_{\circ} : T_1^1(V) \to T_0^2(V)$ is an isomorphism from $T_1^1(V)$ to $T_0^2(V)$. In coordinate notation, we have

$$w^{ij} = \sum_{k=1}^{n} g^{ik} w^j{}_k.$$

(2.11)

The isomorphism $\Pi^{\circ\circ}_{\downarrow} : T_0^2(V) \to T_1^1(V)$ is called **lowering the index**, because in the coordinate expression Eq. 2.10 one index is lowered. The isomorphism $\Pi^{\circ\uparrow}_{\circ} : T_1^1(V) \to T_0^2(V)$ is called **raising the index** because one index is raised in the coordinate expression Eq. 2.11.

Since all the tensor spaces $T_0^2(V)$, $T_1^1(V)$ and $T_2^0(V)$ are isomorphic to each other, we can raise or lower more than one index. For example, lowering indices twice

$$w_{ij} = \sum_{k,l=1}^{n} g_{ik} g_{jl} w^{kl}$$

defines an isomorphism $\Pi_{\downarrow\downarrow}^{\circ\circ} : T_0^2(V) \to T_2^0(V)$. Raising indices twice

$$w^{ij} = \sum_{k,l=1}^{n} g^{ik} g^{jl} w_{kl}$$

establishes an isomorphism $\Pi_{\circ\circ}^{\uparrow\uparrow} : T_2^0(V) \to T_0^2(V)$.

In the case of orthonormal basis and thus $g_{ij} = \delta_{ij}$, the components of all different (p, q) types of tensor with equal $p + q$ are the same. For example, $w^{ij} = w_j^i = w_{ij}$ and we do not even need to distinguish the upper indices from the lower indices.

When we deal with higher degree tensor powers, the order of indices is important and we need to be specific about which index is raised or lowered to avoid ambiguity. In general we can have a tensor power of V and V^* in any order. For example,

$$w^i{}_j{}^{kl} = \sum_{p,q=1}^{n} g_{jp} g^{kq} w^{ip}{}_q{}^l \tag{2.12}$$

defines an isomorphism $\Pi_{\downarrow\circ}^{\circ\circ\uparrow\circ} : V \otimes V \otimes V^* \otimes V \to V \otimes V^* \otimes V \otimes V$.

Remark 15. Cross Link — Active View vs. Passive View

We made remarks about the active view and passive view of linear transformations and the raising and lowering of indices for vectors in Chap. 1. The active view and passive view apply to the raising and lowering of indices for tensors as well. The above discussion is the active view. That is to view the raising and lowering of indices as linear transformations (isomorphisms). In the passive view, the raising and lowering of indices is considered different coordinates of the same tensor under different bases. The same tensor w has coordinates in the form of w^{ijkl} under basis $\{e_i \otimes e_j \otimes e_k \otimes e_l\}_{i,j,k,l=1}^{n}$, but has coordinates $w^{ip}{}_q{}^l$ under basis $\{e_i \otimes e_p \otimes \hat{e}_q \otimes e_l\}_{i,p,q,l=1}^{n}$, and coordinates $w^i{}_j{}^{kl}$ under basis $\{e_i \otimes \hat{e}_j \otimes e_k \otimes e_l\}_{i,j,k,l=1}^{n}$, where $\{\hat{e}_j\}_{j=1}^{n}$ is the reciprocal basis of $\{e_i\}_{i=1}^{n}$ (see Chap. 1 Definition 20).

Remark 16. Look Ahead — Riemann Curvature Tensor of type (1,3) and type (0,4)

In Riemannian geometry, (see Part III Chap. 2), the Riemann curvature tensor has two common forms, either as a type $(1, 3)$ tensor or a type $(0, 4)$ tensor. They are related by

$$R_{ijkl} = \sum_{s=1}^{n} g_{ls} R_{ijk}{}^s,$$

$$R_{ijk}{}^l = \sum_{s=1}^{n} g^{ls} R_{ijks}.$$

§5   Tensor Algebras

5.1   Product of Two Tensors

Let $u \in T_0^p(V)$ and $v \in T_0^r(V)$. Since $T_0^p(V)$ and $T_0^r(V)$ are linear spaces, we can form the tensor product space of them. $T_0^p(V) \otimes T_0^r(V)$ is isomorphic to $T_0^{p+r}(V)$. The mapping $\otimes : T_0^p(V) \times T_0^r(V) \to T_0^{p+r}(V)$ assigns $u = u_1 \otimes \cdots \otimes u_p$ and $v = v_1 \otimes \cdots \otimes v_r$ to

$$u \otimes v = u_1 \otimes \cdots \otimes u_p \otimes v_1 \otimes \cdots \otimes v_r.$$

Similarly we can define the tensor product of two covariant tensors. The tensor product $T_q^0(V) \otimes T_s^0(V)$ is isomorphic to $T_{q+s}^0(V)$.

In the most general case, the tensor product $T_q^p(V) \otimes T_s^r(V)$ is isomorphic to $T_{q+s}^{p+r}(V)$.

The tensor product of two linear spaces $U \otimes V$ is also called the "outer product" because $U \otimes V$ is a different linear space. It is "out of" U and it is "out of" V. Tensor spaces $T_0^p(V)$ of different degrees are different linear spaces and their vectors cannot be added together. The tensor product mapping $\otimes : T_0^p(V) \times T_0^r(V) \to T_0^{p+r}(V)$ is not a binary operation within one space. We really wish to make the mapping $\otimes$ a binary operation within one space though. To do so, we resort to the construction of direct sum of all these tensor power spaces $T_0^p(V)$.

5.2   Tensor Algebras

In Chap. 1, we defined the direct sum $U \oplus V$ of two linear spaces.

We now define the direct sum of tensor spaces $T_q^p(V)$, $p, q = 0, 1, 2, \ldots$ to be

$$T(V) = \bigoplus_{p,q=0}^{\infty} T_q^p(V) = T_0^0(V) \oplus T_0^1(V) \oplus T_1^0(V) \oplus T_0^2(V) \oplus T_1^1(V) \oplus T_2^0(V) \oplus \cdots .$$

Then $\otimes$ becomes a binary operation $\otimes : T(V) \times T(V) \to T(V)$. $T(V)$ is an algebra over field F regarding the tensor multiplication $\otimes$ (see Chap. 1 Section 6). It is called the **tensor algebra** on V. Now tensors of different degrees can be added and the sum is understood as the direct sum. Each tensor space $T_q^p(V)$ is a linear subspace of $T(V)$. The product of a tensor in subspace $T_0^p(V)$ with a tensor in subspace $T_0^r(V)$ is a tensor in subspace $T_0^{p+r}(V)$. An algebra with properties like this is called **graded algebra**.

5.3   Contraction of Tensors

We start with an example. Let $w = u \otimes v \in T_1^1(V)$ be a type $(1,1)$ tensor. From the unique factorization property of tensor product (see Chap. 1 Appendix A2), we know that there exists a unique linear mapping $C_1^1 : T_1^1(V) \to \mathbb{R}$ such that for any $u \in V$ and $v \in V^*$,

$$C_1^1(u \otimes v) = v(u),$$

where $v(u)$ is the action of linear function v on u.

In the coordinate form, if w has coordinates w_j^i under a certain basis, then

$$C_1^1(w) = \sum_{k=1}^{n} w_k^k,$$

which is equal to the trace of $[w_j^i]$ as a matrix.

$C_1^1(w)$ so defined is called the **contraction** of tensor w with respect to (the 1st) upper index and (the 1st) lower index. This leads to the general definition of contraction of tensors.

Definition 11. Contraction of a tensor

Let $T_q^p(V)$ be a tensor space of type (p,q). For any $1 \le s \le p$ and $1 \le t \le q$, from the unique factorization property of the tensor product (see Appendix A2), there exists a unique linear mapping $C_t^s : T_q^p(V) \to T_{q-1}^{p-1}(V)$ such that for any $u_1, ..., u_p \in V$ and $v_1, ..., v_q \in V^*$,
$$C_t^s(u_1 \otimes \cdots \otimes u_s \otimes \cdots \otimes u_p \otimes v_1 \otimes \cdots \otimes v_t \otimes \cdots \otimes v_q)$$
$$= [v_t(u_s)]\, u_1 \otimes \cdots \otimes u_{s-1} \otimes u_{s+1} \cdots \otimes u_p \otimes v_1 \otimes \cdots \otimes v_{t-1} \otimes v_{t+1} \cdots \otimes v_q,$$
where $v_t(u_s)$ is the action of linear function v_t on vector u_s. The mapping $C_t^s : T_q^p(V) \to T_{q-1}^{p-1}(V)$ is called the **contraction** of a tensor of type (p,q) with respect to the sth upper index and t^{th} lower index.

The contraction of a tensor of type (p,q) results in a tensor of type $(p-1, q-1)$.

Theorem 9. *Let $w \in T_q^p(V)$. Then $C_t^s(w)$ can be obtained using coordinates by identifying the sth contravariant index with the tth covariant index and sum over them. Namely,*

$$C_t^s(w) = \sum_{k=1}^{n} w^{\cdots k \cdots}_{\cdots k \cdots}.$$

The result $C_t^s(w)$ does not depend on the choice of basis.

The contraction of tensors can be viewed as a single argument operator in the tensor space $T(V)$, namely $C_t^s : T(V) \to T(V)$.

If we write the decomposable tensors $u \otimes v$ in the form of Gibbs dyadics $\mathbf{uv}$, then the Gibbs dot product notation $(\mathbf{uv}) \cdot \mathbf{w}$ and $\mathbf{u} \cdot (\mathbf{vw})$ are actually the tensor contractions. This can be generalized to higher degree tensors, which can be called multiadics.

The Gibbs dot product of a dyad and a vector is defined as follows.

Definition 12. Dot product of a dyad and a vector

$$(\mathbf{uv}) \cdot \mathbf{w} \overset{\text{def}}{=} \mathbf{u}(\mathbf{v} \cdot \mathbf{w}) \overset{\text{def}}{=} \langle \mathbf{v}, \mathbf{w} \rangle \mathbf{u},$$
$$\mathbf{u} \cdot (\mathbf{vw}) \overset{\text{def}}{=} (\mathbf{u} \cdot \mathbf{v})\mathbf{w} \overset{\text{def}}{=} \langle \mathbf{u}, \mathbf{v} \rangle \mathbf{w}.$$

In the above, the dot product of two vectors $\mathbf{u} \cdot \mathbf{v}$ is just an alternative notation for the inner product $\langle \mathbf{u}, \mathbf{v} \rangle$.

Gibbs also introduced a double dot product for dyadics,

$$(\mathbf{uv}) : (\mathbf{xy}) \overset{\text{def}}{=} (\mathbf{v} \cdot \mathbf{x})(\mathbf{u} \cdot \mathbf{y}).$$

This actually results in an inner product being defined in $T_0^2(V)$, but it is slightly different from what we defined as the induced inner product (see Definition 10). To compare, the induced inner product is defined to be

$$\langle \mathbf{uv}, \mathbf{xy} \rangle = \langle \mathbf{u}, \mathbf{x} \rangle \langle \mathbf{v}, \mathbf{y} \rangle.$$

Exercises

1. Give one example of linear spaces U, V and W and a bilinear mapping $\varphi : U \times V \to W$, such that $\dim W = \dim U \cdot \dim V$ but (W, φ) fails to be a tensor product of U and V.
2. Show that if for some $v_i = 0$, then $v_1 \otimes \cdots \otimes v_i \otimes \cdots \otimes v_m = 0$.
3. Show that if $v_1, v_2 \in V$ are linearly independent, then $v_1 \otimes v_2 + v_2 \otimes v_1$ is not a decomposable tensor.

4. Let $\mathbf{u} = 3\mathbf{e}_1 - 2\mathbf{e}_2 + \mathbf{e}_3$ and $\mathbf{v} = 2\mathbf{e}_1 + 5\mathbf{e}_2 + 7\mathbf{e}_3$. Find the Gibbs dyadics $\mathbf{uv}$.

5. Let $\mathbf{u} = (5, -9) \in \mathbb{R}^2$ and $\mathbf{v} = (2, -1, 3) \in \mathbb{R}^3$. Find $\mathbf{u} \otimes \mathbf{v}$ in the form of a 2×3 matrix.

6. Let

$$M_1 = \begin{bmatrix} 1 & -1 \\ 0 & 2 \end{bmatrix}, M_2 = \begin{bmatrix} 2 & 0 & -3 \\ 1 & 4 & 7 \end{bmatrix}.$$

Find the Kronecker product of M_1 and M_2.

7. Let $\mathbf{u} = 3\mathbf{e}_1 + \mathbf{e}_2 - \mathbf{e}_3$, $\mathbf{v} = -\mathbf{e}_1 + \mathbf{e}_2 + -2\mathbf{e}_3$. Find
   (1) $\xi_1 = \mathbf{u} \otimes \mathbf{u}$
   (2) $\xi_2 = \mathbf{v} \otimes \mathbf{v}$
   (3) $\xi_3 = \mathbf{u} \otimes \mathbf{v}$
   (4) $\xi_4 = \frac{1}{2}(\mathbf{u} \otimes \mathbf{v} + \mathbf{v} \otimes \mathbf{u})$
   (5) $\xi_5 = \frac{1}{2}(\mathbf{u} \otimes \mathbf{v} - \mathbf{v} \otimes \mathbf{u})$
   (6) $\xi_1 \otimes \xi_2$
   (7) $\xi_3 \otimes \xi_3$
   (8) $\xi_5 \otimes \xi_5$

8. Let $\mathbf{u} = \mathbf{e}_1 - \mathbf{e}_2 + 2\mathbf{e}_3 - \mathbf{e}_4$, $\mathbf{v} = 3\mathbf{e}_1 + 5\mathbf{e}_2 - \mathbf{e}_3 + \mathbf{e}_4$. Find
   (1) $\xi_1 = \mathbf{u} \otimes \mathbf{u}$
   (2) $\xi_2 = \mathbf{v} \otimes \mathbf{v}$
   (3) $\xi_3 = \mathbf{u} \otimes \mathbf{v}$
   (4) $\xi_4 = \frac{1}{2}(\mathbf{u} \otimes \mathbf{v} + \mathbf{v} \otimes \mathbf{u})$
   (5) $\xi_5 = \frac{1}{2}(\mathbf{u} \otimes \mathbf{v} - \mathbf{v} \otimes \mathbf{u})$
   (6) $\xi_1 \otimes \xi_2$
   (7) $\xi_3 \otimes \xi_3$
   (8) $\xi_5 \otimes \xi_5$

9. Let $\{\mathbf{e}_1, \mathbf{e}_2, \mathbf{e}_3\}$ be a basis for a linear space V. $\xi \in T_0^2(V)$ and $\xi = \mathbf{e}_1 \otimes \mathbf{e}_1 + \mathbf{e}_1 \otimes \mathbf{e}_2 + \mathbf{e}_2 \otimes \mathbf{e}_2 + \mathbf{e}_2 \otimes \mathbf{e}_3 + \mathbf{e}_3 \otimes \mathbf{e}_3 + \mathbf{e}_3 \otimes \mathbf{e}_1$. Is ξ a decomposable tensor? If yes, decompose it in the form of $\xi = u \otimes v$, where $u, v \in V$.

10. Let $\xi = 14\mathbf{e}_1 \otimes \mathbf{e}_1 + 8\mathbf{e}_1 \otimes \mathbf{e}_2 - 6\mathbf{e}_1 \otimes \mathbf{e}_3 - 21\mathbf{e}_2 \otimes \mathbf{e}_1 - 12\mathbf{e}_2 \otimes \mathbf{e}_2 + 9\mathbf{e}_2 \otimes \mathbf{e}_3 + 35\mathbf{e}_3 \otimes \mathbf{e}_1 + 20\mathbf{e}_3 \otimes \mathbf{e}_2 - 15\mathbf{e}_3 \otimes \mathbf{e}_3$. Is ξ a decomposable tensor? If yes, decompose it in the form of $\xi = u \otimes v$, where $u, v \in V$.

11. Show that if all components of a tensor are zero in one coordinate system, then they are all zero in any coordinate system.

12. Show that if the components of two tensors are equal in one coordinate system, they they are equal in any coordinate system.

Appendix

A1. A Brief History of Tensors

Tensor was a term first used by William Rowan Hamilton to denote the modulus of a quaternion. He also defined many other terms, including "versor" and "right versor" for the quaternion terminology. This meaning of tensor is not related to the modern sense and was abandoned.

The dyadics of Gibbs and the absolute differential calculus of Ricci were the two major threads which led to the modern theory of tensors.

The dyadics that Gibbs defined is exactly the tensor product in the modern sense without the modern jargon to make it rigorous, although Gibbs was limited to 3-dimensional spaces. A dyad is the juxtaposition of two vectors. A dyadic is the formal combination of dyads. Gibbs used the term dyadics instead of tensors. He did define the terms "versor" and "right tensor" as special types of dyadics. He used dyadics as linear transformations by way of dot multiplication with a vector. When a dyadic is applied (dot product) on a vector, he called the effect, or the resulting vector a displacement or strain. His intuition was that the linear transformation was like some elastic deformation in the shape and/or position of the body caused by some physical force. Rotation, elongation and shearing are some of the examples. He defined a "versor" (similar to versor quaternion of Hamilton) as a dyadic that results in a rotation. He defined a "right tensor" as a dyadic in the form $a\mathbf{e}_1\mathbf{e}_1 + b\mathbf{e}_2\mathbf{e}_2 + c\mathbf{e}_3\mathbf{e}_3$. The word "tensor" is used in the sense of stretching because a "right tensor" consists of three elongations.

The tensors of Ricci are constructed on the tangent spaces of a differentiable manifold. The tangent spaces are linear spaces. Ricci defined tensors (tensor fields) in terms of components and properties of coordinate change. Nowadays we understand that the coordinate change of tensors in the tangent space is caused by the basis change of the tangent space, which in turn is caused by the local coordinate change on the manifold.

Much later mathematicians realized tensor is really an algebraic concept in linear spaces and can be disentangled and distilled from differentiable manifold context. (The dyadics of Gibbs are purely algebraic.)

Nowadays, the learning path for a student is just the opposite, which is the logical way—he learns the tensor algebra first and uses that in tensor analysis or differentiable manifolds. The algebraic essence of tensor is really multilinear mapping and the coordinate change property is only the consequence of multilinear mapping.

Tensor product in the form in modern text was defined by H. Whitney [Whitney (1938)]. N. Bourbaki used a constructive definition by using free algebra and quotient algebra [Bourbaki (1942)], and this is one of the popular equivalent modern definitions used today. It is exactly the idea of Gibbs dyadics, but in a polished and rigorous language.

The tensor analysis is part of the theory of differentiable manifolds and it was made clear when the concepts in tensor algebra were made clear.

A2. Alternative Definitions of Tensor

For the reader's reference, we compare the old-fashioned definition, as well as other equivalent alternative modern definitions.

(1) Old-fashioned Definition

The following definition is often seen in physics and engineering books, especially in general relativity. It follows the definition originally given by Ricci in his absolute differential calculus, now known as tensor analysis.

Let $T^{ij}(x^1, \ldots, x^n)$, $i, j = 1, 2, \ldots, n$ be a set of quantities, each is a function of $x^1, \ldots, x^n$. T^{ij} is said to be the components of a **contravariant tensor** (of degree 2), if they transform according to the following law:

$$\overline{T}^{ij} = \sum_{r,s=1}^{n} \frac{\partial \bar{x}^i}{\partial x^r} \frac{\partial \bar{x}^j}{\partial x^s} T^{rs},$$

when the coordinates $x^1, \ldots, x^n$ are transformed to

$$\bar{x}^1 = \bar{x}^1(x^1, \ldots, x^n),$$
$$\cdots \qquad\qquad\qquad (2.13)$$
$$\bar{x}^n = \bar{x}^n(x^1, \ldots, x^n).$$

A set of quantities T_{ij} is said to be the components of a **covariant tensor** (of degree 2), if they transform according to the following law:

$$\overline{T}_{ij} = \sum_{r,s=1}^{n} \frac{\partial x^r}{\partial \bar{x}^i} \frac{\partial x^s}{\partial \bar{x}^j} T_{rs},$$

when the coordinates $x^1, \ldots, x^n$ are transformed as in Eq. 2.13.

A set of quantities T_j^i is said to be the components of a **mixed tensor** (of degree 2), if they transform according to the following law:

$$\overline{T}_j^i = \sum_{r,s=1}^{n} \frac{\partial \bar{x}^i}{\partial x^r} \frac{\partial x^s}{\partial \bar{x}^j} T_s^r,$$

when the coordinates $x^1, \ldots, x^n$ are transformed as in Eq. 2.13.

Remark 17. This rather defines a tensor field in $\mathbb{R}^n$, or on a differentiable manifold in the most general context. $(x^1, \ldots, x^n)$ is the local coordinates of a point on the manifold and a change in local coordinates induces a basis change in the tangent space,

$$\frac{\partial}{\partial \bar{x}^i} = \sum_{k=1}^n \frac{\partial x^k}{\partial \bar{x}^i} \frac{\partial}{\partial x^k}.$$

(see Part III Chap. 2).

We could distill the concept of tensor for a single point, instead of in the context of a tensor field. The following distilled version of the old-fashioned definition is also seen in some physics and engineering books. It keeps the essence in Ricci's definition, which is the coordinate transformation law for the components, without using arbitrary local coordinate change Eq. 2.13, but using linear transformation instead.

A set of quantities T^{ij} is said to be the components of a **contravariant tensor** (of degree 2), if they transform according to the following law:

$$\overline{T}^{ij} = \sum_{r,s=1}^n [A^{-1}]_r^i [A^{-1}]_s^j T^{rs},$$

when the coordinates $x^1, \ldots, x^n$ are transformed to

$$\bar{x}^i = A_j^i x^j.$$

A set of quantities T_{ij} is said to be the components of a **covariant tensor** (of degree 2), if they transform according to the following law:

$$\overline{T}_{ij} = \sum_{r,s=1}^n A_i^r A_j^s T_{rs}.$$

A set of quantities T_j^i is said to be the components of a **mixed tensor** (of degree 2), if they transform according to the following law:

$$\overline{T}_j^i = \sum_{r,s=1}^n [A^{-1}]_s^i A_j^s T_s^r.$$

Remark 18. The coordinate transformation laws are the same as those in Theorem 7. However, what is not made clear here is that how the components of the tensor are related to the basis. What is missing in this definition is exactly the bilinear mapping $\otimes : V \times V \to V \otimes V$ in the modern definition, which both Ricci and Gibbs assumed implicitly.

(2) Axiomatic Definition Using the Unique Factorization Property

---

Definition 13. (Equivalent Definition) Tensor product

Let U, V and W be linear spaces over a field F. $(W, \otimes)$ is called a **tensor product space** of U and V, if $\otimes : U \times V \to W$; $(u, v) \mapsto u \otimes v$ is a bilinear mapping and satisfies the following universal property: For any linear space X and bilinear mapping $\psi : U \times V \to X$, there exists a *unique* linear mapping $T : W \to X$ such that

$$\psi = T \circ \otimes.$$

We denote $W = U \otimes V$. The vectors in W are called **tensors** over U and V.

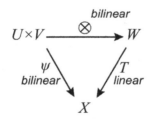

Figure 2.3   Unique factorization property of tensor product.

Remark 19. Some authors use this definition and claim that we are interested in linearizing bilinear mappings. In fact, we have very little interest in linearizing bilinear mappings. It is just an economical workaround to characterize the maximal span and generating properties given in Definition 3.

There are quite some similarities between a tensor product mapping $\otimes$ and a non-singular linear mapping T but there are also differences. If we look at the statements about nonsingular linear mappings in Theorem 9, all the statements are equivalent and we can use any one of them as the definition of a nonsingular linear mapping. We list some of the properties in Theorem 9 in the following.

Let V and W be finite dimensional linear spaces and let $T : V \to W$ be a linear mapping.

(L1) T is nonsingular.

(L2) T is injective.

(L4) $Tv = \mathbf{0} \Rightarrow v = \mathbf{0}$.

(L5) T maps linearly independent sets in V to linearly independent sets in W.

(L6) $\dim(\mathrm{im}(T)) = \dim V$. ($T$ has full rank).

(L8) Factorization property: for any linear space X and any linear mapping $\psi : V \to X$, there exists a linear mapping $\Psi : W \to X$ such that $\psi = \Psi \circ T$.

Now let us compare with tensor product mappings. We list some properties of tensor product mappings as follows. A tensor product mapping has similarities to a nonsingular linear mapping, but as a bilinear mapping, it is also different from a linear mapping.

Let U, V and W be finite dimensional linear spaces and let $\otimes : U \times V \to W$ be a tensor product mapping.

Most tensor product mappings are neither injective or surjective. So there is nothing similar to (L1).

(T1) $x \neq 0$ and $y \neq 0 \Rightarrow x \otimes y \neq 0$. (Theorem 4)

(T2) Linearly independent sets are mapped to linearly independent sets. (Definition 3)

(T3) $\dim(\mathrm{span}(\mathrm{im} \otimes)) = \dim U \cdot \dim V$. (Definition 3)

(T4) Factorization property: For any linear space X and bilinear mapping $\psi : U \times V \to X$, there exists a linear mapping $T : W \to X$ such that

$$\psi = T \circ \otimes.$$

(T1) is analog to (L4). A tensor product mapping has no zero divisors. However, although (T1) is true for tensor product mappings, it is not a characterizing property. It is a necessary condition but not a sufficient condition. The bilinear mapping in Example 5, the product of complex numbers, is a counterexample. The product of complex numbers has no zero divisors but is not a tensor product mapping.

(T2) is condition (1) in Definition 3. It is analog to (L5).

(T3) appears in Definition 4 and says span(im⊗) has the maximal dimension. It is analog to (L6).

(T2), (T3) and (T4) are equivalent to each other. Any of these, combined with condition (2) in Definition 3 is equivalent to the unique factorization property in Definition 13.

(3) Definition by Construction—Dyadics

Definition 14. (Equivalent Definition) Tensor product

Let U and V be linear spaces over a field F. We construct a linear space as follows and shall call it the **tensor product** of U and V, denoted by $U \otimes V$.

Let $\mathscr{V}_F \langle U \times V \rangle$ be the free vector space generated by the set $U \times V$. Let Z be the subspace of $\mathscr{V}_F \langle U \times V \rangle$ generated by all the elements of the form

$$a(u_1, v) + b(u_2, v) - (au_1 + bu_2, v) \tag{2.14}$$

and

$$a(u, v_1) + b(u, v_2) - (u, av_1 + bv_2) \qquad (2.15)$$

for all $a, b \in F$, $u, u_1, u_2 \in U$ and $v, v_1, v_2 \in V$.

The quotient space

$$U \otimes V = \frac{\mathscr{V}_F \langle U \times V \rangle}{Z}$$

is called the **tensor product** of U and V. The elements in $U \otimes V$ are called **tensors** over U and V.

Define a mapping $\otimes : U \times V \to U \otimes V$ such that for all $u \in U$ and $v \in V$, $(u, v) \mapsto u \otimes v \overset{\text{def}}{=} [(u, v)]$, where $[(u, v)]$ is the equivalence class for (u, v) in $\mathscr{V}_F \langle U \times V \rangle$ defined by the subspace Z. This mapping is a bilinear mapping and is called the **canonical bilinear mapping**.

This definition [Bourbaki (1942); Roman (2005)] seems abstract but the idea is really simple. This is nothing but Gibbs dyadics in the new clothes of modern language. See Example 10. Gibbs introduced the dyadics in 1884. The terms "multilinear mapping" and "linear combination" were too modern for Gibbs. He had all the intuitive ideas but he did not make them explicit. In the modern language, the dyad, juxtaposition of two vectors **uv**, is nothing but the ordered pair $(\mathbf{u}, \mathbf{v})$. The set of all the dyads, is just the Cartesian product $U \times V$ in modern language. The "free vector space generated by a set X" is a very ingenious way to make the intuitive "formal finite linear combination" precise.

Remark 20. The term "canonical bilinear mapping" here is the same as the "tensor product mapping" we defined in Section 3 in this chapter. It should not be confused with the "canonical mapping", or "canonical surjection" in the context of quotient set defined in Chap. 0. Tensor product mapping, or canonical bilinear mapping is neither injective nor surjective in general.

(4) Definition Using a Model—Bilinear Forms

Definition 15. (Equivalent Definition) Tensor product

Let U and V be linear spaces over a field F, and U^* and V^* be their dual spaces. Let $W = L(U, V; F)$ be the linear space of all bilinear forms $\xi : U \times V \to F$. (See Example 11.) We define a mapping $\otimes : U^* \times V^* \to W$; $(f, h) \mapsto \xi = f \otimes h$ such that for all $x \in U$ and

$y \in V$,

$$\xi(x, y) \overset{\text{def}}{=} f(x)h(y).$$

The linear space of all bilinear forms $U^* \otimes V^* = L(U, V; F)$ is called the **tensor product** of U^* and V^*.

The **tensor product** of linear spaces U and V is defined as the linear space $L(U^*, V^*; F)$ of all bilinear forms $\eta : U^* \times V^* \to F$. We denote $U \otimes V = L(U^*, V^*; F)$. The vectors in $x \in U$ and $y \in V$ are viewed as linear functions on U^* and V^*. So for any $f \in U^*$ and $h \in V^*$, $x \otimes y(f, h) = x(f)y(h) = f(x)h(y)$.

A3. Bilinear Forms and Quadratic Forms

Bilinear forms and quadratic forms are important in defining additional structures in linear spaces. If the bilinear form is symmetric and positive definite, the space is called an **inner product space** (a finite dimensional inner product space is called a **Euclidean space**). When the positive definite condition is weakened to nondegenerate, it is called a **Minkowski space**. Clifford algebra $Cl(V)$ over linear space V requires V having a nondegenerate symmetric bilinear form. Riemannian manifold is a differentiable manifold whose tangent space at each point is an inner product space. Pseudo-Riemannian manifold is a differentiable manifold whose tangent space at each point is a Minkowski space.

A bilinear form is defined as special case of bilinear mapping in Definition 1. Let $\Phi : V \times V \to F$ be a bilinear form and $\{e_1, \ldots, e_n\}$ be a basis for V. For $x = x_1 e_1 + \cdots + x_n e_n$ and $y = y_1 e_1 + \cdots + y_n e_n$,

$$\Phi(x, y) = \sum_{i,j=1}^{n} a_{ij} x_i y_j.$$

The matrix $[a_{ij}]$ is called the **matrix associated with the bilinear form** with respect to basis $\{e_1, \ldots, e_n\}$.

Definition 16. Degenerate, nondegenerate bilinear form

A bilinear form $\Phi : V \times V \to F$ is said to be **degenerate**, if there exists $v \neq 0 \in V$, such that for all $x \in V$, $\Phi(v, x) = 0$, or for all $x \in V$, $\Phi(x, v) = 0$. If Φ is not degenerate, then Φ is said to be

nondegenerate.

Equivalently, Φ is called nondegenerate if
for all $x \in V$, $\Phi(v, x) = 0 \Rightarrow v = 0$, and
for all $x \in V$, $\Phi(x, v) = 0 \Rightarrow v = 0$.

Definition 17. Quadratic form

Given a linear space V over a field F, a **quadratic form** is a mapping $Q : V \to F$ satisfying the following two conditions.

(1) $Q(ax) = a^2 Q(x)$ for all $a \in F$ and $x \in V$.

(2) $\Phi(x, y) \stackrel{\text{def}}{=} Q(x + y) - Q(x) - Q(y)$ is a symmetric bilinear form on V.

Φ is called the symmetric bilinear form associated with Q.

This definition is equivalent to the old-fashioned definition of a quadratic form, as a quadratic homogeneous polynomial with coefficients in a field F:

$$Q(x_1, \ldots, x_n) = \sum_{i,j=1}^{n} a_{ij} x_i x_j,$$

where the matrix $[a_{ij}]$ is a symmetric matrix. The symmetric matrix $[a_{ij}]$ is called the **matrix associated with quadratic form** Q.

Conversely, given any symmetric bilinear form Φ, $Q(x) \stackrel{\text{def}}{=} \Phi(x, x)$ defines a quadratic form Q, called the quadratic form associated to Φ.

Definition 18. Positive definite, negative definite, indefinite

A quadratic form Q is said to be **positive definite**, if for all $x \neq 0$, $Q(x) > 0$. Q is said to be **negative definite**, if for all $x \neq 0$, $Q(x) < 0$. Q is said to be **indefinite**, if it is neither positive definite nor negative definite.

A symmetric bilinear Φ form is said to be **positive definite**, (**negative definite, indefinite**) if the associated quadratic form Q is positive definite (negative definite, indefinite).

A quadratic form Q is said to be **degenerate (nondegenerate)**, if the associated symmetric bilinear form Φ is degenerate (nondegenerate).

Chapter 3

Exterior Algebra

It is not now possible for me to enter into those thoughts; I become dizzy and see sky-blue before my eyes when I read them.

> — *Heinrich Baltzer writing to Möbius after reading Grassmann's book*

If as you write me, you have not relished Grassmann's Ausdehnungslehre, *I reply that I have the same experience. I likewise have managed to get through no more than the first two sheets of his book.*

> — *August Möbius writing back to Baltzer*

Reading Guide. Exterior algebra, also known as Grassmann algebra, has really simple intuitions in geometry, although it may look abstract. Using tensor concept to define Grassmann algebra is certainly a laconic and rigorous approach but it is not the most intuitive approach. In fact, when Hermann Grassmann introduced his new algebra in his book *Theory of Extensions (Ausdehnungslehre)* in 1844, the modern language of tensors was not available. We start with the intuition in geometry in §1. We adopt a more intuitive, less rigorous approach by constructing Grassmann algebra using "formal wedge product" and "formal linear combinations" in §2. We give a special treatment of exterior forms in Appendix A1, which is the dual case of exterior vectors. We include the tensor approaches in Appendix A2 and A3 for comparison.

§1   Intuition in Geometry

1.1   Bivectors

First let us have a review of analytic geometry. Let $\{e_1, e_2\}$ be a basis for the Euclidean plane $\mathbb{R}^2$, and $a, b \in \mathbb{R}^2$ be two vectors in the plane.

If $a = a_1 e_1 + a_2 e_2$ and $b = b_1 e_1 + b_2 e_2$, the directed area of the parallelogram spanned by vectors a and b is

$$\begin{vmatrix} a_1 & a_2 \\ b_1 & b_2 \end{vmatrix} = a_1 b_2 - a_2 b_1,$$

where $\begin{vmatrix} a_1 & a_2 \\ b_1 & b_2 \end{vmatrix}$ denotes the determinant. We use $a \wedge b$ to denote the parallelogram spanned by a and b, and call it the **wedge product** of a and b. We associate the directed area of the parallelogram to $a \wedge b$. The directed area of $a \wedge b$ is positive if the angle from a to b is counterclockwise. Otherwise, it is negative. Apparently $a \wedge b = -b \wedge a$.

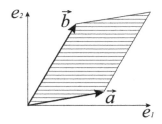

Figure 3.1   Wedge product of two vectors in the plane.

Let $u, v \in \mathbb{R}^2$ be two other vectors and $u \wedge v$ be the parallelogram spanned by u and v. Since the two parallelograms $a \wedge b$ and $u \wedge v$ are in the same plane, we associate the sum of the directed areas of the two parallelograms to $a \wedge b + u \wedge v$.

Next, suppose we have two vectors $a, b \in \mathbb{R}^3$ in the 3-D space. Let $a = a_1 e_1 + a_2 e_2 + a_3 e_3$, and $b = b_1 e_1 + b_2 e_2 + b_3 e_3$. We also define $a \wedge b$ to be the parallelogram spanned by a and b in space and associate the directed area of this parallelogram to $a \wedge b$. Let $u, v \in \mathbb{R}^3$ be two other vectors and $u \wedge v$ be the parallelogram spanned by u and v. Now $a \wedge b$ and $u \wedge v$ are in different planes. How do we define $a \wedge b + u \wedge v$?

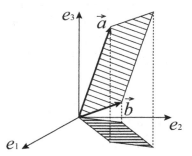

Figure 3.2   Wedge product of two vectors in space.

Recall that $a \wedge b$ represent the parallelogram spanned by a and b. So $a \wedge b$ is no longer a vector in $\mathbb{R}^3$. To find a solution to define $a \wedge b + u \wedge v$, we first make projections of the vectors a, b onto the coordinate planes. $a_1 e_1 + a_2 e_2$ and $b_1 e_1 + b_2 e_2$ are the projections of a and b in the $e_1 \wedge e_2$ plane. The area of the parallelogram which is the projection of $a \wedge b$ onto $e_1 \wedge e_2$ is $\begin{vmatrix} a_1 & a_2 \\ b_1 & b_2 \end{vmatrix} = a_1 b_2 - a_2 b_1$. Similarly, the area of the projection of $a \wedge b$ onto $e_2 \wedge e_3$ plane is $\begin{vmatrix} a_2 & a_3 \\ b_2 & b_3 \end{vmatrix} = a_2 b_3 - a_3 b_2$. The area of the projection of $a \wedge b$ onto $e_3 \wedge e_1$ plane is $\begin{vmatrix} a_3 & a_1 \\ b_3 & b_1 \end{vmatrix} = a_3 b_1 - a_1 b_3$. We use a 3-tuple (A_{12}, A_{23}, A_{31}) to denote $a \wedge b$, where A_{12}, A_{23} and A_{32} are the areas of the projections of $a \wedge b$ in three coordinate planes, $e_1 \wedge e_2$, $e_2 \wedge e_3$ and $e_3 \wedge e_1$ respectively,

$$a \wedge b = (a_1 b_2 - a_2 b_1) e_1 \wedge e_2 + (a_2 b_3 - a_3 b_2) e_2 \wedge e_3 + (a_3 b_1 - a_1 b_3) e_3 \wedge e_1$$
$$= A_{12} e_1 \wedge e_2 + A_{23} e_2 \wedge e_3 + A_{31} e_3 \wedge e_1.$$

Similarly, we can make the three components (B_{12}, B_{23}, B_{31}) to represent

$$u \wedge v = (u_1 v_2 - u_2 v_1) e_1 \wedge e_2 + (u_2 v_3 - u_3 v_2) e_2 \wedge e_3 + (u_3 v_1 - u_1 v_3) e_3 \wedge e_1$$
$$= B_{12} e_1 \wedge e_2 + B_{23} e_2 \wedge e_3 + B_{31} e_3 \wedge e_1.$$

We add them component-wise, and define

$$a \wedge b + u \wedge v \stackrel{\text{def}}{=} (A_{12} + B_{12}) e_1 \wedge e_2 + (A_{23} + B_{23}) e_2 \wedge e_3 + (A_{31} + B_{31}) e_3 \wedge e_1.$$

So all the wedge products of vectors like $a \wedge b$ and $u \wedge v$ form a linear space of its own, outside $\mathbb{R}^3$, which we call the **wedge product** (or **exterior product**) of $\mathbb{R}^3$ and itself, denoted by $\Lambda^2(\mathbb{R}^3)$. It is easy to see that the dimension of $\Lambda^2(\mathbb{R}^3)$ is 3. Vectors in $\Lambda^2(\mathbb{R}^3)$ are called **bivectors** (or **2-vectors**).

The wedge product has the following properties.

(1) Bilinear

$$(\lambda_1 a_1 + \lambda_2 a_2) \wedge b = \lambda_1 a_1 \wedge b + \lambda_2 a_2 \wedge b, \tag{3.1}$$

$$a \wedge (\lambda_1 b_1 + \lambda_2 b_2) = \lambda_1 a \wedge b_1 + \lambda_2 a \wedge b_2, \tag{3.2}$$

for all $a, a_1, a_2, b, b_1, b_2 \in \mathbb{R}^3$ and $\lambda_1, \lambda_2 \in \mathbb{R}$.
(2) Antisymmetric

$$a \wedge b = -b \wedge a. \tag{3.3}$$

Note that Eq. (3.1) and Eq. (3.3) imply Eq. 3.2.

Eq. (3.3) is equivalent to

$$a \wedge a = 0.$$

This is because $a \wedge a = -a \wedge a$ and hence $2a \wedge a = 0$. (We assume the ground field is $\mathbb{R}$ and we are not dealing with fields of characteristic 2).

Remark 1. Cross Link — Wedge Product and Cross Product
    The wedge product defined here is similar to the cross product of two vectors in $\mathbb{R}^3$. They are isomorphic to each other. They are related through Hodge dual. However, this is a coincidence. Cross product can be defined only in three dimensional linear spaces, not for any other dimension.

1.2   Trivectors

Let $a, b, c \in \mathbb{R}^3$ be three vectors. We use $a \wedge b \wedge c$ to denote the directed volume of the parallelepiped spanned by a, b and c. The directed volume is positive if a, b, c are oriented in a right-handed way. Otherwise it is negative. $a \wedge b \wedge c$ is called the **wedge product** of a, b and c. Let $a = a_1 e_1 + a_2 e_2 + a_3 e_3$,

$b = b_1 e_1 + b_2 e_2 + b_3 e_3$ and $c = c_1 e_1 + c_2 e_2 + c_3 e_3$. Then the directed volume associated to $a \wedge b \wedge c$ is

$$\begin{vmatrix} a_1 & a_2 & a_3 \\ b_1 & b_2 & b_3 \\ c_1 & c_2 & c_3 \end{vmatrix}.$$

We define the wedge product of a bivector $a \wedge b$ and a vector c to be $a \wedge b \wedge c$, the directed volume of the parallelepiped spanned by a, b and c, and we define the wedge product of a vector a and a bivector $b \wedge c$ the same as $a \wedge b \wedge c$,

$$a \wedge (b \wedge c) \stackrel{\text{def}}{=} (a \wedge b) \wedge c \stackrel{\text{def}}{=} a \wedge b \wedge c.$$

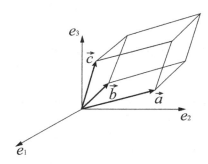

Figure 3.3   Wedge product of three vectors.

Since any three vectors a, b, c can make a parallelepiped (some have zero volume if a, b, c are in the same plane). If we have three other vectors, $u, v, w \in \mathbb{R}^3$, it makes sense to add $a \wedge b \wedge c$ to $u \wedge v \wedge w$. We just add the directed volume of the two. Hence all the trivectors form a one dimensional linear space, denoted by $\Lambda^3(\mathbb{R}^3)$. Vectors in $\Lambda^3(\mathbb{R}^3)$ are called **trivectors** (or **3-vectors**).

Does it make sense to add a vector and a bivector, or to add a bivector and a trivector? They do not make sense before we define them. We can make it to make sense as long as we can find applications. We give the field $\mathbb{R}$ a nickname $\Lambda^0(\mathbb{R}^3)$. We give $\mathbb{R}^3$ a nickname $\Lambda^1(\mathbb{R}^3)$. These $\Lambda^0(\mathbb{R}^3)$, $\Lambda^1(\mathbb{R}^3)$, $\Lambda^2(\mathbb{R}^3)$, $\Lambda^3(\mathbb{R}^3)$ are all different linear spaces with dimensions 1, 3, 3, 1 respectively. It does not make sense to add vectors in different spaces (in our case, scalars, vectors, bivectors and trivectors). However we have developed the direct sum technique in Chap. 1 and we can certainly construct a direct sum of all these space as follows,

$$\Lambda(\mathbb{R}^3) = \Lambda^0(\mathbb{R}^3) \oplus \Lambda^1(\mathbb{R}^3) \oplus \Lambda^2(\mathbb{R}^3) \oplus \Lambda^3(\mathbb{R}^3).$$

This is a 8-dimensional space. We can extend the wedge product to any two elements in $\Lambda(\mathbb{R}^3)$ by using the associative law.

For $\lambda \in \mathbb{R}$ and any $w \in \Lambda(\mathbb{R}^3)$, we define $\lambda \wedge w \overset{\text{def}}{=} w \wedge \lambda \overset{\text{def}}{=} \lambda w$, the same as scalar multiplication of w by scalar λ. The wedge product of a vector and a trivector is always zero. The wedge product of a bivector and a trivector is always zero. This way we have made the wedge product $\wedge : \Lambda(\mathbb{R}^3) \times \Lambda(\mathbb{R}^3) \to \Lambda(\mathbb{R}^3)$ a binary operation on $\Lambda(\mathbb{R}^3)$. Hence $\Lambda(\mathbb{R}^3)$ becomes an algebra over $\mathbb{R}$, called the **exterior algebra**, or **Grassmann algebra**.

We will discuss this in the context of a more general setting in the n-dimensional space $\mathbb{R}^n$ in the next section.

§2   Exterior Algebra

Exterior algebra is an algebra over a field. We recall that an algebra over a field F is a linear space with vector addition, scalar multiplication, and vector multiplication (see Chap. 1 Section 6). In the exterior algebra, this vector multiplication is the **wedge product**.

Let V be a real linear space and $\{e_1, \ldots, e_n\}$ be a basis for V. As we have seen from last section, for vectors $u, v \in V$, the wedge product of u and v is no longer in space V, but rather in a different space $\Lambda^2(V)$. To construct the exterior algebra, we first need to construct the exterior space of degree 2, $\Lambda^2(V)$, as well as the exterior spaces of all other degrees $\Lambda^k(V)$. We construct the exterior algebra on V in the following steps:

Step 1. Construct all the exterior spaces $\Lambda^k(V)$ for $k = 0, 1, 2, ..., n$.

The elements in $\Lambda^k(V)$ shall be called k-vectors. We first consider the "formal wedge product" $u \bar{\wedge} v$, where $u, v \in V$.

Definition 1. Formal wedge product, formal combination, 2-blade, 2-vector

Let $u, v \in V$ be vectors. The **formal wedge product** $u \bar{\wedge} v$ is the concatenation of u, the symbol $\bar{\wedge}$ and v.

The **formal scalar multiplication** of $u \bar{\wedge} v$ and a scalar $k \in F$ is the concatenation of k and $u\bar{\wedge}v$ in the form of $k(u\bar{\wedge}v)$. It is also called a **2-blade**.

The **formal linear combination** of two or more 2-blades $k_1(u_1\bar{\wedge}v_1),\ldots,k_m(u_m\bar{\wedge}v_m)$ with scalar coefficients $k_1,\ldots,k_m \in F$, is defined to be the concatenation of these 2-blades connected by the symbols "+", in the form of

$$k_1(u_1\bar{\wedge}v_1) + \cdots + k_m(u_m\bar{\wedge}v_m).$$

A formal linear combination of 2-blades is called an **exterior vector** of degree 2, or **2-vector**.

Remark 2. Caution — Formal vs. Real

Note that $\bar{\wedge}$ for the formal wedge product is just a symbol without any meaning. The real wedge product $\wedge$ has yet to be defined. The symbol "+" has no meaning either. That is why they are called "formal". We only use them as the "form" of a string of symbols. It is an abuse of notation that we used the same symbol "+" for formal addition and real addition, which is yet to be defined. We did distinguish the formal wedge product $\bar{\wedge}$ from the real wedge product $\wedge$. It is a little inconsistent. This will not cause any confusion because it will turn out that the real wedge product and the formal wedge product, the real sum and the formal sum, are in fact the same.

Remark 3. Cross Link — Formal Linear Combinations

We have already used the method of formal linear combinations in one example of tensor product construction, namely, the Gibbs dyadics (see Chap. 2 Example 10).

Let $\Lambda^2(V)$ be the set of all 2-vectors. Define the sum of two 2-vectors to be the formal sum (two strings connected by a symbol "+") of two 2-vectors. Define the scalar multiplication of a 2-vector and a scalar to be the formal scalar multiplication.

We stipulate that the formal wedge product obey the following laws:

(1) Bilinear: for all $u,\ u_1,\ u_2, v,\ v_1,\ v_2 \in V$ and $\alpha, \beta \in F$,

$$(\alpha u_1 + \beta u_2)\bar{\wedge}v = \alpha(u_1\bar{\wedge}v) + \beta(u_2\bar{\wedge}v),$$
$$u\bar{\wedge}(\alpha v_1 + \beta v_2) = \alpha(u\bar{\wedge}v_1) + \beta u\bar{\wedge}v_2.$$

(2) Anticommutative:

$$u\bar{\wedge}v = -v\bar{\wedge}u. \tag{3.4}$$

$\Lambda^2(V)$ is a linear space with respect to addition and scalar multiplication, called the **exterior space of V of degree 2**. It follows from (2) that

$$v\bar{\wedge}v = 0.$$

So $\{e_i \bar\wedge e_j\}_{i<j}^n$ will be a basis for $\Lambda^2(V)$ and the dimension of $\Lambda^2(V)$ is $\binom{n}{2}$.

In general, we can construct the **formal wedge product** $v_1 \bar\wedge \cdots \bar\wedge v_k$ of vectors $v_1, \ldots, v_k$ and k-**blades** in a similar way. A formal linear combination of k-blades is called an **exterior vector** of degree k, or k-**vector**, or **multivector**. $\Lambda^k(V)$ is the linear space consists of all the k-vectors subject to the following laws:

(1) Multilinear: for all $v_1, \ldots, u_i, v_i, \ldots, v_k \in V$ and $\alpha, \beta \in F$,

$$v_1 \bar\wedge \cdots \bar\wedge (\alpha u_i + \beta v_i) \bar\wedge \cdots \bar\wedge v_k$$
$$= \alpha (v_1 \bar\wedge \cdots \bar\wedge u_i \bar\wedge \cdots \bar\wedge v_k) + \beta (v_1 \bar\wedge \cdots \bar\wedge v_i \bar\wedge \cdots \bar\wedge v_k).$$

(2) Anticommutative:

$$v_1 \bar\wedge \cdots \bar\wedge v_i \bar\wedge \cdots \bar\wedge v_j \bar\wedge \cdots v_k = -v_1 \bar\wedge \cdots \bar\wedge v_j \bar\wedge \cdots \bar\wedge v_i \bar\wedge \cdots \bar\wedge v_k.$$

$\Lambda^k(V)$ is a linear space with respect to addition and scalar multiplication, called the **exterior space over** V **of degree** k. $\{e_{i_1} \bar\wedge \cdots \bar\wedge e_{i_k}\}_{i_1 < \cdots < i_k}^n$ forms a basis for $\Lambda^k(V)$. $\Lambda^k(V)$ has dimension of $\binom{n}{k}$.

We define $\Lambda^0(V) \overset{\text{def}}{=} F$ and $\Lambda^1(V) \overset{\text{def}}{=} V$ as two special cases of $\Lambda^k(V)$.

Step 2. Construct the direct sum of these exterior spaces

$$\Lambda(V) \overset{\text{def}}{=} \Lambda^0(V) \oplus \Lambda^1(V) \oplus \Lambda^2(V) \oplus \cdots \oplus \Lambda^n(V).$$

$\Lambda(V)$ is called the **Grassmann space** over V. The dimension of $\Lambda(V)$ is

$$\binom{n}{0} + \binom{n}{1} + \binom{n}{2} + \cdots + \binom{n}{n} = 2^n.$$

Step 3. In $\Lambda(V)$, define wedge product of a p-vector and a q-vector.

First we define the wedge product of a p-blade and a q-blade. Let $\xi = u_1 \bar\wedge \cdots \bar\wedge u_p$ be a p-blade and $\zeta = v_1 \bar\wedge \cdots \bar\wedge v_q$ be a q-blade. The wedge product of ξ and ζ is defined to be the formal wedge product of $u_1, \ldots, u_p, v_1, \ldots, v_q$, which is a $(p+q)$-blade,

$$\xi \wedge \zeta \overset{\text{def}}{=} u_1 \bar\wedge \cdots \bar\wedge u_p \bar\wedge v_1 \bar\wedge \cdots \bar\wedge v_q.$$

In general, p-vectors are linear combinations of p-blades and q-vectors are linear combinations of q-blades. So the definition of wedge product can be extended to a p-vector and a q-vector by multilinearity.

It can be proved that the wedge product is associative. Furthermore, for vectors $v_1, \ldots v_k \in V$,

$$v_1 \wedge \cdots \wedge v_k = v_1 \bar\wedge \cdots \bar\wedge v_k.$$

So we do not need to distinguish the real wedge product "$\wedge$" from the formal wedge product "$\bar\wedge$" and simply use the symbol "$\wedge$" afterward.

The wedge product has become a binary operation $\wedge : \Lambda(V) \times \Lambda(V) \to \Lambda(V)$ and $\Lambda(V)$ has become an algebra over F.   (End of Step 3. Phew!)

$\Lambda(V)$ with the wedge product as a binary operation is called the **exterior algebra** , or **Grassmann algebra** on linear space V. You may want to compare this lengthier but more intuitive approach to the more concise but abstract approaches to the definition of exterior algebra in Appendix A2 and A3.

Remark 4. Caution — k-blades and k-vectors
k-blades are k-vectors but k-vectors are linear combinations of k-blades and may not be able to be expressed as a single k-blade. The k-blades are also called k-monomials while the general k-vectors are like "polynomials". A k-blade is also called a **decomposable k-vector**. There are **nondecomposable** k-vectors, which cannot be expressed as a single k-blade. For example, let $(e_1, e_2, e_3, e_4\}$ be a basis for V and $\xi = e_1 \wedge e_2 + e_3 \wedge e_4$ is a nondecomposable 2-vector.

The following theorems describe the properties of the wedge product.

Theorem 1. *Let V be a linear space. For all vectors $u, v \in V$,*

(1) $u \wedge v = -v \wedge u$.
(2) $v \wedge v = 0$.

Remark 5. Elaboration — Equivalence of $u \wedge v = -v \wedge u$ and $v \wedge v = 0$
Properties (1) and (2) in this theorem are equivalent if the characteristic of the ground field F of V is not 2. Here is a brief sketch of the proof of this equivalence when $\mathrm{char}(F) \neq 2$.
(1) $\Rightarrow$ (2):

$$u \wedge v = -v \wedge u$$
$$\Rightarrow v \wedge v = -v \wedge v$$
$$\Rightarrow v \wedge v + v \wedge v = 0$$
$$\Rightarrow 2v \wedge v = 0$$
$$\Rightarrow v \wedge v = 0.$$

$(2) \Rightarrow (1)$:

$$v \wedge v = 0$$
$$\Rightarrow (u + v) \wedge (u + v) = 0$$
$$\Rightarrow u \wedge u + u \wedge v + v \wedge u + v \wedge v = 0$$
$$\Rightarrow u \wedge v + v \wedge u = 0$$
$$\Rightarrow u \wedge v = -v \wedge u.$$

Theorem 2. *Let $\xi, \xi_1, \xi_2 \in \Lambda(V)$ be p-vectors, $\eta, \eta_1, \eta_2 \in \Lambda(V)$ be q-vectors and $\zeta \in \Lambda(V)$ be an r-vector. Then*

(1) Associative law:
$(\xi \wedge \eta) \wedge \zeta = \xi \wedge (\eta \wedge \zeta)$.

(2) Distributive law:
$(\xi_1 + \xi_2) \wedge \eta = \xi_1 \wedge \eta + \xi_2 \wedge \eta$,
$\xi \wedge (\eta_1 + \eta_2) = \xi \wedge \eta_1 + \xi \wedge \eta_2$.

(3) Supercommutative law:

$$\xi \wedge \eta = \begin{cases} -\eta \wedge \xi & \text{if } pq \text{ is odd} \\ \eta \wedge \xi & \text{if } pq \text{ is even}, \end{cases} \tag{3.5}$$

To put these two cases together, we have

$$\xi \wedge \eta = (-1)^{pq} \eta \wedge \xi. \tag{3.6}$$

Remark 6. Caution — Anticommutative Law

The properties $\xi \wedge \eta = -\eta \wedge \xi$ and $\xi \wedge \xi = 0$ are not always true for multivectors $\xi, \eta \in \Lambda(V)$ in general. They are true only in the special case when $\xi, \eta \in V$ are vectors in V. For example, let $(e_1, e_2, e_3, e_4\}$ be a basis for V and $\xi = e_1 \wedge e_2 + e_3 \wedge e_4$. Then

$$\xi \wedge \xi = (e_1 \wedge e_2 + e_3 \wedge e_4) \wedge (e_1 \wedge e_2 + e_3 \wedge e_4)$$
$$= 2e_1 \wedge e_2 \wedge e_3 \wedge e_4$$
$$\neq 0.$$

So the exterior algebras are not anticommutative, nor are they commutative. Algebras with the property of Eq. 3.5 are called **supercommutative algebras**. The exterior algebras are supercommutative algebras.

Remark 7. Comparison — Wedge Product and Cross Product

There are similarities between the wedge product and the cross product but there are also differences. The cross product is defined as $\times : V \times V \to V$. The wedge product can be used in two different senses. The first is the wedge product of two vectors, $\wedge : V \times V \to \Lambda^2(V)$. The second is the wedge product of two multivectors in The exterior algebra, $\wedge : \Lambda(V) \times \Lambda(V) \to \Lambda(V)$.

First compare the cross product with the wedge product of two vectors. Both of them are anticommutative.

Next compare the cross product with the wedge product of two multivectors in $\Lambda(V)$. The wedge product of two multivectors is not always anticommutative. The cross product is not associative while the wedge product of two multivectors is always associative.

The wedge product and determinant are closely related.

Example 1. Let $V = \mathbb{R}^3$, $a = a_1e_1 + a_2e_2 + a_3e_3$, $b = b_1e_1 + b_2e_2 + b_3e_3$ and $c = c_1e_1 + c_2e_2 + c_3e_3$ Using the rules for wedge product, we find,

$$a \wedge b = (a_1e_1 + a_2e_2 + a_3e_3) \wedge (b_1e_1 + b_2e_2 + b_3e_3)$$
$$= (a_1b_2 - a_2b_1)e_1 \wedge e_2 + (a_2b_3 - a_3b_2)e_2 \wedge e_{23} + (a_3b_1 - a_1b_3)e_3 \wedge e_1$$
$$= \begin{vmatrix} a_1 & a_2 \\ b_1 & b_2 \end{vmatrix} e_1 \wedge e_2 + \begin{vmatrix} a_2 & a_3 \\ b_2 & b_3 \end{vmatrix} e_2 \wedge e_3 + \begin{vmatrix} a_3 & a_1 \\ b_3 & b_1 \end{vmatrix} e_3 \wedge e_1.$$

$$a \wedge b \wedge c = (a_1e_1 + a_2e_2 + a_3e_3) \wedge (b_1e_1 + b_2e_2 + b_3e_3) \wedge (c_1e_1 + c_2e_2 + c_3e_3)$$
$$= (a_1b_2c_3 + a_2b_3c_1 + a_3b_1c_2 - a_1b_3c_2 - a_2b_1c_3 - a_3b_2c_1)e_1 \wedge e_2 \wedge e_3$$
$$= \begin{vmatrix} a_1 & a_2 & a_3 \\ b_1 & b_2 & b_3 \\ c_1 & c_2 & c_3 \end{vmatrix} e_1 \wedge e_2 \wedge e_3. \qquad \clubsuit$$

In general, we have the wedge product expressed in coordinate form.

Theorem 3. *Let $v_i \in V$ and $v_i = a_{i1}e_1 + \cdots + a_{in}e_n$, $i = 1, \ldots, k$. Then*

$$v_1 \wedge \cdots \wedge v_k = \sum_{1 \leq i_1 < \cdots < i_k \leq n} \begin{vmatrix} a_{1i_1} & \cdots & a_{1i_k} \\ \cdots & \cdots & \cdots \\ a_{ki_1} & \cdots & a_{ki_k} \end{vmatrix} e_{i_1} \wedge \cdots \wedge e_{i_k}.$$

As a special case, when $k = n$,

$$v_1 \wedge \cdots \wedge v_n = \begin{vmatrix} a_{11} & \cdots & a_{1n} \\ \cdots & \cdots & \cdots \\ a_{n1} & \cdots & a_{nn} \end{vmatrix} e_1 \wedge \cdots \wedge e_n.$$

The following is an application of the wedge product in linear algebra.

Theorem 4. *Let V be a linear space and $v_1, \ldots, v_k \in V$. The vectors $v_1, \ldots, v_k$ are linearly dependent if and only if*

$$v_1 \wedge \cdots \wedge v_k = 0.$$

This theorem provides an algorithm to test whether any group of vectors $v_1, \ldots, v_k$ are independent or not. For a special case, when $k = n$, which is the dimension of V, then $v_1, \ldots, v_n$ are linearly dependent if and only if

$$\begin{vmatrix} a_{11} & \cdots & a_{1n} \\ \cdots & \cdots & \cdots \\ a_{n1} & \cdots & a_{nn} \end{vmatrix} = 0.$$

Exercises

1. Let $v_1 = (1, 2)$ and $v_2 = (-1, 3)$. Find the area of the parallelogram spanned by v_1 and v_2, by calculating $v_1 \wedge v_2$.

2. Let A, B, C be three points in the plane with coordinates $(3, -1)$, $(2, 2)$ and $(-1, 1)$ respectively. Find the area of the triangle $\triangle ABC$ by computing a wedge product. (Hint: Let $v_1 = \mathbf{B} - \mathbf{A}$, $v_2 = \mathbf{C} - \mathbf{A}$. Then the area $\triangle = \frac{1}{2} |v_1 \wedge v_2|$.

3. Let $v_1 = (4, 1, 5)$ and $v_2 = (-3, 0, 2)$. Find the area of the parallelogram spanned by v_1 and v_2. (Hint: calculate $v_1 \times v_2$).

4. Let $v_1 = (2, -1, 0)$, $v_2 = (1, 1, 2)$ and $v_3 = (0, 1, 1)$. Find the volume of the parallelepiped spanned by v_1, v_2 and v_3.

5. Let $v_1 = (2, -1, 0, 3)$, $v_2 = (5, 0, 1, -1)$ and $v_3 = (3, 1, 2, 1)$. Find $v_1 \wedge v_2 \wedge v_3$. Use Theorem 4 to test whether v_1, v_2 and v_3 are linearly independent.

6. Let $\{e_1, e_2, e_3, e_4\}$ be a basis for $\mathbb{R}^4$. Let $u = 2e_1 + 3e_2 - e_3$, $v = -e_2 + 4e_3 + 5e_4$. Find $u \wedge v$.

7. Let $\xi = -e_1 + 2e_2 - 3e_3 + e_4$ and $\eta = 2e_1 \wedge e_2 \wedge e_3 - e_2 \wedge e_3 \wedge e_4$. Find $\xi \wedge \eta$.

8. Let $\xi = 1 - 2e_3 + 5e_1 \wedge e_3 - e_2 \wedge e_4 + 3e_2 \wedge e_3 \wedge e_4$ and $\eta = 2e_1 \wedge e_2 \wedge e_3 - e_2 \wedge e_3 \wedge e_4$. Find $\xi \wedge \eta$.

9. Let V be a linear space and $v_1, v_2, v_3, v_4 \in V$. Find if the 2-vector $v_1 \wedge v_2 + v_2 \wedge v_3 + v_3 \wedge v_4 + v_4 \wedge v_1$ is decomposable. If yes, decompose it in the form of $u_1 \wedge u_2$ where $u_1, u_2 \in V$.

10. Let V be a linear space and $v_1, v_2, \ldots, v_p \in V$. We want to test whether $v_1, v_2, \ldots, v_p$ are linearly independent. Theorem 4 provides a testing algorithm by computing the wedge product of p vectors. Here we give another method. If $p > n$, then they are dependent. If $p \leq n$, make the p vectors an $n \times p$ matrix M. Compute $\det(M^T M)$. The vectors

$v_1, v_2, ..., v_p$ are linearly dependent if and only if $\det(M^T M) = 0$. Compare the two algorithms to see which is faster. Think about all other possible algorithms to determine the linear dependency of a set of vectors. What is the fastest algorithm?

11. Show that if $\xi \in \Lambda^k(V)$ and k is odd, then $\xi \wedge \xi = 0$.

Appendix

A1. Exterior Forms

We constructed the exterior algebra $\Lambda(V)$ of linear space V in Section 2. Now we consider the dual space V^* of V, which consists of all the linear forms on V. The dual space V^* is a linear space after all. So the general theory of exterior algebra $\Lambda(V)$ of linear space V should apply to V^* as well. We can have an exterior algebra $\Lambda(V^*)$ of V^*. The **exterior vectors** in $\Lambda(V^*)$ are the **exterior forms**. Exterior forms are very important in the study of differentiable manifold, as a theory of differential exterior forms developed by Élie Cartan. Because of their special importance, we give an alternative special treatment of the exterior forms here.

In Section 2, when we developed the exterior algebra $\Lambda(V)$, we made use of "formal wedge product" and "formal linear combinations", which is rather informal when "formal" means rigorous in a different sense. Because the linear forms are more concrete functions, we are able to construct the exterior algebra of exterior forms without resorting to the "formal wedge product" and "formal linear combinations". Everything can be developed concretely. (Compare with an alternative definition of tensor product using bilinear forms in Chap. 2 Appendix A2).

A1.1. Exterior Forms

First let us recall the definitions of linear functions, bilinear functions and multilinear functions, defined in Chap. 1 Section 3, Chap. 2 Section 2. They are also called linear forms, bilinear forms and multilinear forms. For reader's convenience, we duplicate them here.

Definition 2. Linear form

Let V be a linear space over a field F. An element $\varphi \in V^*$ in the dual space V^*, namely a linear function $\varphi : V \to F$ is also called a **linear form**.

Definition 3. Bilinear form

Let U and V be linear spaces over a field F. A bilinear mapping $\varphi : U \times V \to F$ is called a **bilinear form**.

Definition 4. Multilinear form

Let $V_1, \ldots, V_k$ be linear spaces over a field F. A multilinear mapping $\varphi : V_1 \times \cdots \times V_k \to F$ is called a **multilinear form** (or **k-linear form**).

Remark 8. Why Is It Called So? — "Form"

We have seen the word "form" used in several different terms in the abstract sense, defined as a real valued function or mapping, like linear forms, bilinear forms, quadratic forms, multilinear forms, exterior forms (which we are going to define next). We will also see first and second fundamental forms (see Part II Chap. 2) and differential forms (see Part III Chap. 2). Why are they called "forms"? Of course, they are just definitions and you can name them anything you want. You could name them "*linear witzelsucht*" and "*multilinear witzelsucht*" and say "Don't ask me what '*witzelsucht*' means. Only '*linear witzelsucht*', treated as a single word with a space inside, has a meaning." However, as a matter of fact, there is a namesake for the term "form".

In the old days, the term "form" was used to mean an algebraic expression, especially a homogeneous polynomial, like in "quadratic forms", and the "first fundamental form" and "second fundamental form" in differential geometry of surfaces, which are the quadratic forms in the tangent plane of a surface. In fact in the old days, functions were understood as those "expressions" and the expressions only, not the same understanding in the modern sense[1]. A polynomial can represent a function, for example, $f : \mathbb{R} \times \mathbb{R} \to \mathbb{R}$; $(x, y) \mapsto f(x, y) = ax^2 + bxy + cy^2$. In the modern language, $f(x, y)$ denotes the value but the function itself is denoted by f. But in the old days, there was an abuse of notation. We use $f(x, y) = ax^2 + bxy + cy^2$ to denote both the value corresponding to (x, y), and the function itself. When we use $f(x, y) = ax^2 + bxy + cy^2$ to represent the function itself, x and y are deemed as place holders, rather than specific values. In this sense, $ax^2 + bxy + cy^2$ is treated as a "form", instead of a single value and this form represents the function f. This gives us a clue why the "quadratic functions", "linear functions" and "multilinear functions" are also called "forms".

Definitions 2 and 3 are the modern definitions of linear forms and bilinear forms. You can compare them with the old-fashioned definitions in the following:

A linear form is a function of first degree with respect to each variable, in the form $f(x_1, \ldots, x_n) = a_1 x_1 + \cdots + a_n x_n$.

A bilinear form is a function in the form $f(x_1, \ldots, x_n, y_1, \ldots, y_n) = \sum_{i,j=1}^{n} a_{ij} x_i y_j$.

A quadratic form is a homogeneous polynomial of degree 2. For example, $ax^2 + bxy + cy^2$ is a quadratic form of two variables. A quadratic form of n variables has the form $\sum_{i,j=1}^{n} a_{ij} x_i x_j$.

The old-day approach defines these functions using the components of these vectors, for example, a quadratic form is a homogeneous quadratic polynomial of components $(x_1, \ldots, x_n)$, while the modern approach defines them using vectors without referring to components.

---

[1]The difference between the old-day and modern-day understanding of the concept of function is reflected in a quote by Henri Poincaré: "In the old days when people invented a new function they had something useful in mind. Now, they invent them deliberately just to invalidate our ancestors' reasoning ..."

Next we define exterior forms. An exterior form is an antisymmetric multilinear form.

Definition 5. Exterior form of degree 2 (2-form)

Let V be a linear space over a field F. An **exterior form** of degree 2 (or 2-**form**), is defined to be a bilinear form $\varphi : V \times V \to F$ which is antisymmetric. Namely,

$$\varphi(u, v) = -\varphi(v, u),$$

for all $u, v \in V$.

Definition 6. Exterior form of degree k (k-form)

Let V be a linear space over a field F. An **exterior form** of degree k (or k-**form**), is defined to be a multilinear form $\varphi : V \times \cdots \times V \to F$ which is antisymmetric. Namely,

$$\varphi(v_1, \ldots, v_i, \ldots, v_j, \ldots, v_k) = -\varphi(v_1, \ldots, v_j, \ldots, v_i, \ldots, v_k),$$

for all $v_1, \ldots, v_i, \ldots, v_j, \ldots, v_k \in V$ and $i \neq j$.

A linear form $\varphi : V \to F$ is also called a 1-**form**.

It is easy to see, if for any $i \neq j$, $v_i = v_j$, then $\varphi(v_1, \ldots, v_i, \ldots, v_j, \ldots, v_k) = 0$.

Definition 7. Exterior space $\Lambda^k(V^*)$ of degree k

The set of all k-forms (k being a fixed constant) constitutes a linear space, called **exterior space of degree** k, denoted by $\Lambda^k(V^*)$.

A1.2. k-Blades

Definition 8. 2-blade

Let $\omega_1, \omega_2 \in V^*$ be 1-forms. We define a mapping $\bar{\wedge} : V^* \times V^* \to \Lambda^2(V^*)$,

$$\bar{\wedge}(\omega_1, \omega_2)(v_1, v_2) = \omega_1(v_1)\omega_2(v_2) - \omega_2(v_1)\omega_1(v_2).$$

We also denote $\bar{\wedge}(\omega_1, \omega_2) \overset{\text{def}}{=} \omega_1 \bar{\wedge} \omega_2$. An element in $\Lambda^2(V^*)$ in the form of $\omega_1 \bar{\wedge} \omega_2$ is called a 2-**blade** (or 2-**monomial**).

Definition 9. k-blade

Let $\omega_1, \ldots, \omega_k \in V^*$ be 1-forms. We define a mapping $\bar{\wedge} : V^* \times \cdots \times V^* \to \Lambda^k(V^*)$,

$$\bar{\wedge}(\omega_1, \ldots, \omega_k)(v_1, \ldots, v_k) \overset{\text{def}}{=} \det[\omega_i(v_j)]$$

$$\overset{\text{def}}{=} \begin{vmatrix} \omega_1(v_1) & \cdots & \omega_1(v_k) \\ \cdots & \cdots & \cdots \\ \omega_k(v_1) & \cdots & \omega_k(v_k) \end{vmatrix}. \tag{3.7}$$

We also denote $\bar{\wedge}(\omega_1, \ldots, \omega_k) \overset{\text{def}}{=} \omega_1 \bar{\wedge} \cdots \bar{\wedge} \omega_k$ and call it a k-**blade** (or k-**monomial**).

Remark 9. Caution — k-blades and k-forms

k-Blades are k-forms but the converse is not true. In general, a k-form is the linear combination of k-blades. The k-blades are also called k-monomials while the general k-forms are like "polynomials". A k-blade is also called a **decomposable k-form**. There are **nondecomposable** k-forms, which cannot be a k-blade.

Remark 10. Caution — The Notation $\omega_1 \bar{\wedge} \cdots \bar{\wedge} \omega_k$

The notation $\omega_1 \bar{\wedge} \cdots \bar{\wedge} \omega_k$ is convenient but could be misleading. Note that $\bar{\wedge}$ is defined as a k-ary operation instead of a binary operation. While $\omega_1 \bar{\wedge} \omega_2 \bar{\wedge} \omega_3$ is defined, $(\omega_1 \bar{\wedge} \omega_2) \bar{\wedge} \omega_3$ and $\omega_1 \bar{\wedge} (\omega_2 \bar{\wedge} \omega_3)$ have not been defined yet. It is meaningless to write the latter two for now.

Theorem 5. *Let V be a linear space of dimension n, $\{e_1, \ldots, e_n\}$ be a basis of V and $\{f_1, \ldots, f_n\}$ be the dual basis in V^*. Then*

$$\dim \Lambda^k(V^*) = \binom{n}{k}.$$

The set of k-blades $\{f_{i_1} \bar{\wedge} \cdots \bar{\wedge} f_{i_k} | i_1 < \cdots < i_k\}$ form a basis for $\Lambda^k(V^*)$.

Corollary. *For any k-blade, if $k > \dim V$, then*

$$\omega_1 \bar{\wedge} \cdots \bar{\wedge} \omega_k = 0.$$

This is because any $\omega_1 \bar{\wedge} \cdots \bar{\wedge} \omega_k$ can be expressed as linear combination of $e_{i_1} \bar{\wedge} \cdots \bar{\wedge} e_{i_k}$, where each of $e_{i_1}, \ldots, e_{i_k}$ is one of the basis vectors $e_1, \ldots, e_n$ for V. If $k > n$, two of them must be the same by the pigeonhole principle. Hence $e_{i_1} \bar{\wedge} \cdots \bar{\wedge} e_{i_k} = 0$ and $\omega_1 \bar{\wedge} \cdots \bar{\wedge} \omega_k = 0$.

The space $\Lambda^k(V^*)$ is spanned by all the k-blades. We also denote $\Lambda^0(V^*) \overset{\text{def}}{=} F$ and $\Lambda^1(V^*) \overset{\text{def}}{=} V^*$.

We construct the direct sum of these spaces

$$\Lambda(V^*) \overset{\text{def}}{=} \Lambda^0(V^*) \oplus \Lambda^1(V^*) \oplus \Lambda^2(V^*) \oplus \cdots \oplus \Lambda^n(V^*).$$

$\Lambda(V^*)$ is a linear space over F of dimension 2^n, called the **Grassmann space** of exterior forms. $\Lambda(V^*)$ is the dual space of $\Lambda(V)$, which we discussed in Section 2.

A1.3. Wedge Product of a p-Form and a q-Form

Definition 10. Wedge product of a p-form and a q-form

Let $\omega \in \Lambda^p(V^*)$ be a p-form and $\varphi \in \Lambda^q(V^*)$ be a q-form. The wedge product of ω and φ is defined to be a $(p+q)$-form, $\omega \wedge \varphi \in \Lambda^{p+q}(V^*)$, such that for any $v_1, \ldots, v_p, v_{p+1}, \ldots, v_{p+q} \in V$,

$$\omega \wedge \varphi(v_1, \ldots, v_{p+q})$$

$$\overset{\text{def}}{=} \sum_{\substack{\sigma(1) < \cdots < \sigma(p) \\ \sigma(p+1) < \cdots < \sigma(p+q)}} \text{sgn}(\sigma)\omega(v_{\sigma(1)}, \ldots, v_{\sigma(p)})\varphi(v_{\sigma(p+1)}, \ldots, v_{\sigma(p+q)}),$$

$$(3.8)$$

where the summation is over all the permutations σ of the numbers $(1, \ldots, p+q)$ such that $\sigma(1) < \cdots < \sigma(p)$ and $\sigma(p+1) < \cdots < \sigma(p+q)$.

In this definition we used the notation

$$\text{sgn}(\sigma) = \begin{cases} 1 & \text{if } \sigma \text{ is even permutation}, \\ -1 & \text{if } \sigma \text{ is odd permutation}. \end{cases}$$

In Eq. 3.8, if we lift the restrictions and make the summation over all the permutations σ of the numbers $(1, \ldots, p+q)$, each term in the summation will be repeated $p!q!$ times. So equivalently, Eq. 3.8 can also be written as

$$\omega \wedge \varphi(v_1, \ldots, v_{p+q})$$
$$\stackrel{\text{def}}{=} \frac{1}{p!q!} \sum_{\sigma} \text{sgn}(\sigma)\omega(v_{\sigma(1)}, \ldots, v_{\sigma(p)})\varphi(v_{\sigma(p+1)}, \ldots, v_{\sigma(p+q)}), \quad (3.9)$$

where the summation is over all the permutations σ of the numbers $(1, ..., p+q)$. For practical calculation purposes, Eq. 3.8 without repeating terms is simpler.

Remark 11. A Special Case

As a special case when $p = q = 1$, the wedge product of two 1-forms ω and φ is

$$\omega \wedge \varphi(v_1, v_2) \stackrel{\text{def}}{=} \omega(v_1)\varphi(v_2) - \varphi(v_1)\omega(v_2) = \begin{vmatrix} \omega(v_1) & \omega(v_2) \\ \varphi(v_1) & \varphi(v_2) \end{vmatrix}, \quad (3.10)$$

which coincides with $\omega \bar{\wedge} \varphi$ in Definition 8.

The wedge product $\wedge$ can be viewed as a binary operation in $\Lambda(V^*)$, namely $\wedge : \Lambda(V^*) \times \Lambda(V^*) \to \Lambda(V^*)$. The wedge product $\wedge$ has the following properties.

Theorem 6. *Let* $\omega, \omega_1, \omega_2 \in \Lambda(V^*)$ *be p-forms,* $\varphi, \varphi_1, \varphi_2 \in \Lambda(V^*)$ *be q-forms and* $\psi \in \Lambda(V^*)$ *be an r-form. Then*

(1) Associative law:
   $(\omega \wedge \varphi) \wedge \psi = \omega \wedge (\varphi \wedge \psi)$.
(2) Distributive law:
   $(\omega_1 + \omega_2) \wedge \varphi = \omega_1 \wedge \varphi + \omega_2 \wedge \varphi$,
   $\omega \wedge (\varphi_1 + \varphi_2) = \omega \wedge \varphi_1 + \omega \wedge \varphi_2$;
(3) Supercommutative law:

$$\omega \wedge \varphi = \begin{cases} -\varphi \wedge \omega & \text{if } pq \text{ is odd} \\ \varphi \wedge \omega & \text{if } pq \text{ is even}, \end{cases} \quad (3.11)$$

   To put these two cases together, we have

$$\omega \wedge \varphi = (-1)^{pq}\varphi \wedge \omega. \quad (3.12)$$

This theorem can be viewed either as a counterpart of Theorem 2, or as a special case of it.

Because of the associativity of the wedge product, we can write $\omega \wedge \varphi \wedge \psi$ without parenthesis and we are not feared of any ambiguities.

Theorem 7. *Let* $\omega_1, \ldots, \omega_k \in V^*$ *be 1-forms. Then*

$$\omega_1 \wedge \cdots \wedge \omega_k = \omega_1 \bar{\wedge} \cdots \bar{\wedge} \omega_k.$$

Now we see the k-blade $\omega_1 \bar{\wedge} \cdots \bar{\wedge} \omega_k$ is the same as the wedge product $\omega_1 \wedge \cdots \wedge \omega_k$ and hence there is no need for the symbol $\bar{\wedge}$. We shall just use $\wedge$ instead. With this identification in Theorem 7, the calculation of the wedge product of a p-form ω and a q-form φ is made easier. We know every k-form is the linear combination of k-blades. Hence $\omega \wedge \varphi$ is the linear combination of $(p + q)$-blades. We only need to use Eq. 3.7, which is the definition of k-blades, and we do not need to use Eq. 3.8.

The space $\Lambda(V^*)$ forms an algebra over F with the wedge product as the vector multiplication. It is called the **exterior algebra** (or **Grassmann algebra**) of exterior forms. It is the exterior algebra on linear space V^*, a special case, or the dual case, of exterior algebra, which we discussed in Section 2.

A2. Exterior Algebra as Subalgebra of Tensor Algebra

The development of wedge product and exterior algebra parallels that of tensor product and tensor algebra in many ways. Since we have invested effort on developing tensor algebra in Chap. 2, we can make use of tensor algebra and make the path of developing exterior algebra shorter. We give yet another different treatment of exterior algebra in the context of tensor algebra here. We construct exterior product spaces as subspaces of the tensor product spaces.

We look at one example first. Let $T_0^2(V)$ be the tensor space of degree 2 on V. We showed in Example 12 that the matrix space $M_{n,n}$ is a model for tensor space $T_0^2(V)$. The matrices in $M_{n,n}$ are the tensors over V. Consider all the antisymmetric matrices $[a_{ij}] \in M_{n,n}$ with properties $a_{ij} = -a_{ji}$ for all i, j. An antisymmetric matrix in $M_{n,n}$ is called an antisymmetric tensor. All the symmetric tensors make a linear subspace of the tensor space $M_{n,n}$. The dimension of this subspace is $n(n-1)/2$.

Definition 11. Antisymmetric tensor

We say a contravariant tensor $w \in T_0^p(V)$ is an **antisymmetric**

tensor if

$$w^{\sigma(i_1\ldots i_p)} = \operatorname{sgn}(\sigma)w^{i_1\ldots i_p},$$

where $\sigma(i_1\ldots i_p)$ is a permutation of the indices $(i_1\ldots i_p)$.

Namely, for an antisymmetric tensor, its coordinates are antisymmetric with respect to the permutation of its indices. For example, if $z \in T_0^3(V)$ is an antisymmetric tensor and V is a 5-dimensional linear space, we would have $z^{2,3,5} = -z^{3,2,5}$ but $z^{2,3,5} = z^{3,5,2}$ because $(3,2,5)$ is an odd permutation of $(2,3,5)$ but $(3,5,2)$ is an even permutation of $(2,3,5)$.

Definition 12. Exterior space of degree p

All the antisymmetric tensors in $T_0^p(V)$ form a linear subspace of $T_0^p(V)$, called **exterior space** of V of degree p, denoted by $\Lambda^p(V)$. The elements in $\Lambda^p(V)$ are called **multivectors**, or p-**vectors**.

If $p > \dim V$, there is no antisymmetric tensor other than zero vector in $T_0^p(V)$.

Definition 13. Antisymmetrizer

Let $w^{i_1\ldots i_p}$ be the coordinates of a tensor $w \in T_0^p(V)$. We can define a mapping $A_p : T_0^p(V) \to \Lambda^p(V)$ such that

$$A_p(w) = \frac{1}{p!}\sum_\sigma \operatorname{sgn}(\sigma)w^{\sigma(i_1\ldots i_p)}.$$

$A_p(w)$ is an antisymmetric tensor and A_p is called the **antisymmetrizer**.

We make the direct sum of these exterior spaces.

$$\Lambda(V) \overset{\text{def}}{=} \Lambda^0(V) \oplus \Lambda^1 V) \oplus \Lambda^2(V) \oplus \cdots \oplus \Lambda^n(V).$$

We define the wedge product of two multivectors as follows.

Definition 14. Wedge product of two multivectors

Let $\xi \in \Lambda^p(V)$ be a p-vector, $\eta \in \Lambda^q(V)$ be a q-vector. The wedge product of ξ and η is defined as $\wedge : \Lambda^p(V) \times \Lambda^q(V) \to \Lambda^{p+q}(V)$:

$$\xi \wedge \eta = A_{p+q}(\xi \otimes \eta).$$

The wedge product is actually defined on $\Lambda(V)$, namely $\wedge : \Lambda(V) \times \Lambda(V) \to \Lambda(V)$. The space $\Lambda(V)$ forms an algebra over F, called the **exterior algebra** or **exterior algebra** on linear space V.

The wedge product so defined can be proved to be associative and Theorem 2 can be proved using this tensor approach. Due to the associativity, we can have wedge product like $\xi \wedge \eta \wedge \zeta$ without confusion. Especially, the wedge product of vectors $v_1, \ldots, v_p \in V$ are the antisymmetrized tensor product.

Theorem 8. *For all* $v_1, \ldots, v_p \in V$,

$$v_1 \wedge v_2 = \frac{1}{2}(v_1 \otimes v_2 - v_2 \otimes v_1), \tag{3.13}$$

$$v_1 \wedge \cdots \wedge v_p = \frac{1}{p!} \sum_\sigma \mathrm{sgn}(\sigma) v_{\sigma(1)} \otimes \cdots \otimes v_{\sigma(p)}. \tag{3.14}$$

A3. Exterior Algebra as Quotient Algebra of Tensor Algebra

Definition 15. (Equivalent Definition) Exterior algebra

Let V be a linear space over a field F and $T(V)$ the tensor algebra on V with the tensor product $\otimes$. The **exterior algebra** (or **exterior algebra**) on V is defined to be the quotient algebra,

$$\Lambda(V) \stackrel{\text{def}}{=} T(V)/I,$$

where I is the ideal generated by all elements of the form $x \otimes x$ such that $x \in V$. The mapping $\wedge : \Lambda(V) \times \Lambda(V) \to \Lambda(V)$; $(x, y) \mapsto x \wedge y$ such that $x \wedge y \stackrel{\text{def}}{=} x \otimes y \bmod I$ is called the wedge product.

Chapter 4

Geometric Algebra

Old MacDonald had a form, $e_i \wedge e_i = 0$.

— Michael Stay

Reading Guide. Grassmann algebra can be further generalized to geometric algebra, or Clifford algebra, named in honor of William K. Clifford. Clifford used the name "geometric algebra" in his paper published in 1878, which was one year before his death at age 33, and one year after Hermann Grassmann's death. This new algebra was intended for the applications in geometry, especially in spacial rotations.

Just like tensor algebra and Grassmann algebra, there are different approaches to geometric algebra. The most laconic way to define geometric algebra is to use the quotient algebra of the tensor algebra but it is not the most pedagogical approach. We take a more intuitive approach while we compare with the tensor approach in Appendix A1.

§1   Construction from Exterior Algebra

We all know that we cannot compare apples with oranges. We cannot add apples to oranges either. It is a common trick that adults use to tease a kid. "What is 2 apples plus 3 apples?" The kid would say 5. "What is 2 apples plus 3 oranges?" The kid would be baffled. He may say 5 and you would ask, "5 apples or 5 oranges?" Well, the correct answer is "2 apples and 3 oranges". We can add apples to oranges. The key is to keep them separated. We use a pair of numbers (a, b). a represents the number of apples and b represents the number of oranges. In mathematics, the answer to the above problem is $(2, 0) + (0, 3) = (2, 3)$. This is the idea of vectors.

We also learned that we cannot add two vectors of different dimensions. We cannot add scalars to vectors for the same reason. They are different kinds of objects. We cannot add an inner product to a cross product because the inner product is a scalar but a cross product is a vector. If you insist that you want to add vectors of different dimensions, or scalars and vectors, you can do so. However it has to make sense though. The way to do this is to make a direct sum (see Chap. 1). Say vector $u \in U$ lives in a space of dimension 3 and vector $v \in V$ lives in a space of dimension 4. We make a direct sum space $U \oplus V$, which is made of all the pairs $\{(u, v)|u \in U, v \in V\}$. So the addition becomes $(u, 0) + (0, v) = (u, v)$. We have already applied this idea in Grassmann algebras where scalars, vectors and k-vectors can be added together freely.

Let V be an n-dimensional inner product space. Now we work in the same Grassmann space

$$\Lambda(V) = \Lambda^0(V) \oplus \Lambda^1(V) \oplus \Lambda^2(V) \oplus ... \oplus \Lambda^n(V),$$

but we want to define a new vector multiplication to replace the wedge product.

Let $\xi, \eta \in \Lambda(V)$. We now define a new product of ξ and η, called the **geometric product** of ξ and η denoted by $\xi\eta$. Note that we use the juxtaposition of ξ and η to denote the geometric product of ξ and η. This is not to be confused with Gibbs' dyads for vectors. We have to distinguish them in the context.

For all vectors $u, v \in V$, the new product is defined to be the sum of the scalar product and the wedge product:

$$uv = u \cdot v + u \wedge v, \qquad (4.1)$$

where $u \cdot v$ is the inner product of u and v, and $u \wedge v$ is the wedge product. We know the inner product is symmetric $u \cdot v = v \cdot u$ and the wedge product is antisymmetric $u \wedge v = -v \wedge u$.

Remark 1. Caution — Geometric Product for Any Two Multivectors

Note that the geometric product in Eq. 4.1 is defined for vectors $u, v \in V$ only but not for general multivectors $\xi, \eta \in \Lambda(V)$, although we intend to build a new algebra on the Grassmann space $\Lambda(V)$ and we need to define the geometric product of any two multivectors $\xi, \eta \in \Lambda(V)$, that is a binary operator $\pi : \Lambda(V) \times \Lambda(V) \rightarrow \Lambda(V)$; $(\xi, \eta) \mapsto \xi\eta$. It is not a trivial task to constructively define the geometric product for any two multivectors $\xi, \eta \in \Lambda(V)$. In general the geometric product $\xi\eta$ of $\xi, \eta \in \Lambda(V)$ is not the inner product of ξ and η plus the wedge product $\xi \wedge \eta$. We would rather take a round-about approach, to define geometric algebra using a set of axioms and it can be proved that there exists a unique associative algebra satisfying the axioms up to isomorphism. This was also the approach Clifford himself used when he published his new algebra, not using the modern language though.

Let us recall the definition of an algebra over a field F, in Chapter 1 Definition 22. An algebra over a field F is a linear space over F with a vector multiplication. The new algebra, geometric algebra which we shall develop in the following is an algebra over a field F in this sense.

In a broader context, when we define geometric algebra, we generally relax the requirement for the inner product $\Phi(u, v)$ on V. An inner product is a symmetric positive definite bilinear form. We relax the requirement of positive definiteness but only require $\Phi(u, v)$ to be a symmetric and nondegenerate bilinear form. We still use the notation $u \cdot v$ for $\Phi(u, v)$ but keep in mind that $u \cdot u$ now is allowed to take a negative value.

Definition 1. Geometric algebra

Let V be n-dimensional real linear space with a symmetric non-degenerate bilinear form $\Phi(u, v) = u \cdot v$ defined. Let $\Lambda(V) = \Lambda^0(V) \oplus \Lambda^1(V) \oplus \Lambda^2(V) \oplus ... \oplus \Lambda^n(V)$ be the Grassmann space over V

of multivectors.

A **geometric algebra** (or **Clifford algebra**) on linear space V with respect to the bilinear form Φ is defined to be an associative algebra $Cl(V)$ with the vector multiplication $\pi : \Lambda(V) \times \Lambda(V) \to \Lambda(V)$; $(\zeta, \eta) \mapsto \zeta\eta$, satisfying the following conditions: for all vectors $u, v \in V$,

$$uv = u \cdot v + u \wedge v. \tag{4.2}$$

Geometric algebra was invented and named by William K. Clifford [Clifford (1876)]. In most of the context today, geometric algebra refers to $Cl(V)$ where V is a real linear space, but Clifford algebra $Cl(V)$ is used in a more general sense where V may have any ground field F.

In Definition 1, Eq. 4.2 can be replaced by

$$u^2 \overset{\text{def}}{=} uu = \Phi(u, u) \overset{\text{def}}{=} u \cdot u, \text{ for all } u \in V.$$

It can be proved that the geometric algebra on V with respect to the bilinear form Φ is unique, up to isomorphism.

Remark 2. Comparison — Algebras over $\mathbb{R}$

Note that geometric algebra is associative but not commutative. Furthermore, not all the elements are invertible under geometric product. That means division cannot be defined in geometric algebra. In the following table, we compare the properties of geometric algebra to other algebras over $\mathbb{R}$, including Grassmann algebra, the cross product algebra of $\mathbb{R}^3$, quaternions, octonians (generalization of quaternions developed by Arthur Cayley).

	geometric algebra	exterior algebra	cross product algebra of $\mathbb{R}^3$	quaternion algebra	octonian algebra
associative	Yes	Yes	No	Yes	No
commutative	No	No, but super-commutative	No, but anti-commutative	No	No
division algebra	No	No	No	Yes	Yes

We are going to use the axiomatic definition when working with geometric algebra, instead of constructively defining the geometric product $\xi\eta$

for any two multivectors $\xi, \eta \in \Lambda(V)$, which could be a tedious labor.

We choose an orthonormal basis $\{e_1, \ldots, e_n\}$ for V, such that $e_i \cdot e_j = \delta_{ij}$. We know that

$$\{e_{i_1} \wedge \cdots \wedge e_{i_k} \mid 1 \leq i_i < \cdots < i_k \leq n \text{ and } 0 \leq k \leq n\} \qquad (4.3)$$

is a natural basis for $\Lambda(V)$ as well as for $Cl(V)$. This basis consists of the blades

$$0\text{-blade} \quad 1,$$

$$1\text{-blades} \quad e_1, \ldots, e_n,$$

$$2\text{-blades} \quad e_1 \wedge e_2, \ldots, e_{n-1} \wedge e_n,$$

$$3\text{-blades} \quad e_1 \wedge e_2 \wedge e_3, \ldots, e_{n-2} \wedge e_{n-1} \wedge e_n,$$

$$\cdots \cdots$$

$$n\text{-blade} \quad e_1 \wedge \cdots \wedge e_n.$$

We also know that to define the geometric product, it suffices to define the geometric product on these basis vectors and then extend it to all the elements in $Cl(V)$ using the associativity and distributivity.

Let us first figure out the geometric products of these orthonormal basis vectors $\{e_1, \ldots, e_n\}$ for V.

Theorem 1. *Let $\{e_1, \ldots, e_n\}$ be an orthonormal basis for V. Then*

$$e_i^2 = 1,$$

$$e_i e_j = -e_j e_i, \text{ for } i \neq j.$$

This is because $e_i \cdot e_j = \delta_{ij}$, $e_i \wedge e_j = -e_j \wedge e_i$. When $i = j$, we have $e_i \cdot e_i = 1$ and $e_i \wedge e_i = 0$. Hence

$$e_i^2 = e_i \cdot e_i + e_i \wedge e_i = e_i \cdot e_i = 1$$

$$e_i e_j = e_i \cdot e_j + e_i \wedge e_j = e_i \wedge e_j = -e_j \wedge e_i = -e_j e_i \text{ for } i \neq j.$$

Even though we do not intend to give explicit constructive definition of the geometric product of two general multivectors, the following theorem about geometric product is helpful, when $v \in V$ is a vector and ξ is a k-blade.

Theorem 2. *Let $v \in V$ be a vector and $\xi \in \Lambda^k(V)$ be a k-blade. Then,*

$$v\xi = v \cdot \xi + v \wedge \xi,$$

where $a \cdot \xi$ is tensor contraction.

Note that in general $v \cdot \xi$ is not a scalar. $v \cdot \xi$ is a $(k-1)$-blade and $v \wedge \xi$ is a $(k+1)$-blade.

Remark 3. Caution — Dot Product of Multivectors

There are several different and nonequivalent generalizations of the "dot product" to multivectors, which in general results in another multivector of different grade. They are all tensor contractions in nature. The "dot product" $v \cdot \xi$ used here, is the same as $v \lrcorner \xi$ in Dorst's notation [Dorst (2002)]. Just beware that we have been shying away from defining the geometric product for a general p-vector $\xi \in \Lambda^p(V)$ and a q-vector $\eta \in \Lambda^q(V)$ directly and constructively, in which case $\xi\eta$ is a multivector of mixed grades ranging from $|p-q|$ to $|p+q|$.

Let us reexamine the k-blades in the basis 4.3. Using Theorem 2, we find that

$$e_{i_1} \wedge \cdots \wedge e_{i_k} = e_{i_1} \cdots e_{i_k},$$

when $i_1, \ldots, i_k$ are all distinct. Here $e_{i_1} \cdots e_{i_k}$ is the geometric product of $e_{i_1}, \ldots, e_{i_k}$. So the basis for geometric algebra $Cl(V)$ can be written as

$$\{e_{i_1} \cdots e_{i_k} \mid 1 \le i_i < \cdots < i_k \le n \text{ and } 0 \le k \le n\}, \qquad (4.4)$$

and we do not have to use the wedge product explicitly.

In the following, we show two examples to work out the multiplication table for the basis multivectors for $\dim V = 2$ and $\dim V = 3$.

Example 1. (Geometric algebra on $\mathbb{R}^2$) An orthonormal basis for $\mathbb{R}^2$ is $\{e_1, e_2\}$ with $e_i \cdot e_j = \delta_{ij}$. A basis for $Cl(\mathbb{R}^2)$ is 1, e_1, e_2, and $e_{12} \stackrel{\text{def}}{=} e_1 e_2$.

It is easy to see $e_1^2 = e_2^2 = 1$, $e_1 e_2 = e_{12}$ and $e_2 e_1 = -e_{12}$. We work out the rest of the products in the following.

$$e_1 e_{12} = e_1(e_1 e_2) = e_1^2 e_2 = e_2,$$
$$e_2 e_{12} = e_2(e_1 e_2) = -e_1 e_2^2 = -e_1,$$
$$e_{12} e_1 = (e_1 e_2) e_1 = -e_2 e_1^2 = -e_2,$$
$$e_{12} e_2 = (e_1 e_2) e_2 = e_1 e_2^2 = e_1,$$
$$e_{12} e_{12} = (e_1 e_2)(e_1 e_2) = -e_2 e_1 e_1 e_2 = -e_2 e_2 = -1.$$

We fill these values in the multiplication table.   ♣

	1	e_1	e_2	e_{12}
1	1	e_1	e_2	e_{12}
e_1	e_1	1	e_{12}	e_2
e_2	e_2	$-e_{12}$	1	$-e_1$
e_{12}	e_{12}	$-e_2$	e_1	-1

Example 2. (Geometric algebra on $\mathbb{R}^3$) The situation for $Cl(\mathbb{R}^3)$ is similar. Let $\{e_1, e_2, e_3\}$ be an orthonormal basis for $\mathbb{R}^3$. In addition to 1, e_1, e_2, e_3, other basis vectors for $Cl(\mathbb{R}^3)$ are

$$e_{12} \stackrel{\text{def}}{=} e_1 e_2,$$
$$e_{23} \stackrel{\text{def}}{=} e_2 e_3,$$
$$e_{31} \stackrel{\text{def}}{=} e_3 e_1,$$
$$e_{123} \stackrel{\text{def}}{=} e_1 e_2 e_3.$$

We only choose a few multiplications to work out and leave the rest as exercises.

$$e_1 e_{23} = e_1 e_2 e_3 = e_{123},$$
$$e_1 e_{31} = e_1 e_3 e_1 = -e_3 e_1 e_1 = -e_3,$$
$$e_1 e_{123} = e_1 e_1 e_2 e_3 = e_{23},$$
$$e_{12} e_{12} = e_1 e_2 e_1 e_2 = -e_2 e_1 e_1 e_2 = -e_2 e_2 = -1,$$
$$e_{12} e_{31} = e_1 e_2 e_3 e_1 = (-e_2 e_1)(-e_1 e_3) = e_2 e_1 e_1 e_3 = e_2 e_3,$$
$$e_{12} e_{123} = e_1 e_2 e_1 e_2 e_3 = -e_2 e_1 e_1 e_2 e_3 = -e_3.$$

The following is the multiplication table for $Cl(\mathbb{R}^3)$.   ♣

	1	e_1	e_2	e_3	e_{12}	e_{23}	e_{31}	e_{123}
1	1	e_1	e_2	e_3	e_{12}	e_{23}	e_{31}	e_{123}
e_1	e_1	1	e_{12}	$-e_{31}$	e_2	e_{123}	$-e_3$	e_{23}
e_2	e_2	$-e_{12}$	1	e_{23}	$-e_1$	e_3	e_{123}	e_{31}
e_3	e_3	e_{31}	$-e_{23}$	1	e_{123}	$-e_2$	e_1	e_{12}
e_{12}	e_{12}	$-e_2$	e_1	e_{123}	-1	$-e_{31}$	e_{23}	$-e_3$
e_{23}	e_{23}	e_{123}	$-e_3$	e_2	e_{31}	-1	$-e_{12}$	$-e_1$
e_{31}	e_{31}	e_3	e_{123}	$-e_1$	$-e_{23}$	e_{12}	-1	$-e_2$
e_{123}	e_{123}	e_{23}	e_{31}	e_{12}	$-e_3$	$-e_1$	$-e_2$	-1

In our discussion, we know that the geometric algebra $Cl(V)$ is defined with respect to a bilinear form Φ, which is defined on V. Every symmetric bilinear form is associated with a quadratic form Q. They are related as follows.

$$Q(x) = \Phi(x, x),$$
$$\Phi(x, y) = Q(x + y) - Q(x) - Q(y).$$

So the geometric algebra is also said to be defined with respect to a quadratic form Q.

Let $x \in V$ be a vector with coordinates $(x_1, ..., x_p, x_{p+1}, ...x_{p+q})$ be the coordinates under an orthonormal basis for V, where $p + q = n = \dim V$. Let

$$Q(x) = x_1^2 + \cdots + x_p^2 - x_{p+1}^2 - \cdots - x_{p+q}^2$$

with p positive square terms and q negative square terms. (p, q) is called the **signature** of the quadratic form Q and it is independent of the choice of basis.

Definition 2. Geometric algebra $Cl_{p,q}(V)$ with signature (p, q)

We denote $Cl_{p,q}(V)$ for the geometric algebra on V with respect to a quadratic form with a signature (p, q).

The geometric algebra with some low p, q values are isomorphic to some familiar algebras over $\mathbb{R}$.

Theorem 3.

$$Cl_{0,0}(\mathbb{R}) \cong \mathbb{R},$$
$$Cl_{0,1}(\mathbb{R}) \cong \mathbb{C},$$
$$Cl_{0,2}(\mathbb{R}^2) \cong \mathbb{H}.$$

Here we demonstrate the last isomorphism $Cl_{0,2}(\mathbb{R}^2)$ with $\mathbb{H}$, the algebra of quaternions, by comparing the multiplication tables of $Cl_{0,2}(\mathbb{R}^2)$ and $\mathbb{H}$. Example 1 is a geometric algebra on $\mathbb{R}^2$. However, the signature of Q is $(2, 0)$. For $Cl_{0,2}(\mathbb{R}^2)$, the signature of Q is $(0, 2)$. That means $e_1^2 = e_2^2 = -1$. The multiplication table of $Cl_{0,2}(\mathbb{R}^2)$ is as follows.

	1	e_1	e_2	e_{12}
1	1	e_1	e_2	e_{12}
e_1	e_1	-1	e_{12}	$-e_2$
e_2	e_2	$-e_{12}$	-1	e_1
e_{12}	e_{12}	e_2	$-e_1$	-1

We compare this multiplication table with the multiplication table of quaternions (see Part IV Chap. 3).

	1	i	j	k
1	1	i	j	k
i	i	-1	k	$-j$
j	j	$-k$	-1	i
k	k	j	$-i$	-1

We can immediately identify the isomorphism $\varphi : Cl_{0,2}(\mathbb{R}^2) \to \mathbb{H}$, by assigning $e_1 \mapsto i$, $e_2 \mapsto j$ and $e_{12} \mapsto k$.

§2 Construction from Tensor Algebra

Definition 3. Clifford algebra

Let V be an n-dimensional linear space over a field F and Q a nondegenerate quadratic form on V. Let $T(V)$ be the tensor algebra on V with the tensor product $\otimes$. Let $I(Q)$ be the ideal of $T(V)$ generated by all elements of the form $x \otimes x - Q(x) \cdot 1$ such that $x \in V$. The quotient associative algebra

$$Cl(V) \overset{\text{def}}{=} T(V)/I(Q)$$

is called the **Clifford algebra** with respect to the quadratic form Q.

Exercises

1. Show that $Cl_{0,0}(\mathbb{R}) \cong \mathbb{R}$ and $Cl_{0,1}(\mathbb{R}) \cong \mathbb{C}$.
2. Let $\{e_1, e_2, e_3\}$ be a basis for an inner product space V and $e_i \cdot e_j = \delta_{ij}$. Let $u, v \in V$ and $u = e_1 - e_2$, $v = e_1 + 2e_2 - e_3$. Find
   (1) $u \cdot v$
   (2) $u \wedge v$
   (3) u^2
   (4) v^2
   (5) uv
   (6) vu

(7) $u^2 v$

(8) $v^2 u$

3. Let $\{e_1, e_2, e_3\}$ be a basis for an inner product space V and $e_i \cdot e_j = \delta_{ij}$. Let $\xi, \eta \in Cl(V)$ and $\xi = 1 - e_1 + e_3 + 2e_{12}$, $\eta = 3e_1 - e_{12} + 2e_{23} - 5e_{123}$. Find $\xi\eta$.

4. Let $\xi \in Cl_{0,2}(\mathbb{R}^2)$ and $\xi = 3 - e_1 + 2e_2 - e_{12}$. Find ξ^{-1}.

5. Let $x, y, z \in \mathbb{R}^3$ and $x = 2e_1 - e_1 + e_3$, $y = e_1 + e_3$, $z = -e_1 + 2e_2 + e_3$. Find

   (1) $x \wedge y \wedge z$

   (2) xyz

   (3) yxz

   (4) yzx

   (5) zyx

   (6) zxy

   (7) xzy

6. Show that for all $x, y, z \in \mathbb{R}^3$, $x \wedge y \wedge z = \frac{1}{3!}(xyz - yxz + yzx - zyx + zxy - xzy)$, where xyz is the geometric product of x, y and z.

PART II
GEOMETRY

Leon B. Alberti
(1404 – 1472)

August Möbius
(1790 – 1868)

Carl F. Gauss
(1777 – 1855)

Nikolai Lobachevsky
(1792 – 1856)

Eugenio Beltrami
(1835 – 1899)

Henri Poincaré
(1854 – 1912)

Chapter 1

Projective Geometry

Q: What's green and really far away?
A: The lime at infinity.

— *name unknown*

Reading Guide. This book is not intended to be read from the first page to the last page in the sequential order. You can feel free to skip around. See the chapter dependency chart in the front of the book.

We live in a 3-D world. However, human retinas are 2-D surfaces. We perceive this 3-D world on our 2-D retinas. This perception is called perspective. The fundamental principle of perspective is central projection, which is used in perspective drawing. Artists first discovered the principles of perspective drawing in Renaissance. Mathematicians then picked up and carried on with the study of projective geometry. Today projective geometry is an essential tool in computer graphics and computer vision.

In §1 we start the introduction with perspective drawing. In §2 we discuss the concepts of projective plane, projective coordinates and projective transformations. §2.1 gives a very brief introduction to synthetic projective geometry. The main approach to projective geometry in this chapter is analytic, through the introduction of the ray model and projective coordinates. In §3 we discuss 3-dimensional and higher dimensional projective spaces.

§1   Perspective Drawing

Projective geometry has its origin in perspective drawing, first studied by artists. In the primitive times, our ancestors did not have sophisticated drawing and painting skills. Objects are usually not drawn to proportion, not to mention the representation of depth. Children's paintings in modern days are just like the ancient paintings of our ancestors. This corroborates Sigmund Freud's point of view that in the course of its development, the individual mind repeats our racial history.

In the middle ages, artists started explorations of perspective drawing. Their perspective drawings were approximately correct but with various mistakes. Figure 1.1 (a) is a painting *Humilitas Reads in the Refectory* by Pietro Lorenzetti (1316). You may try to find the mistakes in it. Again, in modern days, it is likely that you have seen children's art just similar to that of medieval artists, with various perspective mistakes.

The discovery of the principles of perspective is due to Filippo Brunelleschi and Leon B. Alberti, early Renaissance architects in Florence, Italy. Alberti wrote the first book on perspective drawing—*On Painting* [Alberti (1435)], in which he laid out the theory and rules of perspective drawing. He was also the first to use the term "vanishing point".

The most important principle of perspective drawing is that a family of parallel lines converge to a single point. If we look at the painting in Figure 1.1 (a), we find that this principle is not observed. Figure 1.1 (b) is the perspective analysis of this painting to show the perspective mistakes. Some lines in white color are marked on the painting. These lines are supposed to be parallel in space. They are all horizontal and in the depth direction. Their images in the painting are supposed to meet at a single point, but in fact they do not. These perspective mistakes make the objects in the painting look tilted. This mistake is common in medieval art, in which different parts of the same painting are views from different view points, instead of having a single view point for the entire painting.

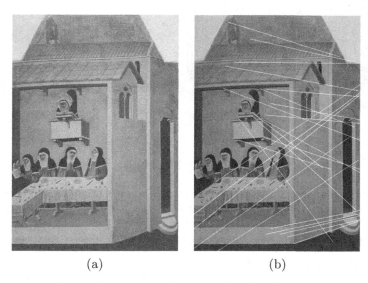

(a)   (b)

Figure 1.1   (a) Perspective mistakes in a painting by Pietro Lorenzetti (1316). (b) Analysis: all the white lines are supposed to be parallel in space and are supposed to meet at one point in the picture. Image source: public domain.

If we make a drawing of a 3-D scene, what does it mean that "the drawing looks real"?

If the projection on our retina of this 2-D drawing is the same as the projection on our retina of the original 3-D scene, then the drawing looks real. To make it look real, the 2-D drawing itself needs to be a central projection of the 3-D scene. Alberti considered the picture plane as a window through which the viewer sees the 3-D world. The key to perspective drawing is central projection. With the principles of perspective understood, artists were able to create realistic looking drawings and paintings. As an example, Figure 1.2 shows such a painting of *Interior of St. Peter's, Rome*, by Giovanni Paolo Panini.

Figure 1.2   Painting: *Interior of St. Peter's, Rome*, by Giovanni Paolo Panini (1731). Image source: public domain.

The German artist and mathematician Albrecht Dürer (1471 – 1528) visited Italy and introduced the principles of perspective to northern Europe. He introduced the term "perspective" (the Latin word for "see through") in his book *The Painter's Manual* in 1525, which included a series of engravings depicting a draftsman drawing with a drawing frame, or perspective machine, now known as Dürer frame or Dürer grid. It consists a wooden frame with black threads forming a grid. Using the grid as coordinate lines, an artist can trace the objects on a gridded sheet of paper. If you place a glass pane with a translucent paper sheet in the frame, you can draw directly on this window. This is also known as Alberti's window or Alberti's veil because Alberti first described it. The image on this window is nothing but the central projection of the 3-D scene with the artist's eye as the center of projection (COP). Figure 1.3 depicts an artist drawing directly on a translucent glass window.

Figure 1.4 illustrates the geometry of central projection with point O as the COP. The plane π is called the **picture plane**, or **image plane**, which is the plane of Alberti's window, or the artist's canvas. Let S be a scene point in 3-D space. Its image S' on the picture plane is the intersection of OS with π.

Let AM and BN be two lines in a family of parallel lines in the ground plane γ. The images of these parallel lines in the picture plane π seem to converge to a single point C. The point C is a vanishing point. If you imagine that AM and BN are two railroad tracks and a train is moving away on the railroad, the image of the train in the picture plane will become smaller and smaller and it seems to vanish at point C. In fact, the point C is not an image of any point in plane γ. If we have a different family of parallel lines in the ground plane γ, in a different direction, their images on the picture plane π also converge to one point, which is different from C. That will be another vanishing point. All the vanishing points in the picture plane π fall on one line, the vanishing line, which is also the horizon line. The horizon line is the apparent line that separates the earth from the sky. It is the line where the sun appears to rise over the sea and where all the ships appear to vanish when they are sailing away.

Figure 1.3 Perspective drawing using Dürer frame, in *The Practical Perspective* by Jean Dubreuil (1642). Image source: public domain.

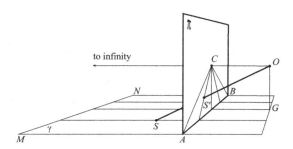

Figure 1.4 Perspective drawing.

With the invention of cameras in 1820s, the principles of perspective are automatically guaranteed in photography by the working mechanism of the camera—the central projection of light rays through the center of the lens of the camera, or the pinhole for a pinhole camera.

In computer graphics, the 3-D world scene is modeled and stored in the computer and rendered to the 2-D screen through computation of central projection utilizing the fast matrix processing power of the graphics hardware, the GPU. Hence projective geometry is very important in computer graphics and computer vision applications.

§2   Projective Planes

Mathematicians took over the study of perspective drawing and central projection from the artists. They carried it further and developed the theory of projective geometry. Johannes Kepler and Girard Desargues introduced the concept of point at infinity. Desargues is also known for an importance theorem named after him. Jean-Victor Poncelet developed much of synthetic projective geometry in a Russian prison after he was captured while serving as a French officer in Napoleon's campaign against Russia. August Möbius and Julius Plücker introduced homogeneous coordinates. Michel Chasles, Karl von Staudt, Arthur Cayley and Felix Klein are among other major contributors in this field.

Intuitively the projective plane is the picture plane, or the Dürer frame, or the artist's canvas onto which the 3-D world is projected. It is a 2-D plane but it is not an ordinary 2-D plane. It is related to the 3-D world. It is the image plane of the 3-D world. Sometimes it is the illusion of the 3-D world. The illusion is caused by the visual ambiguity—many points (all the points on a straight line passing through the COP) are projected to the same point on the picture plane, or the projective plane.

The projective plane can be defined using different models. All the models are equivalent to each other. We start with the extended Euclidean plane model. (Precisely it should be extended affine plane, but we avoid using the term affine plane for now just to make things simple. Simply put, an affine plane is a Euclidean plane where we refrain from speaking about distances.)

2.1   Extended Euclidean Plane Model

When we look at the railroad tracks, they seem to converge to a point on the horizon, as in Figure 1.5.

Intuition. (Point at infinity) A family of parallel lines meet at a point at infinity.

Figure 1.5   Point at infinity.

In a Euclidean plane, if two lines are parallel, alternatively we may say that the two lines "meet at a point at infinity". At the first sight, this alternative saying does no harm but does no good either. "The two lines meet at a point at infinity" is just a euphemism of "The two lines do not meet". In analogy, when we say that "someone is between jobs", it is just a euphemism for "someone is unemployed."

Johannes Kepler and Girard Desargues independently introduced the points at infinity. With the points at infinity introduced, many statements can be simplified because we never need to discuss different cases whether the lines meet or the lines are parallel. Any two lines always meet, either at an ordinary point, or at a point at infinity.

We also introduce one line at infinity and stipulate that all the points at infinity lie on this line at infinity. In the case of the railroad tracks picture, the horizon line is the line at infinity.

With the addition of points at infinity, the Euclidean plane is extended and is called a projective plane.

Definition 1. Projective plane—extended Euclidean plane model

---

Let π be a Euclidean plane. To construct a **projective plane**, denoted by $\bar{\pi}$, we add additional points and one additional line to π as follows:

(1) Add an additional set Γ of points, called **points at infinity**, (or **ideal points**). Retrospectively the points in π are called **ordinary points** of $\bar{\pi}$. It is stipulated that each family of parallel lines in π intersect at a unique point at infinity.

(2) Add one additional line l_∞, which is called the **line at infinity** (or the **ideal line**). It is stipulated that all the points at infinity lie on this line at infinity.

Ordinary points and points at infinity are treated equally and they are just called points of the projective plane. It is easy to see that any two distinct lines intersect at a unique point in the projective plane.

In the projective plane, we do not use the concept of distance. This is because distance is not preserved under central projection. In projective geometry, we only have the **incidence relation**. Namely, we only care about the relation that which points lie on which lines. Projective geometry is an incidence geometry. From now on we will just say extended plain for short. With this extended plane model, it is easy to see that it satisfies the following axioms.

Axioms. (Projective plane)
(1) *Any two distinct points lie on one and only one line.*
(2) *Any two distinct lines meet at a point.*
(3) *There exist at least four points of which no three are collinear.*

If several points lie on the same line, they are said to be **collinear**. If several lines intersect at the same point, they are said to be **concurrent**. Another way of saying that point P lies on line l is that point P is **incident** with line l. We also say line l is **incident** with point P. Using the term "incident", the above axioms can be rewritten in a more "symmetric" form.

Axioms. (Projective plane—alternative form)

($1'$) *Any two distinct points are incident with a unique line.*

($2'$) *Any two distinct lines are incident with a unique point.*

($3'$) *There exist at least four points of which no three are incident with the same line.*

Synthetic projective geometry starts from axioms and studies the projective properties of geometric figures using logical inference. We will have a slight touch of synthetic projective geometry in this subsection and then we switch to the analytic approach in the next subsection with the ray model and projective coordinates. The above axioms of projective plane as an axiom system is not complete. That means it does not completely characterize the extended plane model. The projective plane defined by the extended plane model is called the **real projective plane**. Other alternative models may satisfy these axioms as well. These alternative models include projective planes which have finite number of points, known as finite projective planes. More axioms need to be added to the above axioms in order to uniquely characterize the real projective plane. The following is one axiom which can be added to the system. Historically it was known as Desargues' Theorem because a similar version was proved by Desargues in Euclidean geometry.

Axiom. (Desargues) *Given two triangles, if the three lines joining the three pairs of corresponding vertices are concurrent, then the three intersection points of the three pairs of corresponding sides are collinear.*

We restate the Desargues Axiom in the following referring to Figure 1.6. Given two triangles $\triangle A_1 B_1 C_1$ and $\triangle A_2 B_2 C_2$, let $A_1 B_1$ and $A_2 B_2$ meet at Q; $B_1 C_1$ and $B_2 C_2$ meet at R; $A_1 C_1$ and $A_2 C_2$ meet at S. Desargues' Axiom states, if $A_1 A_2$, $B_1 B_2$ and $C_1 C_2$ meet at a single point P (in such a case, we say that the corresponding vertices of $\triangle A_1 B_1 C_1$ and $\triangle A_2 B_2 C_2$ are in perspective), then Q, R and S are on a single line (in such a case, we say that the three sides of $\triangle A_1 B_1 C_1$ and $\triangle A_2 B_2 C_2$ are in perspective). Hence the following is an alternative way to state the Desargues Axiom.

Axiom. (Alternative form of Desargues Axiom) *Given two triangles, if their corresponding vertices are in perspective, then the three corresponding sides are also in perspective.*

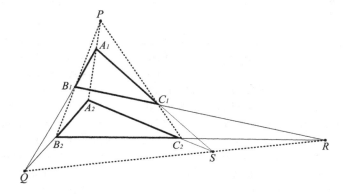

Figure 1.6   Desargues' axiom.

If a projective geometry (satisfying Axiom (1), (2) and (3)) also satisfies Desargues Axiom, it is called **Desarguesian geometry**. Otherwise, it is called **non-Desarguesian Geometry**.

It can be proved that the real projective space $\mathbb{R}P^n$ (see §3) constructed out of a real linear space $\mathbb{R}^{n+1}$ is Desarguesian. It can also be proved that in projective spaces of dimension three and above, Desargues Axiom is not independent, but rather a theorem. When the dimension is two, there exist non-Desarguesian models, like the **Moulton plane** (see [Moulton (1902)] and [Hilbert (1899)] p. 74).

By simply adding points at infinity to the Euclidean plane, we obtained a set of axioms which are different from those of the Euclidean plane. There is an interesting observation. Namely, the points and lines are symmetric in the axioms of the projective plane. This leads to the concept of duality. We say that the line is the dual of the point, and the point is the dual of the line.

Definition 2. Dual proposition

If $\mathscr{P}$ is a proposition about points and lines in a projective plane, by exchanging the terms "point" and "line" in $\mathscr{P}$, we obtain a new proposition $\overline{\mathscr{P}}$. $\overline{\mathscr{P}}$ is called the **dual proposition** of $\mathscr{P}$.

Theorem 1. (Principle of duality) A proposition $\mathscr{P}$ about points and lines in a projective plane is true, if and only if its dual proposition $\overline{\mathscr{P}}$ is true.

This principle of duality can be simply proved by inspecting the dual proposition of each axiom of the projective plane and they turn out to be equivalent to the original axioms.

The principle of duality is actually a metatheorem (a theorem about the theorems). If we know any proposition is true, then from the principle of duality, we know its dual proposition also must be true.

The dual proposition of Desargues Axiom is its converse. From the Desargues Axiom and principle of duality, we obtain the converse of the Desargues axiom.

Theorem 2. (Converse of Desargues Axiom) *Given two triangles, if the three corresponding sides are in perspective, then their corresponding vertices are also in perspective.*

2.2   The Ray Model

In last subsection, by adding new points—points at infinity—we extended the Euclidean plane to a projective plane. Here we introduce another model of the projective plane—the ray model. The ray model is a different approach but it is related to the extended plane model, and basically the two models are the same. They are equivalent to each other and there is a simple one-to-one correspondence between the two models.

The ray model is closely related to the perspective drawing, which we discussed in §1. Figure 1.4 is duplicated here as Figure 1.7, for the reader's convenience, illustrating perspective drawing process. O is the COP and π is the image plane. S is a scene point in the 3-D Euclidean space. Its image under central projection is S' in the image plane π. If Q is any point (not shown in the figure) on the line OS, the image of Q under central projection is also S'. In fact, all the points on line OS are mapped to the same point S' under central projection. Each point S' in the image plane π corresponds to a line OS' under central projection. We may call each ray OS' a point in the projective plane as well. What if a ray, for example, OG is parallel to the image plane π? Then it does not intersect with π. In such a case, we say the ray represents a point at infinity, along the direction of ray OG. This leads to the ray model of the projective plane. It is more convenient to use vectors to represent rays. All the vectors on the same line OS' represent the same ray, and hence the same point in the projective plane. If two vectors v_1 and v_2 are on the same line OS', we say that they are equivalent. In the ray model, a point in the projective plane is represented by a ray passing through O, or the entire equivalence class of a vector v.

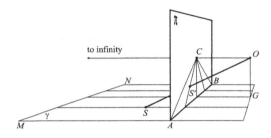

Figure 1.7   Projective plane—the ray model.

Definition 3. Projective plane—the ray model

Let V be the 3-D Euclidean space. We define an equivalence relation $\sim$ in V: $v_1 \sim v_2$ if and only if $v_1 = kv_2$ for some $k \neq 0 \in \mathbb{R}$. Each of these equivalence classes $[v]$ is called a **ray**. A ray represents a straight line passing through the origin of V. The set of all rays is called a **projective plane**, denoted by $P^2(V)$, or simply P^2. A ray $[v]$ is called a point in P^2.

Intuition. (The projective plane) The projective plane P^2 is a 2-D plane but it is related to a 3-D world by way of central projection. When we think of the projective plane, we should think of ourselves as the painter. The projective plane is the painter's canvas, or the glass pane of Alberti's window, or the Dürer frame for perspective drawing. We stand in front of the projective plane and view the projective plane. The view point is outside the projective plane in the 3-D world. Each point in the projective plane corresponds to a line of sight. This is the ray model.

This is the extrinsic view of the projective plane and this view is easier to understand than the intrinsic view like the axiomatic system or the extended Euclidean plane model.

Figure 1.8   Street pavement illusion art of Julie Kirk-Purcell. Image source: Hongyu Guo.

The points on a ray passing through the COP are projected on the same point on the picture plane and hence the depth information of the object in 3-D is lost. This phenomenon is called **depth ambiguity** (or **projective ambiguity**). Artists exploit the depth ambiguity to create 3-D illusions, known as *trompe l'œil* (French for "deceive the eye"). The 3-D illusions of street pavement art have the origin in 1500s in Italy and now are experiencing a revival and have become particularly popular, thanks to the improvement of color chalk quality. Figure 1.8 is a street pavement art work created by artist Julie Kirk-Purcell. The 3-D illusion is good only when the picture is viewed from a particular angle. Figure 1.9 shows the same picture on the ground when viewed from the opposite direction. Notice the drawing of the bear on the ground is so elongated and distorted. The principle of street pavement illusion is the same as that of perspective drawing—central projection. The only difference is that in the conventional art, the artist's canvas, or the picture plane, is in vertical position while in the street pavement art, the picture plane is horizontal. Julie Kirk-Purcell is an art professor and she has published a book, *Sidewalk Canvas: Chalk Pavement Art at Your Feet* [Kirk-Purcell (2011)]. In addition to vibrant pictures of street pavement illusions, the book also reveals the secret and provides practical guides on how to create these 3-D illusions, even with the mathematics explained.

Figure 1.9   The same art viewed from opposite direction. Image source: Hongyu Guo.

2.3   Projective Coordinates for Points

We want to establish coordinates for the projective plane so that we can use the analytic method to study the projective plane. In the Euclidean plane, we use pairs of real numbers (x, y) as the coordinates of points. However, in the projective plane, because of the addition of extra points—points at infinity—we have to come up with a way to provide coordinates for the points at infinity as well.

If we use the extended plane model, we can use a pair of numbers (x, y) to represent an ordinary point. For a point at infinity, we can use a pair of numbers (p, q) to indicate the direction, where $(p, q) \neq (0, 0)$. Also, if p and q are multiplied by a nonzero factor t, then (pt, qt) and (p, q) represent the same direction and hence the same point at infinity. Doing it this way, the ordinary points and points at infinity are treated differently. Given a pair of numbers, we have to indicate it is an ordinary point or a point at infinity. We could use a triple (x, y, z) to represent any point, where $z = 1$, or 0 is used as a Boolean flag. $z = 1$ indicates an ordinary point, while $z = 0$ indicates a point at infinity. This treatment is not uniform with ordinary points and points at infinity and hence it is not convenient. As mentioned earlier, we would prefer a uniform treatment with all the points. The ray model provides a way to do this naturally. We redraw Figure 1.7 but we rotate the figure so that the picture plane π is displayed in a horizontal position (Figure 1.10). O is the COP, or the eye of the artist. The space $\mathbb{R}^3$ with the origin at O has a coordinate system (x, y, z). Any point S in $\mathbb{R}^3$ has coordinates (x, y, z), which can be used to represent the ray OS. If we multiply the vector (x, y, z) by a factor $t \neq 0$, then (tx, ty, tz) represents the same ray.

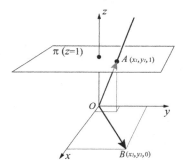

Figure 1.10   Homogeneous coordinates for the projective plane.

Definition 4. Projective coordinates

In the ray model of the projective plane, let (x, y, z) be the coordinates of any point on the ray. Because a ray is considered a point in the projective plane, (x, y, z) are called the **projective coordinates**, or the **homogeneous coordinates** of the point. It is understood that (x, y, z) and (xt, yt, zt) represent the same point, for all $t \neq 0$.

The reason why they are called homogeneous coordinates will be revealed in Remark 3.

We may choose to place the picture plane at $z = 1$. For any point $(x, y, z) \in \mathbb{R}^3$, with $z \neq 0$, (x, y, z) and $(x/z, y/z, 1)$ represent the same ray. $(x/z, y/z, 1)$ is the coordinate of the point A, where the ray intersects the plane π. The ordinary points are points in plane π and they all have $z = 1$. An ordinary point can be represented using two coordinates $X = x/z$, $Y = y/z$. (X, Y) are called the **inhomogeneous** coordinates of an ordinary point.

If $z = 0$, then $(x, y, 0)$ represents a point at infinity. Hence the homogeneous coordinates coincide with the idea of coordinates with Boolean flags ($z = 1$ or 0), but much easier to work with.

The homogeneous coordinates (x, y, z) of a point S is relative to a basis $\{e_1, e_2, e_3\}$ for linear space $\mathbb{R}^3$. If the basis is changed to a new basis $\{\bar{e}_1, \bar{e}_2, \bar{e}_3\}$, the point S will have new homogeneous coordinates $(\bar{x}, \bar{y}, \bar{z})$. If the two bases are related by

$$\bar{e}_i = \sum_{k=1}^{3} A_{ki} e_k, \tag{1.1}$$

namely

$$\begin{bmatrix} \bar{e}_1 & \bar{e}_2 & \bar{e}_3 \end{bmatrix} = \begin{bmatrix} e_1 & e_2 & e_3 \end{bmatrix} A, \tag{1.2}$$

then the new coordinates for P is

$$\begin{bmatrix} \bar{x} \\ \bar{y} \\ \bar{z} \end{bmatrix} = A^{-1} \begin{bmatrix} x \\ y \\ z \end{bmatrix}, \tag{1.3}$$

where A^{-1} is the inverse matrix of A.

2.4   Projective Frames

Any four points A, B, C, D in a projective plane are said to be **in general position**, if no three points lie on the same line.

Theorem 3. (Projective frame) *Given any four points A, B, C, E in general position in a projective plane $P^2(V)$, we can choose a basis for V in such a way that A, B, C, E have homogeneous coordinates $(1, 0, 0)$, $(0, 1, 0)$, $(0, 0, 1)$ and $(1, 1, 1)$ respectively, and the projective coordinates of any other point is uniquely determined up to a scaling factor.*

In a projective plane $P^2(V)$, we choose any four points A, B, C and E in general position and we choose a basis for V determined in such a way by these four points A, B, C and E, as described in Theorem 3. We say we have established a **projective coordinate system**, or **projective frame**, in the projective plane. A, B and C are called the **fundamental points** and E is called the **unit point**. Hence in a projective plane, any four points in general position uniquely determine a projective coordinate frame.

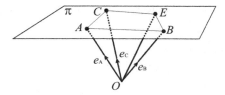

Figure 1.11   Projective frame.

Remark 1. Question — Why Are Four Points Needed in a Projective Frame?

Figure 1.11 shows the ray model with O being the COP. Obviously, if we choose a basis for $\mathbb{R}^3$ such that $e_1 = \overrightarrow{OA}$, $e_2 = \overrightarrow{OB}$ and $e_3 = \overrightarrow{OC}$, the points A, B and C will have coordinates $(1,0,0)$, $(0,1,0)$, $(0,0,1)$ respectively. Why do we need the fourth point E to determine the projective frame? This is because given three points A, B and C, each basis vector of $\mathbb{R}^3$ is only determined up to a scaling factor. If we choose $\bar{e}_1 = a_1 e_1$, $\bar{e}_2 = a_2 e_2$ and $\bar{e}_3 = a_3 e_3$ as a new basis, points A, B and C would have the same homogeneous coordinates, but the coordinates of other points would be different. The vector representing E is

$$v_E = x a_1 e_1 + y a_2 e_2 + z a_3 e_3.$$

By requiring the point E having coordinates $(1, 1, 1)$, we can fix the relative ratio $a_1 : a_2 : a_3$ of the three basis vectors $\overrightarrow{OA}$, $\overrightarrow{OB}$ and $\overrightarrow{OC}$.

Remark 2. Question — Can We Erect a Projective Coordinate System Within the Projective Plane Starting from Scratch?

So far we have been using a model approach, relying on the existence of a 3-dimensional linear space behind the projective plane. Can we start from scratch within the projective plane, relying only on the axioms, performing certain operations and establishing a coordinate system, so that we can study analytic projective geometry? Recall we have discarded the concept of distance in projective geometry. What is the meaning of those coordinates if they do not represent lengths? Karl von Staudt devised a theory and filled this gap. Starting in the projective plane, he only uses line intersections. However, he defined two operations of line segments geometrically—addition and multiplication. These two operations can be proved to form a field. An element in a field is considered a number. Therefore, each point in the projective plane can be represented by a triple of numbers from a certain field F, up to a scaling factor, which are the homogeneous coordinates. However, this field is not necessarily isomorphic to the real field $\mathbb{R}$. That is why we may have other models of projective plane, like finite geometry with finite number of points, corresponding to a finite field F, investigated by O. Veblen [Veblen and Young (1938)]. Only when we impose the axiom of continuity on the projective plane, the field becomes isomorphic to the real field $\mathbb{R}$ and the plane is then called the real projective plane.

2.5   Relation to Terminology in Art, Photography and Computer Graphics

Next let us relate the different choices of projective frames to the terminology in perspective drawing —one-point perspective, two-point perspective and three-point perspective.

The three fundamental points in a projective frame are the vanishing points in perspective drawing, or photography.

Many perspective drawings in art are about buildings and streets, which have many straight line elements. For the buildings and streets, there are often three families of parallel lines which are perpendicular to each other. It is natural to set up a coordinate system (x, y, z) along these three directions. To be consistent with our convention of coordinate frames, we keep the convention that z is in the direction of depth, although it is horizontal now.

Basically there are three types of perspective drawings in art: one-point perspective, two-point perspective and three-point perspective. This applies to photography as well. These three types of perspective which differ in the relative angle of the picture plane to this x, y, z coordinate system. In other words, they are determined by the different viewing angles relative to the buildings and streets. In projective geometry, we think the picture plane is fixed but we change the directions of the basis vectors in the x, y, z frame.

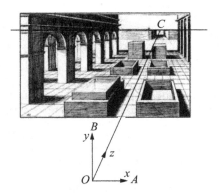

Figure 1.12   One-point perspective, in *Perspective* by Jan Vredeman de Vries, 1604. Image source: public domain.

(1) One-point perspective (or parallel perspective)

In one-point perspective, the picture plane is parallel to the x-y plane.

Equivalently this means we choose the projective frame so that the fundamental point C is an ordinary point in the picture plane. The other two fundamental points A and B are points at infinity. For lines parallel to z-axis, their images converge at the vanishing point C in the picture plane. For lines parallel to the x-axis and lines parallel to the y-axis, their images are still parallel in the picture plane. In one-point perspective, we have one family of converging lines, and two families of parallel lines, as in Figure 1.12 (a).

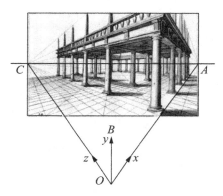

Figure 1.13   Two-point perspective, in *Perspective* by Jan Vredeman de Vries, 1604. Image source: public domain.

(2) Two-point perspective (or angular perspective)

In two-point perspective, the picture plane is still in vertical position. It is parallel to y-axis but not parallel to x or z. It is an angular view of the buildings and streets. Equivalently this means we choose the projective frame so that two fundamental points A and C are ordinary points while B is a point at infinity. The vertical lines still appear to be parallel in the picture, while lines parallel to the x-axis and lines parallel to z-axis converge at the vanishing points A and C, respectively. In two-point perspective, there are two family of converging lines, and one family of (vertical) parallel lines, as in Figure 1.12 (b).

(3) Three-point perspective (or inclined perspective)

In three-point perspective, the picture plane is no longer vertical. This represents an upward view or downward view. Equivalently this means we choose the projective frame so that all three fundamental points A, B and

C are ordinary points. All three families of parallel lines converge to the respective vanishing points A, B and C, as shown in Figure 1.14. The line joining A and C is the horizon line. In an upward view, B is above the horizon line and is called the **zenith**. In a downward view, B is below the horizon and is called the **nadir**.

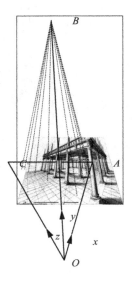

Figure 1.14   Three-point perspective. Image source: public domain.

2.6   Projective Coordinates for Lines

In the ray model, a projective line l is the intersection of a plane γ passing through O, and the picture plane π, as illustrated in Figure 1.15. Namely the line l is represented by the plane γ. The equation of plane γ will serve as the equation of a projective line in the projective plane $\bar{\pi}$.

Let $n = (a, b, c)$ be the normal vector of plane γ. If a point in the plane γ is represented by vector $p = (x, y, z)$, then p is perpendicular to n. Using the inner product, this means $n \cdot p = 0$. Recall the definition of the inner product is $n \cdot p = ax + by + cz$, we have the following theorem.

Theorem 4. (Equation of a line) *Let (x, y, z) be the homogeneous co-ordinates of any point on a line l. Then (x, y, z) satisfies the following* *equation*

$$ax + by + cz = 0,\qquad\qquad (1.4)$$

where a, b, c are some constants.

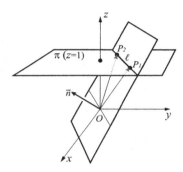

Figure 1.15   Line in the projective plane.

Remark 3. Why Is It Called So? — "Homogeneous Coordinates"

If a function $f(x_1, x_2, \ldots, x_n)$ is a polynomial of variables $x_1, x_2, \ldots, x_n$ and each term has the same degree, then f is called a **homogeneous function** of $x_1, x_2, \ldots, x_n$. The left-hand-side of Eq. 1.4 is a homogeneous function of degree one in terms of variables x, y, z and hence Eq. 1.4 is a homogeneous equation. If we replace (x, y, z) by (xt, yt, zt), Eq. 1.4 still holds. By contrast, the equation of a line in the Euclidean plane is $aX + bY + c = 0$, which is not homogeneous. That is why (X, Y) are called inhomogeneous coordinates.

Because the line equation is homogeneous, we realize that to represent a line, we do not even need to write out the entire equation. The line is uniquely determined by the normal vector (a, b, c), with the understanding that (a, b, c) and (at, bt, ct) $(t \neq 0)$ represent the same line. The triple (a, b, c) is called the projective coordinates, or homogeneous coordinates of the line.

Definition 5. Projective coordinates of a line

Suppose a line has equation $ax + by + cz = 0$, where $(a, b, c) \neq (0, 0, 0)$. (a, b, c) are called the **projective coordinates**, or **homogeneous coordinates of the line**, with the understanding that

(at, bt, ct) represents the same line, for all $t \neq 0$.

We did some reform on the Euclidean plane by introducing the points at infinity. This effort at first seems to be burdensome but now for the first time it has paid off: the line equations are homogeneous and it is much easier to represent a line using homogeneous coordinates, which is just a triple of numbers.

There are even more benefits. The equation of the line passing through two given points is also easier. Let P_1 and P_2 be two points in the projective plane with homogeneous coordinates (x_1, y_1, z_1) and (x_2, y_2, z_2) respectively. $\mathbf{p}_1 = (x_1, y_1, z_1)$ and $\mathbf{p}_2 = (x_2, y_2, z_2)$ are the two representative vectors in $\mathbb{R}^3$ for the two rays OP_1 and OP_2 respectively. The line l passing through the two points P_1 and P_2 is represented by the plane OP_1P_2. The normal vector of this plane is simply

$$\mathbf{n} = \mathbf{p}_1 \times \mathbf{p}_2.$$

So the equation of the line l passing through points P_1 and P_2 is

$$n_1 x + n_2 y + n_3 z = 0,$$

and $\mathbf{n} = (n_1, n_2, n_3)$ is the homogeneous coordinates of l.

Theorem 5. (Line passing through two points) *If $[\mathbf{p}_1]$ and $[\mathbf{p}_2]$ are two points in $P^2(V)$, then the line l passing through $[\mathbf{p}_1]$ and $[\mathbf{p}_2]$ is represented by vector $\mathbf{p}_1 \times \mathbf{p}_2 \in V$. The equation of l is*

$$(\mathbf{p}_1 \times \mathbf{p}_2) \cdot \mathbf{v} = 0,$$

where $[\mathbf{v}]$ is any point on l.

Let $\mathbf{p}_1 = (x_1, y_1, z_1)$, $\mathbf{p}_2 = (x_2, y_2, z_2)$, $\mathbf{v} = (x, y, z)$ be the homogeneous coordinates of $[\mathbf{p}_1]$, $[\mathbf{p}_2]$ and $[\mathbf{v}]$. Then the above equation can be written as

$$\begin{vmatrix} x & y & z \\ x_1 & y_1 & z_1 \\ x_2 & y_2 & z_2 \end{vmatrix} = 0.$$

Remark 4. Cross Link — Point-Line Duality

Now that a point and a line have the same form of representation — a triple, or the homogeneous coordinates, we have to make the context clear when we have a triple, whether it represents a point, or a line.

Furthermore, Eq. 1.4 really has two different interpretations. It can be interpreted as the point (x, y, z) lies on the line (a, b, c), or the point (a, b, c) lies on the line (x, y, z). Hence we have the following theorem.

Theorem 6. (Principle of duality) *The point (x, y, z) lies on the line (a, b, c), if and only if the point (a, b, c) lies on the line (x, y, z).*

Theorem 6 is a special version of Theorem 1, which is the general version of principle of duality.

Remark 5. Historical Note/Cross Link — Homogeneous Coordinates

The homogeneous coordinates were introduced by August Möbius and Julius Plücker independently while Möbius was credited as being the first. Möbius introduced homogeneous coordinates in the form of barycentric coordinates in 1827, while Plücker introduced the homogeneous coordinates in the form of trilinear coordinates in 1835.

2.7   Projective Mappings and Projective Transformations

Let V and V' be two 3-dimensional linear spaces and $P^2(V)$ and $P^2(V')$ be two projective planes. We know that all the linear spaces of the same dimension are isomorphic to each other. Let $\varphi : V \to V'$ be a linear mapping. Because φ is linear, for all $k \in \mathbb{R}$ and $v \in V$, $\varphi(kv) = k\varphi(v)$. Linear mappings map subspaces into subspaces. They map a ray in V to a ray in V'. When the rays in V are interpreted as points in $P^2(V)$, the mapping φ induces a mapping $\psi : P^2(V) \to P^2(V')$. It maps a point in $P^2(V)$ to a point in $P^2(V')$.

Definition 6. Projective mapping

Let $P^2(V)$ and $P^2(V')$ be two projective planes, and $\varphi : V \to V'$ be a linear mapping. A **projective mapping** is defined to be a mapping $f : P^2(V) \to P^2(V')$ such that $f([v]) \mapsto [\varphi(v)]$. A projective mapping $f : P^2(V) \to P^2(V)$ from a projective plane to itself is called a **projective transformation** on $P^2(V)$.

In the above definition, $[v]$ denotes the ray represented by vector v (the equivalence class of v).

Remark 6. Intuition/Cross Link — Projective Mapping

The intuition of projective mappings is central projection, but this intuition is not apparent in the above definition. However, we cannot talk about central projections from one plane π to another plane λ yet because we are studying a projective plane from within. To define the projective mappings as central projections, we need to jump into 3-D space P^3 out of the plane, where the two projective plane π and λ are embedded as subspaces. We will make this connection when we introduce the 3-D projective space P^3 in §3.

It is easy to see that a projective mapping preserves the projective structure. Namely, under a projective mapping, a line is mapped to a line, in the nondegenerate case. Furthermore, if a point P is on a line l in $P^2(V)$ and if P is mapped to P'; l is mapped to l' in $P^2(V')$, then P' is on l'. This means that a projective mapping preserves the incidence relation in a projective plane. A projective mapping is also called a **projective isomorphism**, if the mapping $\varphi : V \to V'$ is a linear isomorphism. All the projective planes are isomorphic to each other (assuming the ground field F is the same).

Definition 7. Collineation

A mapping $f : P^2(V) \to P^2(V')$ is called a **collineation** if for any three collinear points $P_1, P_2, P_3 \in P^2(V)$, their images $f(P_1), f(P_2), f(P_3) \in P^2(V')$ are also collinear.

Remark 7. Question — Is a Collineation Always a Projective Mapping?

The key structure of a projective plane is the incidence relation, namely, the relation that a point is on a line. Collineation is the isomorphism between two projective planes (or projective spaces in general, which we will define later). It is easy to see that a projective mapping is a collineation. Is a collineation necessarily a projective mapping? The answer is yes, if $P^2(V)$ is a real projective plane. The answer in general is no. For example, the answer is no if V is a complex linear space [MSJ (1993)].

Theorem 7. (Fundamental theorem of projective geometry) *A projective mapping from a projective plane to another is uniquely determined by the images of four points in general position.*

To be more specific, let $P^2(V)$ and $P^2(V')$ be two projective planes. Given any four points A, B, C, D in general position in $P^2(V)$, and given any four points A', B', C', D' in $P^2(V')$, there is a unique projective mapping $f : P^2(V) \to P^2(V')$, such that $f(A) = A', f(B) = B', f(C) = C'$ and $f(D) = D'$.

Let us find the analytical expression of a projective mapping in terms of homogeneous coordinates. Let $\varphi : V \to V'$ be a linear mapping and it has a matrix

$$[T] = \begin{bmatrix} \tau_{11} & \tau_{12} & \tau_{13} \\ \tau_{21} & \tau_{22} & \tau_{23} \\ \tau_{31} & \tau_{32} & \tau_{33} \end{bmatrix}.$$

If $[v] \in P^2(V)$ has homogeneous coordinates (x, y, z) and $[\varphi(v)] \in P^2(V')$ has homogeneous coordinates (x', y', z'), then we have

$$\begin{bmatrix} x' \\ y' \\ z' \end{bmatrix} = \begin{bmatrix} \tau_{11} & \tau_{12} & \tau_{13} \\ \tau_{21} & \tau_{22} & \tau_{23} \\ \tau_{31} & \tau_{32} & \tau_{33} \end{bmatrix} \begin{bmatrix} x \\ y \\ z \end{bmatrix}.$$

Theorem 8. *(Projective transformation formulas) Let $f : P^2(V) \to P^2(V); (x, y, z) \mapsto (x', y', z')$ be a projective transformation, where (x, y, z) and (x', y', z') are the homogeneous coordinates of a point and its image in $P^2(V)$. Then*

$$x' = \tau_{11}x + \tau_{12}y + \tau_{13}z$$
$$y' = \tau_{21}x + \tau_{22}y + \tau_{23}z \qquad (1.5)$$
$$z' = \tau_{31}x + \tau_{32}y + \tau_{33}z,$$

where τ_{ij} are constants.

If both (x, y, z) and (x', y', z') are ordinary points and suppose they have inhomogeneous coordinates (X, Y) and (X', Y'), then

$$X' = \frac{\tau_{11}X + \tau_{12}Y + \tau_{13}}{\tau_{31}X + \tau_{32}Y + \tau_{33}}$$

$$Y' = \frac{\tau_{21}X + \tau_{22}Y + \tau_{23}}{\tau_{31}X + \tau_{32}Y + \tau_{33}}, \qquad (1.6)$$

where $(X, Y) = (\frac{x}{z}, \frac{y}{z})$, $(X', Y') = (\frac{x'}{z'}, \frac{y'}{z'})$, with $z \neq 0$ and $z' \neq 0$.

The projective mapping in terms of inhomogeneous coordinates (X', Y') in Eq. 1.6, are rational functions of X and Y, but in general they are not linear functions of X and Y. This equation is a very useful and practical formula when we perform calculations on projective transformations, especially in computer graphics, computer vision and image processing. Most image processing software and some photo editing software provide projective transformation tools.

Remark 8. Intuition/Cross Link — Active View vs. Passive View

There are also the active view and passive view on projective transformations, similar to those on linear transformations (see Part I Chap. 1 Remark 9). In the active view, the point (x, y, z) changes to another point (x', y', z'), as in central projection. In the passive view, the change of the point is relative to the projective frame. If the point does not change but the frame changes, then the projective coordinates of the same point change. We see the coordinate change formula in Eq. 1.3 and the projective transformation formula in Eq. 1.5 are basically the same.

2.8   Perspective Rectification of Images

Many image editing software packages, like Adobe Photoshop, provide a projective transformation tool. Perspective rectification of images has already become a common practice of digital light room, architectural design, photogrammetry and computer vision. That is to use software to change the view angle of the camera after the photograph has been taken. For example, the camera was pointing upward when the photograph in Figure 1.16 (a) was taken. This is often the case when the camera is too close to the building but the photographer still wants the entire building to be contained in the photograph. The buildings have a feeling of being tilted, or falling down. A one-point perspective or two-point perspective is often considered more aesthetic and desirable, with the camera pointing horizontally, as in the pictures in those coffee table magazines.

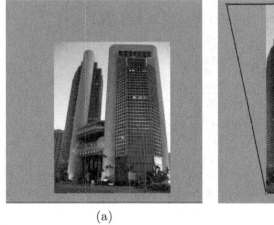

(a)   (b)

Figure 1.16   Projective rectification of an image. Image source: Hongyu Guo.

The fundamental theorem of projective geometry states that a projective transformation from a projective plane to another projective plane (or itself) is uniquely determined by the images of four points in general position. Using Adobe Photoshop, one can select four points in general position, most often the four corners of the photograph, and drag them to the desired new positions, and the projective transformation of the image can be performed instantly with the aid of the software, as shown in Figure 1.16 (b). Projective transformations have the property of mapping straight lines to straight lines.

§3   Projective Spaces

The construction of a 3-dimensional projective space P^3 is very similar to a projective plane. We can use the extended Euclidean space model, or the ray model.

3.1   Extended Euclidean Space Model

We start with the 3-dimensional Euclidean space but add additional points, additional lines and one additional plane. Those added points are called points at infinity, or ideal points. The added lines are called lines at infinity, or ideal lines; the added plane is called the plane at infinity, or the ideal plane. We define that a family of parallel lines meet at one point at infinity; a family of parallel planes meet at one line at infinity; all points at infinity and all the lines at infinity lie in the plane at infinity. The Euclidean space with points at infinity, lines at infinity and one plane at infinity so defined, together with their incidence relations form the projective space P^3.

3.2   The Ray Model

The ray model of projective space P^3 is similar to the ray model for the projective plane, but it is more abstract now because we are projecting the 4-dimensional space onto a 3-dimensional canvas. Phew!

Let V be a 4-dimensional linear space. A **ray** $[v]$ is a straight line passing through the origin in the 4-D space V, represented by vector $v \in V$. When a ray is considered a point (imagining after projected onto the 3-D canvas), we have a 3-dimensional projective space, denoted by $P^3(V)$. The coordinates of a representative vector $v = (x, y, z, w)$ is called the **homogeneous coordinates** of point $[v]$. (xt, yt, zt, wt) and (x, y, z, w) represent the same point for all $t \neq 0$. If $w \neq 0$, the point $[v]$ is called an **ordinary point** and $(X, Y, Z) \stackrel{\text{def}}{=} (\frac{x}{w}, \frac{y}{w}, \frac{z}{w})$ are the **inhomogeneous coordinates** of point $[v]$. If $t = 0$, $(x, y, z, 0)$ represents a **point at infinity**.

3.3   Projective Subspaces

Definition 8. Projective subspace

A **projective subspace** of $P^3(V)$ is defined to be a subset $X \subseteq P^3(V)$ such that if any two points A_1 and A_2 are in X, then the entire line containing A_1 and A_2 is contained in X.

The **projective planes** are 2-dimensional subspaces of the projective space P^3, and the **projective lines** are 1-dimensional subspaces of P^3.

3.4   Projective Mappings Between Subspaces

The study of projective planes started with the idea of central projection, which is also known as perspective mapping. The idea behind the ray model of the projective plane is central projection. The root idea of projective mapping is also central projection. However, in the previous section, we defined a projective mapping as mappings induced by a linear mapping in $\mathbb{R}^3$. We did not use perspective mapping to define projective mapping. This was not intuitive. This was because we constructed the projective planes abstractly. Different projective planes are isolated because they are not embedded in a space as subspaces. In the definition of a projective transformation from a projective plane to itself, we only have one plane and that is our entire world. To make a perspective projection, we need to have two projective planes. The center of projection needs to be outside of both planes in the 3-D space. We cannot do perspective projection if we do not jump out of the plane.

It is the projective space P^3 that provides a stage to discuss central projection from one plane to another plane, with each projective plane being a subspace of the projective space P^3.

Definition 9. Perspective mapping

Let π and λ be two projective planes in a projective space P^3, and $O \in P^3$ be a point which is not on either π or λ. Let r be any line passing through O. Let r meet π at point A and r meet λ at point A'. We construct a mapping $\Phi : \pi \to \lambda$ such that $A \mapsto A'$. The mapping Φ is called a **perspective mapping** (as shown in Figure 1.17).

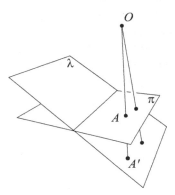

Figure 1.17   Perspective mapping between two projective planes.

Remark 9. Insight — The Need for "Points at Infinity" in the Construction of Projective Planes

In §2, we were prompted by the intuition that parallel railroad tracks seem to intersect at infinite distance and hence we constructed the projective plane by adding these points at infinity to a Euclidean plane. This construction of projective plane indeed provides convenience by eliminating different cases whether two lines intersect or not. Here we see another justification of adding points at infinity. If we discuss perspective mapping between two Euclidean planes, when the ray OA is parallel to plane λ, the image of A is not defined. Hence the perspective mapping cannot be defined on a whole Euclidean plane. Adding points at infinity in projective planes makes a perspective mapping a well-defined mapping between two projective planes.

It is easy to see a perspective mapping from plane π to λ is also a projective mapping from π to λ in the sense of Definition 6. To see this, we use the ray model. Without loss of generality, we can assume the origin of the linear space coincide with O. The point $A \in \pi$ is defined as the ray OA while the point $A' \in \lambda$ is defined as the ray OA', which is the same ray as OA, denoted by r. We define the linear transformation $\varphi : V \to V; r \mapsto r$ as the identity mapping. The projective mapping induced by φ is exactly the same as the perspective mapping Φ that maps A to A'.

Let π and λ be two projective planes in P^3. Is a projective mapping

$\xi : \pi_1 \to \pi_2$ always a perspective mapping? The answer to this question is no. This is easy to see. Let A_1, B_1, C_1 and D_1 be any four points in general position in plane π_1 and A_2, B_2, C_2 and D_2 be any four points in general position in plane π_2. From the fundamental theorem of projective geometry, Theorem 7, we know there exists a unique projective mapping $\varphi : \pi_1 \to \pi_2$ such that $A_1 \mapsto B_1$, $A_2 \mapsto B_2$, $A_3 \mapsto B_3$ and $A_4 \mapsto B_4$. If φ is a perspective mapping, the lines connecting the points in π_1 and their corresponding images in π_2 should all intersect at one point O, which will be the center of projection. However, if the four points in π_1 and four points in π_2 are arbitrary, in general the four lines A_1A_2, B_1B_2, C_1C_2 and D_1D_2 do not intersect at the same point, as shown in Figure 1.18.

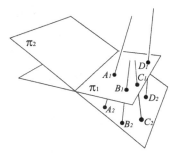

Figure 1.18   A projective mapping may not be a perspective mapping.

Theorem 9. *Let π_1 and π_2 be two projective planes in a projective space P^3 and suppose π_1 and π_2 meet at line l. A projective mapping $f : \pi_1 \to \pi_2$ is a perspective mapping if and only if any point on l is a fixed point under f. Namely, $f(A) = A$ for all A on l.*

Theorem 10. *Let π_1 and π_2 be two projective planes in a projective space P^3. A projective mapping $f : \pi_1 \to \pi_2$ can be expressed as the composition of three or fewer perspective mappings.*

3.5   Central Projection Revisited

Now let us revisit the perspective drawing problem, which we discussed in Section 1. How do we describe the central projection from 3-D space to the

2-D plane (the artist's canvas)? If we discuss this in the realm of Euclidean geometry, we can set up a coordinate system x, y, z for the space with the origin at the COP O, as in Figure 1.19. We use coordinates X, Y for the image plane with the origin at C, which is the intersection of Oz and the image plane. If a point in space has coordinates (x, y, z), then its image on the canvas has coordinates (X, Y) and they are related by

$$X = f\frac{x}{z},$$

$$Y = f\frac{y}{z}.$$

(1.7)

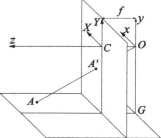

Figure 1.19   Central projection.

However, this is not a well-defined mapping from $\mathbb{R}^3$ to $\mathbb{R}^2$, because if OA is parallel to the image plane, then its image is not defined. This difficulty can be overcome by studying central projection in the context of projective mappings. The 3-D Euclidean space $\mathbb{R}^3$ is completed (by adding points at infinity) to become a 3-D projective space $P^3(\mathbb{R}^4)$ and the 2-D Euclidean canvas plane is completed (by adding points at infinity) to become a 2-D projective plane $P^2(\mathbb{R}^3)$. Similar to Definition 6, we can define a more general projective mapping $f : P^m(V) \to P^k(V')$ from any projective space $P^m(V)$ to any projective space $P^k(V')$ induced by a linear mapping $\varphi : V \to V'$. Here we restrict m and k to 1, 2 and 3, but soon we can see in the next subsection such a restriction is not necessary when the projective space is generalized to higher dimensions, so that m and k can be any natural number.

The terms central projection and perspective mapping are often used interchangeably. The perspective mapping that we defined in Definition 9 is from a plane to a plane. It is bijective and invertible. Similarly, for two lines l_1 and l_2 in the same plane, we can define a perspective mapping from l_1 to l_2 and it will be bijective and invertible. The situation of central projection from 3-D space to a 2-D plane, as in perspective drawing is a little different, which needs some distinction. There has not been accepted terminology in literature to emphasize this distinction. So I will coin some terms as follows. I call the central projection from 3-D space to a 2-D plane a **lossy perspective mapping** because you lose the depth information after the projection. The lossy perspective mapping is surjective but not injective and that is why it may cause illusions. I prefer "lossy" to "non-injective" because "lossy" is more intuitive and "non-injective" is awkward. Retrospectively, the perspective mapping from a plane to a plane, or from a line to a line is called a **bijective perspective mapping**. It is possible to generalize perspective mappings from any dimensional subspace to any dimensional subspace in a higher dimensional projective space. We do this briefly in the next subsection. So a generalized perspective mapping can be bijective (as in the 2-D to 2-D case), surjective but not injective (as in the 3-D to 2-D case) or injective but not surjective (as in the 1-D to 2-D case. Yes, we can project a line into a plane and the image is a line in the plane). The non-invertibility of the lossy perspective mapping explains the depth ambiguity of human visual perception as well as the working mechanism of all 3-D illusion art. We will discuss more on perspective analysis in Part IV Chap. 2 relating to depth ambiguity.

The 3-D to 2-D central projection, or non-injective perspective mapping $f : P^3(\mathbb{R}^3) \to P^2(\mathbb{R}^3)$ is induced by a linear mapping $\varphi : \mathbb{R}^4 \to \mathbb{R}^3$. Both f and φ can be represented by a 4×3 matrix

$$\begin{bmatrix} \tau_{11} & \tau_{12} & \tau_{13} & \tau_{14} \\ \tau_{21} & \tau_{22} & \tau_{23} & \tau_{24} \\ \tau_{31} & \tau_{32} & \tau_{33} & \tau_{34} \end{bmatrix}.$$

If we use homogeneous coordinates (x, y, z, w) for a point A in space $P^3(\mathbb{R}^4)$ and homogeneous coordinates (X, Y, Z) for the image point A', the central projection can be expressed in the matrix form

$$\begin{bmatrix} X \\ Y \\ Z \end{bmatrix} = \begin{bmatrix} \tau_{11} & \tau_{12} & \tau_{13} & \tau_{14} \\ \tau_{21} & \tau_{22} & \tau_{23} & \tau_{24} \\ \tau_{31} & \tau_{32} & \tau_{33} & \tau_{34} \end{bmatrix} \begin{bmatrix} x \\ y \\ z \\ w \end{bmatrix}. \tag{1.8}$$

With special choices of coordinate systems as in Figure 1.19, for an ordinary point in P^3, Eq. 1.8 takes a simpler form

$$\begin{bmatrix} X \\ Y \\ Z \end{bmatrix} = \begin{bmatrix} f & 0 & 0 & 0 \\ 0 & f & 0 & 0 \\ 0 & 0 & 1 & 0 \end{bmatrix} \begin{bmatrix} x \\ y \\ z \\ 1 \end{bmatrix}, \tag{1.9}$$

where f is a constant, which is the image distance. Note that Eq. 1.7 is not linear, but when the perspective projection is discussed in projective space using homogeneous coordinates, Eq. 1.9 is linear. The perspective projection is reduced to matrix multiplication. This is a big advantage of using homogeneous coordinates in the projective space. In computer graphics, the central projection is computed with a dedicated graphics processor GPU, which is optimized with fast matrix manipulation power for the need of 3-D animation and video games.

3.6   Higher Dimensional Projective Spaces

Projective spaces can be generalized to dimension n and the ray model is the easiest approach.

Definition 10. Projective space $P^n(V)$

Let V be a linear space over a field F and $\dim V = n + 1$. A **ray** $[v]$ represented by vector $v \in V$ is the set of all vectors kv for all $k \in F$. Two vectors v_1 and v_2 are said to be equivalent, denoted by $v_1 \sim v_2$ if and only if they are in the same ray. The quotient space $(V - \{0\})/ \sim$ is called a **projective space of dimension** n **associated with** V, denoted by $P^n(V)$. Each ray $[v]$ is called a point in $P^n(V)$. The coordinates of v, which is an $(n + 1)$-tuple, are called the **projective coordinates**, or **homogeneous coordinates** of point $[v]$.

We have already discussed two special cases: $P^2(V)$ and $P^3(V)$. $P^2(V)$ is a projective plane. $P^3(V)$ is a three dimensional projective space. $P^2(V)$ can be a projective subspace of $P^3(V)$. It is also easy to understand that $P^1(V)$, which we call a projective line, is a projective subspace of $P^2(V)$.

We discuss the generalized perspective mappings briefly. Let P^n be a projective space of dimension n, A^r and B^s be two projective subspaces of P^n, of dimensions r and s respectively. A projective mapping from A^r to B^s can always be defined. However, to define a perspective mapping from A^r to B^s, some condition on the COP O and A^r and B^s needs to be satisfied. Let $O \in P^n$ be a point, which will be the COP. For every point $p \in A^r$, draw a line connecting O and p. The condition is that the line Op intersects B^s at a unique point $q \in B^s$. Then we can define a perspective mapping $f : A^r \to B^s$ and define $f(p) = q$. This generalized perspective mapping can be bijective if $r = s$, or surjective but not injective if $r > s$, or injective but not surjective if $r < s$.

Exercises

1. Search online and find the classical paintings by the following artists and find the perspective mistakes in them:
   (1) Duccio di Buoninsegna, *The Last Supper* (1311). Compare this with *The Last Supper* (1498) by Leonardo da Vinci, which has the correct perspective.
   (2) Giotto di Bondone, *Annunciation to St. Anne* (1306).
   (3) Pietro Lorenzetti, *Humilitas Brings a Child Back to Life* (1316).
   (4) Bernardo Daddi, *Annunciation* (1335).
   (5) Jan Van Eyck, *The Arnolfini Portrait* (1434).
   (6) John Gipkyn, *Old St. Paul's* (*Sermon at St. Paul's Cross*) (1616).
2. Street pavement illusion: Let O be the viewpoint and the coordinate system x, y, z is set up as in the figure. The ground plane is equipped with coordinates (X, Z) with $X = x$ and $Z = z$. Suppose a point A on the ground plane represents a point in the illusionary 3-D space with coordinates (x, y, z). Given (x, y, z), find where the point A should be drawn on the ground. Namely, find the coordinates (X, Y) for A.

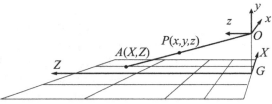

3. Show that the Axioms (1), (2) and (3) of the projective plane admit planes with finite set of points. The following is a model with seven points and seven lines (Fano plane). Show that the Fano plane satisfies

Axioms (1), (2) and (3).

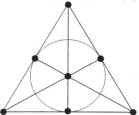

4. Show that Axiom (2) of the projective plane can be weekend to: Any two distinct lines have at least one point in common. To show this, you just need to show that Axiom (1) implies: Any two distinct lines have at most one point in common.

5. Formulate the dual proposition of the Pappus' theorem: Let A_1, A_2, A_3 be three distinct points on a line and B_1, B_2, B_3 be three distinct points on another line. Suppose $A_1 B_2$ and $A_2 B_1$ intersect at M; $B_1 C_2$ and $B_2 C_1$ intersect at N; $C_1 A_2$ and $C_2 A_1$ intersect at P. Then M, N, P are collinear.

6. Use the analytic method (the ray model with homogeneous coordinates) to prove Pappus' theorem.

7. Use the analytic method to prove Desargues' theorem for the real projective plane $\mathbb{R}P^2$.

8. The following are the homogeneous coordinates (x, y, z) of points in the projective plane.

$A\,(2, 3, -1)$
$B\,(1, 0, 0)$
$C\,(1, -1, 0)$
$D\,(1, 0, 1)$
$E\,(4, 6, -2)$
$F\,(-1, 0, 0)$
$G\,(0, 0, -1)$
$H\,(1, 1, 0)$
$I\,(0, 1, 0)$
$J\,(1, 0, -1)$
$K\,(3, -3, 0)$
$L\,(0, 0, 1)$

(1) Some homogeneous coordinates represent the same point. Classify these homogeneous coordinates into groups such that each group represent the same point in the projective plane.

(2) What points are ordinary points and what points are points at infinity?

(3) For the ordinary points, find their inhomogeneous coordinates (X, Y).

9. In the Euclidean plane, a line is represented by the equation $3x - 5y + 2 = 0$. Now the Euclidean plane is extended to the projective plane. By adding one point at infinity, this line becomes a line in the projective plane. Find the equation of the line in the projective plane using homogeneous coordinates (x, y, z).

10. In the projective plane, point P_1 has homogeneous coordinates $(3, 1, 2)$. Point P_2 has homogeneous coordinates $(1, 0, -1)$. Let l be the line passing through P_1 and P_2.

(1) Find the homogeneous coordinates of the line l.

(2) Find the equation of the line l.

11. Let P be a point in the projective plane with homogeneous coordinates $(3, 3, 4)$. Find its new homogeneous coordinates in the following projective frames:

(1) a frame with fundamental points $A = (1, 0, 0)$, $B = (0, 1, 0)$, $C = (0, 0, 1)$ and unit point $E = (1, 1, 1)$ (one-point perspective).

(2) a frame with fundamental points $A = (1, 0, 1)$, $B = (0, 1, 0)$, $C = (-1, 0, 1)$ and unit point $E = (0, 1, 1)$ (two-point perspective).

(3) a frame with fundamental points $A = (1, 0, 1)$, $B = (0, 2, 1)$, $C = (-1, 0, 1)$ and unit point $E = (0, 1, 1)$ (three-point perspective).

12. Find the projective transformation $f : P^2 \to P^2$ such that the given points are mapped to the given points in the following ways.

(1) $(1, 0, 0) \mapsto (-1, 1, 1)$, $(0, 1, 0) \mapsto (1, -1, 1)$, $(0, 0, 1) \mapsto (1, 1, -1)$ and $(1, 1, 1) \mapsto (1, 2, 3)$;

(2) $(1, 0, 0) \mapsto (0, 1, 0)$, $(-1, 1, 1) \mapsto (1, -1, 1)$, $(1, 0, -1) \mapsto (0, 0, -1)$ and keeps $(1, -1, 0)$ fixed.

Chapter 2

Differential Geometry

Euclid alone has looked on Beauty bare.

— Edna St. Vincent Millay

When a man is attracted to a pretty woman, he is attracted by her extrinsic geometry of surfaces.

— Hongyu Guo

Reading Guide. In this chapter we discuss the classical theory of surfaces, mainly due to Gauss, with an emphasis on the intrinsic view, also known as the intrinsic geometry. We keep the discussion of curves to the minimum, because the intrinsic geometry of curves is trivial: all the curves are intrinsically identical. A bug crawling on a curved wire is as happy as one crawling on a straight one. The lowest dimension where intrinsic curvature really occurs is two, which is the case of surfaces.

There are many applications of the theory of surfaces in computer graphics and computer vision. The surfaces are also the prototype of differentiable manifolds and Riemannian manifolds, which become more and more important in computer science, physics and engineering, as well as in mathematics itself. The logical exposition of manifold theory does not depend on the theory of surfaces but the intuition about manifolds is really here. The readers are advised to read this chapter before they read the manifold theory (Part III Chap. 2). Some students in science and engineering tend to take a shortcut by learning manifold theory without leaning the theory of surfaces first, but it is really unfortunate to learn the manifold theory in a parrot's way without first developing intuitions in a more tangible world.

§1   What is Intrinsic Geometry?

To us 3-dimensional beings, surfaces naturally exist in 3-dimensional space. This is because they are naturally embedded in space. However, we can gain a different perspective if we imagine that we are bugs that are restricted on the surface. The bug can make all kind of the measurements on the surface using a measuring tape but it cannot leave the surface and fly into space. We gain a new perspective using this analogy. This method of studying surfaces is called intrinsic geometry. We will elaborate this idea throughout this chapter.

Let us take a short digression. The following is a short fiction that I contrived.

> A psychologist is giving an IQ test to four people: a boy, a girl, a biologist, and a poet. The question is:
> Which one of the four animals is least like the other three?
> A. Bear
> B. Cat
> C. Bat
> D. Ant
> The boy says the answer is C because a bat can fly but others cannot. The girl says the answer is B because a cat is a pet but others are not. The biologist chooses D because an ant is an insect while others are mammals. The poet says the answer is A because Bear has four letters while all others have three and they all end with letter "t".

Many IQ test questions are as silly as this, because the answers to those questions can be arbitrary, especially the types of finding patterns, or continuing sequences. Is one answer better than others? It might, depending on the context, or the perspective. Answer D makes more sense in the context of biology.

Next is another short fiction that I contrived.

A math professor gives a boy a test, similar to the IQ test above. He shows four shapes as in Figure 2.1 and asks the boy:

Which one of the four shapes is least like the other three?

A. Plane

B. Cylinder

C. Cone

D. Sphere

The boy answers A because a plane is flat while all others are curved surfaces. The professor says: "That is a good answer. However, I would prefer choosing D, because if you cut open a cylinder or a cone, they can be 'flattened' to a piece of plane without being stretched. So A, B, C are all flat in my point of view but a sphere can never be flattened without stretching. For example, if you want to 'flatten' an orange peel, you will have to rip it apart (Figure 2.2)."

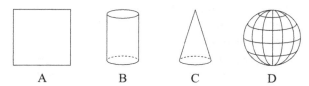

A   B   C   D

Figure 2.1   Classification of surfaces.

In fact, even many adults share the boy's point of view about what is flat and what is curved. Back in history, math professors had held the same view of the boy, until Gauss made his great observation and discovery in 1827. He stated in his seminal paper [Gauss (1827)]:

"From this point of view, a plane surface and a surface developable on a plane, e.g., cylindrical surfaces, conical surfaces, etc., are to be regarded as essentially identical."

Gauss gave a definition of the curvature of a surface, now known as Gaussian curvature. If you calculate the Gaussian curvature of the cylinder or the cone you find it to be zero, the same as the plane, while the sphere has a non-zero curvature. This result is certainly counter-intuitive to the boy in the above story. This view is called the intrinsic view and we will emphasize this intrinsic view in this chapter, as well as in the manifold theory (Part III Chap. 2).

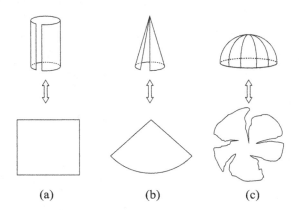

Figure 2.2   A cylinder and a cone can be "flattened" while a sphere cannot.

When it comes to the classification of surfaces, it is similar to those classification questions in an IQ test. There is no absolute right or wrong answer. Gauss brought up an alternative point of view, which provides deeper insight in the study of surfaces. The properties of a surface that do not change after the "bending", or isometric transformation, are called intrinsic properties. So intrinsically, the cylinder and the cone are flat and they are the same as a plane because you can bend a piece of plane to make a cylinder or a cone. For bugs living on a cylinder surface, they will not be able to tell the difference from a plane by just measuring with strings on the surface without leaving the surface. However, a bug living on a sphere is able to find out that they are living on a curved surface. One test is to measure the sum of the interior angles of a triangle. On a sphere, the sum of the interior angles of a triangle is always greater than 180 degrees.

When we talk about extrinsic and intrinsic, we are talking with respect to the surface of interest. If you investigate the surface from outside the surface, it is the extrinsic view. If you investigate the surface from inside the surface, (you have to imagine yourself as a bug which lives on the surface), it is the intrinsic view.

We end this section with a disclaimer. The intrinsic view is not the only approach to geometry. The extrinsic geometry has wide applications as well. However, the intrinsic geometry is the winner in the history of evolution of mathematical theories. The intrinsic view and the extrinsic view are unified through the embedding theorems of Whitney, Nash and others, and the study of embedding of manifolds is still an active research area now.

§2   Parametric Representation of Surfaces

When we discuss surfaces in $\mathbb{R}^3$, we assume that they are smooth surfaces— the functions defining the surfaces are differentiable at least to the second order.

A surface in $\mathbb{R}^3$ can be represented by the graph of a function

$$z = f(x, y), \tag{2.1}$$

which is called an **explicit representation**.

A surface can also be defined by a function $F(x, y, z)$ with the equation

$$F(x, y, z) = 0, \tag{2.2}$$

which is called an **implicit representation**.

Oftentimes we find it is convenient to use two real parameters (u, v) to represent a point P on the surface. We can use these two parameters to represent

$$
\begin{aligned}
x &= x(u, v), \\
y &= y(u, v), \\
z &= z(u, v),
\end{aligned}
\tag{2.3}
$$

where $x(u, v)$, $y(u, v)$ and $z(u, v)$ are smooth functions of u and v. If we use vector notation $\mathbf{r} = (x, y, z)$, Eqs. 2.3 can be combined in the vector form

$$\mathbf{r} = \mathbf{r}(u, v). \tag{2.4}$$

Eq. 2.4 is called a **parametric representation** (or **parametrization**) of the surface. The pair (u, v) is also called the **local coordinates** of the point on the surface. Each explicit representation is also a parametric representation $\mathbf{r} = \mathbf{r}(x, y, f(x, y))$, if we consider (x, y) as parameters. Because (x, y) is the orthogonal projection of (x, y, z) onto the x-y plane, this form of parametric representation is called **Monge parametrization** (or **Monge patch**, or **Monge coordinates**).

The equation $u = constant$ describes a family of curves, called v-**lines** (v varies while u is constant). The equation $v = constant$ describes another family of curves, called *u*-**lines** (*u* varies while *v* is constant). These two families of curves are called **coordinate curves** (or **coordinate lines**) and they form a mesh, called coordinate mesh, or a **curvilinear coordinate system**. At any point P on the surface, the two coordinate curves $u = const$ and $v = const$ do not have to be orthogonal. If they are orthogonal at all points in a neighborhood, it is called an orthogonal curvilinear coordinate system. However, if at any point P, the coordinate curves $u = const$ and $v = const$ are tangent to each other, it is an unpleasant situation. In such a case, the point P is called a **singular point**. A point on the surface is called a **regular point** if it is not a singular point. Whether a point is singular or regular does not depend on the choice of parametrization, but rather depends only on the surface itself.

A plane is a special case of a surface. A plane can be described using a Cartesian coordinate system but it can be described using curvilinear coordinate systems as well. The plane polar coordinate system (r, φ) is one example.

Remark 1. Look Ahead — Patches and Local Coordinates for Differentiable Manifolds

Sometimes, the explicit or implicit representation may be either impossible or inconvenient. The parametric representation is more preferable. Representing a surface by two parameters is what justifies a surface to be called a 2-dimensional space or 2-dimensional manifold. Euler started to use parametric presentations of surfaces and Gauss used it extensively. Using parametrization, or local coordinates, is a key step toward the generalization to differentiable manifolds. Many times it is impossible to represent the entire surface with one parametrization, but we can always represent a local neighborhood using parametrization. This local parametrization is called a **patch** (or **chart**), and we can cover the entire surface with overlapping patches. This leads naturally to the concept of differentiable manifolds (see Part III Chap. 2). In this chapter, we are only interested in the local properties of a surface in a small neighborhood, represented by a single patch.

Example 1. (Sphere, Monge parametrization) The surface of a sphere with radius a and the center at $(0, 0, 0)$ can be represented in the implicit form

$$x^2 + y^2 + z^2 = a^2.$$

The sphere cannot be covered by a single patch. The upper hemisphere can be represented in the explicit form

$$z = \sqrt{a^2 - x^2 - y^2}.$$

This provides a parametrization for the upper hemisphere,

$$\mathbf{r} = \begin{bmatrix} x \\ y \\ z \end{bmatrix} = \begin{bmatrix} x \\ y \\ \sqrt{a^2 - x^2 - y^2} \end{bmatrix}. \tag{2.5}$$

♣

Example 2. (Sphere, spherical coordinates) We can find another parametrization by using spherical polar coordinates,

$$\mathbf{r} = \begin{bmatrix} x \\ y \\ z \end{bmatrix} = \begin{bmatrix} a \sin\theta \cos\varphi \\ a \sin\theta \sin\varphi \\ a \cos\theta \end{bmatrix}, \tag{2.6}$$

where θ is the colatitude angle (or zenith angle) and φ is the azimuth angle (Figure 2.3). Note the spherical polar coordinates cannot cover the entire sphere either. The north pole ($\theta = 0$) and the south pole ($\theta = \pi$) are not covered, where φ is not defined.   ♣

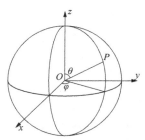

Figure 2.3   Spherical polar coordinate parametrization for the sphere.

Example 3. (Sphere, stereographic projection) Another possible parametrization of the sphere is stereographic projection (Figure 2.4). Set up a coordinate system (x, y, z) such that the south pole of the sphere is at the origin O with coordinates $(0, 0, 0)$. Let a be the radius of the sphere. We use the north pole $N = (0, 0, 2a)$ as the projection center. For any point P on the sphere, draw line NP and project it to point P' on the x-y plane. Let P have coordinates (x, y, z) and P' have coordinates $(X, Y, 0)$. (X, Y) will be used as parameters for point P.

It is easy to see in Figure 2.4, $X = OF$, $Y = OG$ and

$$NP'^2 = ON^2 + OP'^2 = 4a^2 + X^2 + Y^2.$$

Because $\angle OPN$ is a right angle, $\triangle OPN \sim \triangle P'ON$. Hence

$$\frac{NP}{ON} = \frac{ON}{NP'}.$$

Notice $ON = 2a$. Then,

$$NP = \frac{4a^2}{NP'}.$$

Because $\triangle NQP \sim \triangle NOP'$,

$$\frac{x}{X} = \frac{y}{Y} = \frac{2a - z}{2a} = \frac{OP}{OP'} = \frac{NP}{NP'} = \frac{4a^2}{NP'^2} = \frac{1}{1 + \frac{1}{4a^2}(X^2 + Y^2)}.$$

We can find

$$\mathbf{r} = \begin{bmatrix} x \\ y \\ z \end{bmatrix} = \frac{1}{1 + \frac{1}{4a^2}(X^2 + Y^2)} \begin{bmatrix} X \\ Y \\ \frac{1}{2a}(X^2 + Y^2) \end{bmatrix}. \qquad (2.7)$$

♣

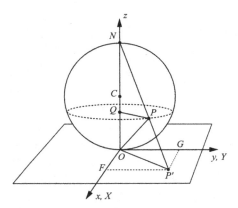

Figure 2.4   Stereographic projection parametrization for the sphere.

Example 4. (Helicoid) Helicoid is a surface which can be considered as generated by a helix. Take a point P on the helix and draw a line that intersects the z-axis at point Q at a right angle. When the point P moves on the helix, the line PQ generates the helicoid surface. A helicoid can have a parametrization (r, θ),

$$\mathbf{r} = \begin{bmatrix} x \\ y \\ z \end{bmatrix} = \begin{bmatrix} r\cos\theta \\ r\sin\theta \\ a\theta \end{bmatrix}, \qquad (2.8)$$

where r is the distance of the point to the z-axis and θ is the angle shown in Figure 2.5.

♣

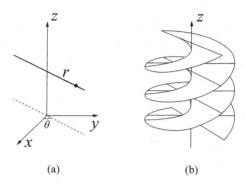

(a)   (b)

Figure 2.5   A helicoid surface.

Example 5. (Catenoid) The catenoid is a surface formed by a catenary curve

$$x = a \cosh \frac{z}{a}$$

rotating around the z-axis. It has a parametrization (r, θ),

$$\mathbf{r} = \begin{bmatrix} x \\ y \\ z \end{bmatrix} = \begin{bmatrix} r \cos \theta \\ r \sin \theta \\ a \cosh^{-1}(\frac{r}{a}) \end{bmatrix}, \tag{2.9}$$

where r is the distance from the point to z-axis and θ is the azimuthal angle of rotation.   ♣

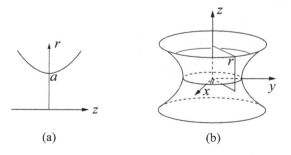

(a)   (b)

Figure 2.6   A catenoid surface.

Theorem 1. (Change of parameters) *Let* $\mathbf{r} = \mathbf{r}(u, v)$ *and* $\mathbf{r} = \mathbf{r}(s, t)$ *be two different parameterizations in a neighborhood on surface* S *in* $\mathbb{R}^3$. *We can define a mapping from a neighborhood of* $\mathbb{R}^2$ *to a neighborhood of* $\mathbb{R}^2$, *such that* $(u, v) \mapsto (s, t)$. *This can be represented by two real functions*

$$s = s(u, v),$$
$$t = t(u, v).$$

Then the above functions are differentiable and have differentiable inverses.

Remark 2. Look Ahead — Differentiable Manifolds

In the definition of a differentiable manifold, the condition of compatibility of the atlas is modeled on this theorem. For abstract differentiable manifolds, this condition has to be imposed as an axiom. See Part III Chap. 2.

§3   Curvature of Plane Curves

It is intuitive that at a point on a curve, the faster the direction of the tangent changes, the more curved it appears at that point. This gives us an idea of how to define and measure the curvature of a plane curve.

Definition 1. Curvature of a plane curve

Let P be a point on a plane curve and Q is a point on the curve near P. Let $\triangle\theta$ be the angle between the tangent line at Q and the tangent line at P; $\triangle s$ be the arc length between P and Q. The **curvature** of the curve at point P is defined to be

$$\kappa \overset{\text{def}}{=} \lim_{\Delta s \to 0} \left| \frac{\Delta\theta}{\Delta s} \right| = \left| \frac{d\theta}{ds} \right|.$$

The **radius of curvature** at point P is defined to be

$$r \overset{\text{def}}{=} \frac{1}{\kappa}.$$

A straight line has zero curvature at any point. A circle with radius a has a constant curvature $\kappa = 1/a$ at any point.

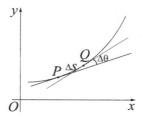

Figure 2.7   Curvature of a plane curve.

Theorem 2. (Curvature of plane curves) *A plane curve represented by* $y = f(x)$ *has curvature*

$$\kappa = \frac{|y''|}{(1 + y'^2)^{3/2}}. \tag{2.10}$$

In calculus, when we study the behavior of a curve in a neighborhood of a point, we often use the tangent to approximate the curve. We say this approximation is the first order. In the second order, the curve can be approximated by a circle. In general, let two curves Γ_1 and Γ_2 have a common point P_0. Let $\mathbf{r}_1$ and $\mathbf{r}_2$ represent a point on curve Γ_1 and Γ_2 respectively. Let s be the arc length and $\mathbf{r}_1(s)$ and $\mathbf{r}_2(s)$ are the parametric forms of the two curves. Assume $s = 0$ at point P_0. If $\dot{\mathbf{r}}_1(0) = \dot{\mathbf{r}}_2(0)$, we say the two curves have **contact of the first order**. This means that the two curves have the same tangent line and the two curves are tangent to each other. If in addition, if the two curves also have $\ddot{\mathbf{r}}_1(0) = \ddot{\mathbf{r}}_2(0)$, we say the two curves have **contact of the second order**.

At any point P_0 on the curve, we can find a circle as a second order approximation of the curve. At point P_0, there are infinitely many circles that are tangent to the curve. However, there is a unique circle that have contact of the second order with the curve. This circle is called the **osculating circle**. It was first named **circulum osculans** by Leibniz, which means "kissing circle" in Latin.

Theorem 3. (Osculating circle of a curve) *Let* (x, y) *be a point on a plane curve represented by* $y = f(x)$. *The osculating circle of the curve* at point (x, y) has its center at (a, b), where

$$a = x - \frac{y'(1 + y'^2)}{y''},$$

$$b = y + \frac{1 + y'^2}{y''}.$$

The radius of the osculating circle is the same as the radius of curvature at (x, y).

For this reason, the center of the osculating circle is also called the **center of curvature**. The osculating circle is also called the **circle of curvature**.

§4   Curvature of Surfaces—Extrinsic Study

When we try to study the curvature of surfaces, the situation is much more complicated than curves. However, we may start with studying the curvature of curves on the surface.

Definition 2. Normal section and normal curvature

Let **n** be the unit normal vector and **w** be a tangent vector at a point P on a surface S. Let N be a normal plane passing **n** and **w**. The intersection of N and S is a curve σ. σ is called a **normal section** determined by tangent vector **w**. The curvature of the normal section is called the **normal curvature** of the surface at point P in the direction of **w**. The normal curvature is signed. If the normal section curves "away" from the surface normal vector, it is defined to be positive. Otherwise, it is negative.

The sign of normal curvature is relative to the surface orientation, namely which direction we define to be the outward direction of the surface. If we flip the direction of the surface normal vector **n**, the sign of the normal curvature will be changed.

A normal section at a point P on the surface is uniquely determined by the direction of the tangent vector **w**. Given a reference direction in the tangent plane at P, the direction of the tangent vector **w** can be defined with an angle φ, which varies from 0 to 2π. The normal curvature in the direction of $\mathbf{w}$ at point P is then uniquely determined by this angle φ.

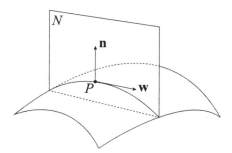

Figure 2.8   Normal curvature.

Theorem 4. (Euler) *At a point P on surface S, there are two directions perpendicular to each other in the tangent plane, where the normal curvature takes a maximum and a minimum value. Let κ_1 and κ_2 be the maximum and minimum normal curvature and $\kappa_1 \geq \kappa_2$. Take the direction of the maximum curvature as a reference direction. Let φ be the angle from the reference direction ($\varphi = 0$) to any direction, then the normal curvature in the direction of φ is*

$$\kappa_\varphi = \kappa_1 \cos^2 \varphi + \kappa_2 \sin^2 \varphi.$$

A special case of this theorem is $\kappa_1 = \kappa_2$. In this case, the normal curvature κ is the same in all directions. Such a point is called an **umbilical point**. All the points on a plane and all the points on a sphere are umbilical points.

Definition 3. Principal curvatures and principal directions

The maximum and minimum normal curvatures κ_1 and κ_2, are called **principal curvatures** at point P. The corresponding directions are called **principal directions** at P.

§5   Intrinsic Geometry—for Bugs that Don't Fly

Distance is an important structure in Euclidean geometry. It is also very important in studying the surfaces, which are viewed as subsets of points in the Euclidean space $\mathbb{R}^3$. The Euclidean distance between two points $P_1 = (x_1, y_1, z_1) \in \mathbb{R}^3$ and $P_2 = (x_2, y_2, z_2) \in \mathbb{R}^3$ is defined to be

$$\rho(P_1, P_2) \overset{\text{def}}{=} \sqrt{(x_1 - x_2)^2 + (y_1 - y_2)^2 + (z_1 - z_2)^2}. \qquad (2.11)$$

The concept of distance can be generalized to abstract metric spaces (see Part III Chap. 1). Here we give a brief introduction of metric spaces.

Definition 4. Metric space

A nonempty set X together with a mapping $\rho : X \times X \to \mathbb{R}$ is called a metric space, if the following **axioms** are satisfied.

(1) $\rho(P_1, P_2) = 0$ if and only if $P_1 = P_2$.
(2) $\rho(P_1, P_2) = \rho(P_2, P_1)$ (symmetry).
(3) $\rho(P_1, P_2) + \rho(P_2, P_3) \geq \rho(P_1, P_3)$ (triangle inequality).

$\rho(P_1, P_2)$ is called the **distance** between the two points P_1 and P_2 in the abstract sense.

The Euclidean distance in $\mathbb{R}^3$ is a prototype, a special case, of the distance ρ. A surface S itself is a metric space with the Euclidean distance ρ defined in Eq. 2.11. A mapping from a surface S to another surface S' preserving the distance ρ between and two points on the surface is called a **congruence**, which is a key concept in Euclidean geometry.

A congruence preserves the 3-dimensional Euclidean distance ρ between any pair of points. A **rigid transformation**, or **rigid motion** (or simply **motion**) is a composition of a rotation and a translation in $\mathbb{R}^3$. A rigid motion is a congruence. Rigid motion is an intuitive concept, representing the motion of a rigid body. A congruence in general can be the composition of a rigid motion and a reflection. A reflection, where the mirror image of a left hand, for example, becomes a right hand, cannot be achieved by a rigid motion (in 3-dimensional space, but possible via a rotation in 4-dimensional space).

There are situations where we use a different definition of distance between points on a surface. We are the inhabitants on the earth. When we talk about distances between cities, we use the distance measured on the earth's surface. The distance between Jaén, Spain and Tauranga, New Zealand is 19939 km. This is the shortest distance on the surface of the earth, the shortest possible distance of air travel. In fact, these two cities are antipodal points on earth, meaning they are exactly opposite each other on the globe. The shortest distance in 3-dimensional Euclidean space would be the diameter of the earth, but we are never concerned with this distance because the current technology is still far away from tunneling through the center of the earth.

Let γ be a curve on surface S, and P_1, P_2 be two points on the curve. The length of the curve between P_1 and P_2 is defined by $\int_{\substack{p_1 \\ \gamma}}^{p_2} ds$, where ds is the infinitesimal arc length on the surface along γ.

Definition 5. Intrinsic distance

The **intrinsic distance** (or **geodesic distance**) between points P_1 and P_2 on the surface S is defined to be the infimum of the curve lengths among all the curves connecting P_1 and P_2,

$$\tilde{\rho}(P_1, P_2) \stackrel{\text{def}}{=} \inf_{\gamma} \int_{\substack{p_1 \\ \gamma}}^{p_2} ds.$$

The new distance $\tilde{\rho}$ is also called the **distance on the surface**. Intuitively, if we connect the two points P_1 and P_2 with a flexible but not stretchable string (a measuring tape) on the surface, the distance $\tilde{\rho}$ is the length of the segment of the taut string between P_1 and P_2. It is straightforward to verify that this new distance $\tilde{\rho}$ satisfies the axioms in Definition 4 and hence we can make the surface S a new metric space with the intrinsic distance $\tilde{\rho}$.

Remark 3. It is easy to see that $\rho(P_1, P_2) \leq \tilde{\rho}(P_1, P_2)$. The reason is that $\rho(P_1, P_2)$ is the shortest length among all the possible paths in $\mathbb{R}^3$, while $\tilde{\rho}(P_1, P_2)$ is the shortest length among all the possible paths restricted on the surface S. The geodesics in $\mathbb{R}^3$ are straight lines. The straight line connecting P_1 and P_2 in $\mathbb{R}^3$ is like a tunnel under the surface.

Definition 6. Geodesic line

A curve γ is called a **geodesic line** (or **geodesic curve**, or simply **geodesic**) if for any two points P_1 and P_2 on the curve, when their distance $\tilde{\rho}(P_1, P_2)$ is sufficiently small,

$$\tilde{\rho}(P_1, P_2) = \int_{\substack{P_1 \\ \gamma}}^{P_2} ds.$$

This definition means that locally a geodesic line realizes the shortest distance between any two points on itself. In a plane, the geodesics are straight lines and on a sphere, the geodesics are great circles. The intrinsic distance $\tilde{\rho}(P_1, P_2)$ measured on the surface is also called geodesic distance, because this distance is the arc length of a geodesic curve connecting the two points. To study the surfaces, we will focus on the intrinsic distance structure $\tilde{\rho}$, instead of the Euclidean distance ρ.

Definition 7. Isometric mapping

Let S_1 and S_2 be two surfaces in $\mathbb{R}^3$. S_1 and S_2 are said to be **isometric** to each other if there exists a mapping $\varphi : S_1 \to S_2$ such that $\tilde{\rho}(\varphi(P_1), \varphi(P_2)) = \tilde{\rho}(P_1, P_2)$ for all points $P_1, P_2 \in S_1$. The mapping φ is called an **isometric mapping**, or simply **isometry**.

Note that the difference between a congruence and an isometry between two surfaces is that the congruence preserves the distance ρ in 3-D space $\mathbb{R}^3$ while an isometry preserves the distance $\tilde{\rho}$ measured on the surface. Obviously, a congruence is an isometry but the converse is not necessarily true. The term rigid transformation is intuitive itself to describe congruence. The intuitive picture of isometry is the flexible bending of a surface without stretching.

Intuition. (Intrinsic geometry vs. extrinsic geometry) In the study of surfaces with an **intrinsic view**, we focus on the **intrinsic distance** $\tilde{\rho}(P, Q)$ **on the surface**, and **isometric mappings** between surfaces, which preserve $\tilde{\rho}(P, Q)$. Surfaces isometric to each other are considered identical. They are only embedded differently in $\mathbb{R}^3$.

By contrast, in the study of surfaces with an **extrinsic view**, we focus on the **distance** $\rho(P,Q)$ **in the 3-D space** and **congruences**, which preserve $\rho(P,Q)$ in $\mathbb{R}^3$.

In terms of the bug analogy, a bug on the surface is able to measure the distance $\tilde{\rho}(P,Q)$ on the surface, but is not able to measure the distance $\rho(P,Q)$ in space without leaving the surface.

Remark 4. Analogy/Comparison — Congruence, Isometry and Homeomorphism

The following analogies are helpful: the intrinsic geometry of surfaces is the geometry for bugs that don't fly; the extrinsic geometry is the geometry for bugs that can fly. We further compare three different types of transformations using an analogy of three different materials. For congruence, we can think of a surface made of adamant materials like steel. You can move a steel surface from one place to another place in space and this transformation is a congruence, or rigid motion. For isometry, we think of a surface made of paper. An isometric mapping allows flexible bending of the surface without stretching. For topological transformation, or homeomorphism (see Part III Chap. 1), the surface is a rubber sheet. Continuous stretching is allowed.

If we use the parametric representation of a surface in Eq. 2.4, we take the differentiation of the vector function $\mathbf{r}(u,v)$,

$$d\mathbf{r} = \mathbf{r}_u du + \mathbf{r}_v dv\,, \tag{2.12}$$

where $\mathbf{r}_u \overset{\text{def}}{=} (\frac{\partial x}{\partial u}, \frac{\partial y}{\partial u}, \frac{\partial z}{\partial u})$ and $\mathbf{r}_v \overset{\text{def}}{=} (\frac{\partial x}{\partial v}, \frac{\partial y}{\partial v}, \frac{\partial z}{\partial v})$ are the vectors tangent to the coordinate lines $u = const$ and $v = const$. The square of the infinitesimal arc length is

$$ds^2 \overset{\text{def}}{=} (d\mathbf{r}) \cdot (d\mathbf{r}) = \mathbf{r}_u^2 du^2 + 2\mathbf{r}_u \cdot \mathbf{r}_v dudv + \mathbf{r}_v^2 dv^2\,. \tag{2.13}$$

Definition 8. First fundamental form, first fundamental quantities

The quadratic form of tangent vectors

$$\Phi_1 \overset{\text{def}}{=} Edu^2 + 2Fdudv + Gdv^2, \tag{2.14}$$

is called the **first fundamental form** (or **line element**) of the surface at point P, where $E \overset{\text{def}}{=} \mathbf{r}_u^2$, $F \overset{\text{def}}{=} \mathbf{r}_u \cdot \mathbf{r}_v$ and $G \overset{\text{def}}{=} \mathbf{r}_v^2$ are called the **first fundamental quantities** at point P.

Remark 5. Intuition — Meaning of the First Fundamental Form

The result $\Phi_1(\mathbf{w})$ of the first fundamental form Φ_1 acting on a tangent vector $\mathbf{w}$ is the inner product of $\mathbf{w}$ with itself, namely $\mathbf{w} \cdot \mathbf{w}$, or the square of its length. This is the abstract definition of the first fundamental form. That is, it is a quadratic form, which maps each tangent vector to a real number. Eq. 2.14 is this quadratic form expressed in local coordinates u and v. When the tangent vector is infinitesimal, $\Phi_1(\mathbf{w})$ is the square of the infinitesimal arc length.

Given a tangent vector $\mathbf{w}$ in the tangent plane at point P with components (w_u, w_v) under the basis $\{\mathbf{r}_u, \mathbf{r}_v\}$, $\Phi_1(\mathbf{w}) = Ew_u^2 + 2Fw_uw_v + Gw_v^2$ is the square of the length of $\mathbf{w}$. The matrix $\begin{bmatrix} E & F \\ F & G \end{bmatrix}$ is the matrix representation of the inner product of vectors in the tangent plane at point P under the basis $\{\mathbf{r}_u, \mathbf{r}_v\}$. The basis $\{\mathbf{r}_u, \mathbf{r}_v\}$ for the tangent plane vary from point to point on the surface. Therefore, E, F and G vary from point to point on the surface and are functions of u and v. Given a curve $\gamma = \gamma(t)$ on the surface in parametric form, the curve length of can be written as

$$s = \int_{t_1}^{t_2} \frac{ds}{dt}dt = \int_{t_1}^{t_2} \sqrt{E\left(\frac{du}{dt}\right)^2 + 2F\frac{du}{dt}\frac{dv}{dt} + G\left(\frac{dv}{dt}\right)^2}\, dt$$

u and v are functions of t on γ. At the end points P_1 and P_2, parameter t takes values t_1 and t_2.

Knowing the first fundamental form or the first fundamental quantities, even without knowing the original definition of the surface in the parametric form, we are able to calculate curve lengths and hence the distances $\tilde{\rho}$ between points.

Remark 6. Look Ahead — Riemannian Geometry

When this is generalized to Riemannian geometry, we use the first fundamental form (also known as the Riemann metric tensor) as the starting point, without assuming the knowledge of the parametric form of the surface or manifold, which is only the embedding of the manifold into a higher dimensional Euclidean space.

Example 6. (First fundamental form of a sphere) First, for a sphere with radius a in Monge parametrization (x, y) given in Example 1, the first fundamental form is

$$ds^2 = \frac{(a^2 - y^2)dx^2 + 2xy\,dx\,dy + (a^2 - x^2)dy^2}{a^2 - x^2 - y^2}. \tag{2.15}$$

With the spherical polar parametrization (θ, φ) given in Example 2, the first fundamental form is

$$ds^2 = a^2 d\theta^2 + a^2 \sin^2\theta\, d\varphi^2. \tag{2.16}$$

If we use the stereographic projection (X, Y) given in Example 3, the first fundamental form becomes

$$ds^2 = \frac{dX^2 + dY^2}{\left[1 + \frac{1}{4a^2}(X^2 + Y^2)\right]^2}. \tag{2.17}$$

♣

Remark 7. Cross Link — Manifolds of Constant Curvature

Riemann generalized the theory of surfaces to n-dimensional manifolds. He considered manifolds of constant curvature K and gave a metric

$$ds^2 = \frac{\sum_{i=1}^n dx_i^2}{\left(1 + \frac{K}{4} \sum_{i=1}^n x_i^2\right)^2},$$

in a suitable coordinate system, in his inauguration speech at University of Göttingen, *On the hypotheses that lie at the foundations of geometry*, delivered in 1854 ([Chern et al. (1999)] and [Kline (1972)] p. 892). When $n = 2$, this suitable coordinate system for a sphere is the stereographic projection given in Example 3.

Theorem 5. (Fundamental theorem of intrinsic geometry of surfaces — Gauss) *Two surfaces S_1 and S_2 in $\mathbb{R}^3$ are isometric to each other if and only if, with choice of parameters, they have the same first fundamental form.*

Corollary. *Any quantity that is a function of the first fundamental quantities only, is invariant under isometric mappings.*

Example 7. (First fundamental forms of a plane and a cylinder) The first fundamental form for the plane is

$$ds^2 = dx^2 + dy^2. \tag{2.18}$$

For the cylinder with radius a, we take the parametric form

$$\begin{bmatrix} x \\ y \\ z \end{bmatrix} = \begin{bmatrix} a\cos\varphi \\ a\sin\varphi \\ z \end{bmatrix}.$$

The first fundamental form of the cylinder is

$$ds^2 = a^2 d\varphi^2 + dz^2. \tag{2.19}$$

If we make parameter transformation

$$u = a\varphi,$$
$$v = z,$$

with the new parameters u and the v, the first fundamental form of the cylinder can be rewritten as

$$ds^2 = du^2 + dv^2, \tag{2.20}$$

which is the same as that of the plane. Locally a cylinder is isometric to a plane.   ♣

Definition 9. Developable surface

A surface is called a **developable surface** if it is isometric to a plane.

With a developable surface, we can always develop (flatten) it on a plane, or we can bend a piece of plane to make a developable surface. Cylinders and cones are developable surfaces while a sphere is not a developable surface.

Example 8. (First fundamental forms of a helicoid and a catenoid) Helicoid is defined by parametric equations Eq. 2.8. The first fundamental form of the helicoid is

$$ds^2 = du^2 + (u^2 + a^2)dv^2.$$

The catenoid is defined by Eq. 2.9. The first fundamental form of this catenoid is

$$ds^2 = \frac{r^2 dr^2}{r^2 - a^2} + r^2 d\varphi^2. \tag{2.21}$$

We make a parameter transformation

$$u = \sqrt{r^2 - a^2} \tag{2.22}$$
$$v = \varphi,$$

then

$$du = \frac{r dr}{\sqrt{r^2 - a^2}}$$
$$dv = d\varphi.$$

The first fundamental form of the catenoid with u and v as parameters can be written as

$$ds^2 = du^2 + (u^2 + a^2)dv^2.$$

Hence the first fundamental forms of the catenoid and the helicoid become the same. Eq. 2.22 is the isometric mapping to bend a piece of helicoid to be pasted on a catenoid.   ♣

§6   Extrinsic Geometry—for Bugs that Can Fly

In last section, we used an analogy of bugs living on the surface to describe the intrinsic geometry of surfaces. The bug can measure the distances $\tilde{\rho}$ on the surface using a taut string but it cannot measure the distances ρ in space because it cannot leave the surface. The bug does not feel the bending of the surface because the distance measured on the surface between any two points is not changed during the bending. In intrinsic geometry, the first fundamental form determines a surface up to isometry. That means a surface can be bent in space without changing the first fundamental form.

There are situations and applications where a surface after bending is considered different. This is the extrinsic view. Using the bug analogy again, now consider a bug that can fly off the surface, and measure the Euclidean distance ρ in 3-D space. In extrinsic geometry, we use the Euclidean distance ρ in 3-D space and the central concern in extrinsic geometry is congruence, which preserves distance ρ in 3-D space.

Let the surface be represented by parameters u and v. We study the properties of the surface in a neighborhood of a regular point P_0 with position vector $\mathbf{r}_0(u, v)$. Let P be a nearby point in this neighborhood on the surface with a position vector $\mathbf{r}(u, v)$, and $\Delta\mathbf{r} = \mathbf{r} - \mathbf{r}_0$.

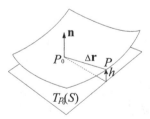

Figure 2.9   Second fundamental form of a surface.

When $\Delta\mathbf{r}$ becomes infinitesimal, it is represented by the differential

$$dr = \mathbf{r}_u du + \mathbf{r}_v dv \,, \tag{2.23}$$

where $\mathbf{r}_u \overset{\text{def}}{=} (\frac{\partial x}{\partial u}, \frac{\partial y}{\partial u}, \frac{\partial z}{\partial u})$ and $\mathbf{r}_v \overset{\text{def}}{=} (\frac{\partial x}{\partial v}, \frac{\partial y}{\partial v}, \frac{\partial z}{\partial v})$ are the tangent vectors tangent to the coordinate lines $v = const$ and $u = const$. They are also in the tangent plane $T_{p_0}(S)$ at P_0.

Look at the distance h from P to the tangent plane $T_{p_0}(S)$ at P_0. Take this distance as signed distance, given an orientation of the surface. If the perpendicular line from the tangent plane to P is in the same direction of the normal vector $\mathbf{n}$, then h takes positive sign. Otherwise, h is negative. h is a second order infinitesimal, when du and dv are infinitesimals. Using Taylor expansion, we find the first order terms vanish. The expansion of h up to the second order is

$$h = \frac{1}{2}\mathbf{n} \cdot d^2\mathbf{r},$$

where $d^2\mathbf{r}$ is the second order differential of $\mathbf{r}$. We have

$$d\mathbf{r} = \mathbf{r}_u du + \mathbf{r}_v dv,$$
$$d^2\mathbf{r} = \mathbf{r}_{uu}du^2 + 2\mathbf{r}_{uv}dudv + \mathbf{r}_{vv}dv^2 + \mathbf{r}_u d^2u + \mathbf{r}_v d^2v.$$

Notice $\mathbf{n} \cdot \mathbf{r}_u = \mathbf{n} \cdot \mathbf{r}_v = 0$ because $\mathbf{r}_u$ and $\mathbf{r}_v$ are tangent vectors and they are perpendicular to the normal vector $\mathbf{n}$. Therefore,

$$h = \frac{1}{2}\left(\mathbf{n} \cdot \mathbf{r}_{uu}du^2 + 2\mathbf{n} \cdot \mathbf{r}_{uv}dudv + \mathbf{n} \cdot \mathbf{r}_{vv}dv^2\right).$$

This is a quadratic form of tangent vectors.

Definition 10. Second fundamental form, second fundamental quantities

The quadratic form of tangent vectors

$$\Phi_2 \overset{\text{def}}{=} Ldu^2 + 2Mdudv + Ndv^2, \tag{2.24}$$

is called the **second fundamental form** of the surface at point P, where $L \overset{\text{def}}{=} \mathbf{n} \cdot \mathbf{r}_{uu}$, $M \overset{\text{def}}{=} \mathbf{n} \cdot \mathbf{r}_{uv}$ and $N \overset{\text{def}}{=} \mathbf{n} \cdot \mathbf{r}_{vv}$, are called the **second fundamental quantities** at point P.

Remark 8. Intuition — Meaning of the Second Fundamental Form

Φ_2 is a quadratic form of tangent vectors. In an infinitesimal neighborhood of P_0, given an infinitesimal tangent vector $\mathbf{w}$ with components (w_u, w_v) under basis $\{\mathbf{r}_u, \mathbf{r}_v\}$ for the tangent plane $T_{P_0}(S)$ at P_0, the second fundamental form $\Phi_2(\mathbf{w}) = Mw_u^2 + 2Lw_uw_v + Nw_v^2$ gives two times the distance from point P on the surface to the tangent plane at P_0.

Using the normal vector

$$\mathbf{n} = \frac{\mathbf{r}_u \times \mathbf{r}_v}{|\mathbf{r}_u \times \mathbf{r}_v|},$$

the second fundamental quantities can be expressed as

$$L = \frac{1}{\sqrt{EG - F^2}} \mathbf{r}_{uu} \cdot (\mathbf{r}_u \times \mathbf{r}_v) = \frac{1}{\sqrt{EG - F^2}} \begin{vmatrix} x_{uu} & y_{uu} & z_{uu} \\ x_u & y_u & z_u \\ x_v & y_v & z_v \end{vmatrix},$$

$$M = \frac{1}{\sqrt{EG - F^2}} \mathbf{r}_{uv} \cdot (\mathbf{r}_u \times \mathbf{r}_v) = \frac{1}{\sqrt{EG - F^2}} \begin{vmatrix} x_{uv} & y_{uv} & z_{uv} \\ x_u & y_u & z_u \\ x_v & y_v & z_v \end{vmatrix},$$

$$N = \frac{1}{\sqrt{EG - F^2}} \mathbf{r}_{vv} \cdot (\mathbf{r}_u \times \mathbf{r}_v) = \frac{1}{\sqrt{EG - F^2}} \begin{vmatrix} x_{vv} & y_{vv} & z_{vv} \\ x_u & y_u & z_u \\ x_v & y_v & z_v \end{vmatrix},$$

where $x_u \overset{\text{def}}{=} \frac{\partial x}{\partial u}$, $x_v \overset{\text{def}}{=} \frac{\partial x}{\partial v}$, $x_{uu} \overset{\text{def}}{=} \frac{\partial^2 x}{\partial u^2}$, $x_{uv} \overset{\text{def}}{=} \frac{\partial^2 x}{\partial u \partial v}$, $x_{vv} \overset{\text{def}}{=} \frac{\partial^2 x}{\partial v^2}$ and the partial derivatives of y and z are denoted similarly.

The normal curvature of a surface can be expressed in terms of the second normal form and the first normal form.

Theorem 6. (Normal curvature) *At a point P on the surface, the normal curvature in the direction represented by tangent vector $\mathbf{w}$ is*

$$\kappa(\mathbf{w}) = \frac{\Phi_2(\mathbf{w})}{\Phi_1(\mathbf{w})}.$$

If $\mathbf{w}$ is a unit tangent vector, then $\Phi_1(\mathbf{w}) = 1$. The following corollary gives an interpretation of the meaning of the second fundamental form.

Corollary. (Normal curvature) *If $\mathbf{w}$ is a unit tangent vector, then the normal curvature in the direction of $\mathbf{w}$ is $\kappa(\mathbf{w}) = \Phi_2(\mathbf{w})$.*

It is obvious that both the first fundamental quantities and the second fundamental quantities are invariant under congruences. The following theorem says the converse is also true. Namely, a surface can be uniquely determined by the first fundamental quantities and the second fundamental quantities, up to congruence.

Theorem 7. (Fundamental theorem of extrinsic geometry of surfaces—Bonnet) *Two surfaces S_1 and S_2 in $\mathbb{R}^3$ are congruent to each other if and* *only if they have the same first fundamental form and the same second fundamental form after appropriate choice of parameters.*

Remark 9. A stronger version of Theorem 7 states that, given any two quadratic forms

$$\Phi_1 = E(u,v)du^2 + 2F(u,v)dudv + G(u,v)dv^2,$$
$$\Phi_2 = L(u,v)du^2 + 2M(u,v)dudv + N(u,v)dv^2,$$

provided $E > 0$, $G > 0$, $EG - F^2 > 0$, and Φ_1, Φ_2 satisfy certain conditions (Gauss equation and Mainardi-Codazzi equations), there exists a unique surface (in a local neighborhood) up to congruence that have Φ_1 and Φ_2 as its first fundamental form and second fundamental form respectively.

§7   Curvature of Surfaces—Intrinsic Study

We studied the curvature of surfaces in Section 4 by studying the normal curvatures of the normal sections of a surface. Euler had a remarkable discovery which reduced infinitely many normal curvatures to a pair of principal curvatures (κ_1, κ_2). We know the normal curvatures of a surface are extrinsic properties because if we bend the surface, the normal curvatures, including the principal normal curvatures will change.

Is it possible that we find a single number to characterize the curvature of a surface at a point, instead of using two numbers (κ_1, κ_2)? An immediate thought would be that we use some number that combines κ_1 and κ_2. Out of infinitely many possibilities, the following are a few candidates that we may consider:

(1) $\kappa_1 + \kappa_2$,

(2) $|\kappa_1 - \kappa_2|$,

(3) $\kappa_1\kappa_2$,

(4) $\sqrt{\kappa_1^2 + \kappa_2^2}$,

(5) $\dfrac{1}{\frac{1}{\kappa_1} + \frac{1}{\kappa_2}}$.

Two of these have been tried out in history. (3) is called the total curvature, or Gaussian curvature, named for K. F. Gauss. (1) with a factor of $\frac{1}{2}$, is called the mean curvature. (4) and (5) are in fact also related to some forms of means of two principal curvatures. (4) is related to the root mean square. (5) is related to the harmonic mean.

A definition is just a short name to substitute a longer phrase. You can define something whatever way you want. However, good definitions reflect some essence and have meaningful applications.

One simple intuition to guide us for the choice is that the Euclidean plane $\mathbb{R}^2$ is flat and it should have zero curvature. If a surface is curved, it should have non-zero curvature. Immediately we see that (2) is not a good choice because for a sphere, $\kappa_1 = \kappa_2$ and $|\kappa_1 - \kappa_2| = 0$. (5) will have difficulty if κ_1 or κ_2 is zero.

Definition 11. Gaussian curvature, mean curvature

Let P be a point on surface S and κ_1 and κ_2 be the two principal curvatures at P. $K = \kappa_1 \kappa_2$ is called the **Gaussian curvature** (or **total curvature**) of the surface at point P.

$H = \frac{1}{2}(\kappa_1 + \kappa_2)$ is called the **mean curvature** of the surface at point P.

For the Euclidean plane, both principal curvatures are zero, $\kappa_1 = \kappa_2 = 0$. Therefore, both Gaussian curvature and the mean curvature are zero, $K = H = 0$. Apparently both definitions passed this test.

Let us test the two definitions on a cylinder with radius a. The two principal curvatures for any point on the cylinder are $\kappa_1 = \frac{1}{a}$ and $\kappa_2 = 0$. The Gaussian curvature $K = 0$ while the mean curvature $H = \frac{1}{2a}$. Which better reflects our intuition? Our intuition seems to tell us that the cylinder is curved and should deserve a nonzero curvature.

The choice by Gauss[1] was $K = \kappa_1 \kappa_2$. The mean curvature was introduced by Sophie Germain in 1831 [Kline (1972)]. It turns out that the Gaussian curvature is an intrinsic invariant but the mean curvature is not.

It is not to say that intrinsic geometry is superior to extrinsic geometry. There are many applications of the mean curvature. However, we will focus mainly on the intrinsic geometry and Gaussian curvature here.

The Gaussian curvature and the mean curvature can be expressed using the first fundamental form and the second fundamental form.

---

[1]The original definition of curvature by Gauss was not a wild guess. He defined the curvature through mapping the surface to a sphere, now called Gauss map (see Theorem 13). Then he proved this curvature is an intrinsic invariant and is also equal to the product of the two principal curvatures discovered by Euler.

Theorem 8. *The Gaussian curvature is equal to*

$$K = \frac{\det \Phi_2}{\det \Phi_1} = \frac{LN - M^2}{EG - F^2}, \tag{2.25}$$

where $\det \Phi_1$ *and* $\det \Phi_2$ *are the determinants of the matrices of the first and the second fundamental form respectively.*

The mean curvature is equal to

$$H = \frac{1}{2} \frac{EN - 2FM + GL}{EG - F^2}. \tag{2.26}$$

Apparently from this theorem, both the mean curvature H and the Gaussian curvature K depend on both the first fundamental quantities and the second fundamental quantities. However, Gauss had a great discovery that the Gaussian curvature K is determined solely by the first fundamental quantities and therefore, by Theorem 5, is an isometric invariant. Gauss was very excited with this discovery and he called this theorem Theorema Egregium (Latin for "Remarkable Theorem").

Theorem 9. (Theorema Egregium — Gauss) *The Gaussian curvature of a surface at point* P *is determined completely by the first fundamental form and hence is invariant under isometric mappings. The Gaussian curvature can be expressed as*

$$K = \frac{1}{2\sqrt{g}} \left\{ \frac{\partial}{\partial u} \left[\frac{1}{\sqrt{g}} \left(\frac{FE_v}{E} - G_u \right) \right] + \frac{\partial}{\partial v} \left[\frac{1}{\sqrt{g}} \left(2F_u - E_v - \frac{FE_u}{E} \right) \right] \right\},$$

where $g \overset{def}{=} \det \Phi_1 = EG - F^2$.

The above formula is known as **Gauss' formula**. It can be written in many different forms, for the convenience of different situations of calculation, which are given in the following.

Corollary 1. (Gaussian curvature — Brioschi's formula) *The Gaussian curvature is equal to*

$$K = \frac{1}{g^2} \left(\begin{vmatrix} F_{uv} - \frac{1}{2}E_{vv} - \frac{1}{2}G_{uu} & \frac{1}{2}E_u & F_u - \frac{1}{2}E_v \\ F_v - \frac{1}{2}G_u & E & F \\ \frac{1}{2}G_v & F & G \end{vmatrix} - \begin{vmatrix} 0 & \frac{1}{2}E_v & \frac{1}{2}G_u \\ \frac{1}{2}E_v & E & F \\ \frac{1}{2}G_u & F & G \end{vmatrix} \right).$$

If we choose some special parametrization, the formulas may have a simpler form.

Corollary 2. (Gaussian curvature — orthogonal curvilinear coordinates) *If the coordinate lines are orthogonal, i.e., $F = 0$ in the first fundamental form, then the Gaussian curvature is equal to*

$$K = -\frac{1}{2\sqrt{EG}} \left(\frac{\partial}{\partial u} \frac{G_u}{\sqrt{EG}} + \frac{\partial}{\partial v} \frac{E_v}{\sqrt{EG}} \right).$$

The Gaussian curvature can also be written in the following form using Christoffel symbols. To put it in a more concise form, we use the indexed notation of parameters $u_1 = u$, $u_2 = v$.

Corollary 3. (Gaussian curvature — Liouville's formula) *The Gaussian curvature is equal to*

$$K = \frac{1}{\sqrt{g}} \left[\frac{\partial}{\partial u_1} \left(\frac{\sqrt{g}}{G} \Gamma_{22}^1 \right) - \frac{\partial}{\partial u_2} \left(\frac{\sqrt{g}}{G} \Gamma_{12}^1 \right) \right]$$

$$= \frac{1}{\sqrt{g}} \left[\frac{\partial}{\partial u_2} \left(\frac{\sqrt{g}}{E} \Gamma_{11}^2 \right) - \frac{\partial}{\partial u_1} \left(\frac{\sqrt{g}}{E} \Gamma_{12}^2 \right) \right],$$

where $\Gamma_{ij}^m = \frac{1}{2} \sum_{k=1}^2 g^{mk} \left(\frac{\partial g_{ik}}{\partial u^j} + \frac{\partial g_{jk}}{\partial u^i} - \frac{\partial g_{ij}}{\partial u^k} \right)$, $i, j, m = 1, 2$, are called Christoffel symbols.

Example 9. (Gaussian curvature of a cylinder) For a cylinder with radius a, the maximal principal curvature is $\kappa_1 = 1/a$. The minimal principal curvature is $\kappa_2 = 0$ along the direction of the ruling. The Gaussian curvature is $K = \kappa_1 \kappa_2 = 0$. This corroborates the fact that a plane and a cylinder are locally isometric. ♣

Example 10. (Gaussian curvature of a sphere) On a sphere, both principal curvatures are equal to $1/a$ at any point. Hence the Gaussian curvature of a sphere is a constant $K = \frac{1}{a^2}$ at any point. ♣

Example 11. (Gaussian curvature of a pseudosphere) A pseudosphere is a surface obtained by rotating a plane curve called tractrix around z-axis.

It has a parametrization

$$\begin{bmatrix} x \\ y \\ z \end{bmatrix} = \begin{bmatrix} \rho \cos \varphi \\ \rho \sin \varphi \\ a \cosh^{-1} \dfrac{a}{\rho} - \sqrt{a^2 - \rho^2} \end{bmatrix},$$

where a is a constant. We can find

$$\mathbf{r}_\rho = (\cos \varphi, \sin \varphi, -\frac{\sqrt{a^2 - \rho^2}}{\rho}),$$
$$\mathbf{r}_\theta = (-\rho \sin \varphi, \rho \cos \varphi, 0).$$

The first fundamental form is

$$ds^2 = a^2 \rho^2 \left[\frac{d\rho^2}{\rho^4} + \frac{d\varphi^2}{a^2} \right].$$

Making parameter transformation,

$$u = \frac{\varphi}{a}, \ \ 0 \le u < \frac{2\pi}{a},$$
$$v = \frac{1}{\rho}, \ \ v \ge \frac{1}{a},$$

the first fundamental form becomes

$$ds^2 = \frac{a^2}{v^2}(du^2 + dv^2).$$

Using the formula in Corollary 2, we find the Gaussian curvature on the surface is a constant

$$K = -\frac{1}{a^2}.$$

We know a sphere has a constant positive curvature. Pseudosphere gets its name because it has a constant negative curvature. ♣

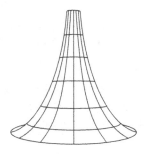

Figure 2.10   A pseudosphere.

All the surfaces in the above examples have constant Gaussian curvatures. In the general case, the Gaussian curvature varies on the surface from point to point. If the two principal normal curvatures at the point have the same sign, meaning both principal sections curve toward the same side of the tangent plane, then the Gaussian curvature is positive. If they curve toward the opposite sides of the tangent plane, the Gaussian curvature is negative. The Gaussian curvature is not affected by the surface orientation. A point on the surface with positive, zero and negative Gaussian curvature is called an **elliptic, parabolic** and **hyperbolic** point respectively. The local geometric properties of the surface is quite different in the neighborhood of an elliptic point, a parabolic point, and a hyperbolic point.

§8   Meanings of Gaussian Curvature

In this section we discuss the intrinsic properties of surfaces as effects of nonzero Gaussian curvature. We will gain more geometric intuition about the Gaussian curvature.

8.1   Effects on Triangles—Interior Angle Sum

We first look at a geodesic triangle on a surface. A geodesic triangle is a triangle with three sides being geodesic lines. In the context, when we say triangles on a surface, we mean geodesic triangles.

Theorem 10. (Gauss-Bonnet) *Let Δ be a geodesic triangle and $\alpha_1, \alpha_2, \alpha_3$ be its interior angles. Then*

$$\alpha_1 + \alpha_2 + \alpha_3 = \pi + \iint_\Delta K dS,$$

where the integration is over the region enclosed by the triangle and K is the Gaussian curvature at a point inside the triangle.

Remark 10. This is only a special case of the general Gauss-Bonnet theorem. In the general Gauss-Bonnet theorem, the figure is not limited to a triangle, but can be any polygon or closed curve.

Definition 12. Angle excess, angle defect of a triangle

Let Δ be a geodesic triangle on a surface with interior angles $\alpha_1, \alpha_2, \alpha_3$.

$$\varepsilon \stackrel{\text{def}}{=} (\alpha_1 + \alpha_2 + \alpha_3) - \pi$$

is called the **angle excess** of the triangle.

If ε is negative, $\delta \stackrel{\text{def}}{=} -\varepsilon = \pi - (\alpha_1 + \alpha_2 + \alpha_3)$ is called the **angle defect** of the triangle.

Corollary. *On a surface of constant curvature K, the angle excess ε is proportional to the area A of the triangle.*

$$\varepsilon = KA.$$

It is easy to see, if the surface has a zero curvature everywhere, the sum of interior angles of a triangle is always π. If the surface has a positive curvature everywhere, the sum of interior angles of a triangle is always greater than π, as in the case of a sphere. If the surface has a negative curvature everywhere, the sum of interior angles of a triangle is always less than π, as in the case of a saddle surface or a pseudosphere.

Using the bug analogy, a bug on the surface has a way to test whether its world it lives in is flat or curved, without leaving the surface. That is to measure the sum of interior angles of a triangle and compare it with π.

The angle excess ε is proportional to the area of the triangle. The larger the area of the triangle, the bigger the angular excess is. Gauss was a land surveyor and he once measured the angle sum of big triangles on earth, formed by peaks of mountains far apart, to decide whether the space was flat or curved. Unfortunately, the triangle he measured is still too small in order to see any deviation from flat space, limited by the precision of the measurements. For a good test, large triangles of astronomical scale are needed. It is the belief of cosmologists nowadays that our universe is curved, and also finite, as described by Riemannian geometry, instead of being flat as describe by Euclidean geometry.

8.2   Effects on Circles—Circumference and Area

The set of points that have a constant geodesic distance r from a given point P is called a **geodesic circle** of radius r at center P. The circumference

C and the area A of this geodesic circle with radius r is related to the Gaussian curvature given by the following theorem.

Theorem 11. *The circumference of a geodesic circle with infinitesimal radius r is*

$$C(r) = 2\pi r - \frac{\pi}{3}Kr^3 + \cdots, \tag{2.27}$$

and the area is

$$A(r) = \pi r^2 - \frac{\pi}{12}Kr^4 + \cdots, \tag{2.28}$$

where r is infinitesimal and $\cdots$ means higher order terms.

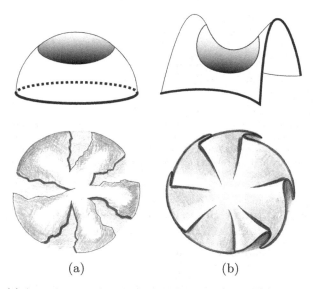

(a)   (b)

Figure 2.11   (a) A patch on a sphere is ripped when "flattened". (b) A patch on a saddle surface is wrinkled when "flattened".

In a Euclidean plane, the Gaussian curvature $K = 0$. The circumference of a circle is $2\pi r$ and the area is πr^2. If the circle is on a surface with a positive Gaussian curvature, then its circumference is less than $2\pi r$ and its area is less than πr^2. If the circle is on a surface with a negative Gaussian curvature, then its circumference is greater than $2\pi r$ and its area is greater than πr^2. This is why when we try to flatten an orange peel, we have to rip it (Figure 2.11 (a)) . The disk with positive curvature has less area than πr^2 to cover the flat disk with same radius r. When we try to flatten a disk on the saddle surface, it will be wrinkled (Figure 2.11 (b)) because a disk with negative curvature has excess area over πr^2 to cover the flat disk with the same radius r.

A bug living on the surface can find out whether it lives on a curved surface or on a plane by simply measuring the circumference or the area of some circle using a string without leaving the surface. By measuring the circumferences or areas of circles and some calculation, the bug can even determine the curvature of the surface without leaving the surface.

Theorem 12. *From Eqs. 2.27 and 2.28, we obtain*

$$K = \frac{3}{\pi} \lim_{r \to 0} \frac{2\pi r - C(r)}{r^3}$$

and

$$K = \frac{12}{\pi} \lim_{r \to 0} \frac{\pi r^2 - A(r)}{r^4}.$$

Remark 11. Curvature Is the Second Order Effect.

In calculus, a curved surface can be approximated locally in a small neighborhood by the tangent plane. So locally a curved surface is similar to a Euclidean plane. But this is the first order approximation. It does not mean all the surfaces are the same. The second order approximation reveals the differences of the surfaces. Gaussian curvature is the second order effect.

8.3   Gauss Mapping—Spherical Representation

Definition 13. Gauss mapping

Let D be an open neighborhood on a surface $S \subset \mathbb{R}^3$ and $P \in D$ is a point in D. Let $S^2 \subset \mathbb{R}^3$ be a unit sphere with center O. Let $\mathbf{n}$ be the unit normal vector of surface S at point P. We can find a unique point Q on the sphere S^2 such that the vector $\overrightarrow{OQ} = \mathbf{n}$. The mapping $g : D \to S^2$; $P \mapsto Q$ is called the **Gauss mapping** (or **Gauss map**, or the **spherical representation**) of surface S.

The following theorem gives another interpretation of Gaussian curvature, namely the limit of the ratio of the area of $\bar{D}$, the image of the region on the sphere, to the area of D itself.

Theorem 13. (Gauss mapping) *Let the image of D under Gauss mapping g be $\bar{D}$ on the sphere. Let the area of D be $\Delta\sigma$ and the area of $\bar{D}$ be $\Delta\bar{\sigma}$. Then at point P,*

$$K = \lim_{\Delta\sigma \to 0} \frac{\Delta\bar{\sigma}}{\Delta\sigma}.$$

Figure 2.12   Gauss mapping.

Remark 12. Elaboration

In Theorem 13, the area $\Delta\bar{\sigma}$ is viewed as signed area. Let a point run on the boundary of D, then its image runs on the boundary of $\bar{D}$. If K is positive, then the point and its image run in the same direction and we say that $\Delta\bar{\sigma}$ and $\Delta\sigma$ have the same sign. If K is negative, they run in the opposite directions and we say that $\Delta\bar{\sigma}$ and $\Delta\sigma$ have opposite signs.

Remark 13. Comparison

Theorem 13 is an analogy of the definition of curvature of a plane curve in Definition 1. Take a section on a plane curve and map it to a unit circle in a similar way of Gauss mapping for surfaces. The curvature of the curve is the limit of the ratio of the arc length of its image on the unit circle (which is equal to the change of angle of the normal vector, or the tangent line) to the arc length on the curve.

8.4   Effects on Tangent Vectors—Parallel Transport

Gaussian curvature is also related to a concept of parallel transport of tangent vectors. In fact, when the surfaces are generalized to higher dimensional manifolds in Riemannian geometry, parallel transport of tangent vectors is the easiest approach to define the curvature on the manifolds.

Let P_1 be a point on the surface and T_1 be the tangent plane at P_1. Let P_2 be a nearby point and T_2 be the tangent plane at P_2. Suppose $v_1 \in T_1$ is a tangent vector at P_1 and $v_2 \in T_2$ is a tangent vector at P_2. Does it make sense to define the two tangent vectors at different points parallel to each other? When v_1 and v_2 are viewed as vectors in the surrounding 3-D space $\mathbb{R}^3$, the usual sense of parallel is $v_1 = v_2$. But this definition does not make sense for the tangent vectors of a surface at different points, because, if v_1 is in the tangent plane T_1 and $v_2 = v_1$, v_2 is not in the tangent plane T_2. It will stick out of the tangent plane T_2. If we still desire to define the parallelism of tangent vectors at different points on the surface, we need to seek a new definition.

Instead of comparing two tangent vectors at two points far away, we introduce a differentiable vector field. Namely, the vector changes from point to point smoothly, with only small changes between nearly points.

Definition 14. Vector field along a curve

Let $\alpha(t)$ be a one parameter curve on a surface S. A vector field $\boldsymbol{w}(t)$ along this curve is a tangent vector assigned at each point P on the curve. A vector field $\boldsymbol{w}(t)$ is called a smooth vector field if it is differentiable with respect to t.

We view the vector $\boldsymbol{w}(t)$ as a vector in the surrounding 3-D space $\mathbb{R}^3$. At each point P on surface, the three vectors $\mathbf{r}_u$, $\mathbf{r}_v$ and $\mathbf{n}$ form a basis for the vectors in $\mathbb{R}^3$, where $\mathbf{r}_u$ and $\mathbf{r}_v$ are in the tangent plane, tangent to the u-line and the v-line, and $\mathbf{n}$ is the normal vector. These bases vary from point to point and they are called moving frames. The tangent vector field $\boldsymbol{w}(t)$ only has components in the tangent plane and its normal component is always zero, i.e.,

$$\boldsymbol{w} = w^1 \mathbf{r}_u + w^2 \mathbf{r}_v. \tag{2.29}$$

Note here we use the superscripts notations w^1, w^2 to denote the components of a vector, according to tensor analysis conventions (superscripts for contravariant components while subscripts for covariant components).

Now we look at the variation of $\boldsymbol{w}(t)$ from a point to a nearby point, or the differential of $\mathbf{w}(t)$, $d\mathbf{w}$. In general, $d\mathbf{w}$ has a non-zero normal component.

$$d\boldsymbol{w} = [d\boldsymbol{w}]_T + [d\boldsymbol{w}]_n,$$

where $[d\boldsymbol{w}]_T$ represents the tangent component of $d\boldsymbol{w}$, and $[d\boldsymbol{w}]_n$ represent the normal component of $d\boldsymbol{w}$.

Definition 15. Covariant differential

Let $w(t)$ be a smooth vector field along curve $\alpha(t)$ on a surface. The tangent component $[dw]_T$ of the differential dw is called the **absolute differential** of the vector field $w(t)$, denoted by Dw. That is,

$$Dw \overset{\text{def}}{=} [dw]_T. \tag{2.30}$$

It is also called **covariant differential** of $w(t)$, for a reason that we will see shortly.

When we try to parallel-transport a tangent vector on a surface, the best we can do is to require the tangent component does not change.

Definition 16. Parallel transport

Let $w(t)$ be a smooth vector field along curve $\alpha(t)$ in a neighborhood on a surface S. $w(t)$ is said to be **parallel**, if its covariant differential is zero, $Dw = 0$. In such a case, a vector $w(t_2)$ at point P_2 is called the **parallel transport** of vector $w(t_1)$ at P_1 along curve $\alpha(t)$.

Note that a parallel vector field is defined along a curve. On any curve, parallel vector fields always exist. Smooth vector fields in a neighborhood on the surface can certainly be defined. However, in general, unless the surface is locally flat (Gaussian curvature identically zero in the neighborhood), such parallel vector fields do not exist in a neighborhood on the surface.

Also note that parallel transport of a tangent vector is defined with respect to a given curve. The parallel transport of a vector from the same starting point to the same ending point could be different, if the paths of the parallel transport are different.

Calculate dw from Eq. 2.29 and we obtain

$$dw = r_u dw^1 + r_v dw^2 + w^1(r_{uu}du + r_{uv}dv) + w^2(r_{uv}du + r_{vv}dv). \tag{2.31}$$

As we mentioned before, the three vectors r_u, r_v and $\mathbf{n}$ form a basis for the vector space $\mathbb{R}^3$ at each point P on the surface.

Definition 17. Connection coefficients

$\boldsymbol{r}_{uu}$, $\boldsymbol{r}_{uv}$ and $\boldsymbol{r}_{vv}$ can be written as the linear combinations of three basis vectors $\mathbf{r}_u$, $\mathbf{r}_v$ and $\mathbf{n}$.

$$\boldsymbol{r}_{uu} = \Gamma_{11}^1 \mathbf{r}_u + \Gamma_{11}^2 \mathbf{r}_v + L\mathbf{n},$$
$$\boldsymbol{r}_{uv} = \Gamma_{12}^1 \mathbf{r}_u + \Gamma_{12}^2 \mathbf{r}_v + M\mathbf{n},$$
$$\boldsymbol{r}_{vv} = \Gamma_{22}^1 \mathbf{r}_u + \Gamma_{22}^2 \mathbf{r}_v + N\mathbf{n}. \tag{2.32}$$

Γ_{ij}^m with $i, j, m = 1, 2$, defined in Eq. 2.32 are called **connection coefficients** (or **Christoffel symbols**).

In Eq. 2.32, we named components in the normal direction L, M, N, while L, M, N have been used for the second fundamental quantities. This is not an abuse of symbols. In fact, L, M, N in Eq. 2.32 are exactly the second fundamental quantities (see Definition 10).

Theorem 14. (Connection coefficients) *The connection coefficients can be expressed in the first fundamental quantities as follows:*

$$\Gamma_{11}^1 = \frac{GE_u - 2FF_u + FE_v}{2(EG - F^2)}, \ \Gamma_{11}^2 = \frac{2EF_u - EE_v - FE_u}{2(EG - F^2)},$$
$$\Gamma_{12}^1 = \frac{GE_v - FG_u}{2(EG - F^2)}, \qquad \Gamma_{12}^2 = \frac{EG_u - FE_v}{2(EG - F^2)}, \tag{2.33}$$
$$\Gamma_{22}^1 = \frac{2GF_v - GG_u - FG_v}{2(EG - F^2)}, \ \Gamma_{22}^2 = \frac{EG_v - 2FF_v + FG_u}{2(EG - F^2)}.$$

In tensor analysis, we use indexed parameters $u^1 = u$, $u^2 = v$ and indexed notations for the first fundamental quantities:

$$\begin{bmatrix} g_{11} \ g_{12} \\ g_{21} \ g_{22} \end{bmatrix} \overset{\text{def}}{=} \begin{bmatrix} E \ F \\ F \ G \end{bmatrix}.$$

The matrix $[g_{ij}]$ is called the metric tensor. The inverse matrix of $[g_{ij}]$ is denoted as

$$\begin{bmatrix} g^{11} \ g^{12} \\ g^{21} \ g^{22} \end{bmatrix} = \frac{1}{EG - F^2} \begin{bmatrix} G \ -F \\ -F \ E \end{bmatrix}.$$

We also introduce $\Gamma_{ji}^m \overset{\text{def}}{=} \Gamma_{ij}^m$. With these notations, the connection coefficients can be expressed in terms of the derivatives of the metric tensor.

Theorem 15. (Connection coefficients)

$$\Gamma_{ij}^m = \frac{1}{2} \sum_{k=1}^{2} g^{mk} \left(\frac{\partial g_{ik}}{\partial u^j} + \frac{\partial g_{jk}}{\partial u^i} - \frac{\partial g_{ij}}{\partial u^k} \right), \, m, i, j = 1, 2. \qquad (2.34)$$

All the connection coefficients Γ_{ij}^m are functions of the first fundamental quantities and their derivatives. Any function of the connection coefficients Γ_{ij}^m is an intrinsic invariant.

The covariant differential $D\boldsymbol{w}$ can be represented using the components under basis $\{\boldsymbol{r}_u, \boldsymbol{r}_v\}$ as follows,

$$D\boldsymbol{w} = \boldsymbol{r}_u Dw^1 + \boldsymbol{r}_v Dw^2,$$

where

$$Dw^i = dw^i + \sum_{j,k=1}^{2} \Gamma_{jk}^i w^j du^k, \, i = 1, 2.$$

Let $\boldsymbol{w}(t)$ be a vector field on a curve $\alpha(t)$ with parameter t. $\frac{D\boldsymbol{w}(t)}{dt}$ is called the **covariant derivative** of $\boldsymbol{w}(t)$.

$$\frac{Dw^i}{dt} = \frac{dw^i}{dt} + \sum_{j,k=1}^{2} \Gamma_{jk}^i w^j \frac{du^k}{dt}, \, i = 1, 2. \qquad (2.35)$$

The covariant differential has the following properties:

Theorem 16. (Properties of covariant differential) *Let $\boldsymbol{w}(t)$ and $\boldsymbol{z}(t)$ be two vector fields, $f(t)$ be a scalar field, along a curve $\alpha(t)$ on a surface.*

(1) $D[\boldsymbol{w}(t) + \boldsymbol{z}(t)] = D\boldsymbol{w}(t) + D\boldsymbol{z}(t)$,
(2) $D[f(t)\boldsymbol{w}(t)] = \boldsymbol{w}(t)df(t) + f(t)D\boldsymbol{w}(t)$ *(Leibniz rule).*

If a vector field $\boldsymbol{w}(t)$ is parallel-transported along curve $\alpha(t)$, then $D\boldsymbol{w}(t) = 0$. We have the parallel transport equation

$$\frac{dw^i}{dt} = - \sum_{j,k=1}^{2} \Gamma_{jk}^i w^j \frac{du^k}{dt}, \, i = 1, 2.$$

Theorem 17. (Properties of parallel transport)

(1) Suppose a tangent vector w at point P is parallel-transported to point P' on a surface along a curve $\gamma(t)$ and becomes w'. Then $\|w\| = \|w'\|$, where $\|w\|$ and $\|w'\|$ are the lengths of w and w'.

(2) Let w_1 and w_2 be two vectors at point P. When they are parallel-transported to P' along a curve $\gamma(t)$ and become w_1' and w_2', the angle between w_1 and w_2 is the same as the angle between w_1' and w_2'.

(3) Putting these two properties together, the parallel transport preserves the inner product of tangent vectors. Namely, $w_1 \cdot w_2 = w_1' \cdot w_2'$.

(4) Parallel transport is isometric invariant, and hence an intrinsic property.

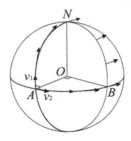

Figure 2.13   Parallel transport on a sphere.

As we have mentioned before, the parallel transport of a tangent vector is defined with respect of a given curve and in general the resulting vector is different even if the starting point and the same ending point are the same, but the path connecting the two points are different. Especially, after a parallel transport along a closed curve, when a tangent vector comes back to the starting point, it is usually different from the original vector. This is the effect of non-zero intrinsic Gaussian curvature of the surface. On a flat surface where the Gaussian curvature is zero everywhere, the tangent vector remains the same after parallel transport along any closed curve. Figure 2.13 shows an example on a sphere. A vector v_1 at point A on the equator is tangent to the meridian. It is parallel-transported to the north pole N along the meridian, and is then transported to a point B on the equator along another meridian which is at right angle with the first, and then transported back to A along the equator. When it comes back to A, it becomes v_2 and has rotated an angle of $-\pi/2$.

Theorem 18. *Let $\alpha(t)$ be a simple closed curve that encircles a simply connected region Σ on a surface. Let $\boldsymbol{w}$ be a tangent vector at point P on $\alpha(t)$. Starting at point P, $\boldsymbol{w}$ is parallel-transported along $\alpha(t)$ finishing a complete loop back to P. Let the resulting vector be $\boldsymbol{w}'$ and $\Delta\theta$ be the angle between $\boldsymbol{w}'$ and $\boldsymbol{w}$. Then*

$$\Delta\theta = \iint_{\Sigma} K \, d\sigma,$$

where $d\sigma$ is the area element.

In the above example of the parallel transport on the sphere, the region Σ enclosed by the curve is big, so that the angle shift $\Delta\theta$ is big. If Σ is small, then $\Delta\theta$ is small. In the limit, we have the following theorem which gives another interpretation of the Gaussian curvature using parallel transport. This may serve as an equivalent definition of Gaussian curvature.

Theorem 19. *In the limit, when the simple closed curve $\alpha(t)$ continuously shrinks to a point and the area $\Delta\sigma$ enclosed by the curve tends to zero, we get another expression for the Gaussian curvature,*

$$K = \lim_{\Delta\sigma \to 0} \frac{\Delta\theta}{\Delta\sigma}.$$

Remark 14. Look Ahead — Parallel Transport in Riemannian Geometry

Covariant differential and parallel transport are defined extrinsically in Definitions 15 and 16 because we move the tangent vectors in the surrounding space $\mathbb{R}^3$, out of the tangent space, and then project back onto the tangent space. With Theorem 20 in the next section, parallel transport can be defined intrinsically. We first define parallel transport of a tangent vector along a geodesic line, which is to keep the length of the vector and the angle of the vector with the geodesic line. To define parallel transport along an arbitrary curve, we approximate the curve with small segments of geodesics and take the limit of the length of each segment to zero. This is one way to define parallel transport on Riemannian manifolds (see Part III Chap. 2).

§9   Geodesic Lines

Geodesic lines play an essential role in differential geometry. We defined the geodesic line in Definition 6 using the length minimizing property, which is a metric property. The geodesic line so defined is called a metric geodesic line.

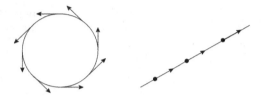

Figure 2.14   Tangent vectors of a circle and tangent vectors of a straight line.

A geodesic line on a surface is the generalization of a straight line in a plane. A straight line has many properties that can be used to characterize a geodesic line, metric properties and affine properties. Let us look at the circle in a plane in Figure 2.14. When a point moves along the circle, the vector tangent to the circle changes directions, while on a straight line, the tangent vectors are all parallel. Using this observation, we can give an alternative but equivalent definition of geodesic lines using the concept of parallel transport of tangent vectors.

Definition 18. (Equivalent Definition) — Geodesic line

Let γ be a curve on a surface S. If the tangent vectors of γ are parallel along γ itself, then γ is called a **geodesic line**.

The geodesic line defined this way is called an affine geodesic line, because it does not use the metric concept. It can be shown that this definition of affine geodesic line agrees with Definition 6, where the concept of distance is used.

If γ is any curve, instead of a geodesic line, after a tangent v is parallel-transported along γ, the angle between v and the curve γ may change. This is because, although v keeps its direction (being parallel), the curve γ may change its own direction (just being a curve). In a special case, if the angle between vector v and the curve γ is not changed after parallel transport of

v along γ, then the curve γ is a geodesic line. The definition of the metric geodesic line in Definition 6 says a geodesic line is the "shortest" line. The definition of the affine geodesic line in Definition 18 says a geodesic line is the "straightest" line on a surface, which does not change its directions to the left or to the right. (Euclid's "definition" of a straight line in the *Elements* certainly gives us some insight: "A straight line is a line which lies evenly with the points on itself.")

Theorem 20. *If a vector v is parallel-transported along a geodesic line γ, the length of v, as well as the angle between v and γ is preserved.*

A surface S embedded in $\mathbb{R}^3$ has a surplus of structures. It has a metric structure of its own with the intrinsic distance on the surface, and an affine structure of its own. It also has the metric structure and affine structure of $\mathbb{R}^3$ as a subset of $\mathbb{R}^3$.

A geodesic line can be defined using the metric structure intrinsically, as in Definition 6, as the metric geodesic line. It can also be defined using the affine structure (use parallelism only without referring to distances), either intrinsically (without referring to $\mathbb{R}^3$), or extrinsically.

The affine geodesics and metric geodesics on a surface coincide. The two definitions also coincide for Riemannian manifolds but they may depart in further generalizations. For example, in the affinely-connected manifolds developed by E. Cartan, it has only affine structures but no metric structures and hence they have only affine geodesics.

By Definition 18, a geodesic line is a curve whose tangent vectors are parallel along itself. Let $\gamma(t)$ be a geodesic line. Its tangent vectors form a vector field

$$\boldsymbol{w}(t) = \frac{du}{dt}\mathbf{r}_u + \frac{dv}{dt}\mathbf{r}_v.$$

In the following we use the indexed notation $u^1 = u$, $u^2 = v$. This corresponds to the former notation

$$w^1 = \frac{du^1}{dt} = \frac{du}{dt},$$
$$w^2 = \frac{du^2}{dt} = \frac{dv}{dt}.$$

When the tangent vectors (w^1, w^2) are parallel along γ, the covariant differential, or the covariant derivatives are zero.

$$\frac{Dw^i}{dt} = 0.$$

Using Eq. 2.35, we obtain the equations for the geodesic line.

Theorem 21. (Equation of geodesic line) *The equations for the geodesic line are*

$$\frac{d^2 u^i}{dt^2} + \sum_{k,l=1}^{2} \Gamma_{kl}^i \frac{du^k}{dt} \frac{du^l}{dt} = 0, \, i = 1, 2, \tag{2.36}$$

where the connection coefficients Γ_{kl}^i are defined affinely in Eq. 2.32, which can be calculated according to Eq. 2.34.

We also use one dot and two dots to denote the derivatives of first order and second order with respect to parameter t. Eq. 2.36 becomes

$$\ddot{u}^i + \sum_{k,l=1}^{2} \Gamma_{kl}^i \dot{u}^k \dot{u}^l = 0. \tag{2.37}$$

When the curve is thought of a trajectory of a particle in motion, t is considered the time parameter and Eq. 2.36 is the equation of motion of the particle.

On a surface, if we go back to tradition of using (u, v) instead of (u^1, u^2), the geodesic equations become

$$\frac{d^2 u}{dt^2} + \Gamma_{11}^1 \left(\frac{du}{dt}\right)^2 + 2\Gamma_{12}^1 \frac{du}{dt}\frac{dv}{dt} + \Gamma_{22}^1 \left(\frac{dv}{dt}\right)^2 = 0,$$

$$\frac{d^2 v}{dt^2} + \Gamma_{11}^2 \left(\frac{du}{dt}\right)^2 + 2\Gamma_{12}^2 \frac{du}{dt}\frac{dv}{dt} + \Gamma_{22}^2 \left(\frac{dv}{dt}\right)^2 = 0.$$

§10   Look Ahead—Riemannian Geometry

What is Riemannian geometry? Short answer: Riemannian geometry is the geometry of curved spaces. The first reaction of many people is: "How can I imagine a curved space?" The answer is, "You don't imagine it. Chances are that you live in it." In a small scale, on the earth or in the solar system, the geometry of our space is approximately Euclidean, but in a large scale, the inter-galaxy space might well be curved, instead of Euclidean.

Bernhard Riemann generalized the intrinsic theory of surfaces initiated by Gauss. The generalized theory is known as Riemannian geometry. The generalizations are in two aspects. Firstly, it is generalized to higher dimensions. Secondly, it is made thoroughly intrinsic.

In fact, curved spaces are not hard to understand. A curved surface is a curved 2-D space. For example, the 2-D sphere S^2 in 3-D Euclidean space can be represented by

$$x^2 + y^2 + z^2 = 1,$$

with coordinates (x, y, z). Higher dimensional curved spaces are not any more difficult either. The 3-D sphere S^3, which is a curved 3-D space embedded in 4-D Euclidean space, can be represented by

$$x^2 + y^2 + z^2 + w^2 = 1,$$

where a point is represented by four coordinates (x, y, z, w).

What is hard is to describe a curved space from within itself, without referring to the surrounding higher dimensional Euclidean space. Riemannian geometry is the intrinsic geometry of curved spaces. Riemannian geometry is the study of surfaces when the surrounding space $\mathbb{R}^3$ is stripped off, as well as higher dimensional curved spaces without being contained in a Euclidean space $\mathbb{R}^k$. Relating to the poem by Millay cited in the epigraph of this chapter, the surface with the surrounding space stripped off should be the "Beauty bare" in the poem, but the first person who has looked on it is not Euclid, but rather Riemann. The precise term for "curved space" is Riemannian manifold. We discuss the general theory of differentiable manifolds and Riemannian manifolds in Part III Chap. 2. Both differentiable manifolds and Riemannian manifolds are defined and studied intrinsically and that is why students feel they are difficult.

Even when Riemannian geometry restricted to 2-D surfaces, there is still a difference between the 2-D Riemannian geometry and the intrinsic theory of surfaces initiated by Gauss. Gauss was the first to discover the intrinsic geometry of surfaces in $\mathbb{R}^3$. However, all human beings are 3-D creatures and Gauss was a 3-D creature as well. Gauss did not and could not flatten himself onto the 2-D surface and study the surface totally from within. In the intrinsic geometry of Gauss, a surface is treated as a subset of the 3-D Euclidean space. A point on the surface is represented by a 3-D vector $\mathbf{r} = (x, y, z)$. The Gaussian curvature is defined extrinsically but proved to be invariant under isometric mappings. The definition of Gaussian curvature (either using principal curvatures or Gauss mapping) involves the surrounding 3-D space.

Riemannian geometry is thoroughly intrinsic. A surface is defined completely as what a bug living on the surface can feel. A point on the abstract surfaces has two coordinates (u, v) instead of three coordinates (x, y, z). Any reference to the surrounding 3-D Euclidean space $\mathbb{R}^3$ is abandoned. In the theory of surfaces in $\mathbb{R}^3$, the first fundamental form is derived from the definition of the surface $\mathbf{r} = \mathbf{r}(x, y, z)$ in 3-D, with $E = \mathbf{r}_u^2$, $F = \mathbf{r}_u\mathbf{r}_v$ and $G = \mathbf{r}_v^2$. In Riemannian geometry, the first fundamental form, also known as the metric, is endowed and serves as the starting point, or the definition of the surface itself. The 2-D surfaces so intrinsically described in Riemannian geometry are called **abstract geometric surfaces**. Any surfaces in $\mathbb{R}^3$ studied by Gauss can be studied as abstract geometric surfaces. However, Riemannian geometry admit abstract geometric surfaces that are not even surfaces embedded in $\mathbb{R}^3$, like the hyperbolic plane, the elliptic plane (projective plane with metric), the flat torus and the Klein bottle.

Exercises

1. Suppose the earth is a sphere. Four cities A, B, C and D are located at the same latitude $\lambda = 40°$, and the longitudes $0°$, $90°$, $120°$ and $180°$ respectively. Airplanes fly between these cities. They have a choice to fly along the geodesic lines or along the latitude circle. Assume the radius of the earth is $a = 6371$ km. Calculate the geodesic distance, and the distance along the latitude circle
   (1) between A and B.
   (2) between A and C.
   (3) between A and D.
   Hint: the key to find the great circle distance between A and B is to find $\angle AOB$, where O is the center of the sphere. You can find this geometrically or algebraically. Geometrically, you can first find AB by studying a triangle in the plane of the latitude circle, and then study $\triangle AOB$. Algebraically, convert the polar coordinates of A and B to Cartesian coordinates (x, y, z). $\angle AOB$ can be found from the dot product of vectors $\overrightarrow{OA}$ and $\overrightarrow{OB}$.

2. Use Definition 1 to verify the curvature of the circle with radius a is $\kappa = 1/a$.

3. Find the curvature, and center of curvature for each point on the parabola $y = x^2$.

4. Find the curvature, and center of curvature for each point on the hyper-bola $y^2 - x^2 = 1$.

5. The saddle surface (hyperbolic paraboloid) is described by $z = 2xy$ in the explicit form. Find the first fundamental form of the saddle surface.

6. The saddle surface can have another coordination in the form of $z = y^2 - x^2$. Find the first fundamental form. Find the rigid transformation in $\mathbb{R}^3$ that maps surface $z = 2xy$ to $z = y^2 - x^2$.

7. The surface $z = x^3 - 3xy^2$ is called a monkey saddle because in addition to room for legs, it also has room for the monkey to rest his tail com-fortably. Suppose the monkey does not know the first fundamental form of his saddle. You find it for him.

8. Find the Gaussian curvature for any point on the saddle surface in the form of $z = 2xy$. Notice that the saddle surface has negative Gaussian curvature everywhere.

9. Find the Gaussian curvature for any point on the saddle surface in the form of $z = y^2 - x^2$.

10. Suppose the monkey cannot find the Gaussian curvature of his monkey saddle. You find it for him.

11. Find the Gaussian curvature for any point on the torus,

$$\begin{bmatrix} x \\ y \\ z \end{bmatrix} = \begin{bmatrix} (b + a\cos v)\cos u \\ (b + a\cos v)\sin u \\ a\sin v \end{bmatrix}.$$

Find its elliptic, parabolic and hyperbolic points on the surface.

12. A surface is represented by the graph of a function $z = f(x, y)$ (Monge parametrization). Find the Gaussian curvature of the surface in terms of $f_x = \dfrac{\partial f}{\partial x}$, $f_y = \dfrac{\partial f}{\partial y}$, $f_{xx} = \dfrac{\partial^2 f}{\partial x^2}$, $f_{xy} = \dfrac{\partial^2 f}{\partial x \partial y}$ and $f_{yy} = \dfrac{\partial^2 f}{\partial y^2}$.

13. In Monge parametrization of a surface $z = f(x, y)$, show that

$$\Gamma^1_{11} = \frac{f_x f_{xx}}{1 + f_x^2 + f_y^2}, \ \Gamma^1_{12} = \frac{f_x f_{xy}}{1 + f_x^2 + f_y^2}, \ \Gamma^1_{22} = \frac{f_x f_{yy}}{1 + f_x^2 + f_y^2},$$

$$\Gamma^2_{11} = \frac{f_y f_{xx}}{1 + f_x^2 + f_y^2}, \ \Gamma^2_{12} = \frac{f_y f_{xy}}{1 + f_x^2 + f_y^2}, \ \Gamma^2_{22} = \frac{f_y f_{yy}}{1 + f_x^2 + f_y^2}.$$

14. Use the formula in the above problem, calculate the connection coeffi-cients Γ^k_{ij}, $i, j, k = 1, 2$, for the sphere with Monge parametrization.

15. In Monge parametrization of a surface $z = f(x, y)$, find the equations of the geodesic lines on the surface.

16. On the sphere of radius $a = 1$, find the circumference and area of a geodesic circle with geodesic radius ρ (arc length measured on the sphere)

for

(1) $\rho = \frac{\pi}{2}$ (great circle) and compare with the circumference and area of a circle in the plane with radius $r = \frac{\pi}{2}$.

(2) $\rho = \frac{\pi}{4}$ (small circle) and compare with the circumference and area of a circle in the plane with radius $r = \frac{\pi}{4}$.

17. Let $N, A, B \in S^2$ be three points on the unit sphere and N be the north pole. Let A have spherical coordinates $(\theta, \varphi) = (\frac{\pi}{4}, 0)$ and B have spherical coordinates $(\theta, \varphi) = (\frac{\pi}{4}, \frac{\pi}{4})$, where θ is the colatitude and φ is the longitude.

(1) Find the circumference of geodesic triangle $\triangle NAB$.

(2) Find the area of this triangle.

(3) Find the angle excess of this triangle.

18. Find the geodesics on a cylinder.

19. Find the geodesics on the helicoid (Example 4).

20. Show that a surface that admits two families of orthogonal geodesics is isometric to the plane.

21. Show that on a surface of revolution:

(1) The meridians are geodesics.

(2) A parallel circle at $z = z_0$ is a geodesics if and only if $\frac{dr}{dz}|_{z_0} = 0$.

22. Suppose surface S_1 has the first fundamental form

$$ds_1^2 = e^{2v}[du^2 + a^2(1 + u^2)dv^2],$$

surface S_2 has the first fundamental form

$$ds_2^2 = e^{2v}[du^2 + b^2(1 + u^2)dv^2],$$

where $a^2 \neq b^2$. Show that S_1 and S_2 have point-wise equal Gaussian curvature but they are not isometric.

Chapter 3

Non-Euclidean Geometry

One geometry cannot be more true than another; it can only be more convenient.

— *Henri Poincaré*

As far as the laws of mathematics refer to reality, they are not certain; and as far as they are certain, they do not refer to reality.

— *Albert Einstein*

Reading Guide. For two thousand years since Euclid wrote his *Elements* till the beginning of the nineteenth century, people had firmly believed that the Euclidean geometry was the true geometry that described our space, namely the space of our universe. The discovery of non-Euclidean geometry was a great revolution in the long history of evolution of mathematical concepts about space as well as the relationship between mathematics and reality. Even many years after the discovery of non-Euclidean geometry, people thought that Euclidean geometry was still the only true geometry for our space, and non-Euclidean geometry was just a logical game and had no applications in the real world. That view turned out to be wrong. Does non-Euclidean geometry have applications in computer graphics and vision? Absolutely. The applications of non-Euclidean geometry are far and wide. Shape analysis is just one example [Small (1996)]. More importantly, non-Euclidean geometry is a special example of the more general geometry—Riemannian geometry, which will be discussed in Part III Chap. 2. The intuition we gain in this chapter will pave the way to the study of differentiable manifolds and Riemannian manifolds in Part III Chap. 2. For further reading on non-Euclidean geometry, the reader is referred to [Greenberg (2007); Sommerville (2005); Coxeter (1998)].

§1   Axioms of Euclidean Geometry

The story starts like this: Long long time ago, there was a man named Euclid. He wrote a book—the *Elements*. The book started a new tradition in the study of geometry, and henceforth a tradition in mathematics. In the beginning of the book, he gave the definitions of the terms that he was going to use, like point, line, plane, etc. (see Chap. 0 Section 3). He also laid out the fundamental assumptions—postulates and axioms. He considered the axioms as evident truth about quantities, and postulates as evident truth about geometrical elements. Literally Euclid used the term "common notions" for axioms. Today we do not distinguish axioms from postulates and just call them axioms. The following is the list of his postulates and axioms [Euclid (1925)].

Postulates. (Euclid) *Let the following be postulated:*

(1) *To draw a straight line from any point to any point.*
(2) *To produce a finite straight line continuously in a straight line.*
(3) *To describe a circle with any center and distance.*
(4) *That all right angles are equal to one another.*

(5) *That, if a straight line falling on two straight lines make the interior angles on the same side less than two right angles, the straight lines, if produced indefinitely, meet on that side on which are the angles less than two right angles.*

Axioms. (Euclid)

(1) *Things which are equal to the same thing are also equal to one another.*

(2) *If equals be added to equals, the wholes are equal.*

(3) *If equals be subtracted from equals, the remainders are equal.*

(4) *Things which coincide with one another are equal to one another.*

(5) *The whole is greater than the part.*

Remark 1. Euclid's axiomatic system is not rigorous in today's standard. Many modern axiomatic systems have been proposed and investigated, including Hilbert's system in his book *Foundations of Geometry* [Hilbert (1899)]. We do not intend to go in that direction. Exercise 3 in this chapter provides an example to illustrate some shortcoming of Euclid's system.

Euclid took the point of view that the axioms and postulates are the truth that are self evident and they do not need to be proved. All other truth needs and should be proved using these axioms and postulates. The proved truth is known as theorems.

Remark 2. The influence of Euclid's axiomatic method is profound, in mathematics, science and beyond. Physics makes extensive use of mathematical concepts and tools and it has been a continuous effort to put the theory of physics into axiomatic systems, as manifested in the sixth problem in the twenty three Hilbert's problems. Benedict de Spinzoza (1632-1677) even emulated the style of the *Elements* in his work Ethics. He started with definitions, axioms and postulates about God and human mind, etc., and proceeded to prove propositions and corollaries. The following are some examples in Ethics.

Axiom 2. Man thinks.

. . .

Postulate 2. Of the individuals of which the human body is composed, some are fluid, some soft, and some hard.

. . .

Prop. 39. If a man hates another, he will endeavour to do him evil, unless he fears a greater evil therefrom arise to himself; and, on the other hand, he who loves another will endeavour to do him good by the same rule.

. . .

Prop. 43. Hatred is increased through return of hatred, but may be destroyed by love.

...
Corol. No one envies the virtue of a person who is not his equal.

For almost two thousand years, people never doubted the truth of Euclid's axioms and postulates. However, there were speculations that the fifth postulate might be a theorem instead of an axiom. Apparently the fifth postulate looks much lengthier and more complicated than the first four postulates. Something that lengthy and complicated should not be considered self evident.

There are many equivalent propositions to Euclid's axiom of parallels. Proving any of the equivalent propositions would mean the proof of Euclid's axiom of parallels.

Theorem 1. *Euclid's fifth postulate is true, if and only if the interior angle sum is* π *for all the triangles.*

Theorem 2. *Euclid's fifth postulate is true, if and only if there exists one triangle whose interior angle sum is* π.

John Playfair provided another equivalent, but apparently simpler version of the fifth postulate, now known as Playfair's axiom[1].

Axiom. (Playfair's axiom of parallels) *In a plane, through a given point P not on a line l, there exists at most one line that does not intersect l.*

In the attempt of proving this proposition, most people took the approach of proof by contradiction. Namely, to start with the assumption that the parallel axiom is false, then try to demonstrate a contradiction. Many mathematicians published attempted proofs of the fifth postulate, only to be found later by others that their proofs had various flaws and there was no success in this direction. See Exercise 2 of this chapter for a seemingly feasible proof by Legendre. You are supposed to find the flaws in the proof.

---

[1] This axiom was given in almost the same form: "Two intersecting lines cannot be both parallel to a third line", by Proclus (fifth century), Joseph Fenn (1769) [Kline (1972)] and Ludlam (1785) [Sommerville (2005)] prior to Playfair (1795).

If we want to prove Euclid's axiom of parallels from his first four postulates, it is necessary to reexamine the theorems in Euclidean geometry to see what theorems are the consequences of the first four postulates without evoking the axiom of parallels. This way we can avoid a cyclic path of proof.

The theory with all the theorems provable by the Euclid's first four postulates is known as the **absolute geometry**. We give two theorems in absolute geometry, in the following.

Theorem 3. (Saccheri-Legendre) *In absolute geometry, the interior angle sum of a triangle is not greater than* π.

Remark 3. Clarification — Euclid's Axiom of Parallels

It is a common misconception to take Euclid's axiom of parallels in the form "In the plane, through a given point P not on a line l, there exists *exactly one* line that does not intersect l". In fact, Euclid's axiom of parallels in Playfair's form says "*at most one*", which means "*one or zero*". The existence of parallels is a theorem of absolute geometry, namely a consequence of the first four postulates of Euclid.

Theorem 4. (Existence of parallels) *In absolute geometry, in a plane, through a given point P not on a line l, there exists at least one line which does not intersect l.*

Theorem 4 together with Euclid's axiom of parallels imply the following corollary.

Corollary. *In Euclidean geometry, in a plane, through a given point P not on a line l, there exists exactly one line which does not intersect l.*

§2   Hyperbolic Geometry

In the attempts to prove Euclid's axiom of parallels, it was a popular approach to prove it in the Playfair's form, using proof by contradiction. This starts with assuming the opposite of of Euclid's fifth postulate in the Playfair's form: In a plane, through a given point P not on a line l, there exists at least two distinct lines which do not intersect l. As we already mentioned in Section 1, no contradiction was ever found, despite the great effort of great minds in mathematics. Through many years of investigation, Lobachevsky and Bolyai were the first mathematicians to believe, that no contradictions would ever be found because there are no contradictions if we replace Euclid's fifth postulate by its negation, which we call it a new axiom:

Axiom. (Lobachevsky's axiom of parallels) *In a plane, through a given point P not on a line l, there exists at least two distinct lines which do not intersect l.*

Euclid's Postulates (1) through (4), together with Lobachevsky's axiom of parallels, give rise to a new geometry, known as **non-Euclidean geometry**, or **hyperbolic geometry**, or Lobachevskian geometry. Lobachevsky's axiom is also known as the hyperbolic axiom of parallels.

On the way of proving Playfairs' axiom, starting from its negation in the hope of finding a contradiction, Lobachevsky and Bolyai found (independently) many trigonometric formulas under this supposedly absurd assumption. What led them to the faith that there is no contradiction, was the fact that the trigonometric formulas they discovered are very similar to the trigonometric formulas in Euclidean geometry on a sphere. However, a faith is nothing more than a guess supported by limited experiences. Belief is not proof. Mathematics is not a religion and mathematicians do not believe in faiths without proof. Without proof, things could go wrong and do go wrong. Without finding a contradiction in 2000 years does not mean someone may not find a contradiction in the 2001st year. What if some contradiction is found in the new geometry, say a million years later?

Then we have a proof of Euclid's fifth postulate and everyone should cheer!

Mathematicians do not like uncertainties like this in mathematics, or on their minds. This kind of uncertainties are like time bombs. You do not know when they may explode. "As a matter of fact", according to Morris Kline, "though Bolyai proudly published his non-Euclidean geometry, there is evidence that he doubted its consistency because in papers found after his death he continued to try to prove the Euclidean parallel axiom" ([Kline (1972)] p. 914).

There is a joke[2] about a physicist, an engineer and a mathematician traveling on a train in Scotland. They saw a black sheep out of the window.

---

[2]This is a public domain joke on the Internet, but I modified it a bit.

The physicist claimed excitedly: "I predicted the black sheep in my new theory of supersymmetry and now we observed it in experiment." The engineer said: "We are going to develop black sheep in the next project." The mathematician murmured, after a long time working with a pencil on paper, "There exists at least one sheep which is black on at least one side."

When it comes to geometry in 1820s, Gauss did see the black sheep and the possibility of the sheep being black on both sides, but he did not say anything about it publicly because he was not sure about the color of the other side of the sheep. There is evidence that Gauss discovered the same formulas that Lobachevsky and Bolyai did and had the same thoughts that they had, but Gauss did not publish anything on this, because this faith was not supported by logic at that time. Gauss was a perfectionist and he wouldn't publish anything with a tiny bit of doubt. Doing something blunt like this could have his fame tainted. The credit that Lobachevsky and Bolyai deserved is actually the courage of a faith without support by logical proof, and even more—the courage to rebel against the conventional truth.

The case was finally settled in about forty years to come, starting in 1868 with the work of Beltrami, followed by Poincaré, Klein, Cayley and the geometry was generalized even further by Riemann. The consistency of the new geometry was proved using the method of models (see Chap. 0). Consistency means that there is no contradiction in the new geometry. It also means that Euclid's fifth postulate is not possible to be proved using the first four postulates. It is independent of other postulates. Unfortunately, none of Lobachevsky (1793–1856), Bolyai (1802–1860) and Gauss (1777–1855) lived long enough to know this result and have the eternal peace on their minds.

Remark 4. Other Geometries — Elliptic Geometry

After the revolution led by Lobachevsky and Bolyai, geometry was liberated from Euclid's doctrines. People explored other alternatives of Euclid's axiom of parallels. One possibility is to replace the Euclid's axiom with the axiom "In a plane, through a given point P not on a line l, there exists no line parallel to l", or simply, "In a plane, any two distinct lines intersect at a point." This is called the elliptic axiom of parallels and the resulting geometry is called elliptic geometry. We recognize the elliptic axiom of parallels is one of the axioms of projective geometry. We also realize that we cannot study elliptic geometry by simply replace Euclid's fifth postulates by the elliptic axiom of parallels in the Euclidean geometry, because the elliptic axiom of parallels contradicts with the first four postulates of Euclid, namely absolute geometry. Theorem 4 of absolute geometry affirms the existence of parallels. To study elliptic geometry, the first four postulates of Euclid also need to be modified. There are two different models of an elliptic plane—the Euclidean sphere, proposed by Riemann, and the projective plane with a metric. The geometry of the sphere is called double elliptic geometry because any two distinct lines intersect at two points, while the geometry of the projective plane is called single elliptic geometry because two distinct lines intersect at one point.

We discuss the models and the consistency of hyperbolic geometry in the next section. In the rest of this section, we briefly summarize some basic consequences of Lobachevsky's axiom.

The situation of parallel lines in hyperbolic geometry is more complex than that in Euclidean geometry, where the parallel line passing through a point is unique. We need more terminology about parallelism in hyperbolic geometry.

Definition 1. Asymptotically parallel line, ultraparallel line

In a plane, let A_1, A_2 and B_1, B_2 be any two points on lines $A_1 A_2$ and $B_1 B_2$ respectively. Line $A_1 A_2$ is called an **asymptotically parallel line**, (or simply **parallel line**) of $B_1 B_2$ in the direction of $B_1 B_2$, if the following conditions are satisfied.
(1) $A_1 A_2$ and $B_1 B_2$ do not intersect.
(2) Any line lying in the angle $\angle B_1 A_1 A_2$ intersects with $B_1 B_2$.

If line $A_1 A_2$ satisfies (1) but does not satisfy (2), then $A_1 A_2$ is called an **ultraparallel line** of $B_1 B_2$.

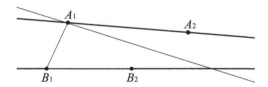

Figure 3.1   Asymptotically parallel line.

Remark 5. Elaboration — The Relation "Asymptotically Parallel" Is Symmetric

In the context of hyperbolic geometry, when we say two lines are parallel, we mean asymptotically parallel. "Ultraparallel" will be stated explicitly. It is easy to show that the "asymptotically parallel" relation is symmetric, that is, if $A_1 A_2$ is asymptotically parallel to B_1B_2 in the direction of B_1B_2, then B_1B_2 is asymptotically parallel to A_1A_2 in the direction of A_1A_2. We may say that A_1A_2 and B_1B_2 are asymptotically parallel in the common direction of A_1A_2 and B_1B_2. It is even easier if we view the lines as directed lines with directions. That is, directed line A_1A_2 is asymptotically parallel to directed line B_1B_2 while A_2A_1 is not asymptotically parallel to B_1B_2.

Definition 2. Angle of parallelism

Let P be a point which is not on the line l (Figure 3.2). Passing P, suppose APA' is an asymptotically parallel line of l in the direction of AA'. From P drop a perpendicular PQ to l. The angle $\Pi \overset{\text{def}}{=} \angle QPA'$ is called the **angle of parallelism** (or **parallel angle**) of AA' at point P with respect to l.

By Lobachevsky's axiom of parallels, passing P, there are at least two lines that do not intersect with l. By symmetry, BPB' is an asymptotically parallel line in the direction of BB' and $\angle QPB' = \angle QPA' = \Pi$. Any line passing P lying in $\angle APB'$ is an ultraparallel line to l. With respect to a given line l, any other line is either an intersecting line, asymptotically parallel line, or ultraparallel line.

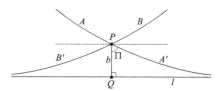

Figure 3.2   Angle of parallelism.

The angle of parallelism is a function of the distance b from P to l, which was first studied by Lobachevsky.

Theorem 5. (Lobachevsky's formula) Let b *be the distance from point* P *to line* l. *The angle of parallelism* Π *at point* P *with respect to line* l, *is determined by*

$$\cos \Pi = \tanh b, \tag{3.1}$$

or equivalently

$$\tan \frac{\Pi}{2} = e^{-b}, \tag{3.2}$$

$$\Pi = 2\tan^{-1}(e^{-b}). \tag{3.3}$$

When $b \to 0$, $\Pi \to \frac{\pi}{2}$. This means that in a small scale, Euclidean geometry is an approximation to hyperbolic geometry. However, in a large scale, when b is large, hyperbolic geometry is very different from Euclidean geometry. When $b \to \infty$, $\Pi \to 0$. In general, we have

Corollary. *The angle of parallelism Π is always less than $\pi/2$.*

Remark 6. Philosophy — What Is the Geometry of Our Universe?

The Corollary of Theorem 5 shows an essential difference between hyperbolic geometry and Euclidean geometry, as a consequence of the hyperbolic axiom of parallels. In Euclidean geometry the angle of parallelism is always $\pi/2$. The Corollary of Theorem 5 is counter-intuitive to most people who have not traveled out of the solar system. Intuition is a belief gained through experience. Our experience on the earth gives us intuition of Euclidean geometry. In our experiences, Π is approximately equal to $\pi/2$. This is because the distance b in our experience is too small, compared to k, the unit distance in space, which is still unknown, but is very large compared with any distance on earth or in the solar system. In the above discussion, we have assumed that $k = 1$. You may argue that when Π is less than $\pi/2$, your straight line is actually a curve. Then what is a straight line and what is a curved line? We agree that a tightened string (which assumes the shortest length) takes the shape of a straight line. We then tie a string between two points and tighten it. Nobody has done such an experiment in the cosmological scale but the possibility of acute angles of parallelism does exist. So the geometry of the universe is really determined by the physical properties of materials. Such a long string in cosmological scale is not even feasible. Light is the only feasible choice for geometrical measurement in large scale. So the geometry of the universe is determined by the physical properties of light and how light interacts with matter.

Euclidean geometry is the summary of our experience on and around the earth in a small region in the universe. Euclidean geometry is only an approximation of the geometry of our universe in a small region. It is dangerous to generalize the laws observed in a small region to the entire universe. Is the geometry of the universe Euclidean, hyperbolic, or something else? The answer depends on the matter distribution in the universe, which we still do not know.

The parallel lines have the following properties in hyperbolic geometry.

Theorem 6. (Properties of asymptotic parallels)

(1) *If l is parallel to m, them m is parallel to l. (symmetry)*

(2) *If m is parallel to n, and n is parallel to l in the same direction, then m is parallel to l in the common direction.* (transitivity)

(3) *If m is parallel to l in one direction, the distance between l and m tends to zero in this direction. The distance increases without bound in the opposite direction.*

(4) *If m is parallel to l, there does not exist any common perpendicular of m and l.*

(5) *If m is ultraparallel to l, there is a unique common perpendicular of m and l. The distance between m and l on both sides of the common perpendicular increases without bound.*

By Theorem 6, the distance between two asymptotic parallels is not constant. The distance between two ultraparallel lines is not constant either. This is another difference between Euclidean geometry and hyperbolic geometry. By proposition (3) in Theorem 6, the distance between two asymptotically parallel lines tend to zero in one direction. This is the reason why they are called asymptotically parallel lines.

Definition 3. Equidistance curve

Let l be a straight line. The locus of points that have the same distance to l is not a straight line but a curve, which is called an **equidistant curve**.

This is easier to understand if we compare with the geometry on a sphere. On the sphere, the great circles can be considered straight lines. Let us take l to be the great circle of the equator. The set of points which have equal distance to the equator is a latitude circle, which is not a great circle, and hence not a straight line.

Theorem 7. *The sum of interior angles of any triangle is less than π.*

Corollary. *There does not exist any rectangle.*

A rectangle is defined to be a quadrilateral (a figure consists of four straight lines) with all the four interior angles being right angles. The corollary of Theorem 7 is a direct consequence of Theorem 7. If the angle sum of a triangle is less than π, then the angle sum of a quadrilateral is less than 2π. Hence the angle sum of any quadrilateral is less than four right angles.

In hyperbolic geometry the closest quadrilaterals to a rectangle are Saccheri quadrilaterals and Lambert quadrilaterals.

A Saccheri quadrilateral $ABCD$ is a quadrilateral, where $\angle A$ and $\angle B$ are right angles and $AD = BC$ (Figure 3.3 a).

Theorem 8. (Saccheri) *In a Saccheri quadrilateral $ABCD$ (Figure 3.3 a), $\angle C$ and $\angle D$ are equal and both are acute angles.*

A Lambert quadrilateral $ABCD$ is a quadrilateral with three right angles $\angle A$, $\angle B$ and $\angle D$ (Figure 3.3 b).

Theorem 9. (Lambert) *In a Lambert quadrilateral $ABCD$ (Figure 3.3 b), the fourth angle $\angle C$ is an acute angle.*

If we take the midpoint P of AB, and midpoint Q in CD in a Saccheri quadrilateral $ABCD$, then PQ is the common perpendicular of AB and CD. The Saccheri quadrilateral $ABCD$ is then divided into two congruent Lambert quadrilaterals $PBCQ$ and $PADQ$.

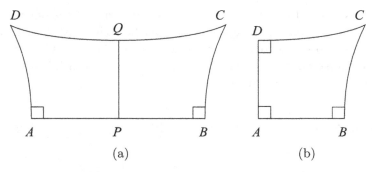

Figure 3.3   (a) Saccheri quadrilateral. (b) Lambert quadrilateral.

The following theorem summaries more facts in hyperbolic geometry.

Theorem 10.

(1) *If the corresponding angles of two triangles are equal, then the two triangles are congruent.*

(2) *There do not exist any two triangles that are similar to each other but not congruent.*

(3) *The three altitudes of a triangle may not intersect at the same point.*

(4) *Given any three points not on the same line, there may not exist a circle passing through the three points.*

Definition 4. Angle defect of a triangle

Let Δ be a triangle with interior angles $\alpha_1, \alpha_2, \alpha_3$. The **angle defect** of the triangle is defined to be $\delta \overset{\text{def}}{=} \pi - (\alpha_1 + \alpha_2 + \alpha_3)$.

Theorem 11. *There exists a universal constant $k > 0$ such that for any triangle with angle defect δ and area A,*

$$\delta = \frac{A}{k^2}. \tag{3.4}$$

This theorem reminds us of Gauss-Bonnet theorem for surfaces in $\mathbb{R}^3$ (Corollary of Theorem 10 in Chap. 2). It gives us a strong hint about the similarity between triangles in hyperbolic plane and geodesic triangles on a curved surface. The constant $1/k^2$ is the analogy of constant Gaussian curvature K except the sign. If we use the unified notation with the Corollary of Theorem 10 by using angle excess ε instead of angle defect ($\varepsilon = -\delta$), Eq. 3.4 becomes

$$\varepsilon = -\frac{A}{k^2},$$

and Theorem 11 coincide with the Gauss-Bonnet theorem on a surface with constant negative Gaussian curvature

$$K = -\frac{1}{k^2}.$$

This foreshadows the interpretation of hyperbolic plane as a curved surface of constant negative Gaussian curvature, first discovered by Eugenio Beltrami in 1868. The constant k has the unit of distance and is called the

space constant. It is the analog of the radius of the sphere in the case of the geometry on a sphere. Its value is relative to the unit of distance we choose. The angle of parallelism in Theorem 5 is expressed in a way such that the distance b is measured using the space constant k as a unit, or simply by taking $k = 1$. The value of k can be interpreted as the distance whose corresponding angle of parallelism is $\Pi(k) = 2\tan^{-1}(e^{-1})$, which is approximately $40°24'$.

Corollary. *For any triangle, its area $A < k^2\pi$.*

Remark 7. Intuition — Upper Bound to the Area of a Triangle

The above corollary states that there is an upper bound to the area of any triangle in the hyperbolic plane. This seems to be against our intuition. In fact, in a small scale, the Euclidean geometry is an approximation of the hyperbolic geometry. This upper bound $k^2\pi$ could be very big because the space constant k is in the astronomical scale. Therefore, in our everyday experience, we do not feel the limit of any upper bound of the area of the triangles.

In the large scale, the intuition to explain the existence of an upper bound to the area of the triangle is the following. There are two ways to increase the area of a triangle: one, to make the vertices further apart; two, to make the sides further apart. When we make the vertices further apart, the triangle seems to gets larger. However, it gets skinnier at the same time. When we try to make the sides further apart, the sides will not meet any more.

Theorem 12. *Let r be the radius of a circle. The circumference of the circle is*

$$C = 2\pi k \sinh \frac{r}{k}.$$

The area of the circle is

$$A = 4\pi k^2 \sinh^2 \frac{r}{2k}.$$

Remark 8. Comparison — Circles on a Sphere

Compare with the formulas of circumference and area of a circle on a sphere:

$$C = 2\pi k \sin \frac{r}{k},$$

$$A = 4\pi k^2 \sin^2 \frac{r}{2k},$$

where r is the geodesic radius (distance measured on the sphere) of the small circle on the sphere and k is the radius of the sphere.

§3 Models of the Hyperbolic Plane

Lobachevsky and Bolyai advocated a new geometry, the hyperbolic geometry, which is drastically different from Euclidean geometry, based on their intuition and faith that a contradiction would not be found in this new geometry. However, the new geometry was still not put on solid foundations. After the discovery of the new geometry, people still held the belief that Euclidean geometry is the only true geometry about the real world. Gauss conducted measurements trying to verify the angle sum of a big triangle consisting of the summits of three mountain peaks, in order to settle the question whether Euclidean geometry or non-Euclidean geometry is true. A breakthrough in the development of non-Euclidean geometry, as well as the entire mathematics, came in 1868, when the Italian mathematician Eugenio Beltrami published two memoirs. Beltrami gave an interpretation of non-Euclidean geometry on a curved surface of constant negative curvature—the pseudosphere. Other models of hyperbolic geometry were constructed later and the consistency problem of hyperbolic geometry was settled. In this section we discuss the models of the hyperbolic plane: Beltrami pseudo sphere model, Gans whole plane model, poincaré half plane model, poincaré disk model, Beltrami-Klein disk model, Weierstrass hyperboloid model and models in Riemannian geometry. We do not go through the verification process for each model here but this has been done in history. All the models satisfy the axioms of hyperbolic geometry—meaning the axioms of absolute geometry plus the hyperbolic axiom of parallels. All the models are equivalent to each other (except a minor issue with the Beltrami pseudo sphere model, see the following subsection) and there is a transformation from one model to another. The significance of these models exceeds the consistency proof. In fact, each model is a different parametrization of the hyperbolic plane. They provide different working coordinates in analytic hyperbolic geometry.

Remark 9. Philosophy — Mathematics and Reality

In geometry, points, straight lines and planes are undefined terms. The concept of points, lines are mathematical abstractions. A point has no size. A line has no width. A triangle is not made of any physical material, like wood or strings. Then how can we do experiment to verify the theorems in geometry? When Gauss tried to measure the angle sum of a big triangle, he needed some operational definition of a straight line. In practice, we use tightened strings and light rays. Flexible but unstretchable strings embody the concept of shortest distance. That way, we define a straight line using the concept of distance. Namely a straight line is a geodesic line. For large distances, like between mountain peaks or even between stars and galaxies, strings are no longer practical and light is the only tool for measurement. We assume that light rays travel along the shortest path, and hence straight line. How can we be sure about that? We are not. We define distance using light. Everything comes back in a circle.

From Hilbert's point of view, a formal axiomatic system consists a set of undefined terms, or primitive terms, governed by a set of axioms. The set of axioms can be viewed as the definition of these primitive concepts. You can interpret a point as a mug, or anything else. An interpretation is called a model of the axiom system. Albert Einstein had a comment, *"As far as the laws of mathematics refer to reality, they are not certain; as far as they are certain, they do not refer to reality."* Henri Poincaré also had a remark: *"One geometry cannot be more true than another; it can only be more convenient."*

3.1   Beltrami Pseudosphere Model

A pseudosphere is a bugle shaped surface in $\mathbb{R}^3$ and we have studied this surface in Example 11 in Chap. 2. The following describes Beltrami's interpretation of the hyperbolic plane:

Hyperbolic points: The points of $\mathbb{H}^2$ are interpreted as the points on a pseudosphere in $\mathbb{R}^3$,

$$\mathbb{H}^2 \stackrel{\text{def}}{=} \{(x, y, z) \in \mathbb{R}^3 \,|\, r < 1,\ z > 0,\ \text{and}\ z = \ln \sqrt{\frac{1 - r^2}{r^2}} - \sqrt{1 - r^2}\},$$

where $r = \sqrt{x^2 + y^2}$. Note the pseudosphere was introduced in Example 11 in a parametric form. Here it is given in the explicit form.

Hyperbolic lines: Beltrami interprets the straight lines in the hyperbolic plane as the geodesics on the pseudosphere. The distance in the hyperbolic plane is interpreted as the distance along a geodesic on the pseudosphere. Then Lobachevsky's axiom of parallels is satisfied on the pseudosphere.

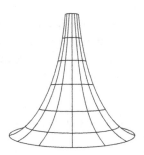

Figure 3.4   Beltrami pseudosphere model.

We know that on the pseudosphere, all the meridians are geodesics. The parallels (or latitude circles) are not geodesics. Other non-meridian geodesics may start from the edge of the bugle, spirals up the bugle surface and comes down back to the edge.

Any statements in the hyperbolic plane can be translated to statements in Euclidean geometry on the pseudosphere. Any possible contradiction in the hyperbolic geometry would be translated to a contradiction in Euclidean geometry. So if Euclidean geometry is consistent, then hyperbolic geometry is consistent.

However, there is a shortcoming of this model. First there is a boundary in the pseudosphere at the bottom. If you go up along a meridian, the geodesic is infinitely long. However, if you go down along a meridian toward the edge, you can reach the edge in finite time. Andrew Pressley has a good analogy, "A bug walking at constant speed along such a geodesic would reach the edge in a finite time, and thus would suffer the fate feared by ancient mariners of falling off the edge of the world." [Pressley (2012)]. There is a remedy to this problem. That is to glue two such bugle surfaces together edge to edge. Even with this remedy, two problems still remain. First, the glued boundaries now becomes a sharp edge. There is not a tangent plane at a point on the edge. Second, the pseudosphere is not topologically equivalent to the hyperbolic plane. In fact, it is rather a hyperbolic cylinder. Namely, it is a strip of the hyperbolic plane rolled up into a cylinder.

Hilbert proved later, that there does not exist a surface in $\mathbb{R}^3$ which is isometric to the entire hyperbolic plane. This means we must give up something in seeking the representation of hyperbolic plane in $\mathbb{R}^3$. If we insist that the surface in $\mathbb{R}^3$ is smooth and topologically equivalent to $\mathbb{H}^2$, then we must distort the distance. We discuss other models of $\mathbb{H}^2$ in the following in this direction—smooth, but not isometric embeddings of $\mathbb{H}^2$ in $\mathbb{R}^3$, in which the distance is distorted.

3.2   Gans Whole Plane Model

Gans model interprets the points in the hyperbolic plane as all the points in the Euclidean plane. However, the distance is redefined so that the hyperbolic lines are the Euclidean hyperbolas.

Hyperbolic points: $\mathbb{H}^2 \stackrel{\text{def}}{=} \mathbb{R}^2 = \{(x, y) \mid x, y \in \mathbb{R}\}$. The points in $\mathbb{H}^2$ are interpreted as the points in the entire Euclidean plane.

Hyperbolic lines: Choose any point O in the Euclidean plane to be the origin. The lines in $\mathbb{H}^2$ are interpreted as hyperbolas with the center at O. Straight lines passing through O are viewed as degenerate hyperbolas.

So they also represent lines in $\mathbb{H}^2$. To clarify, we take a single branch of a hyperbola to represent a line in $\mathbb{H}^2$, since each hyperbola has two separate branches (Figure 3.5).

Asymptotically parallel lines: Two hyperbolic lines are asymptotically parallel if the two hyperbolas share one common asymptote.

Ultraparallel lines: Two hyperbolic lines are ultraparallel if the two hyperbolas do not intersect and do not share any common asymptote.

We shall call this model **Gans whole model** [Gans (1966)]. This model gives an intuitive meaning for the name "hyperbolic geometry", although Felix Klein coined the term from a different perspective.

Hyperbolic distance: The hyperbolic distance between points (x_1, y_1) and (x_2, y_2) in the Gans plane is represented by

$$\rho_H((x_1, y_1), (x_2, y_2)) \stackrel{\text{def}}{=} \cosh^{-1}\left[\sqrt{(1 + x_1^2 + y_1^2)(1 + x_2^2 + y_2^2)} - x_1 x_2 - y_1 y_2\right].$$
$$(3.5)$$

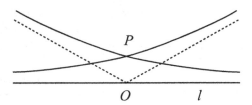

Figure 3.5   Gans plain model.

Remark 10. Cross Link — Independence of Axioms of Linear Spaces

See Part I Chap. 1 Remark 5 about the independence of the axioms of linear spaces in the Peano system and "non-Peano linear spaces". There we used a model to demonstrate the independence of axiom (7) in the axiomatic system (Part I Chap. 1 Definition 3), which is in the same spirit of demonstrating the independence of Euclid's axiom of parallels and the consistency of hyperbolic geometry.

We did not establish the absolute consistency of hyperbolic geometry but rather the relative consistency contingent on the consistency of Euclidean geometry, which we have relatively stronger faith, based on our experience. Hilbert demonstrated the relative consistency of Euclidean geometry in his book *Foundations of Geometry* [Hilbert (1899)] using the model of Cartesian analytic geometry. Namely, if the real number system is consistent, then Euclidean geometry is consistent.

3.3   Poincaré Half Plane Model

The Poincaré half plane model uses half of a Euclidean plane.

Hyperbolic points: $\mathbb{H}^2 \overset{\text{def}}{=} \{(x, y) \in \mathbb{R}^2 \mid y > 0\}$. In this model, the points in $\mathbb{H}^2$ are interpreted as points in the upper half of the Euclidean plane.

Hyperbolic lines: Hyperbolic lines in $\mathbb{H}^2$ are interpreted as the half circles whose centers are on the boundary $y = 0$. Straight vertical lines are considered degenerate cases of circles and also represent hyperbolic lines.

Asymptotically parallel lines: Two hyperbolic lines are asymptotically parallel if the two half circles are tangent at a point on the boundary line $y = 0$.

Ultraparallel lines: Two hyperbolic lines are ultraparallel if the two do not intersect and are not tangent to each other.

Hyperbolic distance: The distance between points (x_1, y_1) and (x_2, y_2) is represented by

$$\rho_H\left((x_1, y_1), (x_2, y_2)\right) \overset{\text{def}}{=} \cosh^{-1}\left[1 + \frac{(x_2 - x_1)^2 + (y_2 - y_1)^2}{2y_1 y_2}\right]. \qquad (3.6)$$

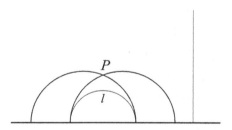

Figure 3.6   Poincaré half plane model.

3.4   Poincaré Disk Model

Another model of $\mathbb{H}^2$ is credited to Poincaré, known as Poincaré disk model.

Hyperbolic points: $\mathbb{H}^2 \overset{\text{def}}{=} \{(x, y) \in \mathbb{R}^2 \mid x^2 + y^2 < 1\}$. The points of $\mathbb{H}^2$ are interpreted as points (x, y) in the interior of a unit circle $x^2 + y^2 < 1$ in the Euclidean plane.

Hyperbolic Lines: Hyperbolic lines are interpreted as the arcs of circles that are perpendicular to the boundary circle C, $x^2 + y^2 = 1$.

Asymptotically parallel lines: Two hyperbolic lines are asymptotically parallel if the two arcs are tangent at a point on the boundary C (Figure 3.7).

Ultraparallel lines: Two hyperbolic lines are ultraparallel if the two arcs do not intersect in the interior of the disk and they are not tangent on the boundary.

All the theorems in hyperbolic geometry can be translated to theorems in Euclidean geometry regarding points and arcs in the unit disk and vice versa. If there is a contradiction in the hyperbolic geometry, it will be translated as a contradiction in Euclidean geometry. If Euclidean is consistent, then hyperbolic geometry is consistent.

Hyperbolic distance: The distance between two points (x_1, y_1) and (x_2, y_2) is represented by

$$\rho_H\left((x_1, y_1), (x_2, y_2)\right) \stackrel{\text{def}}{=} \cosh^{-1}\left[1 + 2\frac{(x_2 - x_1)^2 + (y_2 - y_1)^2}{(1 - x_1^2 - y_1^2)(1 - x_2^2 - y_2^2)}\right]. \quad (3.7)$$

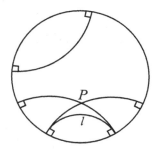

Figure 3.7   Poincaré disk model.

The Dutch artist M. C. Escher (1898 – 1972) created many artworks that illustrate hyperbolic geometry concepts. *Circle Limit IV (Heaven and Hell)* is one example. It demonstrates the tessellation of patterns in the hyperbolic plane represented in the Poincaré disk model. The figures— angels and devils—in the patterns are supposed to be congruent in the hyperbolic plane. The diminishing appearance of the figures toward the boundary of the circle is due to the distance distortion in the Poincaré disk representation, because the embedding is not isometric.

3.5   Beltrami-Klein Disk Model

The Beltrami-Klein disk model also uses the unit disk in the Euclidean plane. It is also known as the projective geometry model.

Hyperbolic points: $\mathbb{H}^2 \stackrel{\text{def}}{=} \{(x, y) \in \mathbb{R}^2 \,|\, x^2 + y^2 < 1\}$. The points of $\mathbb{H}^2$

are interpreted as points (x, y) in the interior of a unit circle $x^2 + y^2 < 1$ in the Euclidean plane, which is the same as the points in Poincaré disk model.

Hyperbolic lines: Hyperbolic lines in $\mathbb{H}^2$ are interpreted as chords (straight line segments) of the circle (not including the end points).

Asymptotically parallel lines: Two hyperbolic lines are asymptotically parallel if the two chords intersect at a point on the boundary circle.

Ultraparallel lines: Two hyperbolic lines are ultraparallel if the two chords do not intersect inside the circle or on the boundary of the circle.

Hyperbolic distance: The distance between points (x_1, y_1) and (x_2, y_2) is represented by

$$\rho_H\left((x_1, y_1), (x_2, y_2)\right) \stackrel{\text{def}}{=} \cosh^{-1}\left[\frac{1 - x_1 x_2 - y_1 y_2}{\sqrt{(1 - x_1^2 - y_1^2)(1 - x_2^2 - y_2^2)}}\right]. \qquad (3.8)$$

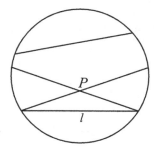

Figure 3.8   Beltrami-Klein disk model.

This distance was first suggested by Cayley in a different form to be a distance for the projective plane. The circle C is a special case of a conic section, in the projective plane. This conic section is called the **absolute figure**, or **absolute conic** (or simply the **absolute**). The points in the interior of the absolute is considered a subset of the projective plane. The chords in the circle are portions of projective lines in the projective plane. By choosing different absolute figures, we obtain different geometries. If the absolute is real, we have **hyperbolic geometry** as discussed above. If the absolute is imaginary, the interior of this imaginary absolute includes all the points in the projective plane. This projective plane with this metric is the elliptic plane and the geometry is called **elliptic geometry**. When the absolute degenerates to a line (two lines that coincide), the interior of the absolute is exactly the projective plane minus one projective line with a metric, which is Euclidean geometry, also called by Klein the **parabolic geometry**.

3.6   Weierstrass Hyperboloid Model

The Weierstrass model uses one sheet of a two-sheet hyperboloid. It is a good working tool for the calculations, especially trigonometry calculations in the hyperbolic plane. Trigonometry problems in the hyperbolic plane can be solved using an analogy on a Euclidean sphere, and then transferred back with the correspondences $\sin\theta \to \sinh\theta$, $\cos\theta \to \cosh\theta$ and $\tan\theta \to \tanh\theta$. This similarity between hyperbolic geometry and Euclidean spherical geometry was also exactly what led Lobachevsky and Bolyai to the belief that hyperbolic plane is a sphere with an imaginary radius and hyperbolic geometry is consistent without contradictions.

The Gans whole plane model is the orthographic projection of the hyperboloid model onto the x,y plane. The following are the interpretation of the elements in the hyperbolic plane in the Weierstrass hyperboloid model.

Hyperbolic points: $\mathbb{H}^2 \overset{\text{def}}{=} \{(x, y, z) \in \mathbb{R}^3 \mid z^2 = 1 + x^2 + y^2, \textbf{ and } z > 0\}$. The hyperbolic plane $\mathbb{H}^2$ is represented by the upper sheet of a two-sheet hyperboloid

$$z^2 = 1 + x^2 + y^2. \qquad (3.9)$$

Hyperbolic lines: Hyperbolic lines in $\mathbb{H}^2$ are interpreted as the intersection of the hyperboloid and a plane passing $(0, 0, 0)$, which are single branches of hyperbolas.

Asymptotically parallel lines: Two hyperbolic lines are asymptotically parallel if the two hyperbolas share one common asymptote.

Ultraparallel lines: Two hyperbolic lines are ultraparallel if the two hyperbolas do not intersect and do not share any common asymptote.

Hyperbolic distance: The hyperbolic distance between point $\mathbf{r}_1 = (x_1, y_1, z_1)$ and $\mathbf{r}_2 = (x_2, y_2, z_2)$ on the hyperboloid is defined to be

$$\rho_H\left((x_1, y_1), (x_2, y_2)\right) \overset{\text{def}}{=} \cosh^{-1}\left[z_1 z_2 - x_1 x_2 - y_1 y_2\right]. \qquad (3.10)$$

Using hyperbolic spherical coordinate parametrization of the hyperboloid,

$$\begin{aligned}
x &= k\sinh\theta\cos\varphi, \\
y &= k\sinh\theta\sin\varphi, \\
z &= k\cosh\theta,
\end{aligned} \qquad (3.11)$$

this model demonstrates a striking similarity to the sphere,

$$x = k \sin \theta \cos \varphi,$$
$$y = k \sin \theta \sin \varphi, \qquad (3.12)$$
$$z = k \cos \theta.$$

There is a nice correspondence between Euclidean spherical geometry and hyperbolic geometry. When we change $\sin \theta$, $\cos \theta$ and $\tan \theta$ to the corresponding hyperbolic functions $\sinh \theta$, $\cosh \theta$ and $\tanh \theta$, the trigonometric formulas on the Euclidean sphere become corresponding formulas in hyperbolic geometry.

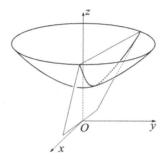

Figure 3.9   Weierstrass hyperboloid model.

3.7   Models in Riemannian Geometry

The hyperbolic plane is a metric space. There is no global isometry from the hyperbolic plane to any surface in $\mathbb{R}^3$. If we want to have a surface as a model of the hyperbolic plane, then this surface is an abstract geometric surface in Riemannian geometry, which cannot be isometrically embedded in $\mathbb{R}^3$. This abstract geometric surface is defined by a Riemannian metric. The models we have studied in last subsection are just different parametrizations of this abstract geometric surface $\mathbb{H}^2$. There is an isometric mapping, or coordinate transformation between any two models. In the following we give the Riemannian metric for each of these models.

Gans whole plane:
$$ds^2 = \frac{(1 + y^2)dx^2 - 2xydxdy + (1 + x^2)dy^2}{1 + x^2 + y^2}. \qquad (3.13)$$

Poincaré half plane:
$$ds^2 = \frac{dx^2 + dy^2}{y^2}. \qquad (3.14)$$

Poincaré disk:

$$ds^2 = \frac{4(dx^2 + dy^2)}{(1 - x^2 - y^2)^2}. \tag{3.15}$$

Beltrami-Klein disk:

$$ds^2 = \frac{(1 - y^2)dx^2 + xydxdy + (1 - x^2)dy^2}{(1 - x^2 - y^2)^2}. \tag{3.16}$$

This is known as Cayley-Klein-Hilbert metric.

Weierstrass hyperboloid:

Using (x, y) parametrization, the hyperboloid model has the same Riemannian metric as that of Gans whole plane.

Using polar coordinates, it becomes

$$ds^2 = d\theta^2 + k^2 \sinh^2 \theta d\varphi^2. \tag{3.17}$$

If we use three coordinates (x, y, z), the line element can be written as

$$ds^2 = dz^2 - dx^2 - dy^2. \tag{3.18}$$

Note this is a quadratic form in $\mathbb{R}^3$ but it is not positive definite. $\mathbb{R}^3$ equipped with this indefinite quadratic form is called a **Minkowski space**. So the hyperboloid model sometimes is also called **Minkowski model**.

§4   Hyperbolic Spaces

The hyperbolic plane can be easily generalized to higher dimensions. A 3-dimensional hyperbolic space $\mathbb{H}^3$ is a space topologically equivalent to $\mathbb{R}^3$ but has a different metric than $\mathbb{R}^3$. An n-dimensional hyperbolic space $\mathbb{H}^n$ is a space topologically equivalent to $\mathbb{R}^n$ but has a different metric than $\mathbb{R}^n$. Any of the six models in last section can be generalized to dimension n. We choose the hyperboloid model.

A point in $\mathbb{H}^n$ is a point $(x_1, \ldots, x_{n+1}) \in \mathbb{R}^{n+1}$ that is on a hypersurface

$$x_{n+1}^2 = 1 + x_1^2 + \cdots + x_n^2.$$

The hyperbolic distance between two points $(x_1, \ldots, x_{n+1})$ and $(y_1, \ldots, y_{n+1})$ is defined to be

$$\rho_H \overset{\text{def}}{=} \cosh^{-1} \left[x_{n+1}y_{n+1} - (x_1 y_1 + \cdots + x_n y_n) \right].$$

The line element is defined to be

$$ds^2 = dx_{n+1}^2 - (dx_1^2 + \cdots + dx_n^2).$$

Exercises

1. The surface of a sphere is not a model of the absolute geometry (hence not model of Euclidean or hyperbolic geometry). If we interpret the great circles on the sphere as straight lines, what axiom of the absolute geometry does the sphere violate?

2. Find the flaw in the following proof of Euclid's axiom of parallels attempted by Adrien-Marie Legendre (1752-1833):

   Given a line l and a point P not on l. Drop perpendicular PQ from P to l at Q. Draw line m through P perpendicular to PQ. Let h be a line through P, distinct from m and PQ. Our goal is to show that h intersects l. Let A be a point on h between lines m and l. $\angle QPA$ is an acute angle. Draw a line k through P symmetric to h with respect to PQ. Let A' be a point on k between m and l. Then $\angle QPA = \angle QPA'$. Therefore Q lies in the interior of $\angle APA'$. Since l passes through a point interior to $\angle APA'$, it must intersect one of its sides. If l intersects PA, then the proof is done. Otherwise, suppose l meets PA' at B'. Find a unique point B on PA such that $PB = PB'$. Then $\triangle PQB' \cong \triangle PQB$ (SAS). Hence $\angle PQB$ is a right angle. Therefore B is on l and h meets l at B.

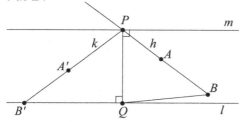

3. Find what is wrong in the following proof of the statement in Euclidean geometry: "Every triangle is an equilateral triangle."

   Proof: Let $\triangle ABC$ be any triangle. It suffices to prove that $AB = AC$. The same way can be used to prove $BC = AC$.

   Draw the angle bisector of $\angle A$ and the perpendicular bisector of side BC. If these two lines are parallel, then the angle bisector of $\angle A$ coincides with the perpendicular bisector of side BC. Hence $AB = AC$.

   Otherwise, assume they intersect at O. Draw the perpendiculars OM to AB, and ON to AC.

   First look at $\triangle AMO$ and $\triangle ANO$. We have $\triangle AMO \cong \triangle ANO$ (AAS). Therefore $AM = AN$ and $OM = ON$.

   Next look at $\triangle OPB$ and $\triangle OPC$. Because OP is the perpendicular bisector of BC, we have $\triangle OPB \cong \triangle OPC$. Hence $OB = OC$.

Next look at $\triangle OMB$ and $\triangle ONC$. They are right triangles and they have two sides equal. Therefore $\triangle OMB \cong \triangle ONC$ and $MB = NC$.

Finally $AB = AM + MB = AN + NC = AC$.

(Note that this problem does not have to do with non-Euclidean geometry (see [Kline (1972)] p. 1006).)

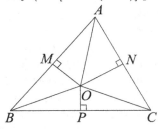

4. Show that if the sum of interior angles of a triangle is the same for all triangles, then the sum is π and hence the Euclid's axiom of parallels holds.

5. Show that the following statement is equivalent to Euclid's axiom of parallels: Let l_1, l_2, l_3 be distinct lines. If l_1 is parallel to l_2 and l_2 is parallel to l_3, then l_1 is parallel to l_3.

6. Calculate the angle of parallelism for the following distances:

   (1) $b = 1$
   (2) $b = \frac{1}{2}$
   (3) $b = \frac{1}{100}$
   (4) $b = \frac{1}{1000}$

   Note the distance is measured with the unit of the space constant $k = 1$.

7. In the hyperbolic plane, find the circumference of a circle with radius $r = k$, where k is the space constant and you can assume $k = 1$. Also find the ratio of this circumference to that of a circle with the same radius $r = k = 1$ in the Euclidean plane. (Remind, a circle with radius $r = k = 1$ is huge!)

8. In the hyperbolic plane, find the area of a circle with radius $r = k$ and find the ratio of this area to that of a circle with the same radius in the Euclidean plane.

9. Prove Theorem 6 using the Poincaré disk model (Hint: Poincaré disk model is conformal and preserves angles).

10. Derive the formula for the angle of parallelism using the Poincaré disk model.

PART III
TOPOLOGY AND MORE

Maurice Fréchet
(1878 – 1973)

Felix Hausdorff
(1868 – 1942)

Bernhard Riemann
(1826 – 1866)

Élie Cartan
(1869 – 1951)

David Hilbert
(1862 – 1943)

Henri Lebesgue
(1875 – 1941)

Chapter 1

General Topology

All men are created equal.   — *Thomas Jefferson*

All men are created topologically equivalent.   — *Hongyu Guo*

Reading Guide. This chapter provides an introduction to general topology, also known as point-set topology. You might be new to topology, but you are sure familiar with Euclidean spaces. Euclidean spaces are the prototypes of general topological spaces. In §2, we start with the topological concepts in the Euclidean spaces. In §3, Euclidean spaces are generalized to metric spaces and in §4 they are further generalized to topological spaces. The following is a Venn diagram showing the relationships between different structures. The structures in the shaded area are the focus of this chapter. See also a brief discussion of structures in Chap. 0.

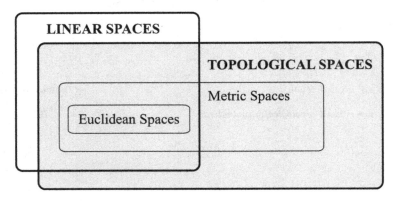

§1   What is Topology?

Topology is a relatively newer area in mathematics compared to algebra and geometry. It has its roots partly in geometry and partly in analysis. The concept at the center of topology is continuity. "Continuous deformations" of shapes in geometry and continuous functions in analysis are just two examples.

Topology started with the study of properties of geometrical shapes that do not change when the shapes are undergoing "continuous deformations", like stretching or twisting. It is the job of topology to make the concept "continuous deformation" precise. The appropriate term corresponding to this intuition is "homeomorphic mapping", which we will see in Section 4. For now, we will use this loose term "continuous deformation".

The term "topology" was first introduced by Johann Listing in the German language in his book *Introductory Studies in Topology* (*Vorstudien zur Topologie*) in 1847. It has the Greek roots "topo-" meaning "place" and "-logy" meaning study. We can guess from the name that topology is concerned with the relative positions of points in a shape, regardless of the length or measurement properties. Historians like to trace the first appearance of the topological ideas back to 1736 when Leonhard Euler studied the problem of the seven bridges of Königsberg, because stretching the bridges, or the river, or the land will not change the answer whether the seven bridges can be traversed or not.

We have discussed some examples of transformations in geometry in Part II. A rigid transformation in $\mathbb{R}^3$ preserves the distance between any two points. There can be other transformations, like affine transformations, projective transformations. Felix Klein observed these different types of transformations form groups under the composition of transformations. In his Erlangen Program, he proposed a view that different geometries are about the study of invariant properties under different transformation groups. Here we can consider more general transformations — "continuous deformations". A property is considered a topological property if it is preserved after continuous deformation. The shapes related by a continuous deformation is considered topologically equivalent. This is why topology is often described as "rubber sheet" geometry. Think of a cube made of rubber sheet. We can continuously deform it to a sphere, or an ellipsoid. Therefore, the cubes, spheres and ellipsoids of different sizes are all topologically equivalent. However, there is no way to stretch and deform a sphere into a torus. Hence a sphere is not topologically equivalent to a torus.

Although some topological properties of figures have been obtained within the study of geometry, we cannot always rely on the analogy of "rubber sheet" to do mathematics. We need to be considerate to people in a country where there are no rubber products and hence no experience with rubber sheet. We need to define the concept of "continuous deformation" precisely. We find that the ideas in analysis provide the right tools to define this term precisely. The key to describe continuity is the concept of "near", or "neighborhood". "Approach" is also a common word used in analysis. "Approach" means "get near". From Newton, Leibniz to Euler, they used the tool of "infinitesimals", which was vaguely described as a nonzero quantity which is smaller than any positive real number, to describe the concept of one point is getting infinitely close to another. If we have two numbers, x and y, and if y is equal to x plus or minus an infinitesimal, then x is "near" y. We can say y is in the infinitesimal neighborhood of y. However, it is very hard to make the concept of infinitesimal logically consistent and hence there was criticism against the concept of infinitesimals, most remarkably from Bishop Berkeley in 1734.

As an alternative to describing "nearness" as a static concept, we may choose to use the concept of "approach", which is an infinite dynamic procedure. It is in the realm of philosophy whether this infinite procedure can be "completed" in finite time and whether we can grasp this "completed infinity" as a whole. In late 1800s, Cauchy, Weierstrass, Dedekind, Cantor and other mathematicians made effort to make the concept precise and rigorous. They avoided using infinitesimals, but used distance and limit instead. The concept of distance was further generalized by Fréchet in 1906. A space with a distance function defined in the abstract sense is called a metric space. In metric spaces, an open set can be defined using the concept of distance. A neighborhood of a point x can be defined as an open set that contains x. If X is the space, it is even possible to "hand pick" a family of subsets of X, to be designated as open sets. Of course we must require that this family of open sets to satisfy some axioms for the theory to be meaningful. We get these axioms from our experiences with the open sets in Euclidean spaces $\mathbb{R}^n$. This further generalization was the work done by Hausdorff, Kuratowski and others in early 1900s. The family of "hand-picked" open sets $\mathbf{O} \subseteq \mathbf{P}(X)$ endows the space a topological structure. $(X, \mathbf{O})$ is called a topological space. The family of open sets $\mathbf{O} \subseteq \mathbf{P}(X)$ is called a topology on X. In this chapter, we will go through the experience of generalization from Euclidean spaces, to metric spaces and finally to topological spaces.

§2   Topology in Euclidean Spaces

2.1   Euclidean Distance

We follow our philosophy that abstract structures come out of everyday concrete examples. Before we delve into the more abstract structures in the following sections, we discuss the topological concepts regarding to the point sets in Euclidean spaces $\mathbb{R}^n$.

The distance between two points $x = (x_1, \ldots, x_n), y = (y_1, \ldots, y_n) \in \mathbb{R}^n$ is defined to be $d(x, y) \stackrel{\text{def}}{=} \sqrt{(y_1 - x_1)^2 + \cdots + (y_n - x_n)^2}$. The distance has the following properties:

Theorem 1. *For all $x, y, z \in \mathbb{R}^n$,*

(1) $d(x, y) \geq 0$.
(2) $d(x, y) = 0$ *if and only if $x = y$.*
(3) $d(x, y) = d(y, x)$ (symmetry).
(4) $d(x, y) + d(y, z) \geq d(x, z)$ (triangle inequality).

2.2 Point Sets in Euclidean Spaces

Using the concept of distance, we can define the concept of an open ball, which is the prototype of a neighborhood. Let $x_0 \in \mathbb{R}^n$ and δ be a real positive number. An **open ball** of radius δ centered at x_0 is defined to be $\{x \in \mathbb{R}^n \mid d(x_0, x) < \delta\}$, denoted by $B_\delta(x_0)$.

Let $A \subseteq \mathbb{R}^n$ be any point set. We now investigate the positions of all points in $\mathbb{R}^n$ relative to A. Relative to a given set $A \subseteq \mathbb{R}^n$, all the points in $\mathbb{R}^n$ can be classified into the following categories: **interior points, exterior points, boundary points, accumulation points, isolated points**. These categories may overlap.

Definition 1. Interior point, exterior point, boundary point

A point $x_0 \in A$ is called an **interior point** of A, if there exists an open ball $B_\delta(x_0) \subseteq A$.

A point $x_0 \in A^c$ is called an **exterior point** of A, if there exists an open ball $B_\delta(x_0) \subseteq A^c$.

A point $x_0 \in \mathbb{R}^n$ is called a **boundary point** of A, if in any open ball $B_\delta(x_0)$, there always exists a point $x_1 \in A$ and a point $x_2 \in A^c$.

Here A^c is the complement of A relative to $\mathbb{R}^n$. By this definition and simple inference, we know that an interior point of A is always an element of A; an exterior point of A is never an element of A; a boundary point of A may or may not be an element of A.

Definition 2. Accumulation point, isolated point

A point $x_0 \in \mathbb{R}^n$ is called an **accumulation point** (or **cluster point**, or **limit point**) of A, if in any open ball $B_\delta(x_0)$, there is always a point x other than x_0 in A.

A point $x_0 \in A$ is called an **isolated point** of A, if there exists an open ball $B_\delta(x_0)$ in which there is no point x other than x_0 in A.

An accumulation point of A may or may not be an element of A. An interior point is always an accumulation point. An exterior point can never be an accumulation point. A boundary point may or may not be an accumulation point. If x is a boundary point of A but not an accumulation point, then x is an isolated point. An isolated point is always an element of A.

Figure 1.1 illustrates a point set $A \subset \mathbb{R}^2$. $x_1 \in A$ is an interior point, and also an accumulation point. $x_2 \in A$ is a boundary point, also an accumulation point. $x_3 \notin A$ is a boundary point, also an accumulation point. Notice that it is possible that some boundary points and accumulation points are not elements of A. $x_4 \in A$ is a boundary point, and an isolated point, but not an accumulation point. $x_5 \notin A$ is an exterior point.

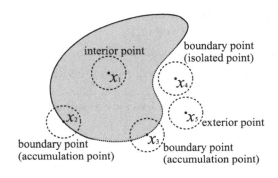

Figure 1.1   A point set in Euclidean space.

Definition 3. Interior, exterior, boundary, derived set, closure

Let $A \subseteq \mathbb{R}^n$. The set of all interior points of A is called the **interior** of A, denoted by A°.

The set of all exterior points of A is called the **exterior** of A, denoted by A^e.

The set of all boundary points of A is called the **boundary** of A, denoted by ∂A.

The set of all accumulation points is called the **derived set** of A, denoted by A'.

The union of A and its boundary $A \cup \partial A$ is called the **closure** of A, denoted by $\bar{A}$.

The following theorems are straightforward.

Theorem 2. *Let $A \subseteq \mathbb{R}^n$. Then*

(1) $A^\circ \subseteq A$.

(2) $A^e \subseteq A^c$.

(3) $A^\circ \subseteq A' \subseteq \bar{A}$.

Theorem 3. *For any point set $A \in \mathbb{R}^n$, its interior A°, boundary ∂A and exterior A^e make a disjoint partition of the space,*

$$\mathbb{R}^n = A^\circ \cup \partial A \cup A^e.$$

Definition 4. Open set, closed set

A point set $A \subseteq \mathbb{R}^n$ is called an **open set**, if for all $x \in A$, there is an open ball $B_\delta(x) \subseteq A$.

A point set $A \subseteq \mathbb{R}^n$ is called a **closed set**, if it contains its entire boundary, namely, $\partial A \subseteq A$.

Theorem 4. *Let $A \subseteq \mathbb{R}^n$.*

(1) *A is an open set if and only if $A \cap \partial A = \varnothing$.*

(2) *A is an open set if and only if $A = A^\circ$.*

(3) *A is a closed set if and only if $A = \bar{A}$.*

Remark 1. Intuition/Elaboration — Open Sets and Closed Sets

Theorem 4 states that A is an open set if and only if A does not contain any part of its boundary. A is a closed set if and only if A contains its entire boundary. A set A is neither open or closed if it contains part but not the entirety of its boundary. Most sets are neither open, nor closed.

The concept of open set and closed set is also relative to the space $\mathbb{R}^n$. For example, in $\mathbb{R}^2$, the disk $\{(x_1, x_2)|x_1^2 + x_2^2 < 1\}$ is an open set. While in $\mathbb{R}^3$, the disk $\{(x_1, x_2, x_3)|x_1^2 + x_2^2 < 1, x_3 = 0\}$ is neither open nor closed.

Remark 2. Historical Note — Open Set and Closed Set

Open set is an important concept that we distilled from analysis on $\mathbb{R}^n$ and will be generalized in the study of general topological spaces. Historically (see [Moore (2008)]), Georg Cantor introduced the closed set in 1884. Lebesgue first introduced the term open set in his doctoral dissertation in 1902. The concept of limit point is due to Weierstrass.

An open set $A \subseteq \mathbb{R}^n$ containing x is called an **open neighborhood** (or simply **neighborhood**) of x.

Theorem 5. (Properties of open sets)

(1) $\varnothing$ and $\mathbb{R}^n$ are open sets.

(2) If A_1 and A_2 are open sets, then $A_1 \cap A_2$ is an open set.

(3) If $\{A_\alpha\}$ is a family of open sets, then the union $\underset{\alpha}{\cup} A_\alpha$ is an open set.

In Theorem 5 property (3), by a family of sets, we mean a family of any cardinality (including uncountable infinity) of sets. Property (2) can be generalized to

Corollary. *The intersection of finite number of open sets is an open set.*

In general it is not true that "The intersection of any number (including infinite number) of open sets is an open set." The following is a counterexample to illustrate this.

Example 1. (A counterexample involving open sets) For each $n = 1, 2, 3, ...$, $G_n = \left(-\frac{1}{n}, 1 + \frac{1}{n}\right)$ is an open set in $\mathbb{R}$. The intersection

$$\bigcap_{n=1}^{\infty} G_n = [0, 1]$$

is a closed set, not an open set.   ♣

Theorem 6. (Properties of closed sets)

(1) $\varnothing$ and $\mathbb{R}^n$ are closed sets.

(2) If $\{A_\alpha\}$ is a family of closed sets, then the intersection $\underset{\alpha}{\cap} A_\alpha$ is a closed set.

(3) If A_1 and A_2 are closed sets, then $A_1 \cup A_2$ is a closed set.

Corollary. *The union of finite number of closed sets is a closed set.*

In general it is not true that "The union of any number (including infinite number) of closed sets is a closed set." The following counterexample illustrates this.

Example 2. (A counterexample involving closed sets) For each $n = 3, 4, 5, ...$, $F_n = \left[\frac{1}{n}, 1 - \frac{1}{n}\right]$ is a closed set in $\mathbb{R}$. The union

$$\bigcup_{n=3}^{\infty} G_n = (0, 1)$$

is an open set, not a closed set.   ♣

Theorem 7.

(1) $\varnothing$ and $\mathbb{R}^n$ are the only subsets of $\mathbb{R}^n$ that are both open and closed.
(2) A is an open set if and only if its complement A^c is a closed set.
(3) A is a closed set if and only if its complement A^c is an open set.

Compact set is another important concept in analysis. It plays an important role in topology. A concept "cover" or "covering" is used to define compactness.

Let $A \subseteq \mathbb{R}^n$ and $\{O_\alpha\}$ be a family of subsets of $\mathbb{R}^n$. $\{O_\alpha\}$ is called a **cover** of A if $A \subseteq \cup_\alpha O_\alpha$. $\{O_\alpha\}$ is called an **open cover** if each of O_α is an open set. $\{O_\alpha\}$ is called a finite cover if it has finite number of subsets O_α. If a subfamily of a cover $\{O_\alpha\}$ is also a cover, it is called a subcover of $\{O_\alpha\}$.

Definition 5. Compact set

A set $A \subseteq \mathbb{R}^n$ in called a **compact set**, if for any open cover $\{O_\alpha\}$ of A, there is always a finite subcover of $\{O_\alpha\}$ that covers A. Otherwise it is called a non-compact set.

The intuition of a compact set A is, that the points of A are "compactly" placed in space and they are not too "spread out". A set can be "spread out" because it stretches to infinity, or it can be "spread out" because it has missing pieces on the boundary. If the boundary is not entirely included in A, a point sequence in A could "sneak" out of A and converge to a boundary point which is not an element of A. This limit procedure is an infinite procedure and hence it prevents some infinite open cover of A from having a finite subcover.

Example 3. (Compact sets in $\mathbb{R}$) Any closed interval $[a, b]$ is a compact set in $\mathbb{R}$. ♣

Example 4. (Non-compact sets in $\mathbb{R}$) Consider $\mathbb{N} = \{1, 2, \ldots, n, \ldots\}$ as a subset of $\mathbb{R}$. $\mathbb{N}$ is not a compact set because $\{(n - \frac{1}{4}, n + \frac{1}{4}) | n = 1, 2, \ldots\}$ is an open cover of $\mathbb{N}$ but it does not have any finite subcover for $\mathbb{N}$.

Consider another set $A = \{1, \frac{1}{2}, \frac{1}{3}, \ldots, \frac{1}{n}, \ldots\}$ as a subset of $\mathbb{R}$. A is not a compact set because $\{(\frac{1}{n}, 1 + \frac{1}{n}) | n = 1, 2, \ldots\}$ is an open cover for A but it does not have any finite subcover for A.

For similar reasons, $B = (0, 1]$ is not a compact set. In fact, neither A nor B is a closed set. The point sequence $1, \frac{1}{2}, \frac{1}{3}, \ldots, \frac{1}{n}, \ldots$ has a limit point 0, which is not in A or B, in both cases. ♣

The Heine-Borel theorem gives a characterization of compact sets in $\mathbb{R}^n$. For this, we first need the concept of a bounded set.

A set $A \subseteq \mathbb{R}^n$ is called a **bounded set**, if there exists an open ball $B_r(x)$, where $x \in \mathbb{R}^n$ and r is a real positive number, such that $A \subseteq B_r(x)$.

In $\mathbb{R}^n$, the concept of compactness is easier to grasp due to the following theorem. However, this theorem is not true in general metric spaces, which we discuss in the next section.

Theorem 8. (Heine-Borel) *A set $A \subseteq \mathbb{R}^n$ is compact if and only if A is closed and bounded.*

2.3   Limits and Continuity

Limit and continuity are the concepts at the heart of mathematical analysis. We can define the concept of continuity using open set. The following definitions are a review of mathematical analysis.

Definition 6. Convergence, limit

Let $x_1, \ldots, x_n, \ldots$ be a sequence of points in $\mathbb{R}^n$. The sequence is said to **converge** to a point $x \in \mathbb{R}^n$, if for any open neighborhood U of x, there exists $n_0 \in \mathbb{N}$ such that $x_n \in U$ for all $n > n_0$. The point x is called the **limit** of this sequence, denoted by

$$\lim_{n \to \infty} x_n = x.$$

Definition 7. Continuous function

Let $f : \mathbb{R}^n \to \mathbb{R}$ be a function, $x_0 \in \mathbb{R}^n$ be a point in $\mathbb{R}^n$ and $y_0 = f(x_0)$.

f is said to be **continuous** at point x_0, if for any open neighborhood V of y_0, there exists an open neighborhood U of x_0, such that for any point $x \in U$, $f(x) \in V$.

f is called a **continuous function** on $\mathbb{R}^n$ if f is continuous at all points in $\mathbb{R}^n$.

§3 Topology in Metric Spaces

3.1 Metric Spaces

Last section was a review of many important concepts in analysis. We realize that the concept "distance" is the key. Using distance, we can define open set; and using open set, we can define all the concepts in analysis, like convergence, limit and continuity.

The concept of distance comes from Euclidean geometry, which is supposed to describe our experience of measurement in the real world—on the earth. The name "geometry" means the measurement of the earth. Euclidean geometry is really the knowledge of our homeland. It is the cradle of modern mathematics. Starting there, it is generalized in many different directions. In analysis, it is generalized to metric spaces. In geometry, it is generalized to non-Euclidean geometries, Riemannian geometry, topological spaces and manifolds.

We have already discussed the methodology of the generalization process — abstraction. Abstraction means extraction. We extract the most essential properties from the concept of distance, but discard the rest. This is a distilling process.

What are the most essential properties of distance? We go back to Section 2. Theorem 1 describes the most important properties of distance.

Definition 8. Metric space

A nonempty set X together with a mapping $\rho : X \times X \to \mathbb{R}$ is called a **metric space** (or **distance space**), if the **following axioms** are satisfied, for all $x, y, z \in X$.

(1) $\rho(x, y) = 0$ if and only if $x = y$.
(2) $\rho(x, y) = d(y, x)$ (symmetry).
(3) $\rho(x, y) + \rho(y, z) \geq \rho(x, z)$ (triangle inequality).

$\rho(x, y)$ is called the **distance** between x and y. The mapping $\rho : X \times X \to \mathbb{R}$ is called the **distance function** (or the **metric**).

Remark 3. Elaboration — Distance Function Is Nonnegative $\rho(x, y) \geq 0$
 Condition $\rho(x, y) \geq 0$ is not in the axioms in the definition of a metric space, but it is a logical consequence of Axioms (1), (2) and (3). This is because for all $x, y \in X$,

$$2\rho(x, y) = \rho(x, y) + \rho(y, x) \geq \rho(x, x) = 0.$$

Remark 4. Historical Note — Metric Spaces
 We pretended that this generalization was done in such an easy way that the properties of the distance function was just sitting there for us. In fact, this was a pioneering step in history. M. Fréchet first introduced metric spaces in his work Sur quelques points du calcul fonctionnel [Fréchet (1906)].

Let (X, ρ) be a metric space and $S \subseteq X$ is a subset of X. When the distance function is restricted on S, (S, ρ) is also a metric space, called the metric subspace of (X, ρ). Let us look at a few examples of metric spaces, with different distance functions.

Example 5. (Euclidean spaces $\mathbb{R}^n$) The Euclidean space $\mathbb{R}^n$ is the prototype of metric spaces. The Euclidean space $\mathbb{R}^n$ with the distance

$$d(x, y) \stackrel{\text{def}}{=} \sqrt{(y_1 - x_1)^2 + \cdots + (y_n - x_n)^2},$$

is a metric space, which was discussed in last section. ♣

Example 6. (Discrete distance) Let X be a nonempty set. For all $x, y \in X$, we define the distance function to be

$$\rho(x, y) \stackrel{\text{def}}{=} \begin{cases} 1, & \text{if } x \neq y, \\ 0, & \text{if } x = y. \end{cases} \tag{1.1}$$

In this metric space, no point x is near any other point y. So it is called discrete metric.   ♣

Example 7. (Manhattan distance) We consider the points $x = (x_1, x_2)$, $y = (y_1, y_2) \in \mathbb{R}^2$. We define the distance

$$\rho(x, y) \stackrel{\text{def}}{=} |y_1 - x_1| + |y_2 - x_2|.$$

This is called the Manhattan distance because the streets are in a rectangular grid in Manhattan, New York City. Manhattan distance is the shortest distance you can travel from one point x to another point y, going through the streets in Manhattan, if you do not have a helicopter.   ♣

Example 8. (Sphere) We consider the set of points on the sphere $S^2 = \{(x_1, x_2, x_3) \in \mathbb{R}^3 | x_1^2 + x_2^2 + x_3^2 = 1\}$. We use the Euclidean distance in $\mathbb{R}^3$. For points $x = (x_1, x_2, x_3)$, $y = (y_1, y_2, y_3) \in S^2$, we define

$$d(x, y) \stackrel{\text{def}}{=} \sqrt{(y_1 - x_1)^2 + (y_2 - x_2)^2 + (y_3 - x_3)^2}.$$

Then (S^2, d) is a metric space. For $x, y \in S^2$, imagine there is a straight line tunnel in $\mathbb{R}^3$ connecting x and y. $d(x, y)$ is the length of the tunnel. Note that we are still using the 3-D Euclidean distance, but the underlying set S^2 is a subset of $\mathbb{R}^3$. (S^2, d) is a metric subspace of $(\mathbb{R}^3, d)$.   ♣

We briefly discussed metric spaces in Part II Chap. 2, Differential Geometry. A smooth surface in $\mathbb{R}^3$ is a metric space with respect to the intrinsic distance measured on the surface. An abstract geometric surface in Riemannian geometry is also a metric space. The next two examples are metric spaces from differential geometry and non-Euclidean geometry.

Example 9. (Spherical geometry) We consider the same set of points on the sphere $S^2 = \{(x_1, x_2, x_3) \in \mathbb{R}^3 | x_1^2 + x_2^2 + x_3^2 = 1\}$. However, now we define the distance between two points x and y to be shortest distance along any smooth curves connecting x and y on the sphere. For points $x = (x_1, x_2, x_3)$ and $y = (y_1, y_2, y_3)$, we define

$$\rho(x, y) \stackrel{\text{def}}{=} \cos^{-1}(x_1 y_1 + x_2 y_2 + x_3 y_3).$$

Then (S^2, ρ) is a metric space. The shortest distance curves are also called **geodesic lines**. The geodesic lines on a sphere are great circles. Given any points x, y which are not antipodal points, there is a unique great circle connecting them. x, y divide the great circle into two arcs. $\rho(x, y)$ is the length of the shorter arc. If we define a straight line passing through two points x and y to be a geodesic line, we obtain a geometry on the surface of the sphere, which is called spherical geometry, or (double) elliptic geometry. A geometry may or may not have the concept of distance. If it does, it is called a metric geometry.   ♣

Example 10. (Hyperbolic geometry—Poincaré disk model) We take the space as the open unit disk in $\mathbb{R}^2$, i.e., $H = \{(x_1, x_2) \in \mathbb{R}^2 | x_1^2 + x_2^2 < 1\}$. Eq. 3.7 defines the distance between two points (x_1, x_2) and (y_1, y_2). We duplicate it here.

$$\rho \stackrel{\text{def}}{=} \cosh^{-1}\left[1 + 2\frac{(x_2 - x_1)^2 + (y_2 - y_1)^2}{(1 - x_1^2 - y_1^2)(1 - x_2^2 - y_2^2)}\right].$$

(H, ρ) is a metric space. It is the Poincaré disk model of the hyperbolic plane (see Part II Chap. 3).   ♣

Example 11. (Sequence spaces l^p) For $0 < p < \infty$, let l^p be a set of all sequences $x_1, x_2, ..., x_n, ...$ satisfying

$$\sum_{n=1}^{\infty} |x_n|^p < \infty.$$

We define a distance between $x = (x_1, x_2, \ldots, x_n, \ldots)$ and $y = (y_1, y_2, \ldots, y_n, \ldots)$ to be

$$\rho(x, y) \stackrel{\text{def}}{=} \left(\sum_{n=1}^{\infty} |x_n - y_n|^p\right)^{1/p}.$$

(l^p, ρ) is a metric space. Each infinite sequence is considered an abstract point in space. This is a particular example of a Banach space (see Chap. 3).   ♣

Example 12. (Lebesgue spaces $L^p[a, b]$) For $1 \leq p < \infty$, let $L^p[a, b]$ be the set of all real functions f such that $|f(x)|^p$ is integrable on the interval $[a, b]$. For two functions $f, g \in L^p$, we define

$$\rho(f, g) \stackrel{\text{def}}{=} \left(\int_a^b |f(x) - g(x)|^p dx\right)^{1/p}.$$

$(L^p[a, b], \rho)$ is a metric space, called Lebesgue space. Each point in this space is a real function. Lebesgue spaces are also Banach spaces (see Chap. 3).   ♣

With this generalization, we feel our field of vision is greatly enlarged and we feel we are immediate liberated from the constraints imposed by the Euclidean distance. We can use the same definition as Definition 4 to define open sets, and we can use the same definitions as Definition 6 and Definition 7 to define convergence and limit, as well as continuous functions. We can do analysis exactly the same way as we did in Euclidean space but with new freedom. In fact, all the concepts that are defined using the Euclidean distance in the Euclidean spaces can be defined in metric spaces in the same way, except that we must beware that the distance is abstract distance now. Because of this, the convergence behaviors of sequences in an abstract metric space can be quite different from those in Euclidean spaces. For example, in the discrete distance space in Example 6, each singleton set $\{x\}$ is an open set. The only converging sequences are those that all the points are the same $x, x, \ldots$. after a certain term n_0. The sequence is converging to x.

The distance is the structure of the metric space. Suppose we have two metric spaces (X_1, ρ_1) and (X_2, ρ_2). If there is a mapping that preserves the distance, the two metric spaces are considered the same in structure. This is the concept of isometric mapping.

Definition 9. Isometric mapping

Let (X_1, ρ_1) and (X_2, ρ_2) be two metric spaces. A bijection $f : X_1 \to X_2$ is called an **isometric mapping** (or **isometry**), if f preserves the distance, i.e., $\rho_2(f(x), f(y)) = \rho_1(x, y)$, for any points $x, y \in X_1$. X_1 and X_2 are said to be **isometric** to each other, if there exists an isometric mapping from X_1 to X_2.

3.2   Completeness

In the following we define complete metric space using the concept of Cauchy sequence.

Definition 10. Cauchy sequence

A sequence $x_1, x_2, x_3, \ldots$ in metric space (X, ρ) is called a **Cauchy sequence**, if for each real number $\varepsilon > 0$, there is an $N \in \mathbb{N}$ such that $\rho(x_m, x_n) < \varepsilon$ for all $m, n > N$.

Definition 11. Complete metric space

> A metric space (X, ρ) is said to be **complete**, if all Cauchy sequences in X converge. Otherwise it is called **incomplete**.
>
> A subset $A \subseteq X$ is said to be **complete**, if A is complete when it is considered as a metric subspace.

Example 13. (Real numbers $\mathbb{R}$) The metric space of real numbers $\mathbb{R}$ with the distance of $x, y \in \mathbb{R}$ defined by $\rho(x, y) \stackrel{\text{def}}{=} |x - y|$ is a complete metric space. ♣

Example 14. (A counterexample) The metric space of real numbers in the open interval $(0, 1)$ is incomplete, because the Cauchy sequence $1, \frac{1}{2}, \frac{1}{4}, \ldots, \frac{1}{2^n}, \ldots$ does not converge in $(0, 1)$. ♣

Example 15. (A counterexample) The metric space of rational numbers $\mathbb{Q}$ with the distance of $x, y \in \mathbb{Q}$ defined by $\rho(x, y) \stackrel{\text{def}}{=} |x - y|$ is incomplete. Applying the long division algorithm for square root on the number 2, we obtain a sequence of decimals

$$x_1 = 1,$$
$$x_2 = 1.4,$$
$$x_3 = 1.41,$$
$$x_4 = 1.414,$$
$$\cdots$$

It is easy to see that $(x_1, x_2, x_3, \ldots)$ is a Cauchy sequence, and we can show that this Cauchy sequence does not converge in $\mathbb{Q}$. Let us look at the sequence $(x_1^2, x_2^2, x_3^2, \ldots)$ with

$$x_1^2 = 1,$$
$$x_2^2 = 1.96,$$
$$x_3^2 = 1.9881,$$
$$x_4^2 = 1.999396,$$
$$\cdots .$$

The sequence $(x_1^2, x_2^2, x_3^2, \ldots)$ converges to 2. If the sequence $(x_1, x_2, x_3, \ldots)$ converges to a rational number r, then we must have $r^2 = 2$. We know that there exists no rational number r such that $r^2 = 2$ and hence we have one example of Cauchy sequence that does not converge in this metric space $\mathbb{Q}$. ♣

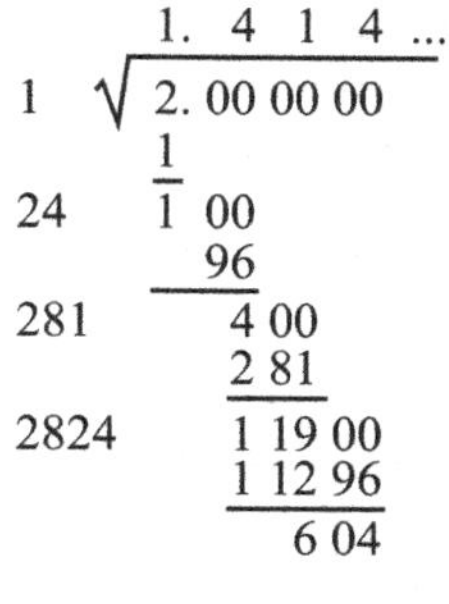

$$
\begin{array}{r}
1.\ 4\ \ 1\ \ 4\ \dots \\
1\ \ \sqrt{2.\ 00\ 00\ 00} \\
\underline{1\ \ \ \ } \\
24\quad \overline{1}\ 00 \\
\underline{96} \\
281\qquad 4\ 00 \\
\underline{2\ 81} \\
2824\qquad 1\ 19\ 00 \\
\underline{1\ 12\ 96} \\
6\ 04
\end{array}
$$

Figure 1.2   Long division to calculate $\sqrt{2}$.

Theorem 9. *If the metric space (X, ρ) is complete, then a subset $A \subseteq X$ is complete if and only if A is closed.*

Theorem 10. *Completeness is invariant under isometric mapping. Let (X, ρ) and (X', ρ') be two metric spaces isometric to each other. (X, ρ) is complete if and only if (X', ρ') is complete.*

The concept of distance is generalized to the distance in the abstract sense and Euclidean spaces are generalized to metric spaces. We have seen that most of the concepts in $\mathbb{R}^n$ can be borrowed in general metric spaces if we use the abstract distance to replace the Euclidean distance. A curious question to ask is, what theorems in last section about $\mathbb{R}^n$ are still true for general metric spaces?

In fact, all the theorem in Section 2 are still true for general metric spaces, with one exception, the last theorem, Theorem 8, the Heine-Borel theorem for $\mathbb{R}^n$. To show this, we just need one counterexample. Let (X, ρ) be a discrete metric space (Example 6) where X is an infinite set. The set X is closed and bounded. For each $x \in X$, $\{B_{\frac{1}{2}}(x) | x \in X\}$ is an open cover for X, but this cover does not have any finite open subcover for X. Therefore X is closed and bounded but not compact. In metric spaces, a similar result about the compactness is a theorem stating: A metric space is compact if and only if it is complete and totally bounded. We do not intend to go further in this direction.

All the theorems in Section 2 except Theorem 8 are even true in the further generalization to topological spaces. In topological spaces, we start with the concept of open set and discard the concept of distance. Theorem 8 does not apply to topological spaces because it uses the concept of bounded set, which is based on distance.

§4   Topology in Topological Spaces

4.1   Topological Spaces

In Section 3, we generalized the concept of distance and we defined abstract metric spaces. We used distance to define an open ball. We used open ball to define open set, closed set, convergence, limit and continuity. These are the important concepts in analysis.

Can we take a shortcut in the chain of definitions? We realize that most of these concepts can be defined using the concept of open set, without directly using the concept of distance.

This is one more step of further generalization from the Euclidean spaces $\mathbb{R}^n$. We give up the concept of distance, but define open set using a set of axioms. Some good properties we have distilled for open sets are in Theorem 5. We use them as the axioms for open sets to define further generalized spaces—topological spaces.

Definition 12. Topological space

Let X be a nonempty set and $\mathbf{O}$ be a family of subsets of X, i.e., $\mathbf{O} \subseteq \mathbf{P}(X)$. $(X, \mathbf{O})$ is called a **topological space** if the following **axioms** are satisfied.

(1) $\varnothing \in \mathbf{O}$ and $X \in \mathbf{O}$.
(2) If $O_1 \in \mathbf{O}$ and $O_2 \in \mathbf{O}$, then $(O_1 \cap O_2) \in \mathbf{O}$.
(3) If $\{O_\alpha\}$ is a family of sets and $O_\alpha \in \mathbf{O}$ for all α, then $\underset{\alpha}{\cup} O_\alpha \in \mathbf{O}$.

If a subset $A \subseteq X$ is an element of $\mathbf{O}$, i.e., $A \in \mathbf{O}$, then A is called an **open set**. The family of all open sets $\mathbf{O}$ is called a **topology**.

In Definition 12, Axiom (1) says that $\varnothing$ and X are open sets. Axiom (2) says the intersection of two open sets is an open set. This implies that the intersection of finite number of open sets is an open set. Axiom (3) says that the union of arbitrary (including infinitely many) number of open sets is an open set.

Remark 5. Historical Note — Topological spaces

Historically, F. Hausdorff first made this abstraction and coined the term "topological space". He gave a set of axioms using "neighborhood" as a primitive concept in his book *Grundzüge der Mengenlehre* in 1914 (*Set Theory*, 2nd ed. New York: Chelsea, 1962). K. Kuratowski published a set of axioms using the closure operator as a primitive concept. The axioms in Definition 12 are equivalent to the Hausdorff's axioms regarding neighborhood, but open set is used as the primitive concept instead. H. Tietze, P. Aleksandrov, W. Sierpiński have contributed to the axioms using open set [Moore (2008)]. N. Bourbaki used exactly the same form of axioms as in Definition 12 using open set in their book *Topologie Générale* (*General Topology*) in 1940 and this became the standard form of the axioms of topological space in the textbooks since then. Any of these axioms are equivalent to each other. They use different primitive concepts: open set, closed set, neighborhood, the closure operator or the interior operator. Given any one as primitive concept, all other concepts can be defined (see chapter exercises).

Example 16. (Euclidean space $\mathbb{R}^n$ as topological spaces) The Euclidean space $\mathbb{R}^n$ with the family of open sets defined by the Euclidean distance $d(x, y) \overset{\text{def}}{=} \sqrt{(y_1 - x_1)^2 + \cdots + (y_n - x_n)^2}$, is a topological space. The topology defined by this distance is called the usual topology or standard topology of $\mathbb{R}^n$. ♣

Example 17. (Metric spaces as topological spaces) A metric space is the prototype of topological spaces. Let (X, ρ) be a metric space. We define an open set to be a set $A \subseteq X$, such that for any $x \in A$, there is an open ball $B_\delta(x)$ contained in A. The topology **O** is the class of all these open sets. It is easy to check that **O** satisfies the axioms in Definition 12 and hence $(X, \mathbf{O})$ is a topological space. **O** is called a **metric topology**, or the topology induced by the metric ρ.

An immediate question to ask is, how far have we gone by generalizing metric spaces to topological spaces? Can any topology be induced by some metric? The answer is no. This is the problem of metrizability of topological spaces. If a topology can be induced from a metric, it is called **metrizable**. Metric spaces have certain properties that a metrizable topological space must share. If a topological space violates one of these properties, then it is not metrizable. The metrizability problems were intensively studied by the Moscow School in Russia, represented by Pavel Aleksandrov and Pavel Uryson. ♣

Example 18. (Discrete topological space) Let X be a nonempty set and let the topology **O** be all subsets of X. i.e., any subset of X is an open set.

This is an example of one extreme, where each singleton set $\{x\}$ is an open set. Obviously this topology can be induced by the discrete metric in Eq. 1.1 and hence it is metrizable. ♣

Example 19. (Indiscrete topological space) It is also known as **trivial topological space**. Let X be a nonempty set. The topology **O** has only two sets, $\varnothing$ and X. This is another extreme example, on the opposite end, compared with discrete topology. In this example, any point sequence is convergent and the limit is not unique. Any point can be the limit of any sequence. ♣

Remark 6. Elaboration — Coarser and Finer Topologies
    Let set X be equipped with two topologies $\mathbf{O}_1$ and $\mathbf{O}_2$. If all open sets in $\mathbf{O}_1$ are open sets in $\mathbf{O}_2$, namely, $\mathbf{O}_1 \subseteq \mathbf{O}_2$, then $\mathbf{O}_1$ is said to be coarser (or weaker) than $\mathbf{O}_2$, and $\mathbf{O}_2$ is said to be finer (or stronger) than $\mathbf{O}_1$, denoted by $\mathbf{O}_1 \leq \mathbf{O}_2$. For any set X, the indiscrete topology is the coarsest topology and the discrete topology is the finest topology.

Example 20. (Examples and a Counterexample of Finite Topological Spaces) Let $X = \{a, b, c\}$. We define a family of subsets
    (1) $\mathbf{O}_1 = \{\varnothing, \{a\}, \{a, b, c\}\}$. Then $(X, \mathbf{O}_1)$ is a topological space.
    (2) $\mathbf{O}_2 = \{\varnothing, \{b\}, \{a, b\}, \{b, c\}, \{a, b, c\}\}$. Then $(X, \mathbf{O}_2)$ is a topological space.
    (3) $\mathbf{O}_3 = \{\varnothing, \{a\}, \{b\}\}$. Then $(X, \mathbf{O}_3)$ is not a topological space.
    Figure 1.3 shows these situations. ♣

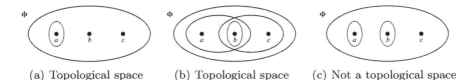

(a) Topological space   (b) Topological space   (c) Not a topological space

Figure 1.3   Examples and a counterexample of topological spaces.

Definition 13. Base

    Let $(X, \mathbf{O})$ be a topological space. A subfamily **B** of **O** is called a **base** for topology **O**, if each open set $U \in \mathbf{O}$ is the union of a subfamily of **B**. The sets in **B** are called **basic open sets**.

Theorem 11. *If* **B** *is a base for the topology* **O** *in topological space* $(X, \mathbf{O})$, *then*

(1) $\bigcup \mathbf{B} = X$.
(2) *For any* $U_1, U_2 \in \mathbf{B}$ *and* $x \in U_1 \cap U_2$, *there is* $U \in \mathbf{B}$ *such that* $x \in U \subset (U_1 \cap U_2)$.

The notation $\bigcup \mathbf{B}$ means the union of all the sets $U_\alpha \in \mathbf{B}$. Let X be any nonempty set and **B** a family of subsets of X. If **B** satisfies the conditions in Theorem 11, then **B** is a base of a unique topology.

Definition 14. Closed set

Let $(X, \mathbf{O})$ be a topological space. $A \subseteq X$ is called a **closed set**, if its complement A^c is an open set.

An open set A containing x is called an **open neighborhood** (or simply **neighborhood**) of x.

Most of the concepts defined in metric spaces can be carried over to topological spaces. All we have to do is to substitute "open neighborhood of x" in the topological space for the "open ball $B_\delta(x)$" in a metric space.

The system of axioms in Definition 12 is not complete. We can add more axioms to this system. One axiom we can add is to describe how the points in the topological space are separated, known as the separation axiom.

Axiom. (Hausdorff) *For any two distinct points* $x, y \in X$, *there exist two disjoint open neighborhoods. That is,* $x \in U$, $y \in V$ *and* $U \cap V = \varnothing$.

In other words, any two distinct points have two disjoint open neighborhoods. The Hausdorff axiom was originally listed by F. Hausdorff together with other axioms regarding the neighborhood concept of topological spaces. Later other researchers have used different separation axioms, $\mathbf{T}_0, \mathbf{T}_1, \mathbf{T}_3, \mathbf{T}_4$, from weaker to stronger respectively, to replace the Hausdorff axiom. The Hausdorff axiom is also known as $\mathbf{T}_2$ axiom. A topological space satisfying the Hausdorff axiom is also called a **Hausdorff space** (or $\mathbf{T}_2$ **Space**).

Theorem 12. *Metric spaces are Hausdorff Spaces.*

Definition 15. Dense

Let X be a topological space. A point set $A \subseteq X$ is said to be **dense** in X, if every open set O in X contains at least one point in A.

A point set $A \subseteq X$ is called a **boundary set**, if the interior of A is empty, i.e., $A^\circ = \varnothing$.

Let $A, B \subseteq X$. A is said to be **dense in** B, if $B = \bar{A}$. If A is dense in X, we just say that A is **dense**.

A point set $A \subseteq X$ is said to be **nowhere dense**, if $\bar{A}$ has empty interior, i.e., $\bar{A}$ is a boundary set.

A point set $A \subseteq X$ is said to be **dense-in-itself**, if A does not possess any isolated point. This condition is equivalent to $A \subseteq A'$.

A point set $A \subseteq X$ is called a **perfect set**, if it is dense-in-itself and closed. This condition is equivalent to $A = A'$.

Example 21. The set of rational numbers $\mathbb{Q}$ is dense in $\mathbb{R}$. The set of irrational numbers $\mathbb{R} - \mathbb{Q}$ is dense in $\mathbb{R}$.   ♣

Example 22. (Cantor set) The Cantor ternary set, or just the Cantor set, is a subset of $\mathbb{R}$. The following is the definition of the Cantor set. Start with $[0, 1]$. Remove the middle third $(\frac{1}{3}, \frac{2}{3})$. Two closed intervals $[0, \frac{1}{3}]$ and $[\frac{2}{3}, 1]$ remain. Remove the middle third of each, $(\frac{1}{9}, \frac{2}{9})$ and $(\frac{7}{9}, \frac{8}{9})$, we have four closed intervals, $[0, \frac{1}{9}]$, $[\frac{2}{9}, \frac{1}{3}]$, $[\frac{2}{3}, \frac{7}{9}]$ and $[\frac{8}{9}, 1]$. This process goes on forever. The remaining points after the infinite process of removal of intervals constitute the Cantor set C. Note the sum of lengths of removed intervals add up to 1. No interval is remaining in the Cantor set. Does the Cantor set contain only those end points of the removed intervals? The answer is no. This is because the cardinality of the end points of the removed intervals is countable, but the cardinality of Cantor set is uncountable. This is easy to see if the points in $[0, 1]$ are represented by decimals of base 3. The Cantor set C corresponds to numbers with all the decimals that only have digit 0 and 2. The interior of C is empty. All the points in C are boundary points but they are also all accumulation points. There are no isolated points.

The Cantor set is

(1) uncountable,

(2) closed,

(3) compact,

(4) nowhere dense,

(5) dense-in-itself,

(6) perfect. ♣

Remark 7. Caution/Clarification — A Is Dense in A Does Not Mean A Is Dense-in-itself

The notions of a set A is dense in set B, and set A is dense-in-itself could have potential confusions. The naming could have been done better but this is already history and accepted convention. A set A is dense in A does not imply that A is *dense-in-itself*. For any closed set A, $A = \bar{A}$ and hence A is dense in A, but A may not be *dense-in-itself*. To be dense-in-itself, A is required not to have any isolated point. J. E. Littlewood had a joking quote: "A linguist would be shocked to learn that if a set is not closed this does not mean that it is open, or again that 'E is dense in E' does not mean the same thing as 'E is dense in itself'".

Definition 16. Separable space

A topological space X is called a **separable space**, if there exists a countable subset of X which is dense in X.

Remark 8. Why Is It Called So?/Historical Note — "Separable Space"

Separable space is not a very suggestive name and should not be confused with the separation axioms T_0 through T_4 of a topological space. F. Hausdorff pointed out in his *Set Theory*, "A set in which a countable set is dense is called separable, an expression due to Fréchet which, although not exactly suggestive, happens to be generally accepted."

4.2 Topological Equivalence

In the informal discussion of topology in Section 1, we used the intuitive terms like "continuous deformation" and "rubber sheet" stretching analogy. Now it is time to make these terms precise. First we define the concept of a continuous mapping and see if this captures the intuition of "continuous deformation" or "continuous stretching".

The definition of a continuous mapping in a topological space is the generalization of Definition 7.

Definition 17. Continuous mapping

Let X_1 and X_2 be topological spaces and $f : X_1 \to X_2$ be a mapping.

Let $a \in X_1$ and $f(a) = b$. f is said to be **continuous at point** a, if for any neighborhood V of b, there exists a neighborhood U of a such that, for any $x \in U$, $f(x) \in V$.

A mapping $f : X_1 \to X_2$ is called a **continuous mapping** if it is continuous at all points in X_1.

Intuition. (Continuous mapping) Let $f : X_1 \to X_2$ be a continuous mapping. This means that if $a \in X_1$ is mapped to $b \in X_2$, the nearby points (in a neighborhood) of a are mapped to the nearby points (in a neighborhood) of b. Another way to think of continuous mapping is that small changes in the input results in small changes in the output.

So the definition of continuous mapping at least partially captures this intuition.

There are other interesting mappings like open mappings and closed mappings.

Definition 18. Open mapping, closed mapping

Let X_1 and X_2 be topological spaces. A mapping $f : X_1 \to X_2$ is called an **open mapping**, if for any open set U in X_1, $f(U)$ is an open set in X_2. A mapping $f : X_1 \to X_2$ is called a **closed mapping**, if for any closed set U in X_1, $f(U)$ is a closed set in X_2.

It turns out that neither open mapping or closed mapping precisely captures our intuition of a continuous stretch that preserves the topological properties.

Putting these together, the topological mapping we have been searching for should be an invertible continuous mapping with a continuous inverse, which we call a homeomorphic mapping, as defined below:

Definition 19. Homeomorphic mapping

Let X_1 and X_2 be topological spaces. An invertible mapping $f : X_1 \to X_2$ is called a **homeomorphic mapping** (or **homeomorphism**, or **topological mapping**), if both f and its inverse f^{-1} are continuous.

Topological spaces X_1 and X_2 are said to be **homeomorphic** (or **topologically equivalent**) to each other, if there exists a homeomorphism between them.

Remark 9. Historical Note — Homeomorphism
The term *homeomorphism* was named by H. Poincaré in 1895, according to EDM [MSJ (1993)].

Example 23. $((0,1)$ is homeomorphic to $\mathbb{R})$ The open interval $X = (0,1)$ is homeomorphic to the open interval $Y = (0,2)$. This can be easily shown with a mapping $f : X \to Y;\ x \mapsto 2x$. This illustrates the intuition that a homeomorphism means continuous stretching.

The open interval $(0,1)$ is also homeomorphic to the real line $\mathbb{R}$. This can be shown with a homeomorphism $f : X \to \mathbb{R};\ x \mapsto \tan\left(\pi(x - \frac{1}{2})\right)$. ♣

Example 24. (A sphere S^2 is homeomorphic to a cube) The sphere S^2 is homeomorphic to any ellipsoid $E = \{(x,y,z) \in \mathbb{R}^3 | \frac{x^2}{a^2} + \frac{y^2}{b^2} + \frac{z^2}{c^2} = 1\}$. The sphere S^2 is even homeomorphic to a cube. When topology is the only concern, we do not have the concept of smoothness or differentiability. We cannot feel the sharp corners on the cube. ♣

Example 25. (The plane $\mathbb{R}^2$ is not homeomorphic to the sphere S^2) The plane $\mathbb{R}^2$ is not homeomorphic to the sphere S^2. However, if we remove a single point on S^2 and let $W = S^2 - \{N\}$, where N is the north pole on S^2. W is homeomorphic to the plane. This can be established with stereographic projection. In Figure 1.4, the north pole N on the sphere is removed. Let P be a point on S^2. From N, we draw a line NP intersecting the plane at P'. The stereographic projection maps P on W to P' on the plane. It is easy to verify that this stereographic projection is a homeomorphism.

If we add one extra point to the plane, which is called the **point at infinity**, then the extended plane is called the completion of the plane, or **Riemann sphere**, because it is homeomorphic to a sphere. The set of complex number $\mathbb{C}$ can be visualized as a plane, called the complex plane. Riemann sphere is viewed as the extended complex plane and used in complex analysis. Riemann sphere is different from the projective completion of the plane, where a projective plane is obtained. In the projective plane, we add infinitely many points at infinity and all those points at infinity lie on a line at infinity. The sphere is not homeomorphic to a projective plane. We will revisit this in next section on manifolds.   ♣

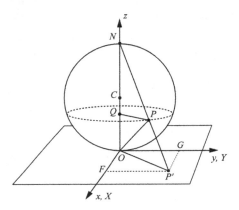

Figure 1.4   Stereographic projection.

Example 26. (The hyperbolic plane $\mathbb{H}^2$ is homeomorphic to the Euclidean plane $\mathbb{R}^2$) They are only different in the metric properties. However, the real projective plane $\mathbb{P}^2$ (see Part II Chap. 1) is not homeomorphic to the Euclidean plane. The real projective plane $\mathbb{P}^2$ is not homeomorphic to the sphere S^2 either. We will discuss more in Chap. 2, since these topological spaces, $\mathbb{R}^2$, $\mathbb{H}^2$, $\mathbb{P}^2$ and S^2 are also 2-dimensional manifolds.   ♣

Example 27. (Topological equivalence classes of English letters) The letters in the English alphabet can be divided into topological equivalence classes as follows. Each row is an equivalence class in which the letters are topologically equivalent to each other.

A, R
B
C, G, I, J, L, M, N, S, U, V, W, Z
D, O
E, F, T, Y

H, K
P
Q
X

Note that this classification is sensitive to the font used. It is also assumed that a letter consists lines with zero width. In printing or handwriting, certain topological deformation (homeomorphism) of the letters is allowed to some extent but we realize that the definition and recognition of each letter is not solely based on topology. Metric characters, like length and angle, are also involved. In handwriting, the letter "z" is easily confused with the digit "2", because they are topologically equivalent, and even metrically very close. Many times we have to distinguish them in the context, especially in the case of handwritten letters.   ♣

4.3 Subspaces, Product Spaces and Quotient Spaces

Definition 20. Topological subspace

Let $(X, \mathbf{O})$ be a topological space and W be a subset of X. The topology $\mathbf{O}$ on X can induce a topology $\mathbf{O}'$ on W in the following way: for any subset $A \subseteq X$, we define $A \cap W$ is an open set in $\mathbf{O}'$ if and only if A is an open set in $\mathbf{O}$. $A \cap W$ is said to be a **relatively open set** in W. The topology $\mathbf{O}'$ on W is called **inherited topology** (or **relative topology**) from X. $(W, \mathbf{O}')$ is called a **topological subspace** (or just **subspace**) of $(X, \mathbf{O})$.

Example 28. (A plane as a subspace of $\mathbb{R}^3$) Consider the plane $W = \{(x, y, z) \in \mathbb{R}^3 | z = 0\}$ as a subset of $\mathbb{R}^3$. W is a subspace of $\mathbb{R}^3$. The disk $D = \{(x, y, z) \in \mathbb{R}^3 | x^2 + y^2 < 1, z = 0\}$ is a relatively open set in W, but it is neither open nor closed in $\mathbb{R}^3$.   ♣

Definition 21. Topological embedding

Let $(X, \mathbf{O})$ and $(Y, \mathbf{O}')$ be two topological spaces. A mapping $f : X \to Y$ is called a **topological embedding** if f is a homeomorphism from X to the subspace $f(X)$. In such case X is said to be **topologically embedded** into Y.

Example 29. (Graph of a continuous real function) Let $f : \mathbb{R} \to \mathbb{R}$ be a continuous real function and G be the graph of f. The mapping $\varphi : \mathbb{R} \to G$ such that $x \mapsto (x, f(x))$ is a homeomorphism. Hence the graph G of f is homeomorphic to $\mathbb{R}$. The graph G of f is a topologically embedding of $\mathbb{R}$ into $\mathbb{R}^2$. ♣

Definition 22. Product space

Let $(X_1, \mathbf{O}_1)$ and $(X_2, \mathbf{O}_2)$ be topological spaces. The family of sets $\mathbf{B} = \{U_1 \times U_2 | U_1 \in \mathbf{O}_1, U_2 \in \mathbf{O}_2\}$ forms a base of a topology $\mathbf{O}$ for $X = X_1 \times X_2$. The topological space $(X, \mathbf{O})$ is called the **product space** of $(X_1, \mathbf{O}_1)$ and $(X_2, \mathbf{O}_2)$.

Remark 10. Elaboration — Product Spaces of Infinitely Many Topological Spaces
The topology for the product space defined above is called the box topology. The product space can also be defined for infinitely many topological spaces. In such cases, box topology can be used for the product space, but more commonly a different topology, called Tychonoff topology is used for the product space. For the product space of infinitely many spaces, the Tychonoff topology is coarser than the box topology. For the product space of two or finitely many spaces, the two topologies coincide.

Example 30. (The plane $\mathbb{R}^2$ as a product space $\mathbb{R} \times \mathbb{R}$) $\mathbb{R}^2$ with the usual topology is the product space $\mathbb{R} \times \mathbb{R}$. Note that an open set in the product topology needs not to be a basic open set. For example, the open disk $\{(x, y) \in \mathbb{R}^2 | x^2 + y^2 < 1\}$ is an open set in $\mathbb{R}^2$ but it is not a rectangular box shaped basic open set. It is the union of infinite number of rectangular boxes. ♣

Definition 23. Quotient space

Let $(X, \mathbf{O})$ be a topological space. Given an equivalence relation $\sim$ on X, let $X/\sim$ be the quotient set and $\pi : X \to (X/\sim); x \mapsto [x]$ be the canonical mapping. We define the **quotient topology** $\mathbf{Q}$ on $X/\sim$ as follows: A subset U of $X/\sim$ is open if and only if $\pi^{-1}(U)$ is open in X. The topological space $(X/\sim, \mathbf{Q})$ is called the **quotient space** of $(X, \mathbf{O})$.

Quotient spaces are useful in constructing new topological spaces. In next chapter, we are going to apply a technique of "gluing" of plane shapes to make new topological spaces. This "gluing" process is actually the process of constructing quotient spaces. When two points are glued together as one point, the new point is viewed as the equivalent class of the two old points.

4.4   Topological Invariants

Definition 24. Compact

A topological space $(X, \mathbf{O})$ is said to be **compact**, if each open cover of X admits a finite open subcover. Otherwise it is said to be **non-compact**.

A subset $A \subseteq X$ is said to be **compact**, if A is compact when it is considered as a topological subspace with relative topology.

Remark 11. Comparison — Metric Properties and Topological Properties

Metric spaces are generalized to topological spaces. The isomorphisms between metric spaces are isometries while the isomorphisms between topological spaces are homeomorphisms. Some properties about metric spaces are also topological properties while others are not. Compactness is defined for both metric spaces and topological spaces. Compactness is topological invariant. Completeness is defined for metric spaces only. Note that completeness is invariant under isometric mappings but in general is not a topological property. One counterexample is that the real numbers $\mathbb{R}$ is homeomorphic to the open interval $(0, 1)$ while $\mathbb{R}$ is a complete metric space but $(0, 1)$ is incomplete.

Theorem 13. *Compactness is a topological invariant. Let $(X_1, \mathbf{O}_1)$ and $(X_2, \mathbf{O}_2)$ be topological spaces and $\varphi : X_1 \to X_2$ a homeomorphic mapping. A subset $A \subseteq X_1$ is compact if and only if $\varphi(A)$ is compact.*

Connectedness is another topological property, which is preserved under homeomorphic mappings.

Definition 25. Connected

A topological space $(X, \mathbf{O})$ is said to be **connected**, if X is not the disjoint union of two open sets. Otherwise it is said to be **disconnected**.

A subset $A \subseteq X$ is said to be **connected**, if A is connected when

> it is considered as a topological subspace with relative topology.

A topological space $(X, \mathbf{O})$ is **connected**, if and only if X is not the disjoint union of two closed sets.

Let $A \subset \mathbb{R}^2$ be the union of two separate closed discs $A = A_1 \cup A_2$, where $A_1 = \{(x, y) | (x + 2)^2 + y^2 \leq 1\}$ and $A_2 = \{(x, y) | (x - 2)^2 + y^2 < 1\}$. Although A_1 is a closed set and A_2 is an open set in $\mathbb{R}^2$, they are relatively open and relatively closed at the same time with the relative topology. Hence the set A is a disconnected set.

Theorem 14. *A topological space $(X, \mathbf{O})$ is connected if and only if that the only subsets that are open and closed are $\varnothing$ and X.*

Theorem 15. *A subset $S \subseteq X$ is connected if and only if S is not the union of two sets $A \neq \varnothing$ and $B \neq \varnothing$ such that*

$$\bar{A} \cap B = \varnothing \text{ and } A \cap \bar{B} = \varnothing.$$

Definition 26. Connected component

The maximal connected subset A of a topological space X is called a **connected component** of the space. Namely,

(1) A is connected; and
(2) if $A \subseteq B$ and B is connected, then $A = B$.

Theorem 16. *Connectedness is a topological invariant. Let $(X_1, \mathbf{O}_1)$ and $(X_2, \mathbf{O}_2)$ be topological spaces and $\varphi : X_1 \to X_2$ a homeomorphic mapping. A subset $A \subseteq X_1$ is connected if and only if $\varphi(A)$ is connected.*

Theorem 17. *Let $(X, \mathbf{O})$ be a topological space. The following statements are equivalent:*

(1) X *is connected.*

(2) X *is not the disjoint union of two closed sets.*

(3) *The only subsets of X that are both open and closed are $\varnothing$ and X.*

(4) *The only continuous functions $f : X \to \{0,1\}$ are constant functions.*

Remark 12. Intuition/Cross Link — Continuous Functions and Connected Graphs of Functions

We have discussed intuitions of continuous functions in subsection 4.2. The graphs of functions can provide more insight about functions themselves. Intuitively the graph of a continuous real function $f : \mathbb{R} \to \mathbb{R}$ has no jumps, no gaps and no holes. You can draw the graph of a continuous function without taking your pencil off the paper. This intuition is correct. In Example 29 we established that the graph of a continuous real function $f : \mathbb{R} \to \mathbb{R}$ is homeomorphic to the real line $\mathbb{R}$. Since $\mathbb{R}$ is connected and a homeomorphism maps a connected set to a connected set, the graph G of a continuous function $f : \mathbb{R} \to \mathbb{R}$ is connected. However, the converse is not true. The function $f(x) = \sin \frac{1}{x}$ when $x \neq 0$ and $f(0) = 0$ is a counterexample to show a real function can have a connected graph but is not continuous. It is true that a real function $f : \mathbb{R} \to \mathbb{R}$ is continuous if and only if the graph G of f is connected and closed. For a mapping $\varphi : X \to Y$ between two arbitrary topological spaces, we always discuss under the context that the domain X is connected. Under this assumption, it is always true that if φ is continuous, then the graph G of φ is connected. The sufficient condition is more complicated. J. Jelinek [Jelinek (2003)] showed a counterexample of a function $f : \mathbb{R}^2 \to \mathbb{R}$ which has connected closed graph but is discontinuous. M. R. Wójcik had his doctoral dissertation (2008) dedicated to this topic. Let X be a connected topological space and G be the graph of $f : X \to \mathbb{R}$. One of the earlier results of M. R. Wójcik and M. S. Wójcik [Wójcik and Wójcik (2007)] established that f is continuous if and only if G is connected and $(X \times \mathbb{R}) - G$ is disconnected. Think of the case when $X = \mathbb{R}$. The intuition behind this result is cutting along the graph with a pair of scissors rather than drawing the graph with a pencil on paper. If the function f is continuous, its graph is connected and the complement $\mathbb{R}^2 - G$ is disconnected. The converse turns out to be also true even when X is an arbitrary connected topological space.

Exercises

1. Let $A \subset \mathbb{R}^2$ be the open unit disc ($A = \{(x,y)|x^2 + y^2 < 1\}$). Find

   (1) A°

   (2) ∂A

   (3) $\bar{A}$

   (4) A'

2. Let $A \subset \mathbb{R}^2$ be the unit circle ($A = \{(x, y) | x^2 + y^2 = 1\}$). Find
   (1) A°
   (2) ∂A
   (3) $\bar{A}$
   (4) A'

3. Let A be the set of rational points in $[0, 1]$. Find
   (1) A°
   (2) ∂A
   (3) $\bar{A}$
   (4) A'

4. Show that the set of rational points in $[0, 1]$ is dense in $[0, 1]$.

5. Let $A \subset \mathbb{R}^2$ be the unit circle ($A = \{(x, y) | x^2 + y^2 = 1\}$). Show that A is dense-in-itself; A is nowhere dense; and A is a perfect set.

6. Let $A \subset \mathbb{R}^2$ be the set of points on the graph of function
$$f(x) = \begin{cases} \sin \frac{1}{x}, & \text{for } x \neq 0 \\ 0, & \text{for } x = 0 \end{cases}.$$
   Find
   (1) A°
   (2) ∂A
   (3) $\bar{A}$
   (4) A'

7. Show that given a finite topological space (the underlying set is a finite set), if it is Hausdorff, then it is discrete.

8. Show that the topology of any finite metric space is discrete topology. The contrapositive of this proposition is that any finite topological space other than the discrete topological space is not metrizable.

9. Show that the Manhattan distance and the Euclidean distance induce the same topology for $\mathbb{R}^2$.

10. Test whether each of the following sequences of real numbers is a Cauchy sequence. If yes, find its limit.
   (1) $x_n = \dfrac{1}{n}$
   (2) $x_n = (-1)^n$
   (3) $x_n = \dfrac{(-1)^n}{n}$
   (4) $x_n = \dfrac{\sin n}{n}$
   (5) $x_n = 1 + \dfrac{1}{2} + \dfrac{1}{3} + \cdots + \dfrac{1}{n}$

11. Alternatively topological space X can be defined using the concept of closed sets. A system of closed sets for the space X is a family $\mathbf{F}$ of subsets of X satisfying the following axioms:

(F1) $\varnothing \in \mathbf{F}$ and $X \in \mathbf{F}$.

(F2) If $F_1 \in \mathbf{F}$ and $F_2 \in \mathbf{F}$, then $(F_1 \cup F_2) \in \mathbf{F}$.

(F3) If $\{F_\alpha\}$ is a family of sets and $F_\alpha \in \mathbf{F}$ for all α, then $\cap_\alpha F_\alpha \in \mathbf{F}$.

Use the concept of closed sets to define open sets. Then use axioms (F1), (F2), (F3) for the closed sets to prove axioms (1), (2), (3) in Definition 12 for open sets.

12. Alternatively topological space X can be defined using the closure operator (Kuratowski). A closure operator on topological space X is a function that assigns to any subset $A \subseteq X$, a subset $\bar{A} \subseteq X$, satisfying the following axioms:

(C1) $\bar{\varnothing} = \varnothing$.

(C2) $\overline{(A \cup B)} = \bar{A} \cup \bar{B}$.

(C3) $A \subseteq \bar{A}$.

(C4) $\bar{\bar{A}} = \bar{A}$.

Use the closure operator to define closed sets and then define open sets. Then use axioms (C1), (C2), (C3), (C4) for the closure operator to prove axioms (1), (2), (3) in Definition 12 for open sets.

13. Alternatively topological space X can be defined using the interior operator. A interior operator on topological space X is a function that assigns to any subset $A \subseteq X$, a subset $A^\circ \subseteq X$, satisfying the following axioms:

(I1) $X^\circ = X$.

(I2) $(A \cap B)^\circ = A^\circ \cap B^\circ$.

(I3) $A^\circ \subseteq A$.

(I4) $(A^\circ)^\circ = A^\circ$.

Use the interior operator to define open sets. Then use axioms (I1), (I2), (I3), (I4) for the interior operator to prove axioms (1), (2), (3) in Definition 12 for open sets.

14. Alternatively topological space X can be defined using the concept of neighborhood (Hausdorff). A neighborhood system for topological space X is a function that assigns to each point $x \in X$ a family of subsets $\mathbf{N}(x)$ satisfying the following axioms:

(N1) $x \in U$ for each $U \in \mathbf{N}(x)$.

(N2) If $U_1, U_2 \in \mathbf{N}(x)$, then $U_1 \cap U_2 \in \mathbf{N}(x)$.

(N3) If $V \in \mathbf{N}(x)$ and $V \subseteq U$, then $U \in \mathbf{N}(x)$.

(N4) Each $U \in \mathbf{N}(x)$ contains some $V \in \mathbf{N}(x)$ such that for all $y \in V$, $U \in \mathbf{N}(y)$.

Use the concept of neighborhood to define open sets. Then use axioms (N1), (N2), (N3), (N4) for the neighborhood to prove axioms (1), (2), (3) in Definition 12 for open sets.

15. Let X be a topological space. Show that the identity function $f : X \to X$; $f(x) = x$ is continuous.

16. Let X, Y be topological spaces. Show that mapping $f : X \to Y$ is continuous if and only if,

   any $A \subseteq Y$ is an open set in $Y \Rightarrow f^{-1}(A)$ is an open set in X.

17. Let X, Y be topological spaces. If $f : X \to Y$ and $g : X \to Y$ are continuous mappings, then the composition $g \circ f$ is a continuous mapping.

18. Show the function $f : \mathbb{R} \to \mathbb{R}$ such that $f(x) = \begin{cases} \sin \frac{1}{x}, & \text{for } x \neq 0 \\ 0, & \text{for } x = 0 \end{cases}$ is discontinuous at $x = 0$.

19. Find a homeomorphism between $(-1, 1)$ and $(0, 7)$.

20. Find a homeomorphism between $(-1, 1)$ and $(0, \infty)$.

21. Show that the real line $\mathbb{R}$ with usual topology is not topologically equivalent to the plane $\mathbb{R}^2$ with usual topology. (Hint: consider to have the point $0 \in \mathbb{R}$ removed and use connectedness argument.)

22. Let X, Y, Z be topological spaces. Show that homeomorphism is an equivalence relation. That is,

   (1) X is homeomorphic to X.

   (2) If X is homeomorphic to Y, then Y is homeomorphic to X.

   (3) If X is homeomorphic to Y and Y is homeomorphic to Z, then X is homeomorphic to Z.

23. Let X, Y be topological spaces. Show

   (1) A bijection $\varphi : X \to Y$ is a homeomorphism, if and only if φ is continuous and open.

   (2) A bijection $\varphi : X \to Y$ is a homeomorphism, if and only if φ is continuous and closed.

24. Let X, Y be topological spaces. Give one example of a mapping $\varphi : X \to Y$ for each of the following cases:

   (1) φ is continuous, open and closed.

   (2) φ is not continuous, not open and not closed.

   (3) φ is continuous, but not open and not closed.

   (4) φ is open, but not closed and not continuous.

   (5) φ is closed, but not open and not continuous.

(6) φ is continuous and open, but not closed.

(7) φ is continuous and closed, but not open.

(8) φ is open and closed, but not continuous.

25. Test whether the topological spaces in Examples (16), (18), (19), (20) are compact.

26. Test whether the topological spaces in Examples (16), (18), (19), (20) are connected.

27. Let $A = A_1 \cup A_2 \cup A_3 \cup A_4 \cup A_5$, where $A_1 = \{(x,y)|x > 0 \text{ and } y > 0\}$, $A_2 = \{(x,y)|x < 0 \text{ and } y > 0\}$, $A_3 = \{(x,y)|x < 0 \text{ and } y < 0\}$, $A_4 = \{(x,y)|x > 0 \text{ and } y < 0\}$, $A_5 = \{(0,0)\}$.

(1) Is A a connected set?

(2) Is A a compact set?

(3) Is A dense-in-itself?

(4) Is A nowhere dense?

(5) Is A a perfect set?

28. Let $A \subset \mathbb{R}^2$ be the set of points on the graph of function

$$f(x) = \begin{cases} \sin\frac{1}{x}, & \text{for } x \neq 0 \\ 0, & \text{for } x = 0 \end{cases}.$$

(1) Is A a connected set?

(2) Is A a compact set?

(3) Is A dense-in-itself?

(4) Is A nowhere dense?

(5) Is A a perfect set?

Chapter 2

Manifolds

It's only when a manifold is compact that life is beautiful[1].

— *Madhav Nori*

Old theorems never die; they turn into definitions[2].

— *Edwin Hewitt*

---

[1]Spoken in a lecture in the University of Chicago in 2013, according to Zev Chonoles.
[2]See Remark 3 for more comments.

Reading Guide. Topology is sometimes described as "rubber sheet" geometry, which studies the properties of geometric shapes that are preserved under continuous stretching. The discussion of general topology in last chapter did study continuous mappings but it did not really give us a flavor of "rubber sheet" geometry. This is because the objects in general topology are general point sets. In fact, the point sets are too general and they may not constitute any sheets in shape. They may include all sorts of jagged fractals. This is why it is called general topology, or point-set topology.

In this chapter we focus on manifolds, which can be visualized as "sheets"—"rubber sheets" or "paper sheets"—in higher dimensions. The topological manifolds in §1 can be considered as the "rubber sheets". The differentiable manifolds in §2 are "smooth rubber sheets", where smooth stretching is allowed but sharp bends like kinks and cusps are disallowed. The Riemannian manifolds in §3 have metric structures. Riemannian manifolds are no longer considered "rubber sheets", but rather "paper sheets", where stretching is disallowed but some flexible bending that preserves the distance is allowed. The affinely-connected manifolds in §4 are generalizations of Riemannian manifolds, where the metric concept of Riemannian manifolds is dropped, but the affine structure is retained.

We should not consider the manifolds in the following four sections as four different "types" of manifolds. Rather, from the structure point of view, they are manifolds endowed with different structures—some with more (richer) structures, some with fewer (poorer) structures. Topological manifolds are the concerns of topology while Riemannian manifolds, as well as manifolds with other geometric structures, are considered modern differential geometry. The differentiable manifolds are somewhere in-between. They have additional differential structures on top of the topological structures, but lack the metric structures compared with Riemannian manifolds. The study of differentiable manifolds is considered differential topology. This chapter is a quick tour through topology, differential topology and modern differential geometry, which is a generalization of classical differential geometry in Part II Chap. 2. The following is a Venn diagram showing the relationships between different structures. The structures in the shaded area are the focus of this chapter. See also a brief discussion of structures in Chap. 0.

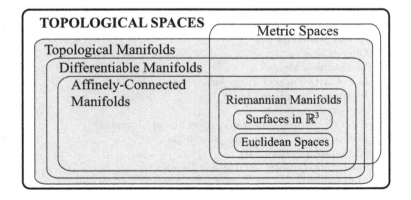

§1   Topological Manifolds

1.1   Topological Manifolds

In last chapter, Euclidean spaces are generalized to topological spaces. There are all sorts of topological spaces. The realm of topological spaces is like a wild jungle. Here we study a particular type of topological spaces—topological manifolds. Topological manifolds can be viewed as the generalization of Euclidean spaces in another direction. Namely, locally, a topological manifold is modeled on, or approximated by, a Euclidean space.

In geometry, we say a straight line is 1-dimensional, a plane is 2-dimensional and the ordinary Euclidean space is 3-dimensional. However, we also say a curve is 1-dimensional, a curved surface is 2-dimensional. What similarities do the curved surfaces have in common with the plane that justify a dimension of 2?

We realize that although a curve is different from a straight line, but when we get to a point on a curve and look with a magnifying glass, a small neighborhood on the curve is similar to a neighborhood on a straight line. A small neighborhood on a curved surface is similar to a small neighborhood on a plane. This is exactly the root idea in calculus, when Newton and Leibniz first discovered it: using a straight line to approximate a curve in a small neighborhood and using a plane to approximate a curved surface in a small neighborhood. From this idea we come to the definition of topological manifolds.

Definition 1. Topological manifold

An n-dimensional **topological manifold** (or simply n-**manifold**) M is defined to be a Hausdorff topological space in which each point $p \in M$ has a neighborhood U_p homeomorphic to an open set of the Euclidean space $\mathbb{R}^n$.

Definition 2. Coordinate patch, atlas

Let M be a topological manifold. A pair (U, ψ) consisting of an open set U of M and a homeomorphism ψ onto an open set of $\mathbb{R}^n$ is called a **coordinate patch** (or **coordinate neighborhood**, or **local coordinate system**, or **chart**) of M. Let $p \in U$ and $\psi(p) =$

$(x_1, \ldots, x_n) \in \mathbb{R}^n$. $(x_1, \ldots, x_n)$ are called the **local coordinates** of point $p \in U$.

A family of coordinate patches $\mathscr{A} = \{(U_\alpha, \psi_\alpha)\}_{\alpha \in \Lambda}$ is called an **atlas** of M if $\{U_\alpha\}_{\alpha \in A}$ forms an open cover of M.

In an atlas $\{(U_\alpha, \psi_\alpha)\}_{\alpha \in \Lambda}$, Λ is the index set. By the definition of a topological manifold M, each point in $p \in M$ has a neighborhood U_p homeomorphic to an open set of $\mathbb{R}^n$. Simply let $\Lambda = M$. Then $\{U_p\}_{p \in M}$ is an open cover of M and $\{(U_\alpha, \psi_\alpha)\}_{\alpha \in M}$ is an atlas of M. However, since more than one points in M may share a neighborhood, it is possible to have an atlas consisting finite number of coordinate patches. Some simple manifolds can be covered by a single coordinate patch (Examples 1 and 2). Most manifolds cannot be possibly covered by a single coordinate patch, for example, the sphere S^2 (Example 3). So a topological manifold can be viewed as overlapping patches of $\mathbb{R}^n$ being glued together. Indeed, in geography, small pieces of paper are glued together to cover a sphere to make a globe. Globally, an n-manifold may or may not be topologically equivalent to $\mathbb{R}^n$. For example, the sphere S^2 and the torus are 2-manifolds but neither is homeomorphic to $\mathbb{R}^2$.

We can have families of coordinate lines in a coordinate patch, which is a grid of curves $x_i(t)$. If a point moves on a coordinate line $x_i(t)$, the value of x_i component changes while all other coordinates x_k $(k \neq i)$ keep constant.

Remark 1. Historical Note — The Term "Manifold"
The term "manifold" (German, Mannigfaltigkeit) was first introduced by B. Riemann.

Example 1. (Euclidean space $\mathbb{R}^n$) As a trivial example, the Euclidean space $\mathbb{R}^n$ itself is the prototype and an example of topological manifolds. $\mathbb{R}^n$ can be covered by a single patch.   ♣

Example 2. (Open submanifold) Let M be an open subset of $\mathbb{R}^n$. With the relative topology as a topological space, M is an n-dimensional manifold. An open submanifold can be covered by a single patch.   ♣

Example 3. (2-Sphere S^2) The 2-sphere S^2 is defined as a surface in $\mathbb{R}^3$:

$$S^2 = \{(x, y, z) \in \mathbb{R}^3 | x^2 + y^2 + z^2 = 1\}.$$

S^2 is a 2-manifold. For each point $p \in S^2$, we can define an open disk

$$U_p = \{q \in S^2 | \tilde{\rho}(q, p) < \delta\},$$

Figure 2.7 shows an immersion of the projective plane into $\mathbb{R}^3$ as a cross-cap. After glue the arcs AC and BD together, and glue AD and BC together on the equator, pinch both of them as one line segment, which coincide with the z axis, as in Figure 2.7 (a) and (b). The cross-cap has self intersections, which cannot be avoided in any immersion of the projective plane in $\mathbb{R}^3$.   ♣

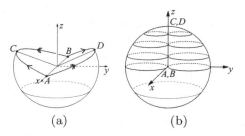

(a)   (b)

Figure 2.7   Cross-cap: immersion of the projective plane in $\mathbb{R}^3$.

Example 10. (3-Sphere S^3) We have defined 2-sphere S^2 as a subset of $\mathbb{R}^3$,

$$S^2 = \{(x, y, z) \in \mathbb{R}^3 | x^2 + y^2 + z^2 = 1\}.$$

The 3-sphere S^3 can be defined as a subset of $\mathbb{R}^4$, which is also called a hypersurface, and particularly a hypersphere in this case.

$$S^3 = \{(x, y, z, u) \in \mathbb{R}^4 | x^2 + y^2 + z^2 + u^2 = 1\}.$$

We want to emphasis on that when study the topological manifolds, we are not limited to subsets, or hypersurfaces of Euclidean spaces. We will show one way of constructing S^3 by gluing. Before that, we first show how to construct S^2 by gluing the boundaries of two identical disks. We start with two identical closed disks,

$$B^2 = \{(x, y) \in \mathbb{R}^2 | x^2 + y^2 \leq 1\}.$$

Then we glue the two boundaries, which are $S^1 = \{(x, y) \in \mathbb{R}^2 | x^2 + y^2 = 1\}$. Then we have a topological manifold equivalent to S^2. It is up to you whether you imagine that you blow air to inflate it or not (see Figure 2.8). With this analogy, we can construct S^3 by gluing as well. We start with two identical closed solid 3-ball B^3 in $\mathbb{R}^3$,

$$B^3 = \{(x, y, z) \in \mathbb{R}^3 | x^2 + y^2 + z^2 \leq 1\}.$$

We then glue the two boundary surfaces S^2 of the two 3-balls together. The resulting 3-manifold is S^3. It is much harder for us to imagine blowing air and inflating it in the 4-dimensional space, but we do not have to. The manifolds have a right to live outside any Euclidean spaces. George Gamow in his book *One, Two, Three, ..., Infinity* [Gamow (1947)], has an intuitive description which helps visualizing S^3. Imagine we have an apple and there are two worms living in it, one black and one white. The worms make tiny, microscopic, intricate and delicate channels in the apple and form two channel systems, which we call black channels and white channels. The two channel systems never meet inside the apple but only meet on the surface. A worm cannot enter the channels of the other worm unless it first comes out on the surface. The surface S^2 seems to be special since it is the inlet and outlet of the two channel systems, but in fact, this space is homogeneous, meaning each point is in the same position compared to other points. There is no center in this space and the points on the surface S^2 are just ordinary points as the points in the interior.   ♣

Figure 2.8 S^2 by gluing.

1.2   Classification of Curves and Surfaces

We describe the classification of curves and surfaces in this section. These are classical results and they are aesthetically pleasing. See Prof. Madhav Nori's comment at the epigraph of this chapter.

We begin with the following definition.

Definition 3. Closed manifold, open manifold

A compact topological manifold is called a **closed manifold**. A topological manifold is called an **open manifold**, if it has no connected component which is compact.

A closed manifold must not be confused with a closed set. The following theorem is the basic result about the topological classification of 1-manifolds.

Theorem 1. (Classification of curves)

(1) *Any compact connected curve is topologically equivalent to a circle S^1.*
(2) *Any non-compact connected curve is topologically equivalent to the real line $\mathbb{R}$.*

The following theorem gives a classification of compact connected surfaces. By surfaces, we mean abstract surfaces, namely 2-manifolds. It uses a term: connected sum, which we define as follows.

Definition 4. Connected sum of two manifolds

Let M_1 and M_2 be topological manifolds of dimension k. Remove a k-dimensional ball from each manifold and glue M_1 and M_2 together along the boundaries. The resulting manifold is called the **connected sum** of M_1 and M_2, denoted by $M_1 \# M_2$.

Figure 2.9 shows the connected sum of two tori.

Figure 2.9   Connected sum of two surfaces.

Theorem 2. (Classification of surfaces)

(1) *Any orientable connected closed surface is topologically equivalent to a sphere or connected sum of n ($n \geq 1$) tori.*
(2) *Any non-orientable connected closed surface is topologically equivalent to a connected sum of n ($n \geq 1$) projective planes.*

A torus is topologically equivalent to a sphere with one handle. The connected sum of two tori is topologically equivalent to a sphere with two handles. In general, the connected sum of n tori is topologically equivalent to a sphere with n handles. Alternatively, Theorem 2 (1) can be stated as follows.

Corollary. *Any orientable connected closed surface is topologically equivalent to a sphere with n ($n \geq 0$) handles.*

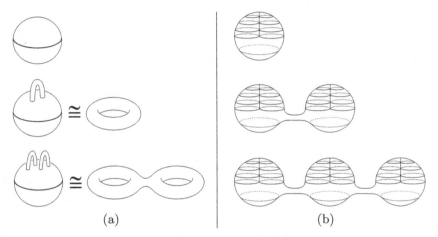

(a)   (b)

Figure 2.10   (a) Classification of orientable closed surfaces. (b) Classification of non-orientable closed surfaces.

For non-orientable closed surfaces, as shown in Figure 2.10 (b), the top is a projective plane and the one in the middle is topologically equivalent to a Klein bottle.

§2   Differentiable Manifolds

Differentiable manifolds are generalizations of smooth surfaces in $\mathbb{R}^n$. There are two ways to come to differentiable manifolds—from topological manifolds, or from curves and surfaces in $\mathbb{R}^n$. Differentiable manifolds have more structures than topological manifolds, but fewer structures than surfaces in $\mathbb{R}^n$. Therefore, we can get differentiable manifolds by starting with topological manifolds and adding differential structures; or by starting with surfaces in $\mathbb{R}^n$ but discarding the requirement of embedding in Euclidean spaces and discarding the concept of distance on surfaces.

In order to model the concept of smoothness on manifolds, we need to add more constraints—the smooth compatibility of overlapping patches. The study of differentiable manifolds is considered differential topology. This is still one step away from geometry, until the metric is added. A differentiable manifold with a metric structure (distance) becomes Riemannian manifold (§3). Until then, curvature cannot be defined, because curvature depends on distance (metric structure, §3), or parallelism (affine structure, §4).

2.1   Differentiable Manifolds

Let $\mathscr{A} = \{(U_\alpha, \psi_\alpha)\}_{\alpha \in \Lambda}$ be an atlas of a topological manifold M. If (U_α, ψ_α) and (U_β, ψ_β) are two overlapping patches, in the overlapping region $U \overset{\text{def}}{=} U_\alpha \cap U_\beta$, each point p has two sets of local coordinates $(x_1 \ldots, x_n)$ and $(y_1, \ldots, y_n)$. There is an induced **local coordinate transformation,** $\Phi :$ $\psi_\alpha(U) \to \psi_\beta(U)$, such that $(x_1, \ldots, x_n) \mapsto (y_1, \ldots, y_n)$. Φ is a mapping from an open set of $\mathbb{R}^n$ to an open set of $\mathbb{R}^n$.

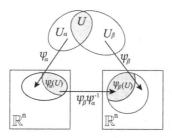

Figure 2.11   Local coordinate transformation.

Let $f : M \to \mathbb{R}$ be a real valued function. We are familiar with the differentiability of functions from $\mathbb{R}^n$ to $\mathbb{R}$, or from $\mathbb{R}^n$ to $\mathbb{R}^n$. Can we define the differentiability of $f : M \to \mathbb{R}$? Although the topological manifold M is different from Euclidean space $\mathbb{R}^n$, it is equipped with local coordinates. We are attempted to define the differentiability of $f : M \to \mathbb{R}$ using local coordinates. Let (U_α, ψ_α) be a local coordinate patch. Let $p \in U_\alpha$ have local coordinates $(x_1, \ldots, x_n)$. The mapping $f : M \to \mathbb{R}; p \mapsto z$ induces a mapping $f \circ \psi_\alpha^{-1}$ from an open set of $\mathbb{R}^n$ to $\mathbb{R}$ such that $(x_1, \ldots, x_n) \mapsto$

z. We could define that f is differentiable at point p, if the coordinate representation $f \circ \psi_\alpha^{-1}$ of the mapping f is differentiable at point p.

One question arises: if p is in the intersection of two coordinate patches (U_α, ψ_α) and (U_β, ψ_β), is this definition of differentiability dependent of the choice of local coordinates? If the answer is no then this attempted definition should fail. However, the good news is, if the local coordinate transformations are all differentiable in the overlapping regions, the definition of differentiability of f does not depend on the choice of local coordinates.

Definition 5. Compatible patches

Two patches (U_α, ψ_α) and (U_β, ψ_β) of a topological manifold M are said to be (**smoothly**) **compatible**, if $U_\alpha \cap U_\beta = \varnothing$, or otherwise, the induced local coordinate transformation $\Phi : \psi_\alpha(U) \to \psi_\beta(U)$ is continuously differentiable to any order, where $U \overset{\text{def}}{=} U_\alpha \cap U_\beta$ (Figure 2.11).

Definition 6. Compatible atlas

An atlas $\mathscr{A}$ of a topological manifold M is called a (**smoothly**) **compatible atlas**, if any two patches in $\mathscr{A}$ are (smoothly) compatible.

By continuously differentiable to any order, we mean the coordinate transformation has continuous partial derivatives up to any order. It is also called C^∞ differentiable.

This condition can be relaxed to C^r differentiable. The coordinate transformation is said to be C^r differentiable if it has continuous derivatives up to the rth order. If the coordinate transformation between any two overlapping patches is C^r differentiable, then the atlas $\mathscr{A}$ is said to be C^r **compatible**.

Example 11. (Counterexample — incompatible atlas of a circle) Most of the atlases of the familiar topological manifolds that we encounter everyday are compatible, like those in the examples in §1. We give a somewhat contrived example of incompatible atlas here. Given the unit circle $S^1 = \{(x, y) \in \mathbb{R}^2 | x^2 + y^2 = 1\}$, let θ be the angle that a point on S^1 makes with the x axis (Figure 2.12). We use four overlapping patches to cover the circle, each being an open arc of half of a circle.

$$U_1 = \{p \in S^1 \mid -\frac{3\pi}{4} < \theta(p) < \frac{\pi}{4}\}, \ \psi_1(p) = \theta,$$

$$U_2 = \{p \in S^1 \mid -\frac{\pi}{4} < \theta(p) < \frac{3\pi}{4}\}, \ \psi_2(p) = \theta^3,$$

$$U_3 = \{p \in S^1 \mid \frac{\pi}{4} < \theta(p) < \frac{5\pi}{4}\}, \ \psi_3(p) = \theta,$$

$$U_4 = \{p \in S^1 \mid \frac{3\pi}{4} < \theta(p) < \frac{7\pi}{4}\}, \ \psi_4(p) = \theta.$$

In the overlapping region $U_1 \cap U_2 = \{p \in S^1 \mid -\frac{\pi}{4} < \theta(p) < \frac{\pi}{4}\}$, the same point p has coordinate θ in patch (U_1, ψ_1) but has coordinate θ^3 in patch (U_2, ψ_2). The induced mapping $\Phi : \psi_2(U_1 \cap U_2) \to \psi_1(U_1 \cap U_2)$ is defined by $\theta \mapsto \sqrt[3]{\theta}$. The real function $\theta \mapsto \sqrt[3]{\theta}$ is not differentiable at $\theta = 0$ and hence patches (U_1, ψ_1) and (U_2, ψ_2) are not compatible. $\{(U_\alpha, \psi_\alpha)\}_{\alpha=1}^{4}$ is an atlas for S^1 as a topological manifold but the atlas is not smoothly compatible. ♣

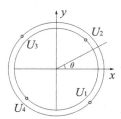

Figure 2.12   An incompatible atlas of a circle.

Definition 7. Differentiable manifold

A topological manifold M together with a compatible atlas $\mathscr{A}$ is called a **differentiable manifold** (or **smooth manifold**), denoted by $(M, \mathscr{A})$. $\mathscr{A}$ is called a **differentiable structure** (or **smooth structure**) on M.

Remark 2. Insight — Intrinsic View vs Extrinsic View

Definition 7 is also known as the definition of an abstract manifold, or the gluing patch construction. A differentiable manifold (as well as a topological manifold) is not defined as a subset of a Euclidean space and hence it is more general and more abstract. Some students have a misconception: a sphere is a differentiable manifold while a cube surface is a topological manifold but not a differentiable manifold because a cube has corners. This is the extrinsic view. The cube can be endowed a smooth structure and hence we will not be able to tell the difference between a cube and a sphere. The difference between a cube and a sphere in $\mathbb{R}^3$ is only the different ways of embedding into $\mathbb{R}^3$. This intrinsic definition of differentiable manifold is the standard definition adopted by almost all the textbooks today, except *Differential Topology* by V. Guillemin and A. Pollack [Guillemin and Pollack (1974)], where the extrinsic definition as subsets of a Euclidean space is used for pedagogical purposes. Due to Whitney's embedding theorem (which says any abstract differentiable manifold can be smoothly embedded in a Euclidean space), the extrinsic definition does not lose much generality. The difference between the intrinsic and extrinsic definition is really the philosophical view. The intrinsic definition reflects the rebellion from the philosophy that the Euclidean space is the God-given space and is a universal container. The intrinsic view says that Euclidean space is nothing but local approximation of the space of the real world. This rebellion started as early as 1930s with the discovery of non-Euclidean geometry.

It is interesting to reflect on our everyday experience on the earth — the sphere we are too familiar with, from the perspective of everyday language. In the English language, the word "sky" is often used in the plural form, like in "You make me happy when skies are gray." This raises a question: "How many skies are there?" Well, we cannot count the exact number of skies because the boundary separating one sky and another is not clearly defined. However, the usage of the word "sky" as a plural form does coincide with the idea of manifold. In this usage, a sky is understood as a patch that covers part of the earth and these patches can overlap. All together, these patches, or skies cover the entire sphere.

Remark 3. Historical Note/Philosophy/Cross Link — Differentiable Manifolds/Old Theorems Turn into Definitions

The idea of manifold with intrinsic construction is due to B. Riemann, which is now known as Riemannian manifold, although Riemann did not have the modern language to make it precise, and Riemann automatically assumed the metric structure on the manifold. The concept of differentiable manifold is the Riemannian manifold with the distance concept stripped and it only appeared explicitly in 1913 in the work of Hermann Weyl ([Kline (1972)] p. 37). The intrinsic nature of descriptions of differentiable manifold and Riemannian manifold is the same. The key in Definition 7 is the smoothness of local coordinate transformations. This definition is due to Whitney in 1930s. For regular surfaces in $\mathbb{R}^3$, this is a theorem (Part II Chap. 2 Theorem 1) but when it is generalized, it must be asserted as an axiom. M. do Carmo offers some insight ([do Carmo (1976)] p. 425), "Historically, it took a long time to appear, probably due to the fact that the fundamental role of the change of parameters in the definition of a surface in $\mathbb{R}^3$ was not clearly understood." We should appreciate Edwin Hewitt's comment (see the epigraph of this chapter): "Old theorems never die; they turn into definitions." Examples of this kind abound. In Part I Chap. 1, Definition 3 (linear space) is modeled on Theorem 1. In Part III Chap. 1, Definition 8 (metric space) is modeled on Theorem 1 and Definition 12 (topological space) is modeled on Theorem 5. Also in this present chapter, you will see that Definition 44 (affinely-connected manifold) is modeled on Theorem 13. If you recognize the connections between the abstract definitions and the old theorems of the concrete systems, your life will be a lot easier.

If a topological manifold M has a C^r compatible atlas $\mathscr{A}$, the pair $(M, \mathscr{A})$ is called a **differentiable manifold of class** C^r (or C^r-

manifold). $\mathscr{A}$ is called a **differential structure** (or **differentiable structure**) **of class** C^r (or C^r-**structure**).

In our context, a smooth structure means a C^∞-structure and a differentiable manifold (or smooth manifold) means a C^∞-manifold.

Definition 8. Equivalent differential structures

Two differential structures $\mathscr{A}$ and $\mathscr{A}'$ are said to be equivalent, if $\mathscr{A} \cup \mathscr{A}'$ is also a compatible atlas.

In such a case we say $\mathscr{A}$ and $\mathscr{A}'$ define the same differential structure. Let $(M, \mathscr{A})$ be a differentiable manifold and $\tilde{\mathscr{A}}$ be the set of all patches that are compatible with $\mathscr{A}$. $\tilde{\mathscr{A}}$ is called the **maximal atlas** containing $\mathscr{A}$.

Remark 4. In the definition of a differentiable manifold, some authors [Chern et al. (1999); Boothby (2002); do Carmo (1992)] also require that the atlas be maximal. This requirement of maximality offers convenience to the discussion but is not essential to the definition of the concept because any atlas $\mathscr{A}$ can be easily extended to a maximal atlas $\tilde{\mathscr{A}}$ by adding all the compatible patches. Our definition agrees with EDM [MSJ (1993)] and Arnold [Arnold (1997)].

In the following, we give some examples of differentiable manifolds.

Example 12. (Euclidean space $\mathbb{R}^n$) This is a trivial case of a smooth manifold. $\mathbb{R}^n$ itself is an open set. So $\mathbb{R}^n$ can be covered by a single patch, which is the Cartesian coordinates. There are alternative atlases to cover $\mathbb{R}^n$, other than the single patch Cartesian coordinates. They are known as curvilinear coordinates. For $\mathbb{R}^2$, some of the familiar curvilinear coordinate systems include polar coordinates, elliptic coordinates, parabolic coordinates, equilateral hyperbolic coordinates and bipolar coordinates. For $\mathbb{R}^3$, cylindrical coordinates, spherical coordinates and ellipsoidal coordinates are often used. ♣

Example 13. (2-sphere S^2) In Example 3, we gave three atlases $\mathscr{A}$, $\mathscr{B}$ and $\mathscr{C}$. Each is a compatible atlas. $\mathscr{A}$, $\mathscr{B}$ and $\mathscr{C}$ are equivalent differential structures and we do not need to distinguish them. They are all part of a maximal atlas. $\mathscr{B}$ and $\mathscr{C}$ with few patches are more convenient for practical use. The sphere S^2 with this differential structure is a differentiable manifold. ♣

Just like homeomorphisms preserve the topological structures, the mappings that preserve the differential structures on differentiable manifolds are called diffeomorphisms, which we will define in the following.

Let M and N be C^∞-manifolds. A mapping $\varphi : M \to N; p \mapsto q$ induces a mapping f from p's coordinate neighborhood to q's coordinate neighborhood. This induced mapping is a mapping from an open set of $\mathbb{R}^n$ to an open set of $\mathbb{R}^m$ and it is called the **coordinate representation** of mapping φ.

Definition 9. Differentiable mapping

Let M and N be C^∞-manifolds. A mapping $\varphi : M \to N$ is called a **differentiable mapping of class** C^r (or C^r-**mapping**) if all the coordinate representations of φ are differentiable mappings of class C^r.

Because the atlas of a C^∞-manifold is C^∞-compatible, we know the definition of differentiable mapping does not depend on what coordinate representation we choose. This justifies the motivation of the smoothness condition of the local coordinate transformation in the definition of differentiable manifold (Definition 7).

Definition 10. Diffeomorphic mapping

Let M and N be C^∞-manifolds. An invertible mapping $\varphi : M \to N$ is called a **diffeomorphic mapping** (or **diffeomorphism**) of class C^r, if both φ and its inverse φ^{-1} are differentiable mappings of class C^r.

Two differentiable manifolds are said to be **diffeomorphic** to each other, if there exists a diffeomorphism between them.

A diffeomorphism is always a homeomorphism, because a differentiable mapping is always a continuous mapping.

Remark 5. Elaboration — Distinct Differential Structures up to Diffeomorphism

Let $\mathscr{A}$ and $\mathscr{A}'$ be two differential structures on differentiable manifold M. The condition $\mathscr{A}$ and $\mathscr{A}'$ being equivalent is stronger than that differentiable manifolds $(M, \mathscr{A})$ and $(M, \mathscr{A}')$ being diffeomorphic. There are examples that differential structures $\mathscr{A}$ and $\mathscr{A}'$ are not equivalent but the differentiable manifolds $(M, \mathscr{A})$ and $(M, \mathscr{A}')$ are diffeomorphic. The condition $\mathscr{A}$ and $\mathscr{A}'$ being equivalent requires the identity mapping being diffeomorphic. For example, in $\mathbb{R}$, the single-patch atlas $x \mapsto x$ and another single-patch atlas $x \mapsto x^3$ are two distinct differential structures that are not equivalent to each other. However, the two differential structures are diffeomorphic to each other. So when we classify differential structures on the same underlying topological manifold, we are concerned with distinct differential structures up to diffeomorphism, instead of being equivalent.

If a topological manifold M has an atlas $\mathscr{A}$, but $\mathscr{A}$ is not a compatible atlas, then $(M, \mathscr{A})$ is not a differentiable manifold. However, this does not rule out the possibility that we can endow M another atlas $\mathscr{A}'$ and make $(M, \mathscr{A}')$ a differentiable manifold. There are topological manifolds that do not admit any smooth structures to become differentiable manifolds [Kervaire (1960)]. There are also topological manifolds that admit more than one distinct differential structures, which are not diffeomorphic to each other. The first such example was the 7-sphere S^7 given by J. Milnor [Milnor (1956)] known as the Milnor exotic sphere. All $\mathbb{R}^n$ ($n \neq 4$) have a unique differential structure up to diffeomorphism. $\mathbb{R}^4$ has exotic differential structures other than the standard differential structure [Donaldson and Kronheimer (1990)].

2.2   Tangent Spaces

Tangent spaces of a differentiable manifold are the high dimensional generalizations of tangent planes of a surface in $\mathbb{R}^3$. However, since the "expulsion from the garden of Eden", things have become more difficult. The garden of Eden refers to the surrounding Euclidean space $\mathbb{R}^n$, which we have been taken for granted. Now we decided to pursue an intrinsic view and not to rely on the surrounding Euclidean space.

Let us first have a review of what life was like in the Garden of Eden — the Euclidean spaces. Look at the 2-sphere S^2 in $\mathbb{R}^3$ defined as a subset of points $(x_1, x_2, x_3) \in \mathbb{R}^3$: $x_1^2 + x_2^2 + x_3^2 = 1$.

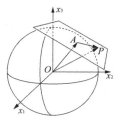

Figure 2.13   Tangent plane of a sphere.

At any point $A = (a_1, a_2, a_3)$ on the sphere, $\mathbf{a} = \overrightarrow{OA} = (a_1, a_2, a_3)$ is a normal vector of the surface. Let $\xi = (\xi_1, \xi_2, \xi_3) \in \mathbb{R}^3$ be a point P in the tangent plane at A. The vector

$$\overrightarrow{AP} = \overrightarrow{OP} - \overrightarrow{OA} = (\xi_1 - a_1, \xi_2 - a_2, \xi_3 - a_3)$$

is called a tangent vector. Any tangent vector in the tangent plane is perpendicular to the normal vector $\mathbf{a}$ and hence $\mathbf{a} \cdot \overrightarrow{AP} = 0$. This is the equation of the tangent plane,

$$a_1(\xi_1 - a_1) + a_2(\xi_2 - a_2) + a_3(\xi_3 - a_3) = 0.$$

This can be simplified to

$$a_1\xi_1 + a_2\xi_2 + a_3\xi_3 = 1.$$

For the tangent plane, if we move the origin to A, and a point in the tangent plane has coordinates $\xi' = (\xi'_1, \xi'_2, \xi'_3)$, then the equation of the tangent plane is

$$a_1\xi'_1 + a_2\xi'_2 + a_3\xi'_3 = 0.$$

When a surface in $\mathbb{R}^3$ is generalized to a hypersurface (differentiable manifold) in $\mathbb{R}^n$, the concept of tangent plane is generalized to tangent space, or tangent hyperplane. For example, we can have a 3-sphere S^3 defined as a subset of points $(x_1, x_2, x_3, x_4) \in \mathbb{R}^4$,

$$x_1^2 + x_2^2 + x_3^2 + x_4^2 = 1.$$

At any point $A = (a_1, a_2, a_3, a_4)$ on S^3, $\mathbf{a} = \overrightarrow{OA} = (a_1, a_2, a_3, a_4)$ is a normal vector. We have a 3-dimensional hyperplane in $\mathbb{R}^4$, called the tangent space of S^3 at point A. Let $\xi = (\xi_1, \xi_2, \xi_3, \xi_4)$ be a point P in the tangent space at A. The vector

$$\overrightarrow{AP} = \overrightarrow{OP} - \overrightarrow{OA} = (\xi_1 - a_1, \xi_2 - a_2, \xi_3 - a_3, \xi_4 - a_4)$$

is called a tangent vector. Any tangent vector in the tangent space is perpendicular to the normal vector $\mathbf{a}$ and hence $\mathbf{a} \cdot \overrightarrow{AP} = 0$. This is the equation of the tangent space, which can be simplified to

$$a_1\xi_1 + a_2\xi_2 + a_3\xi_3 + a_4\xi_4 = 1.$$

It is a 3-dimensional hyperplane in $\mathbb{R}^4$. If we move the origin of space to A, the equation of the tangent space becomes

$$a_1\xi'_1 + a_2\xi'_2 + a_3\xi'_3 + a_4\xi'_4 = 0$$

in the new coordinates.

This is the traditional extrinsic view before Riemann. Riemann steered the direction of differential geometry toward higher dimensions in a completely intrinsic way. In the intrinsic approach, we have abandoned the Euclidean space as a container for the differentiable manifolds. The normal direction or normal vector of the differentiable manifold at a point is forever gone.

Can we still define the tangent space of a differentiable manifold? It turns out that we can still manage to recover the concept of tangent space without going out of the manifold, but we just need to look at them from another perspective.

We start with surfaces in $\mathbb{R}^3$. Higher dimensions are just similar. This alternative perspective is something that we have already happily accepted. That is, in an "infinitesimal neighborhood", the surface is approximately flat, and the tangent plane is the linear approximation of the surface. This agrees with our everyday experience on earth. When you sit on a boat on the lake, the lake looks flat, although you know that Christopher Columbus has discovered that the lake is part of the surface of a sphere. The tangent plane is in fact an infinite plane, but we can linearly extend the "infinitesimal neighborhood" of the surface to make it an infinite tangent plane.

Observe the curves passing a point p on the surface in $\mathbb{R}^3$. Hereafter when we say a curve, we always mean a smooth curve. Each curve has a velocity vector which is tangent to the curve at p. The tangent plane at p consists of all these velocity vectors tangent to various curves passing p. We use a position vector $\mathbf{r} = (x, y, z) \in \mathbb{R}^3$ to represent a point on the surface. A parametrized curve is a smooth mapping $\gamma : \mathbb{R} \to M$, where M is the surface. We are a little sloppy with the notation $\gamma : \mathbb{R} \to M$ because we are only concerned with an infinitesimal segment of the curve centered at p. When you see $\mathbb{R}$, just understand it as a small interval of $\mathbb{R}$. Let $p = \gamma(0) = \mathbf{r}(0)$, and $\mathbf{r}(t) = \gamma(t) = (x(t), y(t), z(t))$ is a nearby point on the curve.

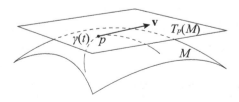

Figure 2.14   Tangent vectors and tangent plane.

The tangent vector at point p which is tangent to curve γ is the velocity vector

$$\mathbf{v} = \frac{d\mathbf{r}(t)}{dt}\Big|_{t=0} = \lim_{t \to 0} \frac{\mathbf{r}(t) - \mathbf{r}(0)}{t}.$$

The tangent vector $\mathbf{v}$ thus defined is a vector in $\mathbb{R}^3$. All the tangent vectors at point p which is tangent to some curve passing p form a plane, which is the tangent plane at p.

For an abstract manifold, we no longer have the containing $\mathbb{R}^3$ or $\mathbb{R}^n$. We can no longer define a tangent vector living in $\mathbb{R}^3$, but we can use the curves $\gamma : \mathbb{R} \to M$ on the manifold. Let $p' = \gamma(t)$ be a nearby point of point $p = \gamma(0)$. We cannot use $\lim_{t \to 0} \frac{\gamma(t) - \gamma(0)}{t}$ or $\frac{d\gamma(t)}{dt}$ anymore. On the abstract manifold, subtraction of two points p and p', as well as the scalar multiplication by a real number $\frac{1}{t}$ is undefined!

Observe a family of curves that are all tangent to each other at point p. What they have in common is that their velocities at p are all in the same direction. How do we define that the two curves having the same velocities? We realized that although we have lost the surrounding Euclidean space $\mathbb{R}^n$, we still have another Euclidean space to our assistance. That is, a manifold is locally modeled on a Euclidean space $\mathbb{R}^k$, which provides the local coordinate system. This is the intuitive idea of the following formal definition.

Definition 11. Equivalent curves

Let M be a differentiable manifold and $p \in M$. Two curves $\gamma : \mathbb{R} \to M$ and $\lambda : \mathbb{R} \to M$ on M are said to be **equivalent** at point p if

(1) $\gamma(0) = \lambda(0) = p$, and
(2) $\lim_{t \to 0} \frac{\mathbf{u}(t)}{t} = \lim_{t \to 0} \frac{\mathbf{v}(t)}{t}$ in some coordinate patch, where $\mathbf{u}(t)$ and $\mathbf{v}(t)$ are the local coordinates of points $\gamma(t)$ and $\lambda(t)$.

It can be verified that this definition does not depend on the choice of local coordinates.

Definition 12. Tangent vector

A **tangent vector** at $p \in M$ is defined to be an equivalence class of curves $\gamma : \mathbb{R} \to M$, with $\gamma(0) = p$. We denote the equivalence class of curve γ by $[\gamma]$.

Remark 6. Cross Link — The Battle of the Curved and the Straight
See a comment in Remark 14 in Section 3.

From the experience with surfaces in $\mathbb{R}^3$, we expect that the set of newly abstractly defined tangent vectors form a linear space. However, we need to overcome a little technical difficulty. For two curves $\gamma_1(t)$ and $\gamma_2(t)$ and real numbers $a \in \mathbb{R}$, neither $\gamma_1(t) + \gamma_2(t)$, nor $a\gamma_1(t)$ is defined on M because M itself is not a linear space. We can make use of the local coordinates to define this.

Definition 13. Tangent space

Let $[\gamma], [\lambda], [\gamma_1], [\gamma_2]$ be tangent vectors on M at point p. Suppose in some coordinate patch, $\gamma(t), \lambda(t), \gamma_1(t), \gamma_2(t)$ have coordinates $\mathbf{x}(t), \mathbf{y}(t), \mathbf{x}_1(t), \mathbf{x}_2(t) \in \mathbb{R}^n$ respectively. If in this patch, $\frac{d}{dt}\mathbf{x}(t)|_{t=0} = \frac{d}{dt}(\mathbf{x}_1(t) + \mathbf{x}_2(t))|_{t=0}$, then we define $[\gamma] \overset{\text{def}}{=} [\gamma_1] + [\gamma_2]$. If for a real number $a \in \mathbb{R}$, $\frac{d}{dt}\mathbf{x}(t)|_{t=0} = a\frac{d}{dt}\mathbf{y}(t)|_{t=0}$, then we define $[\gamma] \overset{\text{def}}{=} a[\lambda]$.

It can be verified the tangent vectors at point $p \in M$ form a linear space of dimension n. This linear space is called the **tangent space** of M at point p, denoted by $T_p(M)$.

We need to validate this definition by verifying the definition is independent of choice of the coordinate patch, and independent of choice of the representatives of the curves. This is left as exercise.

In a local coordinate system $(x_1, \ldots, x_n)$, the coordinate lines passing point p, form a basis for the tangent space at p, which is called the **natural basis**. A coordinate line $\gamma_i(t)$ is the curve on which the value x_i varies while other coordinates x_k ($k \neq i$) keep constant. Namely, the basis vector $\gamma_i(t)$ is defined to be the equivalent class represented by the curve

$$x_k(t) = \begin{cases} t & \text{for } k = i, \\ 0 & \text{for } k \neq i, \end{cases}$$

for $k = 1, \ldots, n$. In natural basis, a tangent vector $[\gamma]$ represented by curve $\gamma(t)$ has components $(\dot{x}_1, \ldots, \dot{x}_n)$, where $\dot{x}_i$ is the shorthand for $\frac{dx_i}{dt}|_{t=0}$.

Tangent vectors are used to define directional derivatives. Recall in calculus, we define the directional derivatives of a scalar field in $\mathbb{R}^n$. A scalar field in $\mathbb{R}^n$ is defined to be a function $f : \mathbb{R}^n \to \mathbb{R}$, which assigns a real number to each point in $\mathbb{R}^n$. Let $x_0 \in \mathbb{R}^n$ be a point in $\mathbb{R}^n$, $v \in \mathbb{R}^n$ be a vector, and $f : \mathbb{R}^n \to \mathbb{R}$ a smooth scalar field. The derivative of f in the direction of v at point x_0 is defined to be

$$\nabla_v f|_{x_0} = \frac{d}{dt} \left(f(x_0 + vt) \right)|_{t=0}.$$

It is easy to show that

$$\nabla_v f|_{x_0} = \sum_{i=1}^{n} v_i \frac{\partial f(x)}{\partial x_i}|_{x_0},$$

where v_i is the ith component of v.

On a surface $M \subset \mathbb{R}^3$, a scalar field on M is defined to be a function $f : M \to \mathbb{R}$, which assigns a real number to each point on the surface. Note that f is defined on the surface M, instead of $\mathbb{R}^3$. Let $x_0 \in M$ be a point on M. Although a tangent vector $v \in \mathbb{R}^3$ of M at p is defined, $x_0 + vt$ is no longer a point on the surface M for any $t \neq 0$ and hence $f(x_0 + vt)$ does not have a definition. To define the directional derivative of a scalar field on a surface, we need to use the curve in an infinitesimal neighborhood of x_0 on the surface to serve as the direction. We do the same for differentiable manifold in general. A scalar field on a differentiable manifold M is defined to be a function $f : M \to \mathbb{R}$, which assigns a real number to each point on the manifold. The tangent vectors have been defined to be the equivalent classes of curves on M. They are just good to serve as directions to define directional derivatives of a scalar field on M.

Definition 14. Directional derivative of a scalar field

Let $f : M \to \mathbb{R}$ be a smooth scalar field on a differentiable manifold M. Let $\gamma(t)$ be a curve on M passing $p = \gamma(0)$ and $p' = \gamma(\Delta t)$, and v be the tangent vector $[\gamma]$. The **directional derivative** of f at point p along vector v is defined to be the real number

$$\nabla_v f|_p \overset{\text{def}}{=} \frac{d}{dt} \left(f(\gamma(t)) \right)|_{t=0} \overset{\text{def}}{=} \lim_{\Delta t \to 0} \frac{f(p') - f(p)}{\Delta t}.$$

When the point p is understood in the context, we also write $\nabla_v f|_p$ as $\nabla_v f$ for short.

Let $\mathcal{F}(M)$ be the set of all smooth scalar fields $f : M \to \mathbb{R}$. The directional derivative $\nabla_v f$ of a smooth scalar field f along a vector field

v can be defined to be another smooth scalar field using the point-wise rule. The directional derivative ∇_v can be viewed as an operator acting on $\mathcal{F}(M)$.

Theorem 3. (Properties of directional derivatives) *Let v be a tangent vector at $p \in M$. Let $a, b \in \mathbb{R}$ and $f, g : M \to \mathbb{R}$ be smooth scalar fields on M. Then*

(1) $\nabla_v(af + bg) = a\nabla_v f + b\nabla_v g$ (ℝ-linear),
(2) $\nabla_v(fg) = f\nabla_v g + g\nabla_v f$ (Leibniz rule).

The tangent vectors v and directional derivative operators ∇_v have a one-to-one correspondence. We can identify the tangent vector v with the directional derivative operator ∇_v. We can even start with defining tangent vectors as operators on $\mathcal{F}(M)$ that satisfy the two rules in Theorem 3, which is a more abstract approach adopted in many books.

Using the local coordinates $(x_1, \ldots, x_n)$, any directional derivative operator can be written in the form

$$\nabla_v = \sum_{i=1}^{n} a_i \frac{\partial}{\partial x_i},$$

where $a_i \in \mathbb{R}$ are real numbers. The operators $\nabla_i \overset{\text{def}}{=} \nabla_{\gamma_i} \overset{\text{def}}{=} \frac{\partial}{\partial x_i}$, $i = 1, \ldots, n$, form a basis for the tangent space, which is the natural basis. $\frac{\partial}{\partial x_i}$ is the operator notation while γ_i is the curve notation of the ith basis vector.

A vector field on a differentiable manifold M is a mapping that assigns a tangent vector to each point on M. The set of all smooth vector fields on M is denoted by $\mathfrak{X}(M)$.

Let $X \in \mathfrak{X}(M)$ be a vector field on M and $f : M \to \mathbb{R}$ a smooth scalar field on M. For each vector $X(p)$ at point $p \in M$, the directional derivative $\nabla_{X(p)} f$ is defined at p. Using this point-wise operation, for all the vectors X, $\nabla_X f$ is a scalar field on M.

It can be shown that, for any two vector fields $X, Y \in \mathfrak{X}(M)$, there is a unique vector field Z, such that for all $f \in \mathcal{F}(M)$, $\nabla_Z f = \nabla_X(\nabla_Y f) - \nabla_Y(\nabla_X f)$.

Definition 15. Lie bracket of two vector fields

Let $X, Y, Z \in \mathfrak{X}(M)$ be vector fields on a differentiable manifold

M. If for all $f \in \mathcal{F}(M)$,

$$\nabla_Z f = \nabla_X(\nabla_Y f) - \nabla_Y(\nabla_X f),$$

we denote $Z = [X, Y]$, and call it the **Lie bracket** (or **Poisson bracket**) of X and Y.

If the tangent vectors X, Y, Z are identified with the directional derivative operators $\nabla_X, \nabla_Y, \nabla_Z$, we come up with an equivalent definition.

Definition 16. (Alternative Definition) Lie bracket of two vector fields

Let $X, Y \in \mathfrak{X}(M)$ be vector fields on a differentiable manifold M. The **Lie bracket** (or **Poisson bracket**) of X and Y is defined to be

$$[X, Y] \overset{\text{def}}{=} XY - YX.$$

Theorem 4. *Let $X, Y, Z \in \mathfrak{X}(M)$ be vector fields on a differentiable manifold M and $Z = [X, Y]$. In local coordinates $(x_1, \ldots, x_n)$, if X, Y, Z have coordinates $(X_1, \ldots, X_n)$, $(Y_1, \ldots, Y_n)$ and $(Z_1, \ldots, Z_n)$ respectively, then*

$$Z_i = \sum_{k=1}^{n} \left(X_k \frac{\partial Y_i}{\partial x_k} - Y_k \frac{\partial X_i}{\partial x_k} \right).$$

Theorem 5. (Properties of Lie bracket) *Let $a_1, a_2 \in \mathbb{R}$ and $f, g \in \mathcal{F}(M)$.*

(1) $\mathbb{R}$-bilinear:
   $[a_1 X_1 + a_2 X_2, Y] = a_1[X_1, Y] + a_2[X_2, Y],$
   $[X, a_1 Y_1 + a_2 Y_2] = a_1[X, Y_1] + a_2[X, Y_2].$
(2) Antisymmetric: $[X, Y] = -[Y, X].$
(3) Jacobi identity: $[X, [Y, Z]] + [Z, [X, Y]] + [Y, [Z, X]] = 0.$
(4) $[fX, gY] = fg[X, Y] + fX(g)Y - gY(f)X.$

Let $\varphi : M \to N$ be a differentiable mapping and γ be a curve on M passing $p \in M$. φ maps the curve γ to a curve γ' on N, where $\gamma' : \mathbb{R} \to N$

and $\gamma' = \varphi \circ \gamma$. Naturally it also maps the velocity vector of γ to the velocity vector of γ'. But rigorously, the latter mapping is not φ itself, but rather a mapping $(d\varphi)_p$ induced by φ, which is called the differential of φ and which we define as follows. Abstractly a tangent vector is defined as an equivalence class of curves, but it always helps to think intuitively that the tangent vectors are velocity vectors, in local coordinates.

Definition 17. Differential of a mapping

Let M and N be C^∞-manifolds and $\varphi : M \to N$ be a differentiable mapping (of class C^r). We define a mapping $(d\varphi)_p : T_p(M) \to T_{\varphi(p)}(N)$ induced by φ as follows: for any tangent vector $[\gamma] \in T_p(M)$ represented by curve $\gamma : \mathbb{R} \to M$,

$$(d\varphi)_p [\gamma] \overset{\text{def}}{=} [\varphi \circ \gamma],$$

where $\varphi \circ \gamma : \mathbb{R} \to N$ is a curve on N passing $\varphi(p)$. $(d\varphi)_p$ thus defined is a linear mapping from $T_p(M)$ to $T_{\varphi(p)}(N)$ and is called the **differential** (or **derivative**, or **tangent mapping**) of φ at point p.

$(d\varphi)_p$ can be extended to the tangent bundle $T(M)$ point-wisely. $d\varphi : T(M) \to T(N)$ is called the **differential** of φ on M. (Tangent bundle will be defined in Definition 18.)

Remark 7. Alternative Notations. Some authors use another notation φ_{*p} for $(d\varphi)_p$ and φ_* for $d\varphi$.

Let $\varphi : M \to N$ be a differentiable mapping, and let $(d\varphi)_p$ be the differential induced by φ at point $p \in M$. Suppose we choose a local coordinate system in a neighborhood of p on M, and a local coordinate system in a neighborhood of $q = \varphi(p)$. Suppose p has local coordinates $(x_1, \ldots, x_m)$ and $q = \varphi(p)$ has local coordinates $(y_1, \ldots, y_n)$. The differentiable mapping φ is represented by n differentiable functions $(F_1, \ldots, F_n)$ from $\mathbb{R}^m$ to $\mathbb{R}^n$, such that

$$y_1 = F_1(x_1, \ldots, x_m),$$
$$\cdots$$
$$y_n = F_n(x_1, \ldots, x_m).$$

Theorem 6. *The differential $(d\varphi)_p$ of differentiable mapping $\varphi : M \to N$ is a linear mapping from $T_p(M)$ to $T_{\varphi(p)}(N)$. In local coordinates, if φ is represented by $(F_1, ..., F_n)$, then its differential $(d\varphi)_p$ is represented by the Jacobian matrix*

$$\begin{bmatrix} \frac{\partial F_1}{\partial x_1} & \cdots & \frac{\partial F_1}{\partial x_m} \\ \cdots & \cdots & \cdots \\ \frac{\partial F_n}{\partial x_1} & \cdots & \frac{\partial F_n}{\partial x_m} \end{bmatrix}.$$

Let us look at some special cases of Definition 17.

Case (1): if $M = N = \mathbb{R}$, then $\varphi : \mathbb{R} \to \mathbb{R}$ is a real function and $(d\varphi)_p$ is the usual derivative of φ at point p. $d\varphi$ is the usual derivative function of φ.

Case (2): if $M = \mathbb{R}^n$ and $N = \mathbb{R}$, then $\varphi : \mathbb{R}^n \to \mathbb{R}$ is a scalar field on $\mathbb{R}^n$ and $(d\varphi)_p$ is the gradient vector of φ at point p. $d\varphi$ is the gradient function of φ, which is a vector field.

Case (3): if M is any smooth manifold and $N = \mathbb{R}$, then $\varphi : M \to \mathbb{R}$ is a scalar field on M and $(d\varphi)_p : T_p(M) \to \mathbb{R}$ is called a **differential form** at point p, which will be discussed more in depth later in this section.

Theorem 7. *Let both M, N be C^∞-manifold of dimension n and $\varphi : M \cdot \to N$ be a differentiable mapping. The following statements are equivalent.*

(1) *$(d\varphi)_p$ is injective.*

(2) *$(d\varphi)_p$ is invertible.*

(3) *$(d\varphi)_p$ is bijective.*

(4) *$(d\varphi)_p$ is linear isomorphism.*

(5) *In any local coordinate system, the Jacobian (the determinant of the Jacobian matrix) of $(d\varphi)_p$ is not equal to zero. Namely,*

$$\left| \frac{\partial F_i}{\partial x_j} \right| \neq 0,$$

*where $F_1, \ldots, F_n$ are the coordinate representation of φ. In such a case, the Jacobian matrix is said to be **non-degenerate**.*

(6) *There exists a neighborhood $U(p)$ of p, such that φ restricted to $U(p)$ is a diffeomorphism.*

Remark 8. Elaboration. In the above theorem, we assumed that the manifolds M and N have the same dimension. If this is not true, then this theorem is not true.

If $\dim M > \dim N$, $(d\varphi)_p$ cannot be injective and non of the properties (1) through (6) is true.

If $\dim M < \dim N$, $(d\varphi)_p$ can be injective, but non of the properties (2) through (6) is true. $\varphi(M)$ is a submanifold of N with dimension $\dim M$, which is less than $\dim N$. If the mapping $\varphi : M \to N$ is restricted to $\varphi : M \to \varphi(M)$, and the differential of φ is restricted to $(d\varphi)_p : T_p(M) \to T_{\varphi(p)}(\varphi(M))$, then all the properties (1) through (6) in Theorem 7 are equivalent again.

2.3 Tangent Bundles

There is a tangent space at each point on a differentiable manifold M. The union of all these tangent spaces has a natural differentiable structure and is an interesting and useful differentiable manifold itself.

Definition 18. Tangent bundle

Let M be a differentiable manifold. The union of tangent spaces at all points on M is a differentiable manifold. It is called the **tangent bundle** of M, denoted by

$$T(M) = \bigcup_{p \in M} T_p(M).$$

If M has a dimension of n, then $T(M)$ is a differentiable manifold of dimension $2n$. We can endow coordinate patches for $T(M)$ as follows. If $(x_1, \ldots, x_n)$ are local coordinates for a point on M, $(\dot{x}_1, \ldots, \dot{x}_n)$ are the coordinates of a tangent vector at p under the natural basis $\{\gamma_1, \ldots, \gamma_n\}$, then $(x_1, \ldots, x_n, \dot{x}_1, \ldots, \dot{x}_n)$ are the local coordinates for a point on the tangent bundle $T(M)$. Recall for a curve $\gamma(t) = \{x_1(t), \ldots, x_n(t)\}$, $\dot{x}_i = \frac{d}{dt}x_i(t)|_{t=0}$.

Locally, the tangent bundle is homeomorphic to $\mathbb{R}^n \times \mathbb{R}^n$. Globally, it may or may not be homeomorphic to $M \times \mathbb{R}^n$. If the tangent bundle $T(M)$ is homeomorphic to $M \times \mathbb{R}^n$, then it is said to be **trivial**.

Remark 9. Cross Link — Tangent Bundle and Lagrangian Mechanics

Tangent bundle may look abstract but the intuitive idea can be traced back to the configuration space in analytic mechanics developed by Lagrange in the 18th century.

Example 14. (Tangent bundle of a circle) The tangent bundle of a circle S^1 consists of all the tangent lines, which form a 2-manifold (Figure 2.15). At first glance, it looks like the plane minus an open disk and it appears to have a boundary, which is the circle. This is not true because the visualization here is not a qualified embedding in $\mathbb{R}^2$. Those tangent lines intersect in $\mathbb{R}^2$. We can continuously rotate each tangent line and make it perpendicular to the plane of the circle. This operation preserves the topological and differential structures of the tangent bundle of the circle and now it is embedded in $\mathbb{R}^3$ as an infinite long cylinder.   ♣

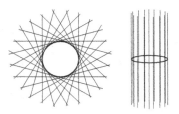

Figure 2.15   Tangent bundle of a circle.

The tangent bundle of the circle is trivial. The tangent bundle of the sphere S^2 is a 4-manifold and it is non-trivial.

On the tangent bundle $T(M)$, for each point $p \in M$, we select a tangent vector in $T_p(M)$. This assignment of a tangent vector to each point $p \in M$ is a vector field. So a vector field on M is also called a **cross section** (or just **section**) **of the tangent bundle** $T(M)$. We are only concerned with smooth vector fields, namely smooth sections of the tangent bundle.

2.4   Cotangent Spaces and Differential Forms

The tangent space $T_p(M)$ of a differentiable manifold M at point p is a linear space of dimension n, where n is the same dimension of M.

Given a linear space V, a linear form (or linear function) is defined to be a mapping $f : V \to \mathbb{R}$, such that for any $v_1, v_2 \in V$ and $a, b \in \mathbb{R}$,

$$f(av_1 + bv_2) = af(v_1) + bf(v_2).$$

All the linear forms in V constitute a linear space, called the dual space (see Part I Chap. 1 Definition 15).

Definition 19. Cotangent vector (differential form), cotangent space

A linear form on the tangent space $T_p(M)$ is called a **cotangent vector** (or **differential form**). All the cotangent vectors constitute the dual space of the tangent space, which is called the **cotangent space** of M at point p, denoted by $T_p^*(M)$.

Definition 20. Differential of a scalar field

Given a differentiable scalar field $f : M \to \mathbb{R}$, we define a differential form $(df)_p : T_p(M) \to \mathbb{R}$, such that for any tangent vector $v \in T_p(M)$,

$$(df)_p(v) \overset{\text{def}}{=} (\nabla_v f)\,|_p.$$

$(df)_p$ is called the **differential** of scalar field f at point p.

When the point p is understood in the context, we also write $(df)_p$ as df for short.

Remark 10. Definition 20 agrees with Definition 17. A scalar field $f : M \to \mathbb{R}$ is a special case of a general mapping $\varphi : M \to N$, when $N = \mathbb{R}$.

Let $p \in M$ be a point in a coordinate neighborhood U with coordinates $(x_1, \ldots, x_n)$, and $\{\gamma_1, \ldots, \gamma_n\}$ be the natural basis of tangent space $T_p(M)$. We define n scalar fields in U, $f_1, \ldots, f_n : U \to \mathbb{R}$, such that

$$f_i(x_1, \ldots, x_n) = x_i, \text{ for } i = 1, \ldots, n.$$

We simply write dx_i for df_i. We find out that dx_i, $i = 1, ..., n$ form the dual basis of $(\gamma_1, \ldots, \gamma_n)$. Namely,

$$dx_i(\gamma_j) = \delta_{ij}.$$

For a tangent vector $\gamma = b_1\gamma_1 + \cdots + b_n\gamma_n$,

$$dx_i(\gamma) = b_i.$$

Theorem 8. *The differential forms $dx_1, \ldots, dx_n$ constitute a basis of the cotangent space. Any differential form ω is the linear combination of these basis vectors,*

$$\omega = a_1 dx_1 + \cdots + a_n dx_n,$$

where $a_1, \ldots, a_n \in \mathbb{R}$.

Theorem 9. *Let $f : M \to \mathbb{R}$ be a smooth scalar field on M. In local coordinates $(x_1, \ldots, x_n)$, the differential (df) of f is represented by*

$$(df)_p = \frac{\partial f}{\partial x_1}\bigg|_p dx_1 + \cdots + \frac{\partial f}{\partial x_n}\bigg|_p dx_n.$$

Remark 11. Under natural basis, the differential (df) of scalar field f is $(\frac{\partial f}{\partial x_1}, \ldots, \frac{\partial f}{\partial x_n})$. In the traditional vector analysis in Euclidean space $\mathbb{R}^n$, we use the notation $\nabla f = (\frac{\partial f}{\partial x_1}, \ldots, \frac{\partial f}{\partial x_n})$ to denote the gradient vector of scalar field f. The directional derivative of f along vector v is the inner product of ∇f and v, namely $\nabla_v f = <\nabla f, v>$. Our new notation here is $\nabla_v f = (df)(v)$, where (df) is actually the gradient vector, but viewed as a covariant vector, or cotangent vector.

Remark 12. Note that not all the differential forms can be written as the differential df of some scalar field f. A differential form has the most general form of $\omega = a_1 dx_1 + \cdots + a_n dx_n$, as stated in Theorem 8. So in the most general form, a differential form is the linear combination of differentials of some scalar fields.

Definition 21. Exact form

If a differential form ω can be written as $\omega = df$ for some scalar field f, then it is called an **exact form**.

The exact forms have an interesting property: the integration does not depend on the path. In such cases, we can introduce the concept of a scalar potential of a differential form (or vector field), such that the differential form becomes the gradient of the potential field. We do not plan to go into the theory of integration of differential forms.

Definition 22. Cotangent bundle

Let M be a differentiable manifold. The union of cotangent spaces at all points on M is a differentiable manifold. It is called the **cotangent bundle** of M, denoted by

$$T^*(M) = \bigcup_{p \in M} T_p^*(M).$$

2.5   Submanifolds and Embeddings

Definition 23. Immersion

Let M and N be C^∞-manifolds. A smooth mapping φ from M into N is called a smooth **immersion** if $(d\varphi)_p : T_p(M) \to T_{\varphi(p)}(N)$ is injective at any point $p \in M$.

The image $\varphi(M)$ is called an **immersed submanifold** of N.

If φ is an immersion, then there is a neighborhood $U(p)$ of M such that U and $\varphi(U)$ are diffeomorphic to each other. U and $\varphi(U)$ are homeomorphic also. But globally, M and $\varphi(M)$ may or may not be homeomorphic to each other. $\varphi(M)$ may have self intersection.

Definition 24. Embedding

If $\varphi : M \to N$ is an immersion and it is also injective, then it is called a (smooth) **embedding**.

The image $\varphi(M)$ is called an **embedded submanifold** of N.

An embedding rules not the possibility of self intersection of the image. An embedding may or may not be a diffeomorphism, or a homeomorphism. A homeomorphism is even not clearly defined without clearly specifying the topology on the image $\varphi(M)$. On one hand, the differentiable structure of M can be carried onto $\varphi(M)$ by the mapping φ so that φ will be a diffeomorphism from M to $\varphi(M)$. On the other hand, the topology of $\varphi(M)$ inherited from M by φ may not be the same as the subset topology inherited from N. This leads to the definition of regular embedding.

Definition 25. Regular embedding and regular submanifold

Let $\varphi : M \to N$ be a smooth embedding. When φ is restricted to $\varphi : M \to \varphi(M)$, if it is a homeomorphism with respect to the subset topology of $\varphi(M)$ inherited from N, then it is called a **regular embedding**.

The image $\varphi(M)$ is called a **regular embedded submanifold** of N.

Definition 26. Submanifolds

Let M and N be C^∞-manifolds and $M \subseteq N$. If the identity map id : $M \to N$ is an immersion, then M is called a **submanifold** of N. If the identity map id : $M \to N$ is an embedding, then M is called a **regular submanifold** of N.

An embedded submanifold does not have self intersection but an immersed submanifold may have self intersection. Locally (in a sufficiently small neighborhood), an immersion is always an embedding.

Theorem 10. (Whitney embedding theorem) *Any n-dimensional C^∞-manifold M with countable basis can always be immersed in $\mathbb{R}^{2n}$ and can be embedded in $\mathbb{R}^{2n+1}$.*

Whitney's theorem unifies the intrinsic view and extrinsic view of differentiable manifolds in some sense. Stretching is still allowed in smooth embeddings. The smooth embeddings do not preserve the distance, as the concept of distance is not even defined for a differentiable manifold without additional structures. When a differentiable manifold is endowed with a metric structure, it becomes Riemannian manifold. For Riemannian manifolds, J. Nash proved a theorem regarding isometric embedding.

Remark 13. Comparison — Topological Embeddings, Smooth Embeddings and Isometric Embeddings

We have defined topological embeddings for topological spaces in Chap. 1, Definition 21. We just defined smooth embeddings for smooth manifolds. We are going to define isometric embeddings for Riemannian manifolds in Section 3, which preserves distances.

In the following, we give examples of embeddings and immersions of some 2-manifolds.

Example 15. (Smooth embedding of torus in $\mathbb{R}^3$) The torus in Example 7 can be smoothly embedded (with stretching) into $\mathbb{R}^3$ in the form $(u, v) \mapsto$

$(x, y, z) \in \mathbb{R}^3$, with

$$\begin{bmatrix} x \\ y \\ z \end{bmatrix} = \begin{bmatrix} (b + a\cos\frac{2\pi v}{a})\cos\frac{2\pi u}{a} \\ (b + a\cos\frac{2\pi v}{a})\sin\frac{2\pi u}{a} \\ a\sin\frac{2\pi v}{a} \end{bmatrix},$$

where $b > a$ can be any constant, which is the major radius of the torus in $\mathbb{R}^3$. This can be put in implicit form

$$T^2 = \{(x, y, z) \in \mathbb{R}^3 | (x^2 + y^2 + z^2 + b^2 - a^2)^2 = 4b^2(x^2 + y^2)\}. \quad \clubsuit$$

Example 16. (Smooth embedding of torus in $\mathbb{R}^4$) The torus can be embedded into $\mathbb{R}^4$ in the form $(u, v) \mapsto (x_1, x_2, x_3, x_4) \in \mathbb{R}^4$, where

$$\begin{bmatrix} x_1 \\ x_2 \\ x_3 \\ x_4 \end{bmatrix} = \begin{bmatrix} a\cos\frac{2\pi u}{a} \\ a\sin\frac{2\pi u}{a} \\ a\cos\frac{2\pi v}{a} \\ a\sin\frac{2\pi v}{a} \end{bmatrix}.$$

An implicit form of this torus in $\mathbb{R}^4$ is

$$T^2 = \{(x_1, x_2, x_3, x_4) \in \mathbb{R}^4 | x_1^2 + x_2^2 = a^2, \ x_3^2 + x_4^2 = a^2\}. \quad \clubsuit$$

When the manifolds are endowed metric structures to become Riemannian manifolds in Section 3, we will see the embedded torus in $\mathbb{R}^4$ in Example 16 has zero Gaussian curvature everywhere, known as the flat torus. The torus embedded in $\mathbb{R}^3$ in Example 15 has non-zero Gaussian curvatures.

Example 17. (Smooth embedding of hyperbolic plane $\mathbb{H}^2$ in $\mathbb{R}^2$ and $\mathbb{R}^3$) The hyperbolic plane $\mathbb{H}^2$ is homeomorphic and diffeomorphic to $\mathbb{R}^2$. The difference between $\mathbb{H}^2$ and $\mathbb{R}^2$ is the metric structure. Geometrically they are different but topologically they are the same. The Gans plane model, Poincaré disk model, Poincaré half plane model and Klein disk model are all smooth embeddings of $\mathbb{H}^2$ in $\mathbb{R}^2$. The hyperboloid model is a smooth embedding in $\mathbb{R}^3$ (see Part II Chap. 3). None of these are isometric embeddings. Hilbert's theorem states that there does not exist any isometric embedding of $\mathbb{H}^2$ in $\mathbb{R}^3$. $\quad \clubsuit$

Example 18. (Smooth immersion and embedding of the Klein bottle) The following is an immersion of Klein bottle in $\mathbb{R}^3$ in the implicit form [Stewart (1991)]:

$$(x^2 + y^2 + z^2 + 2y - 1)\left[(x^2 + y^2 + z^2 - 2y - 1)^2 - 8z^2\right] + \\ 16xz(x^2 + y^2 + z^2 - 2y - 1) = 0.$$

Klein bottle has a smooth embedding in $\mathbb{R}^4$ ([do Carmo (1976)] p. 436):

$$\begin{bmatrix} x_1 \\ x_2 \\ x_3 \\ x_4 \end{bmatrix} = \begin{bmatrix} (r\cos v + a)\cos u \\ (r\cos v + a)\sin u \\ r\sin v\cos\frac{u}{2} \\ r\sin v\sin\frac{u}{2} \end{bmatrix}.$$

♣

Example 19. (Immersion of the projective plane $\mathbb{P}^2$ in $\mathbb{R}^3$) The following is an immersion of the projective plane $\mathbb{P}^2$ into $\mathbb{R}^3$ known as the cross-cap:

$$\begin{bmatrix} x \\ y \\ z \end{bmatrix} = \begin{bmatrix} r(1+\cos v)\cos u \\ r(1+\cos v)\sin u \\ -(\tanh(u-\pi))\,r\sin v \end{bmatrix}.$$

There is also an implicit form of the cross cap ([Hilbert and Cohn-Vossen (1952)] p. 315):

$$(k_1 x^2 + k_2 y^2)(x^2 + y^2 + z^2) - 2z(x^2 + y^2) = 0.$$

Note the cross cap is not strictly an immersion because it has two "pinch points" (singular points). An immersion was found in 1901 by Werner Boy, a student of Hilbert, now known as Boy's surface, or Boy's cap. ♣

Example 20. (Embedding of the projective plane $\mathbb{P}^2$ in $\mathbb{R}^4$) We use the sphere model of the projective plane. On the sphere $S^2 = \{(x,y,z) \in \mathbb{R}^3 \,|\, x^2 + y^2 + z^2 = 1\}$, if we identify the antipodal points (x,y,z) and $(-x,-y,-z)$, then we obtain a model for the projective plane.

We start with a mapping $\varphi : S^2 \to \mathbb{R}^4$; $(x,y,z) \mapsto (x^2 - y^2, xy, xz, yz)$. Because $\varphi(x,y,z) = \varphi(-x,-y,-z)$, this mapping can be viewed as a mapping $\tilde{\varphi} : \mathbb{P}^2 \to \mathbb{R}^4$. If we use x, y parametrization on $\mathbb{P}^2$, and we use the upper hemisphere, we have $z = \sqrt{1 - x^2 - y^2}$. Let $\tilde{\varphi}(x,y) = (u_1, u_2, u_3, u_4)$. Then

$$\begin{bmatrix} u_1 \\ u_2 \\ u_3 \\ u_4 \end{bmatrix} = \begin{bmatrix} x^2 - y^2 \\ xy \\ x\sqrt{1-x^2-y^2} \\ y\sqrt{1-x^2-y^2} \end{bmatrix}.$$

This mapping is a smooth embedding of $\mathbb{P}^2$ into $\mathbb{R}^4$ (see [do Carmo (1976)] p. 437). ♣

§3 Riemannian Manifolds

3.1 Curved Spaces

Geometry, as the name itself suggests, originated from the human activities of measurements on earth. It is a theory about the space relationships in a small local region known as the earth—small in the sense of astronomical scales. After the Greek mathematician Euclid of Alexandria organized geometry into a beautiful logical system, it has been known as Euclidean geometry and people started to make naive generalizations as to think the geometry of the entire universe would be the same. This step of generalization—from "geo-metry" to "cosmo-metry"—is huge. In the 19th century, non-Euclidean geometries as logically consistent theories were discovered. Hence the role of Euclidean geometry as the true geometry of our universe was challenged. It became an open question what is the true geometry of our universe and non-Euclidean geometries became legitimate candidates. It has been realized that the space is determined by matter and the geometry of our space should be tested with experiments. Geometry is the reflection of the material world on the human mind, instead of something hardwired on human mind regardless of the material world. Euclidean geometry is only a good local approximation to describe our space in a very small scale and it may not be valid to generalize this local theory to an indefinite large scale. The geometry of our universe by and large is still unknown.

The quest for the geometry of the universe just parallels the human history of the quest for geometry of the earth. In ancient times, people lived only in a small region on earth. A small region on earth is flat. Hence it was conceived that the earth was flat. When people can travel fast in a larger scale, like flying on a jet plane, it is discovered that the earth is curved!

The surface of a sphere is called a curved surface because the geometry on a sphere is different from that on a Euclidean plane. Likewise, if the possibility is true that our space in the large scale is not described by Euclidean geometry, we call the space "curved space". When we talk about curved spaces, we are talking about geometry instead of topology, because in topology, continuous stretching is allowed and the flat and the curved cannot be distinguished. Differentiable manifolds do not have the concept of distance and they allow smooth stretching. So we cannot discuss geometric properties, like curvature and geodesics, on differentiable manifolds without additional structures. The Riemannian manifold is the mathematical term that describes our intuition of curved spaces. A Riemannian manifold is a differentiable manifold endowed with a metric structure. A small neighborhood on a Riemannian manifold can be approximated by a Euclidean space, but when the numerous patches of Euclidean spaces are glued together, we obtain a curved space. It is a good idea to read Part II Chap. 2, or at least Section 10 of that chapter before reading the rest of this chapter. The reader shall gain more intuition with the surfaces in $\mathbb{R}^3$ as concrete examples of Riemannian manifolds, although the exposition in this chapter does not depend on Part II Chap. 2 in logic.

Remark 14. Philosophy — The Battle of the Curved and the Straight

Time and again we encounter the battle of the curved and the straight. By inventing calculus, Newton and Leibniz offered for the first time, their understanding, insight and also a solution to this battle. That is, in an infinitesimal (just a fancy way to say small, since we cannot make it precise anyway) region, a curve is approximated by a straight line and a curved surface is approximated by a plane (to the first order, although second order effects like curvature can be detected and cannot always be ignored). With the intrinsic view of manifolds, tangent vectors and tangent spaces, we gain even deeper philosophical insight. The Euclidean space with straight lines and planes is nothing but an idealistic local approximation of the real world, which is extended indefinitely in a platonic way. The real world is a manifold where straight lines and planes do not exist. The only thing we can have on a manifold is the notion of distance and geodesic lines. So the notion of distance is more fundamental than the concept of straightness. Straight lines can be defined as the geodesic lines (shortest paths). Geodesics on manifolds are more general and they do not obey all the laws governing straight lines dictated by Euclid. G. Birkhoff even took this approach in 1930's in the Euclidean geometry proper, taking the notion of distance as the basic assumptions in his axioms.

The tangent vector just means an infinitesimal piece of curve and the tangent plane (or tangent space) is just an infinitesimal piece of the manifold itself. Sure this tangent space can be linearly extended indefinitely in our imagination, but the extrinsic picture of an extensive tangent plane (or tangent space) sitting outside the world (the manifold) like Figure 2.13 is rather misleading. Newton had the idea that the curves are approximated by straight lines in an infinitesimal region. The opposite is also true. In the definition of tangent vectors in last section, tangent vectors (straight lines) are approximated by curves in an infinitesimal region. You may argue that you have seen railroad tracks that run in a straight line for miles, but you know that they eventually have to turn. Even if it does not turn left or right, and does the best to lie "evenly with the points on itself" (Euclid's definition of a straight line), it will have to turn down as long as it stays on the surface of the earth. The straightest line on the earth is not a straight line but rather a great circle. Also remember, thousands of miles is considered infinitesimal in the astronomical scope. You may argue that we are not bound to the surface of the earth and we have another degree of freedom going into space. You may have seen a beam of laser light on earth shooting to the surface of the moon and is still pretty straight. How do you know that the laser beam, if not blocked by the moon and anything on the way, will not bend and come back to the earth after traveling billions and billions of years, in a similar way to the first around-the-world navigation on earth made by Ferdinand Magellan?

3.2   Riemannian Metrics

We have discussed the inner product in linear algebra, in Part I Chap. 1. An inner product in linear space V is a symmetric, positive definite bilinear form. Since bilinear forms on V are covariant tensors of degree 2, an inner product $g : V \times V \to \mathbb{R}$ is also called a metric tensor.

Let $T_p(M)$ be the tangent space of a differentiable manifold M at point p. We can endow an inner product, or metric tensor $g_p : T_p(M) \times T_p(M) \to \mathbb{R}$ in the tangent space $T_p(M)$. If we define a metric tensor in the tangent space $T_p(M)$ at each point p, we have a tensor field g on M. If this tensor field g is smooth on M, then we call the manifold a Riemannian manifold.

Definition 27. Riemannian manifold

Let M be a differentiable manifold. Suppose an inner product $\langle w, z \rangle$, also denoted by $g(w, z)$, is defined for all the vectors w, z in the tangent space $T_p(M)$ at each point $p \in M$, then g is a symmetric, positive definite, covariant tensor field on M. Also suppose this tensor field g is smooth on M. The differentiable manifold M together with g is called a **Riemannian manifold** (or **Riemannian space**), denoted by (M, g), and g is called the **Riemannian metric tensor** (field, or simply **Riemannian metric**) on M.

The length of a tangent vector $w \in T_p(M)$ is defined to be $\|w\| = \sqrt{\langle w, w \rangle}$. If in local coordinates, g is represented by matrix $[g_{ij}]$ and w has components w_i in natural basis, then

$$\|w\| = \sqrt{\sum_{i,j=1}^{n} g_{ij} w_i w_j},$$

where n is the dimension of the manifold. The angle between tangent vectors w and z is defined to be

$$\theta = \cos^{-1} \left(\frac{\langle w, z \rangle}{\|w\| \, \|z\|} \right).$$

If two curves λ and γ intersect at point $p \in M$, the angle between the two curves at p is defined to be the angle between the tangent vectors of the two curves at p.

Intuitively, the metric tensor defines the "infinitesimal distance" on the manifold. The tangent vectors are just "infinitesimal displacements" on the manifold. The "infinitesimal distance" ds can be expressed in local coordinates dx_i in the form of

$$ds^2 = \sum_{i,j=1}^{n} g_{ij} dx_i dx_j,$$

which is the first fundamental form of surfaces when the dimension is $n = 2$. Using the language we developed in Section 2 for differentiable manifolds, dx_i are differential forms and they are the dual basis of $\frac{\partial}{\partial x_i}$. ds^2 is a bilinear form, or covariant tensor on $T_p(M)$, namely, $ds^2 \in T_p^*(M) \otimes T_p^*(M)$.

Remark 15. Comparison/Cross Link — Riemannian Manifolds and Surfaces in $\mathbb{R}^3$

The first fundamental form of surfaces in $\mathbb{R}^3$ is the Riemannian metric tensor of the surface, which is a Riemannian manifold of dimension 2. However, to construct a Riemannian manifold, we can endow an arbitrary metric tensor as the starting point. The first fundamental form of a surface is induced (or inherited) from the distance in $\mathbb{R}^3$.

Example 21. (Metric tensor of the Euclidean space) The Euclidean space $\mathbb{R}^n$ with the standard inner product $\langle \cdot, \cdot \rangle$ is a Riemannian manifold. The metric tensor $g_{ij} = \delta_{ij}$, $i, j = 1, \ldots, n$, is the same at every point in $\mathbb{R}^n$. ♣

Example 22. (Metric tensor of the hyperbolic plane $\mathbb{H}^2$, Gans model) In Gans model, the set of points in the hyperbolic plane is the same as the set of points in the Euclidean plane $\mathbb{R}^2$, namely $\mathbb{H}^2 = \{(x,y) | x, y \in \mathbb{R}\}$. The metric tensor of $\mathbb{H}^2$ is

$$[g_{ij}] \stackrel{\text{def}}{=} \frac{1}{1 + x^2 + y^2} \begin{bmatrix} 1 + y^2 & -xy \\ -xy & 1 + x^2 \end{bmatrix}.$$

This is a different metric from the Euclidean metric

$$[g_{ij}] = \begin{bmatrix} 1 & 0 \\ 0 & 1 \end{bmatrix}.$$

So the hyperbolic plane is different from the Euclidean plane. ♣

Example 23. (Metric tensor of the hyperbolic space $\mathbb{H}^n$, Gans model) The hyperbolic plane is easily generalized to dimension n. The points in the hyperbolic space $\mathbb{H}^n$ are the same as the points in the Euclidean space $\mathbb{R}^n$, namely $\mathbb{H}^n = \{(x_1, \ldots, x_n) | x_1, \ldots, x_n \in \mathbb{R}\}$. The metric tensor is

$$g_{ij} \stackrel{\text{def}}{=} \delta_{ij} - \frac{x_i x_j}{1 + \sum_{k=1}^{n} x_k^2}, \quad i, j = 1, \ldots, n.$$

♣

Definition 28. Length of a curve

Let $\lambda : [t_1, t_2] \to M$ be a smooth curve on a Riemannian manifold M and $p_1 = \lambda(t_1)$, $p_2 = \lambda(t_2)$. The length of λ between p_1 and p_2 is defined to be

$$\int_\lambda{}_{p_1}^{p_2} ds \stackrel{\text{def}}{=} \int_{t_1}^{t_2} \left\langle \frac{d\lambda(t)}{dt}, \frac{d\lambda(t)}{dt} \right\rangle^{1/2} dt.$$

In local coordinates $(x_1, \ldots, x_n)$, the length of the curve λ is

$$\int_{t_1}^{t_2} \left(\sum_{i,j=1}^{n} g_{ij} \frac{dx_i}{dt} \frac{dx_j}{dt} \right)^{1/2} dt.$$

Let p_1 and p_2 be two points on a Riemannian manifold M. The distance between p_1 and p_2 is defined to be

$$\tilde\rho(p_1, p_2) \stackrel{\text{def}}{=} \inf_\lambda \widehat{p_1 p_2} \stackrel{\text{def}}{=} \int_\lambda{}_{p_1}^{p_2} ds,$$

where $\inf_\lambda \widehat{p_1 p_2}$ is the infimum of the arc lengths of all smooth curves $\lambda(t)$ connecting p_1 and p_2.

Theorem 11. *A Riemannian manifold with the distance $\tilde\rho$ thus defined forms a metric space.*

Definition 29. Geodesic line

A smooth curve γ on a Riemannian manifold M is called a **geodesic line** (or simply **geodesic**), if for any point p_0 on γ, there exists a sufficiently small neighborhood U of p_0, such that for any point p in the intersection of γ and U,

$$\int_\gamma{}_{p_0}^{p} ds = \tilde\rho(p_0, p).$$

> In other words, a geodesic line is a curve that realizes the shortest distance between any two points in a sufficiently small neighborhood.

It can be shown, such a geodesic line connecting any two points in a sufficiently small neighborhood always exists and is unique.

From variational calculus, the necessary condition for a curve $\gamma(t)$ to be a geodesic line is that it satisfies the Euler-Lagrange equations, as stated in the following theorem.

Theorem 12. (Equations of a geodesic line) *If $\gamma(t)$ is a geodesic line with t being the parameter, then in local coordinates x_i, it satisfies the following equations,*

$$\frac{d^2 x_k}{dt} + \sum_{i,j=1}^{n} \Gamma_{ij}^k \frac{dx_i}{dt} \frac{dx_j}{dt} = 0, \ k = 1, \dots, n, \tag{2.1}$$

where n is the dimension of the manifold and

$$\Gamma_{ij}^k \stackrel{def}{=} \sum_{m=1}^{n} \frac{1}{2} g^{km} \left(\partial_i g_{mj} + \partial_j g_{mi} - \partial_m g_{ij} \right), \tag{2.2}$$

are called Christoffel symbols (of the second kind), in which we used the shorthand ∂_i for $\frac{\partial}{\partial x_i}$.

3.3   Levi-Civita Parallel Transport

We discussed parallel transport, also known as Levi-Civita parallel transport, on surfaces in $\mathbb{R}^3$, in Part II Chap. 2. Parallel transport will be the easiest way to generalize the concept of curvature to higher dimensions. The parallel transport on Riemannian manifolds will be defined intrinsically, while the definition in Part II Chap. 2 is extrinsic. The most popular approach to introduce the parallel transport on Riemannian manifolds is to introduce affine connections through axioms and select one that preserves the Riemannian metric. Parallel transport and covariant derivatives are defined using this Riemannian connection. Riemannian manifolds have a surplus of structures—the metric structures and affine structures. This axiomatic approach uses the affine structure to define a much broader affine connection. This is the most economical approach but it is not intuitive.

We follow a more intuitive and constructive approach used by Vladimir Arnold [Arnold (1997)]. We make use of the concepts of distance and angle on Riemannian manifolds and define parallel transport by construction.

Definition 30. Parallel transport along a geodesic line on a 2-manifold

---

Let γ be a geodesic line on a Riemannian manifold M of dimension 2 and v_p be a tangent vector of M at point p on γ. v_p is transported along γ to a different point q, while its length and its angle with γ are kept constant. At point q, the tangent vector becomes v_q. Then v_q is called the **Levi-Civita parallel transport** (or simply **parallel transport**) of v_p along geodesic line γ.

When the dimension is higher than 2, the situation is a little more complicated, because when a vector is transported along a geodesic line, fixing the length and angle with the geodesic line does not completely fix the vector. The vector can still rotate around the geodesic line. We need to fix the two dimensional plane which contains the newly transported vector and the tangent vector of the geodesic line at that point.

Let p_1, p_2 be two nearby points on a geodesic line γ, separated by a small distance Δ. Let $v_1 \in T_{p_1}(M)$. We make the following construction of parallel transport of v_1 along γ:

If v_1 is tangent to the geodesic line γ at point p_1, the parallel transport of v_1 along geodesic γ is trivial. We just keep v_1 with the same length and always tangent to γ.

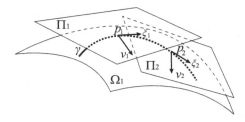

Figure 2.16   Parallel transport along geodesic line on higher dimensional Riemannian manifolds.

Now assume v_1 is not tangent to γ.

Definition 31. Parallel transport along a geodesic line on an n-manifold

---

(cf. Figure 2.16) Let ξ_1 be a vector tangent to the geodesic line γ at p_1, and v_1 be a tangent vector at p_1 not colinear with ξ_1. We make construction of parallel transport of v_1 along γ to a nearby point p_2 as follows:

Let $\Pi_1 \subseteq T_{p_1}(M)$ be the plane in the tangent space spanned by ξ_1 and v_1. Let Ω_1 be the surface (2-D submanifold) consisting of all the geodesics emanating from p_1 and tangent to Π_1. Ω_1 is called a **geodesic surface at** p_1. Let $\Pi_2 \subseteq T_{p_2}(M)$ be the tangent plane of Ω_1 at p_2. We define the **parallel transport** of v_1 from p_1 to p_2 to be the vector in the plane Π_2, with the length of v_1 and its angle to γ kept constant.

Repeat this process and take the limit of $\Delta \to 0$, we can parallel-transport a vector along geodesic line γ from point p_1 over a finite distance.

For the parallel transport of a vector along an arbitrary curve, we use broken geodesics to approximate the curve and we take the limit when each geodesic segment tends to zero.

Definition 32. Parallel transport along arbitrary curve

An arbitrary smooth curve λ can be approximated by broken geodesic arcs. A tangent vector is parallel-transported along these broken geodesic arcs. The parallel transport of the tangent vector along curve λ is defined by the limiting procedure, when the length of each geodesic arc tends to zero.

In the Euclidean space $\mathbb{R}^n$, the parallel transport of tangent vectors coincides with the parallelism of vectors in $\mathbb{R}^n$. If a tangent vector v_2 at p_2 is the parallel transport of v_1 at p_1 along a curve λ, then $v_1 = v_2$ in Cartesian coordinates and this result of parallel transport does not depend on the choice of the path.

Surfaces in $\mathbb{R}^3$ are Riemannian manifolds of dimension 2, with the metric inherited from $\mathbb{R}^3$. The parallel transport of tangent vectors of Riemannian manifolds defined here applies to surfaces in $\mathbb{R}^3$ also and the definition here agrees with Definition 16 in Part II Chap. 2. The difference is, the definition here is intrinsic, while Definition 16 in Part II Chap. 2 is extrinsic, because it refers to the normal direction of the surface in $\mathbb{R}^3$.

Recall the definition of directional derivative of a scalar field f on a differentiable manifold, $\nabla_v f|_p \overset{\text{def}}{=} \lim_{\Delta t \to 0} \frac{f(p') - f(p)}{\Delta t}$ in Definition 14. Similarly we would like to define the directional derivative of a vector field Y. However, we encounter an issue here. Suppose the vector field Y takes value Y_p at point p and value $Y_{p'}$ at point p'. We cannot simply use $Y_{p'} - Y_p$, because the two vectors $Y_{p'}$ and Y_p are tangent vectors at different points and they are not related to each other. The subtraction does not make sense. The solution is to parallel-transport $Y_{p'}$ back to point p, so that it can be compared with Y_p.

Definition 33. Covariant derivative $\nabla_v Y$

Let Y be a vector field on Riemannian manifold M and v be a tangent vector at point p. Choose any curve $\gamma(t)$ passing through p that represents v. Suppose Y has value Y_p at point $p = \gamma(0)$ and value $Y_{p'}$ at point $p' = \gamma(\Delta t)$. Let $\overline{Y}_p$ be the parallel transport of $Y_{p'}$ along curve γ from p' to p. The **covariant derivative** of vector field Y at **point p in the direction** v is defined to be the tangent vector

$$(\nabla_v Y)|_p \overset{\text{def}}{=} \lim_{\Delta t \to 0} \frac{\overline{Y}_p - Y_p}{\Delta t}. \tag{2.3}$$

Let X be another vector field on M. The **covariant derivative** of Y **in the direction** X can be defined point-wisely on the manifold, denoted by $\nabla_X Y$.

Note the definition of covariant derivative of a vector field depends on the notion of parallel transport of tangent vectors, which is defined on Riemannian manifolds but not defined on a differentiable manifold without additional structures, because a differentiable manifold allows free smooth stretching and the concept of parallel vectors cannot be defined.

In the notation $\nabla_X Y$, ∇_X can be viewed as an operator acting on the vector field Y. From another perspective, ∇ can be viewed as an operator acting on two vector fields X and Y, that is, a mapping $\nabla : \mathfrak{X}(M) \times \mathfrak{X}(M) \to \mathfrak{X}(M)$; $(X, Y) \mapsto \nabla_X Y$, where $\mathfrak{X}(M)$ denotes the set of all smooth vector fields on M.

Definition 34. Riemannian connection

Let M be a Riemannian manifold. The mapping

$$\nabla : \mathfrak{X}(M) \times \mathfrak{X}(M) \to \mathfrak{X}(M); (X, Y) \mapsto \nabla_X Y$$

is called the Riemannian connection on M.

Similarly, in the notation $\nabla_X Y$, ∇Y can be viewed as an operator acting on the vector field X. That is, ∇Y is a type type (1,1) tensor field.

Definition 35. Covariant differential ∇Y

Let Y be a vector field on Riemannian manifold M and $p \in M$. We define a type (1,1) tensor $(\nabla Y)|_p : T_p(M) \to T_p(M)$ in the tangent space $T_p(M)$ at point p, such that given any vector $v \in T_p(M)$,

$$(\nabla Y)|_p(v) \overset{\text{def}}{=} (\nabla_v Y)|_p.$$

$(\nabla Y)|_p$ is called the **covariant differential** of vector field Y **at point** p.

Using the point-wise rule, this definition can be generalized to the entire manifold. The **covariant differential** of vector field Y **on manifold** M is defined to be a type (1,1) tensor field, denoted by ∇Y,

$$(\nabla Y)(X) \overset{\text{def}}{=} \nabla_X Y.$$

Hence the covariant derivative of Y in the direction of X is the inner product of X and the tensor covariant differential ∇Y,

$$\nabla_X Y = X \cdot \nabla Y,$$

and this is true in the point-wise sense.

The Riemannian connection ∇, or the covariant derivative $\nabla_X Y$ has the following properties.

Theorem 13. (Properties of the Riemannian connection) *Let X, Y, X_1, X_2, Y_1, Y_2 be smooth vector fields on Riemannian manifold M, and f, f_1, f_2 be smooth scalar fields on M.*

(1) *$\mathcal{F}(M)$-linear on the first variable:*
$$\nabla_{f_1 X_1 + f_2 X_2} Y = f_1 \nabla_{X_1} Y + f_2 \nabla_{X_2} Y.$$
(2) *Additive on the second variable:*
$$\nabla_X (Y_1 + Y_2) = \nabla_X Y_1 + \nabla_X Y_2.$$
(3) *Leibniz rule on the second variable:*
$$\nabla_X (fY) = f \nabla_X Y + (\nabla_X f) Y.$$

Let $\{e_1, ..., e_n\}$ be the natural basis of $T_p(M)$. We can find the coordinate representation of the covariant differential.

Definition 36. Connection coefficients

The covariant derivatives of the natural basis vectors can be expressed in this basis as

$$\nabla_{e_i} e_j = \sum_{k=1}^{n} \Gamma_{ij}^k e_k, \ i, j, k = 1, \dots, n.$$

The coefficients Γ_{ij}^k are called **connection coefficients** of the Riemannian manifold M.

It seems that we have used Γ_{ij}^k for the Christoffel symbols of the second kind in Eq. 2.2 and here we are abusing the symbol. In fact, they are the same as stated in the following theorem.

Theorem 14. *On a Riemannian manifold with metric g, the connection coefficients Γ_{ij}^k defined in Definition 36 are the same as the Christoffel symbols of the second kind,*

$$\Gamma_{ij}^k = \sum_{m=1}^{n} \frac{1}{2} g^{km} \left(\partial_i g_{mj} + \partial_j g_{mi} - \partial_m g_{ij} \right), \ i, j, k = 1, \dots, n.$$

We were familiar with this when we dealt with surfaces in $\mathbb{R}^3$. (see Part II Chap. 2, Equation 2.34.)

Corollary. *Connection coefficients Γ_{ij}^k is symmetric with respect to i and j.*

$$\Gamma_{ij}^k = \Gamma_{ji}^k.$$

When we define torsion tensors in the next section, we will see that this corollary implies that the Riemannian connection is torsion free.

Theorem 15. (Covariant derivative in local coordinates) *Let Y be a smooth vector field on a Riemannian manifold. In local coordinates, the covariant derivative is*

$$\nabla_j Y^i = \frac{\partial Y^i}{\partial x_j} + \sum_{k=1}^n \Gamma_{kj}^i Y^k,$$

where by $\nabla_j Y^i$ we mean $\nabla_{e_j} Y^i$.

Theorem 16. (Coordinate transformation of connection coefficients) *Suppose Γ_{ij}^k are the connection coefficients in local coordinates $(x_1, \ldots, x_n)$. After a local coordinate transformation from $(x_1, \ldots, x_n)$ to $(y_1, \ldots, y_n)$, the connection coefficients are $\overline{\Gamma}_{ij}^k$ in the new coordinate system $(y_1, \ldots, y_n)$. Then*

$$\overline{\Gamma}_{ij}^k = \sum_{p,q,r=1}^n \frac{\partial x_p}{\partial y_i} \frac{\partial x_q}{\partial y_j} \frac{\partial y_k}{\partial x_r} \Gamma_{pq}^r + \sum_{m=1}^n \frac{\partial y_k}{\partial x_m} \frac{\partial^2 x_m}{\partial y_i \partial y_j}. \tag{2.4}$$

Remark 16. Clarification — Connection Is Not a Tensor Field.

Note that the connection Γ_{ij}^k has three indices and n^3 components. The coordinate transformation law of connection coefficients are different from the coordinate transformation laws of tensor fields. From the old-fashioned view of tensors, we know the connection Γ_{ij}^k is not a tensor (field). The set of all smooth vector fields $\mathfrak{X}(M)$ can be viewed as a $\mathcal{F}(M)$-module. From the modern view of tensors, the connection ∇ is not a tensor field because the mapping $\nabla : \mathfrak{X}(M) \times \mathfrak{X}(M) \to \mathfrak{X}(M)$ fails to be $\mathcal{F}(M)$-bilinear. In particular, it fails to be $\mathcal{F}(M)$-linear in the second variable Y (see property (3) in Theorem 13.)

If a tensor is equal to zero, all its components are zero in a coordinate system. If all components of a tensor are zero in one coordinate system, all its components are zero in any other coordinate systems. This is not true for connection coefficients since they are not tensors. It is possible that in one coordinate system, $\Gamma_{ij}^k = 0$ for all i, j, k, at one point p but in another coordinate system, Γ_{ij}^k has non-zero components at point p. Conversely, at any point p, we can always find a coordinate system, in which all $\Gamma_{ij}^k = 0$ at point p. Notice that unless the manifold is flat, we can only transform Γ_{ij}^k away at a single point, not in the entire neighborhood, no matter how small the neighborhood is. In the theory of general relativity, a free-falling reference frame (Einstein's free-fall elevator) is a geodesic coordinate system, where $\Gamma_{ij}^k = 0$ for a single point in the 4-dimensional pseudo-Riemannian spacetime.

3.4   Riemann Curvature Tensor

Locally a Riemannian manifold M is modeled on Euclidean space $\mathbb{R}^n$. In an infinitesimal neighborhood on M, the first order approximation is just a Euclidean space $\mathbb{R}^n$. The deviation from Euclidean space appears to be the second order infinitesimal, which should be quantified by the curvature. This curvature has to be intrinsically defined, without referring to any embedding. Reviewing the theory of surfaces in $\mathbb{R}^3$ (Part II Chap. 2), we find the parallel transport of tangent vectors can be intrinsically defined and is the best way to generalize the concept of curvatures to higher dimensional manifolds.

Definition 37. Curvature operator

Let X, Y be vector fields on Riemannian manifold M. We define a mapping $R(X, Y) : \mathfrak{X}(M) \to \mathfrak{X}(M)$, parametrized by X, Y, such that for all $Z \in \mathfrak{X}(M)$,

$$R(X, Y)Z \stackrel{\text{def}}{=} \nabla_Y(\nabla_X Z) - \nabla_X(\nabla_Y Z) - \nabla_{[Y,X]}Z. \qquad (2.5)$$

The mapping $R(X, Y)$ is called the **curvature operator** in the direction of X and Y at point p. In the abstract form, we write the curvature operator

$$R(X, Y) \stackrel{\text{def}}{=} [\nabla_Y, \nabla_X] - \nabla_{[Y,X]}$$

$$\stackrel{\text{def}}{=} \nabla_Y \nabla_X - \nabla_X \nabla_Y - \nabla_{[Y,X]}. \qquad (2.6)$$

If we use the notion of the second order covariant derivative

$$\nabla^2_{X,Y} Z \stackrel{\text{def}}{=} \nabla_X(\nabla_Y Z) - \nabla_{(\nabla_X Y)} Z,$$

the curvature operator can be written as

$$R(X,Y)Z \stackrel{\text{def}}{=} \nabla^2_{Y,X} Z - \nabla^2_{X,Y} Z,$$

or

$$R(X,Y) \stackrel{\text{def}}{=} \nabla^2_{Y,X} - \nabla^2_{X,Y}.$$

Remark 17. Caution — The Sign of the Curvature Tensor

The reader should be warned about a different definition of this curvature operator in literature. The other differs by a negative sign. The above definition agrees with [Arnold (1997); do Carmo (1992)], but differs from [Chern et al. (1999); Boothby (2002); MSJ (1993)]. When you see the same notation, it may mean different things in different books. Either way is fine as long as it is self-consistent. If you use the other definition, the formulas in many theorems and corollaries should change a sign. With our choice, the Ricci curvature tensor and scalar curvature will be natural averages of the Riemannian curvature tensor, without an extra negative sign. Sectional curvature (Gaussian curvature) does not have an extra negative sign either. See more at Remark 20.

Note, the value $(R(X,Y)Z)|_p$ at any point $p \in M$ depends only on the values of X, Y and Z at p but not their values in a neighborhood. So given vectors X_p, $Y_p \in T_p(M)$, $R(X_p, Y_p) : T_p(M) \to T_p(M)$ is a linear transformation in the tangent space $T_p(M)$.

At point p, imagine an infinitesimal "parallelogram" prescribed by X and Y and we parallel transport vector Z in a loop around this "parallelogram" back to point p. In the limit the sides of this parallelogram tend to zero, $R(X,Y)Z$ is the vector coming back to point p after this parallel transport. See Figure 2.17.

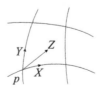

Figure 2.17   Geometric interpretation of curvature tensor.

Using this curvature operator, we can define a curvature tensor of degree four.

Definition 38. Riemann curvature tensor

Let X, Y, Z be vector fields on a Riemannian manifold M. A type (1,3) tensor field, called **Riemann curvature tensor**, is defined to be the mapping

$$R : \mathfrak{X}(M) \times \mathfrak{X}(M) \times \mathfrak{X}(M) \to \mathfrak{X}(M),$$

such that

$$R(X, Y, Z) \stackrel{\text{def}}{=} R(X, Y)Z.$$

The Riemann curvature tensor is also represented by a (0,4) type tensor

$$R : \mathfrak{X}(M) \times \mathfrak{X}(M) \times \mathfrak{X}(M) \times \mathfrak{X}(M) \to \mathcal{F}(M),$$

such that

$$R(X, Y, Z, W) \stackrel{\text{def}}{=} \langle R(X, Y)Z, W \rangle.$$

We use the same symbol for the two different types of tensors when confusion is not feared. There is an isomorphism between these two types of tensors related by raising or lowering an index when in component form.

In a local coordinate system,

$$R(e_i, e_j)e_k = \sum_{l=1}^{n} R^l_{ijk} e_l, \tag{2.7}$$

and

$$R_{ijkl} = R(e_i, e_j, e_k, e_l). \tag{2.8}$$

They are related by

$$R_{ijkl} = \sum_{m=1}^{n} R^m_{ijk} g_{ml}. \tag{2.9}$$

The Riemann curvature tensor R is uniquely determined by n^4 components R^l_{ijk} or R_{ijkl}. The components of Riemann curvature tensor are determined by the connection coefficients.

In local coordinates,

$$R(X, Y)Z = \sum_{i,j,k,l=1}^{n} R^l_{ijk} X^i Y^j Z^k e_l, \tag{2.10}$$

and

$$R(X, Y, Z, W) = \sum_{i,j,k,l=1}^{n} R_{ijkl} X^i Y^j Z^k W^l. \tag{2.11}$$

Remark 18. Caution — Different Indexed Notations of the Curvature Tensor

We use R^l_{ijk} to denote the components of the curvature tensor of type (1,3). I call this form the **implicit ordering of mixed indices** because both upper indices and lower indices are flushed to the very left. By just looking at this symbol, we are not able to determine the order of the upper index l among the lower indices. This could be confusing to the eyes but it does not cause substantial confusion in logic because we can trace back to the very definition in Eq. 2.7 to determine the meaning of each index in R^l_{ijk}, or we can go to Eq. 2.9 to find out that the upper index l in R^l_{ijk} is really the fourth index in R_{ijkl} having been raised. Some books use **explicit ordering of mixed indices**, which adds more clarity to the notation. For example, in our case, R^l_{ijk} is denoted as $R_{ijk}{}^l$, or even $R_{ijk\cdot}{}^l$ with a dot in the position in the lower indices, to indicate that the upper index is the fourth index which has be raised. Some authors even use the notation $\Gamma_{ij}{}^k$ for the Christoffel symbols of the second kind. Again there is a great variety of conflicting conventions. Some books raise the second index as $R_{i\cdot kl}{}^j$, and some books raise the first index as $R^i_{\cdot jkl}$. The reader should be cautious about the different notations and definitions of the components when reading other books.

Theorem 17. *In local coordinates, the Riemann curvature tensor is represented by*

$$R^l_{ijk} = \partial_j \Gamma^l_{ik} - \partial_i \Gamma^l_{jk} + \sum_{m=1}^{n} (\Gamma^m_{ik}\Gamma^l_{mj} - \Gamma^m_{jk}\Gamma^l_{mi}).$$

There are symmetries in R and all of n^4 components are not independent. The Riemann curvature tensor has the following properties.

Theorem 18. (Properties of Riemann curvature tensor)

(1) $R(X,Y) = -R(Y,X)$. (Skew symmetry)
(2) $\langle R(X,Y)W, Z \rangle = -\langle R(X,Y)Z, W \rangle$. (Skew symmetry)
(3) $\langle R(X,Y)Z, W \rangle = \langle R(Z,W)X, Y \rangle$. (Symmetry)
(4) $R(X,Y)Z + R(Y,Z)X + R(Z,X)Y = 0$. (First Bianchi identity)
(5) $\nabla_X R(Y,Z) + \nabla_Y R(Z,X) + \nabla_Z R(X,Y) = 0$. (Second Bianchi identity)

In a local coordinate system, these properties have the following component form.

Corollary. (Properties of Riemann curvature tensor — component form)

(1) $R_{ijkl} = -R_{jikl}$. (Skew symmetry)
(2) $R_{ijkl} = -R_{ijlk}$. (Skew symmetry)
(3) $R_{ijkl} = R_{klij}$. (Symmetry)
(4) $R_{ijkl} + R_{iklj} + R_{iljk} = 0$. (First Bianchi identity)
   This is often written as $R_{i[jkl]} = 0$, where $[jkl]$ represent the rotation of these indices.
(5) $R_{ijkl;m} + R_{ijlm;k} + R_{ijmk,l} = 0$, (Second Bianchi identity)
   where $R_{ijkl;m}$ is a shorthand for $\partial_m R_{ijkl}$. This is also written as $R_{ij[kl;m]} = 0$.

3.5 Sectional Curvature

In the Euclidean space, we have the concept of straight lines and planes. In the hyperbolic space, we still have straight lines and planes—hyperbolic lines and hyperbolic planes. In the general setting of Riemannian manifolds, the concepts of straight lines and planes are gone. On Riemannian manifolds, the closest counterparts of straight lines and planes are geodesic lines and geodesic surfaces. The hyperbolic space is an example of a Riemannian manifold. Hyperbolic lines are geodesics lines and hyperbolic planes are geodesic surfaces in the hyperbolic space.

Definition 39. Plane section, geodesic surface

At a point p on a Riemannian manifold M, a 2-dimensional linear subspace $\pi \subseteq T_p(M)$ is called a **plane section** at point p. A plane section π spanned by two independent tangent vectors X and Y is denoted by $\pi(X, Y)$, or $\pi(X \wedge Y)$.

The geodesics passing p and tangent to a plane section π constitute a surface (2-D submanifold) of M, which is called a **geodesic surface** at p tangent to plane section π.

We have used the concept of geodesic surface to define parallel transport in Definition 31. At any point p, given a plane section π, there exists a unique geodesic surface S at p tangent to π. Let p' be another point on

S and π' be the tangent plane of S at p'. At point p', there is a geodesic surface S' at p' tangent to π'. In general, S and S' do not coincide. If the same surface S is the geodesic surface at all of its points in a neighborhood, then S is called a **totally geodesic surface** [Hadamard (1901); Cartan (1951)]. A totally geodesic surface is the analog in a Riemannian manifold of a plane in the Euclidean space. Many properties of a plane are also true for a totally geodesic surface. For example, if two points on a geodesic line lie in a totally geodesic surface, then all points on the geodesic line lie in this surface. Hyperbolic planes are totally geodesic surfaces in the hyperbolic space.

Definition 40. Sectional curvature

The Gaussian curvature of the geodesic surface at p tangent to plane section $\pi(X \wedge Y)$ is called the **sectional curvature** of M at point p in the section of $\pi(X \wedge Y)$, denoted by $K(\pi)$ or $K(X \wedge Y)$.

Definition 41. Isotropic and constant curvature manifold

A Riemannian manifold M is said to be **isotropic at point** p, if the sectional curvature is the same for all sections $\pi(X \wedge Y)$ at p. M is called **isotropic** if it is isotropic at every point. M is called a **manifold of constant curvature**, if M is isotropic and the sectional curvature is a constant at every point on M.

The hyperbolic space is an example of a manifold of negative constant curvature.

The following theorem gives the relationship between Riemann curvature tensor and the sectional curvature.

Theorem 19. (Sectional curvature) *The sectional curvature $K(X \wedge Y)$ of M, is equal to*

$$K(X \wedge Y) = \frac{\langle R(X,Y)X, Y \rangle}{|X \wedge Y|^2} = \frac{\langle R(X,Y)X, Y \rangle}{\langle X, X \rangle \langle Y, Y \rangle - \langle X, Y \rangle^2},$$

where $|X \wedge Y|$ is the notation for the area of the parallelogram spanned by X and Y, which is equal to $\sqrt{\langle X, X \rangle \langle Y, Y \rangle - \langle X, Y \rangle^2}$.

The sectional curvature $K(X \wedge Y)$ is determined by the point p and section $\pi(X \wedge Y)$. It is independent of the choice of tangent vectors X and Y, as long as they span the same plane section π.

Corollary 1. (Sectional curvature) *If* $\{e_1, e_2\}$ *is an orthonormal basis for section* $e_1 \wedge e_2$, *then the sectional curvature* $K(e_1 \wedge e_2)$ *is equal to*

$$K(e_1 \wedge e_2) = \langle R(e_1, e_2)e_1, e_2 \rangle.$$

Corollary 2. *A Riemannian manifold* M *of dimension 2 is trivially isotropic because there is only one plane section passing a point* $p \in M$. *In such a case, the sectional curvature, or Gaussian curvature is equal to*

$$K = \frac{R_{1212}}{\det g},$$

where $\det g = g_{11}g_{22} - g_{12}g_{21}$ *is the determinant of the matrix* $[g_{ij}]$.

If the basis of the tangent plane is orthonormal, then $g_{ij} = \delta_{ij}$ *and* $\det g = 1$. *Hence*

$$K = R_{1212}.$$

Theorem 20. *The Riemann curvature tensor at point* p *is uniquely determined by the sectional curvatures of all plane sections passing through* p.

Remark 19. Elaboration — Sectional Curvature and Riemann Curvature Tensor

If the dimension of the Riemannian manifold is n, then the tangent space at a point has a dimension n. There are n basis vectors $e_1, \ldots, e_n$ for the tangent space. Any two of the basis vectors span a plane section. These basis vectors can span $\frac{1}{2}n(n-1)$ plane sections. However, the sectional curvatures do not simply work like vector linear combinations. These $\frac{1}{2}n(n-1)$ sectional curvatures cannot determine the sectional curvature for all plane sections completely. From the symmetry of the Riemann curvature tensor, we can find that, out of n^4 components of R_{ijkl}, there are $\frac{1}{12}n^2(n^2-1)$ independent components. This number is much larger than $\frac{1}{2}n(n-1)$. On surfaces, we have $n = 2$. There is only one independent component out of 16 components of R_{ijkl}. We can use R_{1212}, or just the Gaussian curvature K.

Theorem 21. *If Riemannian manifold M is isotropic at point p, then,*

$$R_{ijkl} = K_p(g_{ik}g_{jl} - g_{il}g_{jk}),$$

where K_p is the sectional curvature for all plane sections at point p.

Corollary. *For a constant curvature Riemannian manifold,*

$$R_{ijkl} = K(g_{ik}g_{jl} - g_{il}g_{jk}),$$

where K is the constant sectional curvature, or Gaussian curvature.

3.6 Ricci Curvature Tensor and Ricci Scalar Curvature

The Ricci curvature tensor is the average of the Riemann curvature tensor in some sense.

Definition 42. Ricci curvature tensor

For a fixed pair of vectors X, Y, using the Riemann curvature operator R, we can define a linear mapping $\Omega_{X,Y} : T_p(M) \to T_p(M)$; $Z \mapsto R(X,Y)Z$. We define the **Ricci curvature tensor** to be a mapping $\hat{R} : T_p(M) \times T_p(M) \to \mathbb{R}$, such that

$$\hat{R}(X,Y) \overset{\text{def}}{=} \operatorname{tr}\Omega_{X,Y},$$

where $\operatorname{tr}\Omega_{X,Y}$ is the trace of operator $\Omega_{X,Y}$. In local coordinates,

$$\hat{R}_{ij} = \sum_{m=1}^{n} R_{imj}^m.$$

Theorem 22. *Ricci curvature tensor is symmetric. Namely,*

$$\hat{R}(X,Y) = \hat{R}(Y,X).$$

In local coordinates,

$$\hat{R}_{ij} = \hat{R}_{ji}, \ i,j = 1, \ldots, n.$$

For $X \in T_p(M)$, $Q(X) \overset{\text{def}}{=} \hat{R}(X, X)$ is a quadratic form on $T_p(M)$.

Theorem 23. (Geometric meaning of Ricci curvature tensor) *Let $X \in T_p(M)$ be a unit vector. Then $\hat{R}(X, X)$ is equal to the mean of sectional curvatures of all sections $X \wedge Y$ containing X, for all $Y \in T_p(M)$. $\hat{R}(X, X)$ is called the **Ricci curvature** of direction X at point p.*

We can even define the mean of all Ricci curvature tensors, which is the Ricci scalar curvature.

Definition 43. Ricci scalar curvature

Ricci scalar curvature is defined to be
$$\bar{R} \overset{\text{def}}{=} \text{tr}\hat{R},$$
where $\text{tr}\hat{R}$ is the trace of $\hat{R}$. In local coordinates,
$$\bar{R} \overset{\text{def}}{=} \sum_{i=1}^{n} \hat{R}_i^i = \sum_{i,j=1}^{n} g^{ij}\hat{R}_{ij}.$$

Theorem 24. (Geometric meaning of Ricci scalar curvature) *Ricci scalar curvature $\bar{R}$ is equal to the mean of $\hat{R}(X, X)$ for all the unit tangent vectors $X \in T_p(M)$.*

Since the Ricci curvature tensor and Ricci scalar curvature are averages of the Riemann curvature tensor in some sense, none of them completely determine the Riemann curvature tensor. They are not the complete description of the curvature of the manifold.

Theorem 25. *If Riemannian manifold M is isotropic at point p, then,*
$$\bar{R} = n(n-1)K_p,$$
where n is the dimension of M and K_p is the sectional curvature for all plane sections at point p. Especially if M is a manifold of constant curvature, then
$$\bar{R} = n(n-1)K.$$

Corollary. *Let M be a Riemannian manifold of dimension 2. Then the Ricci scalar curvature and the Gaussian curvature are related by*

$$\bar{R} = 2K.$$

Remark 20. Comparison — Consequences of the Alternative Definition of Curvature Operator with a Negative Sign

If the curvature operator $R(X, Y)$ is defined differently from Definition 37 with an extra negative sign, Theorem 19 should take a different form

$$K(X \wedge Y) = -\frac{\langle R(X,Y)X, Y \rangle}{|X \wedge Y|^2} = \frac{\langle R(X,Y)Y, X \rangle}{|X \wedge Y|^2}.$$

Corollary 1 of Theorem 19 takes a different form

$$K(e_1 \wedge e_2) = -\langle R(e_1, e_2)e_1, e_2 \rangle = \langle R(e_1, e_2)e_2, e_1 \rangle,$$

and Corollary 2 of Theorem 19 also takes a different form $K = -\dfrac{R_{1212}}{\det g} = \dfrac{R_{1221}}{\det g}$ in general, and $K = R_{1221}$ for orthonormal basis. Theorem 21 and its Corollary take different forms of $R_{ijkl} = -K_p(g_{ik}g_{jl} - g_{il}g_{jk})$ and $R_{ijkl} = -K(g_{ik}g_{jl} - g_{il}g_{jk})$. See [Chern et al. (1999); Boothby(2002)]. [MSJ (1993)] (p.1350) defines Ricci curvature tensor with an extra negative sign $\bar{R}_{ij} = -\sum_m R_{imj}^m$. The product of two negative signs is positive one. So their Ricci curvature tensor and scalar curvature agree with ours.

3.7   Embedding of Riemannian Manifolds

Theorem 26. (Nash embedding theorem) *Any smooth n-dimensional compact Riemannian manifold admits a smooth isometric embedding in $\mathbb{R}^k$ for some k.*

The original version of the theorem proved by Nash [Nash (1956)] gave an upper bound of $k = \frac{1}{2}n(3n + 11)$ for compact C^r-manifold ($r \geq 3$) and $k = 2(2n + 1)(3n + 7)$ for noncompact C^r-manifold ($r \geq 3$) (see [MSJ (1993)] p. 1355). With time, researchers were able to make this bound k tighter (lower). There is a lower bound to this upper bound. That is $k \geq s_n$, where $s_n = \frac{1}{2}n(n + 1)$ and is called the Janet dimension ([Janet (1926); Cartan (1927)]).

Hilbert proved that it is impossible to isometrically embed the hyperbolic plane in $\mathbb{R}^3$. Blanuša [Blanuša (1955)] constructed an isometric embedding of the hyperbolic plane in $\mathbb{R}^6$. The real projective plane admits an isometric embedding in $\mathbb{R}^5$. Shing-Tung Yau conjectured that every oriented smooth surface can be isometrically embedded in $\mathbb{R}^4$.

With Nash embedding theorem, the intrinsic view and extrinsic view of geometry are unified. See [Han and Hong (2006)] for more on isometric embedding of Riemannian manifolds.

§4   Affinely-Connected Manifolds

4.1   Curvature Tensors and Torsion Tensors

Differential structures on differentiable manifolds are not rich enough to study the geometric properties like curvature, because the notion of distance is not defined on differentiable manifolds. Geometric concepts, like curvature, are defined for Riemannian manifolds when the concept of metric is introduced. Can we discuss geometry without the concept of distance? We have done so in affine geometry and projective geometry, but not on manifolds yet.

Curvature is a key concept in the geometry of manifolds, which measures how much the manifold deviates from a flat space. We recall in last section, the key to define curvature is to define the concept of parallelism, which is an essential concept in affine geometry. The curvature is defined by the amount a vector has been changed after being parallel-transported around an infinitesimal loop. The change is zero in Euclidean spaces. On Riemannian manifolds, we have metric structures and we defined parallel transport using the concept of lengths and angles. To generalize the geometry to manifolds which do not have the concept of distance, we can axiomize the concept of parallel transport. Properties of Riemannian connections in Theorem 13 prompt us that they can be used as the axiomatic definition of connections. The connection stipulates the concept of what is considered parallel when a tangent vector at one point on the manifold is transported to a nearby point. This is called an affine connection.

Definition 44. Affinely-connected manifold

A differentiable manifold M together with a mapping $\nabla : \mathfrak{X}(M) \times \mathfrak{X}(M) \to \mathfrak{X}(M); (X, Y) \mapsto \nabla_X Y$, is called an **affinely-connected manifold**, if ∇ satisfies the following **axioms**, for all smooth vector fields X, X_1, X_2, Y, Y_1, Y_2 and smooth scalar fields f, f_1, f_2 on M.

(1) $\mathcal{F}(M)$-linear on the first variable:
 $\nabla_{f_1 X_1 + f_2 X_2} Y = f_1 \nabla_{X_1} Y + f_2 \nabla_{X_2} Y.$

(2) Additive on the second variable:
$\nabla_X(Y_1 + Y_2) = \nabla_X Y_1 + \nabla_X Y_2$.

(3) Leibniz rule on the second variable:
$\nabla_X(fY) = f\nabla_X Y + (\nabla_X f)Y$.

$\nabla_X Y$ is called the **covariant derivative** of Y in the direction of X.
∇ is called an **affine connection** on M.

Note that ∇ is $\mathbb{R}$-linear on both X and Y. ∇ is $\mathcal{F}(M)$-linear on X, but not $\mathcal{F}(M)$-linear on Y. From Theorem 13 we know immediately that the Riemannian connections defined in Definition 34 are affine connections.

With the structure of affine connections, most of the discussions about Riemannian manifolds can be carried over, although we do not have a metric structure on the manifold any more.

Remark 21. Historical Note — Affine Connections
The development of affine connections is mainly due to H. Weyl and Élie Cartan. After Einstein geometrized Newton's theory of gravity using Riemannian geometry, H. Weyl was motivated to generalize Riemannian manifolds to affinely-connected manifolds in order to tackle the problem of geometrizing Maxwell's theory of electromagnetic fields. Élie Cartan was motivated to generalize the Erlangen program of Klein to the manifolds of Riemann.

Different names for the manifolds with an affine connection have been seen in literature and they are not quite unified. S. S. Chern used "affinely connected manifold", as well as "affinely-connected manifold" in the same paper [Chern (1947)]. We adopted the one with a hyphen to avoid possible confusion with the concept of connectedness. Other names used in literature include "manifolds with affine connection", "affine connection manifolds" and "affine connection spaces".

Definition 45. Covariant differential

Let X, Y be vector fields on an affinely-connected manifold M with affine connection ∇. The **covariant differential** ∇Y of Y is defined to be a tensor field of type $(1,1)$ $\nabla Y : \mathfrak{X}(M) \to \mathfrak{X}(M)$, such that $\nabla Y(X) \overset{\text{def}}{=} \nabla_X Y$.

Theorem 27. (Affine connections) *Let* $Y, Y_1, Y_2 \in \mathfrak{X}(M)$ *be smooth vector fields and* $f \in \mathcal{F}(M)$ *be a smooth scalar field on* M. Axioms (2) *and* (3) *in* Definition *44 can be rewritten as*

(1) Additive: $\nabla(Y_1 + Y_2) = \nabla Y_1 + \nabla Y_2$.

(2) Leibniz rule: $\nabla(fY) = f\nabla Y + (\nabla f)Y$.

∇ is also called the **nabla** operator because its shape looks like a nabla — a type of harp. It is a vector operator. $(\nabla f)Y$ in property (2) of Theorem 27 means the dyadic product or tensor product of vectors (∇f) and Y.

Now we select a local coordinate system and natural basis $\{e_1, \ldots, e_n\}$ for $T_p(M)$. We can find the coordinate representation of covariant differential.

Definition 46. Connection coefficients

Let $\{e_1, \ldots, e_n\}$ be the field of natural basis at each point on M. The covariant derivatives of the basis vector fields can be expressed as

$$\nabla_{e_i} e_j = \sum_{k=1}^{n} \Gamma_{ij}^k e_k.$$

The coefficients Γ_{ij}^k are called **connection coefficients** (or **Christoffel Symbols**) of M.

Theorem 28. (Covariant derivative in local coordinates) *Let Y be a smooth vector field on an affinely-connected manifold with affine connection ∇. In local coordinates, the covariant derivative is*

$$\nabla_j Y^i = \frac{\partial Y^i}{\partial x_j} + \sum_{k=1}^{n} \Gamma_{kj}^i Y^k,$$

where by $\nabla_j Y^i$ we mean $\nabla_{e_j} Y^i$.

The law of coordinate transformation for connection coefficients take the same form as Eq. 2.4 in Theorem 16 for Riemannian connections.

Let Y be a vector field in a neighborhood U on M with affine connection ∇. Y is called a **parallel vector field** in U, if $\nabla Y = 0$ at all points in U.

For an arbitrary manifold M with affine connection, other than $\mathbb{R}^n$ with the standard affine connection, there do not exist such parallel vector fields in an open neighborhoods. However, we can talk about parallel vector fields on a curve.

Definition 47. Parallel vector field on a curve, parallel transport along a curve

Let γ be a curve on a manifold M with affine connection ∇. Let X be a vector field defined on γ. If $\nabla_v X = 0$ for all vectors v that is tangent to γ, then X is said to be **parallel** on the curve γ. In such a case, a vector in X at one point is called the **parallel transport** of the vector at another point along curve γ.

Definition 48. Geodesic line

Let γ be a curve on a manifold M with affine connection ∇. If the tangent vectors of γ are parallel along γ itself, then γ is called an **affine geodesic line** (or just **geodesic line**) on M.

Intuitively, the geodesic lines are the "straightest" curves. On a general affinely-connected manifold, the concept of distance is absent. On a Riemannian manifold, if we use the Riemannian connection defined in the last section, the affine geodesic lines and metric geodesic lines coincide. The metric geodesics are the "shortest distance" curves. Even on a surface in $\mathbb{R}^3$, geodesics can be defined metrically, or affinely, because a surface in $\mathbb{R}^3$ has both affine and metric structures, and the notions of affine geodesics and metric geodesics coincide.

Theorem 29. (Equations of a geodesic line) *In local coordinates, the geodesic line is described by the following equations:*

$$\frac{d^2 x^k}{dt} + \sum_{i,j=1}^{n} \Gamma_{ij}^k \frac{dx^i}{dt} \frac{dx^j}{dt} = 0, \, k = 1, \ldots, n. \tag{2.12}$$

Eq. 2.12 has the same form as Eq. 2.1 in Theorem 12 for Riemannian manifolds, except that the connection coefficients Γ_{ij}^k are no longer derived from the metric tensor as in Eq. 2.2, because the metric makes no sense now. Γ_{ij}^k are defined in Definition 46. For Riemannian manifolds, the two definitions coincide.

Definition 49. Curvature tensor

Let X, Y, Z be vector fields on a manifold M with affine connection ∇. A type (1,3) tensor field, called the **curvature tensor** of M is defined to be a mapping: $R : \mathfrak{X}(M) \times \mathfrak{X}(M) \times \mathfrak{X}(M) \to \mathfrak{X}(M)$, such that

$$R(X, Y, Z) \stackrel{\text{def}}{=} R(X, Y)Z \stackrel{\text{def}}{=} \nabla_Y(\nabla_X Z) - \nabla_X(\nabla_Y Z) - \nabla_{[Y,X]}Z.$$

This definition is similar to the Riemann curvature tensor except the affine connection ∇ is more general than the Riemannian connection. Ricci curvature tensor and Ricci scalar curvature are defined similarly for an affinely-connected manifold with affine connection ∇ as well. Note the difference between an affinely-connected manifold with general affine connection ∇ and a Riemannian manifold with a Riemannian connection. For a general affine connection ∇, the Ricci curvature tensor may or may not be symmetric, while for a Riemannian connection, the Ricci curvature tensor is always symmetric (see Theorem 22).

Definition 50. Torsion tensor

Let X, Y be vector fields on a manifold M with affine connection ∇. A type (1,2) tensor field, called the **torsion tensor** of M is defined to be a mapping: $T : \mathfrak{X}(M) \times \mathfrak{X}(M) \to \mathfrak{X}(M)$, such that

$$T(X, Y) = \nabla_X Y - \nabla_Y X - [X, Y].$$

In classical differential geometry of curves, the torsion of a space curve is the measure of the degree that the curve deviates from a plane.

In local coordinates,

$$T(X, Y) = \sum_{i,j,k=1}^{n} T_{ij}^k X^i Y^j e_k,$$

where

$$T_{ij}^k = \Gamma_{ji}^k - \Gamma_{ij}^k.$$

Theorem 30. *The torsion tensor for a Riemannian connection is always zero.*

4.2   Metrizability

It is a natural question to ask, from Riemannian manifolds to affinely-connected manifolds, did we really generalize? Namely, for any affine connection ∇ on a manifold, can we find a Riemannian metric such that the affine connection coincide with the Riemannian connection?

For a particular affine connection, if this is true, the affine connection is called **metrizable**. The above question can be put in the form: is any affine connection metrizable?

The answer is no. The following is a counterexample due to A. Vanžurová and P. Žáčková [Vanžurová and Žáčková (2009)], who analyzed the conditions of metrizability of affine connections.

Example 24. (Non-metrizable affine connection) Let M be a 2-D affinely-connected manifold with affine connection ∇. The affine connection is defined by the components in local coordinates
$$\Gamma_{11}^1 = \Gamma_{22}^1 = 1, \ \Gamma_{12}^1 = \Gamma_{21}^1 = 0, \ \Gamma_{11}^2 = \Gamma_{22}^2 = 0, \ \Gamma_{12}^2 = \Gamma_{21}^2 = 2.$$
We can calculate the Ricci curvature tensor $\hat{R}_{11} = -2$, $\hat{R}_{12} = \hat{R}_{21} = 0$, $\hat{R}_{22} = -1$, and the Ricci scalar curvature $\bar{R} = -3$. This affine connection is not metrizable.   ♣

Exercises

1. Show that the set $M \subset \mathbb{R}^3$, $M = \{(x, y, 0)|x, y \in \mathbb{R}\} \cup \{(0, 0, z)|z \in \mathbb{R}\}$ is not a topological manifold.
2. Show that the surface in $\mathbb{R}^3$
$$\begin{bmatrix} x \\ y \\ z \end{bmatrix} = \begin{bmatrix} (a + a\cos v)\cos u \\ (a + a\cos v)\sin u \\ a\sin v \end{bmatrix}$$
is not a topological manifold in $\mathbb{R}^3$.
3. Given two identical squares (including the interiors). What is the topological manifold if the corresponding edges of the two squares are glued together?

4. Given two identical cubes (including the interiors). What is the topological manifold if the corresponding faces of the two cubes are glued together?

5. A Möbius strip has a circular boundary. What is the topological manifold if the boundaries of two Möbius strips are glued together?

6. What is the topological manifold if the boundary of a Möbius strip is glued with the boundary of a circular disk?

7. A cylinder has two circular boundaries. What is the topological manifold if the boundary of a Möbius strip is glued with one circular boundary of a cylinder?

8. Show that the real projective plane $\mathbb{R}P^2$ is a differentiable manifold by providing a compatible atlas.

9. Show that the real projective space $\mathbb{R}P^n$ is a differentiable manifold by providing a compatible atlas.

10. The special linear group $SL(n, \mathbb{R})$ is the group of all the $n \times n$ real matrices with determinant one. Show that $SL(n, \mathbb{R})$ is a differentiable manifold by providing a compatible atlas. What is the dimension of this manifold?

11. Give an example of a mapping $\varphi : M \to N$, where M and N are differentiable manifolds, such that φ is bijective and smooth but not a diffeomorphism.

12. Show the definition of equivalent curves in Definition 11 does not depend on the choice of the coordinate patch.

13. Let a surface S in $\mathbb{R}^3$ be represented by the graph of a function $z = f(x, y)$ (Monge parametrization). A point on the surface is represented by a vector $\mathbf{r} = (x, y, z)$. Denote $\mathbf{r}_x = \frac{\partial \mathbf{r}}{\partial x}$ and $\mathbf{r}_y = \frac{\partial \mathbf{r}}{\partial y}$. They are the tangent vectors at point $\mathbf{r}$. The normal vector at point $\mathbf{r}$ is $\mathbf{r}_x \times \mathbf{r}_y$. Let $\bar{\mathbf{r}} = (\bar{x}, \bar{y}, \bar{z}) \in \mathbb{R}^3$ be a point on the tangent plane $T_{\mathbf{r}}(S)$ of S at $\mathbf{r}$. The equation of the tangent plane $T_{\mathbf{r}}(S)$ is $(\bar{\mathbf{r}} - \mathbf{r}) \cdot (\mathbf{r}_x \times \mathbf{r}_y) = 0$, where $\mathbf{r}$ is considered a fixed point while $\bar{\mathbf{r}}$ is a variable. For the surface of hyperboloid $z^2 - x^2 - y^2 - 1 = 0$, find the equation of its tangent plane at any point.

14. A surface S in $\mathbb{R}^3$ in general can be represented using two parameters u and v such that $\mathbf{r} = \mathbf{r}(u, v)$. Let $\bar{\mathbf{r}} = \bar{\mathbf{r}}(\bar{u}, \bar{v}) \in \mathbb{R}^3$ be a point on the tangent plane $T_{\mathbf{r}}(S)$ of S at $\mathbf{r} = \mathbf{r}(u, v)$. The equation of the tangent plane $T_{\mathbf{r}}(S)$ is $(\bar{\mathbf{r}} - \mathbf{r}) \cdot (\mathbf{r}_u \times \mathbf{r}_v) = 0$. For the surface of hyperboloid in the parametric form
$$x = k \sinh \theta \cos \varphi, \ y = k \sinh \theta \sin \varphi, \ z = k \cosh \theta,$$
find the equation of its tangent plane at any point.

15. Let S^2 be the unit sphere and N be the north pole of S^2. Let $M = S^2 - \{N\}$. The stereographic projection $\psi_1 : M \to \mathbb{R}^2$ is defined in Example 3, with the projection plane touching the south pole. If we use spherical coordinates (θ, φ) for S^2, where θ is the colatitude. and Cartesian coordinates (X, Y) for the plane $\mathbb{R}^2$, then $\psi(\theta, \varphi) = (X, Y)$ with

$$X = \frac{2 \sin \theta \cos \varphi}{1 - \sin \theta},$$
$$Y = \frac{2 \sin \theta \sin \varphi}{1 - \sin \theta}.$$

   (1) Find the Jacobian matrix of the differential mapping $d\psi$.
   (2) Find the Jacobian (determinant) of this matrix.
   (3) Show that ψ is a diffeomorphism.

16. Let $\psi : \mathbb{R}^2 \to \mathbb{R}^3; (x, y) \mapsto (x, xy, y^2)$.
   (1) Find the Jacobian matrix of the differential mapping $d\psi$.
   (2) Show ψ is an immersion except at the origin.

17. Let $f : M \to \mathbb{R}$. In local coordinates (x, y) for M, $f(x, y) = ze^x \cos y$. Find df.

18. Let M be the set of all pairs (v_1, v_2) of mutually orthogonal unit vectors in $\mathbb{R}^3$. Show that M is a differentiable manifold.

19. Let M be the differentiable manifold in the above problem. Show that M is diffeomorphic to the tangent bundle of S^2.

20. The Euclidean space $\mathbb{R}^3$ is a trivial example of a Riemannian manifold. Using the cylindrical coordinate system (ρ, φ, z),
   (1) find the metric;
   (2) calculate the connection coefficients Γ^i_{jk} for $i, j, k = 1, 2, 3$;
   (3) find the equations of geodesics;
   (4) calculate the Riemannian curvature tensor R_{ijkl}, for $i, j, k, l = 1, 2, 3$.

21. Using the spherical coordinate system (r, θ, φ) for the Euclidean space $\mathbb{R}^3$, where r is the radius, θ colatitude and φ longitude,
   (1) find the metric;
   (2) calculate the connection coefficients Γ^i_{jk} for $i, j, k = 1, 2, 3$;
   (3) find the equations of geodesics;
   (4) calculate the Riemannian curvature tensor R_{ijkl}, for $i, j, k, l = 1, 2, 3$.

22. Find the sectional curvature for S^3 with radius a.

23. Schwartzchild spacetime is the spacetime surrounding a center mass, according to the theory of general relativity. The spacetime is not a Riemannian manifold but rather a 4-dimensional pseudo-Riemannian manifold (the metric is not necessarily positive definite). At any time

instant, the space submanifold of Schwartzchild spacetime is a Riemannian manifold with the metric

$$ds^2 = \frac{dr^2}{1 - \frac{r_s}{r}} + r^2(d\theta^2 + \sin^2\theta d\varphi^2),$$

where r_s is a constant called the Schwartzchild radius.

(1) Find connection coefficients Γ^i_{jk}, $i, j, k = 1, 2, 3$.

(2) Find the Riemann curvature tensor R_{ijkl}, $i, j, k, l = 1, 2, 3$.

(3) The surface $\theta = 0$ is a totally geodesic surface, which is called Flamm's surface. Calculate the Gaussian curvature for the Flamm's surface.

Chapter 3

Hilbert Spaces

Each person is a vector in an infinite dimensional space. You can never find two people with the same coordinate in each dimension, especially in a marriage.

— *Hongyu Guo*

Reading Guide. In this chapter, we discuss linear spaces equipped with additional topological structures—Hilbert spaces and Banach spaces. These topics are known as functional analysis. This chapter is placed in Part III because from the structure point of view, the topological structures in Hilbert spaces and Banach spaces play an important role. Hilbert spaces have applications in machine learning, pattern recognition as well as quantum theory in physics. Banach spaces are the generalizations of Hilbert spaces. The following is a Venn diagram showing the relationships between different structures. The structures in the shaded area are the focus of this chapter. See also a brief discussion of structures in Chap. 0.

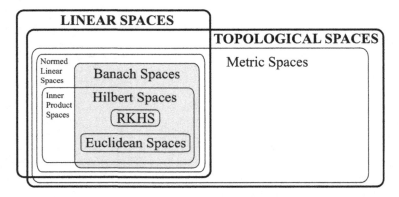

§1   Hilbert Spaces

Let V be a linear space over a field F. Most often we are interested in real or complex linear spaces. In this chapter particularly, we set the stage to be complex linear spaces. If a vector space is equipped with a structure called inner product, we can define distance using the inner product. Using the distance, we can define topology and hence we have a system with much richer structures, including algebraic structure (linear space) and topological structure (metric space). We can discuss all the concepts in analysis, like limit and convergence.

We discussed real inner product spaces in Part I Chap. 1. Here we generalize it to include both real and complex inner product spaces.

Definition 1. Inner product

Let V be a (real or complex) linear space over the field $F = \mathbb{R}$ or

$F = \mathbb{C}$. A mapping $\langle \cdot, \cdot \rangle : V \times V \to F$ is called an **inner product** if it satisfies the following conditions, for all $x, y, x_1, x_2 \in V$ and $a_1, a_2 \in F$.

(1) Linear in the first variable:
$\langle a_1 x_1 + a_2 x_2, y \rangle = a_1 \langle x_1, y \rangle + a_2 \langle x_2, y \rangle$.
(2) Conjugate symmetric: $\langle x, y \rangle = \overline{\langle y, x \rangle}$.
(3) Positive definite: $\langle x, x \rangle \geq 0$ for all $x \in V$, and $\langle x, x \rangle = 0$ iff $x = 0$.

A linear space equipped with an inner product is called a (real or complex) **inner product space**.

In this definition, the notation $\bar{a}$ represents the complex conjugate of complex number a. Condition (2) implies that $\langle x, x \rangle$ is always a real number and that is why $\langle x, x \rangle \geq 0$ always makes sense. Note that real inner product defined in Part I Chap. 1 is a special case of this definition when $F = \mathbb{R}$.

The inner product is linear in the first variable but not linear in the second variable.

Conditions (1) and (2) imply

$$\langle x, y_1 + y_2 \rangle = \langle x, y_1 \rangle + \langle x, y_2 \rangle, \tag{3.1}$$

$$\langle x, ay \rangle = \bar{a} \langle x, y \rangle. \tag{3.2}$$

A mapping $\varphi : V \to \mathbb{C}$, satisfying $\varphi(x + y) = \varphi(x) + \varphi(y)$ and $\varphi(ax) = \bar{a}\varphi(x)$ is called a **semilinear form**. A mapping $\psi : V \times V \to \mathbb{C}$ is called a **sesquilinear form** if it is linear in the first variable and semilinear in the second variable. "*Sesqui*" means "one and half" in Latin. A complex inner product is a sesquilinear form. A real inner product is a bilinear form.

Example 1. ($\mathbb{C}^n$ as an inner product space) Let $\mathbb{C}^n$ be linear space over $\mathbb{C}$ consists all n-tuples $(x_1, \ldots, x_n)$, $x_1, \ldots, x_n \in \mathbb{C}$. We define the inner product of two vectors $x = (x_1, \ldots, x_n)$ and $y = (y_1, \ldots, y_n)$ to be

$$\langle x, y \rangle \overset{\text{def}}{=} x_1 \bar{y}_1 + \cdots + x_n \bar{y}_n.$$

$(\mathbb{C}^n, \langle \cdot, \cdot \rangle)$ is an inner product space.   ♣

Example 2. ($\mathbb{C}^n$ as an inner product space) First consider the linear space $\mathbb{C}^2$. For any $x = (x_1, x_2)$ and $y = (y_1, y_2)$ in $\mathbb{C}^2$, we define

$$\langle x, y \rangle \overset{\text{def}}{=} 3x_1 \bar{y}_1 - x_1 \bar{y}_2 - x_2 \bar{y}_1 + 2x_2 \bar{y}_2.$$

The matrix $\begin{bmatrix} 3 & -1 \\ -1 & 2 \end{bmatrix}$ is positive-definite. $(\mathbb{C}^2, \langle \cdot, \cdot \rangle)$ is an inner product space.

In general, we consider the linear space $\mathbb{C}^n$. Let g be a positive-definite Hermitian matrix (a Hermitian matrix H is a matrix such that $H = \overline{H^t}$, where $\overline{H^t}$ is the conjugate transpose of H). For any two vectors $x = (x_1, x_2, \ldots, x_n)$ and $y = (y_1, y_2, \ldots, y_n)$, we define

$$\langle x, y \rangle \overset{\text{def}}{=} \sum_{i=1}^{n} g_{ij} x_i \bar{y}_j,$$

then $(\mathbb{C}^n, \langle \cdot, \cdot \rangle)$ is an inner product space.   ♣

Example 3. (Sequence space l^2) Let l^2 be a linear space in which each vector is an infinite sequence $x = (x_1, x_2, \ldots, x_n, \ldots)$ such that $\sum_{i=1}^{\infty} |x_i|^2$ converges. The inner product of $x = (x_1, x_2, \ldots, x_n, \ldots)$ and $y = (y_1, y_2, \ldots, y_m, \ldots)$ is defined to be

$$\langle x, y \rangle \overset{\text{def}}{=} \sum_{i=1}^{\infty} x_i \bar{y}_i.$$

Then $(l^2, \langle \cdot, \cdot \rangle)$ is an inner product space.   ♣

Example 4. (Finite sequence space) Consider a linear space V in which each vector is a sequence $x = (x_1, x_2, \ldots, x_n, \ldots)$ such that $x_k \neq 0$ for only finitely many values of k. The inner product of $x = (x_1, x_2, \ldots, x_n, \ldots)$ and $y = (y_1, y_2, \ldots, y_m, \ldots)$ is defined to be

$$\langle x, y \rangle \overset{\text{def}}{=} \sum_{i=1}^{\infty} x_i \bar{y}_i.$$

Then $(V, \langle \cdot, \cdot \rangle)$ is an inner product space. Note the subtle difference between this example and the previous example. Here each vector is a sequence with finite number of non-zero elements. The inner product is always well defined. (In fact, each vector is a sequence that converges to zero.) Due to this subtle difference, we are going to see shortly that this inner product space is not complete and hence is not a Hilbert space, while the inner product space l^2 in the previous example is a Hilbert space.   ♣

Example 5. (Square integrable function space $L^2[a, b]$) Let $L^2[a, b]$ be the linear space of all complex valued functions defined on the closed real interval $[a, b]$ whose square is Lebesgue integrable. Define

$$\langle f, g \rangle \overset{\text{def}}{=} \int_{a}^{b} f(t) \overline{g(t)} dt.$$

$(L^2[a, b], \langle \cdot, \cdot \rangle)$ is an inner product space.   ♣

Using the inner product, the distance and angle between two vectors can be defined.

Definition 2. Length, distance

Let $(V, \langle \cdot, \cdot \rangle)$ be an inner product space. For any $x \in V$, we define the **length** (or **norm**) of the vector x to be $\|x\| \overset{\text{def}}{=} \sqrt{\langle x, x \rangle}$.

For any $x, y \in V$, define the distance between x and y induced by the inner product to be

$$d(x, y) \overset{\text{def}}{=} \|x - y\| = \sqrt{\langle x - y, x - y \rangle}.$$

If $\langle x, y \rangle = 0$, we say that x and y are **orthogonal** to each other. You may try to think if we can generalize the concept of angle between two vectors to a complex linear space.

Theorem 1. *Let $(V, \langle \cdot, \cdot \rangle)$ be an inner product space. For all $x, y \in V$,*

(1) $\|x\| \geq 0$. $\|x\| = 0$ *if and only if $x = 0$.*
(2) $\|ax\| = |a|\, \|x\|$, *for any $a \in \mathbb{C}$, where $|a|$ is the absolute value of a.*
(3) Triangle inequality: $\|x + y\| \leq \|x\| + \|y\|$.

It is easy to verify that distance thus defined satisfies the axioms of metric spaces and hence the inner product space $(V, \langle \cdot, \cdot \rangle)$ becomes a metric space with respect to this distance. We can discuss all the metric properties and topological properties of this space. In metric spaces, completeness is an important property.

Definition 3. Hilbert space

Let $(H, \langle \cdot, \cdot \rangle)$ be a real or complex inner product space. If the metric induced by the inner product is complete, then $(H, \langle \cdot, \cdot \rangle)$ is called a real or complex **Hilbert space** respectively.

We give examples and counterexamples of Hilbert spaces in the following. If the inner product space is finite dimensional, its metric is always complete and hence it is always a Hilbert space. Finite dimensional inner product spaces are called **Euclidean spaces** and finite dimensional complex inner product spaces are called **unitary spaces**. All the Euclidean spaces are isometrically isomorphic to $\mathbb{R}^n$ for some n and all the unitary spaces are isometrically isomorphic to $\mathbb{C}^n$ for some n.

Finite dimensional inner product spaces are well studied and their properties are relatively easier. In this chapter, we are mostly interested in infinite dimensional Hilbert spaces.

Example 6. (Sequence space l^2) The sequence space l^2 in Example 3 is complete. Hence it is a Hilbert space.　　　　　　　　　　　　　♣

Example 7. (Square integrable function space $L^2[a, b]$) The inner product space $L^2[a, b]$ introduced in Example 5 is complete. Hence it is a Hilbert space.　　　　　　　　　　　　　♣

Example 8. (Counterexample—Finite sequence space) The inner product space in Example 4 is not complete and hence not a Hilbert space. Recall the space consists of vectors which are sequences of the form $s = (x_1, x_2, \ldots, x_n, \ldots)$ such that $x_k \neq 0$ for only finitely many values of k. Observe a sequence of vectors $s_1, s_2, s_3, \ldots$ with

$$s_1 = (\tfrac{1}{2}, 0, 0, 0, \ldots),$$
$$s_2 = (\tfrac{1}{2}, \tfrac{1}{4}, 0, 0, \ldots),$$
$$\cdots$$
$$s_n = (\tfrac{1}{2}, \tfrac{1}{4}, \ldots, \tfrac{1}{2^n}, 0, \ldots),$$
$$\cdots \qquad .$$

Clearly this is a Cauchy sequence but it does not converge in this space. ♣

Definition 4. Orthogonal set

Let $(H, \langle \cdot, \cdot \rangle)$ be a Hilbert space and $B \subseteq H$ be a subset of H. If for all $x, y \in B$, $\langle x, y \rangle = 0$ when $x \neq y$, then B is called an **orthogonal set**.

If B is an orthogonal set and in addition for all $x \in B$, $\langle x, x \rangle = 1$, then B is called an **orthonormal set**.

Definition 5. Orthogonal basis

An orthogonal set B of a Hilbert space H is called an **orthogonal basis** (or **Hilbert basis**, or **complete orthogonal set**) if it is maximal, which means for any $x \notin B$, $B \cup \{x\}$ is not an orthogonal set.

An orthogonal basis B of a Hilbert space H is called an **orthonormal basis** (or **complete orthonormal set**) if for all $x \in B$, $\langle x, x \rangle = 1$.

Example 9. (Fourier series) In the Hilbert space $L^2[0,1]$, the set of functions

$$e_k(t) = e^{2\pi i k t}, \ k = 0, \pm 1, \pm 2, \ldots$$

forms an orthonormal basis. Any function $f(t)$ in $L^2[0,1]$ can be expanded as Fourier series

$$f(t) = \sum_{k=-\infty}^{\infty} a_k e^{2\pi i k t}, \tag{3.3}$$

where the coefficient

$$a_k = \langle f(t), e_k \rangle = \int_0^1 f(t) e^{-2\pi i k t} dt.$$

In general, if Hilbert space H has a countable orthonormal basis $\{e_k | k = 1, 2, \ldots\}$, then any vector x can be expanded in terms of this basis

$$x = \sum_{k=1}^{\infty} a_k e_k,$$

where the coefficients are

$$a_k = \langle x, e_k \rangle. \qquad \qquad \clubsuit$$

Theorem 2. (Orthogonal dimension) *Let $(H, \langle \cdot, \cdot \rangle)$ be a real or complex Hilbert space. All the orthonormal bases have the same cardinality, which is called the* **orthogonal dimension** *(or* **Hilbert dimension***) of H.*

Remark 1. Caution — Basis and Dimension of Infinite Dimensional Linear Spaces

Note that for infinite dimensional Hilbert spaces, the orthogonal basis is not a basis for the Hilbert space as a pure linear space. In a Hilbert space, any vector can be written as an "infinite linear combination" of the vectors in the orthogonal basis, like in the case of Fourier series. However, the definition of this infinite sum depends on the notion of convergence, which depends on the topological structure. In a pure linear space without any topological structure, an infinite sum is not defined.

In Part I Chap. 1, the definition of basis is for finite dimensional linear spaces. We have not defined the basis and dimension for infinite dimensional linear spaces, which we are defining now.

Definition 6. Hamel basis

Let V be a linear space over a field F and B be a subset of V. B is called a **Hamel basis** (or **algebraic basis**) if the following conditions are satisfied.

(1) Any finite subset of B is linearly independent.
(2) Any $x \in V$ is a finite linear combination of some finite subset of vectors $\{b_1, \ldots, b_n\} \subseteq B$,

$$x = \alpha_1 b_1 + \cdots + \alpha_n b_n, \ \alpha_1, \ldots, \alpha_n \in F.$$

The cardinality of a Hamel basis is called the **Hamel dimension** (or **algebraic dimension**) of V.

Hamel basis is named after Georg Hamel, a student of Hilbert. Hamel basis applies to both finite and infinite dimensional linear spaces. For finite dimensional linear spaces, Hamel basis and Hamel dimension coincide with the basis and dimension defined in Definitions 8 and 6.

For finite dimensional inner product spaces, an orthogonal basis is also a Hamel basis. The orthogonal dimension and the Hamel dimension coincide. However, for infinite dimensional Hilbert spaces, an orthogonal basis is not a Hamel basis. The orthogonal dimension and Hamel dimension are different. Any infinite dimensional Hilbert space has an uncountable Hamel dimension.

Example 10. (Orthogonal basis and Hamel basis) In the sequence space l^2 in Example 6, the following vectors constitute an orthogonal basis B:

$$
\begin{aligned}
b_1 &= (1, 0, \ldots), \\
b_2 &= (0, 1, 0, \ldots), \\
&\cdots \\
b_n &= (0, \ldots, 0, 1, 0, \ldots), \\
&\cdots
\end{aligned}
$$

However, this is not a Hamel basis, because the vector

$$v = (\frac{1}{2}, \frac{1}{2^2}, \ldots, \frac{1}{2^n}, \ldots)$$

is not a linear combination of any finite subset of vectors in B.   ♣

Theorem 3. *Every linear space has a Hamel basis. All the Hamel bases for the same linear space have the same cardinality.*

Remark 2. Cross Link — Axiom of Choice and Philosophy of Infinite Sets

Theorem 3 is a consequence of the axiom of choice, an axiom in set theory that has quite some controversy. Theorem 3 seems to be pleasing to most people. However, many counterintuitive results, like the existence of non-Lebesgue measurable sets and Banach-Tarsky ball doubling theorem (see Chap. 4, Remark 5), are also consequences of the axiom of choice. It is interesting to compare axiom of choice with Euclid's axiom of parallels. In 1830s, people were asking whether Euclid's axiom of parallels was true. Today, a similar question is still puzzling mathematicians: Is the axiom of choice true? In 1830s, people separated the geometry theorems that do not depend on the axiom of parallels (absolute geometry) from those theorems that do depend on the axiom of parallels (full Euclidean geometry). Today, mathematicians separate the theorems that depend on the axiom of choice (ZFC) from those that do not (ZF). In 1860s it was shown that Euclid's axiom of parallels is independent of other axioms in Euclidean geometry (see Part II Chap. 3). P. Cohen [Cohen (1963, 1964)] showed that the axiom of choice is independent of the axioms of ZF set theory. Poincaré made a comment in the 19th century that axioms are hidden definitions of those undefined concepts. Then today's question really is what axioms should we use to define the concept which we call sets. Finite sets are easy to grasp, but infinite sets are a challenge to the human mind. Poincaré said, "There is no actual infinite; the Cantorians have forgotten this, and that is why they have fallen into contradiction." The founder of set theory G. Cantor later suffered from mental illness, partly because of mathematical worries, like not being able to prove his continuum hypothesis. He died in a mental institution in 1918. Interestingly, P. Cohen [Cohen (1963, 1964)] also proved that the continuum hypothesis is independent of both ZF and ZFC set theory. If we recall that axioms are nothing but hidden definitions of primitive terms, the nature that "the continuum hypothesis is independent of both ZF and ZFC" is the same as what was a quote [MacHale (1993)] by Cohen: "The notion of a set is too vague for the continuum hypothesis to have a positive or negative answer." We indeed have made progress in understanding infinite sets more and more. A final question to ask, after all the nuisances with infinity: has God created infinity, or has man created infinity? An equivalent way to ask the question is, if you are not religious, has man discovered infinity, or has man created infinity?

Theorem 4. *Two Hilbert spaces are isometrically isomorphic if and only if they have the same orthogonal dimension.*

Separability is a property that applies to topological spaces and metric spaces. Recall a topological space X is called a separable space, if there exists a countable subset of X which is dense in X. We are more interested in separable Hilbert spaces.

Theorem 5. *A Hilbert space is separable if and only if it possesses a countable orthogonal basis.*

Corollary. *All infinite dimensional separable Hilbert spaces are isomorphic to l^2.*

Remark 3. Separable Hilbert Spaces — "The Hilbert Space"

Hilbert spaces are the foundation of quantum mechanics in physics. All the quantum states of a single particle form a separable Hilbert space. The space of the quantum states of two particles is the tensor product of the Hilbert spaces of each single particle. Since all the separable Hilbert spaces are isometrically isomorphic (with orthogonal dimension $\aleph_0$), they are often referred to as "the Hilbert space", as if the space is unique. Non-separable Hilbert spaces have applications in quantum field theory.

We recall that the dual space V^* of a linear space V consists of all the linear functionals. For an infinite dimensional linear space, the structure of the dual space is more complicated. The set H' of all continuous linear functionals on a Hilbert space H form a linear subspace of H^*. H' is a Hilbert space with the norm

$$\|f\| \overset{\text{def}}{=} \sup_{\|x\|=1} \{|f(x)|\}.$$

Theorem 6. (Riesz representation theorem) Let H be a Hilbert space. For any continuous linear functional f on H, there is a unique $y \in H$ such that for all $x \in H$,

$$f(x) = \langle x, y \rangle.$$

Based on Riesz representation theorem, we can define an isomorphism $\Phi : H' \to H$, such that $f \mapsto y$, where f and y are defined in the Theorem 6. y is called the **representer** of f in H.

§2 Reproducing Kernel Hilbert Spaces

Kernel methods are a powerful tool with wide applications in machine learning. Its history can be traced back to 1950s. Non-linear support vector machines [Boser et al. (1992); Cortes and Vapnik (1995)] are just one of the applications. We give a brief discussion of the foundation of reproducing kernel Hilbert spaces here and discuss support vector machines in Part IV Chap. 4.

A fundamental task in machine learning is to classify (or separate) two sets of data points in a linear space X. On some occasions, the two point sets can be separated by a hyperplane, which case is called linearly separable. On other occasions the point sets are not linearly separable. If they are not linearly separable, one approach is to embed X in a higher (often infinite) dimensional Hilbert space $(H, \langle \cdot, \cdot \rangle)$, with an embedding $\Phi : X \to H$, so that the data points embedded in H are linearly separable. If we can find a function $K : X \times X \to \mathbb{R}$ such that $K(x, y) = \langle \Phi(x), \Phi(y) \rangle$, the process can be significantly simplified. This is the motivation of kernel methods.

Many concrete Hilbert spaces we deal with are linear spaces of real valued or complex valued functions. In this section, we limit our discussion to Hilbert spaces of real valued functions.

Definition 7. Kernel

Let X be a non-empty set. A function $K : X \times X \to \mathbb{R}$ is called a **kernel** on X if there exists a Hilbert space $(V, \langle \cdot, \cdot \rangle)$ and a mapping $\Phi : X \to V$ such that

$$K(x, y) = \langle \Phi(x), \Phi(y) \rangle,$$

for all $x, y \in X$.

We can call the mapping Φ a lifting from X to H. The meaning is clearer in the context of machine learning (Part IV Chap. 4). When X itself is a Euclidean space, the mapping Φ can be viewed as an embedding (topological embedding or smooth embedding) into H. Note that with the same kernel $K : X \times X \to \mathbb{R}$, X may be lifted to different Hilbert spaces with different mapping Φ. The $(V, \langle \cdot, \cdot \rangle)$ and Φ are not unique.

Definition 8. Reproducing kernel

Let $(H, \langle \cdot, \cdot \rangle)$ be a Hilbert space of functions $f : X \to \mathbb{R}$. A function $K : X \times X \to \mathbb{R}$ is called a **reproducing kernel** of H, if the following conditions are satisfied, for all $x \in X$ and $f \in H$.

(1) $K_x \stackrel{\text{def}}{=} K(\cdot, x) \in H$.
(2) $f(x) = \langle f, K(\cdot, x) \rangle$, (reproducing property).

It is easy to verify, for a reproducing kernel, $K(x, y) = \langle K(\cdot, y), K(\cdot, x) \rangle = \langle K(\cdot, x), K(\cdot, y) \rangle$. It is comforting and intended that every reproducing kernel is a kernel.

Definition 9. Reproducing kernel Hilbert space (RKHS)

Let $(H, \langle \cdot, \cdot \rangle)$ be a Hilbert space of functions $f : X \to \mathbb{R}$. H is called a **reproducing kernel Hilbert space (RKHS)** if the following conditions are satisfied.

(1) H has a reproducing kernel $K(\cdot, \cdot)$,
(2) H can be generated by $K(\cdot, \cdot)$. That is, H is the closure of the span of $K(\cdot, x)$.

Not all the function spaces are RKHS. In the following, we will see that if a Hilbert space of functions has a continuous evaluation functional, then it is an RKHS. First, we need to introduce the **evaluation functional**. The evaluation functional in H at point $x \in X$ is a functional $\delta_x : H \to \mathbb{R}$ defined by,

$$\delta_x(f) \stackrel{\text{def}}{=} f(x),$$

for all $f \in H$ and $x \in X$. The evaluation functional δ_x is also called **Dirac delta functional** (or Dirac delta function), named after physicist Paul Dirac, who used it intensively in quantum mechanics.

Theorem 7. *Let $(H, \langle \cdot, \cdot \rangle)$ be a Hilbert space of functions $f : X \to \mathbb{R}$. H is a reproducing kernel Hilbert space if and only if the evaluation* *functional δ_x is bounded for all $x \in X$, that is, there exists $M \in \mathbb{R}$ such that $|\delta_x(f)| = |f(x)| \leq M \|f\|$ for all $f \in H$.*

The condition that δ_x is bounded is equivalent to that δ_x is continuous. This theorem can be proved using Riesz representation theorem. The Dirac delta functional in any Hilbert space of functions $f : X \to \mathbb{R}$ is always a linear functional. However, it may not be bounded, or continuous in some spaces of functions. If δ_x is continuous, by Riesz representation theorem, δ_x has a representer in H, which we denote by $K_x \in H$, such that for any $f \in H$,

$$f(x) = \delta_x(f) = \langle f, K_x \rangle. \tag{3.4}$$

We define a new function $K : X \times X \to \mathbb{R}$ such that

$$K(x, y) \overset{\text{def}}{=} K_y(x).$$

Hence Eq. 3.4 becomes

$$f(x) = \langle f, K(\cdot, x) \rangle,$$

which is the reproducing property. Therefore $K(\cdot, \cdot)$ is a reproducing kernel and H is a reproducing kernel Hilbert space.

Theorem 8. (Positive definiteness of kernels) *Any kernel $K(\cdot, \cdot)$ is positive definite. That is,*

$$\sum_{i,j=1}^{n} c_i c_j K(x_i, x_j) \geq 0,$$

for all $n \in \mathbb{N}$, $x_1, \ldots, x_n \in X$ and $c_1, \ldots, c_n \in \mathbb{R}$.

Are all the positive definite kernels reproducing kernels for some RKHS? The answer is no. Mercer's Theorem gives a characterization.

Theorem 9. (Mercer) *Let $X \subset \mathbb{R}^n$ be a compact set and $K(\cdot, \cdot) : X \times X \to \mathbb{R}$ be a symmetric function. $K(\cdot, \cdot)$ is a positive definite kernel on X if and only if*

$$\int_X \int_X K(x, y) f(x) f(y) \, dx \, dy > 0$$

for all $f \in L^2(X)$ such that $\int_X |f(x)|^2 \, dx > 0$.

Oftentimes in machine learning applications, we care less about the exact embedding $\Phi : X \to H$. All the operations we need in the higher dimensional Hilbert space is the inner product, which can be produced by a kernel. As long as we know that a symmetric function is a valid kernel, we can proceed with this implicit embedding. The following are known to be valid positive definite kernels: polynomial $K(x,y) = (x \cdot y + 1)^p$, Gaussian: $K(x,y) = e^{-\|x-y\|^2/2\sigma^2}$, hyperbolic $K(x,y) = \tanh(cx \cdot y - d)$ for certain parameters c and d.

§3   Banach Spaces

Let us reflect on the inner product space. With the instrument of inner product, we are able to define the length of vectors. The distance between the two vectors x and y is defined as the length of $x - y$ and from this distance, we can construct a metric space and define all the topological concepts. Can we use the concept of length only, without using the inner product? We distill the properties of the lengths of vectors in an inner product space in Theorem 1 and make generalizations.

Definition 10. Normed linear space

A real or complex linear space V is called a **normed linear space**, if each vector $x \in V$ is associated with a real number $\|x\|$, called the **norm** of x, satisfying the following conditions, for all $x, y, \in V$.

(1) $\|x\| \geq 0$. $\|x\| = 0$ if and only if $x = 0$.
(2) $\|ax\| = |a|\,\|x\|$, for any $a \in \mathbb{C}$, where $|a|$ is the absolute value of a.
(3) Triangle inequality: $\|x + y\| \leq \|x\| + \|y\|$.

In a normed linear space V, the distance between two vectors $x, y \in V$ is defined to be

$$d(x,y) \overset{\text{def}}{=} \|x - y\|.$$

It can be easily verified that the distance so defined makes the normed linear space a metric space.

Example 11. (Inner product space) The inner product space is a prototype of normed linear spaces. Theorem 1 states that any inner product space is a normed linear space with the norm induced by the inner product.   ♣

Example 12. (Non-Euclidean norm for $\mathbb{R}^n$) $\mathbb{R}^n$ is a real linear space. It has the standard norm induced by an inner product

$$\|x\| = (x_1^2 + \cdots + x_n^2)^{\frac{1}{2}}.$$

We can define a different norm, called **p-norm**, (or **non-Euclidean norm**) by

$$\|x\|_p = (|x_1|^p + \cdots + |x_n|^p)^{\frac{1}{p}}, \ 1 \le p < \infty.$$

It can be verified that $\|\cdot\|_p$ is a norm and therefore $(\mathbb{R}^n, \|\cdot\|_p)$ is a normed linear space. This can even be generalized to include $p = \infty$. We define

$$\|x\|_\infty = \max(|x_1|, \ldots, |x_n|).$$

Note that different p-norms with different p define the same topology on $\mathbb{R}^n$.   ♣

Example 13. (Lebesgue spaces $L^p[a, b]$) Let $L^p[a, b]$ be the linear space of all complex valued functions defined on $[a, b]$ whose absolute value raised to pth power is Lebesgue integrable. We define the p-norm for function f to be

$$\|f\|_p = \left[\int_a^b |f(t)|^p \right]^{\frac{1}{p}}, \ 1 \le p < \infty.$$

$(L^p[a, b], \|\cdot\|_p)$ is a normed linear space.   ♣

Definition 11. Banach space

Let $(B, \|\cdot\|)$ be a normed linear space over a field F, where $F = \mathbb{R}$ or $\mathbb{C}$.. If the metric induced by the norm is complete, then $(B, \|\cdot\|)$ is called a **Banach space**.

Hilbert spaces are Banach spaces. Examples 12 and 13 are Banach spaces.

Definition 12. Schauder basis

Let $(B, \|\cdot\|)$ be a Banach space. A **Schauder basis** is defined to be a sequence $(b_1, b_2, \ldots, b_n, \ldots)$ with $b_1, b_2, \ldots, b_n, \ldots \in B$, such that for every $x \in B$ there is a unique sequence (α_n) with $\alpha_1, \ldots, \alpha_n, \ldots \in F$, such that

$$x = \sum_{n=1}^{\infty} \alpha_n b_n,$$

where the convergence is defined with respect to the norm topology.

Every orthonormal basis of a separable Hilbert space is a Schauder basis.

We notice that an inner product can induce a norm. We want to ask the question: given any norm on a linear space, can we find an inner product that induces the norm? This is the same to ask: are normed linear spaces more general than inner product spaces?

To answer this question, we need to observe what characteristics an inner product space has to have, and whether all the normed linear spaces have these characteristics.

Theorem 10. (Parallelogram equality, see Figure 3.1) *Let* $(V, \langle \cdot, \cdot \rangle)$ *be an inner product space and* $\|\cdot\|$ *be the norm induced by the inner product* $\langle \cdot, \cdot \rangle$. *For all vectors* $x, y \in V$,

$$\|x + y\|^2 + \|x - y\|^2 = 2 \|x\|^2 + 2 \|y\|^2.$$

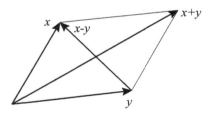

Figure 3.1   Parallelogram equality.

The question has been settled with the Jordan-von Neumann theorem.

Theorem 11. (Jordan-von Neumann) *Let* $(V, \|\cdot\|)$ *be a normed linear space. The norm* $\|\cdot\|$ *can be induced by some inner product* $\langle\cdot,\cdot\rangle$ *if and only if for all* $x, y \in V$, *the following parallelogram equality holds,*

$$\|x + y\|^2 + \|x - y\|^2 = 2\|x\|^2 + 2\|y\|^2.$$

Furthermore, if the norm satisfies the parallelogram equality, the inner product is uniquely determined by the following **polarization identities:**

If V *is a real normed linear space,*

$$\langle x, y \rangle = \frac{1}{4}(\|x + y\|^2 - \|x - y\|^2).$$

If V *is a complex normed linear space,*

$$\langle x, y \rangle = \frac{1}{4}(\|x + y\|^2 - \|x - y\|^2 + i\|x + iy\|^2 - i\|x - iy\|^2).$$

Corollary. *The p-norm on* $\mathbb{R}^n$ *or* $\mathbb{C}^n$ $(n > 1)$ *can be induced by an inner product if and only if* $p = 2$.

Exercises

1. Show that the space of continuous functions $C[a, b]$ on $[a, b]$, with respect to the inner product $\langle f, g \rangle \stackrel{\text{def}}{=} \int_a^b f(t)\overline{g(t)}dt$ is an incomplete inner product space. In fact, this space is a linear subspace of $L^2[a, b]$. Any linear subspace of a Hilbert space which is not topologically closed is incomplete.

2. Decide whether the following sequences in $L^2[0, 1]$ are Cauchy sequences. If yes, find the limit.
   (1) $f_n(x) = x^n$
   (2) $f_n(x) = \sin(nx)$
   (3) $f_n(x) = \dfrac{\sin(nx)}{n}$

3. Suppose a sequence of functions $f_n(x)$ converges to $f(x)$ in $L^2[a, b]$. Does this imply point-wise convergence (for each point $x_0 \in [a, b]$, the sequence

of numbers $f_n(x_0)$ converges to $f(x_0)$)?

4. Let X, Y be normed linear spaces. Show that a linear mapping $\varphi : X \to Y$ is continuous if and only if it is continuous at the origin $0 \in X$.

5. Let X, Y be finite dimensional normed spaces. Show that every linear mapping $\varphi : X \to Y$ is continuous.

6. Let X, Y be normed linear spaces. Give an example of a linear mapping $\varphi : X \to Y$ that is not continuous.

7. Show that the set of functions
$$\{\frac{1}{\sqrt{2\pi}}, \frac{\cos x}{\sqrt{2\pi}}, \frac{\sin x}{\sqrt{2\pi}}, \ldots, \frac{\cos nx}{\sqrt{2\pi}}, \frac{\sin nx}{\sqrt{2\pi}}, \ldots\} \text{ forms an orthonormal basis}$$
for $L^2([-\pi, \pi])$.

8. Show that the set of Legendre polynomials
$$P_n(x) = \frac{1}{2^n n!} \frac{d^n}{dx^n}(x^2 - 1)^n, \ n = 0, 1, 2, \ldots,$$

where $\frac{d^n}{dx^n}$ is the operator to take derivative of nth order, forms an orthonormal basis for $L^2([-1, 1])$.

9. Define the Laguerre polynomials L_n by
$$L_n(x) = \frac{e^x}{n!} \frac{d^n}{dx^n}(x^n e^x), \ n = 0, 1, 2, \ldots.$$

Show that the Laguerre polynomials form an orthonormal basis for $L^2([0, \infty))$.

10. Define the Hermite polynomials H_n by
$$H_n(x) = (-1)^n e^{x^2} \frac{d^n}{dx^n}(e^{-x^2}).$$

Show that $f_n(x) = e^{-x^2/2} H_n(x)$ forms an orthogonal basis for $L^2(\mathbb{R})$.

11. Show that any two norms on a finite dimensional normed space are topologically equivalent.

Chapter 4

Measure Spaces and Probability Spaces

A point is that which has no part. A line is breadthless length. A surface is that which has length and breadth only.

— *Euclid*

Reading Guide. Measure structures are not topological structures. However, in spaces like Euclidean spaces where there are both measure structures and topological structures, they often interact with each other. They are both continuous structures, describing the congregation of points, as opposed to discrete structures, like algebraic structures. Do not confuse measure spaces with metric spaces. Although "measure" and "metric" have very similar meanings in everyday language, measure spaces and metric spaces are quite different. In metric spaces, the key concept is "distance", also known as metric, which is generalized from the Euclidean distance and measures how much the points in space are apart from each other. In measure spaces, the key concept is "measure", which is generalized from the concepts of "length", "area" and "volume" and measures how much the points in space are crammed together.

Of course, distance and length are related in the Euclidean spaces, but they are generalized in different directions to abstract metric spaces and measure spaces. The metric structure (distance) and measure structure (volume, mass, probability) may coexist in harmony: the Lebesgue measure in $\mathbb{R}^n$ is invariant under rigid motions, or isometries, which preserves distances. .

In §1, we discuss the intuitions of length, area and volume in $\mathbb{R}^3$. In §2, Jordan measure is defined in $\mathbb{R}^n$. In §3, Jordan measure is generalized to Lebesgue measure in $\mathbb{R}^n$. In §4, we depart from Euclidean spaces and define abstract measure spaces. The following is a Venn diagram showing the relationships between different structures. The structures in the shaded area are the focus of this chapter. See also a brief discussion of structures in Chap. 0.

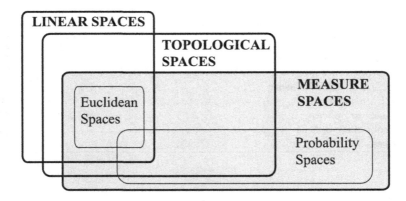

§1   Length, Area and Volume

On the real line $\mathbb{R}$, we have the concept of length. In the plane $\mathbb{R}^2$, we have the concept of area and in the space $\mathbb{R}^3$, we have the concept of volume.

We discuss area in $\mathbb{R}^2$ as an example. Volume is similar except the difference in dimension.

The intuition of the area of a figure is the number of unit squares needed to cover the plane figure. The term "figure" is vague. We agree triangles, rectangles, polygons, circles, ellipses. . . are all figures. In this section, we limit our context of "figures" to polygons. The broadest context for "figures" would be any subsets of $\mathbb{R}^2$. In history, the area for polygons were first studied and precisely defined. With time, the definition of area is generalized to "figures" as a broader and broader family of subsets of $\mathbb{R}^2$—Jordan measure and Lebesgue measure—but the area still cannot be defined for all subsets in $\mathbb{R}^2$ (assuming the axiom of choice is true).

We define the area of polygons with axioms. The areas of polygons are positive real numbers assigned to each polygon satisfying the following axioms.

Axioms. (Area of polygons)

(1) (Finite additivity) *If a polygon P can be decomposed into two non-overlapping polygons P_1 and P_2 with areas A_1 and A_2 respectively, then the area of P is equal to $A = A_1 + A_2$.*
(2) (Unit area) *A square with unit side length has area 1.*
(3) (Isometric invariance) *If two polygons P_1 and P_2 are congruent, then their areas are equal.*

It can be proved that such a mapping $\alpha : \mathbf{G} \to \mathbb{R}$, where $\mathbf{G}$ is the set of all polygons, exists and is unique.

Two polygons P and Q are said to be **equidecomposible** if P can be decomposed into non-overlapping polygons $P_1, \ldots, P_n$, and Q can be decomposed into non-overlapping polygons $Q_1, \ldots, Q_n$, and each P_i is congruent to Q_i, for $i = 1, \ldots, n$.

It follows trivially from the axioms of area that if two polygons are equidecomposible, then they have the same area. The converse is also true.

Theorem 1. (Wallace-Bolyai-Gerwien) *If two polygons have the same area, then they are equidecomposible.*

A rectangle can be covered by squares and we can find that the area of a rectangle is ab, where a is the length and b is the width of the rectangle.

Figure 4.1 shows a triangle ABC. Let AH be the altitude on BC. Let E, F be the midpoints of AB and AC respectively. $EF \parallel BC$ and EF

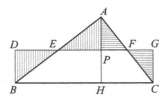

Figure 4.1   Area of a triangle.

intersects AH at P. Then P is the midpoint of AH. Extend PE to D and extend PF to G in the other direction so that $\overline{DE} = \overline{EP}$ and $\overline{PF} = \overline{FG}$. Now $BCGD$ is a rectangle. It is easy to see that $\triangle APE \cong \triangle BDE$ and $\triangle APF \cong \triangle CGF$. So $\triangle ABC$ is equidecomposible to rectangle $BCGD$. Therefore the area of $\triangle ABC$ is equal to $\overline{BC} \cdot \overline{PH}$, which is equal to $\frac{1}{2}ah$, where $a = \overline{BC}$ is the base and $h = \overline{AH}$ is the altitude.

Any polygon can be decomposed into a set of triangles. So the area of a polygon can be defined and computed.

§2   Jordan Measure

The theory of areas of polygons cannot even define the areas of circles, which represent a class of "figures" bounded by curves, instead of straight lines. We need to generalize the definition of area so that it can be applied to a more general class of "figures". The area we are trying to define is called **Jordan measure** (or **Jordan content**). Intuition tells us that when Jordan measure applies to generalized figures, it should also satisfy the axioms of area. When Jordan measure are restricted on polygons, it should agree with the area of polygons we defined in last section.

We will define Jordan measure for the general Euclidean space $\mathbb{R}^n$. The area is a special case when the space is $\mathbb{R}^2$. The Jordan measure in $\mathbb{R}^3$ is the generalization of volume. The Jordan measure in $\mathbb{R}^n$ is the generalization of n-dimensional volume.

By a left-open rectangle in $\mathbb{R}^n$, we mean the point set $\mathrm{R} = (a_1, b_1] \times (a_2, b_2] \times \cdots \times (a_n, b_n]$. We define the (generalized) volume of this left-open rectangle to be

$$v(\mathrm{R}) = |a_1 - b_1| \cdot |a_2 - b_2| \cdot \cdots \cdot |a_n - b_n|. \tag{4.1}$$

The set of all left-open rectangles in $\mathbb{R}^n$ is denoted by Ω.

For the circle, we can use the area of polygons that inscribes the circle to approach the area of the circle. This idea is generalized as the Jordan outer measure.

For any bounded set $A \subset \mathbb{R}^n$, we can find k rectangles $R_1, \ldots, R_k$ such that the union of these rectangles $\bigcup_{i=1}^{k} R_i$ covers A.

Definition 1. Jordan outer measure

Let $A \subset \mathbb{R}^n$ be any bounded set. The **Jordan outer measure** of A is defined to be

$$\overline{m}(A) \stackrel{\text{def}}{=} \inf \sum_{i=1}^{k} v(R_i),$$

where the inf runs over all the possible finite sets of rectangles $R_1, R_2, \ldots, R_k$ such that $A \subseteq \bigcup_{i=1}^{k} R_i$, where $k \in \mathbb{N}$ and inf runs over k as well.

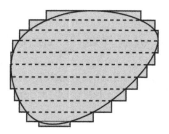

Figure 4.2   Jordan outer measure.

We are happy that the area of polygons is now generalized to the Jordan outer measure and Jordan outer measure applies to any subset of $\mathbb{R}^n$.

Immediately we can show that the Jordan outer measure of a polygon agrees with the area of a polygon defined in last section.

The Jordan outer measure of a circle can be found to be πr^2, where r is the radius of the circle. The Jordan outer measure of an ellipse is πab, where a, b are the semimajor and semiminor axes.

So far so good. However, we do run into some unpleasant problems with Jordan outer measure. First we take an example on the number line $\mathbb{R}$. Let

A be the set of the rational numbers in the interval $[0,1]$ and B the irrational numbers in $[0,1]$. We can find out that $\overline{m}(A) = 1$ and also $\overline{m}(B) = 1$. However, the whole interval $[0,1]$ has a length $\overline{m}([0,1]) = 1$. It is obvious that $A \cap B = \varnothing$ and $[0,1] = A \cup B$, but in this case $\overline{m}(A \cup B) \neq \overline{m}(A) + \overline{m}(B)$.

The same situation happens in the plane $\mathbb{R}^2$. If A is a the set of points (x,y) in the unit square, where both x and y are rational numbers. B is the complement of A in the unit square (points with at least one coordinate being irrational). Then $\overline{m}(A) = \overline{m}(B) = \overline{m}(A \cup B) = 1$.

This means that Jordan outer measure is not additive and it violates axiom (1) of area.

Let us try a different approach.

We recall for a circle, we can also use polygons that are inscribed by the circle to approach its area. This leads to the concept of Jordan inner measure.

Definition 2. Jordan inner measure

Let $A \subset \mathbb{R}^n$ be any bounded set. The **Jordan inner measure** of A is defined to be

$$\underline{m}(A) \overset{\text{def}}{=} \sup \sum_{i=1}^{k} v(\mathrm{R}_i),$$

where the sup runs over all the possible finite sets of rectangles $R_1, R_2, \ldots, R_k$ such that $\bigcup_{i=1}^{k} \mathrm{R}_i \subseteq A$, where $k \in \mathbb{N}$ and sup runs over k as well.

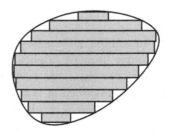

Figure 4.3   Jordan inner measure.

Again, Jordan inner measure works well with those "nice" figures like polygons and circles, and it coincides with Jordan outer measure for those "nice" figures. But it suffers in a similar way on those "jagged" sets, just like the Jordan outer measure does. For the rational points A in $[0, 1]$, $\underline{m}(A) = 0$. The same is true for the irrational points B in $[0, 1]$, $\underline{m}(B) = 0$. This is because, for both A and B, they have no interior. All their points are boundary points. However, $\underline{m}([0, 1]) = 1$. Again we have a counterexample where $\underline{m}(A \cup B) \neq \underline{m}(A) + \underline{m}(B)$, when $A \cap B = \varnothing$. This shows that Jordan inner measure also violates the axioms of area when it is generalized to arbitrary sets.

Both Jordan outer measure and Jordan inner measure fail to serve as the area (or volume) measure because they violates the axioms of area. As humans we have a tendency to deny failures. We can say, "Our definitions are good but those sets are bad." Indeed, both Jordan outer measure and inner measure work quite well with those "nice" point sets, and give us the area we anticipated. It is those badly behaved "jagged", fractal sets that make our definitions fail. We find that it was too ambitious to extend the concept of shapes or figures to all subsets in $\mathbb{R}^n$. We take one step back. We restrain ourselves to the realm of those "nice" sets, which we call Jordan measurable sets.

Definition 3. Jordan measurable set, Jordan measure

A bounded set $A \subset \mathbb{R}^n$ is called **Jordan measurable** if

$$\underline{m}(A) = \overline{m}(A),$$

and in such a case, either $\underline{m}(A)$, or $\overline{m}(A)$ is called the **Jordan measure** (or **Jordan content**) of A, denoted by $m(A)$.

An unbounded set $A \subseteq \mathbb{R}^n$ is said to be Jordan measurable if for any rectangle $R \subset \mathbb{R}^n$, $A \cap R$ is Jordan measurable.

Example 1. (Non-Jordan-measurable sets) The set of rational numbers in $[0, 1]$ is not Jordan measurable. The set of irrational numbers in $[0, 1]$ is not Jordan measurable.   ♣

Remark 1. Cross Link — Relation between Jordan Measure and Riemann Integral
    A bounded set is Jordan measurable if and only if its characteristic function is Riemann integrable.

Theorem 2. *A bounded set $A \subset \mathbb{R}^n$ is Jordan measurable if and only if its boundary ∂A is Jordan measurable and the Jordan measure of its boundary is zero $m(\partial A) = 0$.*

Intuition. (Jordan measurable sets) A set A is Jordan measurable if it has a "thin" boundary.

A set is not Jordan measurable, either because its boundary is not Jordan measurable, or because it has a "fat" boundary, meaning $m(\partial A) > 0$.

Looking at the Jordan outer measure and Jordan inner measure closely, we find the lack precision in some sense, reflected in the following theorem, and this is the cause that a set with a "fat" boundary is not Jordan measurable.

Theorem 3. *For any bounded set $A \subset \mathbb{R}^n$,*

$$\overline{m}(A) = \overline{m}(\bar{A}),$$
$$\underline{m}(A) = \underline{m}(A^\circ).$$

Corollary. *A bounded set $A \subset \mathbb{R}^n$ is Jordan measurable, if and only if $m(A^\circ) = m(\bar{A})$. In such a case,*

$$m(A) = m(A^\circ) = m(\bar{A}),$$

where A° is the interior of A and $\bar{A}$ is the closure of A.

Theorem 4. *A singleton set (set with only one point) is Jordan measurable and its Jordan measure is zero. Any set of finite points is Jordan measurable and its Jordan measure is zero.*

We know immediately that any rectangle R is Jordan measurable and its Jordan measure is the same as its (generalized) volume defined in Eq. 4.1, $m(\text{R}) = v(\text{R})$.

Theorem 5. *A polygon in a plane is Jordan measurable, and its Jordan measure is equal to its area defined in the axioms of the area of polygons.*

A bounded open set is not necessarily Jordan measurable. One counterexample is the complement of a fat Cantor set [Gelbaum and Olmsted (1964)].

Polygons, circles and regions enclosed by "nice" curves are Jordan measurable. These point sets belong to a nice category, know as domains (or regions).

A **domain** (or **region**) in a topological space is defined to be a connected open set.

Remark 2. Question — What Sets Are Jordan Measurable?

Some domains are not even Jordan measurable [Gelbaum and Olmsted (1964)]. In fact, polygons and circles belong to an even nicer subcategory of domains, Jordan domains. But it turns out that some Jordan domains are even not Jordan measurable [Gelbaum and Olmsted (1964)]. In case you ask, a Jordan domain is a domain in the plane enclosed by a Jordan curve. "What is a Jordan curve?" A Jordan curve is a simple closed curve. "Well, curve I know. What is a simple closed curve?" We want to cite Einstein's blind friend story (see Chap. 0) and it is not our plan to continue the discussion in this direction.

The Jordan measure has the following properties.

Theorem 6. (Properties of Jordan measure)

(1) $m(\varnothing) = 0$.

(2) *Finite additivity:*

If $A_1, \ldots, A_k$ are pairwise disjoint Jordan measurable sets, i.e., $A_i \cap A_j = \varnothing$, for $i \neq j$, and for a set $A = \cup_{i=1}^k A_i$, then

$$m(A) = \sum_{i=1}^k m(A_i).$$

(3) *For any rectangle $R = [a_1, b_1] \times [a_2, b_2] \times \cdots \times [a_n, b_n]$,*

$$m(R) = |a_1 - b_1| \cdot |a_2 - b_2| \cdots |a_n - b_n|.$$

(4) *Jordan measure is invariant under congruence in $\mathbb{R}^n$.*

We say that Jordan measure is **finitely additive** because of Property (2) in this theorem.

The Jordan measurable sets have the following properties.

Theorem 7. (Properties of Jordan measurable sets) *Let* **J** *be the family of Jordan measurable sets.*

(1) $\varnothing \in \mathbf{J}$ and $\mathbb{R}^n \in \mathbf{J}$.
(2) $A, B \in \mathbf{J} \Rightarrow A \cup B \in \mathbf{J}$.
(3) $A, B \in \mathbf{J} \Rightarrow A \cap B \in \mathbf{J}$.
(4) $A \in \mathbf{J} \Rightarrow A^c \in \mathbf{J}$.

Note that (2) and (4) imply (1).
(2) and (4) imply (3).
Property (2) can be generalized to

(2)′ $A_1, \ldots, A_k \in \mathbf{J} \Rightarrow \bigcup_{i=1}^{k} A_i \in \mathbf{J}$.

Property (3) can be generalized to:

(3)′ $A_1, \ldots, A_k \in \mathbf{J} \Rightarrow \bigcap_{i=1}^{k} A_i \in \mathbf{J}$.

Remark 3. Cross Link — Algebra of Sets

Let X be a set and **B** is a family of subsets of X. If the members of **B** satisfy the four properties in Theorem 7, then **B** is called an **algebra** (or **Boolean algebra of sets**, or **algebra of sets**). It has nothing to do with the algebra over a field, as in Part I Chap. 1.

§3   Lebesgue Measure

3.1   Lebesgue Measure

Many sets are not Jordan measurable. We would like to extend the measure to a bigger family of point sets.

We know Jordan measure is finitely additive. We are tempted to extend this to infinite additivity. It is easy to realize that this extension can at most go to countable additivity. Extending the additivity to uncountably many sets is impossible. This is the paradox that puzzles school pupils: The length of a point is zero. This was dictated by Euclid two thousand years ago. If we add up the lengths of all the points in $[0, 1]$, the length of $[0, 1]$ should be zero. Why is the length of $[0, 1]$ one, instead of zero?.

School pupils are not mature enough to know the difference between countable infinity and uncountable infinity. But if we cautiously extend the Jordan measure from finite additivity to countable additivity, we can say, the rational points in $[0, 1]$ do have a length, or measure, which is zero. Then the irrational points in $[0, 1]$ also have a measure, which shall be 1. The extended measure is Lebesgue measure. The key difference between Jordan measure and Lebesgue measure is, that in Jordan measure, we use finite number of rectangles to cover the set (although this number can be arbitrarily large), while in Lebesgue measure, we use (countably) infinite number of rectangles to cover the set. As a result, Jordan measure is finitely additive while Lebesgue measure is countably additive. Lebesgue measure applies to a larger family of subsets. When a set is Jordan measurable, Lebesgue measure and Jordan measure coincide.

Following the same idea of covering the point set with rectangles, we first define Lebesgue outer measure, but this time we allow the use of countably infinite number of rectangles to cover the point set.

Definition 4. Lebesgue outer measure

Let $A \subset \mathbb{R}^n$ be a bounded set. Assume A is covered by rectangles $R_1, R_2, \ldots$. The **Lebesgue outer measure** is defined to be

$$\bar{\mu}(A) \stackrel{\text{def}}{=} \inf \sum_{i=1}^{\infty} v(\mathrm{R}_i),$$

where the inf runs over all the possible sequences of rectangles $R_1, R_2, \ldots$ such that $A \subseteq \bigcup_{i=1}^{\infty} \mathrm{R}_i$.

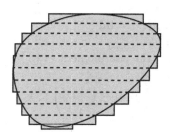

Figure 4.4   Lebesgue outer measure.

We are happy now that Lebesgue outer measure is defined on all subsets of $\mathbb{R}^n$. If a set is Jordan measurable, its Lebesgue outer measure coincides with its Jordan measure.

In general, for any bounded set $A \subset \mathbb{R}^n$, $\underline{\mu}(A) \leq \overline{m}(A)$. This is because Lebesgue measure uses countably infinite covering, while finite covering is also allowed in calculating the infimum. This means that Lebesgue outer measure has better precision than Jordan outer measure.

Let us reexamine some examples that were known to be Jordan non-measurable.

Example 2. (Lebesgue outer measure of rational numbers in $[0, 1]$) Let A be the set of all the rational numbers in the interval $I = [0, 1]$. This is a countable set. We could enumerate the points as $x_1, x_2, \ldots, x_n, \ldots$. Let $\varepsilon > 0$ be a small real number. We use a set of intervals

$U_1 = (x_1 - \frac{\varepsilon}{2}, x_1 + \frac{\varepsilon}{2}],$

$U_2 = (x_2 - \frac{\varepsilon}{2^2}, x_2 + \frac{\varepsilon}{2^2}],$

$\cdots,$

$U_n = (x_n - \frac{\varepsilon}{2^n}, x_n + \frac{\varepsilon}{2^n}],$

$\cdots$

to cover all the points in A. The sum of the lengths of these rectangles is

$$\sum_{i=1}^{\infty} |U_i| = \varepsilon + \frac{1}{2}\varepsilon + \frac{1}{4}\varepsilon + \cdots = 2\varepsilon.$$

Since ε can be arbitrarily small, the infimum of all 2ε would be zero. i.e. $\underline{\mu}(A) = 0$. ♣

Example 3. (Lebesgue outer measure of irrational numbers in $[0, 1]$) Let B be the set of irrational numbers in $I = [0, 1]$. Suppose $V_1, V_2, \ldots, V_n, \ldots$ are countably many intervals such that $V \subseteq \bigcup_{n=1}^{\infty} V_i$. Let $|V_i|$ be the length of the interval V_i. Then $\overline{\mu}(B) = \inf \sum_{i=1}^{\infty} |V_i|$.

In the previous example, $\bigcup_{n=1}^{\infty} U_i$ covers all the rational numbers. Then V should at least contain the complement of $\bigcup_{n=1}^{\infty} U_i$. Namely,

$$\left([0, 1] - \bigcup_{n=1}^{\infty} U_i\right) \subseteq V.$$

Then we have

$$\sum_{i=1}^{\infty} |V_i| \geq 1 - \sum_{i=1}^{\infty} |U_i| = 1 - 2\varepsilon.$$

Since ε can be arbitrarily small, the Lebesgue outer measure of B is

$$\overline{\mu}(B) = \inf \sum_{i=1}^{\infty} |V_i| = 1.$$

♣

Combining these two examples, we have

$$\overline{\mu}(A \cup B) = \overline{\mu}(A) + \overline{\mu}(B). \tag{4.2}$$

So far so good! We can also find that the Lebesgue outer measure works for most other Jordan non-measurable sets. However, Eq. 4.2 only means the axioms of area is checked for Lebesgue outer measure against one particular example and it is good regarding this particular example. We cannot prove that Lebesgue outer measure satisfies axiom (1) of area, namely the finite additivity, in the general case. You are welcome to try to prove it, but here is a warning: it has been proven to be unprovable within ZF set theory. The ZFC set theory (ZF set theory plus axiom of choice) proves it is false (see [Solovay (1970); Vitali (1905)]).

Let us take an alternative approach and define Lebesgue inner measure. The idea is similar to Jordan inner measure, but it is a little different technically. It uses the Lebesgue outer measure of the complement set relative to a rectangle.

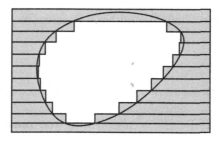

Figure 4.5 Lebesgue inner measure.

Definition 5. Lebesgue inner measure

Let $A \subset \mathbb{R}^n$ be a bounded set and assume A is bounded in a rectangle R , i.e., $A \subseteq R$. The **Lebesgue inner measure** is defined to be

$$\underline{\mu}(A) \stackrel{\text{def}}{=} v(R) - \overline{\mu}(R - A).$$

Intuition. (Jordan outer/inner and Lebesgue outer/inner measures)
The idea of Jordan outer measure is to make the "figure" inscribed in a set of rectangles and gradually shrink the boundary of these rectangles inward.

The idea of Jordan inner measure is to make the "figure" circumscribed by a set of rectangles and gradually expand the boundary of these rectangles outward.

The idea of Lebesgue outer measure is the same as Jordan outer measure, that is to make the "figure" inscribed in a set of rectangles and gradually shrink the boundary of these rectangles inward, but a countably infinite set of rectangles can be used to cover the figure.

The idea of Lebesgue inner measure is different from Jordan inner measure. Lebesgue inner measure is to make the "complement of the figure" $R - A$ inscribed in a set of rectangles and gradually shrink the boundary while keeping $R - A$ covered.

Lebesgue inner measure is defined for all the subsets of $\mathbb{R}^n$, however, similar to the case of Lebesgue outer measure, we cannot prove it satisfies the additivity axiom for all subsets of $\mathbb{R}^n$. So we give up the idea of defining a measure on all subsets of $\mathbb{R}^n$, and restrain ourselves to a smaller class of subsets.

Definition 6. Lebesgue measurable set, Lebesgue measure

A bounded set $A \subset \mathbb{R}^n$ is called **Lebesgue measurable** if

$$\overline{\mu}(A) = \underline{\mu}(A),$$

and in such a case, either $\overline{\mu}(A)$ or $\underline{\mu}(A)$ is called the **Lebesgue measure** of A, denoted by $\mu(A)$.

An unbounded set $A \subseteq \mathbb{R}^n$ is said to be Lebesgue measurable if for any rectangle $R \subset \mathbb{R}^n$, $A \cap R$ is Lebesgue measurable.

Immediately we wonder: what is the relationship between Lebesgue measure and Jordan measure?

Theorem 8. *If a set $A \subseteq \mathbb{R}^n$ is Jordan measurable, then it is Lebesgue measurable and $\mu(A) = m(A)$.*

Theorem 9. *A set $A \subseteq \mathbb{R}^n$ is Jordan measurable if and only if its boundary ∂A is Lebesgue measurable and $\mu(\partial A) = 0$.*

We have realized the limitation of Jordan measure and the newly gained power with Lebesgue measure. The problem with Jordan measure lies on the boundary points. The boundary points are where the points of A and the points of A^c are in infinitely intimate contact. When the boundary is "jagged", with finite covering, Jordan measure is not able to separate the area contributed by points in A and points in A^c, as shown in Theorem 3, while with infinite covering, Lebesgue measure is able to separate the points of A from the points in A^c on the boundary.

Example 4. (Lebesgue measure of Cantor set) See the definition of Cantor set in Chapter 1 Example 22. The Lebesgue measure of all the intervals that have been removed is
$$\frac{1}{3} + \frac{1}{3} \cdot \frac{2}{3} + \frac{1}{3} \cdot \left(\frac{2}{3}\right)^2 + \cdots = 1.$$
So the Lebesgue measure of Cantor set is 0. This is an example that an uncountable set may have zero Lebesgue measure.   ♣

The Lebesgue measure has the following properties.

Theorem 10. (Properties of Lebesgue measure)

(1) $\mu(\varnothing) = 0$.
(2) *Complete additivity (σ-additivity):*
  If $A_1, ..., A_n, ...$ are pairwise disjoint Lebesgue measurable sets, i.e., $A_i \cap A_j = \phi$, for $i \neq j$, and let $A = \cup_{i=1}^{\infty} A_i$, then
$$\mu(A) = \sum_{i=1}^{\infty} \mu(A_i).$$
(3) *For any rectangle $R = [a_1, b_1] \times \cdots \times [a_n, b_n]$,*
$$\mu(R) = |a_1 - b_1| \cdot \cdots \cdot |a_n - b_n|.$$
(4) *Lebesgue measure is invariant under congruence in $\mathbb{R}^n$.*

We say that Lebesgue measure is **completely additive** (or **countably additive**, or **σ-additive**) because of Property (2) in this theorem.

Corollary. *Any countable subset A of $\mathbb{R}^n$ is Lebesgue measurable and $\mu(A) = 0$.*

From this corollary, we know easily that the Lebesgue measure of all rational numbers in $[0, 1]$ is 0.

The Lebesgue measurable sets have the following properties.

Theorem 11. (Properties of Lebesgue measurable sets) *Let $\mathbf{L}$ be the family of Lebesgue measurable sets.*

(1) $\varnothing \in \mathbf{L}$ and $\mathbb{R}^n \in \mathbf{L}$.

(2) $A_1, A_2, \ldots \in \mathbf{L} \Rightarrow \bigcup_{i=1}^{\infty} A_i \in \mathbf{L}$.

(3) $A_1, A_2, \ldots \in \mathbf{L} \Rightarrow \bigcap_{i=1}^{\infty} A_i \in \mathbf{L}$.

(4) $A \in \mathbf{L} \Rightarrow A^c \in \mathbf{L}$.

Remark 4. σ**-algebra.** We know that the family of Jordan measurable sets form an algebra of sets. Theorem 11 implies that the family of Lebesgue measurable sets also form an algebra. In fact, Theorem 11 is stronger than that. It says the union and intersection of *countable* Lebesgue measurable sets are also in this family. A family of sets satisfying conditions (1) through (4) in Theorem 11 is called a σ**-algebra.** σ is the name we use to refer to countable additivity. Countable additivity is also called σ-additivity. σ in the name σ-algebra is the Greek letter for the English letter S, as in "sum". Note the Greek word for sum does not start with σ.

We explicitly state this definition as follows.

3.2 σ-algebras

Definition 7. σ-algebra

Let X be a nonempty set. A nonempty family of subsets $\boldsymbol{\Sigma} \subseteq \mathbf{P}(X)$ is called a σ**-algebra** on X, if the following conditions are satisfied.

(1) $\varnothing \in \Sigma$ and $X \in \Sigma$.

(2) $A_1, A_2, \ldots \in \Sigma \Rightarrow \bigcup_{i=1}^{\infty} A_i \in \Sigma$.

(3) $A_1, A_2, \ldots \in \Sigma \Rightarrow \bigcap_{i=1}^{\infty} A_i \in \Sigma$.

(4) $A \in \Sigma \Rightarrow A^c \in \Sigma$.

Note these conditions are not independent. (2) and (4) imply (1) and (3). The reason we list all of them is that it looks more symmetric and more similar to the definition of a subalgebra of a Boolean algebra, or a subalgebra of a set algebra. The following is an equivalent but more concise definition.

Definition 8. (Equivalent Definition) σ-algebra

Let X be a nonempty set. A nonempty family of subsets $\Sigma \subseteq \mathbf{P}(X)$ is called a σ-**algebra** on X, if the following conditions are satisfied.

(1) $A_1, A_2, \ldots \in \Sigma \Rightarrow \bigcup_{i=1}^{\infty} A_i \in \Sigma$ (closed under countable union).

(2) $A \in \Sigma \Rightarrow A^c \in \Sigma$.

A σ-algebra is a Boolean algebra but the converse is not true. The difference is "closed under countable union" verses "closed under finite union".

Definition 9. Algebra

Let X be a nonempty set and $\Sigma \subseteq \mathbf{P}(X)$ be a nonempty subset of the power set $\mathbf{P}(X)$. Σ is called an *algebra* on X, if the following conditions are satisfied.

(1) $A, B \in \Sigma \Rightarrow A \cup B \in \Sigma$ (closed under finite union).

(2) $A \in \Sigma \Rightarrow A^c \in \Sigma$.

Definition 10. σ-algebra generated by a family of sets **F**

Let X be a nonempty set and **F** be any nonempty family of subsets $\mathbf{F} \subseteq \mathbf{P}(X)$. The least σ-algebra on X containing **F** is called the σ-**algebra generated by F**, denoted by $\sigma(\mathbf{F})$.

Note in this definition, **F** is any family of sets and it may or may not be a σ-algebra itself. If it is, then it is not an interesting case because then we will have $\sigma(\mathbf{F}) = \mathbf{F}$ trivially.

Intuitively we can generate $\sigma(\mathbf{F})$ as follows: initialize $\sigma(\mathbf{F})$ with the sets in **F**. Keep making the complements and countable union of the sets already in $\sigma(\mathbf{F})$ and include them in $\sigma(\mathbf{F})$ until no more sets can be added.

Example 5. (σ-algebra) For any set X, $\boldsymbol{\Sigma} = \{\varnothing, X\}$ is a σ-algebra. This is the smallest σ-algebra. So $\boldsymbol{\Sigma} = \{\varnothing, \mathbb{R}^n\}$ is a σ-algebra on $\mathbb{R}^n$.   ♣

Example 6. (σ-algebra) For any set X, $\boldsymbol{\Sigma} = \mathbf{P}(X)$ is a σ-algebra. This is the largest σ-algebra. So $\boldsymbol{\Sigma} = \mathbf{P}(\mathbb{R}^n)$ is a σ-algebra on $\mathbb{R}^n$.   ♣

Example 7. (σ-algebra) Let $X = \{a, b, c, d\}$ and $\boldsymbol{\Sigma} = \{\varnothing, \{a, b\}, \{c, d\}, X\}$. Then $\boldsymbol{\Sigma}$ is a σ-algebra on X.   ♣

Example 8. (Finite algebras are always σ-algebras) Let Σ be an algebra on X. If Σ is finite, then Σ is also a σ-algebra on X.

Note this is true as long as Σ has finite elements, even if X is infinite. Examples 5 and 7 are all finite algebras. X in Example 7 is finite while X in Example 5 could be infinite.   ♣

Example 9. (Algebra but not σ-algebra) Let $\mathbb{N}$ be the set of all natural numbers. $\boldsymbol{\Sigma} = \{A |\ A$ is finite or cofinite$\}$. Note a set A is said to be cofinite if its complement A^c is finite. Σ is an algebra on $\mathbb{N}$ but it is not a σ-algebra on $\mathbb{N}$. This is because each singleton set of an odd number $\{1\}, \{3\}, \{5\},...$ is in Σ, but the countable union of them, $\{1, 3, 5, \ldots\}$, the set of odd numbers is not in Σ.   ♣

Example 10. (Borel σ-algebra $\mathbf{B}(X)$ and Borel sets) Let $(X, \mathbf{O})$ be a topological space. The σ-algebra containing all the open sets in $\mathbf{O}$ is called **Borel σ-algebra** (or **topological σ-algebra**) on X, denoted by $\mathbf{B}(X)$. A set in the Borel σ-algebra on X is called a **Borel set**. The Borel σ-algebra can be generated by the open sets of X. i.e., starting from open sets, by taking finite or countable union, or intersection, and complement operations, we can construct any Borel set.   ♣

Theorem 12. *In $\mathbb{R}^n$, all Borel sets are Lebesgue measurable.*

Are all the Lebesgue measurable sets also Borel sets? The answer is no. To prove this, first we notice the following.

Theorem 13. *Let $A \subset \mathbb{R}^n$ and $B \subseteq A$. If A has Lebesgue measure $\mu(A) = 0$, then B is Lebesgue measurable and $\mu(B) = 0$.*

Theorem 14. *There exist a set $A \subset \mathbb{R}^n$ such that A is Lebesgue measurable, but A is not a Borel set.*

Take A as any infinite set in $\mathbb{R}^n$ with $\mu(A) = 0$. A has uncountably many subsets and by Theorem 13, all of them are Lebesgue measurable. However, the total number of Borel sets is countable. Therefore, there are Lebesgue measurable sets that are not Borel sets.

Example 11. (Lebesgue σ-algebra $\widetilde{\mathbf{B}}$) Theorem 11 says that all Lebesgue measurable sets form a σ-algebra. We call it **Lebesgue σ-algebra**, denoted by $\widetilde{\mathbf{B}}$. With the discussion above, we know that Lebesgue σ-algebra contains Borel σ-algebra and is strictly larger than Borel σ-algebra. Lebesgue measure restricted to Borel σ-algebra is called **Borel measure**. Historically Émile Borel studied the measure on Borel sets first. His student Henri Lebesgue realized that for a set of Borel measure zero, some of its subsets may not be Borel sets. He extended the Borel σ-algebra to a bigger σ-algebra, now known as Lebesgue σ-algebra. So Lebesgue measure is the extension of Borel measure and Borel measure is the restriction of Borel measure.

A set which has Lebesgue measure zero is called a **null set**. In general, a measure μ is called a **complete measure**, if any subset of any null set is also measurable and has measure zero. Borel measure on $\mathbb{R}^n$ is not complete while Lebesgue measure is complete. Lebesgue measure is the **completion** of Borel measure. Lebesgue σ-algebra is the σ-algebra generated by Borel sets and null sets. Alternatively, Lebesgue σ-algebra is the σ-algebra generated by open sets and null sets.   ♣

Theorem 15. (Structure of Lebesgue measurable sets) *Any Lebesgue measurable set is the union of a Borel set and a null set.*

Remark 5. Non-Lebesgue Measurable Sets and Banach-Tarsky Ball Doubling Paradox. We are a lot happier with Lebesgue measure than Jordan measure because the family of Lebesgue measurable sets is much bigger than the family of Jordan measurable sets. We have seen those sets that are not Jordan measurable are now Lebesgue measurable. Some questions remain. How large is this family of Lebesgue measurable sets? Is every subset of $\mathbb{R}^n$ Lebesgue measurable?

We should be happy that we cannot find a non-Lebesgue measurable set as easy as we find a non-Jordan measurable set. This means the sets we encounter in everyday life are mostly Lebesgue measurable and the Lebesgue measure is much more pleasant to work with. We cannot prove that all subsets of $\mathbb{R}^n$ are Lebesgue measurable. Vitali [Vitali (1905)]first gave an example of a non-Lebesgue measurable set using axiom of choice. R. Solovay [Solovay (1970)] showed that the existence of non-Lebesgue measurable sets is not provable in the ZF Axioms of set theory by constructing a model in which every subset of reals is Lebesgue measurable. This tells us that we can worry less about non-Lebesgue measurable sets! Vitali's example of a non-Lebesgue measurable set shows that it is not provable that all subsets of $\mathbb{R}$ is Lebesgue measurable either, within ZF set theory. So this is one independent statement in the ZF set theory. See Chap. 0 for more on axiomatic systems.

Using axiom of choice, Banach and Tarsky proved a theorem stating a solid ball can be decomposed into five pieces (subsets) and reassembled as two balls of the original size. Precisely the theorem says: Let B be a solid ball. B can be decomposed into five disjoint subsets, $B = S_1 \cup S_2 \cup S_3 \cup S_4 \cup S_5$, ($S_5$ is a singleton set), such that there are five rigid motions R_1, R_2, R_3, R_4, R_5 such that $B \cong R_1(S_1) \cup R_2(S_2)$ and $B \cong R_3(S_3) \cup R_4(S_4) \cup R_5(S_5)$, where $\cong$ means congruent. This gives us the illusion that the volume of one ball is equal the volume of two balls identical to the original. Even though it is called a paradox, the theorem is true, if axiom of choice is true. However, the above interpretation about the volume of two balls is wrong. In fact, the volume of the ball B is not equal to the sum of the volume of S_1, S_2, S_3, S_4, S_5. Out of these five subsets, S_1, S_2, S_3 are non-Lebesgue measurable sets. Their volumes are undefined. See Chap. 4, Remark 2 for more on axiom of choice.

§4   Measure Spaces

We have generalized Jordan measure to Lebesgue measure. Jordan measure is finitely additive but Lebesgue measure is countably additive. How can we further generalize Lebesgue measure? Countable additivity, or σ-additivity is the most we can get. We cannot expect to generalize it to become uncountably additive as we discussed in last section. Uncountable additivity will lead to paradoxes. Because each point in $[0, 1]$ has Lebesgue measure zero, if you add up the "lengths" of all the points in $[0, 1]$, we obtain a paradoxical conclusion that $[0, 1]$ has length zero, as a consequence of uncountable additivity of the measure.

Jordan measure and Lebesgue measure are defined in Euclidean spaces $\mathbb{R}^n$. Both are intended to define the concept of volume in $\mathbb{R}^n$. Further generalization of Lebesgue measure will lead us to depart from Euclidean spaces and define a measure, which should be a set function μ in a general space X. X is just a set. It does not have additional structures like Euclidean spaces do. Given a subset A of X, $\mu(A)$ is a non-negative real number and is called the measure of A.

We have learned a lesson with Lebesgue measure that we may not be able to define such a measure for every subset of X. We must be contended with defining it on a smaller subfamily $\mathbf{M} \subseteq \mathbf{P}(X)$ of subsets. If we insist that the new abstract measure have countable additivity, $\mathbf{M}$ should have some closure properties in order for the countable additivity of the measure function to work. We require $\mathbf{M}$ be a σ-algebra, as in the case of Lebesgue measure.

Definition 11. Measurable space

Let X be a nonempty set and $\mathbf{M}$ be a σ-algebra on X. $(X, \mathbf{M})$ is called a **measurable space**. A set $A \in \mathbf{M}$ is called a **measurable set**.

A measurable space sets the stage for a measure space with a measure function. Now we want to examine what properties of Lebesgue measure we can borrow to be used as axioms governing the abstract measure function in the abstract measure space. We look at Theorem 10. The concepts of length, rectangle and congruence in Properties (3) and (4) in the theorem no longer make sense in the abstract space X. We would adopt the first two properties and they become the axioms of an abstract measure space.

Definition 12. Measure space

$(X, \mathbf{M}, \mu)$ is called a **measure space**, where X is a nonempty set, $\mathbf{M}$ is a σ-algebra on X and $\mu : \mathbf{M} \to \mathbb{R}$ is a nonnegative real valued function called the **measure**, if the following **axioms** are satisfied.

(1) $\mu(\varnothing) = 0$.
(2) Complete additivity (σ-additivity):

If $A = \bigcup_{i=1}^{\infty} A_i$, where $A_1, \ldots, A_n, \ldots \in \mathbf{M}$ are pairwise disjoint measurable sets, i.e., $A_i \cap A_j = \varnothing$, for $i \neq j$, then,

$$\mu(A) = \sum_{i=1}^{\infty} \mu(A_i).$$

In this sense, the Jordan measure is not a measure because it is finitely additive instead of countably additive. That is why some authors prefer to call it Jordan content.

$(\mathbb{R}^n, \widetilde{\mathbf{B}}(\mathbb{R}^n), \mu)$ is the prototype of measure spaces, where $\widetilde{\mathbf{B}}(\mathbb{R}^n)$ is the Lebesgue σ-algebra on $\mathbb{R}^n$ and μ is the Lebesgue measure. You may wonder: what meaning can the abstract measure represent, if it no longer represents volume? We give some examples of measure spaces and we pay special attention to two important measure spaces, mass distributions and probability.

Example 12. (Counting measure) Let X be a nonempty set and $\mathbf{M} = \mathbf{P}(X)$. $\mu : \mathbf{M} \to \mathbb{R}$ is defined as follows: $\mu(A)$ is the number of points in A, if A is finite; $\mu(A)$ is ∞ otherwise. $(X, \mathbf{M}, \mu)$ is a measure space.

For convenience, in some applications, we allow "infinity", or ∞, be treated as a number to be assigned as the measure of some sets. In general, we add two symbols ∞ and $-\infty$ to the real number system $\mathbb{R}$, resulting a system called **extended real numbers**, denoted by $\overline{\mathbb{R}}$. ∞ is also written as $+\infty$. In $\overline{\mathbb{R}}$, we define $x + \infty = \infty$. $x \cdot \infty = \infty$ if $x > 0$.   ♣

Example 13. (Dirac measure) Let $X = \mathbb{R}^n$ and $\mathbf{M} = \mathbf{P}(X)$. $\mu : \mathbf{M} \to \mathbb{R}$ is defined as follows:

$$\mu(A) \stackrel{\text{def}}{=} \begin{cases} 1 & \text{if } \mathbf{0} \in A, \\ 0 & \text{otherwise.} \end{cases}$$

In this example, we suppose there is only one point with unit mass at the origin $\mathbf{0}$ in space $\mathbb{R}^n$ and $\mu(A)$ represents the mass in set A. $(X, \mathbf{M}, \mu)$ is a measure space.   ♣

Example 14. (Point mass distribution) Let $X = \mathbb{R}^n$ and $\mathbf{M} = \mathbf{P}(X)$. Suppose there are k mass points located at $x_1, \ldots, x_k \in \mathbb{R}^n$, with mass m_1, $\ldots$, m_k respectively. $\mu(A)$ is the sum of mass of the mass points contained in A. $(X, \mathbf{M}, \mu)$ is a measure space.   ♣

Example 15. (Mass distribution) Let $X = \mathbb{R}$ and $\mathbf{M} = \mathbf{P}(X)$. Let $I = [0, 1]$. Define $\mu(A) \overset{\text{def}}{=} \mu_L(A \cap I)$, where μ_L is the Lebesgue measure on $\mathbb{R}$. This measure μ describes a uniform mass distribution on $[0, 1]$, where $\mu(A)$ is the mass contained in A. $(X, \mathbf{M}, \mu)$ is a measure space.   ♣

Example 16. (Mass distribution) Let $X = \mathbb{R}^n$ and $\mathbf{M} = \mathbf{P}(X)$. A measure μ is called a **mass distribution** if there is a compact set $D \subset \mathbb{R}^n$ such that $0 < \mu(D) < \infty$, and

$$\mu(A - D) = 0, \text{ for any } A \subseteq \mathbb{R}^n.$$

In this case, the amount of mass $\mu(D)$ is distributed in the set D. $(X, \mathbf{M}, \mu)$ is a measure space.   ♣

The measure structure and topological structure may coexist. A measure can be naturally defined on the topological σ-algebra in a topological space.

Definition 13. Borel measure in a topological space

Let $(X, \mathbf{O})$ be a topological space. The σ-algebra generated by all the open sets in $\mathbf{O}$ is called **Borel σ-algebra** (or **topological σ-algebra**) on X, denoted by $\mathbf{B}(X)$. A set in the Borel σ-algebra on X is called a **Borel set**. $(X, \mathbf{B}(X))$ is a measurable space. A measure defined on the Borel σ-algebra is called a **Borel measure**.

---

§5   Probability Spaces

Striking similarities have been found between probability and measure (not easily though). The origin of the probability theory dates back to the time of Pascal and Fermat in the 17th century. It was motivated by random events like coin flipping or die rolling. With a fair coin, we would think either a head or a tail has a chance of 1/2, and with an unbiased die, each face has a chance of 1/6. However, it has been a difficult endeavor to put the theory of probability on a solid foundation. Multivalued logic was one of the many approaches to the foundation of probability theory. In that approach, the two outcomes in the coin flipping can be represented by true and false values in logic. With the die rolling, it needs six values while for a continuous random variable, we need a logic of real values. That approach turned out to be not so successful. Various approaches had been tried, and finally the Russian mathematician A. Kolmogorov developed a modern axiomatic theory of probability [Kolmogorov (1933)] on the foundation of measure theory.

Definition 14. Probability space, probability measure

A measure space $(X, \mathbf{M}, \mu)$ is called a **probability space**, and the measure μ is called a **probability measure** if $\mu(X) = 1$.

The probability measure is interpreted as the probability distribution of a random variable. The space X is the **sample space** (or **universe**), which contains all the values that the random variable can take. X can be a finite set or an infinite set. Usually a topology is assumed to be endowed on X. If X is a finite set, we do not feel the need of a topology. That is because the discrete topology is implicitly understood. The distribution of a random variable which takes a vector value in $\mathbb{R}^n$ is modeled as a probability measure on $(\mathbb{R}^n, \mathbf{B}(\mathbb{R}^n))$. An **event** is interpreted as a set $A \in \mathbf{B}(\mathbb{R}^n)$. Note an event is a set of points in $\mathbb{R}^n$, instead of a single point. A single point in $\mathbb{R}^n$ is a possible outcome of the random variable. $\mu(A)$ is interpreted as the **probability of event** A. The composite event $A \cup B$ is interpreted as A or B. The composite event $A \cap B$ is interpreted as A and B. $\varnothing$ with $\mu(\varnothing) = 0$ is called **impossible event**. The entire space X with $\mu(X) = 1$ is called **certainty event**. Two events are said to be **independent**, if $\mu(A \cap B) = \mu(A)\mu(B)$.

Example 17. (Finite probability space) Let X bet a finite set. For any $A \subseteq X$, define

$$\mu(A) = \frac{|A|}{|X|},$$

where $|A|$ and $|X|$ are the number of elements in A and X. Then $(X, \mathbf{P}(X), \mu)$ is a probability space. Two concrete examples are:

(1) Tossing a coin: $X = \{0, 1\}$ with 1 representing head and 0 representing tail. $\mu(\text{head}) = \frac{1}{2}$, and $\mu(\text{tail}) = \frac{1}{2}$.

(2) Rolling a die: $X = \{1, 2, 3, 4, 5, 6\}$. The probability of each face is $\frac{1}{6}$. ♣

We do not plan to go too far in the theory of probability but we give one example to illustrate the connection between probability and measure.

In this particular case, it is in dimension two and the measure is the area. A French mathematician Georges Louis Leclerc, Count of Buffon posed a problem in 1733, and solved it later himself in 1777. It is known as Buffon's needle problem: A plane floor is marked with parallel lines with equal distance $2l$ in between. Drop a needle of length l randomly onto the floor (Figure 4.6). What is the probability for the needle to cross a line?

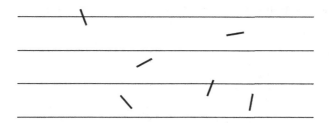

Figure 4.6   Buffon's needle problem.

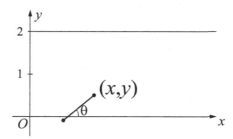

Figure 4.7   Buffon's needle problem in x,y coordinates.

To solve this problem, we set up a coordinate system. We make the x-axis coincide with one of the parallel lines on the floor and the y-axis perpendicular to the parallel lines (Figure 4.7). The position of the needle is determined by two parameters: the distance y from the top end of the needle to the base parallel line and the angle θ from x-axis to the needle. The x position of the needle does not affect the probability of crossing. The parameter l really does not matter because it depends on the unit of length we choose. For simplicity, we take $l = 1$. So the sample space for the configurations of the needle is the rectangle $\{(\theta, y)0 \le \theta \le \pi, 0 \le y \le 2\}|$. The condition for the needle to intersect with the base parallel line is

$$y \le \sin \theta.$$

We draw another diagram (Figure 4.8) to represent the configurations of the needle in the space of θ and y. A curve $y = \sin \theta$ is drawn. The event that the needle crosses a line is represented by the shaded area under this curve. The entire sample space is represented by the rectangle with an area of 2π.

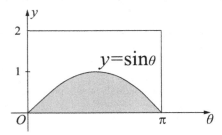

Figure 4.8   Buffon's needle problem in θ, y coordinates.

It is easy to find the area under the curve,

$$S = \int_0^\pi \sin \theta d\theta = 2.$$

Now the problem is converted to this. Drop a small bead onto the rectangle in Figure 4.8. The probability of the needle crossing a line is the same as the probability of the bead falls in the shaded area under the curve in Figure 4.8, which is

$$\frac{S}{2\pi} = \frac{1}{\pi}.$$

This becomes an interesting method for estimating the value of π. If we do this experiment and drop the needle many many times and divide the total number of dropping by the number of crossing, we expect to obtain an estimate of π.

Exercises

1. Show that the bullet-riddled square $[0, 1]^2 - \mathbb{Q}^2$ (points in the unit square with either coordinate being irrational) has Jordan outer measure one and Jordan inner measure zero. Hence the bullet-riddled square is not Jordan measurable.

2. Show that the set of bullets $[0, 1]^2 \cap \mathbb{Q}^2$ (points in the unit square with both coordinates being rational) has Jordan outer measure one and Jordan inner measure zero. Hence the set of bullets is not Jordan measurable.

3. Show that the bullet-riddled square $[0, 1]^2 - \mathbb{Q}^2$ has Lebesgue measure one.

4. Show that the set of bullets $[0, 1]^2 \cap \mathbb{Q}^2$ has Lebesgue measure zero.

5. Show that if a bounded set is Jordan measurable and its interior is empty, then its Jordan measure is zero.

6. Prove Theorem 3.

7. Prove the Corollary of Theorem 3.

8. Show that the Cantor set is Jordan measurable and has Jordan measure zero.

9. The following is the construction of the "fat Cantor set": Start with interval $[0, 1]$. Remove an open interval of length $\frac{1}{4}$ from the middle. Two closed intervals $[0, \frac{3}{8}]$ and $[\frac{5}{8}, 1]$ remain after this. Then remove an open interval of length $\frac{1}{16}$ (note that this is the absolute length, rather than the relative proportion) from the middle of each of the remaining interval. Repeat infinitely. Each time remove an open interval of length $1/2^{2n}$ from the middle of each remaining interval. The resulting set is called a "fat Cantor set". Show that the fat Cantor set

   (1) is uncountable;

   (2) is a perfect set;

   (3) is nowhere dense;

   (4) has nonzero Lebesgue measure.

10. Show that the fat Cantor set is not Jordan measurable. Find its Jordan outer measure and Jordan inner measure.

11. Show that every countable subset of $\mathbb{R}^n$ has Lebesgue measure zero.

12. Let $A_1, \ldots, A_n, \ldots$ be countably many subsets in $\mathbb{R}^n$, each having Lebesgue measure zero. Show that the union $\bigcup_{i=1}^{\infty} A_i$ is Lebesgue mea-

surable and has Lebesgue measure zero. Can this be generalized to the union $\bigcup_\alpha A_\alpha$ of uncountably many sets A_α?

13. Let $A \subset \mathbb{R}$ be any Lebesgue measurable set and $B \subseteq A$ be all the irrational numbers contained in A. Show that B is also Lebesgue measurable and $\mu(A) = \mu(B)$.

14. Let X be an infinite set and $\Sigma = \{A \in \mathbf{P}(X) | A$ is finite, or A^c is finite$\}$. Show that Σ is an algebra but not a σ-algebra.

15. Let X be an uncountable set and $\Sigma = \{A \in \mathbf{P}(X) | A$ is countable, or A^c is countable$\}$. Show that Σ is a σ-algebra.

16. Let X be a topological space. Decide whether the following family of sets are algebras, and whether they are σ-algebras.
    (1) $\Sigma = \{A \in \mathbf{P}(X) | A$ is open$\}$.
    (2) $\Sigma = \{A \in \mathbf{P}(X) | A$ is closed$\}$
    (3) $\Sigma = \{A \in \mathbf{P}(X) | A$ is open or closed$\}$
    (4) $\Sigma = \{A \in \mathbf{P}(X) | A$ is open and closed$\}$

17. In the Buffon's needle problem, find the probability of the needle crossing a line in the general case when the floor line spacing is b and the needle length is l.

PART IV
APPLICATIONS

Chapter 1

Color Spaces

How red is red?

— *Hongyu Guo*

Reading Guide. We live in a colorful world. Thomas Young, Hermann von Helmholtz, James Maxwell and Hermann Grassmann were some of the pioneers developing the color theory in the late 19th century. Today, most of us have some knowledge about colors. There are also many confusions and misconceptions about colors. For example, what is the exact definition of primary colors? When we talk about computer and television screens, we learn that R (red), G (green), B (blue) are the three primary colors. In art however, it has been taught that R (red), Y (yellow) and B (blue) are the three primary colors. Hence there is a confusion and a debate: are the primary colors R, G, B, or R, Y, B? To answer this question and settle the debate, we need to be clear with the precise definition of primary colors, which is absent in most of the books and in literature. We will give the definitions in the subsequent sections.

Some basic prerequisite knowledge of linear algebra (vectors, linear spaces, basis, linear combinations and linear independence, see Part I Chap. 1) is important for a good understanding of the color theory.

Some basic knowledge of projective geometry (homogeneous coordinates, barycentric coordinates, projective frames and projective transformations, see Part II Chap. 1) is helpful for a better understanding of many concepts in the color theory, like the color triangle, the gamut, white point, and white balance.

Some knowledge of Hilbert spaces (infinite dimensional linear spaces, Fourier series, orthogonal basis, See Part III Chap. 3) is not essential to understand this chapter, but may help with a deeper understanding of color phenomena.

§1   Some Questions and Mysteries about Colors

First we need to make one distinction: the distinction of additive color generation systems from subtractive color generation systems. The computer and television screens are light emitting devices. When we deal with paintings in art, things are different. The red pigment used in painting does not emit red light. What it does is to absorb all other colors from illuminating white light, and reflect the red component in it. When we mix colors on television, we add the light intensities of different colors. When we mix pigments in art (or printer ink in printing), we do color subtractions (colors are absorbed by different ingredients in the pigments from white light). So the computer and television screens are additive color generation systems while pigments and printer ink are subtractive color generation systems.

There are many confusions about colors. I agree with K. Nassau ([Nassau (2001)], p. 8) on "If one is not confused by color mixing, one does not really understand it".

For the question whether Red, Green, Blue or Red, Yellow, Blue are primary colors, K. Nassau offers an explanation ([Nassau (2001)], p. 8):

"We learned early in school that we can obtain just about all colors by mixing red, yellow, and blue ... Some of us, but not as many, then learned that there is also additive mixing, ... But if we had exceptionally good instruction, we would have been told rather different details for subtractive color mixing. We would have leaned that the three subtractive primary colors were not red but magenta (a purplish red), not blue but cyan (a bluish green), and yellow. That subtractive color mixing went this way:

. . .

$$\text{cyan+magenta+yellow} \to \text{black}$$

A knowledgeable teacher would have told us that the additive primary colors were red, green, and violet (usually called blue), with these mixing rules:

$$\text{red+green} \to \text{yellow}$$
$$\text{red+blue} \to \text{magenta}$$
$$\text{blue+green} \to \text{cyan}$$
$$\text{blue+green+red} \to \text{white''}$$

I am not picking Nassau as an extremely special case. This is a very popular explanation which can be found in many books as well as online sources. To sum up: RGB are the primary colors for additive color systems while CMY are primary colors for subtractive color systems.

This explanation is plausible but there are several issues.

The first, Nassau seems to attribute the confusions in color related concepts solely to unknowledgeable teachers. The fact is, the confusions are largely due to the current literature. To my best knowledge, there has not been any clear accounts of these concepts in literature, including Nassau's book. The concept of primary colors has never been rigorously defined. Nowadays we have seen more and more use of the concept of color spaces, with many industrial standards of different color spaces established. However, the concept of color spaces has never been precisely defined or described. As the style of many books, highlighting (in boldface or italic) the first appearance of a word serves as its definition, just like "The *cat* has been domesticated for more than 8,000 years" may serve as the definition of the cat. You can find no other definition of primary colors better than this type in most of the books.

The second, while it is true that you find three cartridges, Cyan, Magenta[1] and Yellow for your home printer, artists do not use cyan, magenta

---

[1] The color name magenta comes from a dye, which was named after a historic battle near the city of Magenta, Italy.

and yellow to mix colors. They do use red, blue and yellow and practically they can do great art. Your teacher did not lie and his eyes were not that bad as to call them red and blue when he saw magenta and cyan. If you read through this chapter, you should agree with my argument that your teacher was not wrong teaching red, yellow, blue as three primary colors for paint mixing, although your teacher may not be confident that he was right. Situations like this happen a lot. Someone teaches something because that is what he learned and what he thinks is correct without too many questions asked. With more and deeper questions asked, he is found wrong. While with even more and deeper questions asked, he is found correct again, but this time with better understanding.

The third, one more question remains after Nassau's explanation. In this chapter, to make our life easier, we restrict ourselves to additive color systems. Cyan, Magenta and Yellow are also legitimate colors in additive color systems. According to Nassau (and I agree), $Y = R + G$, $M = R + B$ and $C = B + G$ for additive color systems. People tend to think that the reason that RGB are primary colors is that they add up to white. Now observe the following,

$$C + M + Y = (B + G) + (R + B) + (R + G)$$
$$= 2(R + G + B)$$
$$= 2W.$$

Isn't two times white also white? Now we have seen the hand-waving nature of the previous explanation. You have just seen with your own eyes that in additive color systems, CMY also add up to white, just as good as RGB. Does this mean that CMY are also primary colors for additive color systems? RGB, or CMY, which is correct?

This paradox demands a precise definition of primary colors as well as answers to the following questions:

Why are red, green and blue three primary colors?

Are they primary colors by the laws of nature, or by design choice?

What is the definition of red?

How red is red?

In the following in this chapter, I will try my best to offer precise definitions of primary colors and color spaces, as well as answers to these questions.

Remark 1. Another Paradox about Colors — Why Is the Sky Blue?

To illustrate the confusions about colors, let us look at another question. Why is the sky blue? This is a resolved problem with the standard answer in most of the textbooks.

However, we look at one plausible paradoxical answer[2]: "The main reason is that when you were young, your mother told you that 'Tomatoes are red, grass is green, and the sky is blue', and you certainly had no cause to doubt her word. However, the terms 'red,' 'green,' and 'blue' are just labels that we have collectively chosen to assign to certain portions of the visible spectrum. If our mothers had told us that 'Tomatoes are blue, grass is red, and the sky is green,' then we'd all quite happily use those labels instead." In fact, this is not an answer to the original question. This is rather the answer to a different question: "Why is the word 'blue' used to label the color of the sky?" To avoid this confusion, we might rephrase the original question as "Why is the color of the sky different from that of a tomato?" or "Why is the light from the sky dominated by short wavelengths?" This then has nothing to do with what your mother told you. The answer is in physics. When the light goes through the atmosphere, it is scattered by the molecules in the atmosphere. The molecules in the air scatters the short wavelength light more than the long wavelength (this is known as Rayleigh's law, which states that the scattered light is inversely proportional to the fourth power of the wavelength). At noon, when we look at the sky away from the sun, we only see the scattered light, which has more blue than red. For the same reason, the sky appears red at sunrise and sunset, because at those moments, we are looking in the direction of the sun. More red light penetrates the atmosphere while more blue light is scattered away.

§2   Light, Colors and Human Visual Anatomy

Light is electromagnetic radiation in nature. Electromagnetic radiations span a large range in terms of frequencies or wavelengths. Frequency and wavelength have a one-to-one correspondence. If one is given, the other can be uniquely determined by the formula

$$c = \lambda \nu,$$

where ν is the frequency, λ is the wavelength and c is the speed of light. They are inversely proportional to each other. The higher is the frequency, the shorter is the wavelength.

The wavelengths of electromagnetic radiations span a wide range from thousands of meters to picometers (1 picometer $= 10^{-12}$m). From longer to shorter wavelengths, the electromagnetic radiations are divided into radio waves, microwaves, infrared, visible light, ultraviolet, X-rays and gamma rays. The range of wavelengths from 760 nm to 400 nm are visible to

---

[2]From an article on the Web, Color Vision: One of Nature's Wonders, by Clive Maxfield and Alvin Brown.

human eyes. Red lights have the longest wavelengths (lowest frequencies) and blue lights have the shortest wavelengths (highest frequencies) in the visible spectrum.

The light can be described as an electric field $\mathbf{E}(\mathbf{r}, t)$ which is a vector field that varies in space and time. At a fixed point $\mathbf{r}$ in space, it is a vector function of time $\mathbf{E}(t)$. At any time t, $\mathbf{E}(t)$ is a vector with three components $E_x(t)$, $E_y(t)$ and $E_z(t)$ along three spacial directions x, y and z. Let us just look at its magnitude $E(t)$. It is a continuous function of time t. Using Fourier analysis, $E(t)$ can be decomposed as the superposition of a spectrum of frequencies,

$$E(t) = \int_{-\infty}^{\infty} F(\nu)e^{2\pi i \nu t}d\nu, \qquad (1.1)$$

where ν is the frequency. Most light radiations are a mixture of infinitely many different frequencies, except the laser beams, which have single frequencies. In a rainbow we see the lights of all the different single frequencies because they are separated in space due to refraction by small water droplets in the air after the rain. We also see this rainbow of color lights when a beam of sun light is refracted by a prism, first discovered by Issac Newton, This decomposition of a light into a range of different frequencies is called the **spectrum** of the light.

If we use a narrow slit to separate a thin beam of light in the rainbow, we obtain an approximately single-wavelength light. The color produced by single-wavelength light is called a **spectral color**. Note that the spectral colors are the most vivid colors. Most lights are a mixture of different wavelengths, as shown in Eq. 1.1.

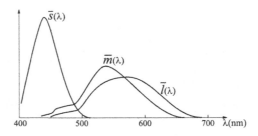

Figure 1.1   Response functions of three types of cones.

All the light radiations form an infinite dimensional Hilbert space. However, the color has to do with both the light and human visual perception.

On the human retina, there are two types of cells—the rods and cones. The rods are responsible for sensing the light intensities (summation over all the wavelengths) while the cones are sensitive to different wavelengths, which give us color vision. There are three types of cones, named L, M and S. They are sensitive to long, medium and short wavelengths respectively. Figure 1.1 shows the response functions (sensitivity) $\bar{l}(\lambda)$, $\bar{m}(\lambda)$ and $\bar{s}(\lambda)$, for L, M and S cones respectively.

Remark 2. A Common Misconception
    A common misconception is that the three types of cones can perceive red, green and blue light respectively, and further more, the three types of cones are called red cones, green cones and blue cones. The fact is, the response functions of three types of cones overlap. The peaks of the response functions of three types of cones fall in long, medium and short wavelength respectively, so that they are called L, M, S cones. We consider the response functions $\bar{l}(\lambda)$, $\bar{m}(\lambda)$ and $\bar{s}(\lambda)$ as vectors in an infinite dimensional Hilbert space of square integrable functions L^2. Although the three response functions overlap, they are independent vectors and they can generate (or span) a three dimensional linear subspace.

When the photoreceptors receive a light with a spectrum $F(\lambda)$, the three types of cones send to the brain three signals

$$L = \int_0^\infty F(\lambda)\bar{l}((\lambda)d\lambda,$$

$$M = \int_0^\infty F(\lambda)\bar{m}(\lambda)d\lambda,$$

$$S = \int_0^\infty F(\lambda)\bar{s}(\lambda)d\lambda.$$

The three types of cones act as three filters, low-pass, medium-pass and high-pass filters, respectively. This is called trichromacy of human visual anatomy. Because of this trichromacy, the human color perception is the projection from the infinite dimensional Hilbert space to a three dimensional linear subspace. Two light sources with different spectrum could be perceived as the same color, if their projections are the same. This phenomenon is called **metamer**.

§3   Color Matching Experiments and Grassmann's Law

In a color matching experiment, we split a circular field of view in an eyepiece into halves. On the left, we project the target color light **Q**, which is to be matched. On the right half of the field, we project three beams of light (usually Red, Green and Blue). We adjust the relative intensities of R, G, B, for example in a ratio of 0.3 of Red, 0.5 of Green and 0.2 of Blue, as shown in Figure 1.2. We keep adjusting the ratio of R, G and B until the eye cannot tell the difference between the colors in the left field and the right field (the boundary line in the middle vanishes), we then examine the amount of R, G, B in the mixing, for example, 0.3 of Red, 0.6 of Green and 0.1 of Blue.

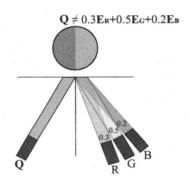

Figure 1.2   Color matching experiment.

Before we go further, we would like to make a new convention about the notations and symbols of the primary colors and the components. In the beginning of this chapter, we used R, G, B to denote three colors— red, green and blue. This is the convention in most of the literature and it is intuitive. However, in the literature, R, G, B are also used to denote the three components of the mixed color $\mathbf{Q}$ in the color matching. In the above example, we would write $R = 0.3, G = 0.6, B = 0.1$. To express the above mentioned example of color matching, we could denote $\mathbf{Q} = 0.3R + 0.6G + 0.1B$. This notation is confusing. Even more confusing notations like $Q = RR + GG + BB$, or $Q = R[R] + G[G] + B[B]$ have been seen in literature. Starting from now, we are going to use boldface letters $\mathbf{E_R, E_G, E_B}$ to represent three primary colors, Red, Green and Blue, because $\mathbf{E}$ is the symbol often used to denote basis vectors in linear algebra. The above color matching equation can be rewritten in the following using this notation: $\mathbf{Q} = 0.3\mathbf{E_R} + 0.6\mathbf{E_G} + 0.1\mathbf{E_B}$.

Note by mixing R, G, B this way, all the coefficients are nonnegative. I shall call this **normal color matching** (or **normal color mixing**) with RGB. Note, by normal color matching, zero coefficients are allowed but negative ones are not. Some vivid, highly saturated colors cannot be matched by normal color matching. Some modification is needed to match those colors. I shall call the modified matching **virtual color matching** (or **virtual color mixing**). In virtual color matching, one or more components of RGB is allowed to be negative, for example. $\mathbf{Q} = -0.3\mathbf{E_R} + 0.5\mathbf{E_G} + 0.8\mathbf{E_B}$. We understand that subtracting light intensity is not possible. What we mean by this is that if we project $0.3\mathbf{E_R}$ on the left field and make it mixed with $\mathbf{Q}$, then $0.3\mathbf{E_R}$ and $\mathbf{Q}$ will match $0.5\mathbf{E_G} + 0.8\mathbf{E_B}$ on the right field. That is, $\mathbf{Q} + 0.3\mathbf{E_R} = 0.5\mathbf{E_G} + 0.8\mathbf{E_B}$. A joke about a physicist, a biologist and a mathematician is pretty much in line with the spirit of virtual color matching: Three of them are sitting in a street cafe watching people going in and coming out of a restaurant across the street. First they see two people going into the restaurant. Then they count three people coming out of the restaurant. The physicist says: "The uncertainty of the measurement is ± 1." The biologist says: "They have reproduced." The mathematician: "If one more person enters the restaurant, the restaurant will be empty." Apparently the mathematician's calculation of the current number of people in the restaurant is $Q = 2 - 3 = -1$. This must be a *virtual restaurant*!

Remark 3. Caution — Do not confuse virtual color matching with subtractive color generation systems. Here we are discussing in the context of additive color generation systems only and we are matching color lights instead of pigments. Virtual color matching only gives a theoretical analysis of the sample color $\mathbf{Q}$, instead of generating it by mixing three colors. When we physically *generate* color light by mixing three color lights, we cannot do subtraction and any negative coefficient is not possible in the mix of three color lights. The reason I used "normal matching" and "virtual matching", instead of "positive matching" and "negative matching", is to avoid confusion with additive color systems and subtractive color systems.

We need the concept of independent colors and we define it in the following.

Definition 1. Independent colors

A set of colors $\mathbf{Q}_1, \ldots, \mathbf{Q}_n$ are called **independent colors** if no color in this set can be matched (normal matching or virtual matching) by the rest of the colors in the set.

Using both normal matching and virtual matching with RGB, we are able to match all colors that physically exist (meaning all the light radiations in nature). This is the experimental foundation of trichromatic color theory.

Hermann Grassmann discovered more quantitative relations in color mixing, now known as Grassmann's law[3].

Grassmann's Law

Let $\mathbf{E}_1$, $\mathbf{E}_2$ and $\mathbf{E}_3$ be three independent colors. In the color matching experiments, suppose the target color $\mathbf{Q}$ is matched (either normal matching or virtual matching) using $\mathbf{E}_1$, $\mathbf{E}_2$ and $\mathbf{E}_3$ with weights a_1, a_2, a_3, and another target color $\mathbf{T}$ is matched using $\mathbf{E}_1$, $\mathbf{E}_2$ and $\mathbf{E}_3$ with weights b_1, b_2, b_3. That is $\mathbf{Q} = a_1\mathbf{E}_1 + a_2\mathbf{E}_2 + a_3\mathbf{E}_3$ and $\mathbf{T} = b_1\mathbf{E}_1 + b_2\mathbf{E}_2 + b_3\mathbf{E}_3$. Then the following is true.

(1) $\mathbf{Q}$ matches $\mathbf{T}$ (denoted by $\mathbf{Q} = \mathbf{T}$) if and only if $a_1 = b_1$, $a_2 = b_2$ and $a_3 = b_3$.

(2) $\mathbf{Q} + \mathbf{T}$ matches $(a_1 + b_1)\mathbf{E}_1 + (a_2 + b_2)\mathbf{E}_2 + (a_3 + b_3)\mathbf{E}_3$, and we denote

$$\mathbf{Q} + \mathbf{T} = (a_1 + b_1)\mathbf{E}_1 + (a_2 + b_2)\mathbf{E}_2 + (a_3 + b_3)\mathbf{E}_3.$$

(3) $k\mathbf{Q}$ matches $ka_1\mathbf{E}_1 + ka_2\mathbf{E}_2 + ka_3\mathbf{E}_3$, and we denote

$$k\mathbf{Q} = ka_1\mathbf{E}_1 + ka_2\mathbf{E}_2 + ka_3\mathbf{E}_3.$$

Hermann Grassmann was also one of the pioneers of the theory of higher dimensional linear spaces (see Part I Chap. 3). Grassmann's law on color matching lays down the foundation of the linear color theory. Basically Grassmann's law state that color mixing is linear and a color can be treated as a vector. Scalar multiplication of a color is defined by a multiple intensity of the light. The addition of two colors is the superposition or mixing of two colors. The equal sign in a color equation means that the two colors on both sides of the equation result in the same stimuli to the human visual system (assuming an individual with normal visual anatomy). Since colors are vectors, we will use boldface uppercase letters to denote colors, to distinguish from their coordinates, which are scalars.

§4   Primary Colors and Color Gamut

Grassmann's law established that the color space is a vector space. The primary colors are simply a basis for this vector space.

---

[3]The following form is the modern interpretation of Grassmann's 1853 publication. Grassmann's original publication was in a much simpler form.

Definition 2. Primary colors

A maximal set of independent colors are called **primary colors**.

By maximal set we mean that, this set of colors $\mathbf{Q}_1, \ldots, \mathbf{Q}_n$ are independent but if we add any one more color $\mathbf{Q}$ in this set, they are no longer independent. This definition basically says that a primary color is a basis vector of the *perceptual color space*.

Remark 4. Elaboration — Why Is the Number of Primary Colors Three?

It is very important to check how we defined *independent colors* in Definition 1, in which *virtual matching* (with possible negative coefficients) is allowed. With this definition, we deal with the *perceptual color space*, which is a three dimensional vector space for humans and this accounts for why there are three primary colors. This is the consequence of human visual anatomy—three types of cones. This is verified by the color matching experiments. Different species of animals have different visual anatomies. For some birds, the *perceptual color space* is four dimensional and there are four primary colors for them. So if we manufacture a color TV for birds, we need four types of phosphors (This is just figurative speaking, CRT and phosphor technology has long been out of date). For some other animals, the perceptual color space is two dimensional, or even one dimensional. One dimensional color space means no color, or monochromatic. For those animals with monochromatic vision, they can perceive the light intensity only, but not the frequency or spectrum difference of light at all. For humans with impaired color vision, the perceptual color space can be two dimensional, or one dimensional, which is very rare though.

If we alter the definition of independent colors in Definition 1 a little bit, so that we allow normal matching only (positive coefficients only) but disallow virtual matching (with possible negative coefficients), then the number of primary colors (basis vectors) is infinite. Each single wavelength light becomes a primary color. In such a case, we deal with the *physical color space*, which is the space of light radiation itself and which is an infinite dimensional vector space, also a Hilbert space. The three dimensional perceptual color space is a subspace of this infinite dimensional Hilbert space. When we deal with colors, we make an orthogonal projection from this Hilbert space to this three dimensional subspace. This projection is the basis for *metamer*. This makes our tasks a lot easier when it come to manufacturing TVs because of the phenomenon of metamer, since we only need three types of phosphors instead of infinitely many. We know the light spectrum of a pixel on TV is not the same as the light spectrum of the scene point, but it is perceived as the loyal production of color because of this projection to a subspace.

Let $\mathbf{E}_1$, $\mathbf{E}_2$ and $\mathbf{E}_3$ be three primary colors, in the terminology of linear algebra, mixing (both normal matching and virtual matching) of colors $\mathbf{E}_1$, $\mathbf{E}_2$, $\mathbf{E}_3$ means forming linear combinations of $\mathbf{E}_1$, $\mathbf{E}_2$, $\mathbf{E}_3$. Just like the basis of a vector space is not unique, the primary colors are not unique but rather a design choice.

In this sense, RGB are primary colors; CMY are primary colors, and

RYB are primary colors too.

To generate colors in practice, we choose three primary colors $\mathbf{E}_1$, $\mathbf{E}_2$, $\mathbf{E}_3$ and mix them just like in the color matching experiments. However, to generate colors by mixing three primaries, we must use nonnegative linear combinations of $\mathbf{E}_1$, $\mathbf{E}_2$, $\mathbf{E}_3$ only, because subtracting light intensity is impossible. This leads to the concept of gamut.

Definition 3. Color gamut

The set of colors that can be generated by **normal mixing** of colors $\mathbf{Q}_1, \ldots, \mathbf{Q}_n$ is called the **color gamut** of $\mathbf{Q}_1, \ldots, \mathbf{Q}_n$.

In practice, it is often desirable that the primary colors meet more conditions in order to generate more colors in the gamut.

Definition 4. Primary colors by design choice

A set of primary colors must be independent. In practice, it is also desirable that

(1) they can generate white color, and
(2) they can generate a practically large gamut.

We often choose R, G and B as primary colors. The reason that CMY are not the choice for primary colors of additive color generation systems is that the gamut of CMY is too small, it is only approximately one quarter of the gamut of RGB. RGB also have a larger gamut than RYB.

Using any primary colors $\mathbf{E}_1$, $\mathbf{E}_2$, $\mathbf{E}_3$ as a basis, we can have a coordinate system for the color space. We show this with R, G, B but it works the same way for any other primary colors. All the colors that R, G, B can generate are in the first octant in the 3-dimensional color space (all three coordinates are nonnegative). Oftentimes we impose an upper limit to the maximum intensity for each of R, G, B. For example, we could make the range to go from 0 to 1, or after digitizing, from 0 to 255, as in digital images. This way we obtain a color cube (Figure 1.3 (a)). We shall use the $[0, 1]$ scale here for simplicity.

If $\mathbf{E_R}, \mathbf{E_G}, \mathbf{E_B}$ are considered basis vectors of this color space, a color

$\mathbf{Q}$ is represented by its coordinates, or its R,G,B components (R, G, B) in the form

$$\mathbf{Q} = R\mathbf{E_R} + G\mathbf{E_G} + B\mathbf{E_B}.$$

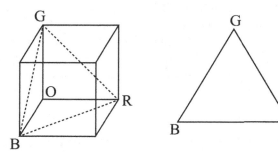

Figure 1.3   The RGB color cube and RGB triangle.

We are often interested in the hue of the color, separated from the brightness. We can use normalized coordinates $R + G + B = 1$. In such a case, we use (r, g, b) instead of (R, G, B). This corresponds to the cross section of the color cube cut by the plane $r + g + b = 1$, which is an equilateral triangle (Figure 1.3 (a) and (b)), called the **RGB color triangle**, or **Maxwell color triangle**, named for James Clerk Maxwell. Given a color in (R, G, B), it can be easily normalized to

$$r = \frac{R}{R + G + B},$$
$$g = \frac{G}{R + G + B}, \tag{1.2}$$
$$b = \frac{B}{R + G + B}.$$

The three vertices R,G,B of the triangle have coordinates $(1, 0, 0)$, $(0, 1, 0)$ and $(0, 0, 1)$ respectively. In this plane, (r, g, b) are the homogeneous coordinates of the point $\mathbf{Q}$. Because the Maxwell color triangle is equilateral, (r, g, b) coincide with the barycentric coordinates, and the trilinear coordinates of point $\mathbf{Q}$.

Nonnegative linear combinations of R,G,B can generate all the colors inside the triangle, including the base lines but nothing outside this triangle. In fact, physical colors outside this triangle do exist, which cannot be mixed by using R, G, B, as illustrated in the CIE chromaticity diagram in Figure 1.6.

Let $\mathbf{E}_1$, $\mathbf{E}_2$, $\mathbf{E}_3$ be three colors represented by three points inside the color triangle. If we choose $\mathbf{E}_1$, $\mathbf{E}_2$, $\mathbf{E}_3$ as a different set of primary colors, the gamut of $\mathbf{E}_1$, $\mathbf{E}_2$, $\mathbf{E}_3$ is the interior (plus boundary) of triangle $\triangle E_1 E_2 E_3$, and hence the gamut of $\mathbf{E}_1$, $\mathbf{E}_2$, $\mathbf{E}_3$ is smaller than that of the original RGB. The gamut of $\mathbf{E}_1$, $\mathbf{E}_2$, $\mathbf{E}_3$ is only a subset of that of RGB. Cyan, Magenta, Yellow are the midpoints of the RGB color triangle. The gamut of CMY is the interior of triangle CMY, which is much smaller (about one quarter) of that of RGB. This is the reason that CMY are not used as primary colors for additive color generation systems, but this is rather a design choice.

§5   CIE RGB Primaries and XYZ Coordinates

Next we need to answer the questions like "what is the definition of the red color".

First we need to realize that each of the color words we use, like red, green, blue, cyan, magenta, yellow and white, does not specify one unique color, but rather a range of similar colors. Suppose we choose a color that our visual system identifies and red. If we change the color a little bit, we would still consider it red. Putting the two colors side by side, the human visual system can easily identify the difference.

Different languages may have different granularity for the color words, meaning the range of colors that one word in one language describes may be divided, described by different words in another language and may be considered different colors. In Russian, there is no single word for blue, but two distinguished words, "голубой" for light blue and "синий" for dark blue. Japanese, Korean and Thai use one word to describe blue and green. In Chinese, there are different words for blue and green. However, there is another word "$q\bar{\imath}ng$", which may mean either green or blue, depending on the context. "$q\bar{\imath}ng$ $c\check{a}o$" means green grass while "$q\bar{\imath}ng$ $ti\bar{a}n$" means blue sky. "$q\bar{\imath}ng$" may even mean black in the older language or literary language, like $q\bar{\imath}ng$ $y\bar{\imath}$ means black clothes. So the word "$q\bar{\imath}ng$" could be really confusing. All natural languages are ambiguous and that is why we need to develop mathematical theories about colors.

Red (Green, Blue respectively) is any color in a range for which the responses from L (M, S respectively) cones on the human retina dominate the other two types of cones. White is any color in a range for which the responses from three types of cones are balanced (approximately equal).

Red, green, blue lights do not have to be single-wavelength light. White light does not have to be equal energy spectrum light.

For the subtle discrimination of two distinct colors, the evaluation and comparison of two colors by the human eyes have to be done side by side simultaneously. For example, placing two slightly different shades of red color in the left view and the right view of the color matching equipment, the eye is able to tell that the colors are different. This means that the eye can compare the difference in three stimuli in great precision given the two colors side by side. Now suppose if the two colors are shown one at a time, of course if the difference is big, like one is red and other other is green (or even pink), the eye can tell the difference. However, if the two colors are very close and are shown one at a time, the eye cannot tell the difference. This means the eye and the brain are not able to save the precise measurement of three stimuli in memory for future reference. The measurement (when two colors are side by side) is in high precision but what is saved in memory is a very rough round-off of the measurement. This low precision round-off corresponds to a color word, like red, or green, or pink.

It is not necessary but we can choose three single-wavelength lights for primary colors. (A light having single frequency also means that it has a single wavelength. Single-wavelength lights are also called monochromatic lights in literature. We avoid using the term "monochromatic" because literally "monochromatic" means "single color", which could be confusing. Each color is not identified with a single wavelength. Single color does not imply single wavelength.) Choosing single-wavelength primaries can give us the largest possible gamut.

In 1931, CIE (International Commission on Illumination, or Commission Internationale de l'Eclairage in French) conducted a serious of color matching experiments and stipulated several standards, which are still in use today. In the CIE 1931 standard, three single-wavelength RGB primary colors are chosen. They are described by the wavelengths as follows:

Red, 700 nm;

Green, 546.1 nm;

Blue, 435.8 nm.

Lasers emit single-wavelength lights. However, lasers were not invented till 1960s. Hence laser technology was not available in 1930s. Even if lasers emit single-wavelength lights, they can only emit light at some selected frequencies, instead of any arbitrary frequency on a continuous spectrum. One easy way to obtain single-wavelength light is to project a continuous spectrum white light through a prism and use a narrow slit to separate a thin beam from the spectrum after the light getting through the prism.

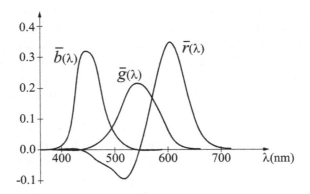

Figure 1.4 $\bar{r}, \bar{g}, \bar{b}$ components of lights of single-wavelength λ.

For single-wavelength light of each wavelength λ, CIE conducted color matching with these three primaries R, G, B. Suppose the target light $\mathbf{F}(\lambda)$ with single wavelength λ and unit intensity is matched by mixing of R, G, B as follows

$$\mathbf{F}(\lambda) = \bar{r}(\lambda)\mathbf{E_R} + \bar{g}(\lambda)\mathbf{E_G} + \bar{b}(\lambda)\mathbf{E_B},$$

where $\bar{r}(\lambda)$, $\bar{g}(\lambda)$ and $\bar{b}(\lambda)$ are the components of R, G, B respectively. We use the bars in the notations to indicate that they are the RGB components for single-wavelength λ.

When we vary the wavelength λ in the target light $\mathbf{F}(\lambda)$ and repeat the color matching, we find that $\bar{r}(\lambda)$, $\bar{g}(\lambda)$ and $\bar{b}(\lambda)$ are functions of λ, as shown in Figure 1.4.

Note that for any single-wavelength λ (other than the R, G, B primaries), virtual matching is needed to match the single-wavelength light $\mathbf{F}(\lambda)$. One of $\bar{r}(\lambda)$, $\bar{g}(\lambda)$ and $\bar{b}(\lambda)$ must be negative, which can be seen in Figure 1.4. This means that the single-wavelength light cannot be matched with normal matching using three primaries R, G, B and it cannot be physically generated by mixing any three primaries.

For a light with a spectrum $F(\lambda)$, which is a mixture of all the frequencies, the R, G, B components can be calculated as follows:

$$R = \int_0^\infty F(\lambda)\bar{r}(\lambda)d\lambda,$$

$$G = \int_0^\infty F(\lambda)\bar{g}(\lambda)d\lambda,$$

$$B = \int_0^\infty F(\lambda)\bar{b}(\lambda)d\lambda.$$

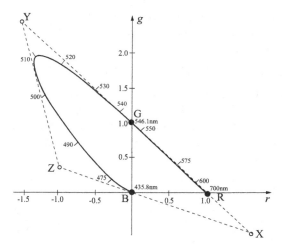

Figure 1.5   Chromaticity diagram in r-g coordinates.

We can use normalized components r, g, b, with $r + g + b = 1$, as in Eq. 1.2. When plotted in the (r, g) coordinates, all the physically existing colors fall in a tongue-shaped region in Figure 1.5. The boundary of this tongue-shaped region is a curve that represents all the **spectral colors**, which have single wavelengths. This boundary curve is called the **spectral locus**, or the **spectral curve**. A spectral color is labeled by its wavelength. The wavelengths vary continuously on the spectral locus, starting from one end with the longest wavelength, about 760 nm, to the other end with the shortest wavelength, about 400 nm. The color also changes continuously on the spectral locus from red, orange, yellow, green to blue. The colors in the interior of the region are called **non-spectral colors**, or **extra-spectral colors**. All the colors that can be mixed with R, G, B lie in a triangle, with (r, g) coordinates $(0, 0)$, $(1, 0)$ and $(0, 1)$. If any of the r, g, b is negative, then the color cannot be physically generated by mixing R, G, B.

We know that $\mathbf{E_R}, \mathbf{E_G}, \mathbf{E_B}$ form a basis for the color space. We also know in a linear space, the basis is not unique. We can easily choose another set of basis vectors. We can define

$$\begin{bmatrix} \mathbf{E_X} \\ \mathbf{E_Y} \\ \mathbf{E_Z} \end{bmatrix} = \begin{bmatrix} 0.4185 & -0.0912 & 0.0009 \\ -0.1587 & 0.2524 & 0.0025 \\ -0.0828 & 0.0157 & 0.1786 \end{bmatrix} \begin{bmatrix} \mathbf{E_R} \\ \mathbf{E_G} \\ \mathbf{E_B} \end{bmatrix} \tag{1.3}$$

as a new basis for the color space. This was the definition made by CIE in 1931 and the new basis vectors $\mathbf{E_X}, \mathbf{E_Y}, \mathbf{E_Z}$ are known as CIE 1931 XYZ primaries. Note that in the definitions of $\mathbf{E_X}, \mathbf{E_Y}, \mathbf{E_Z}$ in Eq. 1.3 there are negative coefficients in the linear combinations of $\mathbf{E_R}, \mathbf{E_G}, \mathbf{E_B}$. Take $\mathbf{E_X}$ for example and write it out:

$$\mathbf{E_X} = 0.4185\mathbf{E_R} - 0.0912\mathbf{E_G} + 0.0009\mathbf{E_B}.$$

This means that $\mathbf{E_X}, \mathbf{E_Y}, \mathbf{E_Z}$ cannot be physically generated by mixing R, G, B lights. In fact, $\mathbf{E_X}, \mathbf{E_Y}, \mathbf{E_Z}$ do not even represent any physically existing colors at all. This is just a mathematical transformation in theory. I shall call $\mathbf{E_X}, \mathbf{E_Y}, \mathbf{E_Z}$ **virtual primary colors**[4] (or **virtual primaries**). Virtual primary colors only make sense in the sense of virtual color matching. Otherwise it does not make sense just like that virtual restaurant with negative number of people in it in the joke.

Suppose a color $\mathbf{Q}$ has components (R, G, B) using primaries $\mathbf{E_R}, \mathbf{E_G}, \mathbf{E_B}$, but components (X, Y, Z) using primaries $\mathbf{E_X}, \mathbf{E_Y}, \mathbf{E_Z}$, that is,

$$\mathbf{Q} = R\mathbf{E_R} + G\mathbf{E_G} + B\mathbf{E_B}$$
$$= X\mathbf{E_X} + Y\mathbf{E_Y} + Z\mathbf{E_Z}.$$

From the theory of linear algebra, we know the (X, Y, Z) coordinates and (R, G, B) coordinates are related by a linear transformation as follows,

$$\begin{bmatrix} X \\ Y \\ Z \end{bmatrix} = \left(\begin{bmatrix} 0.4185 & -0.0912 & 0.0009 \\ -0.1587 & 0.2524 & 0.0025 \\ -0.0828 & 0.0157 & 0.1786 \end{bmatrix}^{-1} \right)^{t} \begin{bmatrix} R \\ G \\ B \end{bmatrix}$$

$$= \begin{bmatrix} 2.7689 & 1.7517 & 0.0009 \\ 1.0000 & 4.5907 & 0.0601 \\ 0.0000 & 0.0565 & 5.5943 \end{bmatrix} \begin{bmatrix} R \\ G \\ B \end{bmatrix}, \tag{1.4}$$

---

[4]In most of the literature, "imaginary primaries" is used. I coined "virtual primaries" because "imaginary" could be confused with complex numbers, which are totally irrelevant in this context. The difference between "virtual" and "imaginary" is what is between -1 and $\sqrt{-1}$.

and

$$\begin{bmatrix} R \\ G \\ B \end{bmatrix} = \begin{bmatrix} 0.4185 & -0.1587 & -0.0828 \\ -0.0912 & 0.2524 & 0.0157 \\ 0.0009 & 0.0025 & 0.1786 \end{bmatrix} \begin{bmatrix} X \\ Y \\ Z \end{bmatrix}. \tag{1.5}$$

With a price that the primary colors X, Y, Z being virtual, the benefit of XYZ primaries is that the coordinates (X, Y, Z) of all physically existing colors are nonnegative.

We can cut the X, Y, Z space by the plane $X + Y + Z = 1$ and look at the cross section. In this cross section, we use x, y, z as the homogeneous coordinates to denote the colors. x, y, z are the normalized X, Y, Z coordinates,

$$x = \frac{X}{X + Y + Z},$$
$$y = \frac{Y}{X + Y + Z},$$
$$z = \frac{Z}{X + Y + Z}.$$

Figure 1.6 is the CIE 1931 chromaticity diagram in x-y coordinates. All the physically existing colors are on or inside the spectral locus, and they all have positive x, y coordinates.

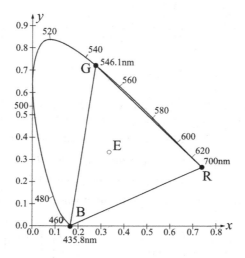

Figure 1.6   CIE 1931 chromaticity diagram in x-y coordinates.

The CIE 1931 R, G, B primary colors are marked as three points on the spectral locus. The colors in the triangle of RGB (including the boundaries) is the gamut of CIE 1931 RGB. For any three points E_1, E_2, E_3 on the chromaticity diagram, they are independent if they are not on the same straight line. The triangle formed by E_1, E_2, E_3 is the gamut of E_1, E_2, E_3. It is easy to see on the chromaticity diagram, that spectral color primaries can span larger gamut than nonspectral primaries. RGB can span a larger gamut than RYB also. CMY span a much smaller gamut, roughly one quarter of that of RGB because C, M, Y are the midpoints of RGB triangle. Now we have finally answered the questions we posed in the beginning of this chapter, like whether RGB or CMY should be primary colors.

Each color word, including red, green, blue, cyan, magenta, yellow, white, burgundy, beige, ..., represents a small region in the CIE chromaticity diagram, instead of a specific single point.

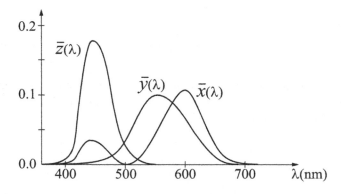

Figure 1.7 $\overline{x}, \overline{y}, \overline{z}$ components of lights of single-wavelength λ.

The color coordinate conversion from R, G, B to X, Y, Z in Eq. 1.4 applies to single-wavelength lights as well. Let $\mathbf{F}(\lambda)$ be a single-wavelength light with wavelength λ, under the two different coordinate systems,

$$\mathbf{F}(\lambda) = \overline{r}(\lambda)\mathbf{E_R} + \overline{g}(\lambda)\mathbf{E_G} + \overline{b}(\lambda)\mathbf{E_B}$$
$$= \overline{x}(\lambda)\mathbf{E_X} + \overline{y}(\lambda)\mathbf{E_Y} + \overline{z}(\lambda)\mathbf{E_Z}.$$

Then we can obtain the color matching functions $\overline{x}(\lambda), \overline{y}(\lambda), \overline{z}(\lambda)$ under the XYZ system as

$$\begin{bmatrix} \overline{x}(\lambda) \\ \overline{y}(\lambda) \\ \overline{z}(\lambda) \end{bmatrix} = \begin{bmatrix} 2.7689 & 1.7517 & 0.0009 \\ 1.0000 & 4.5907 & 0.0601 \\ 0.0000 & 0.0565 & 5.5943 \end{bmatrix} \begin{bmatrix} \overline{r}(\lambda) \\ \overline{g}(\lambda) \\ \overline{b}(\lambda) \end{bmatrix}. \tag{1.6}$$

Figure 1.7 shows the graphs of matching functions $\overline{x}(\lambda), \overline{y}(\lambda), \overline{z}(\lambda)$. For all the wavelengths λ, all the values of $\overline{x}(\lambda), \overline{y}(\lambda), \overline{z}(\lambda)$ are nonnegative.

Given a light with spectrum $F(\lambda)$ which is perceived as color $\mathbf{Q}$, we can find

$$X = \int_0^\infty F(\lambda)\overline{x}(\lambda)d\lambda,$$

$$Y = \int_0^\infty F(\lambda)\overline{y}(\lambda)d\lambda,$$

$$Z = \int_0^\infty F(\lambda)\overline{z}(\lambda)d\lambda.$$

The purpose of the basis change from RGB to XYZ is to have all positive coordinates for all the physical colors. However, infinitely many such transformations can be made to achieve this goal. There were other particular design considerations when the particular basis change as in Eq. 1.3 was chosen by CIE in 1931. In this choice, Y is chosen to be the luminance of the color light $\mathbf{Q}$, hence $\overline{y}(\lambda)$ coincides with the spectral luminance efficiency function of the human eye. The three virtual primaries $\mathbf{E_X}, \mathbf{E_Y}, \mathbf{E_Z}$ have coordinates $(1, 0, 0)$, $(0, 1, 0)$ and $(0, 0, 1)$. We can see that $\mathbf{E_X}$ and $\mathbf{E_Z}$ have Y coordinate zero, which means zero luminance. This explains from another perspective that $\mathbf{E_X}$ and $\mathbf{E_Z}$ are not physically existing lights. Other considerations in the CIE 1931 definition of XYZ primaries include that the line connecting $\mathbf{E_X}$ and $\mathbf{E_Y}$ on the chromaticity diagram is tangent to the spectral locus at the long wavelength end at $\lambda = 650$ nm, and that the line connecting $\mathbf{E_Y}$ and $\mathbf{E_Z}$ on the chromaticity diagram is tangent to the spectral locus at wavelength $\lambda = 504$ nm.

The x, y coordinates are used in the plane $X + Y + Z = 1$. To describe an arbitrary color, the coordinate system (x, y, Y) is also often used as an alternative to (X, Y, Z). The advantage of (x, y, Y) system is the separation of hue and luminance, with (x, y) representing the chromaticity or the hue, and Y representing the luminance. See Norobu and Robertson [Ohta and Robertson (2005)] for more details on the CIE 1931 XYZ standard.

Remark 5. Some Common Misconceptions about Colors

(1) *Misconception*: The primary colors can be mixed to generate any possible color. *Correction*: We can only use nonnegative combinations in color mixing, the gamut of any three primary colors is the interior of a triangle in the chromaticity diagram. Because the spectral locus is convex convex curve, there are always colors out of the gamut of any three chosen primaries. No spectral color can be produced by mixing any other colors.

(2) *Misconception*: A primary color is a color that cannot be decomposed into other colors. (One compares this concept with ancient idea of atoms—atoms cannot be broken

down further but the combination of atoms makes all the materials.) Hence we define a secondary color as a color by mixing two primary colors and a tertiary color as a color by mixing a primary and a secondary color.

Correction: Primary colors are not necessarily single-wavelength colors and hence could be made by mixing other colors. It is true that a single-wavelength light cannot be further decomposed. However, there are infinitely many such single-wavelength lights, instead of three. If we treat each as a primary, or basis vector, then we are working in the physical space of light, which is an infinite dimensional Hilbert space. The color space of human color perception is a three dimensional subspace of this infinite dimensional Hilbert space.

(3) *Misconception*: A primary color must be pure, meaning single-wavelength colors. *Correction*: Primary colors are not necessarily single-wavelength colors. Any three independent colors can serve as primary colors. In practice, we would desire that the three primary colors to span a gamut as big as possible. The three phosphors used on television screens define the RGB primary colors and those colors are are not single-wavelength colors.

(4) *Misconception*: There is only one color that can be defined as absolute red and that can be distinguished from all other red colors. *Correction*: Each color word describes a small region in the chromaticity diagram in stead of a single point.

(5) *Misconception*: If three colors add up to white color, then they are primary colors. *Correction*: This condition is not sufficient, and sometimes even not necessary. To qualify for primary colors, it is necessary that the three colors be linearly independent (any one cannot be mixed by the other two). It is desirable that they can mix white for practical purposes.

(6) *Misconception*: Light with equal energy spectrum defines the absolute white color, or standard white color.

Correction: White color is not a precise color, but rather a small range of colors that produce approximately equal stimuli to the three types of cones on the human retina. Since three types of cones are sensitive to long, medium and short wavelengths respectively, light with balanced spectrum (close to equal energy spectrum) should produce approximately equal stimuli, and hence be perceived as white color.

§6   Color Temperatures

A black body is an idealized object that may emit light, but reflects no radiation. Do not confuse the black body with a black hole. A black body can emit light and can be very bright. A black hole on the contrary, cannot emit any light because of its own strong gravity. The radiation spectrum of a black body is determined uniquely by its temperature. The radiation at each temperature corresponds to a color. Hence the color of the black body radiation can be completely described by its temperature, known as the **color temperature** of the color. A piece of iron heated in a blacksmith's forge can be viewed as an approximation of a black body. When temperature rises, it becomes red hot. If it is continuously heated to even higher temperatures, its color becomes white, and then bluish. When dealing with black body temperatures, we often use Kelvin (K) as the unit. If we denote T as the temperature in Kelvin and t as the same temperature in Celsius, they are related by

$$T = t + 273.15.$$

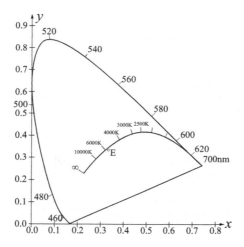

Figure 1.8   Color temperatures.

Figure 1.8 shows the color temperatures of black body radiation in the chromaticity diagram. Note the colors that can be described by color temperatures are limited to black body radiations, which is a curve in the plane of chromaticity diagram, known as the **black body locus**, or **black body curve**. It starts in the red color region with low temperatures, going through the region of white colors and enter a region of bluish color when the temperature is extremely high. In color temperature description, we have only one parameter, which is the temperature, and that is good to describe a curve only. The majority of colors require two parameters (x, y coordinates in the plane) to describe. The black body radiations with temperature around 5000K and 6000K appear to be white and are close to the color of daylight at noon. D50 and D65 are two of the most popular standard illuminants used by CIE. D50 denotes a color of black body radiation with color temperature 5000K, and D65 with a color temperature of

6500K. Sometimes notations D_{50} and D_{65} are used instead. Many commercial fluorescent light bulbs are labeled with color temperatures, like 3200K, 5000K or 6500K. Incandescent lamps have a color temperature range of 2700K to 3300K. Some commercial light bulbs are labeled with descriptive color words, which approximately correspond to the following color temperatures:

Soft white	2700K
Bright white	3500K
Cool white (moonlight)	4100K
Daylight	5000–6500K

Remark 6. A Common Misconception
    Color temperatures are sometimes confused with the concepts of "warm colors" and "cool colors", which are used in art. Color temperatures apply to colors on the black body locus only, while warm colors and cool colors apply to all the colors. The concepts of "warm colors" and "cool colors" are psychological in nature. The colors of red, orange and yellow are considered warm colors because those colors tend to cause a mental association with fire and heat. The colors of green and blue are considered cool colors because those colors psychologically tend to be associated with plants or water. Black body radiation at around 2000K–3000K appears to have red or orange color, which are psychologically warm colors. When the color temperature gets extremely high, for example, above 9000K, the color becomes bluish, which is rather a cool color psychologically.

§7 White Point and White Balance

Some knowledge of homogeneous coordinates and projective frames in projective geometry shall be helpful in understanding the concept of white point. (see Part II Chap. 1).

As we have discussed earlier, each color word in everyday language describes a range of colors. This is true for white color also. White is a range of similar colors that result in approximately equal stimuli to the three types of cones on the retina. It is represented by a small region at the center of the CIE chromaticity diagram, instead of a simple point.

When we choose primary colors (basis vectors for the color space), it is not absolutely necessary but it is aesthetic, intuitive and convenient that the equal amount mixing of R, G, B gives us a color that human eyes perceive as white. That is, R + G + B = W.

In practice, the inverse process is used. We specify a particular color as the white color and stipulate that equal amount of R, G, B mix this white color. This imposes a condition when we select the relative intensity to R, G, B to serve as primary colors.

Starting from the chromaticity diagram in x-y coordinates, we can select any three points not lying on the same line. We can define them as R, G, B and assign coordinates $(1, 0, 0)$, $(0, 1, 0)$ and $(0, 0, 1)$ to them. However, selecting three points this way does not fix the relative intensity of these lights, so that the coordinates of each point (each color) are not fixed. If we recall in projective geometry, four points in general position are needed to determine a projective frame. In addition to the fundamental points R, G, B, we need a unit point which we assign coordinates $(1, 1, 1)$. In the color space, this unit point is called **white point**.

CIE 1931 XYZ system chooses the equal energy point E to be the white point. E has (x, y) coordinates $(1/3, 1/3)$. In practice, we often choose a point on the black body radiation curve that is perceived as white color. For example, D50 or D65 is often selected as the white point. Note that equal energy point E is close to but not on the black body locus.

Color devices like computer screens, digital cameras and image editing software can be calibrated. One of the configurations in color calibration is to set the white point.

Setting white point can be used as a method of color space transformation in image manipulation, known as adjusting the white balance. When shooting pictures indoor with incandescent lighting, the white paper will have a yellowish tint. We can adjust the white balance of the camera. We point the camera to the paper with yellowish tint, and assign this color as the white point, then the camera will adjust its relative R, G, B intensities so that this color will acquire coordinates $(1, 1, 1)$. When the image is displayed on the regular monitor, the paper with a color $(1, 1, 1)$ will appear to be white. Hence the yellowish color bias of incandescent lighting is rectified and the image will look like an image taken under daylight. This white balance adjustment can even be done after the photo was shot, in the photo editing stage. The nature of white balance adjustment is in fact a projective transformation in the color space. As we recall, to determine a projective transformation, we can assign the images to any four points in general position. In this white balance adjustment, we keep the three fundamental points (R, G, B) unchanged but change the unit point (white point). This induces a color transformation for all the colors.

§8   Color Spaces

We have modeled colors as points in a three dimensional vector space. Mixing colors is modeled as the linear combination of these vectors. However, something is special to the colors, which is different from the vectors in general. That is, when we mix colors in an additive color generation system, subtraction can never be used. That is, the coefficients in a linear combination are required to be nonnegative. The set of all physically existing colors does not fill the entire three dimensional vector space, but is rather a convex subset of it. The boundary of this subset is a convex curved surface, which represent all the spectral lights. In the practice of color generation, we use three primary colors and we can only produce a limited gamut of colors. Different sets of primaries may generate different gamut, some bigger, some smaller.

Most of the times we impose a cut off for the maximum light intensity. So the gamut of any system is a bounded region with a finite volume in a 3-dimensional space, which represents all the colors that can be generated in the system, often known as the "color solid". This color solid is also called a particular **color space** generated by this set of primary colors. The color space specifications include the selected primary colors, and often together with the coordinate system used. We can use Cartesian coordinate systems, as in different RGB color spaces, or cylindrical coordinate systems, like in HSV and HSL color systems. The color space specifications also include the choice of a white point and a parameter called gamma, which we will explain shortly. The RGB color spaces, the color solid is a cube, known as the RGB cube. The HSV color space has a shape of a pyramid with a regular hexagon as the base, often called the hexcone. The HSL color space has a shape of two of such hexcones glued together base to base, often called the double cone.

A list of some of the additive color spaces includes: LMS, CIE XYZ, CIE xyY, CIE LAB, CIE LUV, CIE RGB, sRGB, Adobe RGB, Adobe wide-gamut RGB, ProPhoto RGB, ITU-R BT.709 (Rec. 709) RGB, YUV, YIQ, HSV, HSL. Some of the subtractive color spaces include CMY and CMYK. The gamut of these color spaces may partly overlap, with one color space having a bigger gamut than another, as shown in Figure 1.9. If a color lies in the overlapping region of two color spaces, it may have two different sets of coordinates in two different color spaces. We need to handle the coordinate transformation when converting one color space to another. The conversion between different color spaces is known as color management.

LMS color space is based on the three stimulus values L, M, S of three types of cones of the human visual anatomy. The three coordinates L, M, S are always nonnegative. The LMS color space is not often used in color generating devices but can be inferred via a transformation through other color spaces.

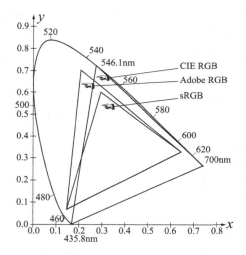

Figure 1.9   Gamuts of different color spaces.

Using all nonnegative coefficients of X, Y, Z, the CIE XYZ color space includes all the physically existing colors. However, the primaries X, Y, Z themselves are non-existing colors. So the CIE XYZ color space is a theoretical color space. The CIE coordinate systems can be used as an absolute reference system. When we specify the primary colors in a color space, we often use their CIE xy coordinates. The white point of a color space is also specified in CIE xy coordinates.

Although we have a linear theory for color spaces, most practical color display devices are nonlinear. The specification of a nonlinear correction coefficient, **gamma**, is also part of the color space specification. For example, on the CRT display, light is emitted from the phosphors coated on the screen when they are hit by high speed electrons from the electron gun. The brightness of the excited phosphor is related to the speed of the electron. The electron is accelerated by a voltage. The relationship between the voltage and the brightness of the phosphor l is nonlinear in genera. If we directly use the RGB values to control the voltage, the colors on the screen will not look correct. Hence we use an empirical nonlinear correction using the power law

$$V_{out} = V_{in}^{\gamma},$$

where γ is a constant which can be approximately determined by experiment. For the CRT displays, a gamma of 2.2 is generally used.

The CMY color space is used in subtractive color generation systems, like printers. Mixing C, M, Y will result in black. Just like the white color may have varying brightness in an additive color system, in a subtractive system, mixing C, M, Y will generate of dark muddy color, instead of an absolute black color with one hundred percent incoming light absorbed. The practice in the printing business, as well as in consumer printers, is to add a fourth color, K for "key", which means black, resulting in a CMYK color space with four primaries. The term "key" comes from the "key plate" in printing terminology.

Even in additive systems, there are more and more systems that adopt four or more primary colors. It could be confusing when we say four primary colors because these colors are no longer independent. We should call them four generators. With four generators, each color has four coordinates. Because the generators are not independent, the coordinates of each color are not unique any more. We just need to make some policy to decide the coordinates but the advantage is that with more generators, we can produce a bigger gamut, which has more vivid, close to spectral colors included.

§9   Hue, Saturation, Brightness and HSV, HSL Color Spaces

In art and in everyday life, we have an intuitive notion of hue, which is sometimes considered a synonym of color, but sometimes considered as one of the multiple aspects of color. Green, light green, dark green have different RGB values and are considered different colors. However, we tend to think that they have the same hue, which is green, but different brightness.

Another perception of color is the saturation, or vividness. We may have two green colors which have the same hue and brightness, but one is more vivid and the other is more dull. We say a color is more saturated if it looks more vivid.

Some quantitative analysis makes these terms from perception more precise. In fact, the hue, saturation and brightness correspond to cylindrical coordinate values in a color space.

Starting from an RGB color space. The line $R = G = B$ describes all the gray shades from black to white. We take this line as the axis and make a cylinder around it. Given any color, we use V as the height measured parallel to this axis, which represent the brightness of the color.

On a plane perpendicular to this axis, which we call the hue plane, we use polar coordinates, the radius S (the distance from the color point to the center gray point) is the saturation. The further away from the center, the higher saturation the color has. The gray is considered completely unsaturated with $S = 0$. The spectral colors have the highest saturation.

If we use the red as a reference line and measure the angle to another color. The angle represents the hue. The red has a hue angle $0°$, green $120°$ and blue $240°$, as shown in Figure 1.10.

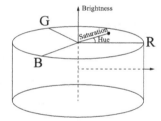

Figure 1.10   Hue, saturation and brightness.

The physics background of color light may explain the human perception of hue, saturation and brightness. Brightness is the total amount of energy emitted. Assume the light has a continuous spectrum. The perception of the hue is the dominant wavelengths in the light. The perception of saturation is actually the bandwidth of the dominant wavelengths in the light. The narrower the bandwidth, the purer, the more saturated, or the more vivid the color appears. To the extreme, a spectral color has a single wavelength, it appears to be the purest, and the most vivid to the eyes.

HSV and HSL are two cylindrical systems in practice. However, these two systems are not just the loyal conversion from Cartesian coordinates to cylindrical coordinates. In the transformation from the Cartesian coordinates to either HSV or HSL system, nonlinear distortion of space is introduced. In the HSV system, H is for Hue, S for Saturation and V for

Value (a name for brightness). In the HSL system, H is for Hue, S for Saturation and L for Lightness (or Luminance).

The HSV color space was first defined by Alvy Smith in 1978. S is defined in the range of $[0, 1]$, V is defined in the range of $[0, 1]$ and H is an angle in $[0°, 360°]$.

Suppose that r, g, b use a scale of $[0, 1]$. Given the (r, g, b) coordinates in a RGB color space, let

$$x_{\max} = \max\{r, g, b\},$$
$$x_{\min} = \min\{r, g, b\}.$$

Define value

$$V = x_{\max},$$

and saturation

$$S = \frac{x_{\max} - x_{\min}}{x_{\max}}.$$

Next we define the hue as an angle. If $S = 0$, then the hue is undefined (gray color). Otherwise define the hue angle as

$$H = \begin{cases} 60°(b' - g') & \text{if } r = x_{\max} \\ 60°(2 + r' - b') & \text{if } g = x_{\max} \\ 60°(4 + g' - r') & \text{if } b = x_{\max}, \end{cases} \quad (1.7)$$

where

$$r' = \frac{x_{\max} - r}{x_{\max} - x_{\min}},$$
$$g' = \frac{x_{\max} - g}{x_{\max} - x_{\min}},$$
$$b' = \frac{x_{\max} - b}{x_{\max} - x_{\min}}.$$

We understand that the H angle in Eq. 1.7 is in a sense of modulo $360°$. If H falls into the negative range, we then add $360°$ to bring it back to the range of $[0°, 360°]$. We simply assign angles $0°$, $120°$ and $240°$ to the three primary colors.

Using the HSV coordinates, the colors R, Y, G, C, B, M and W all have the same V value and hence are placed in the same plane. W has saturation 0 while other six colors have saturation 1. W is located at the center of this plane while R, Y, G, C, B, M form a regular hexagon. The original RGB cube is transformed to a cone with a flat regular hexagon as the cap on the top. Hence this model is also called a **hexcone model**. The hue angles of R, Y, G, C, B, M run from 0° through 300° with a 60° spacing.

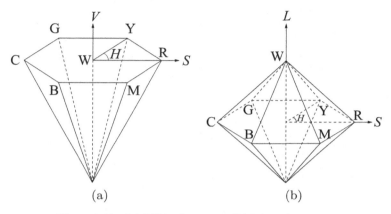

Figure 1.11 (a) HSV color space. (b) HSL color space.

In the HSL color space, the hue, H, is defined the same as in HSV. The S and L values are defined differently. L is defined as

$$L = \frac{x_{\max} + x_{\min}}{2},$$

and

$$S = \begin{cases} \dfrac{x_{\max} - x_{\min}}{2L} & \text{for } 0 < L \leq \frac{1}{2} \\ \dfrac{x_{\max} - x_{\min}}{2(1 - L)} & \text{for } \frac{1}{2} < L < 1. \\ 0 & \text{for } L = 0 \text{ or } L = 1 \end{cases}$$

By this definition, the colors R, Y, G, C, B, M will have the same lightness $L = \frac{1}{2}$ and hence are on the same plane. The white color however, has lightness $L = 1$, which is twice that of the other six colors. After the transformation from RGB to HSL, the original RGB cube becomes a **double cone** (Figure 1.11). For more color space conversions, see [Burger and Burge (2009)].

Remark 7. Color Terms in Art Explained — Hue, Tint, Tone and Shade

When the artists mix colors, the terms hue, tint, tone and shade have special meanings. Hue is referred to the "pure color". In the art terminology, a tint is obtained when a hue is mixed with white. A tone is produced when a hue is mixed with gray. A shade is the result of mixing a hue with black. Quantitative analysis can by applied with these artistic terms. For example, when a color is mixed with white, the hue is unchanged, while the brightness is increased and the saturation is reduced.

Chapter 2

Perspective Analysis of Images

Photographs do not lie ... too often.

— *Hongyu Guo*

Reading Guide. Perspective rectification of images using projective transformations has already become a common practice in photo editing, image processing, architectural design, photogrammetry and machine vision. As early as in Renaissance, in the first treaties on perspective—*On Painting*, Alberti raised questions like what are the relations of the images of the same scene observed from different positions [Alberti (1435); Kline (1972)]. When the scene is planar, the questions have been answered by mathematicians in the early development of projective geometry. There have not been explicit discussions in literature when the scene is 3-dimensional. In this chapter, we will explore these problems and seek the answers. Perspective depth inference from a single image is also investigated. We also discuss perspective diminution and foreshortening. The perspective diminution factor and the perspective foreshortening factor are defined in a rigorous manner and applied to the analysis of perspective distortion. The materials in this chapter are based on two articles that the author has previously published [Guo (2013a,b)].

Photo forensic analysis is one of the applications of perspective depth inference. There have been cases in the court, that both the plaintiff and the defendant provide photo evidences of the scene of interest or dispute. Many people hold the belief that photographs do not lie. However, different photographs of the same scene can give people quite different perceptions. In the court case, the plaintiff and the defendant may provide different photographs, just like the two photos in Figure 2.10, with one being shot with a wide-angle lens and the other with a telephoto lens from different distances. Both the plaintiff and the defendant try to use the photographs to their own advantage to show either the distance in the scene is far or close. Both photos are real and unaltered. However, the spatial perception from the photographs are quite different. The distance in a wide-angle image looks much bigger than in the one with telephoto lens. With perspective depth inference (Sec. 4) on the two images in Figure 2.10, the length of the walkway between the foreground arch and the background arch is calculated to be about 20 meters. The results from the measurements and calculation on the two apparently quite different images agree with each other. Furthermore, the camera position can be inferred by mere measurements on the photograph. It is found that when the photograph in Figure 2.10 (a) was shot, the camera was 4 m away from the scene. When the photograph in Figure 2.10 (b) was shot, the camera was 12 m away from the scene.

§1   Geometric Model of the Camera

The study of projective geometry as a branch in mathematics was motivated by the study of perspective drawing in art. In turn, the study of projective geometry, especially projective transformations find many applications in perspective drawing, photography, camera calibration, photogrammetry, photo forensic analysis, computer graphics, computer vision and robotics.

The simplest camera is a pinhole camera. There is a small pinhole in the front of the camera. Because light travels along straight lines, the light from the object point passes this pinhole and form a point image on the film on the back wall of the camera. The image of the scene is the central projection with the pinhole as the center and the film as the image plane.

Sophisticated cameras use lenses. The formation of images through a thin lens is governed by the laws of optics. Let u be the distance from the 3-D object to the center of the lens and v be the distance from the image point of the object to the center of lens. According to the principles of optics, u and v are related by

$$\frac{1}{u} + \frac{1}{v} = \frac{1}{f},$$

where f is the focal length of the lens. This means if the subject distance u is different, the image distance v is different and hence the image points do not lie in the same plane.

In practice, the image sensor of the camera is a plane. We do not have exactly point images on the sensor. Instead, corresponding to each scene point, a very small circular disk called **circle of confusion** is recorded on the image sensor. When the scene point is within the **depth of field** (DOF), the circle of confusion is so small that it is indistinguishable from a point to the human eyes. This leads to the geometric model, or projective model of a camera. Namely the image of the 3-D scene is the central projection on the image plane.

The distance from the center of projection (COP) to the image plane is called **image distance**. Practically with the cameras for photography, the image distance is slightly bigger than the focal length of the camera lens and the term focal length and image distance are often used interchangeably in photography, when the projective model of the camera, instead of optics is concerned.

The camera lens with a long focal length is called a **telephoto lens** because it is usually focused on far away objects. The long focal lens cameras have a small **field of view**. Given the same size of the sensor, the longer the local length, the smaller the **angle of field** is. A camera lens with a short focal length is called a **wide-angle** lens.

The image plane of a real camera is behind the lens and the image is upside down. When we have a geometric model of the camera, it does not hurt if we place the image plane in front of the COP, just like the canvas of the artist. Everything in theory will be the same, but the image will be upright. In computer graphics, animation and video games, we employ a virtual camera. The image plane is the computer screen, which is the viewing window. The view point (COP) is located in the position of the eye of the user of the computer. The virtual camera looks into this viewing window and sees the 3-D virtual world as projected on the computer screen.

You can find discussion on projective geometry pertaining to the central projection in Part II Chap. 1. We set up a coordinate system (x, y, z) such that the COP is at the origin O. Figure 1.19 in Part II Chap. 1 is duplicated here as Figure 2.1. The image plane is parallel to the x-y plane with an image distance f. Imagine a person is viewing through this virtual camera. It is customary for the viewer to set the positive x to the right direction, the positive y to the upward direction, and z to the forward direction in depth. This convention results in a left-handed coordinate system. In computer graphics applications, Microsoft DirectX adopts this left-handed coordinate system as default for this viewer's convention. On the picture plane, we use X-Y coordinate system. X is parallel to x and Y is parallel to y with C at the origin.

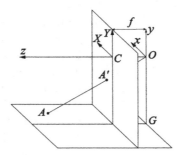

Figure 2.1   Camera coordinate system.

Perspective Projection

For any scene point (x, y, z) in 3-D space, the coordinates of the image point (X, Y) in the image plane are

$$X = f\frac{x}{z},$$
$$Y = f\frac{y}{z}. \tag{2.1}$$

When we discussed projective geometry in Part II Chap. 1, we applied projective transformations in perspective rectification of images. The projective transformation is defined from one projective plane to another projective plane. This applies easily when the image, say a framed photograph or painting hanging on the wall, is viewed from different angles. However, in the perspective rectification practice, as shown in Part II Chap.

1 Figure 1.16, the scene is often a 3-D scene, not planar. Are the images of 3-D scenes viewed from different angles also related by a projective transformation? This will be investigated in the following sections. 2-D scenes and 3-D scenes are investigated as separate cases because there are essential differences in these cases. Some clarification of the terms is needed. By a 2-D scene, we mean that all the scene points lie in a 2-D plane. The scene plane may or may not be parallel to the image plane of the camera. An alternative to the term 2-D scene is "planar scene", which is more accurate. Whenever the term 2-D scene is used, it should be understood as "planar scene". Similarly, the more accurate term for "3-D scene" is "non-planar" scene, which means that all the scene points do not lie in the same plane.

§2   Images Captured From Different Angles

2.1   2-D Scenes

Suppose the scene is 2-D. That is, the scene points are on the same plane. The scene plane is not necessarily parallel to the image plane. This is the case when the scene is a framed photograph or art painting hanging on the wall.

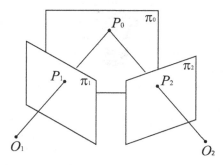

Figure 2.2   A 2-D scene.

In Figure 2.2, π_0 is the plane of a painting on the wall. We take a photograph of it, with O_1 being the COP and π_1 being the image plane of the camera. Now we take another photograph of the same picture π_0 from a different angle, with COP O_2 and image plane π_2. From the theory of projective geometry, the two images are related by a projective transformation, which is the product of two perspective mappings. The transformation is described by Eq. 1.6 in Part II Chap. 1, and we rewrite it in the following:

$$X' = \frac{\tau_{11}X + \tau_{12}Y + \tau_{13}}{\tau_{31}X + \tau_{32}Y + \tau_{33}}$$

$$Y' = \frac{\tau_{21}X + \tau_{22}Y + \tau_{23}}{\tau_{31}X + \tau_{32}Y + \tau_{33}},$$

(2.2)

where (X, Y) are the inhomogeneous coordinates of a point on the image plane π_1, (X', Y') are the inhomogeneous coordinates of the corresponding point on the image plane π_2, and τ_{ij} are constants determined by the positions of O_1, O_2 and the positions of π_0, π_1 and π_2.

2.2   3-D Scenes

When the scene is 3-D in space, as shown in Figure 2.3, are the two images on π_1 and π_2 also related by a projective mapping? The general answer is no. In fact, there is not even a well-defined mapping between the two images.

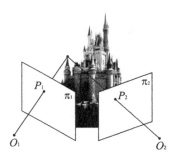

Figure 2.3   Same 3-D scene viewed from different angles.

We only need one counterexample to understand this. Suppose we have a circle in the 3-D scene shown in Figure 2.4, which is described by $y^2 + (z - a)^2 = b^2$, $x = 0$, in the coordinate system of the first camera with O_1 as the origin, where $b > 0$ and $a > f + b$ are constants. The image of this circle on the photograph taken with the first camera is a straight line, because the plane $x = 0$ passes through O_1. It is obvious that the image of the same circle is a curve on the second photograph taken by the second camera, provided that O_1 and O_2 are different and the axes z and z' (optical axes of the two cameras) do not coincide. Because projective transformations always map straight lines to straight lines, the correspondence from image points (X, Y) to image points (X', Y') cannot be a projective transformation. In fact, in the general situation, the correspondence from one photograph to another is not even a well-defined mapping. This fact is evident in epipolar geometry. A single point in one image corresponds to one entire epipolar line in the other image.

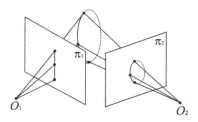

Figure 2.4   Part of a 3-D scene: one image is a straight line while the other is a curve.

Figure 2.5 illustrates another counterexample. It is a sculpture by a Swiss artist Markus Raetz. From one angle, it looks like "YES" while from a perpendicular angle, the word reads "NO".

(a) Front view   (b) Oblique view   (c) Oblique view   (d) Side view

Figure 2.5   3-D scene viewed from different angles. Markus Raetz Zeichnungen, Kunstmuseum Basel ©2013 Artists Rights Society (ARS), New York / ProLitteris, Zurich. Reproduced by permission.

However, as discussed earlier, in practice, given an image of a building, after a projective transformation performed in the image plane, it does look like another image of the same scene from a different angle. In fact, this is an approximation. When the scene is 3-D in space, the relationship between the two images of the same scene can be approximated by a projective transformation, under the following conditions:

(1) The depth of the scene (the maximum difference in depth between any two points in the scene) is small compared with the subject distance (from the COP to the front of the scene);

(2) The difference between the two viewing angles is small;

(3) There are no occlusions (there are no points showing on one image but not on the other because of being blocked by other points).

This explains why the projective approximation fails in the case of the relationship between Figure 2.5 (a) and 2.5 (d). In this case the two viewing angles differ by 90° and there are severe occlusions from these two viewing angles. If the difference in viewing angles is small and there are no occlusions, the projective approximation should also work for the images of this sculpture, like the two views in Figure 2.5 (b) and 2.5 (c).

§3   Images Captured From Different Distances

The next situation is when the two images of the same scene are shot from the same angle but different distances. The axes of the two cameras coincide and the image planes of the two cameras are parallel to each other. The scene can be either 2-D or 3-D. This is really a special case of the situation that was analyzed in the last section. So the results in the last section apply here also. However, because this situation is encountered so frequently in practice, it deserves special attention and treatment. The analysis of this situation is also related to depth inference (discussed in the next section). That is, to infer how far away the camera was from the scene when the photograph was shot, and the relative distances between objects in 3-D, by measurements on the image.

3.1   2-D Scenes

First assume the scene is 2-D. In Figure 2.6 (a), camera one has COP O_1 and camera two has COP O_2. The axes (z-axes) of the two cameras coincide. The image planes π_1 and π_2 are parallel, and both are perpendicular to the line O_1O_2. The scene plane π_0 is not necessarily parallel to π_1 and π_2. In such a setting, the two images on π_1 and π_2 of the same planar scene π_0 are related by a projective transformation. This is a special case of 2-D scenes that we discussed in the last section.

As a special case of the special cases, when the scene plane π_0 is also parallel to π_1 and π_2, as shown in Figure 2.7 (b), the projective transformation becomes a similar transformation. In such a case, by merely looking and measuring on the photograph, there is no way to infer how far away the camera was from the painting hanging on the wall when the photograph was shot.

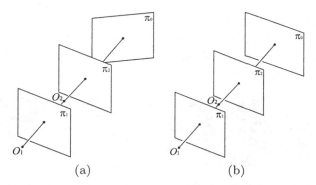

Figure 2.6   2-D scenes shot from the same angle but different distances.

3.2   3-D Scenes

When the scene is 3-D, the situation is more complex. However, there is
a simple case. That is when the two cameras are positioned at the same
point and same direction, as shown in Figure 2.7. The two cameras may
have different focal lengths. In such a case, the two images are related by
a similar transformation (scaling).

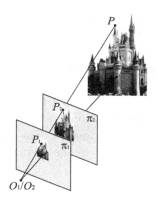

Figure 2.7   3-D scene shot with two cameras at the same distance.

This clarifies the misconception in photography that wide-angle lens
and telephoto lens may cause perspective distortions. What causes the
perspective distortion is not the focal length of the camera, but the subject

distance rather. As an example, Figure 2.8 (a) and (b) are two photographs of the same scene taken at the same position, with one wide-angle lens and one telephoto lens. (The images in Figure 2.8 and Figure 2.10 were taken by the author in the Heritage Park in Corpus Christi, TX.) If the center part in the rectangle frame of Figure 2.8 (a) is cropped and enlarged, it is identical to Figure 2.8 (b).

(a)   (b)

Figure 2.8   Same scene shot from the same distance, 12 m.   (a) Wide-angle lens. (b) Telephoto lens. Image source: Hongyu Guo.

Now suppose two photographs of the same 3-D scene are taken from different distances, as shown in Figure 2.9. Figure 2.9 looks similar to Figure 2.7, but note there is a big difference. In Figure 2.7, the two cameras are located at the same position. O_1 and O_2 are the same point. In Figure 2.9, the two cameras are located at two different locations O_1 and O_2. Let $O_1O_2 = s$ and suppose the two cameras may have different focal lengths f and f'.

The two images of the same scene shot from different distances are not related by a projective transformation. In fact, there is not even a well-defined mapping between the two images. The same 3-D scene point has coordinates (x, y, z) and (x', y', z') in the two camera coordinate systems and they are related by

$$x' = x,$$
$$y' = y,$$
$$z' = z - s.$$

In the image plane π_1, we use coordinates (X, Y) while in image plane π_2 we use coordinates (X', Y'). For a point in space with coordinates (x, y, z), its image point (X, Y) in photograph π_1 is

$$X = f\frac{x}{z},$$
$$Y = f\frac{y}{z}. \tag{2.3}$$

The image point (X', Y') in photograph π_2 of the same scene point is

$$X' = f'\frac{x}{z - s},$$
$$Y' = f'\frac{y}{z - s}. \tag{2.4}$$

The same scene point (x, y, z) in 3-D space is projected in photograph π_1 as point (X, Y) but is projected in photograph π_2 as point (X', Y'). This induces a correspondence $(X, Y) \mapsto (X', Y')$ from π_1 to π_2.

If the two camera shoot from the same place, meaning O_1 and O_2 coincide and $s = 0$, then we have

$$X' = \frac{f'}{f}X,$$
$$Y' = \frac{f'}{f}Y.$$

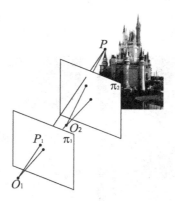

Figure 2.9   3-D scene shot with two cameras at different distances.

This means that the two photographs are similar to each other, even though the cameras may have different focal lengths f and f'. We will further discuss the effect of "perspective distortions" of telephoto lenses and wide-angle lenses in Section 5. Here we have already seen that what "distorts" the perspective is not the focal length of the camera, but rather the subject distance (camera to object distance), because the two photographs taken at the same subject distance ($O_1 = O_2$) are similar to each other regardless of the focal lengths of the cameras.

When we take photographs, as well as in computer graphics 3-D rendering using the virtual camera, we need to have this "perspective distortion" in mind, which is really caused by the subject distance. We can deliberately choose the best subject distance (shooting distance), either to minimize the "perspective distortion" for a better rendering of the object, or to exaggerate the "perspective distortion" for some artistic effects or special effects.

When O_1 and O_2 are different and $s \neq 0$, the correspondence $(X, Y) \mapsto (X', Y')$ is not a similarity transformation. It is not a projective transformation either. In fact, this correspondence $(X, Y) \mapsto (X', Y')$ is not even a well-defined mapping. From Eqs. 2.3 and 2.4, we can obtain

$$X' = \frac{f'z}{f(z-s)}X,$$
$$Y' = \frac{f'z}{f(z-s)}Y.$$

We see that (X', Y') are not uniquely determined by (X, Y). They are also affected by the depth z of the scene point. We could alter the 3-D position (x, y, z) of the scene point so that z is changed but (X, Y) remain the same. But (X', Y') will change because z changes. This is the same topic of depth ambiguity, which we discussed in Part II Chap. 1.

(a)   (b)

Figure 2.10   Same scene shot from different distances (a) From a distance of 4 m with wide-angle lens. (b) From a distance of 12 m with telephoto lens. Image source: Hongyu Guo.

Figure 2.10 (a) and (b) are two photographs of the same 3-D scene. Figure 2.10 (b) is the same as Figure 2.8 (b) and is duplicated here for comparison. Figure 2.10 (a) is shot from a closer distance 4 m with a wide-angle lens while Figure 2.10 (b) is shot from a further distance 12 m with a telephoto lens. Since the image planes of the two cameras are parallel and the z-axes coincide, if the two images were related by a projective transformation, it must be a similar transformation. It is easy to see that these two images are not related by a similar transformation, because when the front arch in the two photographs are registered (aligned), the images of the background arch are not aligned (one is bigger than the other).

§4   Perspective Depth Inference

It must be made clear that no inference of the depth of the 3-D scene can be made from a single image, unless additional prior knowledge about the 3-D scene is available. We know that the process of taking a photograph is to make a central projection from the 3-D scene to the 2-D image plane. In this process, an entire line in 3-D is projected to a single point in the image plane and the depth information is lost. This is the cause of all the depth ambiguities as in the art of 3-D illusions. When we take a photograph of a painting hanging on the wall, suppose the image plane of the camera is parallel to the wall, the depth information is completely lost. Just by examining the photograph, there is no way to find out the original distance from the camera to the wall when the photograph was taken, because all the photographs from different distances are related by a similar transformation. Also, just by examining a photograph of a castle, there is no way to tell whether this is a photograph of a real 3-D castle, or this is a photograph of a framed photograph of a castle hanging on the wall. In the former case, the scene points of the real castle have various depths, while in the latter case, all the scene points in the framed art have the same depth.

However, when we exam a photograph of a 3-D scene in the general situation, if we have partial knowledge of the 3-D scene, we may make some inference about the relative distances and sizes of the 3-D objects by some measurements on the photograph. This partial knowledge about the 3-D scene is known as depth cue. One example of such depth cues is that some object are on the ground, which is a plane perpendicular to the image plane. We first discuss depth inference in one-point perspective images, followed by two-point perspective images.

In the following, we are interested in the depth of objects in the ground plane, assuming the image plane is vertical. We use the x, y, z coordinate system for the scene, and the X, Y coordinate system for the image plane as shown in Figure 2.1.

For any point P on the ground plane, it has coordinates $(x, -h, z)$ and according to the camera projection formula Eq. 2.1, its image (X, Y) on the image plane has

$$Y = -\frac{fh}{z},\tag{2.5}$$

where h is the height of the COP above the ground plane, namely $h = OG$ in Figure 2.1.

4.1   One-Point Perspective

In one-point perspective, the origin C of the image plane X-Y is the principal vanishing point. If the photograph is not cropped, this principal vanishing point is the center of the photograph, assuming the image sensor is centered. We will not rely solely on this in the depth inference because it cannot be always guaranteed. The principal vanishing point can be found as the intersection of a family of lines that are supposed to be parallel in 3-D space.

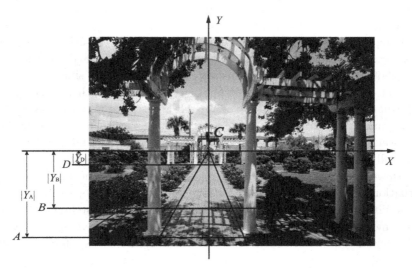

Figure 2.11   Depth inference: image of the same scene shot from a distance of 4m, with wide-angle lens. Image source: Hongyu Guo.

Figure 2.10 (a) was shot with a wide-angle lens from a closer distance while Figure 2.10 (b) was shot with a telephoto lens from a further distance. In Figure 2.10 (a), the brick walkway looks much longer than that in Figure 2.10 (b), although in fact it is the same walkway. This phenomenon gives an illusion and a misconception that a wide-angle lens stretches distance and a telephoto lens compresses distance.

Figure 2.10 (a) is duplicated and enlarged with points and lines marked, and it becomes Figure 2.11. It is in one-point perspective. Point A is the position of the front arch. Point D is the position of the background arch. AD is the distance of the brick walkway. We choose a point B, which is the edge of the broader brick platform under the near arch before the plants. We can count in the image that there are ten brick lengths between A and B. Assume we have the prior knowledge that each brick is 20 cm long (space between two bricks included, as I measured). Then the distance $d_{AB} = 2$ m.

On the image, we draw two lines along the brick lines and they meet at the principal vanishing point C, which will be the origin of the X-Y coordinates in the image plane. In this coordinate system, points on the ground plane have negative Y values. We use $|Y|$ instead. From Eq. 2.5,

$$z = \frac{fh}{|Y|}.$$

Hence

$$z_A = \frac{fh}{|Y_A|},$$

$$z_A + d_{AB} = \frac{fh}{|Y_B|}.$$

The measurements on the image give us

$$|Y_A| = 42,\ |Y_B| = 28,\ |Y_D| = 7.$$

Note that the measurements are done on the computer screen using Adobe Photoshop, instead of on the printed image. The unit of these numbers is the grid spacing, instead of absolute unit like centimeters. However, whatever unit is used should not affect the result. Using these measurements, we obtain

$$fh = \frac{Y_A Y_B}{|Y_B - Y_A|} d_{AB} = 168.$$

Hence

$$z = \frac{168}{|Y|}.$$

It can be calculated that

$$z_A = 4 \text{ m}, \ z_B = 6 \text{ m}, \ z_D = 24 \text{ m}.$$

This means that, the camera was 4 m away from the front arch when the image was shot. The length of the walkway is

$$z_D - z_A = 20 \text{ m}.$$

This was verified by the measurement in the garden. The length of the walkway is indeed 20 m.

Figure 2.12   Depth inference: image of the same scene shot from a distance of 12 m with telephoto lens. Image source: Hongyu Guo.

Figure 2.10 (b) is duplicated and enlarged with points and lines marked, and it becomes Figure 2.12. The same process of depth inference can be applied to the image in Figure 2.12. The same feature points A, B and D are selected in space but their relative positions in the image are different now. The coordinate system (x, y, z) used for the image in Figure 2.12 is different from that for Figure 2.11, because the origin is different now and z for the same scene point is different. The image distance, or the focal length of the camera f' is different too. The camera height h' may be different as well. Measurements on this image indicates,

$$|Y_A| = 42.5, \ |Y_B| = 36.5, \ |Y_D| = 16.$$

It can be found that

$$z = \frac{517.1}{|Y|}.$$

The calculation shows

$$z_A = 12.2 \text{ m}, \; z_B = 14.2 \text{ m}, \; z_D = 32.3 \text{ m}.$$

This means that the camera was 12.2 m away from the front arch with a telephoto lens when this image was shot. This verifies that the camera was indeed further away when the image was shot, compared with the image in Figure 2.11, which was shot from a distance of 4 m, with a wide-angle lens. The length of the walkway is

$$z_D - z_A = 20.1 \text{ m}.$$

Although cameras may cheat the eyes, with the demonstrated calculations in perspective analysis on two quite different looking images, a consistent conclusion about the depth of the background arch is determined.

When we take photographs from a short subject distance, the space seems to be stretched in the depth direction. When we take photographs from a long subject distance, the image of the far away objects seem to be compressed in the depth direction. This is called "**perspective distortion**". We often hear that wide-angle lenses tend to stretch distance while telephoto lenses tend to compress distance. Indeed it is the fact and maybe even a helpful tip that when you are trying to sell your house and taking pictures of the rooms, pictures taken by a wide-angle camera do look more spacious than the rooms actually are. But the explanation of cause is incorrect. What makes the different perspective is the subject distance, rather the focal length. It is a coincidence that we often have a short subject distance when we use wide-angle lenses while we have a long subject distance when use telephoto lenses. Professional photographers are aware of this and have made efforts to correct this misconception in the general public. However, there has not been an analytic and quantitative account of the perspective distortion in the literature, which I am offering here. We will revisit this issue of perspective distortion in Section 6 after analyzing the perspective diminution factor and foreshortening factor in the next section.

4.2   Two-Point Perspective

Figure 2.13 (a) is a two-point perspective drawing by Jan Vredeman de Vries (1604). In a two-point perspective image, there are two vanishing points. The world coordinate line $\tilde{y}$ is parallel to the camera coordinate line y, but $\tilde{x}$ and $\tilde{z}$ are at oblique angles with x and z, as shown in Figure 2.13 (b). Perspective depth inference can work with two-point perspective as well. In Figure 2.13 (a), the two vanishing points on the image plane are V_1 and V_2. The line V_1V_2 is the horizon line. The same coordinate system X, Y can be used in the image plane. Figure 2.13 (b) shows the ground plane in the scene in Figure 2.13 (a). Point G is the station point, which is the perpendicular foot of COP O on the ground as in Figure 2.1. Axis $\tilde{x}$ forms an angle α with axis x. Then,

$$\tilde{z} = \frac{z}{\cos \alpha}.$$

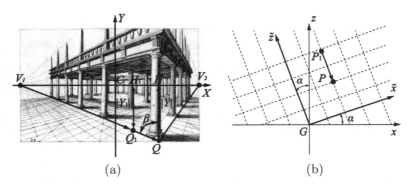

(a)   (b)

Figure 2.13   Depth inference on a two-point perspective image. Image source: public domain.

Let P and P_1 be two points in the ground plane along $\tilde{z}$ direction. Their images are Q and Q_1 in the image plane. The distances of Q and Q_1 to the horizon line V_1V_2 can be measured as $|Y|$ and $|Y_1|$. Suppose V_1Q forms an angle β with the vertical line in the image. Then,

$$V_1Q = \frac{Y}{\cos \beta}.$$

The measurement on the image can use the vertical distance $|Y|$ to the horizon line, or the distance V_1Q to the vanishing point V_1, since they only differ by a constant factor. By Eq. 2.5,

$$|Y| = \frac{fh}{\tilde{z}\cos \alpha}.$$

If the distance P_1P_2 between two points P_1 and P_2 along $\tilde{z}$ direction is known, it can be used to calibrate the parameter $fh/\cos\alpha$, and the depth along $\tilde{z}$ direction can be calculated by

$$\tilde{z} = \frac{|Y_1||Y_2|}{|Y_2 - Y_1|}\frac{P_1P_2}{|Y|}.$$

The depth inference along $\tilde{x}$ direction can be accomplished in a similar way because $\tilde{x}$ is proportional to z, with a simple relationship

$$\tilde{x} = \frac{z}{\sin \alpha}.$$

§5   Perspective Diminution and Foreshortening

Objects close to the viewer appear bigger while objects far away appear to be smaller. This is known as perspective diminution and foreshortening in general. However, the quantitative relationship between the apparent size and depth was not clear until the Renaissance when the principles of perspectives were fully understood. Before and during early Renaissance artists struggled with perspective drawing and made mistakes with inaccurate diminution rate of objects in depth.

Figure 2.14   Perspective diminution and foreshortening, in *Perspective* by Jan Vredeman de Vries, 1604. Image source: public domain.

The terms perspective diminution and foreshortening have been widely used in art. However, the definitions of these terms tend to be vague and confusing. These two terms are often used interchangeably. The architect William Longfellow [Longfellow (1901)] pointed out: "The distinction between mere diminution from distance, and foreshortening, which is diminution from obliquity of view, is not to be forgotten here. If we stand in front of a square or circle, its plane being at right angles to our line of vision, it looks like a square or circle at any distance; it may grow larger or smaller, but its proportions do not change. If we look at it obliquely, the farther parts diminish more than the nearer, the lines that are seen obliquely more than those that are seen squarely, and the shape is distorted. This is foreshortening..." However, Longfellow did not give a quantitative description.

Figure 2.14 is a drawing by Jan Vredeman de Vries, a Dutch artist in the Renaissance, to illustrate the **perspective diminution** and **foreshortening**. When the person stands vertically but moves back in the depth direction, his size diminishes (diminution). The different parts of the body diminish proportionately. When the person is lying down on the ground along the depth direction, the different parts diminish unproportionately. The part in greater depth diminishes much faster (foreshortening). In the following, we define a perspective diminution factor and a perspective foreshortening factor precisely, which have not been defined before in literature. In literature, foreshortening factor has been defined in computer graphics for parallel projections, but not for central projections, or perspective projections. Diminution factor does not apply to parallel projection, because there is no diminution, or shrinking in size with parallel projection. This will be corroborated with perspective diminution factor and we will see this shortly. Because parallel projection can be considered as central projection where the depth z is very large, the diminution factor is close to zero.

5.1   Perspective Diminution Factor

For simplicity, a scene point P in the y-z plane is considered in Figure 2.15. However, this restriction $x = 0$ is not necessary for the theory to hold. It just makes the diagram easier to draw and easier to see. The definition of perspective diminution factor, perspective foreshortening factor apply to any scene point with any (x, y, z).

In perspective projection, the length in 3-D space and the length of its projected image on the image plane have a nonlinear relationship. Locally this relationship can be approximated linearly using differential calculus. It is assumed that the object is a small line segment PQ in the transverse direction. After perspective projection with the center at O, the images of P and Q are P' and Q' respectively. If you imagine that PQ is a small tree on the ground, then $P'Q'$ is its image on the image sensor of the camera. Suppose point P has depth z and vertical coordinate y. Note that y is the vertical coordinate of point P, instead of the size of PQ. The size of the object is denoted by $\Delta y = PQ$. The size of the image is denoted by $\Delta Y = P'Q'$. By Eq. 2.5, when z is kept constant but y is varied by a small amount , the image will change by

$$\Delta Y = P'Q' = \frac{f}{z} PQ = \frac{f}{z} \Delta y.$$

In the limit of $PQ \to 0$, the ratio

$$\lim_{PQ \to 0} \frac{P'Q'}{PQ}$$

is a constant, which shall be defined as the perspective diminution factor.

Definition 1. Perspective diminution factor

The **perspective diminution factor** at depth z is defined to be

$$M_{\parallel} \overset{\text{def}}{=} \lim_{PQ \to 0} \frac{P'Q'}{PQ} \overset{\text{def}}{=} \left| \frac{\partial Y}{\partial y} \right|.$$

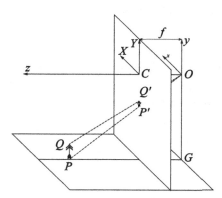

Figure 2.15   Perspective diminution factor.

The symbol $M_{\parallel}$ is used because the transverse direction is parallel to the image plane. It can be found easily that the diminution factor is completely determined by the depth of the object in 3-D space. By taking the derivative in Eq. 2.5, we have the following.

Theorem 1. *The perspective diminution factor at depth z is determined by*

$$M_{\parallel} = \frac{f}{z}.$$

Suppose PQ has unit length. When it is placed at depth z, $M_{\parallel}$ represents the size (height) of the image $P'Q'$. $M_{\parallel}$ is a function of depth z. For the same object PQ, its image size $P'Q'$ is inversely proportional to the depth z. This effect is called **perspective diminution**.

In most of the photographs, for the objects far enough (z big enough), we have $M_{\parallel} < 1$, which means the image is smaller in size than the object, although under certain circumstances, when the depth z is small compared to focal length, it is possible to have $M_{\parallel} > 1$, as in close-up photography and microscopic photography.

5.2   Perspective Foreshortening Factor

The magnification along the depth direction z is different from the transverse magnification (in y direction). Suppose a segment PR is in z-direction, with size $\Delta z = PR$, and the size of its image is $\Delta Y = P'R'$, as shown in Figure 2.16.

Definition 2. Perspective foreshortening factor

The **perspective foreshortening factor** at depth z is defined to be

$$M_{\perp} \stackrel{\text{def}}{=} \lim_{PR \to 0} \frac{P'R'}{PR} \stackrel{\text{def}}{=} \left| \frac{\partial Y}{\partial z} \right|.$$

The symbol $M_{\perp}$ is used because the depth direction is perpendicular to the image plane. From Eq. 2.1 we take the partial derivative of Y with respect to z, and we obtain

$$\lim_{\Delta z \to 0} \frac{\Delta Y}{\Delta z} = \frac{\partial Y}{\partial z} = -\frac{fy}{z^2}.$$

Theorem 2. *The perspective foreshortening factor at depth z is determined by*

$$M_{\perp} = \left| \frac{fy}{z^2} \right|. \tag{2.6}$$

The effect that the size of an object in the depth direction diminishes according to the inverse squared law in Eq. 2.6 is called **perspective foreshortening**.

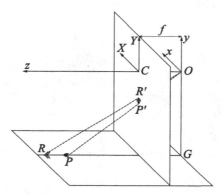

Figure 2.16   Perspective foreshortening factor.

The perspective foreshortening factor is also proportional to y. When y is smaller, $M_\perp$ is smaller, meaning the foreshortening is more dramatic. Notice that $\frac{y}{z} = \tan \alpha$, where $\alpha = \angle COP$ is the view angle of the segment PR. Eq. 2.6 can also be written as

$$M_\perp = \left| \frac{f \tan \alpha}{z} \right|.$$

This means that when the viewing angle α is smaller, the effort of foreshortening is more dramatic.

Similar to diminution, when the depth increases, the size of the image of object PR gets smaller as the effect of foreshortening. However, because the object PR is oriented in the depth direction, the image diminishes obeying an inverse squared law, a rate mush faster than diminution. The effect of foreshortening is more dramatic then diminution. Namely, the depth direction is shortened much faster than the transverse directions. When the depth is doubled, the apparent size of objects with transverse orientation shrinks to one half while the apparent size of objects with longitudinal orientation shrinks to one quarter. This is also the reason that photographs of 3-D objects taken from different distances are not similar to each other.

In Eq. 2.6, when z is very small, $M_\perp$ and the image size can be very big, especially compared to the size of the objects in greater depth. Figure 2.17 shows two photographs of the foreshortening effect, where the length of the person is in the depth direction of the camera. The part of the object (feet or head) are exaggeratedly magnified while the far side is foreshortened dramatically. This effect is exaggerated with wide-angle lenses because one can shoot at very short subject distances with a wide-angle lens.

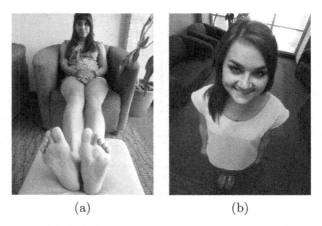

(a)   (b)

Figure 2.17   Foreshortening effect. Image source: Hongyu Guo.

§6   "Perspective Distortion"

We have already discussed a little bit about "perspective distortion" of telephoto and wide-angle lenses and we know it is a misconception. The perspective is not determined by the focal length of the camera, but rather determined by the subject distance. In section 3, we have learned that if we shoot at the same subject distance, using two different cameras, one telephoto and one wide-angle, then the two photographs are similar to each other. Given the same size of the image sensor, the photograph with the telephoto lens have bigger size for the objects but narrower field of view. If we take the wide-angle photograph, crop a small portion around the center, enlarge it proportionally (similar transformation), then it is the same as the photograph shot by a telephoto lens, as shown in Figure 2.8. Using telephoto lenses, we do not do this crop and enlargement manually, but the lens does it automatically. This enlargement is the very reason that the telephoto lenses mislead our eyes. In Figure 2.10 (a) and (b), the depth perception from the two images is quite different. The foreground arch and pillars are about the same size in both photographs. Using this foreground as a reference, the arch and pillars in the background in the Figure 2.10(a) look much smaller than those in Figure 2.10(b). This makes the background objects in Figure 2.10(a) look much further away, while those in Figure 2.10(b) look much closer. The brick walkway in Figure 2.10(a) seems about twice as long as that in Figure 2.10(b). This phenomenon is known as "perspective distortion".

Resizing of the photograph causes "perspective distortion". If the major objects are oriented parallel to the image plane, resizing the photograph will not alter the proportion of the objects but rather change the perception of distance—an enlarged picture causes a perception that the objects are closer while a shrunk picture causes a perception that the objects are further away. Resizing the image can alter the perception of spacing in depth direction between the objects.

If the major objects are oriented along the depth direction of the lens, as in the case of Figure 2.17, resizing the pictures will cause the distortion of relative size of different parts of the same object along depth direction. Figure 2.17(a) looks like a picture of a person with abnormal body proportion (extremely long legs). In fact, if the picture is enlarged enough, it does not seem to be abnormal any more. If one looks with his eyes at the same position as the camera when the picture in Figure 2.17(a) was shot, he sees exactly what the camera sees, which is the photograph itself, and nothing looks abnormal to him. When the photograph is shrunk to a smaller size, as in Figure 2.17(a), the human brain interprets that the model is at a further distance. The human brain is trained and have learned the laws of foreshortening factor $M_\perp$ in Eq. 2.6 unconsciously. When the foreshortening factor $M_\perp$ is applied to objects at larger depth, it results in an interpretation in the brain that the person is out of proportion and hence a perception of "perspective distortion". Figure 2.17(a) and (b) are examples of "perspective distortions" caused by shrinking the images, where distance in the depth direction appears to be longer than it actually is. Figure 2.11(b) is an example of "perspective distortion" caused by enlarging the image, where distance in the depth direction (length of the walkway) appears to be shorter than it actually is. This enlargement can be done by cropping the central part of a wide-angle photograph and editing with software, or by a telephoto lens mechanically and automatically (Figure 2.11(b)).

Using the concept of perspective diminution factor and perspective foreshortening factor, we have a simple explanation of this effect. The perspective foreshortening factor $M \perp$ in Eq. 2.6 is inversely proportional to z^2.

$M_\perp$ equals the image length on the photograph corresponding to unit length object in the depth direction in 3-D. The inverse of $M_\perp$,

$$\frac{1}{M_\perp} = \left| \frac{z^2}{fy} \right|, \qquad (2.7)$$

represents the object size in depth direction in 3-D corresponding to unit length image measured on the photograph. This is a magnifying process that our brains are trained for when interpreting the depth represented in photographs. This magnification is nonlinear in z. The closer to the center in the photograph (larger z), the greater this magnification is. Although our brains do not use formulas to do the calculation, they are trained with experiences. They use the relative size (transverse size, like width and height) as a depth cue to calculate depth unconsciously. When the photograph is enlarged, either manually or by a telephoto lens, our brains are cheated, thinking it is a closer distance and the brain uses this distance to estimate the spacing in the depth dimension in space. As an example in Figure 2.11(b), in the photograph shot with a telephoto lens, the building in the background is perceived as closer in depth than it actually is.

The telephoto lens works the same way as telescopes. They are all long focal length optical systems. The focal length of a telescope should be even longer. The only difference between a telephoto camera lens and a telescope is that a telephoto lens forms a real image on the image sensor, while a telescope forms a virtual image, which is observed by the eye. (Some astronomical telescopes form real images and record the images as photographs too.) If you have the experience watching a far away person walking in the direction of line of sight through a pair of binoculars, you should have noticed that although the person's arms and legs seem to be swinging, the person appears to be marking time without any apparent displacement in the depth direction. Oftentimes, even if the binoculars can make the image bigger, but because the person is far away and the binoculars has limited resolution, you are not able to see whether the person is facing you. Because the depth does not seem to change, you cannot even tell whether the person is walking toward you or away from you. To explain this, we look at how the diminution factor $M_\parallel$ changes with depth z. Given the object size (the person's height) fixed, the diminution factor $M_\parallel$ determines the height of the image of the person. We take the derivative of $M_\parallel$ with respect to z to see how $M_\parallel$ changes with z.

$$\frac{dM_\parallel}{dz} = -\frac{f}{z^2}. \qquad (2.8)$$

When z is very big, $\dfrac{dM_\parallel}{dz}$ is close to zero. This means that the height of the image of the person is almost constant when z changes. This also explains the two pictures of the same scene shot with a wide-angle lens and a telephoto lens from different distances in Figure 2.11. The distance Δz between the pavilion in front and the building in the background is the same in the two pictures. However, because the wide-angle photograph is shot at a closer distance (smaller z), the difference in image size between the front pavilion and the back building is big (bigger $dM_\parallel/dz$). In Figure 2.11 (b), the photograph shot with the telephoto lens, the camera is further away from the scene. The objects have larger depth z. Hence $dM_\parallel/dz$ is smaller and the size difference between the front pavilion and the back building is smaller, giving an illusion that the telephoto lens compresses depth.

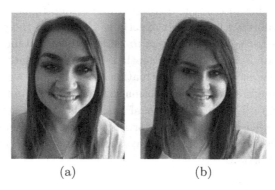

(a)   (b)

Figure 2.18   "Perspective distortion": images of the same model, same pose. (a) Shot from close-up distance of one foot with wide-angle lens. (b) From longer distance. Image source: Hongyu Guo.

Figure 2.18 (a) and (b) are two portraits of the same model, with the same position and the same pose. Figure 2.18 (a) was shot with a 24mm lens (35mm film equivalent) from a distance of one foot, while 2.18 (b) was shot with a 100mm telephoto lens (35mm film equivalent) from a longer distance. Apparently, 2.18 (a) suffers from a distortion. This type of face distortion is very common in the face images in front of Webcams or the built-in cameras of cellphones during a video call. The same type of distortions are in the self-shot portraits with the camera held in one's own hand (the subject distance is one arm's length, if it is shot directly instead of using the reflection of a mirror).

The two images in Figure 2.18 corroborates one of the conclusions we made in Section 3—images of the 3-D scene from different distances are not related by a similar transformation.

Many factors may contribute to the distortions in the left portrait in Figure 2.18. With very short focal length wide-angle lenses, barrel distortions also exist, which is one type of aberration of the lenses known as curvature of field. Curvature of field is not due to perspective. It is a nonlinear aberration of the lens to make it differ from a linear system. The image of a straight line becomes a curve if curvature of field exists with the lens. Even if the distortion of the left portrait is purely perspective, it could be the combined effect of a tilted view angle and short subject distance. The tilted view angle can be rectified by a projective transformation with the help of software tools. A projective transformation on the left portrait may slightly enhance it, but because of the distortion due to depth, we are not able to transform the portrait on the left exactly to the one on the right. There is not an easy fix to the distortion due to short subject distance because this type of distortion is due to varying depth of each scene point. Given the 2-D image only, without the depth information of each point, we cannot rectify the image through a simple transformation. It is the common wisdom in portrait photography that longer focal length and longer subject distance produce more pleasing, attractive portraits. Wide-angle lenses and short subject distances should be avoided in portrait photography to reduce the perspective distortion.

Chapter 3

Quaternions and 3-D Rotations

"The number you have dialed is imaginary. Please rotate your phone 90 degrees and try again."

— *name unknown*

Reading Guide. Quaternions are generalizations of complex numbers. Quaternions provide an alternative representation of 3-D rotations. It is more convenient to make interpolations between rotations represented by quaternions compared with rotations using matrix representations or Euler angles. This advantage can be exploited in computer graphics hardware implementations, resulting faster calculations of the rotations and hence smoother animations. This is one of the compelling reasons that quaternions are applied in computer graphics. We start with a brief review of complex numbers.

§1 Complex Numbers and 2-D Rotations

A complex number is a number in the form of $x + yi$, where x, y are real numbers. x and y are called the **real part** and **imaginary part** of $x + yi$ respectively. i is called the **imaginary unit**.

1.1 Addition and Multiplication

Definition 1. Addition of two complex numbers

$$(x_1 + y_1 i) + (x_2 + y_2 i) \stackrel{\text{def}}{=} (x_1 + x_2) + (y_1 + y_2)i. \tag{3.1}$$

Definition 2. Square of imaginary unit

$$i^2 \stackrel{\text{def}}{=} -1. \tag{3.2}$$

Furthermore, we stipulate the associative law and commutative law for multiplication, distributive laws for multiplication and addition, then the multiplication of any two complex numbers is uniquely determined to be

$$(x_1 + y_1 i)(x_2 + y_2 i) = (x_1 x_2 - y_1 y_2) + (x_1 y_2 + x_2 y_1)i. \tag{3.3}$$

1.2 Conjugate, Modulus and Inverse

Definition 3. Conjugate of a complex number

Given a complex number $z = x + yi$, the **conjugate** of z is defined to be

$$\bar{z} \overset{\text{def}}{=} x - yi. \qquad (3.4)$$

Definition 4. Modulus of a complex number

The **modulus** (or **absolute value**) of $z = x + yi$ is defined by

$$|z| \overset{\text{def}}{=} \sqrt{z\bar{z}} = \sqrt{x^2 + y^2}. \qquad (3.5)$$

In fact, a complex number $z = x + yi$ can be identified as a 2-dimensional vector $(x, y) \in \mathbb{R}^2$. This vector can be represented by an arrow in the plane with the tail at the origin. The plane is called the **complex plane**.

The term modulus is due to J. Argand, who first gave a geometric interpretation of complex numbers, which demystified the "imaginary" aspect of imaginary numbers. The modulus of complex number $x + yi$ is the same as the length (or norm) of vector (x, y).

For $z = x + yi \neq 0$, the inverse of z can be found to be

$$\frac{1}{z} = \frac{\bar{z}}{z\bar{z}} = \frac{\bar{z}}{|z|^2} = \frac{x - yi}{x^2 + y^2}. \qquad (3.6)$$

Complex conjugate and modulus have the following properties.

Theorem 1. (Properties of complex conjugate and modulus) Let z, w be any complex numbers. Then,

(1) $\overline{z + w} = \bar{z} + \bar{w}$.
(2) $\overline{zw} = \bar{z}\,\bar{w}$.
(3) $\bar{\bar{z}} = z$.
(4) $z\bar{z} = \bar{z}z = |z|^2$.
(5) $|z| = |\bar{z}|$.

(6) $|zw| = |z|\,|w|$.

1.3   Polar Representation

Let $z = x + yi$ be a complex number, which is represented by a vector (x, y) in the complex plane. The vector (x, y) has a polar coordinate representation (r, θ), where r is its length and θ is the angle from x-axis to the vector. The angle θ is called the **argument** of z. A complex number z can be represented in the **polar form**

$$z = r(\cos\theta + i\sin\theta),$$

where r is the modulus and θ is the argument of z.

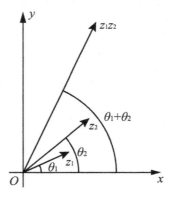

Figure 3.1   Product of two complex numbers.

Given two complex numbers in the polar form, $z_1 = r_1(\cos\theta_1 + i\sin\theta_1)$ and $z_2 = r_2(\cos\theta_2 + i\sin\theta_2)$, the product can be found in the polar form

$$z_1 z_2 = r_1 r_2 \left[\cos(\theta_1 + \theta_2) + i\sin(\theta_1 + \theta_2)\right].$$

This means that the modulus of the product is the product of two moduli and the argument of the product is the sum of the two arguments.

1.4   Unit-Modulus Complex Numbers as 2-D Rotation Operators

A complex number with modulus 1 is called a **unit-modulus complex number**. In the complex plane, all the unit-modulus complex numbers lie on the unit circle S^1. Let u be a unit-modulus complex number with argument θ, and $z = x + iy$ be any complex number. When z is viewed as a vector (x, y) in $\mathbb{R}^2$, the multiplication of u and z results in a vector uz, which is the vector z rotated by an angle θ. The vector rotation in the plane is a linear transformation, which can be represented by a matrix

$$\begin{bmatrix} \cos\theta & -\sin\theta \\ \sin\theta & \cos\theta \end{bmatrix}.$$

Here we have just discovered an alternative way to represent the rotations in a 2-D plane, which is multiplication by a unit-modulus complex number. A unit-modulus complex number can be identified as a rotation operator in the 2-D plane.

§2   Quaternions and 3-D Rotations

The vectors in 2-dimensional spaces and 3-dimensional spaces with operations of addition and scalar multiplication can be easily generalized to n-dimensional spaces. We have seen that complex numbers are represented by 2-dimensional vectors. However, complex numbers also have the multiplication operation defined, which is in the sense of multiplication of two vectors. It is not a trivial task to generalize the complex numbers to higher dimensional spaces so that we keep all the vector addition, multiplication and division operations. At the end of the nineteenth century, a lot of efforts were made to generalize this multiplication (and division) from a 2-dimensional vector space to a 3-dimensional vector space, but all the efforts failed. W. R. Hamilton succeeded in generalizing the complex numbers to a 4-dimensional space, known as quaternions $\mathbb{H}$. $\mathbb{C}$ and $\mathbb{H}$ are examples of division algebras over $\mathbb{R}$. Later in history, more was known about the structures of division algebras over $\mathbb{R}$: The only finite dimensional division algebras over $\mathbb{R}$ (up to isomorphism) are the real numbers $\mathbb{R}$, complex numbers $\mathbb{C}$, quaternions $\mathbb{H}$, and octonians $\mathbb{O}$, which have dimensions 1, 2, 4, 8 respectively. As a price of the generalization, some of the properties of real number multiplication are lost. The multiplication of quaternions is not commutative. The multiplication of octonians is not even associative.

A quaternion is a "number" in the form of $q_0 + q_1 i + q_2 j + q_3 k$, where $q_0, q_1, q_2, q_3 \in \mathbb{R}$. A quaternion can be viewed as a 4-dimensional vector (q_0, q_1, q_2, q_3). i, j, k are called **imaginary units**. Quaternions are generalizations of complex numbers. There is one imaginary unit i in complex numbers, while there are three imaginary units in quaternions. i, j, k can be viewed as three basis vectors with

$$i = (0, 1, 0, 0),$$
$$j = (0, 0, 1, 0),$$
$$k = (0, 0, 0, 1).$$

The scalar 1 can be viewed as the basis vector

$$1 = (1, 0, 0, 0).$$

2.1   Addition and Multiplication

The addition of two quaternions is defined component-wisely. Let

$$p = p_0 + p_1 i + p_2 j + p_3 k,$$
$$q = q_0 + q_1 i + q_2 j + q_3 k. \tag{3.7}$$

Definition 5. Addition of two quaternions

$$p + q \stackrel{\text{def}}{=} (p_0 + q_0) + (p_1 + q_1)i + (p_2 + q_2)j + (p_3 + q_3)k. \tag{3.8}$$

We can define the multiplication of two quaternions so that the quaternions become an algebra over $\mathbb{R}$. To define multiplication for quaternions, it suffices to define the multiplication for the basis vectors and the multiplication can be extended bilinearly to all the quaternions. The multiplication table of basis vectors is shown below.

	1	i	j	k
1	1	i	j	k
i	i	-1	k	$-j$
j	j	$-k$	-1	i
k	k	j	$-i$	-1

This table can be summarized as

Definition 6. Multiplication of imaginary units

$$i^2 = j^2 = k^2 = ijk = -1, \tag{3.9}$$

$$ij = -ji = k$$
$$jk = -kj = i \tag{3.10}$$
$$ki = -ik = j\,.$$

The multiplication of quaternions is associative but not commutative. Given two quaternions p and q in Eq. 3.7, the product of p and q can be found to be

$$
\begin{aligned}
pq = \quad & p_0q_0 - p_1q_1 - p_2q_2 - p_3q_3 \\
& + (p_0q_1 + p_1q_0 + p_2q_3 - p_3q_2)i \\
& + (p_0q_2 + p_2q_0 + p_3q_1 - p_1q_3)j \\
& + (p_0q_3 + p_3q_0 + p_1q_2 - p_2q_1)k\,.
\end{aligned} \tag{3.11}
$$

It is helpful to identify a quaternion $q_0 + q_1 i + q_2 j + q_3 k$ as an ordered pair $(q_0, \mathbf{q})$ of a scalar q_0 and a 3-dimensional vector $\mathbf{q} = (q_1, q_2, q_3)$. We can even write $q = q_0 + \mathbf{q}$ but just keep in mind that this addition means direct sum. q_0 is called the **scalar part** and $\mathbf{q}$ is called the **vector part** of the quaternion. This is the same as identifying q_0 with $(q_0, 0, 0, 0)$, and identifying $\mathbf{q}$ with $(0, q_1, q_2, q_3)$. Using this identification, the product of two quaternions $p = p_0 + \mathbf{p}$ and $q = q_0 + \mathbf{q}$ can be written as

$$pq = p_0q_0 - \mathbf{p}\cdot\mathbf{q} + p_0\mathbf{q} + q_0\mathbf{p} + \mathbf{p}\times\mathbf{q}. \tag{3.12}$$

Notice the scalar part of pq is $p_0q_0 - \mathbf{p}\cdot\mathbf{q}$ while the vector part of pq is $p_0\mathbf{q} + q_0\mathbf{p} + \mathbf{p}\times\mathbf{q}$. If both p and q are vectors (with $p_0 = q_0 = 0$), then the quaternion product in this special case is

$$pq = \mathbf{pq} = -\mathbf{p} \cdot \mathbf{q} + \mathbf{p} \times \mathbf{q}.$$

2.2 Conjugate, Modulus and Inverse

Given a quaternion $q = q_0 + q_1 i + q_2 j + q_3 k$, the **conjugate** of q is defined as follows.

Definition 7. Conjugate of a quaternion

$$\bar{q} \overset{\text{def}}{=} q_0 - q_1 i - q_2 j - q_3 k.$$

Definition 8. Modulus of a quaternion

$$|q| \overset{\text{def}}{=} \sqrt{q\bar{q}} = \sqrt{q_0^2 + q_1^2 + q_2^2 + q_3^2}.$$

The modulus of a quaternion was named in analogy of the modulus of a complex number. Hamilton originally used the term "tensor" for what we mean by modulus now. The modern usage of tensor is totally different from the sense of Hamilton and it is used not in the context of quaternions (See Part I Chap. 2). The modulus of quaternion $q = q_0 + \mathbf{q} = q_0 + q_1 i + q_2 j + q_3 k$ is the same as the length (or norm) of 4-D vector (q_0, q_1, q_2, q_3), or $\sqrt{q_0^2 + \|\mathbf{q}\|^2}$.

For $q \neq 0$, the inverse of q can be found to be

$$\frac{1}{q} = \frac{\bar{q}}{q\bar{q}} = \frac{\bar{q}}{|q|^2} = \frac{q_0 - q_1 i - q_2 j - q_3 k}{q_0^2 + q_1^2 + q_2^2 + q_3^2}.$$

The quaternion conjugate and modulus have the following properties.

Theorem 2. (Properties of quaternion conjugate and modulus) Let p, q be any quaternions. Then,

(1) $\overline{p+q} = \bar{p} + \bar{q}$.
(2) $\overline{pq} = \bar{q}\bar{p}$.
(3) $\bar{\bar{q}} = q$.
(4) $q\bar{q} = \bar{q}q = |q|^2$.
(5) $|q| = |\bar{q}|$.
(6) $|pq| = |p|\,|q|$.

2.3 Polar Representation

A quaternion with modulus 1 is called a **unit-modulus quaternion**. For any quaternion $q = q_0 + q_1 i + q_2 j + q_3 k$, we can always writ

$$q = ru,$$

where $r = |q|$, and $u = \frac{q}{|q|}$ is a unit-modulus quaternion. Let $u = u_0 + \mathbf{u}$ where u_0 is the scalar part and $\mathbf{u}$ is the vector part of u. Since $|u| = 1$, we have

$$u_0^2 + \|\mathbf{u}\|^2 = 1.$$

Let $u_0 = \cos\theta$, where $0 \le \theta < \pi$. Then $\mathbf{u}$ can be written as

$$\mathbf{u} = \mathbf{n}\sin\theta,$$

where $\mathbf{n}$ is a 3-dimensional vector with unit length $\|\mathbf{n}\| = 1$.

Hence any quaternion q can be written as

$$q = r(\cos\theta + \mathbf{n}\sin\theta),$$

where $r = |q|$ is the modulus of q. This is called the **polar representation**, or **polar form** of a quaternion.

2.4 Unit-Modulus Quaternions as 3-D Rotation Operators

All the unit-modulus quaternions lie on a hypersphere S^3, which is embedded in $\mathbb{R}^4$. A unit-modulus quaternion u has a simple inverse $u^{-1} = \bar{u}$.

Let $q = \mathbf{v}$ be a quaternion which has only the vector part (with the scalar part being zero).

Let

$$u = \cos\frac{\theta}{2} + \mathbf{n}\sin\frac{\theta}{2}. \tag{3.13}$$

Then u represents a unit-modulus quaternion with angle $\theta/2$. With some straightforward calculation, we can find, after simplification,

$$uvu^{-1} = \mathbf{v}\cos\theta + (1-\cos\theta)(\mathbf{v}\cdot\mathbf{n})\mathbf{n} + (\mathbf{n}\times\mathbf{v})\sin\theta.$$

This means that uvu is a vector (with the scalar part being zero). It can be checked that the right-hand-side of the above equation is nothing but the vector $\mathbf{v}$ being rotated an angle θ around axis $\mathbf{n}$. Therefore, the unit-modulus quaternion u in Eq. 3.13 can be identified as a rotation operator in 3-D space, which rotates a vector $\mathbf{v}$ around axis $\mathbf{n}$ by an angle θ.

We know that a rotation in 3-D can also be described by a matrix. Let us have a comparison of the quaternion representation with the matrix presentation.

Let $\mathbf{v} = (v_1, v_2, v_3) \in \mathbb{R}^3$ be a 3-D vector. A rotation in 3-D of vector $\mathbf{v}$ is a new vector $A\mathbf{v}$, where A is a matrix

$$A = \begin{bmatrix} A_{11} & A_{12} & A_{13} \\ A_{21} & A_{22} & A_{23} \\ A_{31} & A_{32} & A_{33} \end{bmatrix}.$$

However, a rotation in 3-D that makes $(0,0,0)$ a fixed point has three degrees of freedom (three parameters). The rotation matrix has nine parameters but only three of them are independent. The matrix A must be an orthogonal matrix and satisfy the condition

$$AA^t = E,$$

where A^t is the transpose of A and E is the identity matrix. The direction of the rotation axis $\mathbf{n}$ and the rotation angle θ is not explicit in the matrix elements. Compare with the quaternion representation of rotation. The rotation axis $\mathbf{n}$ and the rotation angle θ are explicit in the quaternion and hence the quaternion representation is more convenient.

Chapter 4

Support Vector Machines and Reproducing Kernel Hilbert Spaces

The question of whether computers can think is like the question of whether submarines can swim.

— *Edsger W. Dijkstra*

Reading Guide. Pattern recognition is closely related to pattern classification. In this chapter, we introduce some fundamental concepts in pattern recognition, classification and machine learning, including supervised learning and unsupervised learning. We give an account of support vector machine—a widely applied learning model in the linear and nonlinear forms. We also make a connection to the kernel methods utilizing reproducing kernel Hilbert spaces.

§1   Human Learning and Machine Learning

Human beings have learning capabilities. More often we learn by examples, rather than by definitions. To teach a young child what is a dog, you never tell the child a dog is "*a highly variable domestic mammal (Canis familiaris) closely related to the gray wolf*". What you do is that you point to a dog and say "Doggie!", and you point to another dog and say "Doggie!" You point to a cat and say "Kitty!", and point to another cat and say "Kitty!" Then the child develops the capability of generalization. Next time when the child sees a new animal, or even just the picture of an animal, like one of those in Figure 4.1, he is able to tell whether it is a dog or a cat.

Figure 4.1   Exercise: Find which is a dog and which is a cat! Image sources: public domain.

We are able to recognize people and distinguish them—our family members, friends, celebrities ..., by looking at their faces. We also notice that the human face recognition may sometimes fail. It is not quite often, but there are some embarrassing moments when you mistaken a stranger as one of your friends. For a European person, if he has not seen many Asian faces in his life, all the Asian faces may look the same to him. It is hard for him to distinguish one from another. The same is true vice versa, for some Asian people to distinguish European faces. All the squirrels look the same to the humans. Maybe all the human faces, Europeans or Asians, look the same to the squirrels too. I hope the squirrels can recognize and identify each other.

How do humans learn? How do humans recognize patterns? Can we make abstractions of this learning process and construct machines that have learning capabilities?

§2   Unsupervised Learning and Supervised Learning

Pattern recognition is closely related to pattern classification. The example in the beginning of Section 1 is to classify (images of) pets into two categories: dogs and cats. The face recognition can be viewed as classification into multiple categories: James (your brother), David (your brother), Chloe (your sister), Michael (your friend), Dr. Wilson (your professor), Arnold Schwarzenegger (celebrity) ...

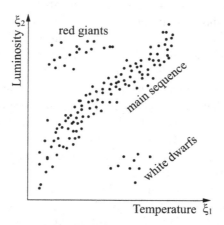

Figure 4.2   Classification of stars—unsupervised learning.

When we deal with classification of objects, each object is represented by a set of parameters $\xi_1, \ldots, \xi_k$, or feature values, which are real numbers. Hence an object is represented by a point $\mathbf{x} = (\xi_1, \ldots, \xi_k)$ in an k-dimensional vector space $\mathbb{R}^k$, which is called the **feature space**.

$\mathbf{x} = (\xi_1, \ldots, \xi_k)$ is also called a **feature vector**. For example, Figure 4.2 is a diagram, known as the Hertzsprung-Russell diagram, showing the classification of stars in astrophysics. The stars have different luminosity (brightness) and they appear in different colors, from reddish to white, to bluish. From the colors we can infer their temperatures. The Hertzsprung-Russell diagram is a scatter graph of stars showing the relationship of the temperature ξ_1 (which determines its color) and its luminosity ξ_2 for each star. Each star is represented by a point, or a vector (ξ_1, ξ_2) in the 2-dimensional ξ_1-ξ_2 plane.

It is natural to our eyes, these points form three groups, or clusters. There are gaps between clusters. Therefore, we can classify them into three categories. We may call the upper left cluster Category A, the middle cluster Category B and the lower right cluster Category C. Oftentimes this is how humans classify. Can machines perform this type of classification? Yes, they can. There are many clustering algorithms. Clustering is known as **unsupervised learning**, because a machine can do it by itself without human intervention. This is opposed to **supervised learning**, or **learning through training**, or **learning by examples**, which we will discuss subsequently.

Further study in astrophysics justifies the above classification. In fact, the three clusters show the different stages in their life cycles of the stars. The temperature and luminosity of each star (as well as the size, which is a parameter not shown in the graph) change through its life cycle. Category B is called the main sequence in astrophysics. This is the stable stage of a star. A star spends about 90% of its life as a main sequence star. Stars in Category A are called red giant stars. A red giant is a star in a late phase in its life. It becomes enormously huge in size, very luminous and colder (red color). Stars in Category C are called white dwarf stars. A white dwarf is a star toward the end of its life, with hot temperature (white color), low luminosity and extremely small size.

A machine can also be trained. This is called supervised learning. In many cases, we have a set of training data. That is, we already know the categories for the individuals in the training data set. We can label each individual in the data set with their categories. Instead of using categories A, B, C, it is more convenient to use numbers. Let us use 1, 0 and -1 in place of A, B, C. We label the data point in category A with 1, category B with 0 and category C with -1. We want to convey this knowledge to the machine, in the hope that in the future when a new object with feature vector $\mathbf{x}$ comes in, the machine will have a capability of generalization to judge what category $\mathbf{x}$ belongs to. How do we teach the machine that certain objects belong to category A and certain objects belong to category B, and make the machine learn? What is the analogy in mathematics of the process that we teach a child "Max is a dog" and "Whiskers is a cat"? When this teaching and learning process is translated to mathematics, we have a mathematical model of supervised learning. The objects are represented by feature vectors $\mathbf{x}$ in a k-dimensional vector space $\mathbb{R}^k$. We assign m categories, represented by real numbers $c_1, \ldots, c_m$. We have a training set of data points $\mathbf{x}_i$, $i = 1, \ldots, n$. That is, we know the categories of these points. We want to find a function $f : \mathbb{R}^k \to \mathbb{R}$ such that it interpolates the given data set. Namely,

$$f(\mathbf{x}_i) = t_i,$$

where $t_i \in \{c_1, \ldots, c_m\}$ is the known label of the category of $\mathbf{x}_i$, for $i = 1, \ldots, N$. For any future test data point $\mathbf{x}$, if $\mathbf{x}$ is close to the points in category c_λ, we expect $f(\mathbf{x}) = c_\lambda$.

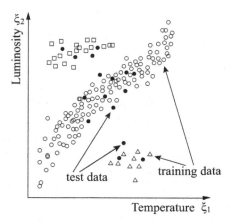

Figure 4.3   Classification of stars—supervised learning.

Figure 4.3 illustrates the supervised learning process, still using stars as example. Suppose the categories of some stars are known. We label them with these known categories. In the figure, we use squares to denote red giants (Category A, or 1), circles for stars in the main sequence (Category B, or 0), and triangles for the white dwarfs (Category C, or -1). We want to find a function f such that $f(\mathbf{x}_i)$ is equal to 1, 0, or -1 for the training data, as the categories that they are assigned to. The dots in the graph represent test data, which we do not have prior knowledge of their classification. If the learning is done right, $f(\mathbf{x})$ should give the correct category for the test data point $\mathbf{x}$.

How about the learning of images, like dogs and cats? With digital pictures, each picture consists of k pixels. An image (gray scale) is defined by the brightness values of k pixels, which is a point in $\mathbb{R}^k$. The learning process is going on in the k-dimensional vector space $\mathbb{R}^k$. Many pictures have millions of pixels. Therefore, the feature spaces usually have very high dimensions. A color picture has R, G, B components. That means a color picture with k pixels is a point in $3k$-dimensional space. The human visual system and the brain are constantly working in high dimensional feature spaces without consciously realizing it.

Of course, if we can do some pre-processing of the image, the dimension of the feature space can be reduced and classification process can be more efficient. We will have more detailed discussion on dimensionality reduction in the next chapter.

§3   Linear Support Vector Machines

Let us start with the simplest case, classification of two categories, just like dogs and cats. It can be easily generalized to multiple categories.

Suppose we have training data points labeled in two categories. Each point is represented by a vector $\mathbf{x}_i$, for $i = 1, \ldots, N$. Figure 4.4 shows an example in the two dimension case, but our discussion will be for the more general case of a k-dimensional feature space $\mathbb{R}^k$. That is, each $\mathbf{x}_i \in \mathbb{R}^k$ is a k-dimensional vector. Each training data point $\mathbf{x}_i$ has a class label t_i, where $t_i \in \{1, -1\}$. If $t_i = 1$, then $\mathbf{x}_i$ is in the first class. If $t_i = -1$, then $\mathbf{x}_i$ is in the second class.

We first assume that the data points are linearly separable, meaning that it is possible to find a hyperplane Π in $\mathbb{R}^k$ such that all the training data points in the first class lie on one side of Π while all the training points in the second class lie on the other side of Π. Suppose the hyperplane has equation

$$\mathbf{w} \cdot \mathbf{x} + b = 0,$$

where $\mathbf{x} \in \mathbb{R}^k$ is any point on this hyperplane, $\mathbf{w} \in \mathbb{R}^k$ and $b \in \mathbb{R}^k$ are constants. $\mathbf{w}$ is the normal vector of the hyperplane Π. The constants $\mathbf{w}$ and b are not uniquely determined, because if $\mathbf{w}$ and b are multiplied by a scaling factor, $\mathbf{w} \cdot \mathbf{x} + b = 0$ represent the same hyperplane.

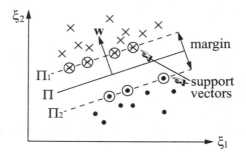

Figure 4.4   Linear support vector machine.

We can define a linear function of $\mathbf{x}$,

$$f(\mathbf{x}) = \mathbf{w} \cdot \mathbf{x} + b.$$

For any data point $\mathbf{x}_i$ in the first class ($t_i = 1$), we require $f(\mathbf{x}) > 0$. Namely,

$$\mathbf{w} \cdot \mathbf{x}_i + b > 0. \tag{4.1}$$

For any data point $\mathbf{x}_i$ in the second class ($t_i = -1$), we require $f(\mathbf{x}) < 0$. Namely,

$$\mathbf{w} \cdot \mathbf{x}_i + b < 0. \tag{4.2}$$

Eqs. (4.1) and (4.2) can be combined into a single equation

$$t_i(\mathbf{w} \cdot \mathbf{x}_i + b) > 0.$$

For the first class data points, there is a minimum value for $f(\mathbf{x}_i)$, which is positive. For the second class data points, there is a maximum value for $f(\mathbf{x}_i)$, which is negative. If we choose a proper scale for $\mathbf{w}$ and b, we can make the minimum value for $f(\mathbf{x}_i)$ for the first class to be 1 while the maximum value for $f(\mathbf{x}_i)$ for the second class to be -1. Therefore,

$$\mathbf{w} \cdot \mathbf{x}_i + b \geq 1, \quad \text{for } t_i = 1, \tag{4.3}$$

$$\mathbf{w} \cdot \mathbf{x}_i + b \leq -1, \quad \text{for } t_i = -1. \tag{4.4}$$

These two inequalities can be combined into one,

$$t_i(\mathbf{w} \cdot \mathbf{x}_i + b) - 1 \geq 0, \text{ for all } i. \tag{4.5}$$

When the equality holds, it represent two hyperplanes Π_1 and Π_2, with Π_1 represented by

$$\mathbf{w} \cdot \mathbf{x} + b = 1,$$

and Π_2 represented by

$$\mathbf{w} \cdot \mathbf{x} + b = -1.$$

Π_1 and Π_2 are parallel to each other and there are no training data points falling in between Π_1 and Π_2. The perpendicular distance between Π_1 and Π_2 is called the **margin** of the separating hyperplane Π.

The perpendicular directed distance from the origin to Π_1 is $(1-b)/\|\mathbf{w}\|$. The perpendicular directed distance from the origin to Π_2 is $(-1-b)/\|\mathbf{w}\|$. Hence the margin of Π is $2/\|\mathbf{w}\|$.

It is easy to see that if there exists such a hyperplane Π that separates the data points in two classes, then Π is not unique. If we translate or rotate Π a little bit, it is still a good separator. We do have room to demand more on the hyperplane Π so that it has some optimal property. We can demand to find a separating hyperplane Π with maximal margin. This means to find a hyperplane Π with minimal $\|\mathbf{w}\|$ subject to constraints (4.5). That is, to minimize

$$\frac{1}{2}\mathbf{w} \cdot \mathbf{w}$$

subject to

$$t_i(\mathbf{w} \cdot \mathbf{x}_i + b) - 1 \geq 0, \text{ for all } i.$$

Note that the optimal separating hyperplane Π is determined by data points lying on the hyperplanes Π_1 and Π_2 only. Those are the data points lying on the frontier of the two classes and are called **support vectors**. This is why implementations of this supervised learning algorithm is called **support vector machines** (SVM) [Boser et al. (1992); Cortes and Vapnik (1995)].

Altering data points that are not support vectors (adding, removing and moving around) does not affect the solution of the optimal separating hyperplane Π, as long as we do not add or move points into the region in between of the two frontier hyperplanes Π_1 and Π_2.

To find the solution for this optimal separating hyperplane Π, we introduce Lagrange multipliers α_i. The problem is transformed to minimize

$$L = \frac{1}{2}\mathbf{w} \cdot \mathbf{w} - \sum_{i=1}^{N} \alpha_i[t_i(\mathbf{w} \cdot \mathbf{x}_i + b) - 1], \tag{4.6}$$

with respect to $\mathbf{w}$, b and maximize it with respect to α_i.

Setting $\dfrac{\partial L}{\partial \mathbf{w}} = 0$ gives

$$\mathbf{w} = \sum_{i=1}^{N} \alpha_i t_i \mathbf{x}_i. \tag{4.7}$$

Setting $\dfrac{\partial L}{\partial b} = 0$, we have

$$\sum_{i=1}^{N} \alpha_i t_i = 0. \tag{4.8}$$

The original optimization problem is equivalent to the dual problem of maximizing

$$L_D = \sum_{i=1}^{N} \alpha_i - \frac{1}{2} \sum_{i,j=1}^{N} \alpha_i \alpha_j t_i t_j \mathbf{x}_i \cdot \mathbf{x}_j, \tag{4.9}$$

subject to

$$\alpha_i \geq 0, \tag{4.10}$$

and

$$\sum_{i=1}^{N} \alpha_i t_i = 0. \tag{4.11}$$

This is a standard quadratic programming problem and can be easily solved. Let $H_{ij} \overset{\text{def}}{=} t_i t_j \mathbf{x}_i \cdot \mathbf{x}_j$ and introduce another Lagrange multiplier λ, we can maximize

$$L'_D = \sum_{i=1}^{N} \alpha_i - \frac{1}{2} \sum_{i,j=1}^{N} H_{ij} \alpha_i \alpha_j - \lambda \sum_{i=1}^{n} \alpha_i t_i,$$

with respect to α_i. Setting $\dfrac{\partial L'_D}{\partial \alpha_i} = 0$, we can solve for α_i in terms of λ. Then substitute solutions for α_i into constraint Eq. 4.11 to solve for λ. After α_i are solved, they are substituted into Eq. 4.7 and we obtain the solution for $\mathbf{w}$.

In the solution, if $\mathbf{x}_i$ is not a support vector (not on the frontier), then $\alpha_i = 0$. That is why $\mathbf{w} = \sum_{i=1}^{N} \alpha_i t_i \mathbf{x}_i$ is determined by those support vectors (with non-zero α_i) only. Interior data points (non support vectors) have no contribution in $\mathbf{w}$. b can be solved from $t_i(\mathbf{w} \cdot \mathbf{x}_i + b) - 1 = 0$ with any support vector $\mathbf{x}_i$, which has a nonzero α_i.

Eq. 4.11 has a physical interpretation. Imagine each data point $\mathbf{x}_i$ exerts a force α_i on the separating hyperplane Π in the direction perpendicular to Π. The points on one side (in the first class) push in one direction while points on the other side (in the second class) push in the opposite direction. Eq. 4.11 shows that the these forces sum up to zero and hence the hyperplane Π will be in equilibrium. Furthermore, only the support vectors lying on the frontier planes Π_1 and Π_2 have non-zero forces α_i. Hence only the support vectors push the hyperplane Π and the result is an equilibrium. This analogy justifies the name of support vector machine even more.

§4   Nonlinear Support Vector Machines and Reproducing Kernel Hilbert Spaces

There are cases in which the data points are not linearly separable. For example, the two classes of data points in Figure 4.5 are not linearly separable. In such cases, we could design a non-linear function $f(\mathbf{x})$ such that for one class, $f(\mathbf{x}_i) > 0$ while for the other class $f(\mathbf{x}_i) < 0$. This is the case in the neural network approach. However, a nonlinear decision boundary is more complex and more challenging than the linear one. There is an alternative approach. That is to embed the data points in a higher dimensional space. In a higher dimensional space, we have more room and hence a chance to linearly separate these data points.

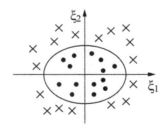

Figure 4.5   Linearly non-separable data.

For the example in Figure 4.5, an ellipse boundary $\dfrac{\xi_1^2}{a^2} + \dfrac{\xi_2^2}{b^2} = 1$ would be able to separate the two classes of data points, but not any linear boundary. We can embed the data points into a 3-dimensional space H with coordinates (η_1, η_2, η_3). We make $(\eta_1, \eta_2) = (\xi_1, \xi_2)$. For the points in the first class (crosses), we make $\xi_3 = 0$, while for the points in the second class (dots), we give them a lift, with $\xi_3 = 1$. Then the embedded data points are linearly separable by a plane $\xi_3 = \dfrac{1}{2}$ in the 3-dimensional space $H = \mathbb{R}^3$, as shown in Figure 4.6.

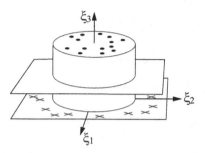

Figure 4.6   Lifting the data points to 3-dimensional space.

In this example, the lifting, which is a mapping from $\mathbb{R}^2$ to $\mathbb{R}^3$, is not continuous. In practice, we want this embedding to be a smooth mapping $\Phi : \mathbb{R}^k \to H$. It may not even be strictly a global topological embedding, it is in general a smooth immersion. It is acceptable if two distinct points are mapped to one point in H, as long as this does not happen to two points in different classes. In general, we will just call it a lifting.

Let us look at one example of such a mapping $\Phi : \mathbb{R}^k \to H$ that immerses the 2-D plane into a 3-D space: $\Phi : \mathbb{R}^2 \to \mathbb{R}^3;\ (\xi_1, \xi_2) \mapsto (\eta_1, \eta_2, \eta_3)$, where

$$\begin{bmatrix} \eta_1 \\ \eta_2 \\ \eta_3 \end{bmatrix} = \begin{bmatrix} \xi_1^2 \\ \sqrt{2}\,\xi_1 \xi_2 \\ \xi_2^2 \end{bmatrix}. \tag{4.12}$$

The immersed image is a cone surface (precisely a nappe, which is half of a double cone) with equation

$$\eta_2^2 = 2\eta_1 \eta_3,$$

with $\eta_1 \geq 0$ and $\eta_3 \geq 0$. This can be seen more easily if we make a transformation (a rotation of angle $\pi/4$ in the plane of η_1-η_3): $\eta_1' = \frac{1}{\sqrt{2}}(\eta_1 + \eta_3)$, $\eta_3' = \frac{1}{\sqrt{2}}(\eta_1 - \eta_3)$. Then the surface equation becomes $\eta_1'^2 = \eta_2^2 + \eta_3'^2$, which is the standard equation of a cone in the coordinates of $(\eta_1', \eta_2, \eta_3')$. It is a nappe (half of a double cone) because $\eta_1' \geq 0$. A plane can separate the data points in the two classes in $\mathbb{R}^3$.

In general, this embedding process could be tedious. However, this particular lifting in Eq. 4.12 has an amazing property. Look at the inner product in $H = \mathbb{R}^3$. Suppose we have two points $\mathbf{x} = (\xi_1, \xi_2), \mathbf{y} = (\xi_1', \xi_2') \in \mathbb{R}^2$, and their images are $\Phi(\mathbf{x}), \Phi(\mathbf{y}) \in \mathbb{R}^3$. Then

$$
\begin{aligned}
\Phi(\mathbf{x}) \cdot \Phi(\mathbf{y}) &= (\xi_1^2, \sqrt{2}\xi_1\xi_2, \xi_2^2) \cdot (\xi_1'^2, \sqrt{2}\xi_1'\xi_2', \xi_2'^2) \\
&= \xi_1^2\xi_1'^2 + 2\xi_1\xi_1'\xi_2\xi_2' + \xi_2^2\xi_2'^2 \\
&= (\xi_1\xi_1' + \xi_2\xi_2')^2 \\
&= (\mathbf{x} \cdot \mathbf{y})^2,
\end{aligned}
$$

where $\Phi(\mathbf{x}) \cdot \Phi(\mathbf{y})$ is the inner product of $\Phi(\mathbf{x})$ and $\Phi(\mathbf{y})$ in $\mathbb{R}^3$ while $\mathbf{x} \cdot \mathbf{y}$ is the inner product of $\mathbf{x}$ and $\mathbf{y}$ in $\mathbb{R}^2$. If we denote $K(\mathbf{x}, \mathbf{y}) = (\mathbf{x} \cdot \mathbf{y})^2$ as a nonlinear function of $\mathbf{x}$ and $\mathbf{y}$, then $\Phi(\mathbf{x}) \cdot \Phi(\mathbf{y}) = K(\mathbf{x}, \mathbf{y})$. Because in the linear SVM algorithm, only the inner products of data points are needed. When we perform a linear SVM learning in the higher dimensional space H, we can do the same as if we were in the original space $\mathbb{R}^k$, except whenever the inner product $\mathbf{x}_i \cdot \mathbf{x}_j$ is needed, we use $K(\mathbf{x}, \mathbf{y}) = (\mathbf{x}_i \cdot \mathbf{x}_j)^2$ instead.

The function $K(\mathbf{x}, \mathbf{y})$ is called a kernel. Oftentimes, we know if some symmetric function $K(\mathbf{x}, \mathbf{y})$ of $\mathbf{x}$ and $\mathbf{y}$ satisfies certain conditions (like those in Mercer's theorem, see Part III Chap. 3), $K(\mathbf{x}, \mathbf{y})$ is guaranteed to be the inner product $\Phi(\mathbf{x}) \cdot \Phi(\mathbf{y})$ of some Hilbert space H, with some mapping $\Phi : \mathbb{R}^k \to H$. The Hilbert space H is called a **reproducing kernel Hilbert space (RKHS)**, with kernel $K(\cdot, \cdot)$. In many algorithms in machine learning including SVM, we do not even need to know the explicit form of the mapping Φ, or the explicit form and dimension of the RKHS. Some of the often used kernels include: polynomial $K(\mathbf{x}, \mathbf{y}) = (\mathbf{x} \cdot \mathbf{y} + 1)^p$, Gaussian $K(\mathbf{x}, \mathbf{y}) = e^{-\|\mathbf{x}-\mathbf{y}\|^2/2\sigma^2}$, hyperbolic $K(\mathbf{x}, \mathbf{y}) = \tanh(c\mathbf{x} \cdot \mathbf{y} - d)$ for certain parameters c and d. For more on RKHS, the reader is referred to Part III, Chap. 3.

Chapter 5

Manifold Learning in Machine Learning

There is only one thing more painful than learning from experience and that is not learning from experience.

— *Archibald MacLeish*

Reading Guide. The goal of manifold learning is to discover a low dimensional submanifold embedded in the feature space, that is, to utilize a lower dimensional curved feature space. It is used for dimensionality reduction and more efficient pattern classification. There are many algorithms for manifold learning. We introduce two of the most important algorithms in this chapter, local linear embedding and Isomap.

§1   The Need for Dimensionality Reduction

In Section 4 of last chapter, we have seen cases where the data points are not linearly separable in lower dimensional spaces $\mathbb{R}^d$, but become linearly separable when they are lifted (embedded) in a higher dimensional space $\mathbb{R}^k$. For example, data points not linearly separable in $\mathbb{R}^2$ can become linearly separable in $\mathbb{R}^3$.

There are other possible situations regarding the data to be classified. It is possible that the feature points live in a k-dimensional space $\mathbb{R}^k$, but these data points do not "occupy" all the k dimensions. That is, all the data points happen to lie in a linear subspace $\mathbb{R}^d$, with a much lower dimension d. If the data points are linearly separable in $\mathbb{R}^k$, then they are linearly separable in $\mathbb{R}^d$. In such a case, we first project the points in $\mathbb{R}^k$ onto a linear subspace $\mathbb{R}^d$ and then solve the classification problem in space $\mathbb{R}^d$ with a much lower dimension, which will be much more efficient.

Another possibility is that the data points are not linearly separable in the original k-dimensional space $\mathbb{R}^k$ but become linearly separable in a lower dimensional subspace. Obviously, this lower dimensional subspace cannot be a linear subspace. It can be a lower dimensional submanifold of dimension d.

We first look at the case of dimension reduction to a linear subspace. Human brains perform pattern classification and recognition in high dimensional spaces. However, the human brain is extremely good at dimensionality reduction in a subconscious way. That is, to throw away irrelevant information and focus on the important features. Take an example of face recognition. Suppose we have an image with 1600×1200, or about two million pixels. If our pattern recognition program takes this image as input, we will work in a space of two million dimensions. However, we know that there is a lot of surplus information in the image. For face recognition, the background as well as the chest in the image is irrelevant. If we just crop the face part of the image, we obtain an image of 600×800 pixels. With this cropping, we can then work in a space of dimension 480,000. If we keep the same cropping area but reduce the resolution to 150×200 pixels, the image is still recognizable to human eyes. Then we can work in a space of dimension 30,000. Dimensionality reduction by cropping an image is only an example for illustration. There are many sophisticated dimension reduction methods, for example, principal component analysis, or PCA (see Appendix A1).

In fact, the human brain works a lot more efficiently than the simple cropping in dimensionality reduction. When it comes to pattern recognition, a small number of features are extracted so that the recognition can be done in a very low dimensional space effectively. The brain is very good as extracting the contours and edges of images. For example, if someone has facial features like a square jaw or big eyes, the brain may use these features to help recognize the face.

Photographer Grancel Fitz published a photograph, *Big Baby*, in 1930s. Apparently the photograph was altered using dark room technology available at that time. In the photograph, a baby is standing by a high chair, while the mother is shrunk in small size, sitting in the high chair. (You can search online to find the photograph). Despite the contrast in absolute sizes, we can easily identity which is a baby and which is an adult.

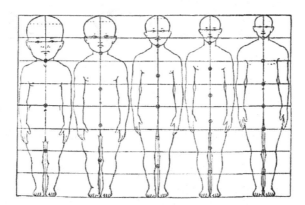

Figure 5.1   Body proportions: The head to body ratio is 1/4 for a baby and 1/8 for an adult. Image source: public domain.

Artists have studied human body proportions since Renaissance. For a one year old baby, his body length is about four times the head length. For an adult, the body length is about eight times the head length, shown in Figure 5.1 (there are variations in individuals as well as in genders and races). The head to body length ratio gets smaller and smaller as the child grows up into adulthood. Even if one has not learned a drawing lesson, his brain has learned the body proportions unconsciously. The head to body length ratio is a feature in only one dimension, but it is very effective in distinguishing children from adults.

Facial proportions can help distinguishing children from adults effectively as well. If we take the length from the hairline to the bottom of the chin as 1, the eyes of a baby lie at 1/2 from the chin while the eyes of an adult lie at 2/3 from the chin (Figure 5.2). When the baby grows older, the eye line moves up from 1/2 to 2/3 gradually. So the classification of child/adult can be done in one dimensional feature space, using either body proportions or facial proportions.

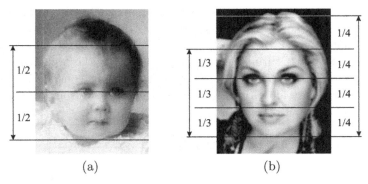

(a)   (b)

Figure 5.2   Facial proportions of baby and adult. Photographs taken from the public domain and cropped.

People can classify images of children and adults subconsciously. This means the classification is done in high dimensional space. As soon as we have learned those characteristic features through study and research, like the body proportions and face proportions, the dimensionality of the feature space is reduced. Take music genre classification as another example. If you have listened to western music and traditional Chinese music, it is very easy to distinguish them without learning any theory. However, as soon as you learn in theory that the traditional Chinese music is pentatonic, meaning using five notes instead of seven, the dimensionality of the feature space is significantly reduced. Yet another example with palm trees. If you have not paid too much attention, all the palm trees may look the same to you, but as soon as you learn the difference between the fan-shaped palms (palmate) and feather-shaped palms (pinnate), the dimension of the feature space for recognition or classification is significantly lowered.

There are also situations that the data points are not contained in any linear subspaces, but rather on a lower dimensional manifold (a curved hypersurface). In Figure 5.3, the data points lie on a "Swiss roll", which is a 2-dimensional surface. If we flatten the "Swiss roll" as a flat strip, the data points are then linearly separable on this 2-dimensional strip.

The idea of manifold learning is to discover an embedded submanifold M in the feature space $\mathbb{R}^k$, on which the data points reside. Locally the manifold is like a patch of a Euclidean space $\mathbb{R}^d$, which has a much lower dimension. Hence the dimensionality is reduced. There are numerous methods and algorithms for manifold learning. In the following sections, we discuss two most popular methods—locally linear embedding and Isomap.

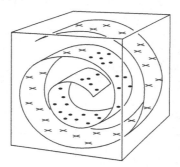

Figure 5.3   The "Swiss roll" as embedded manifold.

§2   Locally Linear Embedding

Locally linear embedding (LLM) makes use of the idea that any manifold can be locally approximated by a linear space—the tangent space.

Suppose M is an embedded d-dimensional submanifold M of a Euclidean space $\mathbb{R}^k$. The problem that LLM tries to solve is to discover this submanifold and provide a d-dimensional local coordinate system for the manifold M (namely, for data points $\mathbf{x}_1, \ldots, \mathbf{x}_N \in M$).

Let $T_{\mathbf{x}_i}(M)$ be the tangent space (tangent plane shown in Figure 5.4(a) and (b)) at $\mathbf{x}_i$ on the manifold M embedded in $\mathbb{R}^k$. Let $\mathbf{x}_{i_1}, \ldots, \mathbf{x}_{i_K}$ be K nearby points on M in a neighborhood of $\mathbf{x}_i$. Note that none of these points $\mathbf{x}_{i_1}, \ldots, \mathbf{x}_{i_K}$ are in the tangent space $T_{\mathbf{x}_i}(M)$. Suppose that $\mathbf{x}_i$ can be written as the linear combination of $\mathbf{x}_{i_1}, \ldots, \mathbf{x}_{i_K}$ as

$$\mathbf{x}_i = \sum_{\alpha=1}^{K} w_{i_\alpha}\mathbf{x}_{i_\alpha}. \tag{5.1}$$

The subsubscript notation in Eq. 5.1 is awkward. We can rewrite this as

$$\mathbf{x}_i = \sum_{\mathbf{x}_j \in U(\mathbf{x}_i)} w_{ij}\mathbf{x}_j, \tag{5.2}$$

where the summation is over the prescribed neighborhood $U(\mathbf{x}_i)$ of $\mathbf{x}_i$, namely, over all the points $\mathbf{x}_j \in U(\mathbf{x}_i)$. This notation can be further simplified as

$$\mathbf{x}_i = \sum_{j=1}^{N} w_{ij}\mathbf{x}_j,$$

by requiring $w_{ij} \overset{\text{def}}{=} 0$ for $\mathbf{x}_j$ not in the nearest neighborhood of $\mathbf{x}_i$. That is, $w_{ij} \overset{\text{def}}{=} 0$ for $\mathbf{x}_j \notin U(\mathbf{x}_i)$.

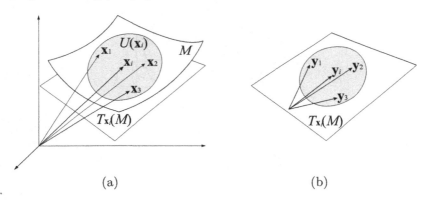

(a)   (b)

Figure 5.4   Locally linear embedding. (a) A neighborhood on the manifold. (b) The tangent space.

This may or may not be possible depending on the value of K and d. If $K = d$ and data points in $U(\mathbf{x}_i)$ are linearly independent, then this linear combination is unique. If $K > d$, it is possible but the weights w_{ij} are not unique. In most of the cases, the dimension d is much less than k but d is still a big number, and d is bigger than K. In such cases, $\mathbf{x}_i$ cannot be written as a linear combination exactly, but only approximately. The best we can do is to find the best approximation such that an error function

$$E(W) = \sum_{i=1}^{N} \left\| \mathbf{x}_i - \sum_{j=1}^{N} w_{ij}\mathbf{x}_j \right\|^2 \tag{5.3}$$

can be minimized. So given N data points $\mathbf{x}_1, \ldots, \mathbf{x}_N \in \mathbb{R}^k$ as input, we can find a solution for w_{ij} to minimize the error function $E(W)$ in Eq. 5.3, where W denotes the matrix of $[w_{ij}]$. In practice, we also impose a constraint

$$\sum_{j=1}^{N} w_{ij} = 1.$$

This constraint has the effect of making the solution of w_{ij} invariant to translations, which intuitively makes sense.

If we make an orthogonal projection of $\mathbb{R}^k$ onto the tangent space $TM_{\mathbf{x}_i}$, then with this projection, in a small neighborhood of $\mathbf{x}_i$, we can obtain a simple local coordinate system in $\mathbb{R}^d$. This is known as the **Monge projection**, or **Monge patch** (see Part II Chap. 2). Let $\Phi : \mathbb{R}^k \to \mathbb{R}^d$ be this projection of Monge patch. Under this projection, $\mathbf{x}_i \mapsto \mathbf{y}_i$, where $\mathbf{x}_i \in \mathbb{R}^k$ is a vector in the higher dimensional space $\mathbb{R}^k$, while $\mathbf{y}_i \in \mathbb{R}^d$ is the local coordinates of $\mathbf{x}_i$.

The key idea that makes the LLE work is the observation that the linear relationship of Eq. 5.1 is preserved under Monge projection. That is, the coordinates of these points are also linearly related,

$$\mathbf{y}_i = \sum_{j=1}^{N} w_{ij} \mathbf{y}_j. \tag{5.4}$$

However, the Monge projection only works for a small patch centered at $\mathbf{x}_i$. To obtain the coordinates for a bigger patch of M, which would cover all the points $\mathbf{x}_1, \ldots, \mathbf{x}_N$, we can use one Monge patch at each point $\mathbf{x}_i$. These patches overlap. That is, each coordinate point $\mathbf{y}_i$ is used in the overlapping patches, and hence Eq. 5.4 is no longer exact for all the overlapping patches, but only holds approximately. That is

$$\mathbf{y}_i \approx \sum_{j=1}^{N} w_{ij} \mathbf{y}_j,$$

again with the understanding $w_{ij} = 0$ if $\mathbf{x}_j$ is not one of the nearest neighbors of $\mathbf{x}_i$. Overall, with the matrix W given, we can find $\mathbf{y}_i$ to minimize an error function

$$e(Y) = \sum_{i,j=1}^{N} \|\mathbf{y}_i - w_{ij}\mathbf{y}_j\|^2,$$

where Y denotes $(\mathbf{y}_1, \ldots, \mathbf{y}_N)$.

The LLE algorithm can be summarized as follows.

Algorithm. (Locally Linear Embedding)

Step 1. *Given the data points $\mathbf{x}_1, \ldots, \mathbf{x}_N \in \mathbb{R}^k$ as input, find the weights w_{ij} to minimize the error function*

$$E(W) = \sum_{i=1}^{N} \left\| \mathbf{x}_i - \sum_{j=1}^{N} w_{ij} \mathbf{x}_j \right\|^2. \tag{5.5}$$

Step 2. *Given the weights w_{ij} found in Step 1, solve for coordinate vectors $\mathbf{y}_i \in \mathbb{R}^d$ to minimize the error function*

$$e(Y) = \sum_{i=1}^{N} \left\| \mathbf{y}_i - \sum_{j=1}^{N} w_{ij} \mathbf{y}_j \right\|^2. \tag{5.6}$$

The optimal solution to Eq. 5.5 is

$$w_{ij} = \begin{cases} \dfrac{\sum_p C_{jp}^{-1}}{\sum_{pq} C_{pq}^{-1}}, & \text{if } \mathbf{x}_j \in U(\mathbf{x}_i), \\ 0, & \text{if } \mathbf{x}_j \notin U(\mathbf{x}_i), \end{cases} \tag{5.7}$$

where

$$C_{pq} = (\mathbf{x}_i - \mathbf{x}_p) \cdot (\mathbf{x}_i - \mathbf{x}_q)$$

is the covariance matrix for point $\mathbf{x}_i$, and the summation for p and q in Eq. 5.7 is over all the nearest neighbors of $\mathbf{x}_i$.

Eq. 5.6 can be written in a quadratic form

$$e(Y) = \sum_{i,j=1}^{N} Q_{ij} \mathbf{y}_i \cdot \mathbf{y}_j,$$

where

$$Q_{ij} = \delta_{ij} - w_{ij} - w_{ji} + \sum_p w_{pi} w_{pj}.$$

The solution for Y is translation invariant. We can impose a constraint

$$\sum_{i=1}^{N} \mathbf{y}_i = 0.$$

We also require that all the points $\mathbf{y}_i$ have unit covariance to avoid degenerate solutions,

$$\frac{1}{N} \sum_i \mathbf{y}_i \mathbf{y}_i^t = I,$$

where I is the $d{\times}d$ identity matrix. The optimal solution for $\mathbf{y}_i$ can be found by computing the bottom $d + 1$ eigenvectors of matrix Q. Discarding the eigenvector corresponding to eigenvalue zero, the remaining d eigenvectors will be the d-dimensional coordinates.

§3   Isomap

We have discussed in Section 1 that the problem of manifold learning is to find a submanifold M of dimension d in the space $\mathbb{R}^k$, on which the given data points reside. That is the general case. Isomap is a special method to find such a submanifold. Furthermore, it is a special case where we look for more and get more properties of this submanifold embedding. We look for and obtain an isometric embedding. The following description makes it more precise.

Problem Statement: Isomap Problem

Input: Given data points $\mathbf{x}_1, \ldots, \mathbf{x}_N \in \mathbb{R}^k$ and a natural number d.
Problem: Find an embedded Riemannian manifold $M \subset \mathbb{R}^k$ of dimension d, and a local isometric embedding $\Phi : \mathbb{R}^d \to M$ such that

(1) all the data points lie on M, that is, $\mathbf{x}_1, \ldots, \mathbf{x}_N \in M$, and
(2) an open region of $\mathbb{R}^d$ is isometrically embedded as a patch on M. That is, if $\mathbf{y}_i, \mathbf{y}_j \in \mathbb{R}^d$ are the d-dimensional local coordinates of $\mathbf{x}_i, \mathbf{x}_j$, then the distance $d(\mathbf{y}_i, \mathbf{y}_j)$ in $\mathbb{R}^d$ is equal to the geodesic distance between $\mathbf{x}_i$ and $\mathbf{x}_j$ on M.

Suppose we have N data points $\mathbf{x}_1, \ldots, \mathbf{x}_N \in \mathbb{R}^k$ that lie on an embedded submanifold M of lower dimension d. Our task is to find this submanifold and an embedding. An embedded manifold can be understood as a d-dimensional curved smooth hypersurface in $\mathbb{R}^k$.

The reason we assume M is a Riemannian manifold is that we care about the geodesic distances between the data points on M. In the general case of machine learning and pattern classification, the distance is not essential, although some times it is. In pattern classification, a smooth mapping in general will suffice, not necessarily isometric (distance preserving). In such cases, providing an isometric mapping does not hurt. In applications where we do care about the distances (like similarity measures), the distance preserving isometric mapping is desirable.

Another point to clarify is the existence of solutions to the problem. This depends on whether we insist that d is an arbitrarily prescribed number, or it is to be learned. If d is to be learned, a solution always exists, with a trivial case $d = k$, and there may be other solutions with lower d. The problem is to find the lowest embedding dimension d. If d is prescribed, as in the above problem statement, the solution may not exist. We know from differential geometry that not all the surfaces can be flattened (isometric to a plane). If this is the case, the problem can be reformatted to finding a smooth embedding that is the closest to an isometric mapping. We can define the "closest" by requiring minimization of a penalty cost function (functional).

For now, suppose we have the smart guess of d and finding such an isometric embedding is possible. This can be done using Tenenbaum-de Dilva-Langford algorithm [Tenenbaum et al. (2000)] in two steps.

Algorithm. (Isomap, Tenenbaum-de Dilva-Langford)
   Step 1. *Find the geodesic distances between every pair of points* $\mathbf{x}_1, \ldots, \mathbf{x}_N$.
   Step 2. *Find the mapping of embedding* $\Psi : \mathbb{R}^k \to \mathbb{R}^d$; $\mathbf{x} \mapsto \mathbf{y}$ *such that the distance between* $\mathbf{y}_i$ *and* $\mathbf{y}_j$ *is equal to the geodesic distance between* $\mathbf{x}_i$ *and* $\mathbf{x}_j$ *on* M. *Also compute* $\mathbf{y}_i = \Psi(\mathbf{x}_i) \in \mathbb{R}^d$ *for all* i *as output.*

In Step 1, an approximation of geodesic distances between each pair of data points is found as follows: for each point, select a set of neighboring points that are the close neighbors of this point. Euclidean distance in $\mathbb{R}^k$ is used with the nearest neighbor selection. We know in a small neighborhood, the Euclidean distance in $\mathbb{R}^k$ can be used as approximation of geodesic distance. A nearest neighbor graph can be constructed. Two points are connected by an edge in the graph if they are nearest neighbors. The geodesic distance between points not directly connected by an edge can be approximated by the shortest distance on the graph, using Dijkstra's algorithm or Floyd's algorithm [Cormen et al. (2009)] to find the shortest path on the graph. The output of Step 1 is a distance matrix $\tilde{D}$, with each entry $\tilde{D}_{ij} = \tilde{d}_{ij}^2$, where $\tilde{d}_{ij}$ is the geodesic distance between $\mathbf{x}_i$ and $\mathbf{x}_j$.

Step 2 can be accomplished by using an algorithm called classical Multidimensional Scaling (MDS), which was introduced by Torgerson [Torgerson (1952, 1958)]. MDS is an algorithm that solves a different problem, but it can be adapted to solve the problem in Step 2 of Isomap. The classical MDS is a special form of principal component analysis (PCA) introduced by Pearson [Pearson (1901)] (see Appendix A1). The procedures of MDS are the same as PCA. Both MDS and PCA solve linear problems. The Isomap problem is a non-linear problem. However, Step 2 in Isomap algorithm can be solved using MDS, if we use the geodesic distances between data points in place of Euclidean distances.

We describe the MDS problem as follows.

Problem Statement: Multidimensional Scaling (MDS) Problem

Input: Given data points $\mathbf{x}_1, \ldots, \mathbf{x}_N \in \mathbb{R}^k$, such that they lie in a d-dimensional linear subspace $S \subset \mathbb{R}^k$. The distance $D(\mathbf{x}_i, \mathbf{x}_j)$ between each pair of points $(\mathbf{x}_i, \mathbf{x}_j)$ in $\mathbb{R}^k$ can be calculated and a distance matrix D with $D_{ij} = D(\mathbf{x}_i, \mathbf{x}_j)$ can be constructed and considered as input.

Problem: Find the dimension d of the linear subspace S that the data points $\mathbf{x}_1, \ldots, \mathbf{x}_N$ span and find a basis $\{\mathbf{e}_1, \ldots, \mathbf{e}_d\}$ for S. Also compute the coordinates of data points $\mathbf{x}_1, \ldots, \mathbf{x}_N$ under this basis $\{\mathbf{e}_1, \ldots, \mathbf{e}_d\}$.

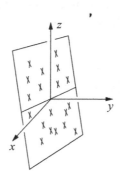

Figure 5.5   Multidimensional scaling.

Figure 5.5 shows an example of the classical MDS problem, where the 3-dimensional data points happen to lie in a plane. This is a special case when $k = 3$ and $d = 2$.

The classical MDS can be considered a special case of PCA. In PCA, we find the directions of the principal components represented by an ellipsoid. If some of the eigenvalues of the covariance matrix of the data are zero in PCA, it means that some axes of this ellipsoid are zero, namely, all the data points lie in a linear subspace, which is the case that classical MDS intend to deal with.

Define $\mathbf{1} \stackrel{\text{def}}{=} [1, 1, \cdots, 1]'$ and $\mathbf{E} \stackrel{\text{def}}{=} \mathbf{11}'$, where $\mathbf{11}'$ denotes matrix multiplication of $\mathbf{1}$ and $\mathbf{1}'$, which yields an $N \times N$ matrix with all the elements being 1. Let $\mathbf{I}$ be the $N \times N$ identity matrix. By defining $\mathbf{H} \stackrel{\text{def}}{=} \mathbf{I} - \frac{1}{n}\mathbf{E}$, we can construct a new matrix

$$L \stackrel{\text{def}}{=} -\frac{1}{2}HDH. \tag{5.8}$$

Multiplying H on both sides of D has the effect of subtracting the mean of the data. Hence the new center of the data points will be at the origin. The following theorem gives a condition of minimum embedding dimension r.

Theorem. *Let $\mathbf{x}_1, \ldots, \mathbf{x}_N \in \mathbb{R}^k$. If the matrix L defined in 5.8 has rank r, then the minimal embedding dimension of $\mathbf{x}_1, \ldots, \mathbf{x}_N \in \mathbb{R}^k$ is r. That is, r is the lowest dimension of any linear subspace of $\mathbb{R}^k$ that contains all points of $\mathbf{x}_1, \ldots, \mathbf{x}_N$.*

When the geodesic distance matrix $\tilde{D}$ is used in place of Euclidean distance matrix D in the MDS algorithm, the local coordinates of the manifold M for points $\mathbf{x}_1, \ldots, \mathbf{x}_N$ can be obtained.

Appendix

A1. Principal Component Analysis

First look at a set of data $x_1, \ldots, x_N \in \mathbb{R}$ drawn from some statistical distribution. Each is a real number. Suppose the number N is big. In statistics, the mean of these numbers measures the average, while the variance measures the spread of the data. The mean is defined to be

$$\mu \overset{\text{def}}{=} \frac{1}{N} \sum_{i=1}^{N} x_i,$$

and the variance is defined to be

$$\sigma^2 \overset{\text{def}}{=} \frac{1}{N} \sum_{i=1}^{N} (x_i - \mu)^2.$$

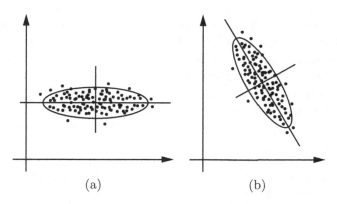

(a)   (b)

Figure 5.6 Principal component analysis.

Now consider a set of data points $\mathbf{x}_1, \ldots, \mathbf{x}_N \in \mathbb{R}^k$. Each $\mathbf{x}_i$ is a k-dimensional vector. These data points form a big cloud in the space $\mathbb{R}^k$. The mean

$$\mu \overset{\text{def}}{=} \frac{1}{N} \sum_{i=1}^{N} \mathbf{x}_i$$

gives the center of the point cloud, which is also called the centroid, or center of gravity. In higher dimensions, the data has more room to spread. They may have different spread along different axes, as in Figure 5.6 (a). The spread may be even in directions other than the coordinate axes, as in

Figure 5.6 (b). In such cases, the covariance matrix can be used to describe the shape of the data. The covariance matrix is defined to be

$$\Sigma \overset{\text{def}}{=} \frac{1}{N} \sum_{i=1}^{N} (\mathbf{x}_i - \mu)(\mathbf{x}_i - \mu)^t,$$

where $(\mathbf{x}_i - \mu)$ is a column matrix and $(\mathbf{x}_i - \mu)^t$ is its transpose, a row matrix. Σ is a $k \times k$ square matrix. In practice, it is always easier to subtract the mean from each data point. This means a coordinate translation and in the new coordinate system, the mean $\mu = 0$ and the covariance matrix is

$$\Sigma \overset{\text{def}}{=} \frac{1}{N} \sum_{i=1}^{N} \mathbf{x}_i \mathbf{x}_i^t.$$

It can be proved that the covariance matrix is a positive definite matrix. We can solve for its k eigenvalues and k orthogonal eigenvectors. Suppose $\lambda_1, \ldots, \lambda_k$ are the eigen values and $\mathbf{e}_1, \ldots, \mathbf{e}_k$ are the corresponding eigenvectors. These eigenvectors are called the principal directions of the data set. The eigenvalues are guaranteed to be nonnegative. The data cloud can be described by an ellipsoid with semiaxes $\lambda_1, \ldots, \lambda_k$. The data cloud may have much bigger spread in some direction than others. We can always sort the eigenvalues. Suppose the eigenvalues $\lambda_1, \ldots, \lambda_k$ have already been sorted in decreasing order, with λ_1 being the largest and λ_k being the least. In the new basis $\{\mathbf{e}_1, \ldots, \mathbf{e}_k\}$, any data point $\mathbf{x}_i$ can be written as $\mathbf{x}_i = \xi_1 \mathbf{e}_1 + \cdots + \xi_d + \cdots + \xi_k \mathbf{e}_k$. ξ_d is called the dth **principal components** of $\mathbf{x}_i$. If the last few eigenvalues $\lambda_{d+1}, \lambda_{d+2}, \ldots, \lambda_k$ are zero, then all the data points live in a d-dimensional linear subspace. We can use the d principal components to represent all the data. Hence the problem can be solved in a lower dimensional space $\mathbb{R}^d$.

Even if none of the eigenvalues is zero, but if the bottom few are close to zero, or very small compared with the largest eigenvalues, we can still project each point in a linear subspace spanned by the first d eigenvectors $\mathbf{e}_1, \ldots, \mathbf{e}_d$, and ignore the other dimensions. This is an effective approximation to reduce the dimensionality and it is known as **principal component analysis** (PCA).

Bibliography

Alberti, L. B. (1435). *On Painting*. Translated by Spencer, J. R., 1956, (Yale University Press).

Arnold, V. I. (1997). *Mathematical Methods of Classical Mechanics*, 2nd ed. (Springer).

Angel, E. and Shreiner D. (2011). *Interactive Computer Graphics: A Top-Down Approach with Shader-Based OpenGL*, 6th ed. (Addison-Wesley).

Berger, M. (2007). *A Panoramic View of Riemannian Geometry*, (Springer).

Blanuša, D. (1955). Uber die Einbettung Hyperbol Ischer Rfiume in Euklidische RSume, *Monatshefte fflr Math*, **59**, 3, pp. 217–229.

Boothby, W. (2002). *An Introduction to Differentiable Manifolds and Riemannian Geometry*, 2nd ed. (Academic Press).

Boser, B. E., Guyon, I. M. and Vapnik, V. N. (1992). A Training Algorithm for Optimal Margin Classifiers, *Proceedings of the Fifth Annual Workshop on Computational Learning Theory*, 5, pp. 144–152.

Bourbaki, N. (1942). *Algebra I: Chapters 1–3 (Elements of Mathematics)*, reprint ed. 1998, (Springer).

Bryant, V. (1971). Reducing Classical Axioms, *The Mathematical Gazette* **55**, 391, pp. 38–40.

Burger, W. and Burge, M. J. (2009). *Principles of Digital Image Processing: Fundamental Techniques, Vol. 1*, (Springer).

Cartan, É. (1927). Sur la Possibilité de Plonger un Espace Riemannien donné Dans un Espace Euclidéen, *Ann. Soc. Polon. Math.*, **6**, pp. 1–7.

Cartan, É. (1951). *Geometry of Riemannian Spaces*, translated by James Glazebrook, 2nd ed., (Math Sci Press).

Chern, S. S. (1947). Note on Affinely Connected Manifolds, Bulletin of American Mathematical Society, **53**, pp. 820–823.

Chern, S. S., Chen, W. H. and Lam, K. S. (1999). *Lectures on Differential Geometry*, (World Scientific).

Clifford, W. K. (1876). Abstract of "On the Classification of Geometric Algebras", *Proceedings of the London Mathematical Society*, **7**, p. 135.

Cohen, P. J. (1963). The Independence of the Continuum Hypothesis, *Proceedings of the National Academy of Sciences of the USA*, **50**, pp. 1143–1148.

Cohen, P. J. (1964). The Independence of the Continuum Hypothesis II, *Proceedings of the National Academy of Sciences of the USA*, **51**, pp. 105–110.

Cormen, T. H., Leiserson, C. E., Rivest, R. L. and Stein, C. (2009). *Introduction to Algorithms*, 3rd ed. (MIT Press).

Cortes, C. and Vapnik, V. N. (1995). Support-Vector Networks, *Machine Learning*, **20**, 3, pp. 273–297.

Coxeter, H. S. M. (1998). *Non-Euclidean Geometry*, 6th ed. (MAA).

Crowe, M. J. (2011). *A History of Vector Analysis: The Evolution of the Idea of a Vectorial System*, (Dover).

Do Carmo, M. P. (1976). *Differential Geometry of Curves and Surfaces*, (Prentice Hall).

Do Carmo, M. P. (1992). *Riemannian geometry*, (Birkhäuser).

Donaldson, S. K. and Kronheimer, P. B. (1990). *The Geometry of Four-manifolds*, (Oxford University Press).

Dorst, L. (2002). The Inner Products of Geometric Algebra, in *Applications of Geometric Algebra in Computer Science and Engineering*, (Birkhäuser).

Euclid, (1925). *The Thirteen Books of Euclid's Elements*, translated from the text of Heiberg with introduction and commentary, (Cambridge University Press).

Forsyth, D. and Ponce J. (2011). *Computer Vision: A Modern Approach*, (Prentice Hall).

Fréchet, M. (1906). Sur Quelques Points du Calcul Fonctionnel, *Rendic. Circ. Mat. Palermo* **22**, pp. 1–74.

Gamow, G. (1947). One, Two, Three ... Infinity, 1988, (Dover). First published by Viking Press, 1947.

Gans, D. (1966). A new model of the hyperbolic plane, *American mathematical monthly*, **73**, 3, pp. 291–295.

Gauss, C. F. (1827). *General Investigations of Curved Surfaces*, translated and edited by Morehead, J. C. and Hiltebeitel A. M., 1902, (Princeton).

Gelbaum, B. and Olmsted, J. (1964). *Counterexamples in Analysis*, 2003, (Dover). First published by Holden-Day, 1964.

Gergonne, J. D. (1818). Essai sur la Theorie des Definitions, *Annales de Mathématique Pure et Appliquée*, **9**, pp. 1–35.

Gibbs, J. W. (1884). *Elements of Vector Analysis: Arranged for the Use of Students in Physics*, (Tuttle, Morehouse & Taylor).

Greenberg, M. (2007). *Euclidean and Non-Euclidean Geometries*, 4th ed. (Freeman).

Greub, W. H. (1967). *Multilinear Algebra*, (Springer-Verlag).

Guillemin, V. and Pollack, A. (1974). *Differential Topology*, (Prentice Hall).

Guo, H. (2013a). Definitions of Perspective Diminution Factor and Foreshortening Factor: Applications in the Analysis of Perspective Distortion. *International Journal of Modern Engineering*, **13**, 2, pp. 78–87.

Guo, H. (2013b). Some Theoretical Results in the Perspective Analysis of Images. *International Journal of Modern Engineering*, **14**, 1, pp. 42–55.

Hadamard, J. (1901). Sur les éleéments linéaires á Plusieurs Dimensions, *Darboux Bull.* **2**, 25, pp. 37–40.

Halmos, P. R. (1941). *Finite-Dimensional Vector Spaces*, (Springer-Verlag).

Han, Q. and Hong, J-X. (2006). *Isometric Embedding of Riemannian Manifolds in Euclidean Spaces*, (American Mathematical Society).

Hilbert, D. (1899). *Foundations of Geometry*, 2nd ed. 1971, (Open Court). Translated from the tenth German ed. First published in 1899.

Hilbert, D. and Cohn-Vossen S. (1952). *Geometry and Imagination*, (Chelsea).

Janet, M. (1926). Sur la Possibilité de Plonger un Espace Riemannien Donné Dans un Espace Euclidien, *Ann. Soc. Polon. Math.* , **5**, pp. 38–43.

Jelinek, J. (2003). A Discontinuous Function with a Connected Closed Graph, *Acta Universitatis Carolinae — Mathematica et Physica*, **44**, 2, pp. 73–77.

Kervaire, M. A. (1960). A Manifold Which Does Not Admit Any Differentiable Structure, *Commentarii Mathematici Helvetici*, **34**, pp. 257–270.

Kirk-Purcell, J. (2011). *Sidewalk Canvas: Chalk Pavement Art at Your Feet*, (Fox Chapel Publishing).

Kline, M. (1972). *Mathematical Thought from Ancient to Modern Times*, (Oxford University Press).

Kolmogorov, A. (1933). *Foundations of Probability Theory*, 1950, (Chelsea). First published in 1933.

Krantz, S. G. (1996). *A Primer of Mathematical Writing*, (American Mathematical Society).

Kühnel, W. (2005). *Differential Geometry: Curves—Surfaces—Manifolds*, (American Mathematical Society).

Lee, J. M. (2011). *Introduction to Topological Manifolds*, 2nd ed. (Springer).

Lee, J. M. (2012). *Introduction to Smooth Manifolds*, 2nd ed. (Springer).

Longfellow, W. P. P. (1901). *Applied Perspective for Architects and Painters*, (Riverside Press).

MacHale, D. (1993). *Comic sections: the book of mathematical jokes, humour, wit, and wisdom*, (Boole Press).

Marcus, M. (1973). *Finite Dimensional Multilinear Algebra, Part I*, (Marcel Dekker).

Milnor, J. W. (1956), On Manifolds Homeomorphic to the 7-Sphere, *Annals of Mathematics*, **64**, 2, pp. 399–405.

Miron, R. and Branzei, D. (1995). *Backgrounds of Arithmetic and Geometry: An Introduction*, (World Scientific).

Moore, G. H. (2008). The Emergence of Open Sets, Closed Sets, and Limit Points in Analysis and Topology, *Historia Mathematica* **35**, 3, pp. 220–241.

Moulton, R. F. (1902). A Simple Non-Desarguesian Plane Geometry, *Transactions of the American Mathematical Society*, **3**, pp. 192–195.

MSJ (Mathematical Society of Japan), (1993). *Encyclopedic Dictionary of Mathematics*, 2nd ed. (MIT Press).

Nash, J. (1956). The Imbedding Problem for Riemannian Manifolds, *Annals of Mathematics*, **63**, 1, pp. 20–63.

Nassau, K. (2001). *The physics and Chemistry of Color*, 2nd ed. (John Wiley & Sons).

Ohta N. and Robertson, A. (2005). *Colorimetry: Fundamentals and Applications*, (Wiley).

Peano. G. (1888). *Geometric Calculus: According to the Ausdehnungslehre of H. Grassmann*, translated by Kannenberg, L., 2000, (Birkhäuser). First published in 1888.

Pearson, K. (1901). On Lines and Planes of Closest Fit to Systems of Points in Space, *Philosophical magazine*, **2**, 6, pp. 559–572.

Poincaré, H. (1899). Des fondements de la géométrie, *Revue de Mëtaphysique et de Morale* **7**, pp. 251–279.

Pressley, A. (2012). *Elementary Differential Geometry*, 2nd ed. (Springer).

Ricci-Curbastro, G. (1892). Résumë de Quelques Travaux sur les Systémes Variables de Fonctions Associés á Une Forme Diffèrentielle Quadratique, *Bulletin des Sciences Mathématiques*, **2**, 16, pp. 167–189.

Ricci-Curbastro, G. and Levi-Civita, T. (1900). Methods of the Absolute Differential Calculus and Their Applications. *Mathematische Annalen*, **54**, pp. 125–201.

Roman, S. (2005). *Advanced Linear Algebra*, 2nd ed. (Springer).

Small, C. G. (1996). *The Statistical Theory of Shape*, (Springer).

Solovay, R. (1970). A Model of Set-Theory in which Every Set of Reals Is Lebesgue Measurable, *Annals of Mathematics*, **92**, 1, pp. 1–56.

Sommerville, D. M. Y. (2005). *The Elements of Non-Euclidean Geometry*, (Dover).

Stewart, I. (1991). *Game, Set and Math.*, (Viking Penguin).

Struik, D. J. (1950). *Lectures on Classical Differential Geometry*, (Addison-Wesley).

Tenenbaum, J. B., de Silva, V. and Langford, J. C. (2000). A Global Geometric Framework for Nonlinear Dimensionality Reduction, *Science*, **290**, 5500, pp 2319–2323.

Torgerson, W. S. (1952). Multidimensional Scaling: I. Theory and Method, *Psychometrika*, **17**, 4, pp. 401–419.

Torgerson, W. S. (1958). *Theory & Methods of Scaling*, (Wiley).

Vanžurová A. and Žáčková, P. (2009). Metrizability of Connections on Two-Manifolds, *Acta Universitatis Palackianae Olomucensis. Facultas Rerum Naturalium. Mathematica*, **48**, 1, pp. 157–170.

Veblen, O. and Young, J. W. A. (1938). *Projective Geometry*, (Ginn & Co.).

Vitali, G. (1905). *Sul Problema Della Misura dei Gruppi di Punti di Una Retta*, (Tip. Gamberini e Parmeggiani).

Voigt, W. (1898). *The Fundamental Physical Properties of the Crystals in an Elementary Representation*, (Leipzig).

Wang, B-Y. (1985). *Foundations of Multilinear Algebra*, (Beijing Normal University Press).

Whitney, H. (1938). Tensor Products of Abelian Groups, *Duke Mathematical Journal*, **4**, 3, pp. 495–528.

Wójcik, M. R. and Wójcik M. S. (2007). Characterization of Continuity for Real-valued Functions in Terms of Connectedness, *Houston Journal of Mathematics*, 33, 4, pp. 1027–1031.

Index